EUROPEAN PRIVATE INTERNATIONAL LAW
AND MEMBER STATE TREATIES WITH THIRD STATES

EUROPEAN PRIVATE INTERNATIONAL LAW AND MEMBER STATE TREATIES WITH THIRD STATES

The Case of the European Succession Regulation

Edited by

Anatol Dutta
Wolfgang Wurmnest

intersentia
Cambridge – Antwerp – Chicago

Intersentia Ltd
Sheraton House | Castle Park
Cambridge | CB3 0AX | United Kingdom
Tel.: +44 1223 370 170 | Fax: +44 1223 370 169
Email: mail@intersentia.co.uk
www.intersentia.com | www.intersentia.co.uk

Distribution for the UK and Ireland:
NBN International
Airport Business Centre, 10 Thornbury Road
Plymouth, PL6 7PP
United Kingdom
Tel.: +44 1752 202 301 | Fax: +44 1752 202 331
Email: orders@nbninternational.com

Distribution for Europe and all other countries:
Intersentia Publishing nv
Groenstraat 31
2640 Mortsel
Belgium
Tel.: +32 3 680 15 50 | Fax: +32 3 658 71 21
Email: mail@intersentia.be

Distribution for the USA and Canada:
Independent Publishers Group
Order Department
814 North Franklin Street
Chicago, IL 60610
USA
Tel.: +1 800 888 4741 (toll free) | Fax: +1 312 337 5985
Email: orders@ipgbook.com

European Private International Law and Member State Treaties with Third States.
The Case of the European Succession Regulation

ISBN 978-1-78068-664-6
D/2019/7849/79
NUR 828

British Library Cataloguing in Publication Data. A catalogue record for this book is available from the British Library.

FOREWORD

Like many other EU regulations, Article 75 of the Succession Regulation contains rules which clarify the relationship between the Regulation and existing multilateral and bilateral conventions.

The Regulation prevails on existing multilateral and bilateral conventions between the Member States. This solution is understandable because it is the only way to create a uniform international succession law between the Member States. The only exception is the Hague Convention of 5 October 1961 on the Conflicts of Laws Relating to the Form of Testamentary Dispositions. The provisions of this Convention apply, instead of Article 27 of the Succession Regulation, with regard to the formal validity of wills and joint wills. The implications of the prevalence of the Regulation are not too significant because, besides some bilateral treaties, the Convention of 1961 is the only important convention on international succession law. The Hague Convention of 2 October 1973 concerning the International Administration of the Estates of Deceased Persons was only ratified by the Czech Republic, Portugal and Slovakia. Other conventions such as the Convention of 16 May 1972 on the Establishment of a Scheme of Registration of Wills and the UNIDROIT Convention of 26 October 1973 providing a uniform law in the form of an international will, deal with substantive succession law which is not covered by the Regulation.

As to treaties between Member States and third States, a distinction is to be made between treaties concerning recognition and enforcement of foreign decisions and treaties concerning jurisdiction and applicable law. Although the first category covers decisions in succession matters, they do not conflict with the Succession Regulation, which is limited to the recognition and enforcement of decisions of the Member States. The second category conflicts with the Succession Regulation, but the Regulation does not affect the application of such treaties. They prevail on the Regulation. This solution is nothing more than the application of an important rule of international law, namely *pacta sunt servanda* as enshrined in Article 351 Treaty on the Functioning of the European Union.

Until now, it has not been easy to get an overview of all the treaties concluded by the Member States with third States. It has been even more difficult to gain an insight into the application of those treaties in the contracting States. These challenges were the driving force behind a working conference organized in Augsburg on 23 and 24 November 2017 by Prof. Anatol Dutta and Prof. Wolfgang Wurmnest, under the auspices of the Universities of Augsburg and Munich. An important merit of this book is that it includes a compilation of all treaties concluded by selected Member States with third States and their English translations, which provide a very convenient tool to make the treaties themselves accessible to a wider readership. It is surprising to see that some of the selected Member States have no treaties with third States, for example Belgium, as the treaties with Switzerland of 29 April 1959 and with the United Kingdom of 2 May 1934 only deal with recognition and enforcement and therefore do not conflict with the Succession Regulation. Other Member States have very few treaties, such as France and Italy, whereas the Czech Republic and Slovakia have many, since the former Czechoslovakia concluded treaties with a large number of third States.

The scope of this book is much broader than a compilation and translation of those treaties. It includes contributions based on the presentations given by distinguished speakers at the Augsburg conference and it brings the project to fruition with a report by Prof. Dutta, who analyzes the treaties from the perspective of the European Union, and a comparative report by Prof. Wurmnest who offers a policy perspective. The contributions analyze the background of the treaties and we learn that, in some cases, they were meant to end the capitulation regimes. Those treaties introduce equal treatment concerning jurisdiction, but in order to facilitate commerce and to offer some protection to the citizens of the contracting States, the conflict rules use nationality as a connecting factor. Other treaties focus on the establishment of consular relations or regional cooperation.

From the perspective of the Succession Regulation, the contributions identify many frictions between the harmonized procedural rules of this Regulation and the Conventions with third States. Further, the Regulation and the treaties do not always have the same scope of application, since some treaties are limited to movable or immovable successions. Nationality is used as connecting factor and choice of law is excluded. From a European perspective, there are few arguments to uphold the treaties because they hamper a uniform international succession law. At first sight, the best solution would be to denounce the treaties, or to at least bring them in line with the Succession Regulation. However, the book is not one sided and it discusses the application and interpretation of the treaties in third States. Here we learn that a large number of the treaties in question are still aligned with the private international law of those third States and that denunciation or attempts to renegotiate the treaties could have an impact on the relationship between Member States and third States. It seems that the treaties will be part of international succession law for a long time.

I am very proud to write the foreword for this unique and fascinating book which offers a cosmopolitan perspective. It covers an almost virgin territory and enables a wide readership to gain an insight into an underestimated part of the Succession Regulation. The high quality of the contributions makes this book a work of outstanding scholarship in the field of comparative private international law. It offers guidance for academics and practitioners and will stimulate and facilitate further comparative research.

Walter Pintens

CONTENTS

LIST OF TREATIES AND CONVENTIONS

The reader should be aware that not all treaties and conventions analyzed in the various country reports are reproduced in the Annex (p. 357). The working group decided to translate and reproduce only those agreements that may affect the Succession Regulation in one way or the other. This list of the reproduced treaty law includes treaties whose scope of application is disputed or not entirely clear, so that frictions with the Succession Regulation cannot be excluded *a priori*. As the treaties and conventions taking precedence over the Succession Regulation are often of a very general nature (legal assistance, friendship treaties, etc.), the translation was restricted to provisions that matter in cross-border inheritance cases. Treaties dealing mainly or even entirely with the recognition and enforcement of judgments of third States in an EU Member State were not translated, as those agreements do not interfere with the Succession Regulation's scope of application. Within the countries, the treaties are listed in alphabetical order following the common name of the Contracting State.

AUSTRIA

CROATIA

---

1 Austrian Bundesgesetzblatt No. 45/1966.

2 Austrian Bundesgesetzblatt No. 21/1960.

3 Austrian Bundesgesetzblatt No. 224/1955.

4 Službeni list Socijalističke Federativne Republike Jugoslavije – Dodatak: Međunarodni ugovori i drugi sporazumi, br. 5/63.

CZECH REPUBLIC

FINLAND

---

5 Vyhláška ministra zahraničních věcí č. 97/1960 Sb.
6 Vyhláška ministra zahraničních věcí č. 80/1981 Sb.
7 Vyhláška ministra zahraničních věcí č. 93/1989 Sb.
8 Vyhláška ministra zahraničních věcí č. 106/1978 Sb.
9 Vyhláška ministra zahraničních věcí č. 95/1983 Sb.
10 Sdělení Ministerstva zahraničních věcí č. 123/2002 Sb.m.s.
11 Sdělení Ministerstva zahraničních věcí č. 133/2003 Sb.m.s.
12 Vyhláška ministra zahraničních věcí č. 98/1984 Sb.
13 Vyhláška ministra zahraničních věcí č. 207/1964 Sb.
14 Suomen asetuskokoelman sopimussarja 21/1935, amendments Suomen säädöskokoelman sopimussarja 60/2015.

FRANCE

GERMANY

ITALY

SWEDEN

---

15 Suomen asetuskokoelman sopimussarja 48/1980.
16 Journal officiel de la République française, 02.02.1958, p. 1266.
17 Reichsgesetzblatt 1930 II, 1002.
18 Bundesgesetzblatt 1959 II, 233.
19 Reichsgesetzblatt 1930 II, 747.
20 Gazzetta Ufficiale del Regno d'Italia, No. 145 of 29.05.1865.
21 Gazzetta Ufficiale del Regno d'Italia, No. 265 of 14.11.1930.

OTHER EU MEMBER STATES

22 Službeni list Federativne Narodne Republike Jugoslavije – Dodatak: Međunarodni ugovori i drugi sporazumi, br. 1/57.

23 Recueil systématique du droit fédéral 0.142.113.721.

24 Resmi Gazete of 27.12.1939, No. 4395.

25 Službeni list Socijalističke Federativne Republike Jugoslavije – Dodatak: Međunarodni ugovori i drugi sporazumi, br. 3/68.

26 Službeni list Socijalističke Federativne Republike Jugoslavije – Dodatak: Međunarodni ugovori i drugi sporazumi, br. 5/63.

27 Službeni list Federativne Narodne Republike Jugoslavije – Dodatak: Međunarodni ugovori i drugi sporazumi, br. 8/61.

LIST OF ABBREVIATIONS

ABGB	Allgemeines Bürgerliches Gesetzbuch
AG	Amtsgericht, Attorney General
AJ Famille	Actualité Juridique Famille
Ankara L. Rev.	Ankara Law Review
ANP	Act on non-litigious procedure
ANPRS	Act on non-litigious procedure of the Republic Srpska
Art.	Article(s)
ATF	Arrêts du Tribunal Fédéral Suisse
ATRIO	Archivio dei trattati internazionali online
AÜHFD	Ankara Üniversitesi Hukuk Fakültesi Dergisi
AußStrG	Außerstreitgesetz
B&H	Bosnia and Herzegovina
BBl.	Bundesblatt
BerGesVR	Berichte der Deutschen Gesellschaft für Völkerrecht
BGB	Bürgerliches Gesetzbuch
BGBl.	Bundesgesetzblatt
BGE	Bundesgerichtsentscheidungen
BGer.	Bundesgerichtshof (Schweiz)
BGH	Bundesgerichtshof
BGHZ	Entscheidungen des Bundesgerichtshofes in Zivilsachen
BOA	Başbakanlık Osmanlı Arşivi
br.	broj
Brussels IIbis, IIa	Council Regulation (EC) No 2201/2003 of 27 November 2003 concerning jurisdiction and the recognition and enforcement of judgments in matrimonial matters and the matters of parental responsibility, repealing Regulation (EC) No 1347/2000
BS	Amtliche Sammlung des Bundesrechts
BVerfG	Bundesverfassungsgericht
BWNotZ	Zeitschrift für das Notariat in Baden-Württemberg
č.	číslo

Cass.	Corte di cassazione
Cass. civ.	Cour de cassation, chambre civile
CC	Civil Code
cf.	confer
Ch.	Chapter
Coll.	Collection
Destatis	Statistisches Bundesamt
DH. EUM. ECB	Dahiliye Nezareti Emniyet-i Umumiye Ecanib Kalemi
DIP	Droit international privé
dir.	director(s)
diss. op.	dissenting opinion
DNotI	Deutsches Notarinstitut
DNotZ	Deutsche Notar-Zeitschrift
DTJV	Deutsch-türkische Juristenvereinigung
EC	European Communities
ECJ	European Court of Justice
ECR	European Court Reports
ed., eds.	edition, editor(s)
e.g.	for example
EGBGB	Einführungsgesetz zum Bürgerlichen Gesetzbuche
ErbR	Zeitschrift für die gesamte erbrechtliche Praxis
esp.	especially
et al.	et alii
et seq., et seqq.	et sequens, et sequentes
etc.	et cetera
EU	European Union
EuErbVO	EU-Erbrechtsverordnung
Eurostat	Statistisches Amt der Europäischen Union
FamFG	Gesetz über das Verfahren in Familiensachen und in den Angelegenheiten der freiwilligen Gerichtsbarkeit
FamRZ	Zeitschrift für das gesamte Familienrecht
Fasc.	Fascicule
FB&H	Federation of Bosnia and Herzegovina
FNRY	Federal National Republic of Yugoslavia
FPRY	Federal People's Republic of Yugoslavia
FRY	Federal Republic of Yugoslavia

GBO	Grundbuchordnung
GP	Gesetzgebungsperiode
GPR	Zeitschrift für das Privatrecht der Europäischen Union
Grdz.	Grundzüge
HE	Hallituksen esitys
i.a.	inter alia
ibid.	ibidem
i.e.	id est
int., int'l	international
IPRax	Praxis des Internationalen Privat- und Verfahrensrechts
IPRspr	Die deutsche Rechtsprechung auf dem Gebiete des Internationalen Privatrechts
Istat	Italian National Institute of Statistics
İÜHFM	İstanbul Üniversitesi Hukuk Fakültesi Mecmuası
Iž	drugostepeni izvršni predmeti
JABl	Amtsblatt der österreichischen Justizverwaltung
JORF	Journal officiel de la République française
JORT	Journal officiel de la République tunisienne
JT	Journal des Tribunaux
LG	Landgericht
lit.	littera
m.	madde
Mac.	Macedonia
MB	Moniteur belge
MHB	Milletlerarası Hukuk ve Milletlerarası Özel Hukuk Bülteni
MittBayNot	Mitteilungen des Bayerischen Notarvereins, der Notarkasse und der Landesnotarkammer Bayern
m.m.	med mera
Mon.	Montenegro
MPI	Max-Planck-Institut
n.	note(s)
NIC	Nordic Inheritance Convention
NJW-RR	Neue Juristische Wochenschrift – Rechtsprechungs-Report
n°	numéro
No., Nos.	number, numbers
OGH	Oberster Gerichtshof

OJ	Official Journal of the European Union
OLG	Oberlandesgericht
p., pp.	page, pages
para.	paragraph(s)
PIL	Private international law
PILA	Private International Law Act
prop.	proposition
PŽ	Drugostepeni parnični predmeti
RCDIP	Revue critique de droit international privé
R.D.C.	Revue de droit commercial
RDIPP	Rivista di diritto internazionale privato e processuale
Rép not.	Répertoire notarial
Rev. Dipr. be.	Revue de droit international privé
RGBl.	Reichsgesetzblatt
RNotZ	Rheinische Notar-Zeitschrift
RS	Recueil systématique du droit fédéral
RS	Republika Srpska
SAFBH	Succession Act of the Federation of Bosnia and Herzegovina
Sb.	Sbírka zákonů
Sb.m.s.	Sbírka mezinárodních smluv
Sec.	Section(s)
SFRY	Socialist Federal Republic of Yugoslavia
SopS	Suomen asetuskokoelman sopimussarja, Suomen säädöskokoelman sopimussarja
SOU	Statens offentliga utredningar
spec.	specifically
SR	Succession Regulation [Regulation (EU) No. 650/2012 of the European Parliament and of the Council of 4 July 2012 on jurisdiction, applicable law, recognition and enforcement of decisions and acceptance and enforcement of authentic instruments in matters of succession and on the creation of a European Certificate of Succession]
SSSR	Savez Sovjetskih Socijalističkih Republika
SÜHFD	Selçuk Üniversitesi Hukuk Fakültesi Dergisi
supp.	supplement
t.	tome

TFEU	Treaty on the Functioning of the European Union
TPA	Treaty between the Republic of Finland with the Union of Soviet Socialist Republics Concerning the Provision of Legal Protection and Legal Assistance in Civil, Family and Criminal Cases of 11 August 1978
Trib.	Tribunale
UK	United Kingdom
UNIDROIT	International Institute for the Unification of Private Law
US	United States
USSR	Union of Soviet Socialist Republics
v.	versus
vol.	volume
vp	valtiopäivät
YbPIL	Yearbook of Private International Law
ZErb	Zeitschrift für die Steuer- und Erbrechtspraxis
ZEV	Zeitschrift für Erbrecht und Vermögensnachfolge

LIST OF CONTRIBUTORS

Davor Babić
Prof. Dr., University of Zagreb, Croatia

Andrea Bonomi
Prof. Dr., University of Lausanne, Switzerland

Slavko Đorđević
Prof. Dr., University of Kragujevac, Serbia

Anatol Dutta
Prof. Dr., M. Jur. (Oxford), Ludwig Maximilians University of Munich, Germany

Stéphanie Francq
Prof. Dr., LL.M. (Berkeley), Catholic University of Louvain, Belgium

Pietro Franzina
Prof. Dr., University of Ferrara, Italy

Samuel Fulli-Lemaire
Dr., (now) Maître de conférences, Panthéon-Assas (Paris II) University, France

Biset Sena Güneş
LL.M. (London), University of Ankara Yıldırım Beyazıt, Turkey

Markku Helin
Prof. em. Dr., University of Turku, Finland

Tena Hoško
Assistant Prof. Dr., University of Zagreb, Croatia

Dirk Looschelders
Prof. Dr., University of Düsseldorf, Germany

Julie Mary
LL.M. (Vienna), Research Assistant, Lawyer, Catholic University of Louvain, Belgium

Zlatan Meškić
Prof. Dr., University of Zenica, Bosnia and Herzegovina

Magdalena Pfeiffer
Associate Prof. Dr., Charles University, Prague, Czech Republic

Walter Pintens
Prof. em. Dr., Catholic University of Leuven, Belgium

Claudia Rudolf
Associate Prof. Dr., University of Vienna, Austria

Wolfgang Wurmnest
Prof. Dr., LL.M. (Berkeley), University of Augsburg, Germany

Nadjma Yassari
PD Dr., LL.M. (SOAS), Max Planck Institute for Comparative and International Private Law, Hamburg, Germany

INTRODUCTION

Anatol DUTTA and Wolfgang WURMNEST

In the last decade, the European Union (EU) has unified large segments of private international law for its Member States. The enacted Regulations take precedence over national private international law rules and also over international treaties concluded between the Member States, as far as EU law does not provide otherwise.[1] However, existing bilateral and multilateral treaties concluded by Member States with third States enjoy priority over European private international law rules. This priority rule, which can be found in most of the private international law Regulations adopted so far, has been described as the 'Achilles heel' of the European conflict-of-law system. It hampers the uniform application of EU law and creates friction with harmonized procedural rules. In addition, the legal relationships for a considerable number of third State citizens and – as far as the treaties are universally applicable – even all covered relationships are not governed by EU private international law but by rules laid down in international treaties, which in part date back to the beginning of the 20th century.

The implications of this pluralism on the functioning of the rather new European private international law rules have not yet been explored in depth. The various international treaties or conventions concluded by the current Member States have neither been comprehensively collected nor has their content been analyzed in a systematic manner. This book, which is the fruit of an international working group set up by the Universities of Augsburg and Munich in 2017, aims to partly fill this gap by starting with a kind of 'test drilling' in the area of succession upon death. Reporters from various EU Member States loosely representing the 'four corners of the EU' analyze the scope and effect of treaties and conventions concluded by their countries with third States in the area of succession law and analyze their impact on the functioning of the European Succession Regulation (Regulation No. 650/2012, hereafter: SR).[2] As

1 Cf. European Union Perspective, A. DUTTA, section 2.

2 Regulation (EU) 650/2012 of the European Parliament and of the Council of 04.07.2012 on jurisdiction, applicable law, recognition and enforcement of decisions and acceptance and enforcement of authentic instruments in matters of succession and on the creation of a European Certificate of Succession [2012] OJ L201/107.

in other EU instruments, Article 75(1)1 SR provides that its rules do not affect bilateral treaties concluded with third States before the Regulation was enacted. The reports contained in this book cover Austria, Belgium, Croatia, the Czech Republic, Finland, France, Germany, Italy and Sweden. The comparative report at the end of this book also takes into account treaties concluded by Estonia[3] and (without claiming completeness) by Greece.[4] In addition, reporters of selected third States represent their views on the treaties and conventions concluded by their countries with EU Member States. The book contains contributions from Iran, Turkey and Switzerland as well as the States succeeding to former Yugoslavia that are not EU Member States (Bosnia and Herzegovina, Serbia, Montenegro and North Macedonia). These countries were chosen as many of their citizens live and work in the EU.

The country reports pursue five goals:

- *Compilation and translation of the relevant legal sources*: Firstly, all bilateral treaties and multilateral conventions concluded by selected Member States with third States which take precedence over the Succession Regulation, especially its conflict rules in Articles 20 et seq. SR, are compiled to provide an overview on the private international law rules applied by courts in the various EU States. Such an overview thus far exists only for individual Member States. In addition, treaty provisions that are relevant for the field of succession upon death have been translated into English in order to lay the foundation for a cross-border analysis of these legal texts.
- *Analyzing the background of these sources*: Secondly, the historical and political background of the bilateral treaties and multilateral conventions are analyzed from the perspective of the nation State. This analysis is important to understand whether and to what extent these treaties or conventions are vital for the Member States.
- *Determination of the scope of application*: Thirdly, the scope of application of these sources is determined (especially *ratione personae* and *ratione materiae*). In addition, the impact of the treaties is assessed. Are its rules applied in practice by courts and notaries when dealing with cases of succession? If so, are many cases affected? Defining the precise scope of application is crucial to the question of whether and how these sources affect the uniform application of EU private international law: the narrower the scope of these treaties and conventions, the less that EU private international law is affected. These issues have so far not been examined at a cross-border level.

---

3 The Estonian reporter could not hand in her final report, but she provided some general information that could be used for the comparative report.

4 The information about one treaty Greece has concluded is taken from the Swiss report.

- *Detecting friction with harmonized procedural rules*: Fourthly, it is to be assessed how the treaties with third States affect – in practice – the functioning of the European procedural rules for succession cases. Problems may arise with regard to the newly introduced European Certificate of Succession (Articles 62 et seq. SR) or with regard to issues of jurisdiction (Articles 4 et seq. SR). Further, it seems likely that courts will deal differently with friction resulting from rules laid down in treaties with third States. In such instances it is determined how to best restore the coherence and uniform application of EU law.
- *Application and interpretation in third States*: Finally, it is important to understand how third States apply and interpret these treaties and conventions. Such a 'bilateral' perspective is important for detecting discrepancies in the interpretation of sources by the courts of Member States and third States which hamper the uniform application of these instruments. If the analysis reveals that the courts of some third States do not apply the relevant bilateral treaties, the Member States that have concluded these treaties would have good arguments for their termination or modification with the aim of strengthening the European private international law system.

The last two points have already made clear that the perspective of nation States, be they EU Member States or third States, is only one facet of the analysis. The EU perspective has also to be considered. The European Union has enacted the European Succession Regulation to unify the rules of private international law. The Regulation also contains rules on jurisdiction and rules for a European Certificate of Succession. The conflict and jurisdiction rules of the Succession Regulation follow mainly the residence principle and use the last habitual residence of the deceased as a connecting factor (Articles 4, 21(1) SR); nationality and the location of the assets play a secondary role only. When the Regulation was negotiated, the EU did not pay too much attention to treaties with third States, which take precedence pursuant to Article 75(1)1 SR, given that many Member States were not ready to terminate or alter those agreements for various reasons and it was more important to put a European order in place. The EU Commission, or more precisely the expert group assembled by the German Notary Institute which prepared the Regulation, took notice of some of the treaties.[5] But the questions of how much these treaties affect the Regulation and how its rules can be reconciled with these treaties were not touched upon by the expert group. Against this background, this book contains two contributions on

5 Deutsches Notarinstitut, 'Rechtsvergleichende Studie der erbrechtlichen Regelungen des Internationalen Verfahrensrechtes und Internationalen Privatrechts der Mitgliedsstaaten der Europäischen Union', p. 232 <ec.europa.eu/civiljustice/publications/docs/testaments_successions_de.pdf> accessed 08.04.2019.

the EU perspective. The first will focus on the powers of the EU to force Member States to terminate these agreements; and the second contains a comparative report on the impact of these instruments on the functioning of the European Succession Regulation.

As to the scope of the book, the focus lies on special national or regional treaties and/or conventions between Member States and third States – i.e. States which do not participate in the Succession Regulation – taking precedence over the Succession Regulation. International conventions that deal with substantive law, such as the UNIDROIT Convention providing a Uniform Law on the Form of an International Will of 26 October 1973 and the Hague Convention Concerning the International Administration of the Estates of Deceased Persons of 2 October 1973, are not analyzed. The same holds true for the Hague Convention on the Conflicts of Laws Relating to the Form of Testamentary Dispositions of 5 October 1961 that has been explicitly accommodated with the Succession Regulation (see Article 75(1)2 SR).

We gratefully acknowledge the help of Lena Franke, Maria Guggemos, Lilian Gutkin, Patricia Jauch, Maximilian Kübler-Wachendorff, Sylvia Lech-Hallwachs, Julia Ranzinger, Katharina Teifel and Simon Zechmann (all Augsburg) for their help in organizing the Augsburg conference in November 2017. The editing process was coordinated by Felix Aiwanger (Munich) and Benedikt Wössner (Augsburg) and supported by Veronika Anselm, Sara Schmidt, Bernhard Brechmann, Philipp Melzer (all Munich) and Merlin Gömann (Augsburg/Berlin). Michael Friedman (Hamburg) read the contributions and translations and suggested stylistic improvements. We are also indebted to Professor Walter Pintens (Leuven/Saarbrücken) and Dr Johannes Weber (German Notary Institute), who participated in the workshop in November 2017, and Maarja Torga (University of Tartu), who provided valuable information about the legal situation in Estonia to the editors, including translations of some treaty rules. We are further grateful to Ann-Christin Maak-Scherpe and Rebecca Moffat of Intersentia's Cambridge office for strongly supporting this book even though some of their colleagues might think that it was made for 'specialists amongst the specialists'. Finally, we want to thank the *Bundesnotarkammer*, which showed no hesitation in very generously supporting the Augsburg conference.

QUESTIONNAIRE

Anatol Dutta and Wolfgang Wurmnest

The contributors were equipped with the following questionnaire in order to structure their reports.

1. INTRODUCTION

Each report should address the following points. The questionnaire should, however, not be regarded as exhaustive. If in a certain jurisdiction or region other problems or challenges arise, those issues should be discussed as well. The draft structure outlined below might be a possible framework, but variations might be necessary for some jurisdictions.

2. TREATIES AND CONVENTIONS TAKING PRECEDENCE OVER THE EUROPEAN SUCCESSION REGULATION

- Has your jurisdiction ratified one or more bilateral treaty/ies or multilateral convention(s) (hereafter: 'treaty' or 'treaties') that take precedence over the rules of the European Succession Regulation (hereafter: 'SR') pursuant to Article 75 SR?
- If so, please provide a comprehensive list of those treaties, describe their (historical, social and/or economic) background and provide an official source (Official Journal or the like).
- Describe for each treaty its scope of application (*ratione materiae*, *ratione personae*). The following issues might in particular be of interest:
  - Which issues of succession law are covered by the treaties (intestate succession, succession by testamentary disposition, forced heirship, testamentary executors, administration, special succession regimes for certain assets)? Are areas of law connected to succession covered, e.g. matrimonial property rights of the surviving spouse, family status, etc.?

- Does the treaty cover assets located solely in the Contracting States or also assets located in other States? Which rules govern the localization of assets, notably intangible assets? If property located in other States is not covered, which rules of private international law would a judge apply to those assets? This latter issue should be discussed in the section on private international law.
- If the treaty applies only to nationals of the Contracting States, please explain how multiple nationalities are dealt with (i.e. instances where a person holds a passport from each of the Contracting States or where a person holds a passport from a Contracting State and also from another State).

3. PRIVATE INTERNATIONAL LAW OF THE TREATY REGIMES

- Describe the private international law rules contained in those treaties in more detail. What are the relevant connecting factors? Does the treaty distinguish between movable and immovable assets? If so, which rules define the movable or immovable nature of an asset, e.g. as to shares in a company which owns immovables? Does the treaty contain special rules on the validity of testamentary dispositions? If not, which rules apply (the general conflict rule of the treaty or the SR)? Are other succession law issues subject to special rules? You may use hypotheticals to illustrate your description or refer to case law (if there is any).
- Describe the differences in the conflict-of-law rules in the treaties and the rules laid down in the SR. Hypotheticals may be used for illustrative purposes.
- Do the courts or other authorities competent to deal with successions in your jurisdiction actually apply the rules of the treaties?
- Do the courts or other authorities competent to deal with successions in your jurisdiction try to interpret the provisions of the treaties narrowly to avoid friction with the SR?
- Do the treaties (potentially) affect many succession cases in your country? To bolster your findings you may add context material (statistics and the like), e.g. where a sizable minority of your country is affected by the treaties.

4. PROCEDURAL ISSUES

- Do the treaties contain rules on jurisdiction in succession matters? If so, please describe those rules.

- Do the treaties contain rules on the recognition and enforcement of decisions in succession matters? If so, please describe those rules. Do those rules apply to succession certificates or comparable documents?
- Do the treaties vest consular staff of the respective foreign Contracting State(s) with special powers as to the administration of the estate?
- Do the courts or other authorities competent to deal with successions in your jurisdiction issue European Certificates of Succession pursuant to Articles 62 et seq. SR if the treaty is applicable and defines the applicable law or jurisdiction?

5. THE FUTURE OF EXISTING TREATIES AND CONVENTIONS WITH THIRD STATES

- Has the government of your country voiced any plans to terminate/modify the treaties based on the aim of strengthening the uniform application of EU law? Alternatively, has the government voiced – or is it your view – that these treaties must remain in force as they are vital for your country, be it for reasons of interior policy (social cohesion, minority policy) or the external relations of your country?
- What is the (majority) view of the local legal community with regard to the existence of the treaties (useful instruments, outdated obstacles to legal harmonization or the like)?
- Can you conceive of modifications to the treaties in order to, on the one hand, fulfil the political exigencies of your country and, on the other hand, diminish the degree to which a uniform application of the SR is being impaired?

6. ANNEX

Please provide the relevant articles of the treaties in their original version and in a translated English version.

PART I

THE PERSPECTIVE OF EU MEMBER STATES

THE EXTERNAL RELATIONS OF AUSTRIA

Claudia RUDOLF*

* I would like to thank Sarah Kohlweg for her support.

1. INTRODUCTION

Austria is bound by the Hague Convention of 5 October 1961 on the Conflicts of Laws Relating to the Form of Testamentary Dispositions[1] and is party to several treaties regarding matters of succession such as legal assistance, consular rights, applicable law, jurisdiction and mutual recognition and enforcement of decisions.[2] Treaties with Member States remain applicable to the extent that they concern matters that do not fall under the scope of the European Succession Regulation (Article 75(2)), e.g. obligations of notification and consular rights of participation.[3] Treaties with third States (within the meaning of the Succession Regulation), on the other hand, take precedence over the Succession Regulation, as is provided by Article 75(1) SR. However, to the extent that treaties with third States covers matters which do not relate to the subjects of the Succession Regulation, e.g. the recognition and enforcement of decisions given in third States, there is no conflict in application triggering the provisions of Article 75(1) SR.

---

1 Bundesgesetzblatt (henceforth referred to as BGBl.) No. 295/1963.

2 The texts of the treaties can be accessed at <http://www.ris.bka.gv.at> accessed 11.06.2019, by entering the respective numbers (Greece (RGBl No. 169/1856, BGBl. No. 139/1921, JABl 1951, 42); United States of America (BGBl. No. 192/1931); Federative People's Republic of Yugoslavia (BGBl. No. 224/1955); Union of Soviet Socialist Republics (BGBl. No. 21/1960); Germany (BGBl. No. 105/1960); Belgium (BGBl. No. 287/1961); Czech Republic (BGBl. No. 309/1962, BGBl. No. 123/1997); Slovak Republic (BGBl. No. 309/1962, BGBl. No. 1046/1994); Switzerland (BGBl. No. 125/1962); United Kingdom of Great Britain and Northern Ireland (BGBl. No. 224/1962, BGBl. No. 416/1980); Netherlands (BGBl. No. 37/1966); Iranian Empire (BGBl. No. 45/1966); France (BGBl. No. 288/1967); Hungary (BGBl. No. 306/1967; BGBl. No. 146/1977); British Columbia (BGBl. No. 314/1970); Poland (BGBl. No. 79/1974); Luxembourg (BGBl. No. 610/1975); Bulgaria (BGBl. No. 342/1976); Tunisia (BGBl. No. 305/1980); Spain (BGBl. No. 373/1985); Italy (BGBl. No. 472/1989); and Turkey (BGBl. No. 571/1992).

3 Cf. for Austria R. Fucik in A. Deixler-Hübner and M. Schauer (eds.), *Kommentar zur EU-Erbrechtsverordnung*, 2nd ed., Manz, Wien 2019, Art. 75 EuErbVO para. 4, 14–21.

1.1. OVERVIEW

The following treaties between Austria and third States take precedence over the Succession Regulation:

- the Agreement between the Republic of Austria and the Federal People's Republic of Yugoslavia on Mutual Legal Assistance Including the Final Protocol (**Treaty 3**);
- the Treaty on Consular Relations between the Republic of Austria and the Union of Soviet Socialist Republics (**Treaty 2**); and
- the Treaty of Friendship and Establishment between the Republic of Austria and the Persian Empire (**Treaty 1**).

The Treaty with the Union of Soviet Socialist Republics and the Treaty with Yugoslavia take precedence over the provisions of the Succession Regulation on international jurisdiction and conflict of laws. The Treaty with Iran takes precedence only over the provisions on conflict of laws. Following the disintegration of Yugoslavia, the Treaty continues to apply to its successor States, namely Bosnia and Herzegovina, Croatia, Kosovo, North Macedonia (henceforth: 'Macedonia'), Montenegro, Serbia and Slovenia. Since Croatia and Slovenia have become EU Member States, the Succession Regulation takes precedence over the Treaty. The Treaty with the Soviet Union on the other hand continues to apply only to Russia and not to any other successor States of the Union of Soviet Socialist Republics.

1.2. TREATY WITH YUGOSLAVIA

1.2.1. Background

Up to 1938, mutual legal assistance between Austria and Yugoslavia was governed by a Treaty signed on 1 May 1928.[4] This Treaty laid down provisions on succession to the estate of a deceased person. After 1945, the changed political, economic and organizational conditions in Yugoslavia prevented the Treaty from being reinstated.[5]

The present Agreement between the Republic of Austria and the Federal People's Republic of Yugoslavia on Mutual Legal Assistance Including the Final

4 Promulgated in BGBl. No. 100/1929.

5 Regierungsvorlage vom 23.03.1955, 489 der Beilagen zu den stenographischen Protokollen des Nationalrates VII. GP, p. 15.

Protocol (**Treaty 3**; henceforth referred to as the Treaty with former Yugoslavia)[6] was signed on 16 December 1954 and entered into force on 12 December 1955. Both the German and the Serbo-Croatian versions are authentic (Article 49 of the Treaty, Final Provision of the Protocol). The Treaty with former Yugoslavia continues to apply to legal relations with Bosnia and Herzegovina,[7] Croatia,[8] Kosovo,[9] Macedonia,[10] Montenegro,[11] Serbia[12] and Slovenia[13] as a bilateral treaty. The Succession Regulation takes precedence over the Treaty to the extent of its scope in relation to the EU Member States of Slovenia[14] and Croatia.

1.2.2. Scope of Application

The Treaty with former Yugoslavia contains provisions on mutual legal assistance in matters of both private and criminal law. Its third part (Articles 29 to 40) is dedicated to matters of succession to the estate of a deceased person and aims to establish equality between nationals and citizens of the other Contracting State in these matters.[15]

The provisions on succession apply to testamentary and intestate succession as well as to reserved shares and legacies. They apply to both contentious and non-contentious proceedings on successions. There are no particular rules laid down for specific goods or matrimonial property.

There is no general rule on whether or not an estate located in a third State falls under the scope of the Treaty with former Yugoslavia. Article 29 of the Treaty, for example, is applicable exclusively to an estate located in the respective 'other' Contracting State. The same is provided for international jurisdiction on the succession to immovable property (Article 30 of the Treaty). Similarly, the provision on recognition and enforcement of decisions and the issuing of movable property (Article 31(2) and (4) of the Treaty) applies only to an estate

---

6 Promulgated in BGBl. No. 224/1955.

7 Regarding relations with Bosnia and Herzegovina, the Treaty with former Yugoslavia applies on the grounds of the principle of continuity under international law. A. Duchek, W. Schütz and I. Tarko, *Zwischenstaatlicher Rechtsverkehr in Zivilrechtssachen*², Manz Verlag, Wien 1998, p. 601; M. Potyka and T. Traar 'Verlassenschaftssachen', in A. Burgstaller, M. Neumayr, A. Geroldinger and G. Schmaranzer (eds.), *Internationales Zivilverfahrensrecht*, LexisNexis, Wien 2014, Chapter 61, para. 39, n. 80; Austrian Supreme Court (henceforth referred to as OGH) 04.04.2000, 10 ObS 347/99y; OGH 21.05.2014, 3 Ob 121/13k.

8 BGBl. No. 474/1996; cf. OGH 10.04.2014, 6 Ob 59/14s.

9 BGBl. III No. 147/2010.

10 BGBl. III No. 92/1997.

11 BGBl. III No. 124/2007.

12 BGBl. III No. 156/1997.

13 BGBl. No. 714/1993.

14 R. Fucik, above n. 3, Art. 75 EuErbVO para. 17.

15 Regierungsvorlage vom 23.03.1955, 489 der Beilagen zu den stenographischen Protokollen des Nationalrates VII. GP, p. 16.

located in the other Contracting State. Article 31(1) of the Treaty, however, does not restrict the international jurisdiction of the courts of the home State of the deceased to an estate located on certain territory in matters concerning movable property. The international jurisdiction of the courts of the State of last domicile, on the other hand, is restricted to movable property located on the territory of this State (Article 36(1) of the Treaty). It can therefore be concluded that where, for example, the estate of a Serbian citizen falls under the jurisdiction of Austrian courts, the jurisdiction of these courts is, in accordance with Article 30 and Article 36(1) of the Treaty, restricted to movable and immovable property located on Austrian territory.[16]

The connecting factor is not the nationality of the heirs or legatees, but the nationality of the deceased. There is no explicit provision on persons possessing multiple nationalities. Articles 32, 33(1), 36(1) and 37 of the Treaty speak of 'citizens of the other Contracting State'; consequently, the Treaty with former Yugoslavia does not apply to deceased possessing the nationalities of both Contracting States. The same can be said for Article 29(1) of the Treaty, which refers alternatively to 'national law' or the law of the 'other Contracting State', for Article 36(2) of the Treaty, which refers to the 'succession law of the State of his nationality', and for Article 38 of the Treaty, which entitles consular representatives to represent citizens of 'their State' in matters of succession. A further argument is that the principle of equal treatment with nationals ceases to have effect if a person is a citizen of both Contracting States. The Treaty with former Yugoslavia therefore does not apply to the estate of a deceased who held the citizenship of both Contracting States.

The provisions mentioned above do not explicitly exclude the application of the Treaty with former Yugoslavia to the estate of deceased possessing the nationality of both a Contracting State and a third State, provided the nationality of the Contracting State is the closest connecting nationality. The principle of equal treatment with nationals is effective in this case as well. However, a prerequisite for the application of the Treaty with former Yugoslavia to matters of multiple nationalities should be that both Contracting States consider the closest connecting nationality to be sufficient and apply the Treaty. In Austrian legal literature[17] the general view is that treaties with third States do not apply to citizens possessing multiple nationalities. The preparatory works reveal nothing on this subject; as far as can be seen, there is no Austrian case law on this subject either.

---

16 See also the statement by the Ministry of Justice, BMJ-Z30.061/0004-I 9/2017.

17 M. Potyka and T. Traar, above n. 7, para. 8; T. Traar in A. Burgstaller, M. Neumayr, A. Geroldinger and G. Schmaranzer (eds.), *Die EU-Erbrechtsverordnung*, LexisNexis, Wien 2016, Art. 75 EuErbVO para. 6.

1.3. TREATY WITH THE SOVIET UNION

1.3.1. Background

The Treaty on Consular Relations between the Republic of Austria and the Union of Soviet Socialist Republics (**Treaty 2**; henceforth referred to as the Treaty with the former Soviet Union)[18] was signed on 28 February 1959 and entered into force on 19 January 1960. On 31 May 1974, a Protocol[19] was added to the Treaty. Both the German and the Russian versions are authentic and have equal significance for interpretation purposes (Article 33(2) of the Treaty, Final Provisions of the Protocol). Pursuant to the Exchange of Notes Concerning Treaty Relations between Austria and the Russian Federation[20] that took place on 15 June 1993 after the disintegration of the Soviet Union, the Treaty continues to apply to relations between Austria and Russia (Group II, 12). The Final Provisions of the Protocol provide that within the context of the Treaty, 'Union of Soviet Socialist Republics', 'USSR' or 'Soviet' is to be read as 'Russian Federation' and 'Russian' respectively. The Treaty with the former Soviet Union does not apply to relations with other successor States of the Union of Soviet Socialist Republics.

The Preamble sets out the regulation of consular affairs between Austria and the Russian Federation as the objective of the Treaty with the former Soviet Union. Consular representatives are to promote, within the scope of their capacity, the strengthening of the friendly relationship as well as the advancement of economic transactions between the Russian Federation and Austria (Article 14 of the Treaty).

1.3.2. Scope of Application

In accordance with its objectives, the Treaty with the former Soviet Union governs the establishment of consular offices, the appointment of consular representatives (including their rights, privileges, immunities, functions and capacities) and also issues concerning consular staff. Its third section, concerning the capacities of consular representatives, contains provisions on international jurisdiction and conflict-of-laws rules for matters of succession.[21] From these provisions it can be inferred that intestate and testamentary succession

---

18 Promulgated in BGBl. No. 21/1960.

19 Protocol to the Treaty of Consular Relations between the Republic of Austria and the Union of Soviet Socialist Republics, promulgated in BGBl. No. 459/1975, entry into force 03.09.1975.

20 Promulgated in BGBl. No. 257/1994. The Exchange of Notes entry into force 09.03.1994.

21 M. Potyka and T. Traar, above n. 7, para. 51 describe this as atypical for a Consular Agreement.

(Article 23(1)) as well as the satisfaction and securing of claims (Article 24(1) and (2)) fall under the scope of the Treaty with the former Soviet Union. Other provisions concern the capacities of consular representatives regarding estates left by citizens of the sending State (e.g. Article 21(2) or Article 22(1) lit. b of the Treaty).

Estate assets located in a third State do not fall under the scope of the provisions on international jurisdiction and on conflict of laws (Article 23(1) and (2), Article 24(3) and Article 26 of the Treaty). The text suggests that the Treaty with the former Soviet Union applies only to movables and immovables left by a citizen of the sending State located in Austria or Russia (as receiving States).[22]

However, a differentiated regime governs the personal scope of the Treaty with the former Soviet Union. To give an example, consular representatives have, on the one hand, within the scope of their competence the power to protect the rights and interests of citizens of the sending State (Article 15(1) of the Treaty) as well as the capacity to draft testaments for citizens of this State (Article 19 Point 2 of the Treaty). On the other hand, their capacity to issue visas is not limited to citizens of the receiving State. They can issue visas to 'their' citizens as well as to citizens of foreign States (Article 17 Point 2 of the Treaty). Moreover, Russian and Austrian consular representatives have, under certain circumstances, the right to draft and authenticate treaties between citizens of the sending State and citizens of the receiving State or of third States (Article 19 Point 4 of the Treaty).

The provisions on international jurisdiction and on conflict of laws – specifically Article 23(1) and Article 26 – refer to 'citizens of the sending State'. Neither the Treaty itself nor the Austrian preparatory works explicitly state whether the Treaty with the former Soviet Union applies to persons possessing multiple nationalities. Assuming that, in general, the capacities of consular representatives serve the protection of the rights and interests of citizens of the sending State on the territory of the 'foreign' receiving State, dual citizens holding both Austrian and a Russian citizenship require consular protection on neither Russian nor Austrian territory. Persons possessing multiple nationalities including that of a third State can, however, enjoy the protection of a Russian consular representative on Austrian territory only if they are considered Russian citizens in the context of the Treaty with the former Soviet Union (and vice versa). As far as can be ascertained, there is no Austrian case law on this subject. In Austrian legal literature[23] the general view is that treaties with third States do not apply to persons possessing multiple nationalities. The provisions on international jurisdiction and conflict of laws require the deceased

22 Likewise, Regierungsvorlage vom 09.09.1959, 39 der Beilagen zu den stenographischen Protokollen des Nationalrates IX. GP, pp. 27 and 29.

23 M. Potyka and T. Traar, above n. 7, para. 8; T. Traar, above n. 17, Art. 75 EuErbVO para. 6.

to be a citizen of the sending State (Article 23(1) and Article 26 of the Treaty).[24] Because the Treaty differentiates between citizens of the sending State, of the receiving State and of third States in other provisions, it can be assumed that the present provisions apply only to deceased who were citizens of exclusively one Contracting State.

1.4. TREATY WITH IRAN

1.4.1. Background

On 23 September 1936, Austria and Iran signed a Treaty of Friendship and Arbitration, and on 1 June 1937 they signed a Treaty of Establishment. However, as a result of the events of 1938 these Treaties never entered into force. Starting in 1950 the present Treaty of Friendship and Establishment (**Treaty 1**; henceforth referred to as the Austrian-Iranian Treaty) was prepared by means of written correspondence (cf. the Preamble). This new Treaty is in large parts based on the Austrian-Iranian Treaties of 1936 and 1937, but it further contains provisions consistent with those found in the Swiss-Iranian Treaty of Establishment as well as the Treaty of Establishment between the UK and Iran. As a novel provision, the principle of equal treatment with the citizens of the most favoured nation was included.[25]

The Treaty of Friendship and Establishment was signed on 9 September 1959 and entered into force on 16 March 1966.[26] The Treaty was composed in German, Persian and French versions, all of which are authentic versions of the Treaty. In the event of disputes in interpretation, the French-language version is binding (Article 16 of the Treaty).

According to the Preamble of the Treaty, its objectives are a tightening of the bond of friendship between the Contracting Parties (Article 1 of the Treaty) and an increase in economic and technological cooperation. Furthermore, the Treaty aims to govern the right of establishment of Austrian and Iranian citizens on the territory of the other Contracting Party. Article 10(3) and (4) as well as Article 11 of the Treaty lay down, among other rules, rules concerning succession to the estates of deceased persons.

The principle of equality provides two ways in which the objects stated in the Preamble are to be achieved. Firstly, citizens of Iran enjoy equal treatment with the citizens of the most favoured nation in Austria and vice versa on the basis

---

24 Regierungsvorlage vom 09 September 1959, 39 der Beilagen zu den stenographischen Protokollen des Nationalrates IX. GP, pp. 27–28.

25 Regierungsvorlage vom 31.05.1960, 217 der Beilagen zu den stenographischen Protokollen des Nationalrates IX. GP, p. 10.

26 Promulgated in BGBl. No. 45/1966.

of reciprocity. Secondly, they enjoy equal treatment with Austrian citizens and vice versa. The first variant, called the most-favoured-nation clause, is predominant. It applies to the treatment accorded members of the diplomatic or consular authorities of the Contracting Parties (Article 2 of the Treaty), on the one hand, and to the treatment of citizens of the Contracting Parties (Article 3(3) of the Treaty) on the other hand. It further applies to the pursuit of self-employed activities carried out by citizens of a Contracting Party (Article 5(1) of the Treaty), to activities of companies (Article 6(3) of the Treaty), to the acquisition of property and to the judicial and official protection of persons and property (Article 8, Article 10(1) of the Treaty). However, the most-favoured-nation clause does not apply to paid employment activities and does not provide equal treatment with citizens of third States who enjoy privileges granted by a multilateral treaty (Article 14 of the Treaty). Equal treatment with nationals – meaning that citizens of Iran enjoy equal treatment with Austrian citizens and vice versa – is provided in matters of internal taxes (Article 7 of the Treaty) and legal aid (Article 5 of the Declaration concerning assistance to the poor and the *cautio judicatum solvi*).

1.4.2. Scope of Application

Further, the Austrian-Iranian Treaty lays down rules regarding succession. Article 10(3) of the Treaty provides that, among other matters,[27] intestate and testamentary succession fall within the material scope of the Treaty. The second sentence of Article 10(4) governs the formal validity of testaments; Article 11 of the Treaty governs the requirements for consular intervention and the powers consular representatives have for this purpose.

The Austrian-Iranian Treaty neither describes the legal matters falling under the scope of 'intestate succession' and 'testamentary succession' nor does it contain a list of matters excluded from the Treaty's scope of application. Under my assessment, this suggests a broad definition of the term 'succession', including in its scope the administration of estates, e.g. the power to represent or responsibility for debts under the succession. This interpretation is supported by Article 11(1) of the Treaty, which provides that consular representatives and administrators appointed for this purpose can, under certain circumstances, carry out the liquidation themselves. The Austrian preparatory works, too, do not contain a clarification of the term 'succession'. Instead, they record in a general manner that the Treaty lays down 'provisions concerning the estate'.[28]

---

[27] Article 10(3) of the Treaty further encompasses matters of marriage, matrimonial property regimes, divorce, legal separation, dowry, paternity, descent, adoption, legal capacity, majority and tutelage.

[28] Regierungsvorlage vom 31.05.1960, 217 der Beilagen zu den stenographischen Protokollen des Nationalrates IX. GP, p. 10.

There is merely one exception. The preparatory works interpret the term 'testament' within the meaning of French legal terminology. Therefore, the term 'testament' includes only unilaterally revocable dispositions of property upon death.[29] This is in accordance with Austrian legal terminology and excludes agreements as to succession from the scope of the Treaty.

As far as can be ascertained, it is not discussed in Austrian legal literature whether or not estate assets located in third States fall under the scope of the Austrian-Iranian Treaty. In general, very little case law exists on the subject of this Treaty – and this specific question is not addressed at all. A statement by the Ministry of Justice[30] suggests that treaties, which take precedence over the European Succession Regulation, do not apply to estates located in a third State. Article 10(3) of the Treaty provides that the citizens of one Contracting Party remain, on the territory of the other Contracting Party, bound by their national law in matters of intestate and testamentary succession. The wording 'on the territory of the other Contracting Party' does not, according to the assessment of the present author, lead to the assumption that the Treaty is limited to estate assets located on Iranian or Austrian territory. Rather, Article 10(3) of the Treaty is merely to be understood in the sense that citizens of Iran remain, on Austrian territory, bound by Iranian law (and vice versa) in the matters mentioned above.[31] From an Austrian perspective, §106 Jurisdiktionsnorm (Act of Court Jurisdiction),[32] which restricts the international jurisdiction of Austrian courts to estates located in Austria, must be taken into account in certain circumstances (cf. the section on procedural issues).

Article 11(1) of the Treaty, on the other hand, includes an explicit territorial restriction of consular intervention concerning an estate. Under certain circumstances, such intervention may be restricted to estate assets of Austrian citizens located in Iran and to estate assets of Iranian citizens located in Austria.

Article 10(3) of the Treaty speaks of 'the citizens of one of the High Contracting Parties'. The question arises whether the Austrian-Iranian Treaty is applicable only to the estate of a deceased who was a citizen exclusively of one

---

29 Regierungsvorlage vom 31.05.1960, 217 der Beilagen zu den stenographischen Protokollen des Nationalrates IX. GP, p. 11.

30 BMJ-Z30.061/0004-I 9/2017.

31 In this spirit, see the (presumably) prevailing view regarding the first sentence of Article 8(3) of the Treaty of Establishment between Germany and the Persian Empire. Cf. W. Wurmnest, 'Der Anwendungsbereich des deutsch-iranischen Niederlassungsabkommens bei erbrechtlichen Streitigkeiten und deutscher ordre public' (2016) 5 *Praxis des Internationalen Privat- und Verfahrensrechts* 447, 450 containing further evidence.

32 §106 Jurisdiktionsnorm reads in translation: 'Domestic jurisdiction to rule on liquidation of succession to an estate located in Austria as well as for proceedings replacing the liquidation (§§153 et seqq. AußStrG) is provided to the extent to which this is required to conform to an international agreement within the meaning of Article 75(1) of the European Succession Regulation.'

Contracting Party. There seems to be no Austrian case law on the subject of multiple nationalities in matters of succession. However, in cases on family law, an area which also falls under the scope of Article 10(3) of the Treaty, it was decided that these matters are covered only if all parties are citizens of the same Contracting State. Where one of the parties possesses multiple nationalities, the Austrian-Iranian Treaty does not apply. This is irrespective of whether the party holds citizenship of the other Contracting State or of a third State.[33]

According to T. Traar[34] and M. Potyka,[35] treaties with third States do not apply to persons holding multiple nationalities, irrespective of whether the deceased was a citizen of both Austria and Iran or a citizen of a Contracting Party and a third State. M. Potyka and T. Traar consider this to be a general rule. They argue that another treaty concerning the estate may exist in relation to third States which may lead to contradictory treaty obligations. Therefore, the relevant treaties concluded with third States should take precedence over the European Succession Regulation only if the deceased was a citizen exclusively of the other Contracting State. Contradictory treaty obligations can, however, only arise if the deceased possesses Austrian or Iranian nationality and also that of a third State. The wording of Article 10(3) of the Treaty is not in itself conclusive.

As mentioned above, the objectives of the Austrian-Iranian Treaty are to be achieved by means of the principle of equal treatment with nationals and equal treatment with the citizens of the most favoured nation. Therefore, these principles must be taken into account when interpreting the Treaty. A dual citizen of Austria and Iran enjoys equal treatment with Austrian nationals on account of his citizenship; the applicability of the Treaty is not necessary to receive equal treatment. Therefore, and to this extent, the opinion of M. Potyka and T. Traar can be subscribed to. If, however, the deceased was a dual citizen of one of the Contracting Parties and also a third State, the opinion of AG Hamburg-St. Georg[36] regarding the German-Iranian Treaty of establishment is convincing. The Austrian-Iranian Treaty should therefore be applicable to dual citizens holding citizenship of Austria or Iran and a third State, provided the Austrian or Iranian citizenship is dominant. In this manner concerns voiced by M. Potyka and T. Traar can be accommodated. A prerequisite to the application of the Austrian-Iranian Treaty to such cases should be, however, that both Contracting States consider a dominant citizenship to be sufficient.

---

33 OGH 29.10.1987, 7 Ob 700/87; OGH 06.06.1989, 2 Ob 536/89; OGH 13.10.2011, 6 Ob 69/11g; OGH 29.01.2019, 2 Ob 170/18s; A. Duchek and F. Schwind, *Internationales Privatrecht*, Manz, Wien 1979, p. 177.

34 T. Traar, above n. 17, Art. 75 EuErbVO para. 6.

35 M. Potyka and T. Traar, above n. 7, para. 8.

36 AG Hamburg-St. Georg, 13.04.2015 – 970 VI 1645/12.

2. PRIVATE INTERNATIONAL LAW

2.1. THE CONFLICT-OF-LAWS RULES OF THE TREATIES

2.1.1. Treaty with Former Yugoslavia

The Treaty with former Yugoslavia (**Treaty 3**) lays down a conflict-of-laws rule regarding movable property. There is, however, no such rule regarding the succession to immovable property. Pursuant to Article 39 of the Treaty, the classification of movables is governed by the laws of the State in which the assets are located. Consequently, this also applies to the classification of immovables.[37]

The conflict-of-laws rule regarding movable property, Article 36(2) of the Treaty, prescribes that the movable property, upon a request in accordance with Article 36(1) of the Treaty, does not fall under the jurisdiction of the home State of the deceased – diverging therefore from the provision of Article 31(1) of the Treaty – but under that of the Contracting State in which the deceased was last domiciled. The movable property located in the State of last domicile is then governed by the succession law of the national law of the deceased (principle of nationality). This is a reference to domestic law, excluding *renvoi*. The Treaty with former Yugoslavia does not provide for a choice of the law applicable to the succession; as far as can be seen the possibility of choice is not discussed in legal literature regarding the Agreement.

Under Article 29(1) of the Treaty, citizens of one Contracting State have the right to make dispositions on all property located on the territory of the other Contracting State by declaration of last will and by testamentary gift. These dispositions are valid if they satisfy the requirements of the citizen's national law or those of the law of the other Contracting State. This provision does not differentiate between movables and immovables. The wording allows for more than one interpretation. The preparatory works[38] call attention to the principle of equal treatment with nationals. The citizens of a Contracting State can dispose of all property they possess in the other Contracting State by declaration of last will (Article 29(1) of the Treaty) and can acquire property rights by succession in the same way as nationals (Article 29(2) of the Treaty).

---

37 A. Blaschke, 'Behandlung jugoslawischer Nachlässe in Österreich auf Grund des Vertrages vom 16 Dezember 1954', (1958) 6 *Österreichische Hefte für die Praxis des internationalen und ausländischen Rechts* 101; Regierungsvorlage vom 23.03.1955, 489 der Beilagen zu den stenographischen Protokollen des Nationalrates VII. GP, p. 19 on Art. 30.

38 Bericht des Justizausschusses vom 29.04.1955, 505 der Beilagen zu den stenographischen Protokollen des Nationalrates VII. GP; Regierungsvorlage vom 23.03.1955, 489 der Beilagen zu den stenographischen Protokollen des Nationalrates VII. GP, p. 16.

The prevailing opinion in Austrian legal literature[39] takes the view that Article 29(1) of the Treaty applies to the formal validity of last wills. According to M. Potyka and T. Traar,[40] this provision no longer has an independent scope since the Hague Convention of 5 October 1961 on the Conflicts of Laws Relating to the Form of Testamentary Dispositions obliges Austria to recognize testaments as valid as to form. A. Blaschke[41] holds the opinion that Article 29(1) of the Treaty covers the capacity of the person to make a disposition. According to Austrian authors,[42] the practical significance of Article 29(1) of the Treaty lies in the fact that it encompasses the Austrian Contract of Inheritance, which is legitimate only under Austrian law.

In my assessment the phrasing '*letztwillig verfügen*' does not include agreements as to succession but only unilateral dispositions like testaments and legacies. In the Serbo-Croatian version, the phrasing '*izjavom poslednje volje*' (declare the last will) is used. In matters regarding formal validity, the Hague Convention supersedes Article 29(1) of the Treaty because both of the Contracting Parties have ratified the Convention.[43] As far as can be seen, there is no case law on the subject of the scope of Article 29(1) of the Treaty. The Treaty with former Yugoslavia does not contain any additional conflict-of-laws rules.

2.1.2. Treaty with the Former Soviet Union

As relating to estate property, the provisions on conflict of laws and on international jurisdiction can be found in the same article – Article 23 of the Treaty (**Treaty 2**) on movable property and Article 26 of the Treaty on immovable property. These provisions ensure a unity of the forum with the applicable law (*ius*). The following paragraphs cover the conflict-of-laws rules.

Neither Article 23 nor Article 26 of the Treaty explicitly state which law governs the classification of goods as movable or immovable. Since the provisions apply only to estates located in a Contracting State, it is reasonable to assume that the classification should be governed by local law. This serves practical purposes as well.

The Treaty with the former Soviet Union does not use nationality or place of residence as a connecting factor, instead steering a 'middle course'.[44] Upon application, the law of the receiving State is to be applied to movable property

---

39 M. Potyka and T. Traar, above n. 7, para. 116; A. Duchek, W. Schütz and I. Tarko, above n. 7, p. 1094.

40 M. Potyka and T. Traar, above n. 7, para. 116, on the respective conflict-of-laws rules in treaties with non-EU Member States in general.

41 A. Blaschke, above n. 37, 101, 105.

42 A. Blaschke, above n. 37, 101, 105; A. Duchek and F. Schwind, above n. 33, p. 179.

43 With the exception of the Republic of Kosovo.

44 Regierungsvorlage vom 09.09.1959, 39 der Beilagen zu den stenographischen Protokollen des Nationalrates IX. GP, p. 27.

located in this State if the deceased was a citizen of the sending State but was last domiciled in the receiving State. The persons entitled to file the application are the statutory or testamentary heirs or legatees domiciled in the receiving State or in a third State. It must be filed within six months of the death of the deceased (Article 23(1) of the Treaty). Therefore, Austrian succession law[45] is applicable to the estate of a Russian citizen who was last domiciled in Austria, provided the statutory or testamentary heirs or legatees domiciled in Austria or in a third State file an application to this effect. The same applies, vice versa, to the estate of Austrian citizens who were last domiciled in Russia. However, it must be noted that movable property located in the receiving State falls under the scope of this provision. Article 23(1) of the Treaty directly refers to substantive succession law; a choice of law regarding movable property located in the receiving State is therefore not possible. A choice of the law applicable to the estate is not addressed in Austrian legal literature on the Treaty with the former Soviet Union.

If the conditions postulated by Article 23 of the Treaty are not met, the relation to the receiving State is considered weak and movable property is to be handed over to a consular representative in accordance with Article 24 of the Treaty. The consular representative then proceeds in accordance with the law of the sending State (Article 23(2) of the Treaty). From an Austrian point of view, this entails movable property located in Austria being handed over to a Russian consular representative in the event the heirs are domiciled in Russia, even if the deceased was last domiciled in Austria. Furthermore, if the deceased was not last domiciled in Austria, it is to be handed over even if he possessed movable property in Austria and the heirs are domiciled in Austria.

The provisions of Article 23(1) of the Treaty give rise to several questions. The persons entitled to file the application are statutory or testamentary heirs or legatees domiciled in the receiving State or in a third State. The text suggests that where a testator bequeaths part of his estate located in the receiving State to a single heir who is domiciled in the receiving State, this heir can by himself file the application with effect for all movable property located in this State. This can be inferred by the use of the term 'or' in the text of the Article. Pursuant to this interpretation, the effect of Article 23(1) of the Treaty can arise against the will of the other heirs. The preparatory works, on the other hand, require all 'heirs' to file the application. The possibility of a 'combination' between testamentary and statutory heirs is not considered in the explanatory remarks to the government bill. Evidently, Article 23(1) of the Treaty is based on the assumption that only either testamentary or statutory heirs or legatees[46]

---

45 M. Potyka and T. Traar, above n. 7, para. 115; Regierungsvorlage vom 09.09.1959, 39 der Beilagen zu den stenographischen Protokollen des Nationalrates IX. GP, p. 27.

46 With regard to legatees, the situation where a deceased has disposed of property that was located in the receiving State by way of a legacy is provided as an example.

are domiciled in the receiving State or a third State. This assumption explains the use of the plural form for each group in the German and in the Russian versions, in combination with the term 'or'. Pursuant to the preparatory works, Article 23(1) of the Treaty requires all heirs to file the application. In the event one heir does not file the application, movable property is to be handed over to a consular representative in accordance with Article 23(2) of the Treaty. The interests of the other heirs who wanted to file the application are safeguarded by the possibility of retaining their share of the estate in accordance with Article 24 of the Treaty (see the explanations to Article 24 of the Treaty). The determination of the share these heirs are entitled to is governed by the law of the sending State.

In this context it must further be established which law is relevant for determining whether a person is an heir or a legatee and whether he or she is therefore entitled to file an application. As will be established in the section on international jurisdiction, forum and *ius* are identical pursuant to Article 23 of the Treaty. The competent authorities of the receiving State are to apply the substantive law of this State to movable property located in the receiving State. In order to uphold the unity of forum with *ius*, the law of the receiving State is relevant in determining the status as a testamentary or statutory heir or legatee.

Article 23(1) of the Treaty does not establish the point in time relevant for determining the domicile of a person. This has significance where a person filing an application transfers his domicile to the sending State or from the sending State to the receiving State or a third State between the time of death of the deceased and the filing of the application. The preparatory works to the Treaty do not cover this issue. The text suggests that the time of death is the relevant point in time.

Article 26 of the Treaty governs the succession to immovable property. It provides that the law of the State in which the property is located applies to the succession to immovable property located in the receiving State. Substantive Austrian law[47] is therefore applicable to the succession to immovable property left by a Russian citizen located on Austrian territory, and vice versa. Unlike Article 23 of the Treaty, this is irrespective of where the deceased was last domiciled and does not depend upon the filing of an application.

The Treaty with the former Soviet Union does not explicitly provide a conflict-of-laws rule governing the substantive or formal validity of a disposition of property upon death. Russia has not ratified the Hague Convention of 5 October 1961 on the Conflicts of Laws Relating to the Form of Testamentary Dispositions. From an Austrian perspective, however, the Hague Convention governs validity as to form. It can be assumed that substantive validity is governed by the substantive law of the receiving State.

Regierungsvorlage vom 09.09.1959, 39 der Beilagen zu den stenographischen Protokollen des Nationalrates IX. GP, p. 28.

47 M. Potyka and T. Traar, above n. 7, para. 115.

Article 23 and 26 of the Treaty are the only Articles containing conflict-of-laws rules.

2.1.3. *Austrian-Iranian Treaty*

Pursuant to Article 10(3) of the Treaty (**Treaty 1**), the citizens of one of the High Contracting Parties remain – when on the territory of the other Contracting Party – bound by their national law in matters of intestate and testamentary succession. The connecting factor is the nationality of the deceased,[48] not the nationality of the successors. Article 10(3) of the Treaty refers to the domestic law of the Contracting States; *renvoi* is not possible.[49] It follows that from an Austrian perspective, a deceased who is an Iranian citizen is not subject to Austrian succession law; instead, Iranian domestic law is applicable. A Contracting Party can derogate from the application of the domestic law of the deceased only in exceptional cases and only to an extent which is in accordance with the general practice exercised in relation to all other foreign States (first sentence of Article 10(4) of the Treaty[50]). Article 10(4) acts as an implicit public policy clause, since even at the time of ratification the non-application of foreign law in case of violation of public policy was common practice.[51] Because of its discrimination between men and women, the application of Iranian succession law may violate Austrian public policy, which includes the equal treatment of men and women as a fundamental value, where there is a sufficient connection to the forum. In its decision 2 Ob 170/18s, the Austrian Supreme Court of Justice ruled that the application of Iranian succession law violated public policy to the extent that it discriminates between men and women. In doing so, it rejected arguments to the contrary, such as maintenance obligations of male descendants under Iranian law and the fact that under Austrian law the deceased had the (theoretical) possibility of making a testament to effect the same result as would be achieved upon applying Iranian law.

Article 10(3) of the Treaty does not explicitly provide for a choice of law. As far as can be ascertained, this topic has not been addressed in Austrian legal literature either.

Article 10(3) of the Treaty does not differentiate between movables and immovables. Hence, the nationality of the deceased is the connecting factor for the succession to both movable and immovable property.

---

48 T. Traar, above n. 17, Art. 75 EuErbVO para. 6; OGH 26.01.2005, 3 Ob 303/04m.

49 According to M. Potyka and T. Traar, above n. 7, para. 114, conflict-of-laws rules in treaties generally refer to the domestic law of a State, excluding rules under which reference would be made to the law of another country.

50 A. Duchek and F. Schwind, above n. 33, p. 178.

51 OGH 29.01.2019, 2 Ob 170/18s.

The second sentence of Article 10(4) of the Treaty establishes the connecting factor for the formal validity of testaments. A testament is valid as to form if it complies with the law of the State whose nationality the testator possessed or with the law of the State in which the disposition was made. Article 10(4) of the Treaty does not specify whether nationality at the time of the making of the testament is decisive or whether the nationality at the time of death is relevant as well. Against the inclusion of the nationality at the time of death, it can be argued that the second sentence of Article 10(4) of the Treaty applies the same rule to the formal validity of marriage; an equivalent to 'time of death' does not exist in the case of marriage. The wording indicates that the time of the making of the testament is decisive.

According to M. Potyka and T. Traar,[52] this provision no longer has an independent scope since the Hague Convention of 5 October 1961 on the Conflicts of Laws Relating to the Form of Testamentary Dispositions obliges Austria to recognize testaments as valid as to form. Unlike Austria, the Islamic Republic of Iran has not (yet) ratified the Hague Convention. For this reason, the second sentence of Article 10(4) of the Treaty applies (cf. Article 30(4) lit. b of the Vienna Convention on the Law of Treaties). For this reason, the additional connecting factors provided for in the Hague Convention, e.g. the habitual residence of the deceased at the time the testamentary disposition was made or at the time of death, do not apply in this case.

The Austrian-Iranian Treaty does not explicitly provide a connecting factor for the substantive validity of a testament. It does not stand to reason that the Contracting Parties considered only the formal validity of a testament and wished for the substantive validity of a testament to remain outside the scope of the Treaty. Instead, it can be assumed that they sought to comprehensively regulate succession and that the term testamentary succession encompasses substantive validity as well.

Apart from the provisions mentioned above, the Austrian-Iranian Treaty does not contain rules concerning conflict of laws.

2.2. COMPARISON WITH THE EUROPEAN SUCCESSION REGULATION

2.2.1. Treaty with Former Yugoslavia

There are two essential differences between the Treaty with former Yugoslavia (**Treaty 3**) and the European Succession Regulation: Firstly, the Treaty contains

52 M. Potyka and T. Traar, above n. 7, para. 116, on conflict-of-laws rules in treaties with third States in general.

a conflict-of-laws rule only on movable property (Article 36(2)), resulting in a fragmentation of successions – with the national law of the deceased applying to the succession to movable property and the succession to immovable property being primarily governed by the law of the State in which the testator had his habitual residence (Article 21(1) SR).[53] Secondly, Article 36(2) of the Treaty does not provide for a choice of law regarding movable property.

2.2.2. Treaty with the Former Soviet Union

A comparison with Article 21(1) SR shows the following differences: Articles 23 and 26 of the Treaty (**Treaty 2**) govern only estates located in the receiving State. The Treaty with the former Soviet Union provides different connecting factors for the succession to movable and immovable property. The succession to immovable property is always governed by the law of the place in which the estate is located (law of the receiving State), without regard to where the deceased was last domiciled. Upon application, the law of the place in which the estate is located applies to movable property in the event the deceased was last domiciled in the receiving State. Otherwise, the law of the sending State is applicable – it further applies if the prerequisites of Article 23(1) of the Treaty are not fulfilled. From this it follows that even in cases where a Russian citizen last domiciled in Austria leaves immovable and movable property, all of which is located on Austrian territory (or vice versa), a fragmentation of successions can result from these divergent rules. A fragmentation will always occur when a Russian citizen last domiciled in Austria leaves, among other estate assets, immovable property in the sending State.

Contrary to Article 22 SR, a person does not have a choice of law since Article 23(1) and Article 26 of the Treaty directly refer to the substantive succession law of the receiving State. Another difference is that the Treaty with the former Soviet Union does not contain provisions on the formal validity of dispositions of property upon death.

2.2.3. Austrian-Iranian Treaty

Unlike Article 21(1) SR, the connecting factor in Article 10(3) of the Austrian-Iranian Treaty (**Treaty 1**) is the citizenship of the deceased. Furthermore, unlike Article 22 SR, a person does not have a choice of law. Another difference is that the second sentence of Article 10(4) of the Austrian-Iranian Treaty provides only the nationality of the deceased and the location of the making of the testamentary disposition as connecting factors for the formal validity of testaments.

---

53 T. Traar, above n. 7, Art. 75 EuErbVO para. 7.

2.3. PRACTICAL SIGNIFICANCE OF THE TREATIES

All three Treaties apply if the deceased was a citizen of one of the Contracting States. It must be noted that the Austrian nationality laws do not, in general, allow for multiple nationalities and derogate from this general rule only in special cases. The following numbers should give an idea of the practical relevance of these Treaties. On 1 January 2019, Austria had a population of 8,859,992 million people: 121,547 (1.37 per cent) of them were Serbian citizens; 95,863 (1.08 per cent) were Bosnian and Herzegovinian citizens; 25,544 (0.28 per cent) were Kosovar citizens; 23,427 (0.26 per cent) were Macedonian citizens; 1,417 (0.01 per cent) were Montenegrin citizens; 32,543 (0.36 per cent) were Russian citizens and 14.457 (0.16 per cent) were Iranian citizens.

These numbers are largely in conformity with the result of the survey carried out in order to ascertain the practical relevance of the Treaties. In Austria, the liquidation of an estate is mainly carried out by notaries as court commissioners. Therefore, a survey on the application of the Treaties by Austrian notaries was carried out in November 2017 with the kind support of the Austrian Chamber of Notaries. A questionnaire comprising five questions was distributed. In total, there were 514 notaries in Austria (status: November 2017), some of which cooperate in office partnerships. In total 64 questionnaires were completed and submitted. Although the results do not claim statistical significance, they do give a good indication of the scale of application of the Treaties.

The first question – do the notaries apply the rules of the Treaties – did not specify a certain period in time. From 64 completed questionnaires, the number of notaries applying the Treaties can be derived. The notaries gave multiple answers. Out of these notaries, 36 have applied the Treaty with Bosnia-Herzegovina, 20 the Treaty with Kosovo, 15 the Treaty with Macedonia, 14 the Treaty with Montenegro, 37 the Treaty with Serbia, 7 the Treaty with Russia and 4 the Treaty with Iran. A total of 19 notaries reported they had never dealt with one of the Treaties; that is almost one-third of the answers.

The notaries were asked to estimate the share of their succession cases affected by the Treaties (out of their total number of succession cases). The Treaties with Bosnia-Herzegovina and Serbia seem to be the most relevant in practice, while the Treaties with Russia and Iran are of minor importance.

The notaries estimate that the Treaty with Bosnia-Herzegovina applies to 0.5–2.5 per cent of their workload on the subject of succession; the Treaty with Kosovo is estimated as applying to 0.5–1 per cent; the Treaty with Montenegro to 0.5 per cent; and the Treaty with Serbia to 0.5–3 per cent. The notaries further state that they dealt with only few cases to which the Treaty with Russia applied and that only a handful of cases concerned the Treaty with Iran.

Another question concerned the interpretation of these Treaties. Of the 64 notaries replying to the questionnaire, 41 per cent stated they interpret the provisions of the Treaties in a narrow fashion; 17 per cent of the notaries interpret them in a broader fashion; 42 per cent did not provide any information.

3. PROCEDURAL ISSUES

3.1. JURISDICTION

3.1.1. Treaty with Former Yugoslavia

The Treaty with former Yugoslavia (**Treaty 3**) contains differentiated provisions on international jurisdiction, making it dependent on the classification of property as movable or immovable. This classification is governed by the laws of the State in which the estate is located (Article 39 of the Treaty).

As to the liquidation of immovable property located in Austria and in contentious proceedings regarding succession, reserved shares or legacies in respect of such immovable property, Austria has exclusive jurisdiction, with the inverse being true as relates to the former Yugoslavia (Article 30 of the Treaty).

In general, matters concerning movable property fall under the jurisdiction of the courts of the national State of the deceased (first sentence of Article 31(1) of the Treaty). Upon request by the authorities of the national State of the deceased, the corporeal movable property must be surrendered to them, unless otherwise provided for in the Treaty with former Yugoslavia (right of retention until the competent courts of the home State of the deceased have passed a final judgment, Article 34(1) of the Treaty[54]) or unless the transfer is prohibited by a ban on exports or exchange restrictions (Article 31(4) of the Treaty).

Article 36(1) of the Treaty contains an exception to the provision of the first sentence of Article 31(1) of the Treaty. From an Austrian perspective, this exception entails, for instance, that where the heirs and forced heirs (excluding legatees) of a Serbian citizen who was last domiciled in Austria are themselves also domiciled in Austria, these heirs can, within a certain period,[55] apply to an Austrian court for the liquidation of an estate located in Austria. The application is to be granted if neither an heir, forced heir nor a legatee enters an objection within a certain period after being notified of the application. The period can amount from one to three months and is to be set by the court. In this case contentious proceedings on succession, reserved shares and

---

54 A. Duchek, W. Schütz and I. Tarko, above n. 7, p. 1095.

55 This period can amount to three to six months; cf. Article 36(1) of the Treaty read in conjunction with Article 35(1) of the Treaty.

legacies fall under the jurisdiction of the courts of this State as well. Pursuant to Article 36(2) of the Treaty, the succession rules of the law of the home State are applicable. In the current author's assessment, the law of this State also governs the determination of the persons who are entitled to the estate.

A further exception to the provisions of the first sentence of Article 31(1) of the Treaty is set out in the second sentence of this article. The liquidation of movable property located in Austria and matters of succession, reserved shares and legacies fall under the jurisdiction of Austrian courts in cases where the recognition and enforcement of decisions of the other Contracting State, as provided for in Article 31(2) of the Treaty, is no longer possible.

3.1.2. Treaty with the Former Soviet Union

As was mentioned above, in regards to property the provisions on conflict of laws and on international jurisdiction can be found in the same Article – in Article 23(1) of the Treaty (**Treaty 2**) on the succession to movable property and in Article 26 of the Treaty on the succession to immovable property. These provisions ensure the unity of the forum with the applicable law (*ius*).

The following paragraphs cover international jurisdiction. The succession to immovable property falls under the jurisdiction of the authorities of the State in which the estate is located (Article 26 of the Treaty). Similarly, movable property located in the receiving State may fall under the jurisdiction of the authorities of the receiving State – provided further prerequisites are met. If these prerequisites are not met, movable property located in the receiving State falls under the jurisdiction of the authorities of the sending State. For this purpose, movable property is to be handed over to a consular representative (Article 23(2) of the Treaty). Heirs, creditors and other 'interested parties' (according to the preparatory works these are legatees and mandatory heirs[56]) domiciled in the receiving State or a third State can file their claims regarding the estate within six months (Article 24(1) of the Treaty). The authorities of the sending State (national State of the deceased) apply the law of 'their' State.[57] A share of the estate that, within nine months, is not used for the purposes of satisfying or safeguarding claims that were filed in accordance with Article 24(1) of the Treaty and that is not linked to these claims is to be surrendered to a consular representative (Article 24(2) of the Treaty). Exchange restrictions must be adhered to when surrendering the estate and in any further transfer by the consular representative (Article 24(3) of the Treaty).

---

56 Regierungsvorlage vom 09.09.1959, 39 der Beilagen zu den stenographischen Protokollen des Nationalrates IX. GP, p. 28.

57 Regierungsvorlage vom 09.09.1959, 39 der Beilagen zu den stenographischen Protokollen des Nationalrates IX. GP, p. 28.

3.1.3. *Austrian-Iranian Treaty*

The Austrian-Iranian Treaty (**Treaty 1**) does not contain provisions on international jurisdiction.

In order not to affect the Austrian-Iranian Treaty (within the meaning of Article 75(1) SR), the Austrian legislature holds the view[58] that a decision or European Certificate of Succession on the estate of an Iranian issued by a court of a Member State applying the law of the State in which the deceased had his last habitual residence (in accordance with Article 21(1) SR) – instead of the national law of the deceased – cannot be enforced. For this reason, §106 Jurisdiktionsnorm (Act of Court Jurisdiction) provides that an estate located in Austria falls under Austrian international jurisdiction.

It is questionable whether this interpretation by the Austrian legislature is accurate.[59] It is arguably impermissible to pass laws in favour of bilateral treaties after adoption of the Succession Regulation. Pursuant to §106 Jurisdiktionsnorm, the estate left by Iranian citizens on Austrian territory falls under the jurisdiction of Austria in proceedings on succession falling, pursuant to the Succession Regulation, under the jurisdiction of the courts of another Member State. According to the explanatory remarks to the government bill,[60] Austria has jurisdiction pursuant to §106 Jurisdiktionsnorm in the event another Member State is conferred jurisdiction by the Succession Regulation, which indicates that international jurisdiction is not intended to be governed by §106 Jurisdiktionsnorm but by the Succession Regulation in cases where the Succession Regulation confers jurisdiction to Austria.

3.2. RECOGNITION AND ENFORCEMENT OF DECISIONS

3.2.1. *Treaty with Former Yugoslavia*

In Article 31(2) of the Treaty (**Treaty 3**), the Contracting States commit themselves to recognizing and enforcing dispositions and decisions on estates and on succession, reserved shares and legacies that were made by the courts of the other Contracting State to the extent to which they concern movable property located on their territory. Such recognition and enforcement is necessary, as the courts of the home State of the deceased can make dispositions on property located on the territory of the other Contracting State. The Contracting States are under no obligation to recognize and enforce a decision

---

58 Regierungsvorlage vom 17.06.2015, 688 der Beilagen XXV. GP, p. 48.

59 A. Tschugguel, 'EU-Erbrechtsverordnung, Zwei spezielle Fragen der gesetzlichen Anpassung' (2015) 6 *Zeitschrift für Familien- und Erbrecht* 260, 261.

60 Regierungsvorlage vom 17.06.2015, 688 der Beilagen XXV. GP, p. 48.

in cases where the Treaty with former Yugoslavia contains provisions to the contrary or where a decision offends the legal principles of the State in which the estate is located (Article 31(2) Point 1 and 2 of the Treaty).

The second sentence of Article 31(1) of the Treaty therefore provides international jurisdiction in the event recognition or enforcement in the other Contracting State is, in accordance with Article 31(2) of the Treaty, not possible.

3.2.2. Treaty with the Former Soviet Union

The Treaty with the former Soviet Union (**Treaty 2**) does not contain provisions on the recognition and enforcement of decisions in respect of an estate. Pursuant to Article 23(1) and Article 26 of the Treaty, only an estate located in Austria falls under the jurisdiction of Austrian courts, with the inverse being true for the former Soviet Union. No bilateral treaty on recognition and enforcement of decisions regarding an estate exists between Austria and Russia; cf. in this context §79(2) of the Austrian Exekutionsordnung (Execution Act).

3.2.3. Austrian-Iranian Treaty

Neither the Austrian-Iranian Treaty (**Treaty 1**) nor any other bilateral agreement between Austria and Iran contains provisions on the recognition or enforcement of decisions;[61] cf. in this context §79(2) of the Austrian Exekutionsordnung.

3.3. CONSULAR RIGHTS

3.3.1. Treaty with Former Yugoslavia

The consular offices of the Contracting States have the following capacities. In the context of securing movable property, the consular office of the other Contracting State must be notified in a timely fashion. Consular representatives can take part in official acts and file applications if the estate is located in the State in which the consular office is located (Article 33(3) of the Treaty (**Treaty 3**)). Upon application, dispositions made for the purpose of securing the estate can be modified or revoked regardless of any rights held by third persons (Article 33(4) of the Treaty).

Another capacity is provided for in Article 37 of the Treaty. When a citizen of one Contracting State dies during travels in the other Contracting State,

[61] OGH 29.01.2019, 2 Ob 170/18s.

the goods he carried with him are to be surrendered to the consular office of his national State, provided the deceased was neither domiciled nor had his habitual residence in the other Contracting State. The consular office must meet liabilities that were incurred during the deceased's stay in the other Contracting State; it is then to proceed in accordance with the law of the national State of the deceased.

Consular representatives are entitled to represent 'their' citizens in proceedings on the estate taking place in the other Contracting State in the event these citizens are absent or have not appointed any other representatives (Article 38 of the Treaty). In such a case, citizenship of the heir or creditor is decisive.

3.3.2. Treaty with the Former Soviet Union

Article 22 of the Treaty with the former Soviet Union (**Treaty 2**) governs the capacities of consular representatives[62] in matters concerning an estate. The Treaty does not differentiate between immovables and movables, and it does not consider the further treatment of the estate (Article 23 to Article 25 of the Treaty). The objective of Article 22 of the Treaty is protection of the rights of heirs who are citizens of the sending State – it is therefore a special right of intervention. Consular representatives are empowered to participate in the drawing up of the inventory and to request certain measures serving the preservation of the estate assets. They are further empowered to request the selling of estate assets, e.g. due to impending spoilage or impending debasement. Since requests of this nature are usually made by representatives like attorneys and notaries, Article 22 of the Treaty explicitly allows for intervention by representatives. The capacity to adopt measures of declaration, safe-keeping and sealing remains with the local authorities (Article 21(3) of the Treaty).

Article 25 of the Treaty contains a special provision for the case where a Russian citizen not domiciled in Austria dies on Austrian territory (or for the opposite situation). In such a case, assets carried by the deceased are to be surrendered to a consular representative. Liabilities the Russian citizen entered into while on Austrian territory are to be repaid to the extent of value of the movable property. Consular representatives must adhere to exchange restrictions imposed by the receiving State.

3.3.3. Austrian-Iranian Treaty

Article 11(1) of the Austrian-Iranian Treaty (**Treaty 1**) grants certain powers regarding the estate to Iranian consular representatives on Austrian territory

---

62 R. Fucik, above n. 3, Art. 75 EuErbVO para. 9.

and to Austrian consular representatives on Iranian territory. The following requirements must be met: A deceased who is an Austrian citizen leaves assets on Iranian territory, or a deceased who is an Iranian citizen leaves assets on Austrian territory. Those entitled to the estate are unknown, absent or not represented and hold the same citizenship as the deceased. Consular intervention becomes inadmissible as soon as it is certain that no person holding the same citizenship as the deceased is entitled to the estate.

The responsible consular representatives possess the right to demand the sealing or unsealing of all furniture, securities and papers. Furthermore, they can undertake the liquidation of the estate and appoint administrators for these proceedings, especially if the estate contains perishable goods. It is explicitly clarified in Article 11(2) of the Treaty that the international jurisdiction of the State in which the property is located is not affected by these powers.[63]

3.4. ISSUING OF A EUROPEAN CERTIFICATE OF SUCCESSION WITHIN THE SCOPE OF BILATERAL TREATIES

The question remains open as to whether Austrian notaries can, as court commissioners, issue a European Certificate of Succession in cases where Austria has jurisdiction pursuant to the Treaty with former Yugoslavia (**Treaty** 3), the Treaty with the former Soviet Union (**Treaty** 2) or the Austria-Iranian Treaty (**Treaty** 1). The Austrian legislature did not provide a general rule on this subject in the course of the adaptation of Austrian laws to the Succession Regulation.

In the course of the survey that was circulated to notaries, the notaries were asked whether or not they issued a European Certificate of Succession in cases where a treaty determines the applicable law or international jurisdiction. Of the 64 notaries who replied to the questionnaire, 11 per cent indicated that they issue European Certificates of Succession; 62 per cent of the notaries stated that they do not issue European Certificates of Succession in such cases, and 27 per cent did not provide any information.

The Treaties which are covered in this report do not lay down any rules on certificates of succession. Therefore, the issue of precedence does not arise and Article 75 Succession Regulation is not applicable.[64] In this context it must be noted that, pursuant to the Treaty with former Yugoslavia, which is by far the most relevant Treaty in practice, Austria has jurisdiction to rule only on property located in Austria.

---

63 R. Fucik, above n. 3, Art. 75 EuErbVO para. 7.
64 T. Traar, above n. 17, Art. 75 EuErbVO para. 7.

On the other hand, the treatment of a European Certificate of Succession issued by a Member State concerning property located in Austria in cases where one of the Treaties is applicable (from an Austrian perspective) is not explicitly regulated. According to M. Traar,[65] the European Certificate of Succession, which establishes a mere presumption (cf. Article 69 (1) SR), should in such cases cease to have effect if it contradicts Austrian law.

The Austrian legislature has adopted §106 Jurisdiktionsnorm (Act of Court Jurisdiction, see above section 3.1.3). The preparatory works[66] set forth that a European Certificate of Succession or other decisions on succession given by the courts of a Member State should not be recognized in matters falling within the scope of the Austrian-Iranian Treaty. For this reason, §106 Jurisdiktionsnorm restricts Austrian jurisdiction to property located in Austria. The preparatory works further set forth that, because the Treaty with former Yugoslavia and the Treaty with the former Soviet Union not only provide rules on the conflict of laws but also on international jurisdiction, §106 Jurisdiktionsnorm is not applicable to matters falling within their scope. This suggests that the legislature does not intend to extend recognition to a European Certificate of Succession or to some other decision on succession falling within the scope of either the Treaty with former Yugoslavia or the Treaty with the former Soviet Union – at least to the extent to which the Certificate or decision contradicts Austrian law.

4. THE FUTURE

In the aforementioned survey notaries were asked to give a personal statement or opinion on the Treaty with former Yugoslavia (**Treaty 3**), the Treaty with the former Soviet Union (**Treaty 2**) and the Austrian-Iranian Treaty (**Treaty 1**). The results show that 18 notaries qualify the Treaties as rather useful, some pointing out their particular usefulness regarding immovables. A total of 19 notaries qualify the Treaties as obstacles or support the termination[67] of the Treaties. Ten notaries endorse a harmonization with the Succession Regulation. There were 16 notaries who did not provide any information or gave a statement saying they had no experience concerning these Treaties.

The government of Austria has not officially voiced any plans to modify or terminate the Treaties with the aim of strengthening the uniform application of the Succession Regulation. An inquiry was made at the Ministry of Justice.

65 T. Traar, above n. 17, Art. 75 EuErbVO para. 7.

66 Regierungsvorlage vom 17.06.2015, 688 der Beilagen XXV. GP, p. 48.

67 S. Frodl and F. Kieweler in W. Rechberger and B. Zöchling-Jud (eds.), *Die EU-Erbrechtsverordnung in Österreich*, Verlag Österreich, Wien 2015, para. 1.35, describe this as an *ultima ratio*.

The Ministry of Justice provided a statement[68] indicating that even if a renegotiation of the Treaty with former Yugoslavia were possible, no changes to the status quo are desired. The provisions on international jurisdiction are well established and are considered to be effective and practical. Cross-border procedural acts or executions remain an exception. Furthermore, the application of foreign law (the law of the home State of the deceased) causes no problems because of long-standing practice. In its statement on the Treaty with the former Soviet Union, the Ministry of Justice again indicated that even if a renegotiation of the Treaty were possible, no changes to the status quo are desired. The main advantage of the Treaty is considered to be the unity of the forum with the applicable law. The statement of the Ministry of Justice as to the Austrian-Iranian Treaty suggests it is of minimal practical importance. For this reason, changes to the Treaty are not being considered.

In the current author's assessment, no modifications to the Treaty with former Yugoslavia will take place in the near future because Serbia, Macedonia and Montenegro are in the process of implementing EU law into their domestic legislation (membership status: candidate countries) and Bosnia and Herzegovina and Kosovo are potential candidates.

Concerning the Austrian-Iranian Treaty, it must be taken into consideration that the main objective of the Treaty is ensuring equal access to justice and rights of establishment for the respective nationals in the other country. Article 10 ((3) and (4)) is merely a minor part of the Austrian-Iranian Treaty and governs not only testamentary and intestate succession but other matters as well, e.g. family law. Even if a renegotiation were to take place (which, due to the minor practical importance of the Treaty, is highly unlikely from a pragmatic standpoint), it should be taken into account that the Iranian conflict-of-laws rules are familiar with neither party autonomy nor 'habitual residence' as a connecting factor. The introduction of these principles would constitute an unknown factor for international successions.

The fundamental difference between the Treaty with the former Soviet Union and the Succession Regulation consists in the separate provisions on movables and immovables. These separate connecting factors, encompassing the last domicile and the location of immovable property, correspond to Russian private international law (Article 1224 Russian Civil Code). The Russian Civil Code does not provide for a way to organize the succession in advance by choosing the law applicable to the succession. A change to the Treaty favouring only one of the Contracting Parties is unlikely. It must be further noted that, for the main part, the Treaty with the former Soviet Union is a treaty on consular relations. The rules concerning the conflict of laws and jurisdiction are provided in its third section, which primarily governs the capacities of consular representatives.

---

68 BMJ-Z30.061/0004-I 9/2017.

5. CONCLUSION

Considering the survey as well as the sparse case law and the few examples in legal literature on the subject of the Treaties, it can be concluded that the application of the Treaties does not pose any (generally known) difficulties. This is especially true in the case of the Treaty with former Yugoslavia (**Treaty 3**), which in practice is the most relevant by far, as confirmed by the statement of the Ministry of Justice.

The question remains open as to whether a European Certificate of Succession is to be issued in cases where international jurisdiction or the applicable law is determined by a treaty with a third State. The same can be said for the recognition of a European Certificate of Succession issued by a Member State which is not bound by such a treaty. These matters require a uniform solution within the Member States of the European Union.

THE EXTERNAL RELATIONS OF BELGIUM

Stéphanie Francq and Julie Mary

1. INTRODUCTION

This contribution presents the private international law rules applicable in Belgium in matters of succession following the entry into force of Regulation (EU) 650/2012 of the European Parliament and of the Council of 4 July 2012 on jurisdiction, applicable law, recognition and enforcement of decisions and acceptance and enforcement of authentic instruments in matters of succession and on the creation of a European Certificate of Succession.[1] In Belgium, the European Succession Regulation currently governs all matters related to succession.

The research project aims at identifying 'frictions' between international conventions (often bilateral conventions) concluded between Member States and third States in the field covered by the European Succession Regulation. Indeed, as underlined in the research project description, existing international conventions between Member States and third States will take precedence over the Regulation as far as they concern matters covered by the Regulation (Article 75(1) SR).

In respect of succession, only two bilateral conventions have been concluded between Belgium and *third* States:[2] the Convention of 2 May 1934 between Belgium and the United Kingdom for the reciprocal enforcement of judgments[3] and the Convention of 29 April 1959 between Belgium and Switzerland on recognition and enforcement of judicial decisions and arbitral awards.[4] These conventions solely concern the matter of recognition and enforcement of a decision and not international jurisdiction and the applicable law in matters of succession. Their influence on the European Succession Regulation is thus minor, and these conventions apply in rare circumstances.

In the first part of the report, the two bilateral conventions signed between Belgium and *third* States (i.e. every State that is not bound by the European Succession Regulation) will be presented (below, section 2). In the second part of the report, the provisions of the Belgian Private International Law Code in matters of succession will be discussed (below, section 3). Finally, the last part of this report will illustrate some of the problems that arise due to the lack of bilateral conventions or treaties concluded with third States (below, section 4).

Because of the specific Belgian context, this report analyzes more specifically the consequences for the European Succession Regulation resulting from the *absence* of bilateral and multilateral treaties or conventions concluded between Member States and third States in matters of succession. Indeed, the lack of bilateral conventions or treaties has consequences in international

---

1 Regulation (EU) 650/2012 of the European Parliament and of the Council of 04.07.2012 on jurisdiction, applicable law, recognition and enforcement of decisions and acceptance and enforcement of authentic instruments in matters of succession and on the creation of a European Certificate of Succession [2012] OJ L201/107.

2 Meaning every State that is not bound by the European Succession Regulation, thus including Denmark, United Kingdom and Ireland.

3 Convention entre la Belgique et le Royaume-Uni pour l'exécution réciproque des jugements du 2 mai 1934, approved by the law of 4 May 1936, *MB*, 27.11.1936, 7682.

4 Convention entre la Belgique et la Suisse sur la reconnaissance et l'exécution des décisions judiciaires et des sentences arbitrales du 29 avril 1959, approved by the law of 21.05.1962, *MB*, 11.09.1962, 7743.

litigations in matters of succession. Tackling this specific problem will hopefully contribute to a better understanding of the hypothesis of this research project by assessing how the absence of international conventions might also challenge the smooth resolution of international successions in the EU. Our hypothesis is that, depending on their wording, bilateral conventions may further the efficiency of EU law (here the European Succession Regulation) and thus also dissolve 'frictions' left open by the Regulation in regards to litigations involving third States litigants.

2. CONVENTIONS TAKING PRECEDENCE OVER THE EUROPEAN SUCCESSION REGULATION

Before the adoption of the European Succession Regulation, international jurisdiction was determined by applying either international conventions (bilateral and multilateral conventions or treaties) or Belgian private international law (i.e. the Private International Law Code,[5] hereinafter 'PIL Code', below, section 3). Because no international convention covered this aspect, the applicable law was determined by the provisions of the PIL Code.

In this contribution, only bilateral conventions concluded with third States are taken into consideration.[6] Multilateral treaties, such as the Convention providing a Uniform Law on the Form of an International Will, the Hague Convention of 5 October 1961 on the Conflicts of Laws Relating to the Form of Testamentary Dispositions and the Convention on the Establishment of a Scheme of Registration of Wills, will not be analyzed. These conventions either contain substantive law and have no impact on the European Succession Regulation, or they have been taken into consideration by the Regulation (as to the Hague Convention of 5 October 1961, see Article 75(1) SR).

As mentioned earlier, the relationship between prior bilateral conventions ratified by Member States and the European Succession Regulation is determined by Article 75 of this Regulation. The Regulation will not preclude the application of conventions concluded by Member States with third States which 'concern matters covered' by the Regulation. Strictly speaking, the recognition and enforcement of *third* State decisions are not 'matters covered' by the Regulation. Indeed, pursuant to Article 39(1) of the European Succession

5 Loi du 16 juillet 2004 portant le Code de droit international privé, *MB*, 27.07.2004, 57344.

6 For an example of convention concluded with a Member State: Traité franco-belge du 8 juillet 1899 sur la compétence judiciaire, sur l'autorité et l'exécution des décisions judiciaires, des sentences arbitrales et des actes authentiques, approved by the law of 31 March 1900, *MB*, 30.07.1900, 3386. On the notion of *third* States, see above n. 2.

Regulation, the latter is concerned only with the recognition and enforcement of decisions given in a *Member* State. Therefore, the substantive scope of application of the two bilateral conventions identified above and the substantive scope of the European Succession Regulation do not overlap, and their interaction does not, as such, trigger the mechanism of Article 75 of the Regulation.

2.1. CONVENTION BETWEEN BELGIUM AND THE UNITED KINGDOM

The Convention concluded in 1934 between Belgium and the UK for the reciprocal enforcement of judgments takes precedence over the Belgian PIL Code in matters of recognition and enforcement of civil and commercial decisions rendered by UK courts. This Convention will be applied by Belgian courts to the recognition of a decision rendered in the UK, a question placed outside the scope of application of the European Succession Regulation, which applies only to the recognition and enforcement of decisions rendered in Member States (Article 39(1) and Recital 82 SR).

The 1934 Convention applies irrespective of the nationality of the litigants.[7] The recognition in Belgium of a decision rendered in the UK in a succession litigation opposing, for instance, a US citizen residing in the UK against German members of the family residing in Belgium would thus be governed by the 1934 Convention.

Article 1(4) of the Convention states that the notion of 'judgment' means 'any decision of a Court however described (judgment, order and the like) by which the rights of the parties are finally determined'. Judgments covered by the Convention are, however, those rendered by a 'Superior Tribunal', meaning for the UK those of the House of Lords (at the time; now the Supreme Court) or the Court of Appeal and the High Court (in England and Wales) and for Belgium those of the 'Cour de Cassation', courts of appeal and courts of first instance (including those of the commercial chambers).[8] As far as recognition and

---

7 Article 2(1) of the 1934 Convention indeed mentions that: '(1) Judgments pronounced after the date of the entry into force of the present Convention by a superior court in the territory of one High Contracting Party, other than judgments rendered on appeal from inferior courts, shall, whatever the nationality of the judgment creditor or debtor, be recognised and enforced in the territory of the other in the cases and upon the conditions laid down in Articles 3 to 8 inclusive of the present Convention.'

8 Article 1(3)(a) of the 1934 Convention. Under the terms of this provision, '... (3) the words "superior court" shall be deemed to mean: (a) in the case of the United Kingdom, the House of Lords, and for England and Wales, the Supreme Court of Judicature (Court of Appeal and High Court of Justice) and the Courts of Chancery of the Counties Palatine of Lancaster and Durham; for Scotland, the Court of Session; and for Northern Ireland, the Supreme Court of Judicature [now the Court of Judicature of Northern Ireland].'

enforcement of decisions is concerned, the substantive scope of the Convention is as wide as it can be: the Convention does not contain a formal rule limiting its substantive scope, except through references to civil and commercial matters, nor any exclusion of specific matters such as family law issues.[9]

---

9 Under Article 3, concerning recognition:
'(1) Judgments in civil and commercial matters, given by any superior court in the territory of one High Contracting Party, and executory in the country of the original court, although still open to proceedings by way of opposition, appeal or setting aside shall, in the courts of the territory of the other, be recognized in all cases where no objection to the judgment can be established on any of the grounds hereinafter enumerated, that is to say unless:
(a) in the case in question the jurisdiction of the original court is not recognised under the rules of Private International Law with regard to jurisdiction observed by the court applied to;
(b) the judgment was given in default, and the judgment debtor did not appear in the proceedings and satisfies the court applied to that he did not actually acquire knowledge of the proceedings in reasonable sufficient time to act upon it. It is understood that in all cases, where it is proved that notice of the proceedings has been duly served on the defendant in conformity with the provisions of Articles 3 or 4 of the Convention signed- between the High Contracting Parties on June 21st 1922, it shall be deemed to be conclusive evidence that the defendant actually acquired knowledge of the proceedings;
(c) the judgment is one which is contrary to the public policy of the country of the court applied to;
(d) the judgment is in respect of a cause of action which had already at the date when it was given as between the same parties, formed the subject of another judgment which is recognised under the law of the court applied to as final and conclusive;
(e) the judgment, has, in the opinion of the court applied to been obtained by fraud;
(f) in the opinion of the court applied to, the judgment was given against a person, defendant in the proceedings, who under the rules of public international law was entitled immunity from the jurisdiction of the original court, and did not submit to the jurisdiction of the original court; or is sought to be enforced against a person who is entitled under the rules of public international law to immunity from the jurisdiction of the court applied to;
(g) the judgment debtor satisfies the court applied to that proceedings by way of appeal, opposition or setting aside have been instituted against the judgment in the country of the original court.

It is understood that if such proceedings have not been actually instituted, but the time for lodging an appeal, opposition or, application to set aside has not expired under the law of the country of the original court, the court applied to may, if it thinks fit, adjourn its decision on the recognition of the judgment so as to allow the judgment debtor a reasonable opportunity of instituting such proceedings.
(2) Recognition of a judgment shall not he refused merely on the ground that the original court has applied in the choice of the system of law applicable to the case, rules of Private International Law different from those observed by the court applied to.
(3) The recognition of a judgmect under paragraph (1) of this Article rneans that such judgment shall be treated as conclusive as to the matter thereby adjudicated upon in any further action as between the parties (judgment creditor and judgment debtor) and as to such matter shall constitute a defence against further action between them in respect of the same cause of action.'

As regards Article 5, concerning enforcement, it states the following:
'(1) Judgments, to which the present Article applies, given by a superior court in the territory of one High Contracting Party shall be enforced by the courts of territory of the other High Contracting Party in the manner and upon the conditions set out in Articles 6 to 8 inclusive.

The Convention deserves a few comments in respect of three issues which could potentially create frictions with the European Succession Regulation: the general grounds for refusing recognition and enforcement, especially indirect jurisdiction (section 2.1.1); the specific issue of irreconcilable decisions and *lis pendens* (section 2.1.2) and Brexit (section 2.1.3).

2.1.1. Grounds for Refusing Recognition and Enforcement: Indirect Jurisdiction

Under Article 3 of the Convention,[10] decisions rendered in the UK are to be recognized in Belgium, unless some ground for refusal is raised. For instance, recognition will be refused if the decision is manifestly contrary to public policy (*'ordre public'*) or is rendered by a court that has no jurisdiction under the private international law rules of the requested State. Articles 7 et seq. of the Convention provide for the rules related to the *exequatur* of such decisions.

In matters of recognition, the Belgian PIL Code generally provides for rules (specifically, Article 22 et seq.) similar to those of the 1934 Convention.[11] Since there are no specific rules (in the PIL Code) about recognition and enforcement of decisions in matters of succession, the general rules apply. Under the general rule stating the grounds for refusing recognition, there is no systematic review of the jurisdiction of the court of origin (Article 25 of the PIL Code).[12] Contradiction of public policy and the existence of irreconcilable decisions are typical grounds for refusing recognition under the 1934 Convention, as under the PIL Code.

The existence in the 1934 Convention of a refusal ground based on indirect jurisdiction is thus worth observing in the Belgian context. Article 4 of the Convention establishes indirect jurisdiction rules and specifies that the jurisdiction of the court of origin is to be recognized in any case where, for instance, the losing

---

(2) The judgments to which the present Article applies are judgments in civil or commercial matters including judgments for the payment of a sum of money as compensation upon the claim of an injured party appearing as «partie civile» in criminal proceedings:
(a) which are capable ot being executed in the country of the original court although still open to proceedings by way of opposition, appeal or setting aside; whereby money is made payable, including judgments for -the -payment of costs in civil or commercial matters;
(b) whereby a definite sum of money is made payable, including judgments for the payment of costs in civil or commercial matters;
(c) to the recognition of which none of the objections set out in Article 3 can be established.
(3) The provisions of this Article do not apply to judgments for the payment of a sum of money for any form of taxation, State or Municipal, or for the payment of penalties.'

10 See above n. 9.

11 See on this matter, L. Barnich, 'Successions internationales en Belgique' in *Les successions*, Bruxelles, Bruylant 2012, 637–648, esp. 639–640.

12 Article 25(1)(7) and (8) of the PIL Code provide that decisions will not be recognized if Belgian courts had exclusive jurisdiction or if the jurisdiction of the court of origin was based on the sole presence of the defendant, or of assets, without any relation to the object of the litigation.

party was the claimant in the proceedings or was the defendant and accepted the international jurisdiction of the court seized of the matter. These rules do not, however, apply to a decision in family or succession matters (see Article 4(3) of the Convention).[13] In such a case, the jurisdiction of the court of origin is to be accepted at the recognition level if the ground of jurisdiction is compatible with the private international law rules of the requested State. A decision in matters of succession rendered in the UK will not be recognized if the UK Court has accepted jurisdiction on grounds that are foreign to Belgian PIL, and it will be recognized if the jurisdiction ground is similar to those supporting international jurisdiction of Belgian courts. For instance, a UK decision will be recognized in Belgium if the deceased had his/her habitual residence or assets in the UK.

The refusal ground which refers to the compatibility of UK jurisdiction rules with Belgian rules on jurisdiction leads to a surprising effect in the current context. In practice, the Belgian PIL rules on succession have been entirely replaced by the European Succession Regulation (below, section 3). As a result, the jurisdiction of UK courts will be assessed at the recognition stage in Belgium on the basis of the European Succession Regulation. The situation is not without irony: Despite the fact that the UK is a 'third State' in regards to the European Succession Regulation, and soon will be a 'third State' in regards to EU law, the wording of the bilateral convention signed (long before the EU) with Belgium indirectly submits the jurisdiction of the UK Court to the European Succession Regulation if this decision needs to be recognized in Belgium.

2.1.2. Lis Pendens *and Irreconcilable Decisions*

The 1934 Convention does not provide for any specific *lis pendens* mechanism but treats the subsequent issue of irreconcilable decisions by giving priority to the decision rendered first in time (Article 3(1)(d) 1934 Convention).[14]

---

13 Under the terms of Article 4 of the 1934 Convention:
'(1) Notwithstanding the provisions of Article 3(1)(a) and without prejudice to the provisions of paragraphs (2) and (3) of the present Article, the original court shall be recognised as possessing jurisdiction in all cases:
(a) where the judgment debtor was in respect of the matter, which is the subject of the judgment, a plaintiff or counter-claimant in the proceedings in the original court;
(b) where the judgment debtor, being a defendant in the proceedings in the original court submitted to the jurisdiction by voluntarily appearing in the proceeding. It is understood that the expression 'voluntarily appearing in the proceedings' does not include an appearance merely for the purpose of protecting property situated within the jurisdiction of the original court from seizure, or of obtaining the release of property seized, or for the purpose of contesting the jurisdiction of the original court; (...)
(3) The provisions of paragraph (1) of this Article do not apply:
(a) to judgments in matters of family law or status (including divorces or other judgments in matrimonial causes);
(b) to judgments in matters of succession, or the administration of the Estates of deceased persons; ....'

14 See above n. 9.

One potential difficulty raised by bilateral conventions signed by Member States concerns indeed the fate of irreconcilable decisions rendered in a third State and in a Member State in the same litigation. The Regulation addresses this issue by giving priority to the decision rendered first in time (Article 40(d) SR). Thus, if a decision has been rendered in Germany before a decision was rendered in the UK, the German decision should, under the European Succession Regulation, have priority over the UK decision when recognition is sought for both decisions in Belgium. The application of the 1934 Convention produces the same result. Indeed, in a case where the recognition or enforcement of a decision rendered in the UK and of a decision rendered in Germany are requested in Belgium at the same period of time, the conflict is solved along similar lines under Article 3(1)(d) of the 1934 Convention:[15] Priority should be given to the decision rendered first in time as long as it fulfils the conditions to be recognized in the requested State (below, section 4.5).

In this case, the Convention is thus compatible with the European Succession Regulation. Had the wording of the Convention given priority to the decision rendered in the contracting State (compare below on the Convention with Switzerland, section 2.2), the Convention would have been in clear conflict with the Regulation. The Convention would take precedence over the Regulation and command the recognition of the UK decision even if rendered after the German decision.

2.1.3. *Brexit*

The 1934 Convention has rarely been applied[16] since the adoption of the 1968 Brussels Convention on jurisdiction and the enforcement of judgments in civil and commercial matters, which superseded the conventions concluded between Member States in matters covered by the 1968 Convention.[17]

Brexit obviously raises the issue of the revival of the 1968 Brussels Convention and of its potential relationship with the 1934 Convention. In respect of the specific problem of successions and wills, the situation is, however, pretty straightforward. The 1968 Convention did not apply to wills and successions (Article 1(1) Brussels Convention) nor will its 'revival'. Moreover, it is very unlikely that a potential agreement between the UK and the EU assuming the role of Brussels I Recast would regulate successions and wills, given that

---

15 See above n. 9.

16 For an example of the application of the 1934 bilateral Convention: Cass., 28 mai 2010, *Rev. Dipr. be.*, 2010/4, 51.

17 See Articles 55 and 56 of the Brussels 1968 Convention and Case C-9-10/77, Bavaria Fluggesellschaft Schwabe & Co. Kg and Germanair Bedarfsluftfahrt GmbH & Co. Kg v. Eurocontrol – References for a preliminary ruling: Bundesgerichtshof – Germany, ECLI:EU:C:1977:132.

they are excluded from the scope of this Regulation (Article 1(2)(f) Brussels I Recast). Brexit thus does not bring any major changes, and the 1934 Convention will remain the sole reference concerning the recognition and enforcement of judgments rendered in the UK concerning a succession.

Due to its limited scope of application (in matters related to recognition and enforcement of decisions) and the content of its provisions, this Convention neither influences nor contradicts the European Succession Regulation.

2.2. CONVENTION BETWEEN BELGIUM AND SWITZERLAND

The 1959 Convention on the recognition and enforcement of judicial decisions and arbitral awards will be applied by Belgian courts to the recognition of a decision rendered in Switzerland. This issue is placed outside the scope of application of the European Succession Regulation, which applies only to the recognition and enforcement of decisions rendered in Member States (Article 39(1) and Recital 82 SR).

The 1959 Convention takes precedence over the Belgian PIL Code in matters of recognition and enforcement of civil and commercial decisions rendered by Swiss courts, including decisions in matters of succession (see Article 2(1)(j)).[18] The 1959 Convention is not superseded by the Lugano Convention (Convention of 21 December 2007 on jurisdiction and the recognition and enforcement of judgments in civil and commercial matters). Pursuant to Article 65 of the Lugano Convention, this Convention takes precedence over bilateral conventions concluded between its Contracting States only in so far as such conventions concern matters governed by the Lugano Convention. Annex VII lists the conventions superseded, among others the Convention concluded between Belgium and Switzerland in 1959. However, since the Lugano Convention does not cover successions and wills (Article 1(2)(a) Lugano Convention), the recognition of Swiss decisions regarding successions and wills in Belgium falls under the scope of the 1959 bilateral Convention.

The 1959 Convention applies irrespective of the nationalities of the litigants (Article 12(1) of the Convention).[19]

Article 1 of the 1959 Convention stipulates that decisions in civil and commercial matters rendered by Swiss courts are to be recognized in Belgium,

18 Article 2(1)(j): 'The courts of the State in which the decision was made shall be deemed to have jurisdiction with the meaning of Article 1, paragraph 1(b) in the following cases: … (j) in the case of actions between the heirs relating to the estate of a person who had his last domicile in the State in which the decision was made, irrespective of whether the estate comprises movable or immovable property.'

19 Article 12 states that: '(1) This Convention shall apply irrespective of the nationality of the parties.'

unless – among other reasons – recognition would be contrary to public policy or the jurisdiction of the court of origin is not compatible with the indirect jurisdiction rules of the Convention.[20]

The rules concerning the enforcement of decisions are contained in Articles 4 to 8 of the Convention.

Again here, two issues deserve a closer examination: the judicial review of jurisdiction of the court of origin as a ground for refusing recognition or enforcement (indirect jurisdiction) (section 2.2.1); *lis pendens* and irreconcilable decisions (section 2.2.2).

2.2.1. Grounds for Refusing Recognition and Enforcement: Indirect Jurisdiction

Under Article 2(1)(j) of the 1959 Convention,[21] international jurisdiction in matters of succession is accepted (at the recognition stage) if the deceased had his/her domicile in the State where the decision was issued. Hence, a decision rendered by a Swiss court will be recognized in Belgium if, among other conditions, the deceased had his/her domicile in Switzerland at the time of death.

Since a similar connecting factor in regards to international jurisdiction was adopted in the European Succession Regulation (i.e. the last habitual residence), the Convention between Belgium and Switzerland and the European Succession Regulation have high chances of co-existing in a harmonious fashion. For instance, if a decision concerning a succession has been rendered in Switzerland, it is probably because the deceased had his/her domicile in this country. Since in most instances, the domicile and the habitual residence coincide, no EU court is likely to be seized of the same matter under Article 4 of the European Succession Regulation. As a result, when a decision is rendered by a Swiss court in a situation relating to a succession, and the recognition of this decision is requested in Belgium under the 1959 Convention, there should

---

20 Under the terms of Article 1 of the 1959 Convention:
'(1) The authority of judicial decisions made in civil and commercial matters in one of the two States, even if made by a criminal court, shall be recognized in the other State if they satisfy the following conditions:
(a) that recognition of the decision is not incompatible with the public policy of the State in which it is applied for;
(b) that the decision was made by a court having jurisdiction under Article 2;
(c) that, under the laws of the State in which the decision was made, ordinary remedies are no longer available against it;
(d) that, in the case of a decision by default, the notice of proceedings or the summons was served on the defendant in accordance with the laws of the State in which the decision was made and the conventions, if any, in force between the two countries, and that it reached him in due time.'

21 See above n. 18.

be no decision rendered by an EU court. *Lis pendens* between Belgium and Switzerland is also unlikely.[22] Should a situation of *lis pendens* between Belgium and Switzerland occur, Article 10 of the 1959 Convention provides that the court second seized should abstain from exercising its jurisdiction if the court first seized has jurisdiction under the indirect jurisdiction grounds of the Convention and if its decision is likely to be recognized in the State second seized.[23]

2.2.2. Lis Pendens *and Irreconcilable Decisions*

As mentioned above, the 1959 Convention provides for an explicit *lis pendens* mechanism, giving priority to the court first seized as long as its decision is likely to be recognized in the contracting State whose courts are second seized. Because the problem is solved *ex ante*, the Convention does not provide for a refusal ground concerning irreconcilable decisions that would give priority to the decision rendered first in time. Between Belgium and Switzerland, if the Convention is properly applied, *lis pendens* should be solved and irreconcilable decisions should not occur.

However, a situation of *lis pendens* between a Member State court and Switzerland cannot entirely be excluded. Therefore, irreconcilable decisions rendered by Swiss courts and by other Member State courts may occur. The European Succession Regulation entitles EU courts to be seized on grounds other than the habitual residence of the deceased (see Articles 5 and 10 in particular). In addition, Swiss courts may also be seized on the basis of jurisdictional grounds other than the domicile of the deceased (see Articles 87 and 88 of the Swiss PIL Code).[24] It can also happen that the domicile and the habitual

---

22 As a matter of principle, Swiss courts have jurisdiction in succession matters when the deceased had his/her last domicile in Switzerland (Art. 86 Swiss PIL Code).

23 Under the terms of this provision:
'(1) The courts of each of the two States shall, on a motion by one of the parties to the proceedings, decline to rule on an application if an application based on the same cause and between the same parties is already pending before a court of the other State which would have jurisdiction under the terms of this Convention and if such application could result in a decision which would have to be recognized in the other State.
(2) The provisional or protective measures provided by the laws of Belgium and Switzerland may in case of emergency be adopted by the authorities of either State, irrespective of the court dealing with the merits of the case.'

24 Under those provisions, in succession matters Swiss courts have jurisdiction over assets located in Switzerland and over any litigation relating to the succession of a Swiss national who was domiciled in another State and whose 'place of origin' is in Switzerland (the place of origin under Swiss law being a different notion than the domicile: the place of origin coincides with the special relationship between a Swiss national and a specific city in Switzerland). These grounds for jurisdiction are used only as far as the foreign authorities do not administer the succession. However, if a Swiss national formulates a choice in favour of

residence of the deceased do not coincide. Therefore, *lis pendens* between Swiss courts and EU courts, if unlikely, cannot be excluded.

In such a case, the *lis pendens* mechanisms provided for by the European Succession Regulation and the 1959 Convention are useless: Article 17 of the European Succession Regulation is limited to *lis pendens* between Member States, and Article 10 of the 1959 Convention[25] covers only *lis pendens* between Switzerland and Belgium. It cannot be excluded that recognition of a Swiss decision and recognition of a decision rendered in another Member State – based on the same factual situation – will be sought in Belgium.

In such a case, two scenarios are possible:

1. The Swiss decision was rendered first and the Member State decision was rendered afterwards: the 1959 Convention would call for recognition of the Swiss judgment only if the deceased was domiciled in Switzerland. This is consistent with Article 40(d) of the European Succession Regulation, which gives priority to the decision rendered first in time, even if rendered in a third State.
2. The Swiss decision was rendered after the decision of a Member State court: the 1959 Convention would call for the recognition of the Swiss judgment only if the deceased was domiciled in Switzerland. The Regulation would, however, call for the recognition of the EU judgment rendered first in time (unless other conditions set by Article 40 of the Succession Regulation are not fulfilled). In this case, Article 75 of the Regulation would prove useful due to its all-encompassing formulation. Indeed, Article 75 states that the 'Regulation shall *not affect the application* of international conventions' in force between Member States and third States. The Regulation should thus give priority to the application of the 1959 Convention, and the Swiss decision should be recognized even if rendered after a decision rendered in another Member State.

Issues concerning recognition and enforcement of incompatible decisions are further developed (below, section 4.5). At this stage, one conclusion can already be drawn from the examples of the two bilateral conventions signed by Belgium: bilateral conventions are most useful when they contain not only a *lis pendens* mechanism but also a refusal ground giving priority to the decision rendered first in time, similar to the refusal ground of Article 40(d) of the European Succession Regulation.

Swiss law in his/her will, Swiss courts always have jurisdiction. The exclusive jurisdiction of a foreign court where immovables are located is always preserved.

25 See above n. 23.

3. PRIVATE INTERNATIONAL LAW CODE

The provisions of the PIL Code in matters of succession were recently modified.[26] The adoption of the European Succession Regulation – which takes precedence over national codifications – led to an adaptation of the Belgian PIL Code.[27] Due to the universal scope of application of the European Succession Regulation, the corresponding national provisions became obsolete and had to be abrogated. Further minor changes were introduced in the PIL Code because of the entry into force of the Regulation. Adapting the PIL Code was a relatively easy task since the European Succession Regulation rests on similar principles as those previously adopted in the Belgian PIL Code on international jurisdiction and applicable law.

3.1. INTERNATIONAL JURISDICTION

Before the recent legislative change, Article 77 of the PIL Code – entitled International Jurisdiction with Respect to Succession – was drafted as follows (free translation):

> In addition to the cases provided for in the general provisions of the present statute, excluding Article 5 [domicile of the defendant], the Belgian courts have jurisdiction to hear actions regarding succession if: (1) the deceased had his/her habitual residence in Belgium at the time of death, or (2) the claim relates to assets that are in Belgium when the action is introduced.

The current Article 77 of the PIL Code now provides that (free translation):

> §1. Jurisdiction of Belgian courts shall be determined by application of Regulation (EU) 650/2012 of the European Parliament and of the Council of 4 July 2012 on jurisdiction, applicable law, recognition and enforcement of decisions and acceptance and enforcement of authentic instruments in matters of succession and on the creation of a European Certificate of Succession.

---

[26] They were introduced by the following legislation: Loi du 6 juillet 2017 portant simplification, harmonisation, informatisation et modernisation de dispositions de droit civil et de procédure civile ainsi que du notariat, et portant diverses mesures en matière de justice, *MB*, 24.07.2017, 75168. For comments on the provisions of the PIL Code before the modifications, see J.-L. van Boxstael, 'Chapitre X. Les successions' in *Rép. not., t. XVIII, Le droit international privé, livre 0, Code DIP – Premiers commentaires*, Bruxelles, Larcier 2010, 171–191.

[27] P. Wautelet and J. Mary, 'Le règlement 650/2012 relatif aux successions internationales. Aperçu et principes généraux' (2010) *JT* 377–390, esp. 377.

§2. By derogation from the general provisions of the present statute, any claim in matters of succession that has been excluded from the scope of application of the Regulation is regulated by provisions on jurisdiction provided for in Articles 4 to 19 of the Regulation aforementioned in paragraph 1.

In short, the Belgian lawmaker made sure that the European Succession Regulation constitutes the sole reference for determining the jurisdiction of Belgian courts in matters of international succession. The first paragraph of the new Article 77 of the PIL Code simply aims at guiding practitioners to the new Regulation.[28] As such, it works as a reminder of the existence and priority of the Regulation. The second paragraph of Article 77 of the PIL Code extends the substantive scope of application of the Regulation and substitutes the Regulation for the former rules of Belgian PIL concerning succession and wills, even for matters excluded from the scope of the Regulation.[29] The provisions of the European Succession Regulation are used in Belgium to assess the international jurisdiction of Belgian courts in any litigation relating to a succession even where such claim would *a priori* fall outside of the scope of the Regulation (and unless it is covered by another EU Regulation, such as Regulation 2016/1103 on matrimonial property).[30]

For instance, the European Succession Regulation does not cover the formal validity of dispositions of property upon death that have been made orally. However, in application of the PIL Code (Article 77(2)), this matter will be covered by the Regulation, and thus the international jurisdiction of Belgian courts will be determined in accordance with the provisions of the European Succession Regulation in the event a litigation occurs about such dispositions. This provision might also be relevant in practice for litigation relating to the transmission of property rights made other than by succession as mentioned in Article 1(2)(g) of the European Succession Regulation. Litigation relating to gifts, transmission of ownership with reserve of *usufruct*, pension plans and other methods used to plan a succession (but not directly relating to succession

---

28 The Belgian legislature proceeded in a similar way in matters related to maintenance obligations. See Article 73 of the PIL Code. Under Article 73(1) of the PIL Code, international jurisdiction of Belgian courts is to be determined by application of Council Regulation (EC) 4/2009 of 18 December 2008 on jurisdiction, applicable law, recognition and enforcement of decisions and cooperation in matters relating to maintenance obligations.

29 A. Bonomi, 'Article 1' in A. Bonomi, I. Pretelli and P. Wautelet (eds.), *Le droit européen des successions. Commentaire du Règlement n° 650/2012 du 4 juillet 2012*, Bruxelles, Bruylant 2016, 75, No. 11 (on the unilateral extension of the scope of EU rules).

30 In the field of maintenance, the Belgian PIL Code still provides for its own subsidiary rule on jurisdiction in cases where the claim falls outside of the scope of the Maintenance Regulation (Regulation 4/2009). Under Article 73(2) of the PIL Code, Belgian courts have jurisdiction when the creditor is habitually resident in Belgium or when the creditor and the debtor are both Belgian nationals. General provisions of the PIL Code also remain applicable when the Regulation does not apply.

issues as described in Article 23 of the Succession Regulation)[31] would thus be treated in Belgium under the provisions of Articles 4 to 19 of the European Succession Regulation in order to determine the jurisdiction of Belgian courts.

Article 77(2) of the PIL Code raises serious questions of interpretation in situations of *lis pendens* with third States courts. We will come back to this point (below, section 4.2).

3.2. APPLICABLE LAW

Concerning the law applicable to succession, before 2017, Article 78 of the PIL Code provided as follows (free translation):

> §1. Succession is governed by the law of the State on the territory of which the deceased had his habitual residence at the time of his death.
>
> §2. Succession to immovable property is governed by the law of the State on the territory of which the immovable is located. However, if foreign law refers to the law of the State on the territory of which the deceased had his habitual residence at the time of his death, the latter will be applied.

Articles 79 to 84 of the same Code were dedicated to wills.

Following the modification of the provisions in matters of succession,[32] the current version of Article 78 of the PIL Code has been drafted in the following terms (free translation):

> §1. The law applicable in matters of succession shall be determined by Regulation (EU) 650/2012 of the European Parliament and of the Council of 4 July 2012 on jurisdiction, applicable law, recognition and enforcement of decisions and acceptance and enforcement of authentic instruments in matters of succession and on the creation of a European Certificate of Succession.
>
> §2. Every matter related to succession, that is not covered by the scope of application of this Regulation, shall be submitted to the applicable law determined in accordance with Articles 20 to 38 of the Regulation.
>
> §3. The provisions of the Hague Convention of 5 October 1961 on the formal validity of wills shall be applied to dispositions upon death that are not covered either by the Regulation or by the Convention.

---

31 On this dividing line, see A. Bonomi, above n. 29, 93, No. 44.

32 Also introduced by the following legislation: Loi du 6 juillet 2017 portant simplification, harmonisation, informatisation et modernisation de dispositions de droit civil et de procédure civile ainsi que du notariat, et portant diverses mesures en matière de justice, *MB*, 24.07.2017, 75168.

The structure of this provision is similar to the structure of Article 77 of the PIL Code analyzed above. The first paragraph has a purely declaratory function, leading practitioners to the application of the Regulation. The second paragraph unilaterally extends the scope of application of the Regulation to matters placed outside of its substantive reach. In short, the law applicable in matters related to succession will be determined in Belgium solely by application of the European Succession Regulation, except for the formal validity of wills.

The law applicable to the formal validity of wills is determined by the Hague Convention of 5 October 1961. Article 78(3) of the PIL Code extends the scope of application of this Convention to the formal validity of dispositions of property upon death that are covered neither by the Regulation nor by the Convention. Examples of application of Article 78(3) of the PIL Code are difficult to find and the *effet utile* of this provision can be questioned.[33]

Finally, all other provisions of the PIL Code concerning wills and successions have been repealed (Article 79 et seq. PIL Code).

The Belgian legislature has also enacted a provision referring practitioners to EU regulations in matters related to maintenance obligations[34] and parental responsibility.[35] For maintenance and parental responsibility (contrary to what has been done in the field of succession), a subsidiary conflict-of-laws rule has been maintained in the PIL Code for situations that are not covered by those regulations, i.e. mainly the situation of adults and maintenance obligations arising outside of family relations.

---

33 Under the terms of the Explanatory Report concerning the law modifying the PIL Code provisions (Projet de loi portant simplification, harmonisation, informatisation et modernisation de dispositions de droit civil et de procédure civile ainsi que du notariat, et portant diverses mesures en matière de justice, doc. No. 54-2259/001, 61), agreements on future successions ('pactes successoraux') are excluded from the scope of the 1961 Convention. Therefore, one could think that Article 78(3) of the PIL Code could be used to extend the scope of the Convention on this point. However, the Explanatory Report points out that the Regulation covers those agreements. Therefore, Article 78(3) is not to be used for agreements on future successions. The formal validity of dispositions of property upon death made orally (excluded from the scope of the Regulation, Art. 1(2) f)) is covered by the 1961 Convention (see Art. 10 of the 1961 Convention) and can therefore not provide an example of application of Article 78(3) of the PIL Code. The Explanatory Report cited above admits that examples of application of Article 78(3) are difficult to find.

34 See Article 74 of the PIL Code, under which the applicable law is to be determined by application of the European Regulation on maintenance obligations (and thus by the 2007 Hague Protocol). For maintenance obligations not deriving from family relationships, the PIL Code has a specific conflict-of-laws rule (Art. 75 PIL Code).

35 See Article 35(3) of the PIL Code, under which the applicable law is to be determined by application of the Convention of 19 October 1996 on Jurisdiction, Applicable Law, Recognition, Enforcement and Co-operation in Respect of Parental Responsibility and Measures for the Protection of Children. A subsidiary conflict-of-laws rule (Art. 35(1) PIL Code) is provided for situations not covered by the Hague Convention.

4. PRACTICAL PROBLEMS RELATED TO THE ABSENCE OF BILATERAL CONVENTIONS OR TREATIES

This part of the contribution critically assesses the lack of bilateral conventions in regards to successions and wills. This section aims at identifying the problems that arise only because Belgium has *not* concluded specific bilateral conventions or treaties in matters of succession. The problems concern jurisdiction, applicable law and recognition of decisions. Some of these questions echo the problem of the 'reflex effect/effet reflex' under Brussels I that have been only partially solved with the Recast version.[36]

4.1. INTERNATIONAL JURISDICTION: CHOICE-OF-COURT AGREEMENTS

Under Article 5 of the European Succession Regulation, the parties can agree that courts of a Member State have jurisdiction to rule on a succession matter if the deceased chose the law of this State to govern his/her succession (pursuant to Article 22 SR). Pursuant to Article 20 of the European Succession Regulation, its application is universal regarding the applicable law, meaning that the deceased can choose the law of a third State to govern his/her succession.

In the event the law chosen by the deceased is the law of a third State and a choice of court designates the courts of this country, the following problem arises: it seems at first sight impossible to use Article 5 of the European Succession Regulation in order to assess the choice of court, since (i) the chosen law is not the law of a Member State; (ii) the chosen courts are those of a third State. This problem obviously recalls the 'effet reflex' issue under Brussels I and its Recast version. As explained in more details below in connection with *lis pendens* (section 4.2), several positions are possible. First, one could consider that the European Succession Regulation should be applied by analogy and that a choice of court formulated in favour of the courts of a third country whose law has been chosen should be respected. Second, the Regulation could be analyzed as leaving the issue outside its scope, so that national conflict-of-jurisdictions rules should be used to assess the choice of court. Third, the Regulation could be read as prohibiting the choice of third country courts. The careful wording of Article 5 of the European Succession Regulation and the limitations imposed on the possibility of electing the competent court could hardly be read as a generous opening in favour of unlimited party autonomy towards third States.

---

36 Regulation (EU) 1215/2012 of 12.12.2012 on jurisdiction and the recognition and enforcement of judgments in civil and commercial matters (recast) [2012] OJ L351/1.

Therefore, when a question arises as to whether the private international law of the Member States can apply in the case at hand and allow such a choice-of-court agreement, the answer depends on the interpretation of the Regulation. A. Bonomi considers that the private international law of Member States should not apply because the Regulation permits a choice-of-court agreement only in specific circumstances (it is thus not a liberal choice) and because it contains an exhaustive list of rules for determining international jurisdiction of Member States courts. The Regulation should thus have the final word on a choice of courts and national law should not offer a more flexible solution.[37]

In Belgium, even if the application of the national conflict-of-jurisdictions rules were allowed, those rules would lead back to the application of the European Succession Regulation. In the absence of any bilateral convention on jurisdiction, Article 77(2) of the PIL Code refers to the Regulation in order to assess any issue of jurisdiction concerning successions, even in the presence of a choice-of-court in favour of the courts of a third State (for more details and nuances on the interpretation of Article 77(2), below, section 4.2). To be sure, applying the Regulation in such a case consists in 'forcing' its application and legislative intent: the use of Article 77(2) of the PIL Code is based on the hypothesis that national conflict-of-jurisdictions rules could apply, and this hypothesis implies that the Regulation does not intend to regulate the issue of a choice of court in favour of third States. The 'forced' application of the European Succession Regulation to a choice of court in favour of third States thus seems very difficult to achieve in practice.

The uncertainty concerning a choice-of-court in favour of a third State could actually be solved by a bilateral convention. If Belgium (or any Member State) had concluded a bilateral convention on international jurisdiction in matters of succession regulating choice-of-court agreements, the questions raised above would be irrelevant. Article 75 of the European Succession Regulation would give priority to the convention, and the bilateral convention would automatically solve the issue of choice-of-court agreements by allowing or prohibiting them. Obviously, the effect given to the choice of a third State court accepted on the basis of a bilateral convention might constitute one of the examples of 'frictions' which this research project aims at identifying. Indeed, if the European Succession Regulation is to be interpreted as prohibiting a choice-of-court in favour of third States (on the basis of the narrow formulation of its Article 5), the priority given to a bilateral convention favouring such clause would contradict the 'effet utile' of the Regulation.

The existence of a bilateral convention would thus make the situation simpler in terms of interpretation and more predictable for the parties, but it would not necessarily further the objectives of the Regulation.

---

[37] A. Bonomi, 'Article 5' in A. Bonomi, I. Pretelli and P. Wautelet, above n. 29, 180–181.

4.2. *LIS PENDENS* BETWEEN BELGIAN COURTS AND THIRD STATE COURTS

Lis pendens with third State courts is not explicitly regulated by the European Succession Regulation. Indeed, Article 17 only regulates *lis pendens* between Member States courts. Just as analyzed above regarding jurisdiction clauses in favour of third State courts, the problem can be dealt with under the heading of 'effet reflex'. Again, three positions can be considered. First, Article 17 of the Regulation could be used by analogy and allow Member States courts to decline jurisdiction in favour of third States courts first seized in a similar fashion as they would do in favour of other Member States courts first seized.[38] Alternatively, because Article 17 limits its effects to the operation of *lis pendens* between Member States, such a situation could be considered as placed beyond the reach of the Regulation and thus left to the national PIL provisions.[39] In Belgium in particular, Article 14 of the PIL Code regulates international *lis pendens*. Potentially, it could also be considered that the Regulation comprises a comprehensive system concerning the jurisdiction of Member State courts, a system which intentionally does not provide for any *lis pendens* provision in relations with third States and thus prohibits national courts from declining to exercise their jurisdiction based on the Regulation in favour of third States courts first seized. Indeed, the EU lawmaker could have decided to (but did not) insert into the European Succession Regulation a provision similar to Article 33 of Regulation 1215/2012 (Brussels I Recast).

Obviously, the difficulty derives from the absence of any explicit provision in the European Succession Regulation on *lis pendens* with third States. Interpretating the legislative intent of EU institutions is complex: did they simply consider that such a problem falls in the sphere of national conflict-of-jurisdictions rules or did they intend to prohibit Member States courts from declining jurisdiction in favour of third States courts? The problem goes beyond the reach of this national report.

The interplay between this problem and bilateral conventions signed by Member States operates at two levels.

Level 1: First, should the European Succession Regulation be interpreted as prohibiting Member States courts from declining jurisdiction in favour of third States courts first seized, a bilateral convention signed with a third State

---

38 On the notion of 'reflex effect', see M. Fallon, 'L'applicabilité du Règlement Bruxelles I aux situations externes après l'avis 1/03' in *Vers de nouveaux équilibres entre ordres juridiques. Liber amicorum H. Gaudemet-Tallon*, Paris, Dalloz 2008, 241–264, esp. 247–248, and S. Francq, 'La refonte du Règlement Bruxelles I. Champ d'application et compétence' (2013) 5 *R.D.C.* 307–333, esp. 312–313.

39 A. Bonomi, 'Article 17' in A. Bonomi, I. Pretelli and P. Wautelet, above n. 29, 258–259, Nos. 7–8.

could derogate from this prohibition. Article 75 of the Regulation would give priority to the specific mechanism of *lis pendens* provided for in the convention. One could consider that such a solution would create 'frictions' with the Regulation. Such a mechanism would, however, ensure a sound prevention of parallel proceedings.

As mentioned earlier, the 1959 Convention between Belgium and Switzerland contains a provision on *lis pendens* (even if the Convention is only concerned with recognition and enforcement). In relation to Switzerland, a Belgian court second seized on the basis of the European Succession Regulation should refrain from exercising its jurisdiction if the Swiss court is first seized and its decision is likely to be recognized.

If the Regulation is to be interpreted as imposing an all-encompassing system of allocation and exercise of jurisdiction,[40] the Regulation thus excludes the possibility of Member States courts considering *lis pendens* with third State courts, except on the basis of a bilateral convention taking precedence on the Regulation. In such a case, the questions analyzed at Level 2 (below) are irrelevant. Those questions arise *only if* the Regulation is to be interpreted as leaving the *lis pendens* question outside of its ambit when third State courts are involved.

Level 2: Second, should it be taken for granted that the issue of *lis pendens* with third States remains within the ambit of national conflict-of-jurisdictions rules, the interpretation of those national conflict rules might as such lead to difficulties. And those difficulties could be prevented in the presence of efficiently drafted conventions. Such is the case for Belgium.

Article 77(1) of the PIL Code refers to the Regulation for all matters relating to succession and covered by the Regulation. Based on the idea that the Regulation does not intend to regulate the issue of *lis pendens* with third States, Article 14 of the PIL Code could be used by Belgian courts to resolve the *lis pendens* issue involving a third State court.

However, Article 77(2) of the PIL Code explicitly states that, in Belgium, the European Succession Regulation applies to any claim in matters of succession that has been excluded from the scope of application of the Regulation ('toute demande en matière de succession que ce règlement exclut de son domaine d'application'). For those claims, Article 77(2) of the PIL Code excludes the application of general provisions of the Belgian PIL Code on jurisdiction. In other words, the Regulation should be applied in Belgium also in respect of matters that it does not intend to regulate, and general provisions on jurisdiction of the PIL Code would not apply in that case.

40 This is how Belgian lawmakers apparently understand the European Succession Regulation: Explanatory Report, above n. 33, 59.

How should the provision be construed?

1. Firstly, the provision could be interpreted as meaning that *any issue/question* relating to successions presented in front of Belgian courts should be dealt with only on the basis of the Regulation and that the use of all general provisions of the Belgian PIL Code is excluded. The European Succession Regulation and its Article 17 would be used, by analogy, for coordinating proceedings in matters of succession brought before the courts of Belgium as well as a third State. Not only would Article 77(2) lead to a unilateral extension of the scope of application of the Regulation, it would also lead to the application of Article 17 beyond the explicit legislative intent of EU lawmakers.

   Such an interpretation does not make much sense because a European provision would be used in situations for which the provision was clearly not conceived. The wording of Article 17 is limited to *lis pendens* between Member States.

   Extending the application of Article 17 SR to relations between Belgium and third States, as a result of the unilateral extension of the scope of the Regulation as accomplished by Article 77(2) of the PIL Code, would also contradict the context of mutual trust between Member States within which Article 17 SR has been adopted. Article 17 SR simply provides that a court is to decline its jurisdiction if another court has been first seized of the same cause of action between the same parties and has established its jurisdiction. By contrast, the coordination of proceedings between Member States and third States usually requires additional procedural guarantees.[41] In the absence of any specific procedural guarantee, Article 17 of the European Succession Regulation may not be appropriate for regulating relations between Belgian courts and third State courts that would not comply with a proper administration of justice (including the rights of defence). However, if Article 17 of the European Succession Regulation is applied in relation to third States by the effect of Article 77(2) of the PIL Code, Belgian courts should decline jurisdiction in favour of a third State court first seized, even if there is a risk of a non-proper administration of justice in the third State concerned.

---

41 For instance, Article 33 Brussels I Recast provides – among other things – that the proceedings will be dismissed in the Member State: '… if the proceedings in the court of the third State are concluded and have resulted in a judgment capable of recognition and, where applicable, of enforcement in that Member State'. This condition relating to the recognition of the foreign decision is also included in Article 14 of the PIL Code, in addition to a guarantee of proper administration of justice.

2. Alternatively, Article 77(2) of the PIL Code could be interpreted as meaning that the reference to the European Succession Regulation covers only *substantive matters* that are excluded from the substantive scope of the European Succession Regulation under Article 1(2). Pursuant to the effect of Article 77(2) of the PIL Code, those matters would be submitted to the jurisdiction provisions of the Regulation. But this would not mean that *any issue* raised in such a litigation would necessarily be dealt with under the Regulation to the exclusion of general provisions of the PIL Code. Also, whereas Article 77(2) of the PIL Code excludes the application of general provisions of the Belgian PIL Code on jurisdiction, it is sensible to construe this provision as excluding general provisions of the PIL Code providing for grounds of jurisdiction and not merely any provision dealing with jurisdictional issues. Thus, under a narrow interpretation of Article 77(2) of the PIL Code, Article 14 of the PIL Code would still be used to solve the issue of *lis pendens* with third States even in matters submitted to the Regulation by effect of Article 77(2) of the PIL Code.

The questions of interpretation raised by Article 77(2) of the PIL Code are extremely complex, whereas *lis pendens* requires a speedy and clear solution. Any bilateral convention signed between Belgium and a third State containing specific *lis pendens* rules would take precedence over Article 77 of the PIL Code and substantially clarify the situation. Indeed, in the hypothesis analyzed here (Level 2), the Regulation is interpreted as leaving the question of *lis pendens* with third States beyond its ambit. International conventions signed with third States could thus regulate the issue without interfering with the Regulation (and without needing the mediation of Article 75 of the European Succession Regulation).

In conclusion, the absence of bilateral or multilateral conventions or treaties concluded with third States in matters of international jurisdiction related to succession raises all sorts of concerns in case of *lis pendens* with third States. An example is Article 10 of the 1959 Convention between Switzerland and Belgium. Such a bilateral mechanism is, however, limited in reach because it involves only the two States parties to the Convention.

Of course, EU lawmakers could have prevented these questions of interpretation by drafting a specific provision in the Regulation on *lis pendens* with third States. Such a provision is lacking, and in fact the Regulation actually increases the chance of *lis pendens* with third States by allowing Member States courts to be seized even if assets are localized in third States (Article 10). The only coordination mechanism provided for by the Regulation is in Article 12, which allows a Member State court not to rule on assets located in third States where it suspects that its decision will not be recognized and enforced in the country where the assets are located.

4.3. *FORUM NECESSITATIS*

Under Article 11 of the European Succession Regulation, the courts of a Member State that have no jurisdiction pursuant to the provisions of the Regulation may, on an exceptional basis, rule on the succession if proceedings cannot reasonably be brought or conducted or would be impossible in a third State with which the case is closely linked.

The need (and practical use) for this provision is more limited in the event of a bilateral convention or treaty concluded between the Member State and the third State involved. Indeed, under a bilateral convention, common jurisdiction rules are provided that should render proceedings possible in the third State concerned. Thus, only unique circumstances will lead to the application of Article 11 of the European Succession Regulation.

Again, in Belgium the absence of bilateral conventions or treaties concluded with third States may increase the potential likelihood of an intervention under Article 11 of the European Succession Regulation.

4.4. APPLICABLE LAW

Pursuant to Article 21(2) of the European Succession Regulation, the law which governs a succession will not apply if, at the time of death, the deceased was manifestly more closely connected with another State. The law of this other State will thus apply.

In the event the law to be applied by the courts of a Member State is the law of a third State that must be set aside due to the existence of closer links with another State, the question arises as to whether the decision will be recognized in the third State whose law has been ruled out. If there are no bilateral conventions or treaties concluded with this third State (i.e. facilitating the recognition of the decision from the Member State at issue), there is no guarantee that the decision will be recognized by this third State. The third State might indeed review the applicable law at the recognition stage.

For instance, pursuant to Article 10 of the European Succession Regulation, Belgian courts may have jurisdiction to settle the succession of a Belgian-Moroccan national whose death occurred in Morocco. In that case, Belgian courts are to apply Moroccan law. However, if the deceased was more closely connected to Belgium, Belgian courts will apply Belgian law under the European Succession Regulation. Under Moroccan private international law, by contrast, the succession is governed by the law of the nationality of the deceased.[42] In the event the parties need to have the Belgian decision recognized and executed

[42] Fasc. 60 – Maroc: Conflits de lois – Conflits de juridictions, f) Successions et libéralités, *LexisNexis*.

in Morocco, nothing ensures that the Belgian decision will be recognized in Morocco. In the absence of a bilateral convention concluded between Belgium and Morocco in matters of succession or as regards the recognition of decisions, Morocco may refuse to recognize the Belgian decision that set Moroccan law aside.[43] In Morocco, a foreign decision will be recognized if the conditions provided for the *exequatur* are met. Among other things, the court of the State of origin must have jurisdiction and its decision must not be contrary to Moroccan public order.[44] Practitioners from Morocco suggested that the chances of getting such a Belgian decision recognized are scarce.

Finally, without bilateral conventions or treaties concluded with third States, there is a risk that a choice of applicable law pursuant to Article 22 of the European Succession Regulation will not be recognized by the courts of a third State. Indeed, if a choice of law in matters of succession is not allowed in that State (which is not bound by the Regulation), there is a high probability that the deceased's choice will be excluded. The possibility of a choice of law has, however, been inserted in the Regulation in order to promote legal certainty and has the potential to further a uniform ruling as to the succession.[45] Indeed, choice of law may assure that the court of a Member State and the court of a third State apply the same law, even if the latter does not permit a *professio juris*.[46] For instance, a Moroccan, domiciled in Belgium, chooses Moroccan law as the law governing his succession. Belgian courts will accept the choice of law (unless it is contrary to public policy), and while Moroccan courts will exclude the choice of law, they will in any event apply the law of the nationality of the deceased, i.e. Moroccan law. The succession would thus be administered under the same law in Belgium and Morocco. Nevertheless, nothing ensures that the Belgian decision would be recognized in Morocco nor that the objectives of the European Succession Regulation in terms of legal certainty will be met.

4.5. RECOGNITION AND ENFORCEMENT OF DECISIONS

Under the terms of Article 10(a) of the European Succession Regulation, Belgian courts have jurisdiction to rule on the succession of a Belgian national

---

43 Belgium concluded a convention with Morocco within the framework of the Hague Convention of 1 March 1954 on Civil Procedure: Convention entre le Royaume du Maroc et le Royaume de Belgique relative à l'entraide judiciaire en matière civile, commerciale et administrative et dans le domaine de l'information juridique, 30 mars 1981, *MB*, 10.01.1984. Under the terms of this Convention, the rules for judicial proceedings are simplified when a litigation involves nationals of one or the other State. However, it does not simplify the recognition of a decision from one State on the territory of the other State.

44 Fasc. 60 – Maroc: Conflits de lois – Conflits de juridictions, B. Effets des jugements étrangers – b) Conditions, *LexisNexis*.

45 A. Bonomi, 'Article 22' in A. Bonomi, I. Pretelli and P. Wautelet, above n. 29, 303.

46 Ibid.

whose habitual residence at the time of death is in a third State (for instance, Morocco) if estate assets are located in Belgium. This will also be the case if a Moroccan national, who had worked in Belgium, returned to Morocco when he retired and died there less than five years following his departure from Belgium (see Article 10(b) SR). In the event the courts of the State in which the Belgian or the Moroccan national died have jurisdiction to rule on this succession, the question of the recognition and enforcement of the Belgian decision will arise. Without any bilateral convention or treaty concluded with this third State, there is a risk that the State will not recognize the decision and consequently take another decision incompatible with the first one.[47]

This risk also exists in the event the Member State concluded a convention with a third State that contains rules contrary to the ones in the European Succession Regulation. For instance, the 1959 bilateral Convention concluded between Belgium and Switzerland provides that a Belgian decision will be recognized in Switzerland if the decision was rendered by courts having jurisdiction (Article 1),[48] in accordance with the indirect jurisdiction rules of the Convention. Pursuant to Article 2 of the 1959 Convention,[49] courts have indirect jurisdiction in litigations between successors if the deceased was domiciled in the State that rendered the decision. In the event international jurisdiction of Belgian courts was based on the location of the assets in Belgium, the decision will probably not be recognized by the Swiss courts.

To prevent this risk, the European Succession Regulation provides in Article 12 that courts of a Member State can decide not to rule on one or more assets located in a third State if there is a risk that the decision will not be recognized and enforced in that third State. Clearly, this provision will be most useful when the Member State has not concluded any bilateral convention or treaty ensuring the recognition and enforcement of decisions in third States. Member States like Belgium may end up applying Article 12 of the European Succession Regulation more often than Member States which have concluded bilateral/international conventions on the recognition of judgments with third States.

Finally, in matters of recognition, Article 40 of the European Succession Regulation provides an explicit rule on the recognition of a decision given in a Member State that is incompatible with a decision rendered earlier in another Member State or in a third State. Pursuant to this Article, the earlier decision is to be recognized if it fulfils the conditions necessary for its recognition in the Member State in which recognition is sought. In this context, depending on their wording, bilateral conventions or treaties may or may not further the

[47] Article 12 of the European Succession Regulation intends to prevent this problem by allowing Member State courts to limit the reach of their decision to assets located in the EU.

[48] See above n. 20.

[49] See above n. 18.

effet utile of the Regulation and provide (or not) for solutions compatible with those offered by the Regulation. If the wording of the convention is similar to the wording of Article 40 of the European Succession Regulation and gives priority to the judgment rendered first in time, the Regulation and the convention will come to identical results. Belgium can illustrate the importance of the careful wording of such conventions (above, section 2).

For instance, proceedings are brought before Belgian courts for the recognition of a decision given in France. During the proceedings, the defendant produces an authentic copy of a Swiss decision (involving the same cause of action and the same parties) given after the French decision. Pursuant to the 1959 bilateral Convention concluded with Switzerland, Belgian courts should recognize the Swiss decision, even if the French decision was given earlier (above, section 2.2).

The solution will be different if the French decision is incompatible with a decision rendered by the United Kingdom's courts. Under Article 3 of the 1934 Convention concluded between Belgium and the United Kingdom,[50] a decision rendered between the same parties and on the same cause of action after another decision was rendered will not be recognized. The 1934 Convention provides for a rule similar to the one contained in Article 40 of the Regulation. Conflicts between incompatible decisions will be avoided in this particular case.

5. CONCLUSION

In Belgium, bilateral conventions apply only to recognition and enforcement of decisions rendered in the United Kingdom and in Switzerland. These Conventions apply to the recognition and enforcement of those third State decisions in Belgium and to the recognition and enforcement in those third States of Belgian decisions adopted under the European Succession Regulation.

Nowadays, Belgian courts apply the European Succession Regulation, even in the event of claims that are not covered by this instrument (Articles 77 and 78 PIL Code), to determine both international jurisdiction and the applicable law. As described above, this technique of a unilateral extension of the scope of the Regulation may lead to complex interpretation issues in respect of (i) a choice-of-court in favour of third State courts; and (ii) *lis pendens* with third States (above, sections 4.1 and 4.2).

International or bilateral conventions could solve these issues and have priority over both the Regulation and Article 77(2) of the PIL Code. As such, they could offer answers in tune with the needs of practice in cases of international succession for issues such as choice-of-court and *lis pendens*. Obviously, these

---

[50] See above n. 9.

problems could have been treated in the Regulation itself. The EU lawmaker could have inserted provisions on *lis pendens* with third States and clearly stated that a choice of third State courts is prohibited.

Finally, while Belgium has developed broad relationships with Morocco, it has surprisingly not concluded any bilateral conventions in matters of succession. Belgium has signed with Morocco a bilateral convention governing matters related to social security (including the distribution of a survival pension of a man who concluded a polygamous wedding) and matters related to legal assistance (the 1981 Convention mentioned above). However, nothing has been negotiated in regards to successions despite the large number of bi-nationals (Belgian Moroccans) who have assets in the two countries.

In addition to a depiction of the Belgian legal context, this contribution has offered a first view of why and how bilateral conventions may actually further the efficiency of EU law, here in particular the European Succession Regulation.

Bilateral conventions can support the *effet utile* of the European Succession Regulation by:

- ensuring the recognition and enforcement in third States of EU court decisions adopted on the basis of the European Succession Regulation and thus furthering both the goal of legal certainty and the principle of universality of succession upon which the European Succession Regulation is based; the recognition of an EU court decision in third States is especially uncertain where the Member State court based its jurisdiction on Article 5 or 10 of the Regulation;
- resolving the problem of incompatible decisions by giving priority to the decision rendered first in time (as does the European Succession Regulation) and thus avoiding that a decision rendered in a third State should be given priority under a bilateral convention over a decision rendered earlier in a Member State (due to the priority of the convention).

Bilateral conventions can complement the Regulation:

- where it lacks appropriate coordination mechanisms with third States (e.g. on the issue of *lis pendens* with third State courts and the choice of third State courts) and thereby circumvent complex issues involving the interpretation of the European Succession Regulation itself ('effet reflex') and potentially national PIL provisions (in Belgium, Article 77 PIL Code);
- where the application of some of its provision depends on what happens in a third State (Articles 11 and 12 SR).

THE EXTERNAL RELATIONS OF CROATIA

Davor BABIĆ and Tena HOŠKO

1. INTRODUCTION

Before the Succession Regulation[1] came into force, Croatian private international law of succession was governed by the Croatian Private International Law Act (hereinafter: Croatian PIL Act),[2] several bilateral treaties and one multilateral treaty, i.e. the Hague Convention of 5 October 1961 on the Conflicts of Laws Relating to the Form of Testamentary Dispositions.[3]

---

1 Regulation (EU) No. 650/2012 of the European Parliament and of the Council of 04.07.2012 on jurisdiction, applicable law, recognition and enforcement of decisions, and acceptance and enforcement of authentic instruments in matters of succession and on the creation of a European Certificate of Succession [2012] OJ L201/107.

2 Act concerning the resolution of conflicts of laws with the provisions of other countries in certain matters, Official Journal (hereinafter: OJ), Nos. 53/1991, 88/2001. For more information on the private international law of succession under that Act see I. MEDIĆ MUSA, 'Kolizijski aspekti nasljeđivanja s međunarodnim obilježjem' (2006) 4 *Aktualnosti građanskog i trgovačkog zakonodavstva i pravne prakse*, 355–374, T. RATKOVIĆ, 'Private international law aspects of succession – the Croatian experience' (2014) 13 *Anali Pravnog fakulteta Univerziteta u Zenici*, 8–32.

3 Official Journal of the Federal People's Republic of Yugoslavia, International Treaties and Other Agreements (hereinafter: OJ FPRY, Int'l Treaties), No. 10/1962. Croatia became a party to the Convention on 08.10.1991 by notification of succession, published in OJ, Int'l Treaties, No. 4/1994.

Amongst all the bilateral treaties dealing with succession matters with an international element, only a few outlived the entrance into force of the Succession Regulation. Most bilateral treaties have been derogated from by the Succession Regulation, by virtue of its Article 75(2), since they were concluded with other EU Member States. Those treaties deal with a wide scope of international legal assistance in civil and even criminal matters. They are, of course, still in force, but the parts dealing with succession matters have been replaced by the Succession Regulation. The majority of such treaties cover jurisdictional issues, conflict of laws, and recognition and enforcement of foreign decisions in succession matters,[4] whereas the minority cover only recognition and enforcement of foreign decisions in succession matters.[5]

Three bilateral treaties were not influenced by the Regulation in any way since they are outside of its scope of application. Treaties with Bosnia and Herzegovina of 1996,[6] (today: North) Macedonia of 1994[7] and Turkey of 1999[8] were concluded to regulate issues of legal assistance in civil (and criminal) matters. They apply to recognition and enforcement of decisions in civil matters, including succession matters. The issue of recognition and enforcement of decisions is also governed by the Succession Regulation, but only between Member States.[9] Seeing that these bilateral treaties apply to recognition and

4 Croatia is a successor to all such treaties as they were concluded by former Yugoslavia (treaties with Austria of 1954, Bulgaria of 1956, Poland of 1960, Czechia and Slovakia of 1964 and Hungary of 1968).

5 Two such treaties were concluded by former Yugoslavia (with Greece in 1959 and with France in 1971), whereas only one, with Slovenia, was concluded by Croatia in 1999.

6 Agreement between the Government of the Republic of Croatia, Government of Bosnia and Herzegovina and Government of the Federation of Bosnia and Herzegovina on legal assistance in civil and criminal matters of 26.02.1996 (Sporazum između Vlade Republike Hrvatske, Vlade Bosne i Hercegovine i Vlade Federacije Bosne i Hercegovine o pravnoj pomoći u građanskim i kaznenim stvarima od 26. veljače 1996.), OJ, Int'l Treaties, Nos. 12/1996, 3/2008, 5/2003, 4/2008.

7 Treaty between the Republic of Croatia and the Republic of Macedonia on legal assistance in civil and criminal matters of 02.09.1994 (Ugovor između Republike Hrvatske i Republike Makedonije o pravnoj pomoći u građanskim i kaznenim stvarima od 2. rujna 1994.), OJ, Int'l Treaties, Nos. 3/1995, 1/1997.

8 Treaty on legal assistance in civil and commercial matters between the Republic of Croatia and the Republic of Turkey of 10.02.1999 (Ugovor o pravnoj pomoći u građanskim i trgovačkim stvarima između Republike Hrvatske i Republike Turske od 10. veljače 1999.), OJ, Int'l Treaties, Nos. 5/2000, 10/2003.

9 Art. 39 of the Succession Regulation. See more in I. Pretelli, 'Chapitre IV Reconnaissance, force exécutoire et exécution des décisions' in A. Bonomi and P. Wautelet (eds.), *Le droit européen des successions*, Bruylant, Bruxelles 2013, p. 567, M. Makowsky, 'Kapitel IV Anerkennung, Vollstreckbarkeit und Vollstreckung von Entscheidungen' in R. Hüßtege and H.-P. Mansel (eds.), *Rom-Verordnungen*, Nomos, Baden-Baden 2015, 2nd ed., margin notes 2–3, U. Bergquist, 'Chapter IV: Recognition, Enforceability and Enforcement of Decisions' in U. Bergquist et al., *EU Regulation on Succession and Wills*, Verlag Dr. Otto Schmidt, Köln 2015, pp. 184–185. A. Dutta, 'Vorbemerkung zu Art. 39 EuErbVO' in F.J. Säcker, R. Rixecker, H. Oetker and B. Limperg (eds.), *Münchener Kommentar zum BGB*, Verlag C.H. Beck, Munich 2015, 6th ed., margin note 3.

enforcement of decisions from non-EU Member States, and do not cover conflict of laws or jurisdiction, they are not in collision with the Regulation. If and when some of those States accede to the European Union, the Succession Regulation will prevail in application between them as well.[10]

The only bilateral treaty that applies in Croatia pursuant to Article 75(1) of the Succession Regulation is the one on legal assistance with the former Soviet Union (**Treaty 4**). That treaty was in force in Croatia when the Succession Regulation came into force; it regulates the issues covered by the Succession Regulation and was not concluded exclusively between Member States. It thus meets all the criteria under Article 75(1), and therefore the Regulation does not influence its application.

2. TREATY WITH THE SOVIET UNION TAKING PRECEDENCE OVER THE EUROPEAN SUCCESSION REGULATION

2.1. BACKGROUND

In the 1950s and 1960s former Yugoslavia concluded several treaties on international legal assistance having a very similar scope of application as well as similar rules. Examples of such treaties are the ones with Austria of 1954[11] (**Treaty 3**), Bulgaria of 1956[12] (**Treaty 22**), Poland of 1960[13] (**Treaty 26**), Romania of 1960[14] (**Treaty 27**), former Czechoslovakia[15] of 1964 (**Treaty 13**)

---

10 North Macedonia and Turkey are candidates for accession to the EU, and Bosnia and Herzegovina is a potential candidate. Information available at <https://europa.eu/european-union/about-eu/countries_en>, accessed 28.03.2019.

11 Treaty between the Federal People's Republic of Yugoslavia and the Republic of Austria on reciprocal legal transactions of 16.12.1954 (Ugovor između Federativne Narodne Republike Jugoslavije i Republike Austrije o uzajamnom pravnom saobraćaju od 16. prosinca 1954.), OJ FPRY, Int'l Treaties No. 8/1955.

12 Treaty between the Federal People's Republic of Yugoslavia and the Republic of Bulgaria on reciprocal legal assistance of 23.03.1956 (Ugovor između Federativne Narodne Republike Jugoslavije i Narodne Republike Bugarske o uzajamnoj pravnoj pomoći od 23. ožujka 1956.), OJ FPRY, Int'l Treaties No. 1/1957.

13 Treaty between Yugoslavia and Poland on legal transactions in civil and criminal matters of 06.02.1960 (Ugovor između Jugoslavije i Poljske o pravnom saobraćaju u građanskim i krivičnim stvarima 6. veljače 1960.), OJ FPRY, Int'l Treaties 5/1963.

14 Treaty between the Socialist Federal Republic of Yugoslavia and the Romanian People's Republic on legal assistance of 18.10.1960 (Ugovor između Socijalističke Federativne Republike Jugoslavije i Rumunjske Narodne Republike o pravnoj pomoći od 18. listopada 1960.), OJ FPRY, Int'l Treaties No. 8/1961.

15 Treaty between Yugoslavia and Czechoslovakia on regulation of legal relations in civil, family and criminal matters of 20.01.1964 (Ugovor između Jugoslavije i Čehoslovačke o regulisanju pravnih odnosa u građanskim, porodičnim i krivičnim stvarima od 20. siječnja 1964.), OJ SFRY, Int'l Treaties No. 13/1964.

and Hungary of 1968[16] (**Treaty 25**). They cover a wide range of issues related to international legal assistance and the private international law of civil, commercial and family matters. In that vein they also contain rules on succession matters. Croatia became a party to those treaties by means of succession, i.e. by notification of succession.[17] However, these treaties do not apply today in succession matters as they have been superseded by the Succession Regulation given that they were concluded with EU Member States.

On the other hand, the Treaty between the Federal People's Republic of Yugoslavia and the Union of Soviet Socialist Republics on legal assistance in civil, family and criminal matters of 24 February 1962 (**Treaty 4**; hereinafter: the Treaty) still applies by virtue of Article 75(1) of the Succession Regulation. The Treaty came into force in Croatia on 8 October 1991 by means of succession.[18] It remains in force only between Croatia and the Russian Federation while it does not apply between Croatia and other former Soviet Union States.[19]

2.2. SCOPE OF APPLICATION

The Treaty has a wide scope of application *ratione materiae*. It applies in civil and criminal matters, providing rules on different areas of legal assistance, including but not limited to legal aid, service of documents, costs of proceedings, security for costs, conflict of laws and jurisdictional rules for different civil matters as well as recognition and enforcement of judgments in civil matters.

In the context of successions having an international element, the Treaty covers conflict-of-laws rules, jurisdictional rules, rules regarding powers of diplomatic and consular staff, and recognition and enforcement rules. First, the principle of equality in succession matters is established, i.e. Russian citizens are given equal rights in succession matters in Croatia as enjoyed by Croatian citizens. Such a rule establishes reciprocity in succession matters, which is important, since without it foreign (non-EU Member State) nationals are not

---

16 Treaty between the Socialist Federal Republic of Yugoslavia and the People's Republic of Hungary on reciprocal legal transactions of 07.03.1968 (Ugovor između Socijalističke Federativne Republike Jugoslavije i Narodne Republike Mađarske o uzajamnom pravnom saobraćaju od 7. ožujka 1968.), OJ SFRY, Int'l Treaties Nos. 3/1968, 1/1987.

17 See OJ, Int'l Treaties, Nos. 9/1995, 1/1997, 11/1997, 13/1997, 4/2002, 1/2005.

18 Treaty between Yugoslavia and the Union of Soviet Socialist Republics on legal assistance in civil, family and criminal matters of 24.02.1962 (Ugovor između FNRY i SSSR-a o pravnoj pomoći u građanskim, porodičnim i krivičnim stvarima od 24. veljače 1962.), OJ FPRY, Int'l Treaties No. 5/1963. Croatia became a party to the Convention on 08.10.1991 by notification of succession published in the OJ, Int'l Treaties, No. 4/1998.

19 Information gathered from the Ministry of Foreign Affairs and European Integration, <http://www.mvep.hr/hr/vanjska-politika/bilateralni-odnosi/pregled-bilateralnih-medunarodnih-ugovora/> accessed 28.03.2019.

able to inherit in Croatia.[20] It is further expressly stated that nationals of one State can dispose by a testament of their assets located in the other country.[21]

Further, and with respect to the substantive scope of application in succession matters in particular, the Treaty covers both succession by testamentary disposition as well as intestate succession, including forced heirship. Also, the issue of *bona vacantia* is regulated by a special provision.[22] Besides succession matters, the Treaty also covers issues pertaining to succession, such as a declaration of death *in absentia* as well as matters that may occur in inheritance proceedings as preliminary questions – legal capacity, establishing or contesting maternity, paternity and adoption.[23]

The Treaty does not, however, necessarily cover all the succession estate. All movable assets are within the Treaty's scope of application, but immovable assets can be outside its scope of application, which is evidenced in the rules on jurisdiction.[24] Since jurisdiction for succession to all movables is given to the authorities of the country of nationality of the deceased, it is clear that even movables situated in a non-contracting State are covered by the Treaty. When it comes to the localization of movable assets, especially intangible ones, the Treaty is silent on the issue. Seeing that the authorities of the deceased person's nationality have jurisdiction, and the same law applies to the succession to movables, their localization is irrelevant in terms of applicability of the Treaty.

Jurisdiction concerning immovables is given to the authorities of the State in which they are situated. Thus, if a Russian national owns immovables in Croatia and in another country, the Treaty does not apply to the succession to immovable property in that other country. Therefore, the competent Croatian authority's decision on its jurisdiction and the applicable law for that property will be taken under the rules of the Succession Regulation. For example, if the person has habitual residence in Croatia, jurisdiction will exist under Article 4 of the Regulation. Still, if the assets are situated in a third, non-EU Member State, the Croatian competent authority may, at the request of one of the parties, decide not to rule on such assets under Article 12 of the Succession Regulation if it may be expected that its decision will not be recognized and declared enforceable in that third State.

---

20 Art. 2 of the Croatian Succession Act, OJ Nos. 48/2003, 163/2003, 35/2005, 127/2013, 33/2015. However, according to Art. 2(2) of the same Act, reciprocity is presumed until proven otherwise. The same was held by the Supreme Court of the Republic of Croatia in Judgment Rev 3341/1993-2 of 23.06.1994, which stated that 'as far as reciprocity in succession with certain states is concerned, the practice starts from a presumption that reciprocity in succession matters exists with all States – until the opposite is proven'.

21 Art. 36 of the Treaty.

22 Art. 46 of the Treaty.

23 Arts. 25–35 of the Treaty. The main connecting factor as well as the jurisdictional criterion for all matters is nationality.

24 Art. 39 of the Treaty.

With respect to the personal scope of application of the Treaty, it applies only to the succession of nationals of the Contracting States, i.e. Russian and Croatian nationals. The Treaty does not address the situation in which a person has dual nationality, i.e. Croatian nationality and another nationality, whether Russian or of another country. The Croatian PIL Act, on the other hand, regulates that situation in its Article 11. Yet it may be doubtful whether the PIL Act would even apply since according to its Article 3 the Act does not apply in situations regulated by an international treaty. Still, since the application of Article 11 of the PIL Act would be used to determine the scope of application of the Treaty, it might be concluded that the provisions of the PIL Act apply if they serve the goal and function of the Treaty.

According to Article 11 of the PIL Act, if a person has dual nationality, one of which is Croatian, he/she is to be considered solely a Croatian national.[25] Therefore, the competent authority would consider dual nationals holding Croatian nationality solely Croatian nationals. With respect to the scope of application of the Treaty, this means that it would not apply in the case of a dual Croatian-Russian national unless that person has immovable property in Russia. In that case, the competent Russian authority would have jurisdiction and would apply Russian law to succession in respect of immovable property under the Treaty.[26] If the competent Croatian authority fails to apply the Treaty and decides upon the inheritance of immovable assets situated in Russia, it would be in breach of its international obligation. On the other side, if a dual Croatian-Russian national has no immovable property in Russia, but has such property in other States, Croatian authorities would apply the Succession Regulation.

If the person has dual nationality, neither of which is Croatian, the law of the country of nationality in which the person is domiciled is to be applied under Article 11(2) of the PIL Act. This means that if a person has Russian nationality as well as that of another country, but is domiciled in Russia, the competent authority would apply the Treaty. If the person is domiciled in that other country, the Treaty would not apply since the competent authority would not consider that person a Russian national. Further, if the person is not domiciled in the country of his/her nationality, the competent authority applies, under Article 11(3) of the PIL Act, the law of that nationality to which the person is most closely connected, i.e. the law of effective nationality.[27] Where a person

---

25 A similar provision can be found in Art. 2 of the Croatian Nationality Act (OJ Nos. 53/1991, 70/1991, 28/1992, 113/1993, 4/1994, 130/2011, 110/2015).

26 Arts. 37(2) and 39(2) of the Treaty.

27 See more in M. Dika, G. Knežević and S. Stojanović, *Komentar zakona o međunarodnom privatnom i procesnom pravu*, Nomos, Belgrade 1991, p. 48., P. Bosnić, *Hrvatsko međunarodno privatno pravo*, Pravni fakultet Sveučilišta u Splitu, Split 1999, p. 66, K. Sajko, *Međunarodno privatno pravo*, Zagreb, Narodne novine 2009, 5th ed., p. 124, T. Varadi et al., *Međunarodno privatno pravo*, Univerzitet u Beogradu – Pravni fakultet, Belgrade 2016, 15th ed., p. 270.

holding Russian and another foreign nationality is domiciled in a country whose nationality the person does not have, the Treaty would apply if the competent authority would consider that the person is most closely connected to Russia, i.e. has the effective nationality of Russia.

The solution of the PIL Act for dual nationals having Russian and another foreign nationality might not be consistent with the Treaty's purpose. For that reason, application of the PIL Act could be avoided by interpreting the Treaty in a way that it always applies to Russian nationals, notwithstanding the fact that they have the nationality of another country. In that way, the personal scope of application of the Treaty would be expanded and the purpose of the Treaty ensured – legal assistance and equal legal protection of nationals of one Contracting State in the other.[28] That would, however, result in a narrowing of the scope of application of the Succession Regulation.

Such interpretation might lead to further complications. For example, a Russian-German national who had his/her last habitual residence in Croatia and who owned movable and immovable property in Croatia would be considered solely a Russian national and his/her succession would be governed by Russian law (for movables) and Croatian law (for immovables) under the Treaty. Under the Regulation, by contrast, the default rule would result in application of Croatian law. However, he/she would also be able to choose as applicable the law of either of his/her nationalities under Article 22 of the Regulation, one of them being German law in this example. It is evident that in such circumstances the application of the Treaty may go against the deceased person's wishes – if he/she chose German law as applicable – as well as the idea of non-discrimination of EU nationals.

3. CONFLICT OF LAWS

The Treaty contains several conflict-of-laws rules: one on succession in general; one on the form of a testamentary disposition and its revocation; and one on *bona vacantia*.

The choice-of-laws rule for succession in general differentiates between the law applicable for movable and immovable property. Succession to movable property is governed by the law of nationality (*lex patriae*) of the deceased at the time of death and the succession to immovable property is governed by law of the place where the property is situated (*lex rei sitae*).[29] By providing different connecting factors for succession to movable and immovable property,

---

28 Art. 1 of the Treaty expressly provides for equal legal protection of nationals of one Contracting State in the other Contracting State.

29 Art. 37 of the Treaty.

the Treaty accepts the scission of the estate and departs in that regard not only from the formerly applicable PIL Act and the Succession Regulation, but also from other bilateral treaties concluded by Croatia which accept the unity of the succession estate.[30] In a hypothetical situation of a Russian national who owned both movable and immovable property in Croatia, the competent authority would apply Russian law for the movable property (if it were competent for those assets) and Croatian law for the immovable assets. If that person, however, had habitual residence in another EU country that has no bilateral treaty with Russia, the competent authority of that country would, as a default rule, have jurisdiction and would apply its own law to the succession as a whole under the Regulation.[31]

The issue regarding the law applicable to the question of whether the assets are movable or immovable is not regulated by the Treaty itself. This is a deviation from other bilateral treaties concluded in the same period under which the law governing that issue is the law of the country where the assets are located.[32] Academic writings suggest that the same approach should be applied in Croatian law in general, although the Croatian PIL Act accepts multi-stage characterization. Under that method, characterization is governed by domestic law as long as the competent authority applies domestic conflict-of-laws. If domestic conflict-of-laws rules lead to the application of foreign law, then characterization is also governed by that law.[33] However, application of *lex rei sitae* is mentioned as an exception to the rule when the issue of the characterization of property as movable or immovable is at hand.[34] Such an exception is also accepted for the characterization of property in the jurisdictional rule for succession matters that differentiates between movable

---

30 Art. 30 of the PIL Act, Art. 21 of the Succession Regulation. See M. Dika, G. Knežević and S. Stojanović, above n. 27, p. 107 for bilateral treaties.

31 Arts. 4 and 21 of the Succession Regulation.

32 Art. 39 of the Treaty with Austria of 1954 (**Treaty 3**), Art. 33 of the Treaty with Bulgaria of 1956 (**Treaty 22**), Art. 48 of the Treaty with Poland of 1960 (**Treaty 26**), Art. 38 of the Treaty with Romania of 1960 (**Treaty 27**), Art. 39(5) of the Treaty with Czechoslovakia of 1964 (**Treaty 13**), Art. 54 of the Treaty with Hungary of 1968 (**Treaty 25**).

33 M. Dika, G. Knežević and S. Stojanović, above n. 27, pp. 40–41, P. Bosnić, above n. 27, pp. 56–57, M. Živković, 'Opšte ustanove međunarodnog privatnog prava i Zakon o rešavanju sukoba zakona sa propisima drugih zemalja – pogled dvadeset godina kasnije i de lege ferenda' in M. Živković (ed.), Dvadeset godina Zakona o međunarodnom privatnom pravu, Centar za publikacije Pravnog fakulteta u Nišu, Niš 2004, pp. 18–19, K. Sajko, above n. 27, pp. 184–185. Cf. A. Jakšić, 'Član 9. ZMPP-a i osnovni pojmovi međunarodnog privatnog prava' in M. Živković (ed.), *Dvadeset godina Zakona o međunarodnom privatnom pravu*, Centar za publikacije Pravnog fakulteta u Nišu, Niš 2004, pp. 66–67.

34 M. Dika, G. Knežević, S. Stojanović, above n. 27, pp. 39–40, P. Bosnić, above n. 27, p. 57, M. Živković, above, n. 33, p. 21. According to K. Sajko, above n. 27, p. 180, connecting factors are only to be interpreted – and not to be classified – but the interpretation is done under the most closely connected law, which in case of assets would be the *lex rei sitae*.

and immovable property.[35] It is thus reasonable to conclude that the same would apply in the context of the Treaty.

The conflict-of-laws rule for the formal validity of a testamentary disposition and its revocation is contained in Article 38 of the Treaty. Two alternative connecting factors are foreseen. The governing law is either the law of the nationality of the deceased at the time of the disposition/revocation, or the law of the country where the disposition/revocation was made. The Treaty thus follows the generally accepted principle of *favor testamenti*, which enables the disposition to be valid in terms of form in more situations. It is, however, not as generous as the Succession Regulation or the Hague Convention of 1961, which both foresee five different connecting factors and ensure formal validity in a very wide number of cases.[36]

The Treaty is silent on the issue of the law applicable to the substantive validity of a testamentary disposition. Other bilateral treaties as well as the Croatian PIL Act contain a rule on capacity to make a will, but such a provision is missing in the Treaty.[37] The question thus arises as to whether the general succession law as determined by the Treaty applies or whether the competent authority may resort to the Succession Regulation in order to determine the law applicable. The answer to the latter question should be in the negative since the Treaty supersedes the Regulation in all succession matters, although that might not be the happiest solution. Application of the law designated under the Treaty for succession in general could lead to the application of two different laws depending on whether the assets were movable or not. While that will most probably turn out to be quite impractical, such an approach is not completely unknown in comparative private international law.[38] On the other hand, application of the Succession Regulation would lead to the application of only one law, but not necessarily the law that would govern other issues under the Treaty. Under the Regulation, the governing law is the one that would be applicable to succession as a whole had the testator died on the day of the making of the will, meaning that the governing law would be either the one of nationality as chosen by the testator or the one of habitual residence of the deceased if no manifestly more closely connected law exists.[39]

---

35 M. Dika, G. Knežević and S. Stojanović, above n. 27, p. 233, 237.

36 See Art. 27 of the Succession Regulation and Art. 1 of the Hague Convention of 1961.

37 Art. 30(2) of the Croatian PIL Act as well as Art. 21 of the Treaty with Bulgaria of 1956 (**Treaty 22**), Art. 37 of the Treaty with Poland of 1960 (**Treaty 26**), Art. 35(1) of the Treaty with Romania of 1960 (**Treaty 27**), Art. 38(1) of the Treaty with Czechoslovakia of 1964 (**Treaty 13**), Art. 43(1) of the Treaty with Hungary of 1968 (**Treaty 25**).

38 E.g. in the UK; see: J. Fawcett and J.M. Carruthers, *Cheshire, North and Fawcett Private International Law*, Oxford University Press, Oxford 2008, 14th ed., p. 1265, 1279, Lord C. of Mapesbury et al. (eds.), *Dicey, Morris and Collins on the Conflict of Laws*, Volume 2, Sweet and Maxwell, London 2012, 15th ed., p. 1419.

39 Art. 24(1) of the Succession Regulation.

Finally, the Treaty contains a special rule on the issue of *bona vacantia*, i.e. an estate without heirs. An estate without heirs usually passes to the State. The difference amongst States is how their legal order views the role of the State in such a circumstance – it can either be an appropriator acquiring the assets located on its territory as a sovereign authority or a residual heir inheriting the assets notwithstanding their location.[40] Under the Treaty, if there are no heirs under the governing law, movable property passes to the country whose nationality the deceased person held, and immovable property passes to the country in which it is located.[41] The Treaty therefore characterizes the issue of movable *bona vacantia* as one of inheritance, which leads to application of the law of nationality of the deceased, and immovable *bona vacantia* as one of occupation, which leads to application of the law of the place where the immovable assets are situated.[42] The Regulation, on the other hand, does not resolve the issue so directly. It only gives States the right to appropriate assets located within its territory, as long as creditors are allowed to seek satisfaction from the estate as a whole.[43]

It can be seen that the rules of the Treaty on the applicable law are quite different from the ones of the Succession Regulation. To what extent this influences the uniformity of the choice of law in succession matters in Croatia in practice is questionable. There have been no published decisions of Croatian courts on the application of the Treaty. How often judges and notaries even have an opportunity to apply the Treaty might be seen through statistical data. According to the last population census from 2011, there were 1,279 Russian nationals in Croatia, which is 0.03 per cent of the population, meaning they constitute the 15th largest minority in Croatia.[44] However, some of these Russian nationals may also have Croatian nationality, and the Treaty might not apply to them. Besides the fact that there is a small number of Russian nationals living in Croatia, one should also bear in mind that Russian nationals are also owners of real estate in Croatia. Russian natural persons have been able to acquire real estate in Croatia from May 2014, when the Ministry of Justice declared that reciprocity with Russia exists with respect to ownership of real estate by natural persons.[45] Russian nationals are showing interest

40 See e.g. I. Medić Musa, above n. 2, p. 369, P. Wautelet, 'Article 33' in A. Bonomi and P. Wautelet (eds.), *Le droit européen des successions*, Bruylant, Bruxelles 2013, p. 502, P. Lagarde, 'Chapter III: Applicable Law' in U. Bergquist et al., *EU Regulation on Succession and Wills*, Verlag Dr. Otto Schmidt, Köln 2015, p. 169.

41 Art. 46 of the Treaty.

42 M. Dika, G. Knežević and S. Stojanović, above n. 27, p. 108.

43 Art. 33 of the Succession Regulation.

44 Data available at <https://www.dzs.hr/> accessed 28.03.2019.

45 See journal articles such as: 'Hrvatske nekretnine opet veliki hit u Rusiji 'U 30 dana dobili smo upit za kupnju marine i par hotela', 07.07.2014, *Jutarnji list*, <http://www.jutarnji.hr/biznis/financije-i-trzista/hrvatske-nekretnine-opet-veliki-hit-u-rusiji-u-30-dana-dobili-smo-upit-za-kupnju-marine-i-par-hotela/674164/> accessed 28.03.2019, 'Miljenić dopušta

in buying real estate in Croatia, especially along the Croatian coastline.[46] Since the Treaty is on occasion applicable to the succession to not only the Croatian-based movable property of a deceased Russian national[47] but also to Croatian-based immovable property of a deceased Russian national, the impact of the Treaty on the private international law of succession in Croatia is not to be disregarded.

4. PROCEDURAL ISSUES

4.1. JURISDICTION

Jurisdiction in succession matters follows the principle of scission of the estate as enshrined in the conflict-of-laws rules of the Treaty. Jurisdiction for succession to movable property is given to the authorities of the State of nationality of the deceased, whereas jurisdiction for succession to immovable assets is given to the authorities of the country where the assets are located.[48] In both cases the competent authority also has jurisdiction over succession disputes.[49] The Treaty further allows an exception for jurisdiction over movable property situated in the country of last domicile of the deceased. In cases where a national of one Contracting State had his/her last domicile in the other Contracting State, heirs and legatees having domicile or residence in that Contracting State may demand that its authorities conduct succession proceedings over movable assets situated in that State. They may make this demand within six months from the time of death, and a further deadline of three months is given to heirs if they wish to object to such jurisdiction. If no objection is raised, the proceedings will be held in the Contracting State of the last domicile of the deceased as regards the movables situated there.[50]

The default rule on jurisdiction thus enables, in principle, a so-called *Gleichlauf* – i.e. situations where the competent authority applies its own law.

Rusima kupnju nekretnina', 14.05.2017, *Večernji list*, <https://www.vecernji.hr/vijesti/ministar-miljenic-dopusta-rusima-kupnju-nekretnina-938788> accessed 28.03.2019.

46 See journal articles such as: M. Brkljača, 'Rusi obožavaju kupovati nekretnine u Hrvatskoj, a iznosi koje troše kreću se u milijunima eura', 16.05.2016, <http://www.vijesti.rtl.hr/novosti/hrvatska/1943463/rusi-obozavaju-kupovati-nekretnine-u-hrvatskoj-a-iznosi-koje-trose-krecu-se-u-milijunima-eura/> accessed 28.03.2019, S. Lukić, 'Slovenci, Nijemci i Rusi kupuju najviše kuća po Hrvatskoj', *Jutarnji list*, 15.05.2016, <http://www.jutarnji.hr/vijesti/hrvatska/slovenci-nijemci-i-rusi-kupuju-najvise-kuca-po-hrvatskoj/4041753/> accessed 28.03.2019. Since 2006 the Ministry of Justice has issued 528 approvals to Russian legal and natural persons for acquisition of ownership of immovables.

47 Art. 39(4) of the Treaty. See more in 4.1. Jurisdiction, nn. 50–51 and accompanying text.

48 Art. 39(1)–(2) of the Treaty. The same is stated in the rules, now inapplicable, of the other bilateral treaties. See M. Dika, G. Knežević and S. Stojanović, above n. 27, pp. 235–236.

49 Art. 39(3) of the Treaty.

50 Art. 39(4) of the Treaty.

Thus, the competent authority of the country of nationality of the deceased will have jurisdiction and apply its own law on succession to movables, whereas the competent authority of the country where the immovable property is situated will have jurisdiction over those assets and will apply its own law. By way of exception, when an authority of the country of the last domicile has jurisdiction over movable property situated in that State, it applies the law of the country of nationality of the deceased and not its own law. The Treaty is in this respect similar to the Succession Regulation, which also tries to ensure that the competent authority applies its own law in most situations.[51]

Besides the general jurisdictional rule for succession, the Treaty also regulates jurisdiction for the opening and reading of wills. Jurisdiction is given to the authorities of the country in which the will is situated.[52] If an authority of one Contracting State has opened and read a will of a national of the other Contracting State, the copy of the will (or its original if needed), a copy of the minutes regarding the reading of the will proceedings and information on the condition of the will is to be delivered to the authority of the country of nationality of the deceased.[53]

The authorities of the Contracting State in which the assets of a national of the other Contracting State are situated have jurisdiction for preservation measures regarding those assets. Those authorities are to make a list of the assets and issue measures in order to secure and administer them in accordance with their own law. They also have to inform the diplomatic or consular staff of the other Contracting State about the measures taken and transfer the movable assets and documents to the staff on its demand. The diplomatic or consular staff may take part in the performance of those measures and may propose that they be changed, revoked or postponed.[54]

4.2. POWERS OF DIPLOMATIC AND CONSULAR STAFF

The Treaty vests the diplomatic and consular staff of the Contracting States with several powers relevant to succession law matters. The diplomatic and consular staff have the power to provide and receive information about the death of nationals of the Contracting States, to transfer and accept the assets of the deceased and to represent their nationals.

---

51 Recital 27 of the Preamble to the Succession Regulation.

52 Art. 43(1) of the Treaty.

53 Art. 43(2) of the Treaty.

54 Art. 42 of the Treaty. Very similar provisions can be found in Art. 51(1)–(3) of the Consular convention between the Socialist Federal Republic of Yugoslavia and the Union of Soviet Socialist Republics of 10.06.1987, OJ SFRY, Int'l Treaties No. 7/1989 (hereinafter: Consular Convention). Croatia became a party to the Convention on 08.10.1991 by notification of succession published in OJ, Int'l Treaties, No. 4/1998.

The diplomatic or consular staff of one Contracting State is to be informed about the death of its national in the other Contracting State or about movables situated in that other State if its national dies in a non-contracting country. The information should also cover knowledge regarding the heirs, the estate and the testament, if any. Also, if the diplomatic and consular staff find out about the death of their nationals sooner than the authorities of the other Contracting State, they are to inform these authorities about the assets situated there so they can secure them if necessary. In all cases, the diplomatic and consular staff are to exchange information if a national of the other Contracting State appears as an interested party in succession proceedings.[55]

Further duties of the diplomatic and consular staff relate to transfer of assets of the deceased national of either of the Contracting States. First, if a national of one Contracting State dies during a trip in the other Contracting State, where he/she had no residence or domicile, his/her assets are to be given to the diplomatic and consular staff of his/her State without any formalities.[56] Second, if after succession proceedings the assets are to be transferred to an heir who is a national of the other Contracting State in which he/she resides or is domiciled, those assets are to be given to the diplomatic and consular staff of that other Contracting State. In order for the transfer to occur, several conditions need to be fulfilled; requirements include that the competent authority has invited creditors to register their claims, claims have been secured or paid, the inheritance tax has been paid and the competent authority approves such transfer.[57]

Last but not least, diplomatic and consular staff have the right to represent their nationals in all succession matters without any special authorization as long as those persons are absent and have not authorized another person to represent them.[58]

4.3. RECOGNITION AND ENFORCEMENT OF FOREIGN DECISIONS

Under the Treaty, one Contracting State is to recognize and enforce decisions from the other Contracting State in civil and family law matters. In relation to succession decisions, the Treaty expressly mentions that decisions issued by notaries are also to be recognized and enforced under the same rules as

---

55 Art. 41 of the Treaty. Very similar provisions can be found in Art. 50 of the Consular Convention.

56 Art. 40 of the Treaty. Very similar provision can be found in Art. 51(3) of the Consular Convention.

57 Art. 45 of the Treaty.

58 Art. 44 of the Treaty. Very similar provisions can be found in Art. 51(4)–(5) of the Consular Convention.

court decisions.[59] In that manner, the Treaty is similar to the Succession Regulation, whose recognition and enforcement rules also apply to decisions of Croatian notaries in succession matters since they can conduct succession proceedings as court delegates.[60]

The Treaty foresees that recognition of a decision is an outcome of a recognition proceeding, meaning that recognition is not automatic.[61] There are only a few exceptions to the rule – decisions on dissolution of marriage, on declaration of death and on legal capacity of nationals of one Contracting State issued in that State that are to be recognized in the other Contracting State automatically, without any review.[62] This is a major difference from the Succession Regulation, which promotes the idea of mutual trust between courts of Member States by providing that decisions are recognized without any special procedure taking place.[63]

Decisions in succession matters are to be recognized and enforced under the Treaty if several requirements are met: if they are confirmed to be final and enforceable; if the authority in the country of origin would have jurisdiction over the matter according to the rules of the country of recognition; if recognition and enforcement is not contrary to the fundamental principles of the law of the State of recognition (public policy clause); if there was no breach of either the right to be heard or the representation rights of the person against whom the decision was brought; if no earlier decision or proceedings between the same parties in the same matter exist in the State of recognition; if the law of the State of recognition had to be applied and it was, or another law was applied that does not essentially deviate from the law of the State of recognition.[64] It is worth noting that similar requirements are also provided for in the treaties with Bosnia and Herzegovina of 1996, (today: North) Macedonia of 1994 and Turkey of 1999. The only major distinction is in the jurisdictional requirement – under those treaties the only reason to reject recognition and enforcement is the fact that the court of the State of recognition had exclusive jurisdiction over that matter, whereas the *Spiegelbildprinzip* applies in the Treaty.[65]

The party seeking recognition and enforcement has to submit, together with the application, a copy of the decision and a confirmation of its finality

---

59 Art. 48(2) of the Treaty.

60 Recital 20 of the Preamble to the Succession Regulation in connection with Art. 176(3) of the Croatian Succession Act.

61 Art. 51(1) of the Treaty.

62 Art. 54 of the Treaty.

63 Art. 39(1) of the Succession Regulation.

64 Art. 49 of the Treaty.

65 Art. 21 of the Treaty with Bosnia and Herzegovina of 1996, Art. 21 of the Treaty with Macedonia of 1994, Art. 18 of the Treaty with Turkey of 1999.

and enforceability, confirmation that the party who did not take part in the proceedings and against whom the decision was brought was invited in time and in accordance with the rules of the State of origin to take part in the proceedings and, finally, an official translation of those documents.[66] The application for recognition and enforcement is to be submitted to the authority that issued the decision that will then transfer it to the court competent for recognition and enforcement in the Contracting State of recognition.[67] If the party has residence or domicile in the State of recognition, it may submit the application to the competent court of that State directly.[68] The court deciding upon recognition and enforcement may seek explanation from the requesting party or the authority that issued the decision.[69] The deciding court conducts the proceedings of recognition and enforcement in accordance with its own law.[70]

5. THE FUTURE OF THE TREATY WITH THE RUSSIAN FEDERATION

The Croatian government has not voiced any plans to either terminate or modify the Treaty. Its termination seems rather unlikely given the fact that Croatia wishes to strengthen its relationship with Russia, especially with regard to economic exchange.[71] Modification of the Treaty is not that unlikely, but it also does not seem to be a top priority from an external relations perspective.

It is interesting that the Treaty regulates conflict-of-laws rules in succession matters differently from both Croatian and Russian private international law. Under Croatian law, i.e. the Succession Regulation, the governing law applies to the succession as a whole, accepting unity of the estate. The applicable law will be the law of nationality of the deceased person if chosen, and if there is no choice, the law of last habitual residence of the deceased applies if there is no manifestly more connected law.[72] Russian private international law provides for scission of the estate by designating the law of last residence of the deceased as governing for movable assets and the *lex rei sitae* as governing for

66 Arts. 51(4) and 52 of the Treaty.
67 Art. 51(2) of the Treaty.
68 Art. 51(3) of the Treaty.
69 Art. 53(2) of the Treaty.
70 Art. 53(1) of the Treaty.
71 See Ministry of Foreign Affairs and European Integration website, <http://www.mvep.hr/hr/mediji/ostale-vijesti/veleposlanik-republike-hrvatske-u-ruskoj-federaciji-tonci-stanicic-predao,46897.html> accessed 28.03.2019.
72 Arts. 21 and 22 of the Succession Regulation.

immovable assets.[73] The main difference when compared to the Treaty is in the connecting factor for the succession to movable property. The Treaty foresees nationality and Russian law the last place of residence as the connecting factor. The Russian law defines residence as the place where a person permanently or habitually resides.[74]

A difference also exists with respect to capacity to make a will as well as the form of the will. Capacity to make a will is, at least according to the authors, governed by *lex rei sitae* and *lex patriae* under the Treaty. The Regulation provides for application of the same law as to the succession in general (nationality if chosen, last habitual residence if no choice was made and an escape clause is not applicable), whereas under Russian law the governing law is the one of residence of the deceased at the time when the will was made.[75] All three approaches are thus different, and a common thread cannot easily be found. The only common ground is the one on which the Regulation and Russian law stand, since in Russia residence could be equated to habitual residence.

The form of a will and will revocation is governed by either of several alternative laws under all three regimes. The Hague Convention of 1961 that is applicable in Croatia foresees the greatest number of connecting factors, five of them in total. The Treaty has only two alternative connecting factors – nationality of the deceased and the place where the will was made – and Russian law foresees the application of the law of residence of the deceased or the law of the place where the will was made or Russian law, thus having three connecting factors.[76]

Modification of the Treaty could thus be made in order to bring the Treaty closer to both Russian and Croatian law. If the scission principle is to remain in the Treaty, the connecting factor for movable property should be habitual residence, and not nationality of the deceased, so as to harmonize the rule with Russian law and approximate it to Croatian law, at least with respect to the choice of the connecting factor. The capacity to make a will should, for reasons of practicality, be governed by one law, preferably the one of habitual residence of the deceased in order to approximate the Treaty to both Croatian and Russian law. The form of testaments, on the other hand, should be governed by as many alternatively applicable laws as possible, modelled after the Hague Convention of 1961, so as to strengthen *favor testamenti*.

---

73 Art. 1224(1) of the Russian Civil Code. English translation published in [2002] *Yearbook of Private International Law*, pp. 349–364.

74 S. Lebedev et al., 'New Russian Legislation on Private International Law', [2002] *Yearbook of Private International Law* 117, 144.

75 For more on the Treaty's rules and those of the Succession Regulation see above, under 3. Conflict of Laws. For Russian Law see Art. 1224(2) of the Russian Civil Code.

76 For more on the Treaty's rules and those of the Succession Regulation see above, under 3. Conflict of Laws. For Russian Law see Art. 1224(2) of the Russian Civil Code.

Such modifications of the Treaty would result in less friction with the Succession Regulation as well as with Russian law and would also be consistent with the contemporary theory of private international law, which favours use of the habitual residence in many areas, including succession, since its application usually fulfils the main task of private international law, namely to find the most closely connected law.

THE EXTERNAL RELATIONS OF THE CZECH REPUBLIC

Magdalena PFEIFFER

1. INTRODUCTION

The Czech Republic is party to a number of bilateral treaties on legal assistance that contain provisions on succession law. A number of these bilateral treaties deal not only with legal assistance in civil matters but also with legal assistance in criminal matters. Apart from national law and the law of the European Union, they represent another source of private international law in the Czech Republic. Pursuant to Article 10 of the Czech Constitution,[1] promulgated treaties, to whose ratification the Parliament of the Czech Republic has given its consent and by which the Czech Republic is bound, form a part of the Czech legal order and take precedence over conflicting national rules. The relationship between international treaties and national law is also explicitly stipulated in Section 2 of the Czech Act on Private International Law (hereinafter 'Czech PILA').[2] According to this provision, the statute is applied when an international treaty by which the Czech Republic is bound does not provide otherwise. Bilateral treaties thus take priority, provided the respective issue is regulated differently than in national law, irrespective of which rule was adopted earlier. The same scheme applies also to multilateral treaties. From the perspective of the Czech Republic the relevance of multilateral treaties in the field of succession is minimal. The Czech Republic is not bound by the 1961 Hague Convention on the Conflicts of Laws Relating to the Form of Testamentary Dispositions.[3] The only multilateral treaty in the field of succession law to which the Czech Republic is a party is the 1973 Hague Convention Concerning the International Administration of the Estates of Deceased Persons.[4] The material scope of this Convention

1 Act No. 1/1993 Coll., Constitution of the Czech Republic.
2 Act No. 91/2012 Coll., on Private International Law.
3 <https://www.hcch.net/en/instruments/conventions/full-text/?cid=40> accessed 28.03.2019.
4 <https://www.hcch.net/en/instruments/conventions/full-text/?cid=83> accessed 28.03.2019.

is not in conflict with the scope of the Succession Regulation. Therefore, this Convention is not considered as relevant within this contribution.

The majority of bilateral treaties on legal assistance were concluded before 1993, the year when the former Czechoslovakia[5] split into two independent States: the Czech Republic and the Slovak Republic. Therefore, in the majority of the bilateral treaties the contracting party is either the Czechoslovak Republic, the Czechoslovak Socialist Republic or the Czech and Slovak Federative Republic, depending on the date of their signature and respective changes in the political arrangement of the Czechoslovak State. The Czech and Slovak Federative Republic was dissolved based upon the Constitutional Act No. 542/1992, Coll. on the Dissolution of the Czech and Slovak Federative Republic, adopted on 25 November 1992. The Czech Republic, as one of the two successor States, was established on 1 January 1993. It assumed all rights and obligations of the Czech and Slovak Federative Republic resulting from international laws as of the date of dissolution of the Czech and Slovak Federative Republic, except for its rights and obligations linked to those territories which are not sovereign territories of the Czech Republic.[6] Given this continuity, the dissolution of the Czechoslovak federation has not jeopardized the validity of the bilateral treaties on legal assistance.

The content of the various bilateral treaties on legal assistance in civil matters binding for the Czech Republic differs substantially. Basically, there are three different groups of bilateral treaties on legal assistance. There is a group of bilateral treaties that, in terms of their material scope, are limited to issues of legal assistance, such as service of documents, the taking of evidence, costs of proceedings, and the validity and evidential value of documents. These treaties are mostly of older date, for example the Treaty with the United Kingdom[7] or with Switzerland,[8] signed in 1926 and 1928, respectively. Another group of bilateral treaties includes, in addition to the above-listed issues of legal assistance, provisions on recognition and enforcement of decisions rendered by judicial authorities of the other contracting party. These kinds of bilateral treaties were concluded mostly with countries with which the former Czechoslovakia had neither close cultural nor economic relations at the time of their signature. The last and most numerous group is constituted by more comprehensive bilateral treaties having an extensive scope of application that, in addition to issues of

---

5 Czech and Slovak Federative Republic.

6 Art. 5 para. 2 of Constitutional Act No. 4/1993 Coll. of the Czech National Council of 15.12.1992 on Measures Related to the Dissolution of the Czech and Slovak Federative Republic.

7 Treaty between Czechoslovak Republic and United Kingdom of Great Britain and Ireland on Legal Assistance in Civil Matters (No. 70/1926 Coll.)

8 Treaty between Czechoslovak Republic and Switzerland on Mutual Legal Assistance in Civil and Commercial Matters (No. 9/1928 Coll.).

legal assistance and recognition and enforcement of decisions, contain special jurisdiction and conflict-of-laws rules for a number of legal acts and relations (legal capacity, family relations, obligations, succession matters and others). Most of these treaties were concluded with former socialist countries from Central and Eastern Europe or with non-European people's democratic countries (e.g. Mongolia (**Treaty 8**), North Korea (**Treaty 7**) or Vietnam (**Treaty 12**)). The discrepancies in the material scope are determined, as indicated above, by historical, political and territorial context. This manner of cooperation in legal matters has survived the dissolution of the Eastern bloc; however, the number of bilateral treaties on legal assistance signed after the year 1989 dropped substantially. Since 1989 only two new relevant treaties have been concluded: with Ukraine in 2001 (**Treaty 10**); and with Uzbekistan in 2002 (**Treaty 11**). One would presume that such comprehensive treaties on legal assistance are being concluded preferably in respect of countries with which a State has very close relations, necessitating the simplification of the legal relations to meet the requirements of practice. There can, however, be other considerations too. In 2002 the Czech Republic concluded such a treaty with Uzbekistan, despite the fact that mutual relations between the Czech Republic and Uzbekistan can hardly be considered close and intensive enough to trigger the necessity of a treaty. The Czech Republic has also concluded various treaties on legal assistance in criminal matters, for example recently with Kazakhstan[9] and Hong Kong.[10]

Even though their provisions may take precedence over both national and EU law, legal practice often neglects those treaties, as knowledge about their scope of application is not so widely spread as in the case of national or EU law.[11] In addition, some of the rules have lost their practical relevance due to political changes that the Contracting States have gone through. A very obvious example of such a non-functioning treaty is the example of the treaty on legal assistance with North Korea (**Treaty 7**).

Bilateral treaties on legal assistance face the same problem as other international conventions – the non-existence of its uniform interpretation. These treaties usually do not contain definitions of the terms applied and although it is expected that treaties are to have a uniform interpretation, the absence of an authority ensuring such uniform interpretation inevitably leads to the practice that courts of contracting parties tend to interpret the treaties pursuant to their national law.

---

9 Treaty with Hong Kong on Mutual Legal Assistance in Criminal Matters (notification of Ministry of Foreign Affairs No. 15/2015 Coll. of Int. Treaties).

10 Treaty with Kazakhstan on Mutual Legal Assistance in Criminal Matters (notification of Ministry of Foreign Affairs No. 55/2014 Coll. of Int. Treaties).

11 J. Valdhans, *Právní úprava mimosmluvních závazků s mezinárodním prvkem*, C. H. Beck, Prague 2012, p. 68.

2. TREATIES AND CONVENTIONS TAKING PRECEDENCE OVER THE EUROPEAN SUCCESSION REGULATION

The Czech Republic has binding bilateral treaties on legal assistance in civil matters that contain special jurisdiction and conflict-of-laws rules on succession with 23 countries: Albania (**Treaty** 5), Belarus (**Treaty** 9), Bosnia and Herzegovina (**Treaty** 13), Bulgaria, Croatia, Cuba (**Treaty** 6), Georgia (**Treaty** 9), Kosovo (**Treaty** 13), Kyrgyzstan (**Treaty** 9), Hungary, (today: North) Macedonia (**Treaty** 13), Moldavia (**Treaty** 9), Mongolia (**Treaty** 8), Montenegro (**Treaty** 13), North Korea (**Treaty** 7), Poland, Romania, Russia (**Treaty** 9), Serbia (**Treaty** 13), Slovenia, Ukraine (**Treaty** 10), Uzbekistan (**Treaty** 11), and Vietnam (**Treaty** 12). These treaties also contain general provisions on recognition and enforcement of decisions rendered by judicial authorities of the other contracting party. Another 12 binding bilateral treaties on legal assistance in civil matters have neither jurisdiction nor conflict-of-laws rules in succession matters but contain general provisions on recognition and enforcement of decisions rendered by judicial authorities of the other contracting party that apply also to decisions in succession matters. This is the case for the treaties with Afghanistan, Algeria, Cyprus, France, Greece, Italy, Slovakia, Spain, Switzerland, Syria, Tunisia and Yemen.

Regarding the relationship of the above-listed bilateral treaties with the Succession Regulation, there is a distinction to be made pursuant to Article 75 of the Succession Regulation between treaties concluded with another EU Member State and with a third country. Given the topic of this book, this report focuses on treaties taking precedence over the Succession Regulation, i.e. treaties concluded with third States on matters covered by the Succession Regulation. From the perspective of the Czech Republic, the Succession Regulation does not affect the application of relevant provisions on succession matters in bilateral treaties with 23 countries: Afghanistan, Albania (**Treaty** 5), Algeria, Belarus (**Treaty** 9), Bosnia and Herzegovina (**Treaty** 13), Cuba (**Treaty** 6), Georgia (**Treaty** 9), Kosovo (**Treaty** 13), Kyrgyzstan (**Treaty** 9), Macedonia (**Treaty** 13), Moldavia (**Treaty** 9), Mongolia (**Treaty** 8), Montenegro (**Treaty** 13), North Korea (**Treaty** 7), Russia (**Treaty** 9), Serbia (**Treaty** 13), Switzerland, Syria, Tunisia, Ukraine (**Treaty** 10), Uzbekistan (**Treaty** 11), Vietnam (**Treaty** 12), and Yemen. Seventeen of them contain, apart from general provisions on recognition and enforcement of decisions rendered by judicial authorities of the other contracting party also applying to decisions in succession matters, special jurisdiction and conflict-of-laws rules on succession matters;[12] six of them

---

12 Albania, Belarus, Bosnia and Herzegovina, Cuba, Georgia, Kosovo, Kyrgyzstan, Macedonia, Moldavia, Mongolia, Montenegro, North Korea, Russia, Serbia, Ukraine, Uzbekistan, and Vietnam.

contain general provisions on recognition and enforcement only.[13] The bilateral treaties on legal assistance concluded with the former Union of Soviet Socialist Republics (hereinafter also 'former Soviet Union') (**Treaty 9**) and the former Socialist Federal Republic of Yugoslavia (hereinafter also 'former Yugoslavia') (**Treaty 13**) apply for a number of successor States.[14] Therefore, there are only 15 relevant bilateral treaties to be analyzed in this chapter. The general provisions on recognition and enforcement of decisions in civil matters given in the territory of the contracting party that are enshrined in all of these bilateral treaties are not dealt with in depth as they are applied in a parallel regime with their counterparts in the Succession Regulation that are applicable to decisions rendered in the territory of Member States, without resulting in any friction.

There is no explicit provision stipulating the personal scope of application in any of these treaties. However, in an introductory general provision, all of them guarantee national treatment to nationals of the other contracting party as regards their individual and property rights. In addition, there is a provision in all respective chapters on succession pursuant to which nationals of one contracting party enjoy equal status as nationals of the other contracting party with respect to their right to acquire property and rights in its territory by testate or intestate succession, as well as with respect to their right to make or revoke a will regarding assets situated in its territory. Based on these general provisions and given the absence of any explicit stipulation, the personal scope of application of the treaties is to be interpreted as limited to cases that involve nationals of contracting parties. Therefore the provisions on matters of succession will apply mainly to proceedings where the deceased is a national of the other contracting party with respect to the property of the deceased that is located in the territory of the forum contracting party. Some of the relevant treaties lay down powers for diplomatic or consular offices to represent their own nationals without special powers of attorney before the authorities of the other contracting party in succession matters, including succession disputes, provided that such nationals are absent and had not issued any power of attorney to any person or agent. These provisions may therefore also apply in cases when a national of one Contracting State is party to succession proceedings opened in the territory of the other contracting party as a potential heir or legatee (irrespective of the nationality of the deceased or of the location of the assets).

None of the treaties addresses possible conflicts of dual or multiple nationalities. Czech judicial authorities are most likely to fill the gap by applying Czech national law. Section 28(1) of the Czech PILA solves dual or multiple

13 Afghanistan, Algeria, Switzerland, Syria, Tunisia, and Yemen.

14 For Belarus, Georgia, Kyrgyzstan, Moldavia and Russia in cases of a treaty with the former Soviet Union; and for Bosnia and Herzegovina, Kosovo, Macedonia, Montenegro and Serbia in cases of a treaty with former Yugoslavia.

nationalities in favour of the Czech nationality[15] and considers dual nationals that hold Czech nationality as Czechs. In a situation where the deceased was at the time of death a national of both contracting parties, Czech authorities would consider him Czech and would not apply the treaty unless the deceased had assets in the territory of the other contracting party. In a situation where the deceased was a dual national of the other contracting party and of a third State, the principle of effective nationality applies, or, in absence of such nationality, the nationality last acquired is decisive pursuant to paragraph (2) of Section 28 of the Czech PILA.[16] Provided the effective nationality or the last acquired nationality of dual nationals that do not hold Czech nationality is the nationality of a third State with which the Czech Republic has no relevant bilateral treaty, the Succession Regulation applies.

There is no provision on the territorial scope of application either. It is beyond doubt that the jurisdiction and conflict-of-laws rules enshrined in these treaties apply to succession to the estate located in the territory of either contracting party; it is, however, questionable whether the same also applies to movable assets of the deceased that are located in the territory of a third State. It is clear from the wording of the respective jurisdiction rules that immovable assets belonging to the deceased that are situated in the territory of a third State are outside of the scope of these treaties. It is less clear with respect to movable assets of the deceased. If we follow a mere linguistic interpretation of the provisions, we might conclude that all movable assets of the deceased irrespective of their location fall within the scope of the bilateral treaties; however, if we follow a systematic and purpose-oriented interpretation, this conclusion does not stand. The territorial scope of application is to be limited to both movable and immovable assets situated in the territory of the contracting parties. A different conclusion could lead to undesirable frictions with the Succession Regulation, resulting in parallel decisions being rendered on succession to movable assets. For example if an Uzbek national domiciled in Uzbekistan with movable and immovable assets in the territory of Uzbekistan, Czech Republic and Germany dies, according to the extensive interpretation both Uzbek judicial authorities pursuant to Article 45(1) of the Czech-Uzbek bilateral treaty[17] **(Treaty 11)**

---

15 Sec. 28(1) of the Czech PILA: 'If someone is in the decisive time period a citizen of the Czech Republic and if such a person is at the same time considered by another state to be its citizen, the nationality of the Czech Republic shall be decisive.'

16 Sec. 28(2) of the Czech PILA: 'If someone is in the decisive time period a citizen of several foreign states, the last acquired nationality shall be decisive provided, considering the person's life situation, the relation of such a person to another state of which he or she is a citizen shall not substantially prevail; in such a case the nationality of that [latter] state shall be decisive.'

17 Treaty between the Czech Republic and the Republic of Uzbekistan on Legal Assistance and Legal Relations in Civil and Criminal Matters, No. 133/2003 Coll. of Int. Treaties.

and German courts by virtue of Article 10(2) of the Succession Regulation would have jurisdiction to rule on movable assets of the deceased situated in Germany.

None of the treaties that lays down jurisdiction and conflict-of-laws rules in succession matters defines their material scope of application. It is to be deduced from the introductory provision in respective chapters on succession which expressly stipulate the equality principle in matters of intestate and testate succession in all relevant treaties that these rules apply to both intestate and testate succession. Due to the absence of a definition, succession matters are likely to be interpreted extensively rather than restrictively and the rules thus applied to all matters of succession.

2.1. TREATY WITH ALBANIA

2.1.1. Background

The treaty between the Czechoslovak Republic and the People's Republic of Albania on Legal Assistance in Civil, Family and Criminal Matters (**Treaty** 5) was concluded on 16 January 1959 and entered into force on 28 May 1960.[18] At the time when this treaty was drafted and signed the People's Republic of Albania was one of the countries of the Eastern bloc with which the former Czechoslovakia had close ties. Therefore, the treaty is relatively comprehensive.

2.1.2. Scope of Application

The treaty covers both civil and criminal matters. In civil matters the treaty contains, among others, provisions on legal assistance; service of documents and the taking of evidence; waiver of security for costs; conflict-of-laws rules on legal capacity; jurisdiction and conflict-of-laws rules on divorce; relations between parents and children; guardianship and curatorship; adoption and succession matters; and provisions on recognition and enforcement of decisions rendered by judicial authorities of the other contracting party.

Relevant provisions on succession matters are enshrined in Articles 31 to 39. With regard to jurisdiction, the treaty stipulates different rules with respect to movable and immovable assets. Pursuant to the rule in Article 34(1), the judicial authorities of the contracting party of which the deceased was a national at the time of his/her death are competent to rule in matters of succession regarding movable assets. However, pursuant to a special rule in Article 34(4), provided

---

18 Decree of the Minister of Foreign Affairs No. 97/1960 Coll.

all movable assets of the deceased national of one contracting party are located in the territory of the other contracting party and provided all heirs agree, the judicial authorities of this contracting party have, upon request of an heir or a legatee, jurisdiction to rule on the succession to the asset. With respect to immovable assets, the judicial authorities of the Contracting State in whose territory the immovable asset is situated have competence to rule on succession to this property (Article 34(2)). It is explicitly stipulated in Article 43(3) that the jurisdiction rules in its paragraphs 1 and 2 apply also in contentious proceedings regarding succession claims. Irrespective of jurisdiction, the authorities of the contracting party in whose territory the assets of the deceased are situated can take all measures necessary to secure and administrate this property according to its own law (Article 38); the authorities are to notify the diplomatic or consular office of the other contracting party, which can request the postponement, modification or revocation of such measures. The treaty grants the diplomatic or consular offices powers to represent their own nationals in succession matters before authorities of the other contracting party without a special power of attorney, provided these nationals are absent and had not issued any power of attorney (Article 36). The conditions on which movable assets or proceeds from the sale of assets are released to heirs or legatees domiciled or resident in the territory of the other contracting party are laid down in Article 39.

With regard to conflict-of-laws rules, the treaty follows a dualist approach, applying different connecting factors to the succession of movable and immovable assets. The law applicable to movable assets is determined based on the connecting factor of the nationality of the deceased at the time of death (Article 32(1)), the law applicable to immovable assets is determined based on the connecting factor of the location of the asset (Article 32(2)). The treaty contains no special provision for cases of dual or multiple nationalities. Nor does it contain any provision on the scope of the applicable law. Choice of law is not permitted. Article 33 contains special conflict-of-laws rule on wills. The capacity to make or revoke a will as well as its validity is governed by the *lex patriae* of the deceased at the time of the disposition (Article 33). For formal validity, it is sufficient if the will complies with the law of the contracting party in whose territory the will was made or revoked (Article 33(2)). The treaty does not explicitly mention other dispositions *mortis causa*, but it stipulates that the *lex patriae* of the deceased at the time of the disposition governs the admissibility of dispositions of property upon death (Article 33(1)). There is no provision on estates without a claimant. With respect to family matters relevant in succession matters, the treaty contains no provision on the matrimonial property rights of a surviving spouse. In Articles 41 to 46 the treaty contains general rules on cross-border recognition and enforcement of final decisions rendered by judicial authorities of the other contracting party, which apply also to decisions in succession matters.

2.2. TREATY WITH FORMER YUGOSLAVIA

2.2.1. *Background*

The Treaty between the Czechoslovak Socialist Republic and the Socialist Federal Republic of Yugoslavia on Legal Relations in Civil, Family and Criminal Matters (**Treaty 13**) was concluded on 20 January 1964 and entered into force on 2 August 1964.[19] Similar to Albania, former Yugoslavia was a befriended State of the then Czechoslovakia. Even though both contracting parties subsequently broke apart, the treaty retains its significance as it continues to apply in bilateral relations of the Czech Republic with all successor States of former Yugoslavia, i.e. Bosnia and Herzegovina, Croatia, Montenegro, Macedonia, Serbia, Slovenia and Kosovo.[20] In relation to Kosovo, the treaty has been in force since 30 November 2010.[21] The bilateral treaty is a comprehensive one and contains, among other provisions, special jurisdiction and conflict-of-laws rules on succession matters that take precedence over the respective provisions of the Succession Regulation in relation to Bosnia and Herzegovina, Montenegro, Macedonia, Serbia and Kosovo.

2.2.2. *Scope of Application*

The treaty covers both civil and criminal matters. In civil matters it contains, among others, provisions on legal assistance; service of documents; the taking of evidence; waiver of security for costs; exchange of documents on civil status of nationals; jurisdiction and conflict-of-laws rules in matters of legal capacity; a jurisdiction rule on proceedings for declaration of death; jurisdiction and conflict-of-laws rules in family matters (marriage, divorce, matrimonial property regime, relations between parents and children, guardianship and adoption), as well as succession matters; and provisions on recognition and enforcement of decisions rendered by judicial authorities of the other contracting party.

Relevant provisions on succession matters are enshrined in Articles 35 to 45. General jurisdiction rules are laid down in Article 39(1) and (2). Judicial authorities of the contracting party of which the deceased was a national at the time of death are competent to rule in matters of succession regarding movable assets, while judicial authorities of the contracting party in the territory of which an immovable asset is located are competent to rule in matters of succession to such an asset. These general rules apply in both contentious and

19 Decree of the Minister of Foreign Affairs No. 207/1964 Coll.

20 Note that the Czech Republic recognized Kosovo as an independent State in May 2008.

21 Notification of the Ministry of Foreign Affairs of the Czech Republic No. 2/2011 Coll. of Int. Treaties.

non-contentious succession proceedings (Article 39(3)). Provided the deceased national of one contracting party had his/her last domicile in the territory of the other contracting party, heirs domiciled in this Contracting State can request no later than six months after the death of the deceased that judicial authorities of this Contracting State rule on the succession to movables located in its territory. If no objections are raised by any of the heirs within three months of notification of such a request, the request is granted (Article 39(4)). Provisions of the *lex rei sitae* apply for the determination of whether the assets are of a movable or immovable nature (Article 39(5)). Diplomatic or consular offices are granted powers to represent their nationals in succession matters before authorities of the other contracting party without a special power of attorney, provided their nationals are absent and had not issued any power of attorney (Article 42). National measures to secure or administrate assets can be taken pursuant to Article 40 by authorities of the contracting party in whose territory such assets belonging to a national of the other contracting party are situated. Diplomatic or consular offices of the other contracting party, which have to be notified, may take part in taking these measures and can request their postponement, modification or revocation. The conditions on which movable assets or proceeds from the sale of movable and immovable assets are released to heirs domiciled or resident in the territory of the other contracting party are laid down in Article 45.

Conflict-of-laws rules are formulated in line with the monist approach; the applicable law governs succession as a whole regardless of the nature of the assets of the estate. The conflict-of-laws rule for succession matters uses the traditional connecting factor of nationality; the law applicable to succession is the *lex patriae* of the deceased at the time of death (Article 36). The treaty does not contain any provision on the scope of the applicable law; no choice of law is admissible. The treaty has no special provision on dual or multiple nationalities. Article 37 contains a special provision on estates without a claimant. If there is no heir according to the law applicable to succession, movable assets pass to the Contracting State of which the deceased was a national at the time of death, and immovable assets pass to the Contracting State in whose territory the assets are situated. With respect to testamentary dispositions, the treaty deals with wills only. Pursuant to Article 38, the legal capacity to make and revoke a will as well as its validity is governed by the *lex patriae* of the deceased at the time of making or revoking the will. For formal validity it is sufficient if the will complies with the law of the contracting party in whose territory the will was made or revoked (Article 38(2)). The treaty is silent on other forms of disposition of property upon death. Jurisdiction and conflict-of-laws rules for the matrimonial property regime are stipulated in Articles 24 and 25 of the treaty. In respect to recognition and enforcement of decisions given in the territory of the other contracting party, general rules in Articles 50 to 60 apply also to decisions in matters of succession. Pursuant to an explicit provision in Article 50(2) of the treaty, these rules apply also to decisions in succession matters rendered by an authority of a contracting party that has jurisdiction to hear matters of succession pursuant to its own law.

2.3. TREATY WITH MONGOLIA

2.3.1. Background

The Treaty between the Czechoslovak Socialist Republic and the Mongolian People's Republic on Legal Assistance and Legal Relations in Civil, Family and Criminal Matters (**Treaty 8**) was concluded on 15 October 1976 in Ulaanbaatar and entered into force on 22 March 1978.[22] At the time when this treaty was drafted and signed, the then Mongolian People's Republic numbered among countries with close ties to the former Czechoslovakia. Therefore the treaty is, as well as the above-mentioned treaties, relatively comprehensive.

2.3.2. Scope of Application

The treaty covers both civil and criminal matters. In civil matters the treaty contains, among others, provisions on legal assistance; service of documents and the taking of evidence; waiver of security for costs; jurisdiction and conflict-of-laws rules in matters of legal capacity; a jurisdiction rule on proceedings for declaration of death; jurisdiction and conflict-of-laws rules in family matters (marriage, divorce, matrimonial property regime, spousal maintenance, relations between parents and children, guardianship, curatorship and adoption); jurisdiction and conflict-of-laws rules with respect to obligations and succession matters; as well as provisions on recognition and enforcement of decisions rendered by judicial authorities of the other contracting party.

Relevant provisions on succession matters are enshrined in Articles 38 to 49. Pursuant to the jurisdiction rule in Article 42, judicial authorities of the contracting party of which the deceased was a national at the time of death have jurisdiction to rule on succession to movable assets with the exception of the situation referred to in Article 42(4) when movable assets of the deceased are situated in the territory of the other contracting party; judicial authorities of the Contracting State in whose territory immovable assets are situated have competence to rule on succession to this property. It is explicitly stipulated in the treaty that the jurisdiction rules in Article 42(1) and (2) apply also in contentious proceedings regarding succession claims. The treaty also contains

[22] Decree of Minister of Foreign Affairs No. 106/1978 Coll.

provisions on powers of the judicial authorities of contracting parties to take measures to secure an inheritance situated in their territory (Article 45), powers of their diplomatic or consular offices to represent nationals in succession matters without a special power of attorney before authorities of the other contracting party (Article 47(1)) and on the conditions under which assets or proceeds from their sale are released to heirs domiciled or resident in the territory of the other contracting party (Articles 48 and 49).

The law applicable to succession to movable assets is determined based on the nationality principle (Article 39(1)), and the law applicable to succession to immovable assets on the *situs* principle (Article 39(2)). *Lex rei sitae* governs the issue of whether the property is movable or immovable (Article 43). There is a special provision in Article 41 with respect to an heirless estate. When there is no heir according to the law applicable to succession, movable assets pass to the Contracting State of which the deceased was a national, and immovable assets pass to the Contracting State in the territory of which they are located. The treaty contains no provision on the scope of the applicable law; no choice of law is admissible. It is silent on dual or multiple nationalities. In respect to testamentary dispositions, *lex patriae* governs the legal capacity to make and revoke a will and its validity. For formal validity it is sufficient if the will complies with the *lex loci actus* provided it is the law of a contracting party. Other forms of dispositions of property upon death are not dealt with. The treaty contains jurisdiction and conflict-of-laws rules for the matrimonial property regime (Articles 20 and 21). With respect to recognition and enforcement, general rules in Articles 55 to 62 apply also for decisions in succession matters. They apply to decisions rendered in succession matters by courts as well as by other authorities of the other contracting party that have jurisdiction pursuant to national law (Article 55(2)).

2.4. TREATY WITH CUBA

2.4.1. Background

The treaty between the Czechoslovak Socialist Republic and the Republic of Cuba on Legal Assistance in Civil, Family and Criminal Matters (**Treaty 6**) was concluded in Prague on 18 April 1980 and entered into force on 11 July 1981.[23] The treaty was signed with the purpose of further development of friendship and mutual cooperation at a time when Cuba and Czechoslovakia, both communist countries, had very close ties. The treaty has a rather broad material scope of application.

---

23 Decree of Minister of Foreign Affairs No. 80/1981 Coll.

2.4.2. *Scope of Application*

The treaty covers both civil and criminal matters. In civil matters the treaty contains, among others, provisions on legal assistance; service of documents and the taking of evidence; waiver of security for costs; jurisdiction and conflict-of-laws rules in matters of legal capacity; a rule on jurisdiction to declare a person dead; jurisdiction and conflict-of-laws rules in family matters (marriage, divorce, matrimonial property regime, relations between parents and children including maintenance, guardianship and adoption); jurisdiction and conflict-of-laws rules regarding property rights and non-contractual obligations; and jurisdiction and conflict-of-laws rules for succession matters; as well as general provisions on recognition and enforcement of decisions rendered by judicial authorities of the other contracting party.

Relevant provisions on succession matters are enshrined in Articles 34 to 41. The treaty's jurisdiction rules allow parallel proceedings in succession matters in the courts of both contracting parties provided the deceased national of a contracting party had movable and immovable assets situated in the territory of both contracting parties, and they apply to both contentious and non-contentious proceedings (with the exception of the rule in Article 38(2)). Pursuant to the rule in Article 38(1), judicial authorities of the contracting party of which the deceased was a national at the time of death are competent to rule in matters of succession to movable assets, with the exception of a situation where the movable assets of the deceased national are situated in the territory of the other contracting party (Article 38(2)). Regarding immovable assets, the judicial authorities of the Contracting State in whose territory the immovable asset is situated have jurisdiction to rule on succession to the asset (Article 38(3)). *Lex rei sitae* determines whether an asset is movable or immovable (Article 38(5)). Pursuant to Article 39(1), authorities of the contracting party in the territory of which the assets of the deceased national of the other contracting party are located may take measures necessary to secure and administrate the estate pursuant its own law regardless of the nationality of potential heirs; the respective diplomatic or consular office is to be notified. The treaty does not vest diplomatic or consular offices with special powers to represent their nationals in succession matters before the authorities of the other contracting party without a special power of attorney, but they can participate in taking measures to secure and administrate assets of their national and request their postponement, modification or revocation (Article 39). Conditions on which movable assets are released to the competent authority or diplomatic or consular office of the other contracting party are set out in Article 41.

The general conflict-of-laws rule for succession upon death follows the monist approach; pursuant to Article 35, the law applicable to succession, the *lex patriae* of the deceased at the time of death, governs succession as a whole. The treaty has no special provision on dual or multiple nationalities. The treaty does not contain any provision on the scope of the applicable law; no choice of law is admissible. Article 37 contains a special rule on estates without a claimant. If according to the applicable law to a succession there is no heir, movable assets pass to the Contracting State of which the deceased was a national, and immovable assets pass to the Contracting State in whose territory they are situated. With respect to testamentary dispositions, there are special conflict-of-laws rules enshrined in Article 36 of the treaty on the legal capacity to make and revoke a will and on its validity. The legal capacity to make or revoke a will and its validity are governed by the *lex patriae* of the deceased at the time of its being made or revoked. For formal validity, it is sufficient that the will complies with the law of the Contracting State in whose territory the will was made or revoked (Article 36(2)). The treaty is silent on other forms of dispositions of property upon death. Jurisdiction and conflict-of-laws rules for the matrimonial property regime, which can be relevant in connection with succession proceedings, are stipulated in Article 19. The general provisions on recognition and enforcement of decisions in civil matters rendered by judicial authorities of the other contracting party in Articles 46 to 55 apply also to decisions in matters of succession.

2.5. TREATY WITH THE FORMER SOVIET UNION

2.5.1. Background

The Treaty between the Czechoslovak Socialist Republic and the Union of Soviet Socialist Republics on Legal Assistance and Legal Relations in Civil, Family and Criminal Matters (**Treaty 9**) was concluded in Moscow on 12 August 1982 and entered into force on 4 June 1983.[24] This treaty replaced the Treaty between the Czechoslovak Republic and the Union of Soviet Socialist Republics on Legal Assistance in Civil, Family and Criminal Matters concluded on 31 August 1957 (promulgated under the No. 29/1958 Coll.). The treaty has not lost its significance with the dissolution of the Soviet Union in 1991; it is being applied in relations between the Czech Republic and some of the successor States of the former Soviet Union: Belarus, Georgia, Kyrgyzstan, Moldavia and Russia. Until 2002, when a new bilateral treaty entered into force (see in detail below), the treaty had been applied also in relations with Ukraine.

2.5.2. Scope of Application

This treaty again covers both civil and criminal matters. In civil matters the treaty contains, among others, provisions on legal assistance; service of documents

[24] Decree of Minister of Foreign Affairs No. 95/1983 Coll.

and the taking of evidence; waiver of security for costs; jurisdiction and conflict-of-laws rules in matters of legal capacity; a rule on jurisdiction for declaring a person dead; provisions on exchange of documents regarding the civil status of nationals; jurisdiction and conflict-of-laws rules in family matters (marriage, divorce, matrimonial property regime, relations between parents and children, determination of paternity, guardianship, curatorship and adoption); a conflict-of-laws rule on the formal validity of legal acts, jurisdiction and conflict-of-laws rules in respect of the right of ownership; non-contractual obligations and succession matters; as well as general provisions on recognition and enforcement of decisions rendered by judicial authorities of the other contracting party.

Provisions on matters of succession upon death are enshrined in Articles 39 to 48. The treaty with the former Soviet Union, unlike the above-analyzed treaties, does not use nationality but the domicile of the deceased as the relevant connecting factor in both its jurisdiction and conflict-of-laws rules. Pursuant to the general jurisdiction rule in Article 43(1), the judicial authorities of the contracting party in whose territory the deceased had his/her last domicile have jurisdiction to rule in matters of succession to movable assets. Jurisdiction in respect of immovable assets is granted to the judicial authorities of the contracting party within whose jurisdiction the immovable asset is situated (Article 43(2)). These jurisdiction rules apply also in contentious proceedings regarding succession claims. Pursuant to Article 45(1), authorities of the contracting party in whose territory the assets of the deceased national of the other contracting party are located may take measures necessary to secure and administrate the assets pursuant to its own law. Diplomatic or consular offices of the other contracting party that have to be notified may take part in taking these measures and request their postponement, modification revocation. They are also vested with special powers to represent their nationals without a special power of attorney in succession matters before the authorities of the other contracting party under conditions set in Article 44. Conditions under which movable assets and proceeds from the sale of movable and immovable assets are released to heirs domiciled or temporarily resident in the territory of the other contracting party are laid down in Article 48.

Conflict-of-laws rules on matters of succession follow the dualist approach resulting in a scission of the applicable law provided the deceased had movable and immovable assets in the territory of both contracting parties. The law applicable to succession to movable assets is the law of the Contracting State where the deceased had his/her last domicile (Article 40(1)); the law applicable to immovable assets is the *lex rei sitae* (Article 40(2)). The treaty has no provision regarding the scope of the applicable law; no choice of law is admissible. *Lex rei sitae* governs whether assets are movable or immovable (Article 40(3)). The treaty contains no special provision on dual or multiple nationalities.

There is a special provision in Article 41 on estates without a claimant. If, in accordance with the law applicable to succession, there is no heir, movable assets pass to the Contracting State of which the deceased was a national and immovable assets to the Contracting State in whose territory they are located. In respect to testamentary dispositions, there is a special conflict-of-laws rule in Article 42 on wills. The legal capacity to make or revoke a will as well as its validity is governed by the *lex patriae* of the deceased at the time of its making or revoking. For formal validity it is sufficient that the will complies with the law of the Contracting State in whose territory the will was made or revoked (Article 42(2)). Other forms of dispositions of property upon death are not considered. The treaty also contains jurisdiction and conflict-of-laws rules for the matrimonial property regime (Article 25). As to the recognition and enforcement of decisions in succession matters rendered by authorities of the other contracting party, general rules in Articles 53 to 66 apply.

2.6. TREATY WITH VIETNAM

2.6.1. Background

The Treaty between the Czechoslovak Socialist Republic and the Socialist Republic of Vietnam on Legal Assistance in Civil and Criminal Matters (**Treaty 12**) was concluded in Prague on 12 October 1982 and entered into force on 16 April 1984.[25]

This treaty, together with the bilateral treaty concluded with Ukraine (**Treaty 10**, see in detail below), belongs to the most frequently applied bilateral treaties on legal assistance binding for the Czech Republic. This can be attributed to the high number of Vietnamese nationals living in the territory of the Czech Republic. At the end of 2016 there were over 58,000 Vietnamese living in the Czech Republic.[26] The Vietnamese started coming to the former Czechoslovakia in the 1970s as students or exchange workers. A second influx in migrants from Vietnam took place after the Velvet Revolution of 1989, when the Vietnamese started to do business in the Czech Republic. Nowadays they represent the third largest minority.[27] Given the very close ties between the contracting parties, the material scope of the bilateral treaty is rather broad.

---

25 Decree of Minister of Foreign Affairs No. 98/1984 Coll.

26 Data of the Czech Statistical Office. Available at <https://vdb.czso.cz/vdbvo2/faces/index.jsf?page=vystup-objekt&pvo=CIZ01&z=T&f=TABULKA&katalog=31032&evo=v57516_!_VUZEMI97-100-nezj_1&c=v23~2__RP2016MP12DP31> accessed 28.03.2019.

27 Following Ukrainians and Russians.

2.6.2. *Scope of Application*

The treaty covers both civil and criminal matters. In civil matters, which pursuant to its Article 1(3) include family and labour matters, the treaty contains, among others, provisions on legal assistance; service of documents and the taking of evidence; waiver of security for costs; jurisdiction and conflict-of-laws rules in matters of legal capacity; a rule on jurisdiction to declare a person dead; jurisdiction and conflict-of-laws rules in family matters (marriage, divorce, matrimonial property regime, relations between parents and children including maintenance obligations, guardianship and adoption); a conflict-of-laws rule on the formal validity of legal acts; jurisdiction and conflict-of-laws rules in respect of non-contractual obligations and succession matters; as well as general provisions on recognition and enforcement of decisions rendered by judicial authorities of the other contracting party.

Relevant provisions on succession matters are enshrined in Articles 34 to 41. Pursuant to Article 38(1), judicial authorities of the contracting party of which the deceased was a national at the time of death are competent to rule in matters of succession to movable assets. In a situation when all movables of the deceased national are situated in the territory of the other contracting party, its judicial authorities have jurisdiction to rule on succession to movable assets upon request of an heir, provided all known heirs agree (Article 38(2)). Judicial authorities of the Contracting State in whose territory immovable assets are situated have jurisdiction to rule on succession upon death to these assets (Article 38(3)). The jurisdiction rules in Article 38(1) and (3) apply also in contentious proceedings regarding succession claims. Authorities of the contracting party in whose territory the assets of the deceased are situated are entitled to take measures necessary to secure and administrate the assets pursuant to its own law regardless of the nationality of potential heirs. The diplomatic or consular office of the other contracting party may participate in taking such measures and request their postponement, modification or revocation. This treaty does not, however, vest diplomatic or consular offices with powers to represent their nationals in matters of succession without a special power of attorney before authorities of the other contracting party. Conditions on which movable assets are released to a judicial authority, diplomatic or consular office of the other contracting party are laid down in Article 41.

The law applicable to succession of movable assets is the *lex patriae* of the deceased at the time of death (Article 35(1)); the law applicable to immovable assets is the *lex rei sitae* (Article 35(2)), which also governs the issue of whether assets are movable or immovable (Article 35(3)). There is no provision regarding the scope of the applicable law; no choice of law is admissible. The treaty contains no special provisions on dual or multiple nationalities. The situation when there is no heir according to the law applicable to succession is dealt with in Article 37: movable assets pass to the Contracting State of which the deceased was a national, and immovable assets pass to the Contracting State in whose territory they are situated. The conflict-of-laws rule in Article 36 deals with legal capacity to make or revoke a will as well as its validity; other forms of dispositions of property upon death are left out. The governing law is the *lex patriae* of the deceased at the time of its making or revoking; for formal validity it is sufficient that the will complies with the *lex loci actus* provided it is the law of a contracting party (Article 36(2)). The treaty also contains jurisdiction and conflict-of-laws rules for the matrimonial property regime (Article 19). The general provisions on recognition and enforcement of decisions rendered in the territory of the other contracting party that are laid down in Articles 46 to 55 apply also to decisions in matters of succession.

2.7. TREATY WITH NORTH KOREA

2.7.1. Background

The Treaty between the Czechoslovak Socialist Republic and the Democratic People's Republic of Korea on Mutual Legal Assistance in Civil, Family and Criminal Matters (**Treaty** 7) was concluded in Pyongyang on 11 September 1988 and entered into force on 16 June 1989.[28] In comparison with the treaties analyzed above, this treaty is less comprehensive and practically non-functional, as the current relations with North Korea are very limited due to the political situation.

2.7.2. Scope of Application

This treaty covers both civil and criminal matters. In civil matters the treaty contains, among others, provisions on legal assistance; service of documents and the taking of evidence; waiver of security for costs; exchange of information on final judgments given against nationals of the other contracting party; a conflict-of-laws rule on legal capacity; a rule on jurisdiction to declare a person dead; provisions on exchange of documents on the civil status of nationals; jurisdiction and conflict-of-laws rules in family matters (marriage, divorce, matrimonial property regime, relations between parents and children, guardianship, curatorship and adoption); jurisdiction and conflict-of-laws rules on succession matters; as well as provisions on recognition and enforcement of decisions rendered by judicial authorities of the other contracting party.

All provisions on succession matters are enshrined in a single article. Article 25 deals with jurisdiction, the applicable law, testamentary capacity and estates without a claimant. Both jurisdiction and conflict-of-laws rules

---

[28] Decree of Minister of Foreign Affairs No. 93/1989 Coll.

follow the dualist principle and lead to a possible scission. Jurisdiction to rule on succession to movable assets is entrusted to the judicial authorities of the contracting party of which the deceased was a national at the time of death; jurisdiction to rule on immovable assets is vested with the judicial authorities of the contracting party in whose territory the immovable asset is situated (Article 25(3)). The *lex patriae* of the deceased at the time of death governs succession to movable assets of the deceased, and *lex rei sitae* governs succession to immovable assets (Article 25(2)). The issue of whether assets are movable or immovable is also governed by *lex rei sitae*. The treaty has no special provision on dual or multiple nationalities. It has no provision on the scope of the applicable law; no choice of law is admissible. If there is no heir in accordance with the law applicable to succession, movable assets pass to the Contracting State of which the deceased was a national, and immovable assets pass to the Contracting State in whose territory the assets are located (Article 25(5)). Pursuant to Article 25(4), the legal capacity to make or revoke a will as well as its validity is governed by the *lex patriae* of the deceased at the time of making or revoking the will. For formal validity it is sufficient that the will complies with the *lex loci actus*. The treaty is silent on other forms of dispositions of property upon death. There are no provisions on measures to secure the inheritance, on releasing assets to the competent authority, diplomatic or consular office of the other contracting party or on special powers for diplomatic or consular offices. The treaty contains jurisdiction and conflict-of-laws rules for the matrimonial property regime (Article 21). The general rules on recognition and enforcement of decisions in civil matters rendered in the territory of the other contracting party that are laid down in Articles 26 to 32 apply also to court decisions in matters of succession.

2.8. TREATY WITH UKRAINE

2.8.1. Background

In relations with Ukraine, one of the successor States of the Union of Soviet Socialist Republics, the bilateral treaty with the former Soviet Union (**Treaty 9**, analyzed above) was applicable until 2002, when it was replaced by a new bilateral treaty. The treaty between the Czech Republic and Ukraine on Legal Assistance in Civil Matters (**Treaty 10**) was concluded in Kiev on 28 May 2001 and entered into force on 8 November 2002.[29] It was amended by a Protocol signed on 14 September 2007,[30] which, however, does not affect provisions relevant to matters of succession.

---

[29] Notification of Ministry of Foreign Affairs No. 123/2002 Coll. of Int. Treaties.

[30] Notification of Ministry of Foreign Affairs No. 77/2008 Coll. of Int. Treaties.

According to statistical data there were roughly 110,000 Ukrainians living in the Czech Republic at the end of 2016.[31] Due to the fact that Ukrainians represent the most numerous group of foreigners living in the Czech Republic, the treaty is of major significance in practice. The number of Ukrainians living in the Czech Republic might have been one of the reasons that led to the conclusion of a new bilateral treaty on legal assistance in 2002. When compared with the treaties analyzed above that were concluded between the 1960s and the 1980s, this treaty is relatively recent and was drafted in a totally different political environment. One would therefore expect a certain progress as to its content and concept, but it does not differ from older bilateral treaties on legal assistance with the exception of some provisions having been formulated more thoroughly.

2.8.2. Scope of Application

This treaty, unlike all other relevant treaties that contain jurisdiction and conflict-of-laws rules on matters of succession, does not cover criminal matters; its scope is limited to legal assistance in civil matters that, pursuant to Article 1(1) lit. a, include family, labour and commercial matters. The treaty contains, among others, provisions on legal assistance; service of documents and the taking of evidence; waiver of security for costs; jurisdiction and conflict-of-laws rules in matters of legal capacity; guardianship and curatorship; a rule on jurisdiction to declare a person dead; jurisdiction and conflict-of-laws rules in family matters (marriage, divorce, matrimonial property regime, paternity determinations, relations between parents and children, including maintenance obligations and adoption); jurisdiction and conflict-of-laws rules on contractual and non-contractual obligations; a conflict-of-laws rule regarding the right of ownership and jurisdiction and conflict-of-laws rules on labour and succession matters; as well as general provisions on recognition and enforcement of decisions rendered by judicial authorities of the other contracting party.

Relevant provisions on succession matters are enshrined in Articles 37 to 47. Judicial authorities of the contracting party of which the deceased was a national at the time of death are entrusted with competence to rule in matters of succession to movable assets (Article 41(1)) with the exception of a situation when all movables are situated in the territory of the other contracting party (Article 41(3)). Judicial authorities of the Contracting State in whose territory immovable assets are situated have competence to rule on succession to these assets (Article 41(2)). *Lex rei sitae* governs the issue of whether assets are

---

31 Data of the Czech Statistical Office. Available at <https://vdb.czso.cz/vdbvo2/faces/index.jsf?page=vystup-objekt&pvo=CIZ01&z=T&f=TABULKA&katalog=31032&evo=v57516_!_VUZEMI97-100-nezj_1&c=v23~2__RP2016MP12DP31> accessed 28.03.2019.

movable or immovable. The jurisdiction rules in Article 41(1) and (2) apply also in contentious proceedings regarding succession claims. Pursuant to Article 45(1), authorities of the contracting party in whose territory the assets of the deceased national of the other contracting party are located are entitled to take all measures necessary to protect or secure the assets pursuant to its own law; the diplomatic or consular offices of the other contracting party may participate in taking these measures and may request their postponement, modification or revocation. The conditions upon which movable assets or proceeds from the sale of movable and immovable assets are released to heirs domiciled or resident in the territory of the other contracting party are laid down in Article 47.

The conception of conflict-of-laws rules on succession matters in this treaty is in line with other relevant treaties. The law applicable to succession to movable assets is determined based on the nationality of the deceased at the time of death (Article 38(1)), and the law applicable to succession to immovable assets is determined based on the location of the assets (Article 38(2)). The issue of whether assets are movable or immovable is determined by the *lex rei sitae* (Article 38(3)). The treaty does not have any special provision on dual or multiple nationalities. There is no provision regarding the scope of the applicable law; no choice of law is admissible. With respect to estates without a claimant, Article 39 stipulates that if there is no heir, movable assets pass to the Contracting State of which the deceased was a national at the time of death, and immovable assets pass to the Contracting State in whose territory the assets are located. With respect to testamentary dispositions, the treaty deals with wills only. Pursuant to Article 40, legal capacity to make or revoke a will as well as its validity is governed by the *lex patriae* of the deceased at the time of making or revoking the will. For formal validity, it is sufficient if the will complies with the law of the contracting party in whose territory the will was made or revoked (Article 40(2)). The treaty is silent on other forms of dispositions of property upon death, but Article 40(3) stipulates that paragraphs 1 and 2 apply to disinheritance accordingly. The treaty contains jurisdiction and conflict-of-laws rules on the matrimonial property regime (Article 29). General rules on recognition and enforcement of decisions rendered in the territory of the other contracting party are enshrined in Articles 52 to 58 of the treaty and apply also to decisions in succession matters.

2.9. TREATY WITH UZBEKISTAN

2.9.1. Background

The Treaty between the Czech Republic and the Republic of Uzbekistan on Legal Assistance and Legal Relations in Civil and Criminal Matters (**Treaty 11**) was concluded in Tashkent on 18 January 2002 and entered into force on 1 December 2003.[32] The bilateral treaty with Uzbekistan is the youngest bilateral treaty on legal assistance in civil and criminal matters that the Czech Republic concluded with a third country and that contains provisions on succession matters. Again, despite the fact that it is a relatively recent treaty, the concept, structure and content does not differ substantially from the treaties concluded in the 1980s.

2.9.2. Scope of Application

The treaty covers both civil and criminal matters. With respect to civil matters, which pursuant to Article 1(1) include family, labour, commercial matters and administrative matters adjudicated by courts, the treaty contains, among others, provisions on legal assistance; service of documents and the taking of evidence; waiver of security for costs; jurisdiction and conflict-of-laws rules on legal capacity; a rule on jurisdiction to declare a person dead; jurisdiction and conflict-of-laws rules in family matters (marriage, divorce, matrimonial property regime, relations between parents and children, including paternity determination, guardianship, curatorship and adoption); a conflict-of-laws rule on the validity of legal acts and jurisdiction and conflict-of-laws rules on the right of ownership; non-contractual obligations and succession matters; as well as provisions on recognition and enforcement of decisions rendered by judicial authorities of the other contracting party.

Relevant provisions on matters of succession are enshrined in Articles 41 to 49. This treaty, similar to the treaty with the former Soviet Union (**Treaty 9**), uses the domicile of the deceased as the relevant connecting factor in rules on the succession to movable assets. Pursuant to Article 45(1), judicial authorities of the contracting party in whose territory the deceased had his/her last domicile have jurisdiction to rule in matters of succession to the movable assets. Pursuant to Article 45(2), judicial authorities of the Contracting State in whose territory immovable assets are situated have competence to rule on succession to the assets. *Lex rei sitae* governs the issue of whether assets are movable or immovable (Article 42(3)). The jurisdiction rules apply to both contentious and non-contentious proceedings regarding succession claims. Pursuant to Article 48(1), the judicial authorities of the contracting party in whose territory the assets of the deceased national of the other contracting party are located may take measures necessary to secure and administrate such assets. The treaty vests diplomatic and consular offices with special powers; they may participate in taking measures to secure and administrate assets of their nationals, and they

[32] Notification of Ministry of Foreign Affairs No. 133/2003 Coll. of Int. Treaties.

may represent their own nationals in succession matters (with the exception of the right to waive the succession) without a special power of attorney before judicial authorities of the other contracting party under conditions laid down in Article 46. The conditions under which movable assets or proceeds from the sale of assets are released to heirs resident in the territory of the other Contracting State are laid down in Article 49.

The conflict-of-laws rule on succession matters in Article 42 stipulates different conflict treatment for movable and immovable property of the estate. The law applicable to succession to movable assets is the law of the Contracting State of the last domicile of the deceased (Article 42(1)). The law applicable to immovable assets is the law of the Contracting State in whose territory the assets are situated (Article 42(2)). There is no provision on the scope of the applicable law; no choice of law is admissible. If there is no heir according to the law applicable to succession, movable assets pass to the Contracting State of which the deceased was a national, and immovable assets pass to the Contracting State on whose territory the assets are located (Article 43). In respect of testamentary dispositions, there is a special conflict-of-laws rule in Article 44 on wills. Legal capacity to make or revoke a will as well as its validity is governed by the *lex patriae* of the deceased at the time of its making or revoking. For formal validity it is sufficient that the will complies with the law of the Contracting State in whose territory the will was made or revoked (Article 44(2)). Other forms of dispositions upon death are not dealt with. The treaty contains jurisdiction and conflict-of-laws rules for the matrimonial property regime (Article 27). As to recognition and enforcement of decisions in succession matters rendered by judicial authorities of the other contracting party, general rules in Articles 50 to 54 of the treaty apply.

2.10. TREATY WITH TUNISIA

The Treaty between the Czechoslovak Socialist Republic and the Republic of Tunisia on Legal Assistance in Civil and Criminal Matters, on Recognition and Enforcement of Judicial Decisions and on Extradition including an Additional Protocol was concluded in Tunis on 12 April 1979 and entered into force on 21 February 1981.[33]

This treaty covers both civil and criminal matters. As to civil matters the scope of the treaty is much more limited compared to all the treaties analyzed above. It does not contain jurisdiction or conflict-of-laws rules. It is limited to matters of legal assistance (service of documents, the taking of evidence, exchange of

[33] Decree of Minister of Foreign Affairs No. 40/1981 Coll.

extracts from documents on civil status) and general rules on recognition and enforcement of decisions given by judicial authorities of the other contracting party, which also apply to decisions in succession matters (Articles 24 to 30). As explicitly stipulated in Article 24(2) of the treaty, the recognition and enforcement rules apply not only to court decisions in succession matters but also to decisions rendered by other authorities of the other contracting party that have jurisdiction in succession matters pursuant to national law.

2.11. TREATY WITH ALGERIA

The Treaty between the Czechoslovak Socialist Republic and the People's Democratic Republic of Algeria on Legal Assistance in Civil, Family and Criminal Matters was concluded in Algiers on 4 February 1981 and entered into force on 23 November 1983.[34]

This treaty covers both civil and criminal matters. The scope of the treaty in civil matters is limited to matters of legal assistance (service of documents, the taking of evidence) and general rules on recognition and enforcement of decisions given by judicial authorities of the other contracting party, which also apply to decisions in succession matters (Articles 24 to 29). Pursuant to Article 24(2) of the treaty, the general recognition and enforcement rules apply not only to court decisions on succession matters but also to decisions on succession matters rendered by other authorities of the other contracting party that have jurisdiction in succession matters pursuant to national law.

2.12. TREATY WITH AFGHANISTAN

The Treaty between the Czechoslovak Socialist Republic and the Democratic Republic of Afghanistan on Legal Assistance in Civil and Criminal Matters was concluded in Prague on 24 June 1981 and entered into force on 8 December 1982.[35]

This treaty is very similar to the treaties concluded with Tunisia, Algeria and Syria. It covers both civil and criminal matters. The material scope of the treaty with respect to civil matters is limited to matters of legal assistance (service of documents, the taking of evidence, waiver of security for costs) and general rules on recognition and enforcement of decisions given by judicial authorities of the other contracting party, which also apply to decisions in succession matters (Articles 25 to 31).

---

34 Decree of Minister of Foreign Affairs No. 17/1984 Coll.

35 Decree of Minister of Foreign Affairs No. 44/1983 Coll.

2.13. TREATY WITH SYRIA

The Treaty between the Czechoslovak Socialist Republic and the Syrian Arab Republic on Legal Assistance in Civil, Family and Criminal Matters was concluded in Damascus on 18 April 1984 and entered into force on 8 November 1985.[36]

The treaty covers both civil and criminal matters. The material scope is limited to matters of legal assistance (service of documents, the taking of evidence, exchange of excerpts from registers regarding the civil status of nationals of the other contracting party) and general rules on recognition and enforcement of decisions given by judicial authorities of the other contracting party, which apply also to decisions in succession matters (Articles 26 to 33). Recognition and enforcement rules apply to both court decisions in succession matters and decisions rendered by other authorities of the other contracting party that have jurisdiction in succession matters pursuant to national law (Article 26(2)).

2.14. TREATY WITH YEMEN

The Treaty between the Czechoslovak Socialist Republic and the People's Democratic Republic of Yemen on Legal Assistance in Civil and Criminal Matters was concluded in Prague on 19 January 1989 and entered into force on 13 February 1990.[37]

This treaty covers both civil and criminal matters. The material scope of the treaty is similarly very limited; it covers only matters of legal assistance (service of documents, the taking of evidence, transmission of excerpts from registers regarding the civil status of nationals of the contracting parties, waiver of security on costs) and general rules on recognition and enforcement of decisions given by judicial authorities of the other contracting party, which also apply to decisions in succession matters (Articles 24 to 31).

2.15. TREATY WITH SWITZERLAND

The Treaty between Czechoslovak Republic and Switzerland on Recognition and Enforcement of Judicial Decisions was concluded in Bern on 21 December 1926 and entered into force on 24 February 1929.[38] It is the oldest treaty with a third country that is relevant in succession matters and that is binding for the Czech Republic. Its material scope is limited to recognition and

36 Decree of Minister of Foreign Affairs No. 8/1986 Coll.
37 Decree of Minister of Foreign Affairs No. 76/1990 Coll.
38 Decree No. 23/1929 Coll.

enforcement of judicial decisions in civil and commercial matters given on the territory of the other contracting party in civil or commercial matters.

3. PRIVATE INTERNATIONAL LAW

Special conflict-of-laws rules on matters of succession are enshrined in the treaties concluded with the following third countries: Albania, former Yugoslavia, Mongolia, Cuba, North Korea, the former Soviet Union, Vietnam, Ukraine and Uzbekistan (**Treaties 5–13**); and in all of them the relevant conflict-of-laws rules follow more or less a similar pattern: they contain a general conflict-of-laws rule on matters of succession, a special provision on estates without a claimant and special conflict-of-laws rules on the capacity to make and revoke a will and its validity.

All of the treaties contain a basic general conflict-of-laws rule to determine the law applicable to succession upon death, but in none of the treaties is there a provision equivalent to Article 23 of the Succession Regulation on its scope. None of them further specifies the scope of the applicable law, providing neither an exhaustive nor a non-exhaustive list. Unlike the Succession Regulation, which is based on the principle of a monist solution for the conflict of laws, the overwhelming majority of the above-listed treaties adopt the dualist approach, resulting in a possible scission of applicable law. Different connecting factors for succession to movable and immovable assets are applied in the general conflict-of-laws rule in the treaties with Albania (**Treaty 5**), Mongolia (**Treaty 8**), the former Soviet Union (**Treaty 9**), Vietnam (**Treaty 12**), North Korea (**Treaty 7**), Ukraine (**Treaty 10**) and Uzbekistan (**Treaty 11**). Consistent with the traditional concept, *lex rei sitae* is the law applicable for succession to immovable assets pursuant to all of these treaties. The connecting factor applied in the general conflict-of-laws rule for succession to movable assets of the deceased is either nationality (applied in the treaties with Albania, Mongolia, Vietnam, North Korea and Ukraine) or domicile (applied in the treaties with the former Soviet Union and Uzbekistan). The notion of domicile is not defined in any of these treaties. Czech courts are likely to interpret the notion in accordance with its national law, which defines domicile in Section 80 of the Czech Civil Code.[39]

---

39 Act 89/2012 Coll., Civil Code: '(1) The place where an individual stays with the intention to live there permanently is his domicile, subject to changes in circumstances; such intention may be evident from his declarations or from the circumstances of the case. If an individual states a domicile other than his actual domicile, anyone may also invoke his actual domicile. No one may claim to have his actual domicile elsewhere against anyone who, in good faith, invokes the actual domicile. (2) An individual with no domicile is considered to reside at the place where he lives. If such a place cannot be determined or if it can be determined only with disproportionate difficulties, the place where an individual has property or the place of his last residence is considered to be his domicile.'

Nationality has been considered for a long time as the traditional connecting factor in matters of succession, which is reflected in its application in the majority of the bilateral treaties. The choice of this criterion corresponds to the social and political circumstances at the time of the treaties' conclusions. At that time, nationality was the decisive connecting factor in most national codifications of private international law, including the then applicable Czech codification.[40] Even in the two treaties that apply domicile as the relevant connecting factor, the nationality of the deceased still plays its role with respect to the treaties' personal scope of application, as the treaties apply to nationals of contracting parties only. As can be expected in matters of succession, in all conflict-of-laws rules the time of death of the deceased is the moment relevant for the determination of the connecting factor. The connecting factor of the habitual residence of the deceased – applied as the default conflict-of-laws rule in Article 21(1) of the Succession Regulation – is not to be found in any of the above-analyzed bilateral treaties; it plays no role at all. Two bilateral treaties (with former Yugoslavia (**Treaty 13**) and with Cuba (**Treaty 6**)) follow the monist approach. The *lex patriae* of the deceased at the time of death governs the succession as a whole, regardless of whether the assets are movable or immovable.

As stated above, with respect to immovable assets the treaties that follow the scission principle apply the traditional *lex rei sitae*. Conflict-of-laws rules using the connecting factor of the location of the immovable asset – together with jurisdiction rules that entrust the judicial authorities of the contracting party where the immovable asset is located with exclusive jurisdiction to rule on succession of immovable assets within its jurisdiction – guarantee that, pursuant to these treaties, judicial authorities of the contracting parties will always rule on succession to immovable assets situated only in their territory and apply only the *lex fori*. However, where one of the treaties follows the monist principle, it does not preclude the judicial authorities that have jurisdiction to rule on succession to immovable assets situated in their jurisdiction from having to apply the law of the other contracting party. For instance, in the case of a deceased national of Macedonia who had immovable assets in the Czech Republic, pursuant to Article 39(2) and Article 36 of the treaty with former Yugoslavia (**Treaty 13**), which also applies in relations with Macedonia, Czech notaries will have jurisdiction to rule on succession to these assets and will have to apply Macedonian law.

Unlike Article 22 of the Succession Regulation, none of the relevant bilateral treaties enables the deceased to choose the law applicable to succession, not even in a limited way. The absence of a choice of law is clearly to be attributed to the era in which the treaties were negotiated and signed. Choice of law in

40 Act No. 97/1963 Coll., on Private International Law and International Procedural Law.

succession matters is a relatively new innovation. It found its way into Czech national law first in 2012[41] with the recodification of private law, including private international law, and its introduction in the Succession Regulation in the same year was considered almost revolutionary.

Logically, there is no *renvoi* provision included in any of the relevant treaties. There would be no space for its application as only the law of either Contracting State is applicable pursuant to the unified conflict-of-laws rules. None of the relevant bilateral treaties contains a substantive public policy provision. Most probably there was no need to include an *ordre public* mechanism because the rules are designed in such a manner that in most cases succession matters are governed by the *lex fori*.

There is no provision on which law is to govern the localization of assets. With respect to immovable assets there is little practical need for an explicit provision, as the judicial authorities of the Contracting State in whose territory the immovable asset is located have exclusive jurisdiction to rule on succession to this asset pursuant to all the relevant bilateral treaties, and these authorities will mostly apply their national law. If necessary, Czech courts will apply their own rules on the localization of assets. In Czech succession proceedings, the notary, who acts as court commissioner, works from the information regarding the assets of the deceased that are located both in the territory of the State of the court and abroad as related by potential heirs. In a situation where the heirs are able to specify property allegedly located abroad (e.g. provide the name of the bank where the deceased supposedly had an account or present an excerpt from the respective registry), the notary proceeds pursuant to the relevant provisions on legal assistance. There are special provisions in the bilateral treaties on the taking of evidence in the territory of the other contracting party. In most cases the request has to be filed via the Ministry of Justice. In a situation where the heirs have no details on assets of the deceased that are purportedly located abroad, the notary refrains from submitting a general request for the taking of evidence. If additional assets are found after the proceedings were declared terminated, they are dealt with in supplementary proceedings.[42]

All treaties, with the exception of Albania (**Treaty 5**), contain the same special conflict-of-laws rule to determine the law applicable to the issue of whether assets are movable or immovable: the *lex rei sitae* is the governing law. This conflict-of-laws rule is to be found also in the treaties concluded with Cuba (**Treaty 6**) and former Yugoslavia (**Treaty 13**), where the nature of the assets is not relevant for the purposes of determining the applicable law, but it is relevant for jurisdiction rules (see below). In the case of the treaty with Albania,

---

[41] Effective from 1 January 2014.

[42] Sec. 193 of the Act No. 292/2013 Coll., on Special Judicial Proceedings.

Czech judicial authorities would fill the gap by applying the national law, which contains the same solution. Pursuant to Section 69(1) of the Czech PILA,[43] the issue of whether an asset is movable or immovable is governed by the *lex rei sitae*. This provision is systematically part of Section 69, which deals with rights in rem; however, this rule may be applied by analogy also in succession matters.

Apart from the general rule on the law applicable to succession, all relevant treaties contain special conflict-of-laws rules regarding the capacity to make or revoke a will, including its validity. All but one treaty deal expressly with wills only, leaving aside other forms of dispositions of property upon deaths. Only the treaty with Albania (**Treaty 5**) contains a special rule determining the law applicable on the admissibility of dispositions upon death other than wills. The capacity to make or revoke a will is governed by the *lex patriae* of the deceased at the time of its making or revoking. This law applies also to the validity of the will. For the formal validity of the will it is, however, sufficient if it complies with the *lex loci actus*, provided it is the law of a contracting party. The requirements for formal validity are rather strict when compared with the generous wording of the corresponding conflict-of-laws rule on the formal validity of dispositions of property upon death in Article 27 of the Succession Regulation, which offers seven (eight in so far as immovable assets are concerned) alternative applicable laws to ensure their formal validity. In addition to the above-mentioned conflict-of-laws rules on wills, the treaty with Ukraine (**Treaty 10**) contains a special conflict-of-laws rule on disinheritance; the provisions on wills apply accordingly. Unlike the Succession Regulation, the relevant treaties do not contain special conflict-of-laws rules to determine the law governing either the validity of dispositions of property upon death other than wills or the capacity to make or revoke them; in the event of, for instance, agreements as to succession, the Succession Regulation is to apply.

All the relevant bilateral treaties, with the exception of the treaty with Albania (**Treaty 5**), contain a special provision on estates without a claimant. If according to the law of one contracting party governing succession upon death there is no heir, movable assets pass to the Contracting State of which the deceased was a national at the time of death, and immovable assets pass to the Contracting State in whose territory the assets are located. The Contracting State thus acquires the immovable assets located in its territory regardless of whether the law applicable to succession upon death considers the State as the final heir. With respect to Albania, the national rule on estates without a claimant in Section 78 of the

[43] Sec. 69(1) of the Czech PILA: 'Rights in rem in immovable properties as well as in tangible movable properties shall be governed, unless otherwise stipulated by this Act or other [Czech] law, by the law of the place where the property is located. The same law shall also apply to determine whether a property is immovable or movable one.'

Czech PILA would apply, and immovable assets of the deceased situated on the territory of the Czech Republic would pass to the Czech Republic.[44]

If we compare the conflict-of-laws rules in succession matters in the relevant bilateral treaties that are binding for the Czech Republic, on one side, and the rules of the Succession Regulation on the other side, it is obvious that the conceptions diverge substantially. While the autonomy of the deceased in the choice of law plays no role in the above-analyzed bilateral treaties, the Succession Regulation enables a limited choice of law in Article 22. The general conflict-of-laws rule in the vast majority of the bilateral treaties is based on the dualist approach, and there are separate rules for the determination of the law applicable regarding the succession to movable and immovable assets. By means of systematic and purpose-oriented interpretation, it may be deduced that the rules apply solely to assets of the deceased located in the territory of the contracting parties. The Succession Regulation follows the monist principle, and there is (with some exceptions of *dépeçage*) a single law applicable to the succession to the estate of the deceased as a whole, irrespective of its nature and location (this including assets situated in the territory of a third State).

4. PROCEDURAL ISSUES

In addition to containing conflict-of-laws rules on matters of succession, nine of the bilateral treaties on legal assistance analyzed above also contain rules on jurisdiction to hear matters of succession. These rules, with the exception of the treaty with North Korea (**Treaty 7**), apply for both non-contentious and contentious proceedings in matters of succession. The rules are drafted in a very similar way in all of the treaties in question, and here again they differ substantially from the jurisdiction rules in the Succession Regulation. The concept set out in the treaties is based on parallel proceedings in the territories of both contracting parties. They contain different rules regarding jurisdiction to rule on succession to movable and immovable assets, unlike the Succession Regulation that has in Article 4 one general provision on jurisdiction so as to rule on succession as a whole, irrespective of the nature of the assets. Pursuant to the general rule in all of the relevant treaties, the judicial authorities of the contracting party in whose territory the immovable assets are situated have jurisdiction to rule on succession to these assets. With respect to immovables,

44 Sec. 78 of the Czech PILA: 'The deceased person's properties and rights located in the territory of the Czech Republic shall accrue to the Czech Republic provided there is no heir; the Czech courts shall have jurisdiction to decide in these matters. A state or another territorial unit or an institution existing for these purposes shall not be deemed as an heir, unless they were appointed an heir in a will.'

it is clear from the wording of the jurisdiction rule that it applies only to assets located on the territory of the contracting parties. The judicial authorities of the contracting parties have no jurisdiction pursuant to the provisions of the bilateral treaties to rule on succession to immovable assets located on the territory of a third State. Competence to rule on succession to movable assets is conferred on the judicial authorities of the contracting party: (i) whose nationality was possessed by the deceased at the time of death (in the case of the treaties with Albania (**Treaty 5**), former Yugoslavia (**Treaty 13**), Cuba (**Treaty 6**), Vietnam (**Treaty 12**), North Korea (**Treaty 7**) and Ukraine (**Treaty 10**)); or (ii) in whose territory the deceased had his/her last domicile (in the case of the treaties with the former Soviet Union (**Treaty 9**) and Uzbekistan (**Treaty 11**)). With respect to succession to movable assets, the connecting factor applied in the jurisdiction rule always correlates with the connecting factor applied in the corresponding conflict-of-laws rule. The treaty with the former Soviet Union and the treaty with Uzbekistan use the connecting factor of domicile to determine both the jurisdiction to rule on succession to movable assets and the law governing succession to movable assets. The treaty with Albania, Cuba, Mongolia, former Yugoslavia, Vietnam, North Korea and Ukraine use the connecting factor of nationality in an identical fashion. Although it is not clear from the wording of these rules whether the judicial authorities of the contracting parties have competence to rule on succession to movable assets situated solely on the territory of Contracting States or also on the territory of third States, the territorial scope of application is to be interpreted as limited to movable as well as immovable assets situated in the territory of Contracting States. The competence to rule on the succession to immovable and movable assets situated in the territory of third States is to be determined pursuant to the provisions of the Succession Regulation that apply to the estate of the deceased regardless of where individual assets of this estate are situated, without prejudice to Article 12. Provided the deceased had immovable and movable assets located in the territory of both contracting parties, succession proceedings have to be initiated in both countries. This principle diverges from the key principle of the Succession Regulation that aims at single succession proceedings rendering a ruling on the succession as a whole. In a situation where the deceased national of one contracting party had assets situated not only in the territory of the contracting parties but also in the territory of a third State, the jurisdiction rules of the relevant bilateral treaty have to be complemented by the jurisdiction rules of the Succession Regulation.

Some of the bilateral treaties contain a special jurisdiction rule that applies in a situation where a deceased who was a national of one contracting party or who was domiciled in that State's territory has movable assets in the territory of the other contracting party. Pursuant to this provision, which is enshrined in the treaties with Albania (**Treaty 5**), former Yugoslavia (**Treaty 13**), Mongolia (**Treaty 8**), Cuba (**Treaty 6**), Vietnam (**Treaty 12**) and Ukraine (**Treaty 10**), the judicial authorities of the contracting party in whose territory the movable assets are situated have jurisdiction to rule on succession to these movable assets. The wordings, however, differ slightly in individual treaties. In most of the treaties this competence is subject, first, to the request of an heir or another person that has rights or claims against the estate and, second, to the consent of all (known) heirs – and possibly also to a time limit. The respective provision in the treaty with Mongolia even stipulates that this competence can be requested by the deceased, which is not logically viable.[45] Pursuant to all treaties, with the exception of the treaty with North Korea (**Treaty** 7), the judicial authorities of one contracting party may take measures to secure and administrate the assets of the deceased national of the other contracting party that are situated in their territory regardless of their competence to rule on the succession to these assets. Diplomatic and consular offices of the other contracting party are to be notified and may participate in taking these measures and request their postponement, modification or revocation. They are also (with the exception of the treaties with North Korea, Cuba and Vietnam) vested with special powers to represent their nationals in succession matters without a special power of attorney before the authorities of the other Contracting State, provided that such nationals are absent and had not issued any power of attorney. This statutory authorization is formulated as a general one with the exception of the treaties with the former Soviet Union (**Treaty** 9), Uzbekistan (**Treaty** 11) and North Korea (**Treaty** 7), which stipulate explicitly that the diplomatic or consular office is not authorized to waive the succession. The treaties with the former Soviet Union and former Yugoslavia contain a special provision stipulating that these powers apply also to contentious proceedings regarding succession claims. The treaties (with the exception of the treaties with Cuba, the former Soviet Union and Vietnam) also stipulate an obligation of the competent authority of one Contracting State to inform the diplomatic or consular office of the other Contracting State of the death of a national of the other contracting party in its territory and to communicate information available on heirs and the estate.

None of the above-analyzed bilateral treaties contains special rules on recognition and enforcement of decisions rendered in the territory of the other contracting party in matters of succession, but the general provisions on recognition and enforcement of decisions rendered in the territory of the other contracting party in civil matters that are a part of all of the relevant treaties apply, among others, to court decisions in succession matters. The competence to deal with succession matters may not be entrusted only to courts; in some countries the national law grants other authorities the competence to rule on succession matters (e.g. notaries in the Czech Republic). Therefore some of the

---

[45] Art. 42(4) of the Treaty with Mongolia.

treaties (the treaty with former Yugoslavia (**Treaty 13**), Mongolia (**Treaty 8**), Syria, Algeria and Tunisia) stipulate within the chapter on recognition and enforcement that decisions on succession matters rendered by judicial authorities of one contracting party that have jurisdiction pursuant to its own law to hear matters of succession are to be considered as court decisions in civil matters under the treaty. Czech courts apply the general rules on recognition and enforcement of decisions as found in the relevant bilateral treaties to decisions in matters of succession rendered in the territory of Contracting States only. Decisions in matters of succession given in the territory of the EU Member States are to be recognized and enforced pursuant to the provisions of the Succession Regulation. A conflict might arise in situations when recognition or enforcement of a decision in matters of succession rendered by courts of an EU Member State is sought in the Czech Republic provided the deceased was a national of a third State with which the Czech Republic has a bilateral treaty covering succession matters. If the deceased national of a third State had his/her last habitual residence in another EU Member State that has no bilateral treaty with the State of his/her nationality, the courts of this EU Member State have jurisdiction by virtue of Article 4 of the Succession Regulation to rule on the succession as a whole, including assets situated in the Czech Republic. Such a decision on the succession to assets situated in the Czech Republic given by courts of an EU Member State would most probably be recognized or enforced in the Czech Republic even if the deceased was a national of a third State with which the Czech Republic has a bilateral treaty covering succession matters.

5. THE FUTURE OF EXISTING TREATIES WITH THIRD STATES

The government of the Czech Republic has not officially voiced any plans to terminate or modify the treaties based on the aim of strengthening the uniform application of the Succession Regulation. Some of these treaties have kept their practical relevance as there are strong minorities of nationals of the other contracting party living in the territory of the Czech Republic, e.g. the treaties with Ukraine (**Treaty 10**) or Vietnam (**Treaty 12**). On the other hand, some of them have little practical relevance, e.g. the treaty with North Korea (**Treaty 7**), due to current political developments. Czech courts have grown accustomed to the application of bilateral treaties on legal assistance in civil matters; the International Department for Civil Law Matters of the Czech Ministry of Justice does not record any substantial difficulties with their application by Czech courts. It is therefore rather unlikely that the Czech Republic would take any steps to terminate all of them or some of them in the near future. The bilateral treaties cover not only succession matters but a range of other civil (and criminal) matters, and their termination solely for the sake of a smooth application of the Succession Regulation is thus not to be expected. The Czech Republic is interested in preserving friendly cultural and economic relations with most of the contracting parties, something that could be hampered by the termination of these treaties or even by a mere attempt to modify the status quo that might be deemed unnecessary by the other contracting party.

6. CONCLUSION

The bilateral treaties on legal assistance in civil (and criminal) matters analyzed in this chapter were concluded between 1959 and 2002. Despite the fact that most of them were negotiated and concluded in the era of communism, they have retained their relevance. There are no official data available on how often Czech courts apply these bilateral treaties, neither in general nor in matters of succession. Their prevailing relevance can be derived from the numbers of respective nationals in the Czech Republic. The treaties with Ukraine (**Treaty 10**), Vietnam (**Treaty 12**) and Russia (**Treaty 9**) belong to the most frequently applied treaties, which can be attributed to the number of nationals of these States living in the territory of the Czech Republic. According to the statistical data available, there were 110,000 Ukrainians, 58,000 Vietnamese and 36,000 Russians living in the Czech Republic at the end of 2016.[46]

The two most recent relevant treaties that are binding for the Czech Republic are the treaty with Ukraine (**Treaty 10**) that was concluded in 2001 and the treaty with Uzbekistan (**Treaty 11**) that was concluded in 2002. It is surprising how little the respective provisions on succession matters in these recent treaties differ from the relevant provisions in the treaties that were concluded almost 30 years earlier under substantially different social and political circumstances. This shows that it would not be an easy task for the Czech Republic to renegotiate the existing treaties (provided EU legislation enabling EU Member States to do so were adopted) with the aim of modifying the provisions on succession matters so as to be compatible with the Succession Regulation.

The jurisdiction and conflict-of-laws rules applied in all of the relevant bilateral treaties diverge substantially from their counterparts in the Succession Regulation. All jurisdiction rules are based on a scission of proceedings in matters of succession dependent on the nature of the assets, which may result in the necessity of initiating parallel succession proceedings in the courts of both contracting parties, while the Succession Regulation – aiming at

46 Data of the Czech Statistical Office. Available at <https://www.czso.cz/documents/11292/56594384/c01R07_2016.pdf/63ace08b-4092-4213-8993-a48eafeabb54?version=1.0> accessed 28.03.2019.

making international succession cases easier – stipulates single proceedings on the succession as a whole. The conflict-of-laws rules in succession matters in the bilateral treaties apply the connecting factor of nationality or domicile for movable assets and location for immovable assets, whereas the Succession Regulation applies habitual residence as the key connecting factor. The Succession Regulation follows a monist approach; the applicable law governs succession to both movable and immovable assets. By contrast, the majority of the relevant bilateral treaties follow the dualist principle, whereby the law applicable to movable and immovable assets may differ. With respect to immovable assets, this solution in the relevant bilateral treaties may be viewed more favourably by the competent courts as both the jurisdiction and conflict-of-laws rules are based on the *situs* principle, which means that the competent authority rules exclusively on the succession to immovable assets situated in its territory, thereby applying always the *lex fori*. This is unlike the Succession Regulation, under which the competent court may also rule on succession to immovable assets situated abroad. The treaties do no admit any choice of the law applicable to succession upon death; the Succession Regulation, for the sake of easier cross-border estate planning, allows the deceased to choose the law of the State of which he/she is a national at the time of the choice or at the time of death.

Czech judges and notaries, as court commissioners in succession proceedings, have thus far very little practical experience with the parallel application of the Succession Regulation alongside a bilateral treaty concluded with a third State. There are no best practices with respect to issuing a European Certificate of Succession when a bilateral treaty is applicable.

THE EXTERNAL RELATIONS OF FINLAND AND SWEDEN

Markku Helin

1. INTRODUCTION

The Treaty of Amsterdam, which gave the EU competence in private international law, entered into force in 1999. Before that many States had for more than a century satisfied their needs in this area by entering into multilateral or bilateral treaties with other States.

When the EU very diligently started to exercise its new competence, the question of the destiny of earlier treaties and conventions arose. Such treaties may have considerable regional or bilateral importance for the State parties. Would the EU tolerate the divergence that follows from the continued application of such treaties? And if so, in what way do the treaties affect the unity that was purported by concluding the EU instrument in question?

In the next section, the treaties which Finland and Sweden have concluded within the sphere of the European Succession Regulation (SR) are examined. After an enumeration and a short description of these treaties, the focus is on the Nordic Inheritance Convention (NIC) (**Treaty 14**), which from the point of view of the theme of this book is by far the most important and most interesting. The historical background of the NIC is outlined first, in order to elucidate its importance for the Nordic States.[1] Thereafter the contents of the NIC are described in order to answer two questions: (1) In what way does the NIC affect the application of the Succession Regulation in Finland and Sweden; and (2) How does the Regulation affect the application of the NIC and the fulfilment of the needs and interests that are behind the conclusion of it?

2. TREATIES AND CONVENTIONS TAKING PRECEDENCE OVER THE EUROPEAN SUCCESSION REGULATION

Finland is a party to three and Sweden to two treaties within the scope of the European Succession Regulation. Both States have ratified the Hague Convention of 1961 on the Conflicts of Laws Relating to the Form of Testamentary Dispositions. They ratified it without any reservations and, in accordance with Article 75(1) SR, apply it instead of the Regulation. This means that Finland and Sweden are a little bit more liberal as regards the acceptable form of a will than the Member States that apply Article 27 SR. The content of the Hague Convention of 1961 is so well known that it is unnecessary to describe it here.

In 1980 Finland concluded a treaty with the Soviet Union Concerning the Provision of Legal Protection and Legal Assistance in Civil, Family and Criminal Cases (hereafter: TPA) (**Treaty 15**).[2] It is now in force between Finland and Russian Federation and between Finland and Ukraine. It covers mainly such matters as service of documents and the taking of evidence in the other Contracting State. But there are two provisions on succession. The first, Article 24 TPA, prohibits any discrimination of citizens of a Contracting State living in another Contracting State as regards their right to inherit. This does not affect the Succession Regulation. The other provision, Article 25 TPA, is about the law applicable to the form of wills. It concerns wills that are made by a citizen of a Contracting State and applies also to the revocation of such wills.

Ukraine ratified the Hague Convention of 1961 in 2011. Because of the reservations Ukraine has made to this Convention, Article 25 TPA may still

1 By Nordic States, I refer to Denmark, Finland, Iceland, Norway and Sweden.

2 The official title in Finnish: Sopimus Suomen Tasavallan ja Sosialististen Neuvostotasavaltojen Liiton välillä oikeussuojasta ja oikeusavusta siviili-, perhe- ja rikosasioissa (SopS 48/1980). 'SopS' refers to the Finnish Treaty Series, where international treaties are published.

in theory become applicable in relations between Finland and Ukraine, but in practice it has relevance only between Finland and the Russian Federation.

Like the Hague Convention of 1961, Article 25 TPA offers a list of laws that may be applied alternatively, but the list is a little bit shorter than the one found in the 1961 Convention. Therefore, it is in theory possible that a will is made in accordance with the law that exists in the list of the Hague Convention of 1961 but not in the list of the TPA. There are no precedents as to how Article 25 TPA is to be interpreted. But it seems that Article 25 TPA only lays down sufficient conditions of validity and does not prevent the Contracting States from deeming the will to be valid as to form even on other grounds. Therefore, in the view of the present author, Finland, in accordance with the obligations based on the Hague Convention of 1961, applies that Convention in every case where the question of the formal correctness of a will arises.

From the point of view of this contribution, the most important of the agreements with third States is the Nordic Inheritance Convention, i.e. the Convention between Denmark, Finland, Iceland, Norway and Sweden Comprising International Private Law Provisions on Succession, Wills and Estate Administration (**Treaty 14**).[3] It was concluded in 1934, but some minor amendments have subsequently been made, the most important changes being accomplished in 2012. The NIC contains all elements that are relevant in private international law, i.e. provisions on jurisdiction, the applicable law and recognition and enforcement of judgments. It also has some provisions on legal assistance with respect to an inventory of the assets belonging to the estate. What follows concentrates on this Convention.

3. THE NORDIC INHERITANCE CONVENTION

3.1. HISTORICAL BACKGROUND

The Nordic States have centuries of partly common political history. Denmark (including Iceland) and Norway formed a union for more than 400 years, having a single monarch until 1814. Also Sweden was part of that union for about a century, until 1520, at that time called the Kalmar Union. When the union between Denmark and Norway collapsed in 1814, Norway and Sweden joined together in a personal union, where the Swedish king was also the king of Norway. That ended in 1905, when Norway became independent. The union between Denmark and Iceland lasted until 1918 and Iceland gained full sovereignty in 1944.

3 Konvention mellan Finland, Danmark, Island, Norge och Sverige undertecknad i Köpenhamn den 19 november 1934 om arv, testamente och boutredning, SopS 21/1935, amended in Sops 36/1976 and SopS 60/2015.

Finland was for more than 700 years an integral part of Sweden, this lasting until 1809. In that year Sweden had to surrender its eastern part to Tsarist Russia, because of an unsuccessful war, and Finland became an autonomous Grand-Duchy in connection with Russia. The autonomy covered, among other things, matters within the sphere of general legislation (e.g. private law and penal law). Accordingly, the Swedish Civil Code of 1734 remained in force in Finland until it was gradually and very slowly replaced by Finnish legislation of its own. Also, the administrative structure of Sweden remained in Finland. Finland became independent in 1917, but even now the way in which administration and society is organized in these two States reflects remarkable similarities.

Common history and a similarity of the societies created appropriate circumstances for legal cooperation between the Nordic States, which started in the 1870s. The similar languages of Denmark, Norway and Sweden, which many Finns and Icelanders understand, made the cooperation easy and smooth. As regards private international law, the heyday of Nordic cooperation was the late 1920s and 1930s. Several treaties were concluded at that time, among them the Nordic Inheritance Convention in 1934 (**Treaty 14**). Other Nordic Conventions from that decade include the Convention on Marriage, Adoption and Guardianship (Marriage Convention),[4] the Convention on Recovery of Maintenance[5] and the Convention on Recognition and Enforcement of Judgments in Matters of Civil Law.[6] The Nordic Conventions of the 1930s were in later decades reformed or in some cases replaced by new instruments. The Nordic Convention on Recognition and Enforcement of Judgments was in 1976 replaced by a new Convention and by uniform laws that were enacted on the basis of that Convention.[7] Also new topics have been taken on board. Uniform laws on recognition of determinations of paternity in other Nordic States were enacted in 1980.[8]

The Nordic States also mutually integrated in other ways. In 1954 it was agreed that citizens of a Nordic State did not need a passport when crossing the borders between the Nordic States. Simultaneously, the citizens of a Nordic State also obtained the liberty to live in another Contracting State without needing a

---

4 Konvention mellan Finland, Danmark, Island, Norge och Sverige den 6 februari 1931 innehållande internationellt privaträttsliga bestämmelser om äktenskap, adoption och förmynderskap m.m., SopS 20/1931 with several later amendments.

5 Konvention angående indrivning av underhållsbidrag avslutad i Oslo den 10 februari 1931 mellan Finland, Danmark, Island; Norge och Sverige, SopS 21/1931.

6 Konvention mellan Finland, Danmark, Island, Norge och Sverige om erkännande och verställighet av domar, SopS 9/1933.

7 Konvention mellan Finland, Danmark, Island, Norge och Sverige om erkännande och verkställighet av domar på privaträttens område, SopS 56/1977.

8 The Swedish title of the Finnish Act is Lag om erkännande av nordiska faderskapsavgöranden (352/1980). The number refers to the Statute Book of Finland, where Acts of Parliament and government decrees are published.

permit of residence for that State. A common labour market was established in the same year and an agreement concerning social security was concluded in 1984. The intention, which has been confirmed in the Helsinki Treaty of 1962,[9] is to create an area covering all the Nordic States, where a private citizen can easily be relocated and where he/she may study and work irrespective of the borders and without losing the benefits he has earned in one State and without having to pay multiple taxes. Thus, many of the objectives that the EU aims to achieve were in fact achieved between the Nordic States several decades ago.

The Nordic private international law treaties have considerably promoted the free movement of Nordic citizens within the North. The most important connecting factor in the instruments as regards both jurisdiction and applicable law is the habitual residence of the person. Because of this, the courts dealing with an inter-Nordic situation may most often apply their own law. The same, of course, holds true with respect to lawyers advising their clients. Seen from the point of view of Nordic citizens, this means that the forum and applicable law often change either immediately or after a short period of time, when a new habitual residence in another Nordic State is established. However, the consequences of such a change are normally not dramatic, because in many cases the laws of the different Nordic States, though different in details, are similar as regards their basic principles.

The conclusion of the Amsterdam Treaty was a major event from the point of view of Nordic cooperation, due to different solutions the different Nordic States have taken with regard to European integration. Finland and Sweden are Member States of the EU. Denmark has long been a Member State, but it does not participate in the cooperation in the area of private law. Norway and Iceland are outside the EU but belong to the European Economic Area. Therefore, it was clear that the unity and coordination in the North, which was achieved by the Nordic Conventions, cannot be retained by EU instruments. The resulting question was whether the coming EU instruments would respect the unity of private international law that had been achieved in the North over a number of decades or whether they would overrule its achievements.

The Nordic States have been willing to keep the Nordic instruments. They are considered to be relatively simple and easy to apply, even though the technical set up, where the same provision may contain rules both on the applicable law and jurisdiction, is somewhat confusing. Because of mutual trust in the administration of justice in each of the Contracting States, it has not been necessary to put every detail into the convention text. The Nordic instruments are also somewhat less abstract than the instruments of private international law normally are because they can rely on the relative similarity of substantive family and inheritance laws in the North.

---

9 Samarbetsöverenskommelse mellan Danmark, Finland, Island, Norge och Sverige, SopS 28/1962.

In order to maintain the coherence brought to the North by the Nordic instruments, the Nordic Member States adopted the policy that, if the general rules in a European instrument concerning relationships with existing conventions do not allow the continued application of the Nordic instruments, exceptions will be sought.[10] Now, 20 years after the Amsterdam Treaty, we know how it went. The policy was successful with regard to earlier Regulations, but after that the results have been modest.[11] The search for unity between the EU Member States has overruled the unity that for decades existed in the North. The Nordic Inheritance Convention will now be examined.

3.2. EFFORTS TO UPDATE THE NORDIC INHERITANCE CONVENTION

In 2006, the Nordic States decided to update the NIC (**Treaty 14**), which had gradually started to suffer from its advanced age. During the decades after its conclusion, the substantive succession laws in the Nordic States had experienced changes, making some provisions in the NIC obsolete. There were also other characteristics in the Convention that were, 60 years after its conclusion, regarded as problematic. One aspect was the complete lack of party autonomy; the citizens within the scope of the NIC had no right to choose the law that was to govern succession. Another problematic feature was a rule according to which an heir could request, with regard to his rights to succession, the application of the home law (national law) of the deceased if the deceased had lived in his/her new Contracting State of habitual residence for less than five years. If only some

10 On this see M. Jänterä-Jareborg, 'The Nordic Input on the EU's Cooperation in Family and Succession Law: Exporting Union Law Through "Nordic Exceptions"', in B. Hess, M. Bergström and E. Storskrubb (eds.), *EU Civil Justice, Current Issues and Future Outlook*, Swedish Studies in European Law, Volume 7, Hart Publishing, Oxford and Portland/Oregon 2016, pp. 143–159.

11 On the Nordic exceptions in the Regulations see Council Regulation (EC) No. 2201/2003 of 27.11.2003 concerning jurisdiction and the recognition and enforcement of judgments in matrimonial matters and the matters of parental responsibility, repealing Regulation (EC) No. 1347/2000 [2003] OJ L338/1 [Brussels IIbis], Art. 59; Council Regulation (EC) No. 4/2009 of 18.12.2008 on jurisdiction, applicable law, recognition and enforcement of decisions and cooperation in matters relating to maintenance obligations [2009] OJ L7/1, Art. 69; Council Regulation (EU) 2016/1103 of 24.06.2016 implementing enhanced cooperation in the area of jurisdiction, applicable law and the recognition and enforcement of decisions in matters of matrimonial property regimes [2016] OJ L183/1, Art. 62. As regards the Nordic exception in Brussels IIbis see M. Helin, 'The Impact and Application of the Brussels II bis Regulation in Finland', in K. Boele-Woelki and C. Gonzáles Beilfuss (eds.), *Brussels II bis: Its Impact and Application in the Member States*, Intersentia, Antwerp 2007, pp. 91–102. See also M. Jänterä-Jareborg, 'A European Family Law for Cross-Border Situations – Some Reflections Concerning the Brussels II Regulation and Its Planned Amendments'(2002) 4 *Yearbook of Private International Law*, 67–82.

of the heirs claimed the application of *lex patriae*, two different laws would be applied to the succession: the *lex patriae* of the deceased with regard to those who claimed the application of it and the *lex domicilii* with regard to the other heirs.

The group of experts that was set up to propose necessary changes gave its report in 2009. It suggested abolishing heirs' right to claim the application of the *lex patriae*. It also proposed a relatively broad party autonomy. According to the expert group, the person should have the following options to designate the law governing the succession of his estate:

1. the law of a Contracting State of which the deceased was a citizen at the time of the provision or at his or her death;
2. the law of a Contracting State in which the deceased had his or her habitual residence at the time of the provision or at his or her death;
3. the law of a Contracting State in which the deceased had previously had his or her habitual residence; or
4. if the person was married or lived in a registered partnership at the time when the provision is made, also the law that is applicable to matrimonial property of the spouses or partners.

Had the deceased not made the choice, the law of the Contracting State in which the deceased was habitually resident at the time of death would have been applicable, but normally only provided that the deceased had lived in that State for at least two years. The purpose of the requirement of two years' residence was to remove problems of evidence with regard to habitual residence in cases where the deceased at a short time before his death had moved from one Contracting State to another. It would also have aligned the Convention with the conflict-of-laws rules on matrimonial property in the Nordic Marriage Convention, where the requirement was instituted some years ago. If the requirement of two years was not fulfilled, the applicable law would have been the law of the Contracting State in which the deceased had most recently had his or her habitual residence and lived there for at least two years. If that requirement was not fulfilled, the law of the closest connection would have been applicable.

Almost at the same time as the report was presented, the European Commission issued its proposal for a European Succession Regulation.[12] After that it was considered to be clear that the principle of loyalty prevented Finland and Sweden from concluding any new treaties within the proposed scope of the future Regulation. Therefore, the proposal of the expert group was put on ice to wait and see what would happen in the negotiations in Brussels.

---

12 COM (2009) 154 final.

When the negotiations in Brussels neared their end, Finland and Sweden asked for an exception to the Regulation, enabling them to apply the NIC in the updated form as suggested by the expert group. The Commission was not delighted with that request. Only a very narrow exception was given a green light. Pursuant to what is now Article 75(3) SR, Finland and Sweden were promised the opportunity to apply the updated NIC insofar as it provides for:

a. rules on the procedural aspects of estate administration as defined by the Convention and assistance in that regard by the authorities of the Contracting Parties to the Convention; and
b. simplified and more expeditious procedures for the recognition and enforcement of decisions in matters of succession.

After this, the Nordic States had in a very short time to decide how to proceed. The amendments to the NIC had to be done before the Regulation was adopted because after that point in time Finland and Sweden would have no power to conclude treaties with third States affecting the Regulation.

Several options were on the table.[13] One option was to abandon the reform and continue the application of the NIC in its existing form. That had been possible because the Succession Regulation allowed the Member States to maintain existing international conventions, where third parties were involved (Article 75(1) SR). Later on Denmark, Iceland and Norway could have perhaps negotiated a treaty with the EU using the Regulation as a model and the Nordic Convention could then be denounced. It was, however, deemed to be unclear how realistic this option would be. Would the EU be interested? Would the Regulation, which is quite complicated in its structure and contents, be attractive enough for Denmark, Iceland and Norway in order to be an appropriate basis for negotiations?

Another option was to accept the report of the expert group as such. The problem with this option was that Finland and Sweden had no power to conclude anything that could affect the application of the Regulation outside the exception that was promised to them. Therefore, this option was possible only provided that Denmark, Iceland and Norway were willing to enter into such agreement, with Finland and Sweden being given the right not to apply those parts of the Convention that would affect the common European rules. From the point of view of the objectives of Nordic cooperation, this was a bad

[13] On this see also the report of The Nordic Council of Ministers on the amendment: *Den nordiska konventionen om arv, testamente och boutredning. En översyn av konventionsregleringen föreslagen av den nordiska expertgruppen för familjerättsfrågor*. TemaNord 2013:528. Nordiska ministerrådet 2013, pp. 29–31.

solution. No coherence of conflict-of-laws rules would be attained because those rules in the Regulation and in the expert group proposal were different.

The option that was chosen was as follows. The proposal of the expert group was changed so that the basic provisions concerning the law applicable to a succession became similar to those in the Regulation. The possibility of choosing the law governing succession was, accordingly, reduced to cover only the *lex patriae* (cf. Article 3 NIC amended version), as in the Regulation. In the absence of a choice of law, as in the Regulation, the law of the Contracting State in which the deceased had his habitual residence at the time of death is applicable (Article 2 NIC amended version). The planned requirement of two years' residence in that State was abolished. An escape clause along the lines of Article 21(2) SR was introduced for situations where the deceased had only a superficial connection to the Contracting State of his last habitual residence.

In addition, it was agreed that Finland and Sweden would apply the Convention only, unless otherwise provided in the Regulation (Article 1 NIC amended version). The most important area – where all Contracting States apply the Convention as such – is the recognition and enforcement of decisions that are given in a non-EU Nordic State. But in several important respects, such as the applicable law and jurisdiction, Finland and Sweden apply the Regulation, i.e. a set of provisions which is different from those applied in the other Nordic States.[14] But the content of these two sets of provisions is similar to such an extent that remnants of the unity that existed before could be maintained. In this way the European rules were exported to those States in Scandinavia which are outside the EU. The Scandinavian States embraced these provisions not because of their high quality, but because the coherence of conflict-of-laws rules in the North could to some extent be safeguarded in this way.

The following section describes the contents of the NIC as it is now – since 1 September 2015 – in force between the Contracting States.

3.3. SCOPE OF APPLICATION OF THE NORDIC INHERITANCE CONVENTION

The material scope of the NIC (**Treaty 14**) is broad. It covers intestate succession as well as succession by testamentary disposition. Also questions relating to the formal and material validity of wills and other dispositions upon death are within its scope, as well as administration and distribution of the estate.

The Convention covers all the property that is situated in the Contracting States (Article 19 NIC). The Convention is silent as regards the property situated

14 See also M. Jänterä-Jareborg, above n. 10 pp. 155–156.

in a third State. The *travaux préparatoires* do not tackle the problem either. A look at the preparatory documents gives the impression that the drafters did not want to take a stand on that question. In legal literature, Bogdan has taken the view that property outside the North is also covered.[15]

As regards the scope *ratione personae*, the NIC is applicable only to citizens of a Nordic State who at the time of death have their habitual residence in one of the Nordic States. The narrow personal scope was adopted because Finland and Sweden, whose own private international law in the 1930s was based on the principle of nationality, wanted to keep their general system untouched. The Nordic system was built as an exception to the general system. An additional reason was that Finland and Sweden wanted to keep open the possibility of concluding treaties on succession with such States that use nationality as the most important connecting factor.[16] That would have become difficult if the NIC was also applicable in situations where the deceased was a national of a third State.[17] Now we know that this possibility was never used.

At the time, when the Convention was concluded, the narrow personal scope was not a problem, because in the 1930s the number of foreigners living in the North and not being citizens of any Nordic State was quite low. Since then the situation has changed. The number of people coming from outside the North and not having a Nordic nationality has increased considerably in every Contracting State and especially in Sweden. As consequence, a growing number of people living in the Nordic States are outside the NIC's personal scope and the practical value of the NIC is, accordingly, somewhat reduced.

However, the expert group that was set up to update the NIC recommended keeping the narrow personal scope. The hidden reason behind the recommendation was that it would be easier to secure an exception from the application of the Succession Regulation if the NIC did not affect the application of the Regulation in situations where the deceased was habitually resident outside the North or was a national of a non-Contracting State. As we saw earlier, the power of this argument in Brussels turned out to be limited.

---

15 M. Bogdan, *Svensk internationell privat- och processrätt*, 7th ed., Norstedts, Vällingby 2008, p. 243.

16 See *Nordisk konvention om arv, testamente och boutredning med därav föranledd svensk lagstiftning*. Nytt Juridiskt Arkiv II 1935. Stockholm 1935, pp. 359–360. See also *Udkast til konvention mellem Danmark, Finland, Island, Norge och Sverige om arv og dødsboskifte*. Copenhagen 1933, p. 25.

17 These reasons behind the narrow personal scope have disappeared over recent decades. International treaties which the drafters of the NIC had in mind have not been concluded. The role of nationality as a connecting factor has considerably diminished both in Finland and in Sweden. The Finnish private international rules on succession since 2001 have been based on habitual residence as the primary connecting factor. See Chapter 26 Inheritance Code (40/1965).

The NIC is silent as to the question of whether it applies in situations where the deceased had multiple nationalities. The objectives of the NIC support, in the view of the present author, the interpretation according to which the Convention does not apply if the deceased, in addition to having the nationality of a Nordic State, was also a national of a third State, whereas situations where the deceased was a national of more than one Nordic State are within the Convention's scope. This conclusion is, however, uncertain because Article 3(3) NIC and its preparatory documents seem to indicate that persons having the nationality of a third State in addition to a Nordic one are within the Convention's scope.[18] Legal scholars have not tackled the issue, and, as far as can be known, there are no precedents clarifying the situation.

3.4. PRIVATE INTERNATIONAL LAW

3.4.1. Conflict-of-Laws Rules in the Nordic Inheritance Convention

The rules in the Convention on the law applicable to succession (*lex successionis*) are enshrined in Articles 2, 3 and 3a NIC (**Treaty 14**). Because of the above-mentioned reasons, they are similar to Articles 21 and 22 SR. Accordingly, if the deceased has not designated the applicable law, the law of the Contracting State in which the deceased was habitually resident at the time of death are to be applied. If, however, it is clear from all the circumstances that the deceased was at the time of death manifestly more closely connected with another Contracting State, the law applicable will be the law of that other Contracting State. As the wording of the escape clause shows, it is not applicable in situations where a deceased within the scope of the NIC was most closely connected with a non-contracting State. The *lex successionis* may only be the law of a Contracting State.

The possibility of designating the applicable law is, as in the Succession Regulation, restricted to the *lex patriae* either at the time of the designation or at the time of death. If the person is a national of more than one Nordic State, he/she may designate the law of any of such States as applicable.

The applicable law covers both movable and immovable property. A narrow exception is, however, made in favour of the *lex rei sitae* in situations where the real property belonging to the estate is of such nature that special rules apply as regards the right to inherit the property (Article 13 NIC).

[18] See also the comments on Article 3, *Den nordiska konventionen om arv, testamente och boutredning. En översyn av konventionsregleringen föreslagen av den nordiska expertgruppen för familjerättsfrågor*. TemaNord 2013:528. Nordiska ministerrådet 2013, p. 44.

An important difference between the NIC and the Succession Regulation concerns the scope of the *lex successionis*. Pursuant to the NIC, the *lex successionis* does not cover questions such as the estate's liability for debts or administration of the estate, these issues having conflict-of-laws rules of their own (Articles 17 and 19 NIC). In other words, the scope of the *lex successionis* is narrower in the NIC than in the Succession Regulation. This means, among other things, that under the NIC the designation of the *lex patriae* as the law applicable to succession does not affect the rules on the law applicable to liability for debts and estate administration.

The reason why the *lex successionis* in the NIC does not cover liability for debts and estate administration is to be found in the substantive succession laws of the Nordic States. In accordance with legislation in those countries, the property of the deceased does not immediately pass on to successors at the time of death. Rather, when a person dies a separate legal person, the estate of the deceased, comes into existence by operation of law. The estate must be administered either by the beneficiaries jointly, by an administrator appointed by the court or by an executor nominated by the deceased in a will. The main purpose of the estate administration is to pay the debts of the deceased, to terminate his/her contracts and then to convey the property which is left, for distribution in accordance with the *lex successionis*.

The administration of the estate is, under the NIC, to be arranged in the Contracting State where the deceased was habitually resident at the time of death (Article 19 NIC). The law of that State, i.e. the *lex fori*, is applicable to administration and also to liability for any debts. This brings with it many advantages, because judges and lawyers involved in those questions may apply their own law. Applying procedures of a foreign law would be much more difficult. The law of the deceased's last habitual residence is normally also the law that creditors, debtors and others who have entered into legal transactions with the deceased know best, and, accordingly, they can defend their interests. The system of the Succession Regulation, under which the person may by designating the law applicable to his succession also designate the law applicable to debts and administration of the estate, is likely to bring unpleasant surprises to creditors.

Because of these advantages, Finland and Sweden suggested that a similar solution or, alternatively, the solution which was adopted in the Hague Convention of 1989 should be incorporated into the Succession Regulation.[19] However, in a rather unsatisfactory discussion in the Council working group,

[19] Under Article 7 of the 1989 Hague Convention, the *lex successionis* does not cover administration of the estate. A Contracting State may, however, enlarge the scope of the *lex successionis* to cover also questions of estate administration, if such questions are considered in that State to be governed by the law of succession.

the suggestion did not get enough support. The Commission stressed the importance of having a single law that is applied from the opening of the succession to the devolution of the deceased's property. As a weak compromise, Article 29 was added to the Succession Regulation. The basic content of this very complicated provision is that a Member State may in certain situations appoint an administrator in accordance with its own law, but normally the *lex successionis* determines the powers and obligations of the administrator.

As with the Succession Regulation, the NIC also has many conflict-of-laws rules concerning death dispositions. The structure of these rules is, however, different in these two instruments. The differences may be shown in a tabular form as in Table 1.

Table 1. The structure of conflict rules in the NIC and SR compared

Law applicable	NIC	SR
to succession (*lex successionis*)	Articles 2, 3, 3a, 3b	Articles 21 and 22
scope of *lex successionis*	None	Article 23
formal validity of wills	Article 8	–
formal validity of death dispositions	–	Article 27
competence to make or revoke a will	Article 9	–
invalidity of the will on certain substantive grounds	Article 10	–
admissibility and substantive validity of wills	–	Article 24
admissibility and substantive validity of agreements as to succession	–	Article 25
validity of agreements as to succession	Article 12	–
time limits on the right to inherit	Article 16	–
liability for debts left by the deceased	Article 17	–
estate administration	Article 19	Article 29
distribution of the property	Article 19	–

Source: Compiled by the author.

Note: In the table 'none' means that a provision on the issue in question is lacking. An empty space (–) means that there is no specific provision on the issue, but the issue at stake belongs to the sphere of another conflict rule in the instrument.

From the comparison it can be seen that the provisions on applicable law in both instruments by and large cover the same issues irrespective of their different structures. To take an example, the Succession Regulation does not have a conflict rule on the power to make a will, but Article 24 SR seems to cover, among other things, the same question. To take another example, the NIC, unlike the SR, does not have a conflict rule on 'formal validity of death dispositions', because the formal validity of a will and the validity (both formal and substantive) of an agreement as to succession have been seen as separate questions deserving separate answers. In spite of this difference, both instruments deal adequately with the questions concerning the law applicable to the formal validity of different kinds of death dispositions.

The conflict-of-laws rules in these two instruments are also similar as to their contents, because in both instruments the habitual residence of the person at the time he/she made the disposition is an important connecting factor. The similarity has the advantage that if, for instance, a Finnish citizen living in Sweden had made a testamentary disposition following the provisions of the Succession Regulation, the disposition normally would remain valid if he/she later moved to Denmark, and the validity of his/her disposition would be assessed in Danish courts on the basis of the NIC. But there are exceptions to this. Thus, it is not possible to rely on this without checking the issue in the case in question. In that respect the situation is worse than it was before the entry into force of the Regulation.

3.4.2. *The Application of the NIC Conflict-of-Laws Rules in Finland and Sweden*

The basic rule is that Finland and Sweden are to apply conflicts rules of the Succession Regulation, not those of the NIC, even where the case falls within the scope of the NIC. The only exception is mentioned in Article 75(3) SR. Pursuant to this rule, Finland and Sweden may apply the NIC 'in so far as it provides for … rules on the procedural aspects of estate administration as defined by the Convention and assistance in that regard by authorities of the States Contracting Parties to the Convention'.

The exception means that if the deceased was within the scope *ratione personae* of the NIC, Article 19 NIC concerning the law applicable to estate administration is to be applied in place of the Succession Regulation. Pursuant to Article 19 NIC, the law applicable to administration of the estate is the law of the Contracting State where the deceased was habitually resident at the time of death. This is also the State where the administration of the estate is to be arranged.

> *Example:* A Norwegian person having habitual residence in Finland dies there after having designated Norwegian law to be applied to succession after him. Pursuant to Article 19 NIC, Finland, as the country where the estate administration is arranged, may apply its own law to the procedural aspects of administration of the estate. Norwegian law, which pursuant to the Succession Regulation is the *lex successionis*, is applied to material questions such as who the heirs are, what their shares are and what assets each of them is entitled to receive from the estate.
>
> The exception also concerns relationships between Finland and Sweden. So, if in the example above the deceased were a Swedish national, the law of Finland would govern the administration of the estate and the *lex successionis* would be applied

only to questions that are regarded to be material and, accordingly, not covered by Article 19 NIC. If, on the contrary, the deceased was outside of the scope of NIC, Finland and Sweden would have to apply the Regulation as a whole, and administration of the estate would take place in accordance with the law that was, in accordance with the Regulation, the *lex successionis*.

The dichotomy between *lex successionis* and *lex administrationis* gives rise to the question of what is meant by 'administration' or by 'procedural aspects of administration' as it is put in the Regulation. According to the wording of the 'Nordic exception', the question is to be answered by interpreting the Convention. The notion of the Convention, and not that of the Regulation, is decisive. The *travaux préparatoires* of the Convention are rather silent as to the content of 'procedural aspects of estate administration', quite probably because the question was regarded as being unproblematic.[20] In the view of the present author, the common understanding is that all the issues with regard to how the estate is to be administered are procedural in their nature and, accordingly, within the scope of the Nordic exception.[21]

Examples of issues of estate administration that are regarded as being procedural and outside the scope of the *lex successionis* include:

- appointment and dismissal of an estate administrator;
- professional and other qualifications that an estate administrator must fulfil;
- the rights and duties of an estate administrator, including situations where the estate is insolvent;
- the need for consent of the beneficiaries in certain situations;
- how the property belonging to the estate is to be taken care of;
- the obligation to compensate loss or damage which the administrator has caused to the estate, to the creditor or to a beneficiary;
- the right to remuneration.

If the administration of the estate is arranged in accordance with Article 19 NIC, the question arises whether a European Certificate of Succession may be issued on the powers of the estate administrator. The answer is not self-evident because in these cases the powers of the administrator do not follow from the *lex successionis* but instead from the law determined by Article 19 NIC. On the

---

20 See *Nordisk konvention om arv, testamente och boutredning med därav föranledd svensk lagstiftning*. Nytt Juridiskt Arkiv II 1935. Stockholm 1935 pp. 392–397. See also *Udkast til konvention mellem Danmark, Finland, Island, Norge och Sverige om arv og dødsoskifte*. Copenhagen 1933, pp. 50–52.

21 See also the report in n. 13 p. 56 and the proposal of the Swedish government, prop. 2014/15: 105 p. 48. This is also the way in which the distinction between the *lex successionis* and the *lex administrationis* has been drawn in Finnish autonomous legislation on private international succession law. See the proposal of the Finnish government HE 44/2001 vp, pp. 76 and 81.

other hand, the Nordic exception that leads to the described situation is part of the Regulation, and there is nothing in the Regulation that clearly prohibits the issuance of the Certificate in these situations. Obtaining the Certificate would be useful if the deceased had property in a non-Nordic EU State.

3.5. PROCEDURAL ISSUES

3.5.1. *Jurisdiction*

Provisions on jurisdiction can be found in Articles 19 and 21 NIC (**Treaty 14**). Under these rules, the Contracting State where the administration of the estate is arranged, i.e. the Contracting State where the deceased was habitually resident, has jurisdiction. However, a limited possibility for prorogation exists in certain situations (Article 21(2) NIC).

Finland and Sweden do not apply the NIC's provisions on jurisdiction. Rather, they have to apply the rules of the Succession Regulation. This means, among other things, that the NIC system, where only one State has jurisdiction, no longer exists. Finnish or Swedish courts may have an obligation to exercise jurisdiction in accordance with Article 10 SR even though, for example, Denmark has exclusive jurisdiction according to the NIC. This may lead to concurrent litigation and may be detrimental to estate administration in the State of the deceased's habitual residence.

3.5.2. *Recognition and Enforcement of Decisions*

The NIC has a specific provision (Article 27 NIC) on recognition of a court order where an estate administrator or estate distributor has been appointed. Pursuant to this rule, the court order is in force in the other Contracting States without any possibility of opposing or challenging it in the State requested.

As regards recognition and enforcement of other decisions in matters of succession, the NIC (Article 28) refers to the Nordic Convention on Recognition and Enforcement of Private Law Judgments[22] and uniform laws enacted on the basis of this Convention. Pursuant to the uniform laws, the decision that has been given in accordance with the NIC is recognized and is – after a certain procedure in the State requested has been completed – enforceable in the requested Nordic State. There are some grounds of refusal, the most important of which concern indirect jurisdiction and parallel proceedings pending in different Contracting States. Also contradiction of the decision with the *ordre public* is a ground of

---

22 SopS 56/1977, see n. 7.

refusal, but it is highly improbable that it could come into question in situations where the *lex causae* is the law of a Nordic State.

Finland and Sweden recognize and enforce judgments coming from Denmark, Iceland and Norway on the basis of those provisions. Similarly, Denmark, Iceland and Norway apply those rules to recognition and enforcement of Finnish or Swedish decisions. In most cases they have to recognize Finnish and Swedish decisions within the scope of the NIC even though jurisdiction was exercised under the Succession Regulation on a ground that is not available under the NIC system. However, if jurisdiction was based on Article 10(2) SR, the decision will not be recognized in the States in question because the inter-Nordic rules contain a provision on indirect jurisdiction prohibiting recognition of a judgment where jurisdiction was based solely on the location of assets in the State of origin.

In Article 75(3) SR, the Nordic EU Member States, i.e. Finland and Sweden, have been given a permission to apply the NIC also in their mutual relations on recognition and enforcement. However, the permission is conditional. The application of the NIC is possible 'in so far as it provides for ... simplified and more expeditious procedures for the recognition and enforcement of decisions in matters of succession'.

Article 27 NIC, providing for automatic recognition of a court order where an estate administrator or estate distributor has been appointed, is clearly simpler than the Succession Regulation's provisions on recognition. As regards other decisions, it is not quite clear whether the Nordic rules are simplified compared to the Succession Regulation.

The Swedish legislature has taken the view that the Nordic rules are simplified and more expeditious compared to the European rules because in the inter-Nordic enforcement system there is no *exequatur*.[23] The Finnish legislature, conversely, has been silent, which in the view of the present author is an unhappy solution because the proceedings concerning recognition and enforcement are very near to each other in the instruments in question. Even though there is formally no *exequatur* in the inter-Nordic system, there is an additional step in the proceedings that closely resembles *exequatur*.

The relevance of this exception is rather limited. It is available only in cases which are within the scope of the NIC. In all other cases where recognition of a Swedish court order is requested in Finland (or vice versa), the Succession Regulation is applicable. Therefore, the exception is rather a complication than a useful tool. The complexity is increased by the fact that the notion 'court order' is narrower in the NIC than in the Succession Regulation. Under the Regulation, the decisions of an estate distributor can be recognized because an

[23] See proposal of the Swedish government prop. 2013/15: 105, pp. 51–52. See also *Internationella rättsförhållanden rörande arv*. SOU 2014:23, Regeringskansliet, Stockholm 2014, p. 241.

estate distributor that fulfils the requirements in Article 3(2) SR is considered to be a court. The NIC, by contrast, does not support a similar enlargement of the concept of 'court', and decisions of an estate distributor are not recognized and enforced under it.

4. CONCLUDING REMARKS

Giving space to international conventions is one of the ways in which the EU can take note of the fact that there is life outside the borders of the Union. Other ways include avoiding overly broad grounds of jurisdiction in the Union Regulations and accepting that proceedings pending in a third State may have *lis pendens* effect within the EU.

In the view of the present author, the EU has not succeeded very well in efforts to be fair to third States in international family and succession law. Grounds of jurisdiction in EU Regulations are quite broad. Therefore, a third State may also have jurisdiction on a justified ground, which increases the risks of forum shopping and parallel proceedings. *Lis pendens* rules taking into account proceedings in a third State exist in the Brussels Ia Regulation but not in the Regulations relating to family and inheritance law. It is unclear whether a Member State may on the basis of its own legislation give *lis pendens* effect to such proceedings.[24] If not, the European rules may destroy proceedings that are pending in a third State on fully acceptable grounds.

From the point of view of continuation of the Nordic cooperation in inter-Nordic situations relating to family and inheritance law, the exceptions that were admitted in the Brussels II Regulation and the Maintenance Regulation were satisfactory, but in the Succession Regulation only a quite narrow exception was granted. That compelled the Nordic States to safeguard the coherence of inter-Nordic rules on private international succession law in a rather unorthodox way. The result that was achieved under a very tight time limit is not ideal in all respects.

From the point of view of the EU, the restrictive policy towards exceptions is understandable. If the objective of legislative work is harmonization of jurisdiction and conflict-of-laws rules in order to facilitate mutual recognition, it is hard to allow exceptions that may later be used as precedents when seeking new exceptions. On the other hand, shouldn't the search for unity be balanced with other interests? Is it really the case that the principle of mutual recognition does not tolerate any differences as to jurisdiction and the applicable law? According to Article 67(1) TFEU, the EU is to respect the different traditions

24 See on this A. Calvo Caravaga, A. Davi and H.-P. Mansel (eds.), *The EU Succession Regulation. A Commentary*, Cambridge University Press, Cambridge 2016, pp. 265–67.

of Member States when constructing the area of freedom, security and justice. Could the feeling of togetherness in the North, which for decades has found expression in private international law instruments, be regarded as a tradition worthy of respect?

States in different corners of the EU may have specific needs to maintain or conclude agreements with those third States with which they have close ties. In order to meet those needs, the EU has in certain areas adopted Regulations authorizing Member States to enter into agreements with third States under certain preconditions.[25] Such provisions would be welcome also in the areas of succession and matrimonial property law. As is true in the case of the Succession Regulation, the new Regulation (EC) 2016/1103 on matrimonial property, with its very narrow 'Nordic exception', is also difficult for the Nordic States and creates problems which resemble those described above.

---

25 See Regulation (EC) No. 662/2009 of the European Parliament and of the Council of 13.07.2009 establishing a procedure for the negotiation and conclusion of agreements between Member States and third countries on particular matters concerning the law applicable to contractual and non-contractual obligations [2009] OJ L200/25 and Council Regulation (EC) No. 664/2009 of 07.07.2009 establishing a procedure for the negotiation and conclusion of agreements between Member States and third countries concerning jurisdiction, recognition and enforcement of judgments and decisions in matrimonial matters, matters of parental responsibility and matters relating to maintenance obligations, and the law applicable to matters relating to maintenance obligations [2009] OJ L200/46.

THE EXTERNAL RELATIONS OF FRANCE

Samuel Fulli-Lemaire

1. INTRODUCTION

Identifying the treaties between France and third States which, under Article 75(1) of the European Succession Regulation, prevail over the Regulation is a task significantly more challenging than it might seem. Only one example stands out, the Hague Convention of 5 October 1961 on the Conflicts of Laws Relating to the Form of Testamentary Dispositions, but the case of this particular instrument is envisioned in the second part of Article 75(1). It can accordingly be excluded from this survey.

France is a party to the 1973 Washington Convention providing a Uniform Law on the Form of an International Will, but, as the name suggests, this convention does not contain choice-of-law rules, but rather a third model for testaments which has taken its place in substantive French law beside the holograph and notarial wills. It need not be addressed, nor do the various consular treaties which contain neither choice-of-law rules nor rules on jurisdiction.[1] Similarly, the innumerable bilateral treaties on judicial cooperation[2] which frequently cover recognition and enforcement of foreign judgments cannot interfere with the Regulation and will thus not be discussed.[3]

1 P. Lagarde, 'Successions' [2017] *Répertoire Dalloz de droit international*, No. 11.

2 Examples include the 28.06.1972 and 27.08.1964 conventions concluded with Tunisia and Algeria respectively. For an overview, see B. Audit and L. d'Avout, *Droit international privé*, 7th ed., Economica, Paris 2017, 556–557.

3 See, however, S. Francq and J. Mary's chapter on Belgium in the present volume, which sets out and analyzes several sophisticated situations where such interference could exist. These situations could be transposed to the French context.

Beyond these examples, the search for treaties that could be relevant is a process that almost irresistibly evokes a fumble in the dark. Nothing is mentioned, as far as France is concerned, in the Regulation commentaries as regards Article 75,[4] not even in those that are written in French.[5] The books[6] or articles[7] written with practitioners in mind are equally silent. This should perhaps not come as a surprise since, in the field of private international family law, the treaties France is party to do not cover succession matters.[8]

Only one author has recently – albeit in a context unrelated to the European Succession Regulation – flagged international instruments that could perhaps be relevant.[9] But whether they actually are relevant is far from clear. The main difficulty, which is addressed in the next section (section 2), stems from the fact that these treaties do not refer specifically to succession matters, but to what is known in French private international law as *statut personnel*, a pivotal concept which in the present context gives rise to considerable uncertainty. The section thereafter will then focus on the only convention that explicitly provides for an interpretation of *statut personnel* that includes matters of succession, the 1957 judicial convention between France and Tunisia (**Treaty 16**), a text which brings its own challenges (section 3). The various *conventions d'établissement* which were concluded between France and its former colonies in Africa in the early

4 H. P. Pamboukis (ed.), *EU Succession Regulation No. 650/2012 – A Commentary*, Nomiki Bibliothiki/C.H. Beck/Hart/Nomos, Athens/Munich/Oxford/Baden-Baden 2017; A.-L. Calvo Caravaca, A. Davì and H.-P. Mansel (eds.), *The EU Succession Regulation – A Commentary*, Cambridge University Press, Cambridge 2016; U. Bergquist et al., *EU Regulation on Succession and Wills – Commentary*, Otto Schmidt, Cologne 2015; G. Biagioni, 'L'ambito di applicazione del regolamento sulle successioni' in P. Franzina and A. Leandro (eds.), *Il diritto internazionale private europeo delle successioni mortis causa*, Giuffrè, Milan 2013.

5 See e.g. A. Bonomi and P. Wautelet (eds.), *Le droit européen des successions*, Bruylant, Brussels 2013; C. Nourrissat, 'Le champ d'application du règlement' in G. Khairallah and M. Revillard (eds.), *Droit européen des successions internationales*, Defrénois, Issy-les-Moulineaux 2013, esp. Nos. 67–71; P. Lagarde, 'Les principes de base du nouveau règlement européen sur les successions' [2012] *RCDIP* 691; M. Revillard, 'Successions internationales : le règlement du Parlement européen et du Conseil du 4 juillet 2012 en matière de successions' [2012] *Defrénois* 743.

6 H. Péroz and É. Fongaro, *Droit international privé patrimonial de la famille*, 2nd ed., LexisNexis, Paris 2017; S. Benquet, *Le notaire et la succession du conjoint ou du partenaire en droit international*, Bruylant, Brussels 2017; A. Marmisse-d'Abbadie d'Arrast, *Droit international privé et droit notarial*, Ellipses, Paris 2017.

7 R. de Gourcy, 'Une convention (ou un règlement) peut en cacher un autre … Des conventions bilatérales en droit international privé' [2016] 11 *Les Cahiers du CRIDON* 34. Most tellingly, a special issue of the *AJ Famille* journal (2014, pp. 340 et seq.) dedicated to bilateral conventions in the field of private international family law, is silent on the topic of successions.

8 See e.g. the 10.08.1981 French-Moroccan convention and the 18.05.1971 French-Yugoslav convention, which is still in force with regard to Serbia, Montenegro, Kosovo, and Bosnia-Herzegovina. On this point, see R. de Gourcy, above n. 7, 38.

9 M. Revillard, *Droit international privé et européen : pratique notariale*, 8th ed., Defrénois, Issy-les-Moulineaux 2014, 856–860.

1960s will then be analyzed (section 4). Other treaties will also be alluded to briefly (section 5) before some closing remarks are provided (section 6).

2. THE AMBIGUOUS REFERENCE TO *STATUT PERSONNEL* IN INTERNATIONAL TREATIES

The traditional position of French private international law is quite clear: *statut personnel*, a category which could tentatively be translated as 'personal and family status', does not include matters related to succession.[10] The reason is that *statut personnel* is governed by the *loi personnelle*, that is to say the law of nationality, which in the French tradition does not apply to succession. Succession involving immovables has long been subject to the *lex rei sitae*, while as far as movables are concerned, the applicable law is the law of the deceased's last domicile.[11]

This of course raises an issue whenever France enters into a treaty with a State that defines *statut personnel* more expansively, unless of course the wording of the treaty defines exactly the topics it is intended to regulate. Unfortunately, it appears that an overwhelming majority of treaties do not include such a definition. Several examples, which include treaties concluded with Islamic countries and various French former colonies, will be discussed below.

This difficulty is not by any stretch a new problem: Jean-Paulin Niboyet's treatise on private international law from 1948[12] had already raised precisely this point with regard to various treaties concluded in the 1920s.[13] The intervening decades have, however, seen little in the way of clarification, as an overview of how this terminological ambiguity plays out with regard to the issue at hand will show. For this purpose, the 1957 judicial convention between France and Tunisia (**Treaty 16**) must be addressed separately.

3. THE 1957 JUDICIAL CONVENTION BETWEEN FRANCE AND TUNISIA

This convention (**Treaty 16**) is unusual because its main aim was to regulate a transition period after Tunisian independence and safeguard French interests in

10 See H. Batiffol and P. Lagarde, *Droit international privé*, vol. II, 7th ed., LGDJ, Paris 1983, No. 392; I. Fadlallah, 'Statut personnel' [2003] *Répertoire Dalloz de droit international.*

11 See Cass. civ., 19 juin 1939, *Labedan*, Dalloz périodique, 1939, 1, 97. On this case, see also B. Ancel and Y. Lequette, *Les grands arrêts de la jurisprudence civile de droit international privé*, 5th ed., Dalloz, Paris 2006, No. 18.

12 J.-P. Niboyet, *Traité de droit international privé français*, t. V, Sirey, Paris 1948, Nos. 1481 et seq.

13 One of these treaties will subsequently be alluded to, see below n. 29.

the newly independent Tunisia – this explains why its single provision dealing with private international family law applies only to French citizens, a feature which might otherwise appear baffling in a bilateral instrument. Yet in so doing, the treaty also sought to lay the groundwork for future judicial cooperation between the two countries. This may explain why, even though many provisions were only meant to apply during a five-year period of time, the treaty itself was not drafted in a way that made it clear that, as a whole, it would remain in force only for that specific period of time.

The provision at the heart of the debate is Article 2, according to which 'in matters of personal [and family] status, as defined by the 12 July 1956 decree of the [ruling] Bey, persons of French nationality are governed by French law'.[14] The 12 July 1956 decree of the Bey, in turn, lists succession matters among those included in the 'personal and family status' category.[15] In other words, the convention provides that the successions of French citizens are to be governed by French law. This suggests that the 1957 judicial convention between France and Tunisia should be regarded as a bilateral treaty that prevails over the European Succession Regulation pursuant to Article 75(1).

This first assessment must, however, be qualified because of the peculiarities of this convention. Indeed, its current relevance is widely questioned on both sides of the Mediterranean. In Tunisia, an influential view seems to be that the convention was meant to apply only during the five-year transition period over the course of which Tunisian courts would progressively take over from French courts. After that period ended, the convention should have been discontinued and, in effect, it was replaced in Tunisian law by a subsequent reform.[16] In France, the convention is sometimes ignored under the pretext of its having been replaced by the 1972 convention concluded between France and Tunisia.[17]

Neither of these views appears wholly convincing, inasmuch as the 1957 convention is formally still in force and should accordingly apply.[18] In practice however, it does not seem to be applied, at least as far as successions are concerned.

---

14 Author's translation.

15 See Art. 2 of the Decree of 12.07.1956 on the *statut personnel* of non-Muslim and non-Jewish Tunisians, Journal Officiel Tunisien, 13.07.1956, p. 987. On this provision, see P. Lagarde, 'Successions' [1969] *Répertoire Dalloz de droit international*, No. 207.

16 S. Ben Achour, 'La loi française du 17 mai 2013 ouvrant le mariage pour tous et les relations franco-maghrébines' in S. Ben Achour and L. Chedly (eds.), *Actualités du droit international privé de la famille en Tunisie et à l'étranger*, Latrach Éditions, Tunis 2015, 150–151.

17 M. Revillard, above n. 9, No. 857. Regarding the 1972 convention, see above n. 2.

18 Furthermore, it has recently been mentioned in connection with the implications held for private international law by the 2013 reform entitling same-sex couples to marry, see e.g. D. Bureau, 'Le marriage international pour tous à l'aune de la diversité' in *Mélanges en l'honneur du Professeur Bernard Audit*, Lextenson Éditions/LGDJ, Issy-les-Moulineaux 2014, off-print, Nos. 16–19.

4. THE *CONVENTIONS D'ÉTABLISSEMENT* CONCLUDED BETWEEN FRANCE AND ITS FORMER COLONIES IN AFRICA

The phrase *conventions d'établissement* can be translated as 'conventions on residence and trade' or 'conventions on establishment'. The treaties themselves revolve around such issues as access to the labour market, access to courts and establishment of legal persons, and they do not deal with family or succession matters in a systematic way. However, they often include an isolated provision according to which *statut personnel*, which is not otherwise defined, should be governed by the law of nationality.

Many such conventions were concluded between France and its former African colonies in 1960, that is to say, immediately after the latter became independent.[19] The conventions contain an identical Article 7,[20] the §2 of which provides that 'the personal status of French citizens on the territory of the [other Party] is governed by French law and the personal status of [citizens of the other Party] on the territory of the French Republic is governed by [the law of that State]'.[21] These conventions are of particular interest because there is a specific reason why, in this context, *statut personnel* should be interpreted more broadly than it normally is in French private international law.

The reason harkens back to the colonial era. Before these countries gained independence, the French approach to colonization gave rise to so-called 'inter-personal conflicts': 'there were conflicts between the laws of the mainland and those of the colonies, as well as among those of different colonies. Article 75 of the current French Constitution, which claims to be directly inherited from this period, constitutionalizes the various personal statuses'.[22]

The traditional solution to these inter-personal conflicts was to include succession matters in *statut personnel*, and that is indeed the interpretation that most if not all of these countries have subsequently adopted in their own private international law rules.[23] Because the same extensive understanding of

---

19 A lesser-known provision of the 1962 Évian agreements which ended the Algerian war (*Déclaration des guaranties, 3ème partie*) provides that the succession of French citizens established in Algeria is to be governed by French law, see P. LAGARDE, above n. 15, No. 208. Like Art. 2 of the 1957 judicial convention between France and Tunisia (see above), that provision is unilateral.

20 J. FOYER, 'Problèmes de droit international privé dans les relations entre la France et les nouvaux États africains d'expression française' [1962] *Travaux du comité français de droit international privé* 139, esp. 161–162.

21 Author's translation.

22 V. PARISOT, 'Internal Conflicts of Laws', [2013/2014] 15 *Yearbook of Private International Law* 541, 545.

23 F. BOULANGER, 'Essai comparative sur la notion de statut personnel dans les relations internationals des pays d'Afrique noire' [1982] *RCDIP* 647, at No. 9.

the notion of *statut personnel* had been applied by French colonial courts under French rule, some authors have suggested that it should be maintained when interpreting the bilateral conventions on establishment.[24]

This seemingly promising discussion, however, appears to be largely outdated. Many of the treaties have been replaced over time and the new versions do not refer to *statut personnel*,[25] others have simply been repealed,[26] and the status of several more remains unclear.[27] In any event, there do not seem to be any cases where any of the conventions on establishment were ever applied to succession matters.

5. OTHER POSSIBLY RELEVANT CONVENTIONS

Provisions according to which personal and family status are governed by the law of nationality can be found in other conventions on establishment, in particular the 24 June 1964 treaty between France and Iran on navigation and establishment.[28] Whether this treaty, like others which may contain similar provisions, applies to succession matters depends again on the question of whether a broad or narrow interpretation of *statut personnel* should be favoured. Absent a post-colonial context, however, the rationale for favouring the extensive interpretation appears markedly weaker.

It should be noted that Jean-Paulin Niboyet himself discussed the issue with regards to a previous treaty between France and Iran, a temporary agreement dated 11 May 1928 which also contained the same rule. In his treatise on private international law, Niboyet berated the drafters for forgetting to specify how *statut personnel* should be understood within the meaning of the 1928 convention, and he suggested a solution which in his view would safeguard

---

24 P. Lagarde, above n. 15, No. 210. J. Foyer, above n. 20, esp. 163, also favours this outcome, but out of pragmatism and not principle: it would spare French courts from having to apply the laws of these States – which at that time were extremely unclear – to the successions of French citizens who died domiciled abroad or with immovable property abroad.

25 See in particular the France-Togo convention of 10.07.1963, which was replaced by the convention of 13.06.1996, and the France-Gabon convention 17.08.1960, which was replaced by the convention of 11.03.2002.

26 For instance, the France-Madagascar convention of 27.06.1960, which was repealed on 18.03.1975.

27 Notably, the France-Chad convention of 11.08.1960, the France-Congo convention of 15.08.1960, and the France-Central African Republic convention of 13.08.1960.

28 Art. 2, §2: 'The applicable law is designated by choice-of-law rules. In any case, the personal [and family] status of French citizens on the territory of the Iranian Empire is governed by French law and the personal [and family] status of Iranians on the territory of the French Republic is governed by Iranian law'.

the status quo: applying the narrow interpretation to Iranian citizens in France and the broad interpretation to French citizens in Iran.[29] Here again, there is no case law.

6. CLOSING REMARKS

The search for treaties concluded between France and third States which, under Article 75(1) of the European Succession Regulation, prevail over the Regulation has turned out to be a fascinating if brief foray into the recent history of private international law and the issues raised by the interpretation of international conventions. At the end of the day, however, this probe has yielded only meagre pickings since it is impossible to argue conclusively that – apart from the Hague Convention of 1961 naturally – any single treaty takes precedence over the Regulation. It has furthermore proved impossible to find case law applying any of the possibly relevant treaties, either before or after the entry into force of the Regulation.

The clearest sign of the fruitlessness of the endeavour, perhaps, is that Paul Lagarde's *Répertoire Dalloz de droit international* entry on succession, which in its earlier incarnations[30] was arguably the source of this discussion or at least the reason why it has not vanished completely over the decades, no longer refers to any treaty of interest for the purpose of the present study.[31]

---

29 J.-P. Niboyet, above n. 12, No. 1482.
30 Particularly the 1969 version, see P. Lagarde, above n. 15.
31 P. Lagarde, above n. 1, No. 10.

THE EXTERNAL RELATIONS OF GERMANY

Dirk Looschelders

1. INTRODUCTION

With effect from 17 August 2015,[1] the European Succession Regulation has led to a unification of the international law of succession in the Member States of the EU – with the exception of Denmark, Ireland and the United Kingdom.[2] However, there is no full harmonization since, according to Article 75(1) SR, the Regulation does not affect the application of international agreements to which one or more Member States were parties at the time of the adoption of the Regulation and which relate to the subjects covered by the Regulation. Bilateral treaties concluded between individual Member States and third States take precedence over the Regulation, too.[3] Treaties of this kind exist in many Member States. As these agreements are often based on traditional legal principles, such as the principle of nationality, the *lex rei sitae* rule for succession to immovable property and the exclusion of party autonomy, their application can lead to significant tensions with the European Succession Regulation.[4]

---

1 See Article 83(1) and Article 84 SR.

2 See Recitals 82 and 83 SR.

3 A. Dutta, 'Zur international-privatrechtlichen Qualifikation des §1371 Abs. 1 BGB', [2013] *FamRZ*, 452; L. Kunz, 'Der Referentenentwurf für ein Internationales Erbverfahrensgesetz – Überblick und Problemaufriss', [2014] *GPR* 285, 292; P. Mankowski, 'Gelten die bilateralen Staatsverträge der Bundesrepublik Deutschland im Internationalen Erbrecht nach dem Wirksamwerden der EuErbVO weiter?', [2013] *ZEV* 529 et seq.; D. Lehmann, 'Der Referentenentwurf für ein Begleitgesetz zur EuErbVO', [2014] *ZEV* 232, 233.

4 A. Dutta, in: F. J. Säcker, R. Rixecker, H. Oetker, and B. Limperg (eds.), *Münchener Kommentar zum BGB*, Vol. 11, 7th ed., C. H. Beck, München 2018, Article 75 EuErbVO; D. Looschelders, in: B. Dauner-Lieb, T. Heidel and G. Ring (eds.), *NomosKommentar BGB*, Vol. 6, 3rd ed., Nomos-Verlagsgesellschaft, Baden-Baden 2019, Preliminary statement to Article 1 EuErbVO para. 26; P. Mankowski, above n. 3, 529, 530, 534; C. F. Majer, 'Das deutsch-türkische Nachlassabkommen: ein Anachronismus', [2012] *ZEV* 182 et seq.; R. Süß, 'Der Vorbehalt zugunsten bilateraler Abkommen mit Drittstaaten' in: A. Dutta and S. Herrler (eds.), *Die Europäische Erbrechtsverordnung*, C. H. Beck, München 2014, pp. 181 et seq. para. 14; M. Gebauer, 'Das deutsch-türkische Nachlassabkommen im Sog des Europäischen Kollisionsrechts', [2018] *IPRax* 345, 347 et seq.

2. TREATIES AND CONVENTIONS TAKING PRECEDENCE OVER THE EUROPEAN SUCCESSION REGULATION

2.1. OVERVIEW

Germany has entered into three bilateral treaties with third States which concern matters covered by the European Succession Regulation. These are in the order of conclusion:

- the German-Iranian Treaty on Establishment of 17 February 1929 (**Treaty 17**);
- the German-Turkish Consular Treaty of 28 May 1929 with an Agreement on Succession Matters (**Treaty 19**); and
- the German-Soviet Consular Treaty of 25 April 1958 (**Treaty 18**).

A number of other consular treaties binding for Germany concern questions relevant to the law of succession, such as consular rights, most-favoured treatment rules or the mutual recognition and enforcement of decisions. However, since the European Succession Regulation does not cover the aforementioned matters,[5] these agreements cannot conflict with the European Succession Regulation.[6] This also applies to the Treaty between the United States of America and Germany on Friendship, Commerce and Consular Rights of 8 December 1923[7] and the Treaty on Friendship, Commerce and Navigation between the Federal Republic of Germany and the United States of America of 29 October 1954.[8]

2.2. TREATY ON ESTABLISHMENT BETWEEN GERMANY AND THE PERSIAN EMPIRE

2.2.1. Background

The Treaty on Establishment between Germany and the Persian Empire of 17 February 1929[9] (**Treaty 17**), along with the Final Protocol to Article 8(3)

---

5 For example, the European Succession Regulation concerns only the recognition and enforcement of decisions given in other Member States and not the recognition and enforcement of decisions given in third States.

6 A. Dutta, above n. 4, Article 75 EuErbVO para. 33; A. Zanobetti, in: A. Calvo Caravaca, A. Davì and H. Mansel (eds.), *The EU Succession Regulation*, Cambridge University Press, Cambridge 2016, Article 75 para. 3.

7 RGBl. 1925 II, 795; RGBl. 1935 II, 743; BGBl. 1954 II, 722.

8 BGBl. 1956 II, 487.

9 RGBl. 1930 II, 1002.

of the Treaty, entered into force on 11 January 1931.[10] After the Second World War, it was reinstated on 4 November 1954.[11] The purpose of the Treaty is to ensure that the nationals of each Contracting State in the territory of the other Contracting State enjoy the same treatment as that State's nationals with regard to judicial and official protection of their person and goods (Article 8(1)).[12] In particular, the persons concerned are to have free and unrestricted access to the courts of the other Contracting State and be able to appear before these courts on the same terms as nationals (Article 8(2)). On the other hand, in respect of the law of persons, family and succession, the nationals of each State in the territory of the other State will not be subject to the local law but to their national law (Article 8(3)).[13]

2.2.2. Scope of Application

2.2.2.1. Material Scope of Application

The material scope of Article 8(3) of the German-Iranian Treaty on Establishment extends to the entire law of persons, family and succession. These terms are explained in the Final Protocol to Article 8(3) of the Treaty, according to which the term 'law of succession' covers both intestate and the testamentary succession as well as the administration and distribution of the estate. With respect to the purpose of the Treaty, all matters of succession law are to be included.[14] However, there is an exception with regard to the formal validity of dispositions of property upon death.[15] As the Final Protocol limits the scope of Article 8(3) of the Treaty to the personal statute, the form of dispositions of property upon death is not covered.[16] This question is traditionally not a subject of the personal statute of the deceased.[17]

Article 8(3) of the German-Iranian Treaty on Establishment also covers some areas of law connected to succession. This applies in particular to matrimonial

---

10 RGBl. 1931 II, 9.

11 Announcement of 15.08.1955, BGBl. II, 829.

12 BVerfG 04.12.2006, *NJW-RR* 2007, 577; OLG München 01.02.2010, *ZEV* 2010, 255.

13 H. Dörner, in: J. v. Staudinger (ed.), *Kommentar zum Bürgerlichen Gesetzbuch*, revised ed., Sellier-de Gruyter, Berlin 2007, Preliminary statement to Article 25 et seq. EGBGB para. 149.

14 H. Dörner, above n. 13, Preliminary statement to Article 25 et seq. EGBGB para. 155.

15 S. Lorenz, in: H. G. Bamberger, H. Roth, W. Hau and R. Poseck (eds.), *Beck'scher Online Kommentar BGB*, 48th ed., date: 01.05.2018, C. H. Beck, München, Article 25 EGBGB para. 11; G. Hohloch, in: B. Grunewald, G. Maier-Reimer and H. P. Westermann (eds.), *Erman Bürgerliches Gesetzbuch*, 14th ed., Otto Schmidt, Köln 2014, Article 25 EGBGB para. 4a; L. Kroiß, in: B. Dauner-Lieb, T. Heidel and G. Ring (eds.), *NomosKommentar BGB*, Vol. 1, 3rd ed., Nomos-Verlagsgesellschaft, Baden-Baden 2016, Article 25 EGBGB para. 4; H. Dörner, above n. 13, Preliminary statement to Article 25 et seq. EGBGB para. 153.

16 G. Hohloch, above n. 15, Article 25 EGBGB para. 5.

17 H. Dörner, above n. 13, Preliminary statement to Article 25 et seq. EGBGB para. 155.

property rights[18] of the surviving spouse and to all questions concerning family status including the effectiveness of a marriage. However, Article 8(3) of the Treaty is limited to the nationals of each Contracting State 'in the territory of the other State'. Therefore the provision applies only to Iranian married couples in Germany or German married couples in Iran, but not to marriages between two Iranian nationals in Iran or marriages occurring in a third State.[19] According to the prevailing opinion, Article 8(3) of the German-Iranian Treaty is also not applicable to German-Iranian married couples.[20] The connection to nationality, as found in the provision, is in any event insufficient to determine the law applicable to mixed-nation marriages.

2.2.2.2. Territorial Scope of Application

Whether the German-Iranian Treaty on Establishment solely covers property located in the Contracting States or also assets located in other States is disputed. Before the entry into force of the European Succession Regulation, it was a widely shared view that the Treaty did not preclude the application of Article 3a(2) of the EGBGB (old version), pursuant to which the special regulations of the State in which the property is located prevail over the general succession rule.[21] Other authors assumed that Article 8(3) of the German-Iranian Treaty on Establishment applied to the entire estate of the deceased irrespective of its location, thereby Article 3a(2) EGBGB (old version) would be inapplicable.[22]

After the entry into force of the European Succession Regulation, with regard to successions it is no longer possible to refer to the precedence of the special regulations of the State in which the property is located pursuant to Article 3a(2) of the EGBGB (old version). Henceforth, the decisive question is whether the

---

18 D. Looschelders, *Internationales Privatrecht*, Springer Verlag, Berlin 2004, Article 15 EGBGB para. 49.

19 OLG München 01.02.2010, *ZEV* 2010, 255.

20 BVerfG 04.12.2006, *NJW-RR* 2007, 577, 578; BGH 20.12.1972, *BGHZ* 60, 68, 74; BGH 15.01.1986, *FamRZ* 1986, 345, 346 et seq.; BGH 18.10.1989, *NJW* 1990, 636, 637; D. Looschelders, above n. 18, Article 14 EGBGB para. 39; G. Kegel, in: H. Soergel, *Bürgerliches Gesetzbuch*, 12th ed., Kohlhammer, Stuttgart 1996, Preliminary statement to Article 3 EGBGB para. 46; C. v. Bar, *Internationales Privatrecht*, Vol. 2, C.H. Beck, München 1991, para. 210; R. Sieghörtner, 'Folgen der gleichheitswidrigen Erbbeteiligung von Ehemann und Ehefrau nach iranischem Recht' [2016] *MittBayNot* 264, 265.

21 AG Hamburg St. Georg 13.04.2015, *ZEV* 2015, 580; H. Dörner, above n. 13, Preliminary statement to Article 25 et seq. EGBGB para. 152; F. Odersky, in: R. Hausmann and F. Odersky, *Internationales Privatrecht in der Notar- und Gestaltungspraxis*, 3rd ed., C. H. Beck, München 2016, §15 para. 363.

22 S. Lorenz, above n. 15, Article 25 EGBGB para. 11; A. Dutta, in: F. J. Säcker, R. Rixecker, H. Oetker, and B. Limperg (eds.), *Münchener Kommentar zum BGB*, Vol. 11, 6th ed., C. H. Beck, München 2015, Article 25 EGBGB para. 297; F. Bauer, in: A. Dutta and J. Weber, *Internationales Erbrecht*, C. H. Beck, München 2016, Appendix I to Article 75 EuErbVO para. 4.

scope of Article 8(3) of the German-Iranian Treaty on Establishment is limited to assets which are located in one of the Contracting States. For a territorial limitation of the scope of application, one can point to the phrases 'in the territory of the other State' in Article 8(1) and (3) of the Treaty.[23] But, since the phrases in question refer only to the persons concerned – nationals of the Contracting States – and not to their assets, this argument appears rather weak. The more convincing reasoning is that the purpose of the German-Iranian Treaty on Establishment is to improve the legal position of the deceased and his heirs in the other Contracting State.[24] Thus, to extend the territorial scope to property located in a third State would go beyond the protective purpose of Article 8(3) of the German-Iranian Treaty on Establishment.[25] After the entry into force of the European Succession Regulation, the restrictive interpretation of the territorial scope of the German-Iranian Treaty also has the advantage of minimizing possible conflicts with the European Succession Regulation.[26]

2.2.2.3. Personal Scope of Application

The German-Iranian Treaty on Establishment applies only to nationals of the Contracting States.[27] In the case of succession law, only the nationality of the deceased is relevant.[28] According to the prevailing opinion, the Treaty is not applicable to German-Iranian dual nationals.[29] This is based on the consideration

---

23 AG Hamburg St. Georg 13.04.2015, *ZEV* 2015, 580, 581; H. Dörner, above n. 13, Preliminary statement to Article 25 et seq. EGBGB para. 152.

24 R. Süß, above n. 4, pp. 181 et seq. para. 21.

25 See, for the parallel problem of marriages in a third State, OLG München 01.02.2010, *ZEV* 2010, 255.

26 R. Süß, above n. 4, pp. 181 et seq. para. 23.

27 I. Ludwig, in: M. Herberger, M. Martinek, H. Rüßmann, S. Weth and M. Würdinger (eds.), *juris Praxiskommentar BGB*, Vol. 6, 8th ed., Juris GmbH, Saarbrücken 2017, Article 25, 26 EGBGB para. 19.

28 H. Dörner, above n. 13, Preliminary statement to Article 25 et seq. EGBGB para. 156; A. Dutta, above n. 4, Article 75 EGBGB para. 10.

29 BVerfG 04.12.2006, *NJW-RR* 2007, 577, 578; OLG München 01.02.2010, *ZEV* 2010, 255; G. Hohloch, above n. 15, Article 25 EGBGB para. 4a; S. Lorenz, above n. 15, Article 25 EGBGB para. 11; G. Kegel, above n. 20, Preliminary statement to Article 3 EGBGB para. 46; L. Kroiß, above n. 15, Article 25 EGBGB para. 4; A. Köhler, in: L. Kroiß, C. Horn and D. Solomon (eds.), *NomosKommentar Nachfolgerecht*, Nomos-Verlagsgesellschaft, Baden-Baden 2015, Preliminary statement to Articles 20–38 EuErbVO para. 45; D. Martiny, in: H. Prütting, G. Wegen and G. Weinreich (eds.), *BGB Kommentar*, 12th ed., Luchterhand Verlag, Köln 2017, Private International Law Appendix 9 Article 75 EuErbVO para. 4; R. Süß, above n. 4, pp. 181 et seq. para. 4; F. Bauer, above n. 22, Appendix I to Article 75 EuErbVO para. 2; W. Wurmnest, 'Der Anwendungsbereich des deutsch-iranischen Niederlassungsabkommens bei erbrechtlichen Streitigkeiten und deutscher ordre public', [2016] *IPRax* 447, 449; see also, via recourse to Article 5(1)(2) EGBGB H. Dörner, above n. 13, Preliminary statement to Article 25 et seq. EGBGB para. 157.

that the Treaty obliges the Contracting States to grant nationals of the other State the same rights and obligations as their own nationals. German-Iranian dual nationals, however, have the same rights and obligations as any other national in both States anyway. Therefore, the protective purpose of the Treaty does not apply to German-Iranian dual nationals.[30] The opposing view refers to the law of the State with which the deceased had the closest connection (so-called effective nationality) in accordance with Article 5(1)(1) EGBGB.[31] The purpose of Article 8(3) of the German-Iranian Treaty to ensure that the nationals of a Contracting State in the territory of the other State remain subject to their national law in regards to the personal statute is an argument in favour of this view. Indeed, this purpose applies also to German-Iranian dual nationals who are located in Germany but who have a closer connection to Iran.

On the other hand, the choice-of-law rule contained in Article 8(3) of the German-Iranian Treaty on Establishment has to be viewed within the context of the Treaty. The primary objective of the Treaty is to provide national treatment to nationals of the other Contracting State. The conflict-of-laws objective of making the persons affected subject to their own law is subordinate.[32] Therefore, the systematic link between Article 8(3) and Article 8(1) and (2) of the German-Iranian Treaty on Establishment supports the prevailing opinion.

However, in accordance with Article 5(1)(1) of the EGBGB, the prevailing opinion refers to the law of the State with which the deceased had the closest connection if he or she died in Germany as a national of both a third State and Iran.[33] In this case, Article 8(3) of the German-Iranian Treaty is (only) applicable if the deceased had his or her closest connection to Iran. The German-Iranian Treaty on Establishment is not applicable to Iranian nationals who have refugee status under the Geneva Refugee Convention or who are entitled to asylum under Sections 2 or 3 of the German Asylum Act.[34] Thus, the European Succession Regulation is not supplanted in that respect.

---

30 BVerfG 04.12.2006, *NJW-RR* 2007, 577, 578; OLG München 01.02.2010, *ZEV* 2010, 255; L. Kroiß, above n. 15, Article 25 EGBGB para. 4.

31 A. Dutta, above n. 22, Article 25 EGBGB para. 296; but see A. Dutta, above n. 4, Article 75 EuErbVO para. 10.

32 W. Wurmnest, above n. 29, 447, 449.

33 AG Hamburg St. Georg 13.04.2015, *ZEV* 2015, 580 et seq.; A. Dutta, above n. 4, Article 75 EuErbVO para. 10; S. Lorenz, above n. 15, Article 25 EGBGB para. 11; H. Dörner, above n. 13, Preliminary statement to Article 25 et seq. EGBGB para. 157; A. Köhler, above n. 29, Preliminary statement to Articles 20–38 EuErbVO para. 45 et seq.; I. Ludwig, above n. 27, Article 25, 26 EGBGB para. 20; W. Wurmnest, above n. 29, 447, 449; contra F. Bauer, above n. 22, Appendix I to Article 75 EuErbVO para. 3.

34 H. Dörner, above n. 13, Preliminary statement to Article 25 et seq. EGBGB para. 157; G. Hohloch, above n. 15, Article 25 EGBGB para. 4a; S. Lorenz, above n. 15, Article 25 EGBGB para. 11; A. Köhler, above n. 29, Preliminary statement to Articles 20–38 EuErbVO para. 45; I. Ludwig, above n. 27, Article 25, 26 EGBGB para. 21; F. Bauer, above n. 22, Appendix I to Article 75 EuErbVO para. 3.

2.3. CONSULAR TREATY BETWEEN GERMANY AND TURKEY

2.3.1. Background

The German-Turkish Consular Treaty of 28 May 1929[35] (**Treaty 19**) entered into force on 18 November 1931[36] and was reinstated after the Second World War with effect from 1 March 1952.[37] The Treaty mainly provides rules on consular rights in the event of the death of a national of the State represented by the consul.[38] Concerning the estates of deceased nationals of one of the Contracting States in the territory of the other Contracting State, Article 20 of the Consular Treaty grants the consul the rights set out in the Annex to the Treaty. The Annex contains an Agreement on Succession Matters with rules on private international law, jurisdiction and the recognition of decisions.

The purpose of the Treaty is to protect the estate of the nationals of one of the Contracting States and the rights of their heirs if the deceased died in the territory of the other Contracting State. This is based on the notion that the estate of one's own nationals and the rights of their heirs would, otherwise, not be adequately protected in the other Contracting State.[39] In the academic literature it is reasonably emphasized that the German-Turkish Consular Treaty and the Agreement on Succession Matters date back to a time when only a few people had their residence in the other Contracting State; moreover, their residence in the other State was in most cases only temporary.[40] This background has to be taken into account when interpreting the Agreement.

2.3.2. Scope of Application

2.3.2.1. Material Scope of Application

The conflict-of-laws rules of the German-Turkish Agreement on Succession Matters are applicable to the succession as a whole.[41] Section 16 of the Agreement provides a special regulation with respect to the formal validity of dispositions of property upon death, but it is widely superseded by the 1961 Hague Convention on the Form of Wills.[42]

---

35 RGBl. 1930 II, 747.

36 RGBl. 1931 II, 539.

37 BGBl. 1952 II, 608.

38 C. F. Majer, above n. 4, 182, 185 et seq.

39 H. Krüger, 'Zur staatlichen Verantwortlichkeit für das Leben – Ein Beitrag zum deutsch-türkischen Rechtsdialog' in: S. Arkan and A. Yongalik (eds.), *Festschrift – Liber Amicorum Tugrul Ansay*, Kluwer Law International, Alphen aan den Rijn 2006, pp. 139, 151; M. Gebauer, above n. 4, 345, 346; C. F. Majer, above n. 4, 182, 183.

40 H. Krüger, above n. 39, 139, 150; C. F. Majer, above n. 4, 182, 185.

41 H. Dörner, above n. 13, Preliminary statement to Article 25 et seq. EGBGB para. 172.

42 For details see section 3.1.2.

The regulation in Section 15 of the Agreement regarding jurisdiction has a quite limited scope of application. It applies only to actions concerning a declaratory judgment on the entitlement to an estate, claims to an inheritance, claims arising from a legacy and claims to a reserved share.[43]

2.3.2.2. Territorial Scope of Application

Regarding the territorial scope, the conflict-of-laws rules of the Agreement on Succession Matters are to be applied, pursuant to Article 20 of the German-Turkish Consular Treaty, if the estate of a deceased national of one Contracting State is located in the other Contracting State.[44] The application of the Agreement on Succession Matters principally requires that the deceased died in the Contracting State in whose territory the movable or immovable property of which the estate in question consists is located.[45] However, according to Section 18, the regulations of Sections 1–17 apply *mutatis mutandis* if the deceased died in another State. Whether the deceased had his habitual residence in one of the Contracting States or in a third State is also irrelevant.[46]

According to the prevailing opinion, the German-Turkish Agreement on Succession Matters is not applicable to property located in the home State of the deceased or in a third State.[47] The opposing view holds that the restriction to estates in the other Contracting State as prescribed in Article 20 of the Consular Treaty concerns only consular rights.[48] The systematic link between the regulations of the Agreement, however, supports the prevailing opinion. In addition, the German-Turkish Agreement on Succession Matters as well as the German-Iranian Treaty on Establishment merely aims to resolve conflicts between the legal systems of the Contracting States.[49] To apply the conflict-of-laws rules to property located in third States would go beyond the protective purpose

---

43 For details see section 4.1.

44 'Deutsch-türkisches Nachlassabkommen – Gesetzliche Erbfolge nach einem türkischen Staatsangehörigen', [2016] *DNotI-Report*, 103, 104.

45 F. Bauer, above n. 22, Appendix II to Article 75 EuErbVO para. 4.

46 S. Lorenz, above n. 15, Article 25 EGBGB para. 6; F. Odersky, above n. 21, §15 para. 352.

47 H. Dörner, above n. 13, Preliminary statement to Article 25 et seq. EGBGB para. 163; S. Lorenz, above n. 15, Article 25 EGBGB para. 6; A. Köhler, above n. 29, Preliminary statement to Articles 20–38 EuErbVO para. 52; I. Ludwig, above n. 27, Articles 25, 26 EGBGB para. 42; F. Odersky, above n. 21, §15 para. 355; H. Dörner, 'Das deutsch-türkische Nachlaßabkommen' [1996] *ZEV* 90, 96; R. Süß, above n. 4, 181 et seq. para. 19; C. Rumpf, in: M. Ferid, K. Firsching, H. Dörner and R. Hausmann, *Internationales Erbrecht, Türkei* (date: 01.05.2013), C. H. Beck, München 2013, Grdz. C para. 97; C. F. Majer, above n. 4, 182, 184; with regard to the immovable part of the estate F. Bauer, above n. 22, Appendix II to Article 75 EuErbVO para. 4.

48 A. Dutta, above n. 4, Article 75 EuErbVO para. 20; J. Fetsch, 'Auslandsvermögen im Internationalen Erbrecht' [2006] *RNotZ* 77, 114; P. Mankowski, above n. 3, 529, 530; W. Wurmnest, above n. 29, 447, 450; cf. M. Gebauer, above n. 4, 345, 346 et seq.

49 C. F. Majer, above n. 4, 182, 184.

of the Agreement. Therefore, the European Succession Regulation is applicable to an estate located in the home State of the deceased or in a third State.

2.3.2.3. Personal Scope of Application

The personal scope of application of the German-Turkish Agreement on Succession Matters is limited to nationals of the Contracting States.[50] The legal position of dual nationals is not regulated in the Agreement.[51] In order to assess their position, it is necessary to distinguish whether the deceased had the nationality of both Contracting States or the nationality of a third State in addition to the nationality of the other Contracting State.

If the deceased had the nationality of both Contracting States at the time of death, the prevailing opinion in literature assumes that the German-Turkish Consular Treaty, consistent with its purpose, is not applicable.[52] In this case, the deceased and the heirs would not need special protection by the Consular Treaty. An opposing view applies the law of the State with which the deceased had the closest connection.[53] According to another differentiating view, at least the *lex rei sitae* rule provided for in Section 14(2) of the Agreement on Succession Matters is applicable to German-Turkish dual nationals.[54]

The systematic link with the regulations on consular rights militates against the application of the Agreement on Succession Matters to German-Turkish dual nationals. Dual nationals indeed do not require special protection. Even though Section 14(2) of the Agreement on Succession Matters does not explicitly take nationality into account, its application requires that the deceased falls within the personal scope of the German-Turkish Consular Treaty.[55] By not applying the Consular Treaty to dual nationals, the principle of mutual recognition of judicial decisions and certificates relating to succession pursuant to Sections 15 and 17 of the Agreement is admittedly restrained. On the other hand, a narrow interpretation ensures that conflicts with the European Succession Regulation are limited to the unavoidable minimum.[56] If the German-Turkish Consular

[50] A. Dutta, above n. 4, Article 75 EuErbVO para. 19; F. Bauer, above n. 22, Appendix II to Article 75 EuErbVO para. 3; J. Fetsch, above n. 48, 77, 114.

[51] Z. Kaya, 'Der Nachlass eines deutsch-türkischen Doppelstaaters' [2015] *ZEV* 208, 209.

[52] A. Dutta, above n. 4, Article 75 EuErbVO para. 19; K. Schurig, in: *Soergel, BGB*, 12th ed., Kohlhammer, Stuttgart 1996, Article 25 EGBGB para. 108; F. Bauer, above n. 22, Appendix II to Article 75 EuErbVO para. 7; F. Bauer, 'Internationale Zuständigkeit türkischer Gerichte' [2007] *FamRZ* 1252, 1255; C. F. Majer, above n. 4, 182, 183; H. Krüger, above n. 39, 131, 151.

[53] J. Fetsch, above n. 48, 77, 115.

[54] H. Dörner, above n. 13, Preliminary statement to Article 25 EGBGB et seq. para. 174; A. Köhler, above n. 29, Preliminary statement to Articles 20–38 EuErbVO para. 52.

[55] C. F. Majer, above n. 4, 182, 184.

[56] Cf. M. Gebauer, above n. 4, 345, 349 et seq.

Treaty does not apply, the applicable law is to be determined by the European Succession Regulation.

Dual nationals who in addition to Turkish nationality have the nationality of a third State are subject to the German-Turkish Consular Treaty in accordance with Article 5(1)(1) EGBGB as long as they were most closely connected to Turkey.[57] Again, the Treaty is not applicable to Turkish nationals who have refugee status under the Geneva Refugee Convention or who are entitled to asylum under German law.[58]

2.4. CONSULAR TREATY BETWEEN GERMANY AND THE SOVIET UNION

2.4.1. Background

The Consular Treaty between Germany and the Soviet Union of 25 April 1958[59] (**Treaty 18**) entered into force on 24 May 1959.[60] The Treaty contains rules on consular rights and on measures preserving a deceased's estate as well as a conflict-of-laws rule regarding the succession to the immovable part of an estate (Article 28(3)). This conflict rule also applies to cases which do not relate to the administration of the estate by a consul.[61] The German-Soviet Consular Treaty of 1958 does not contain a conflict-of-laws rule regarding the succession to the movable part of the deceased's estate. In contrast, the former German-Russian Consular Treaty of 6 January 1926[62] included a separate Agreement on Succession Matters, which contained conflict-of-laws rules regarding succession to the movable as well as the immovable part of an estate.[63]

After the dissolution of the Soviet Union, the German-Soviet Consular Treaty of 1958 remained in force due to corresponding agreements with Russia and most of the other successor States of the Soviet Union.[64] Estonia, Latvia and Lithuania are not to be considered as successor States of the

---

57 AG Bad Homburg 13.7.1977, *IPRspr.* 1977 No. 103, p. 292, 294; H. Dörner, above n. 13, Preliminary statement to Article 25 et seq. EGBGB para. 173; A. Dutta, above n. 4, Article 75 EuErbVO para. 19; contra F. Bauer, above n. 22, Appendix II to Article 75 EuErbVO para. 3.

58 F. Bauer, above n. 22, Appendix II to Article 75 EuErbVO para. 3.

59 BGBl. 1959 II, 233.

60 BGBl. 1959 II, 469.

61 H. Dörner, above n. 13, Preliminary statement to Article 25 et seq. EGBGB para. 196; A. Dutta, above n. 4, Article 75 EuErbVO para. 31; K. Schurig, above n. 52, Article 25 EGBGB para. 106.

62 RGBl. 1926 II, 1.

63 H. Dörner, above n. 13, Preliminary statement to Article 25 et seq. EGBGB para 193.

64 A. Dutta, above n. 4, Article 75 EuErbVO para. 28; H. Dörner, above n. 13, Preliminary statement to Article 25 et seq. EGBGB para. 194; D. Lehmann, above n. 3, 232, 234.

Soviet Union since these States had been occupied by the Soviet Union contrary to international law since 1940.[65] The Kyrgyz Republic proclaimed by a notice dated 19 December 2014 that it would no longer apply the German-Soviet Consular Treaty.[66] In relation to Turkmenistan, the legal situation remains unclear, as there has not been any agreement or announcement on the maintenance of the German-Soviet Consular Treaty of 1958.[67]

2.4.2. *Scope of Application*

2.4.2.1. Material Scope of Application

With regard to the immovable part of an estate, the law determined pursuant to Article 28(3) of the German-Soviet Consular Treaty governs the succession as a whole.[68] However, questions regarding the formal validity of dispositions of property upon death are outside its scope.[69]

2.4.2.2. Territorial Scope of Application

With respect to its territorial scope, the German-Soviet Consular Treaty only applies to cases in which a national of one of the Contracting States has bequeathed immovable assets located in the other Contracting State.[70] Thus, the Treaty does not apply to an immovable part of the estate which is located in the home State of the deceased or in a third State.[71]

2.4.2.3. Personal Scope of Application

The personal scope of application of the German-Soviet Consular Treaty confines itself to nationals of one of the Contracting States.[72] The Treaty

---

65 A. Dutta, above n. 4, Article 75 EuErbVO para. 28; H. Dörner, above n. 13, Preliminary statement to Article 25 et seq. EGBGB para. 195; D. Lehmann, above n. 3, 232, 234; cf. D. Looschelders, in: J. v. Staudinger (ed.), *Kommentar zum Bürgerlichen Gesetzbuch*, revised ed. 2019, Sellier-de Gruyter, Berlin 2019, Preliminary statement to Private International Law para. 376.

66 BGBl. II 2016, 128.

67 A. Dutta, above n. 4, Article 75 EuErbVO para. 28; H. Dörner, above n. 13, Preliminary statement to Article 25 et seq. para. 195; I. Ludwig, above n. 27, Articles 25, 26 EGBGB para. 50.

68 F. Bauer, above n. 22, Appendix III to Article 75 EuErbVO para. 11; H. Dörner, above n. 13, Preliminary statement to Articles 25 et seq. EGBGB para. 197.

69 See section 3.1.3.

70 A. Dutta, above n. 4, Article 75 EuErbVO para. 31; F. Bauer, above n. 22, Appendix to Article 75 EuErbVO para. 7.

71 F. Bauer, above n. 22, Appendix III to Article 75 EuErbVO para. 7; I. Ludwig, above n. 27, Article 25, 26 EGBGB para. 48; F. Odersky, above n. 21, §15 para. 366; R. Süß, above n. 4, 181 et seq. para. 20.

72 F. Bauer, above n. 22, Appendix III to Article 75 EuErbVO para. 7.

does not explicitly regulate whether it applies to dual nationals. Due to the systematic link with the regulations on consular rights, it is to be assumed that German-Russian dual nationals fall outside the scope of the Treaty.[73] In the event the deceased had possessed the nationality of a third State in addition to Russian nationality, the Treaty applies only if the deceased was most closely connected with Russia.[74] The German-Soviet Treaty is not applicable to Russian nationals who have refugee status under the Geneva Refugee Convention or who are entitled to asylum under Sections 2 or 3 of the German Asylum Act.[75]

3. PRIVATE INTERNATIONAL LAW

All three Treaties provide conflict-of-laws rules. However, the connecting factors are heterogeneous.

3.1. THE CONFLICT-OF-LAWS RULES OF THE TREATIES

3.1.1. German-Iranian Treaty on Establishment

The connecting factor in Article 8(3) of the German-Iranian Treaty (**Treaty 17**) on Establishment is the law of the deceased's home State. The provision is applicable to the succession as a whole. There is no differentiation between movable and immovable property. The Treaty applies to intestate succession as well as to testamentary succession. However, the formal validity of dispositions of property upon death is not regulated by the Treaty.[76] In this respect, the 1961 Hague Convention on the Form of Wills or Article 27 SR is applicable before German courts.[77]

3.1.2. German-Turkish Agreement on Succession Matters

The German-Turkish Agreement on Succession Matters (**Treaty 19**) distinguishes between movable and immovable property.[78] According to Section 14(1) of the

---

73 F. Bauer, above n. 22, Appendix III to Article 75 EuErbVO para. 7; F. Odersky, above n. 21, §15 para. 367.

74 Contra F. Bauer, above n. 22, Appendix III to Article 75 EuErbVO para. 7: inapplicability of the Treaty to dual nationals.

75 F. Bauer, above n. 22, Appendix III to Article 75 EuErbVO para. 7; F. Odersky, above n. 21, §15 para. 367.

76 See above section 2.2.2.1.

77 For the differentiation, D. Looschelders, above n. 4, Article 27 EuErbVO para. 1.

78 See OLG Karlsruhe 27.02.2018, *NJW-RR* 2018, 713; K. Thorn, in: O. Palandt (ed.), *Bürgerliches Gesetzbuch*, 78th ed. 2019, Article 75 EuErbVO para. 2; F. Odersky, above n. 21,

German-Turkish Agreement the succession to movables is governed by the law of the State of which the deceased was a national at the time of his death. On the other hand, Section 14(2) of the Agreement provides that the succession to immovables is governed by the law of the State in which they are located. According to Section 12(3) of the German-Turkish Agreement, the law of the State in which the property is located determines whether it is to be qualified as movable or immovable.

The formal validity of dispositions of property upon death is regulated by Section 16 of the German-Turkish Agreement on Succession Matters. Section 16(1) of the Agreement provides that a disposition of property upon death is formally valid if its form complies with the law of the State in which the disposition was drawn up or with the law of the State whose nationality the deceased had at the time of its having been drawn up. According to Section 16(2) of the Agreement, the same applies to the revocation of such a disposition. As Germany and Turkey are Member States of the 1961 Hague Convention on the Form of Wills, Section 16 is inapplicable for wills or joint wills drafted subsequent to the Convention's entering into force in Turkey on 21 October 1983.[79] The 1961 Hague Convention, however, is not applicable to agreements as to succession. Therefore, in that respect, Section 16 of the Agreement on Succession Matters is still relevant.[80]

The German-Turkish Agreement on Succession Matters does not contain special rules on the material validity of dispositions of property upon death. Hence, the material validity of a disposition of property upon death is determined by Section 14 of the Agreement.[81] In the event of a change of nationality, the connection to the law of the home State of the deceased at the time of his death can lead to the problem that a disposition of property upon death – being initially valid under the testator's national law at the time it was drawn up – subsequently becomes invalid. Similar problems can arise with regard to the binding effect of an agreement as to succession or a joint will. These results are inappropriate given the aim of promoting legal certainty

§15 para. 365; M. Gebauer, above n. 4, 345 et seq.; D. Looschelders, above n. 65, Preliminary statement to Private International Law para. 600.

79 S. Lorenz, above n. 15, Article 25 EGBGB para 7; H. Dörner, above n. 13, Preliminary statement to Article 25 et seq. EGBGB para. 183; G. Hohloch, in: B. Grunewald, G. Maier-Reimer and H. P. Westermann (eds.), *Erman Bürgerliches Gesetzbuch*, 15th ed., Otto Schmidt, Köln 2017, Article 75 EuErbVO para. 10; A. Dutta, above n. 4, Article 75 EuErbVO para. 22; A. Köhler, above n. 29, Preliminary statement to Article 20–38 EuErbVO para. 53; F. Bauer, above n. 22, Appendix II to Article 75 EuErbVO para. 15; H. Dörner, above n. 47, 90, 95.

80 H. Dörner, above n. 13, Preliminary statement to Article 25 et seq. EGBGB para. 185; S. Lorenz, above n. 15, Article 25 EGBGB para 7; G. Hohloch, above n. 79, Article 75 EuErbVO para. 10.

81 F. Odersky, above n. 21, §15 para. 350.

and protecting legitimate expectations.[82] Following the regulatory concept of Section 16 of the Agreement, one solution to the problem might be to consider it sufficient that the disposition was materially valid under the law of the State whose nationality the deceased had at the time of its having been drawn up.[83] Alternatively, depending on when the disposition of property upon death was drawn up, the gap could be filled by recourse either to Article 26(5) EGBGB (old version) or to Articles 24 and 25 SR.

3.1.3. *German-Soviet Consular Treaty*

The German-Soviet Consular Treaty (**Treaty 18**) provides a conflict-of-laws rule only with regard to the succession to immovables. According to Article 28(3) of the German-Soviet Consular Treaty the succession to immovables is governed by the law of the State in which the property is located. The law of the State in which the property is located also regulates the question of whether the property is movable or immovable.[84] On the other hand, from the point of view of the German courts the succession to movables is governed by the law which is determined by the European Succession Regulation.[85]

The German-Soviet Consular Treaty does not contain rules on the formal validity of dispositions of property upon death. Therefore, before German courts the 1961 Hague Convention on the Form of Wills and Article 27 SR are applicable.[86]

3.2. COMPARISON WITH THE EUROPEAN SUCCESSION REGULATION

3.2.1. *Principles of Unity and Universality of the Succession versus Scission System*

Section 14(2) of the German-Turkish Agreement on Succession Matters (**Treaty 19**) and Article 28(3) of the German-Soviet Consular Treaty (**Treaty 18**)

82 Crit. H. Dörner, above n. 13, Preliminary statement to Article 25 et seq. para. 175; H. Dörner, above n. 47, 90, 93.

83 H. Dörner, above n. 47, 90, 93.

84 Cf. KG Berlin 05.10.2010, *ZEV* 2011, 132, 133; A. Dutta, above n. 4, Article 75 EuErbVO para. 31; F. Bauer, above n. 22, Appendix III to Article 75 EuErbVO para. 8; I. Ludwig, above n. 27, Articles 25, 26 EGBGB para. 47.

85 F. Bauer, above n. 22, Appendix III to Article 75 EuErbVO para. 10; G. Hohloch, above n. 79, Article 75 EuErbVO para 14.

86 A. Dutta, above n. 4, Article 75 EuErbVO para. 31; H. Dörner, above n. 13, Preliminary Question to Article 25 et seq. EGBGB para. 199; S. Lorenz, above n. 15, Article 25 EGBGB para. 13; A. Dutta, above n. 4, Article 75 EuErbVO para. 22; L. Kroiß, above n. 15, Article 25 EGBGB para. 16.

contain special rules on the succession to immovables. On the other hand, the succession to movables is governed by the law of the State whose nationality the deceased possessed at the time of death (Section 14(1) of the German-Turkish Agreement on Succession Matters) or by the law of the State in which he had his habitual residence at the time of death (Article 21(1) SR). The result of this distinction can be a fragmentation of succession, which is regarded as an obstacle to the free movement of persons in the Union.[87] Therefore, Article 23(1) SR establishes the principles of unity and universality of the law governing the succession as determined by Article 21 or Article 22 SR.[88]

3.2.2. Guiding Objective Connecting Factors

According to Article 21(1) SR the most important objective connecting factor is the habitual residence of the deceased at the time of death. Additionally, Article 21(2) SR contains a so-called escape clause referring exceptionally to the law of another State in cases where it is clear from all circumstances that, at the time of death, the deceased was manifestly more closely connected with this other State.[89] By contrast, Article 8(3) of the German-Iranian Treaty on Establishment (**Treaty 17**) and Section 14(1) of the German-Turkish Agreement on Succession Matters (**Treaty 19**) strictly refer to the law of the State whose nationality the deceased possessed at the time of death.

3.2.3. Choice of Law

The bilateral treaties between Germany and Iran, Turkey and the successor States of the Soviet Union do not provide rules on the choice of law. By contrast, Article 22 SR provides that a person may choose as the law to govern his succession as a whole the law of the State whose nationality he possesses at the time of making the choice or at the time of death.

With respect to the German-Iranian Treaty on Establishment (**Treaty 17**), some German courts and scholars assumed that Iranian nationals have the ability to choose a law pursuant to Article 25(2) EGBGB (old version).[90] However,

---

87 Recital 37 SR.

88 E. Castellanos Ruiz, in: A. Calvo Caravaca, A. Davì and H. Mansel (eds.), *The EU Succession Regulation*, Cambridge University Press, Cambridge 2016, Article 23 SR para. 1; D. Looschelders, above n. 4, Article 23 EuErbVO para. 1; C. F. Nordmeier, in: M. Weller, *Europäisches Kollisionsrecht*, Nomos-Verlagsgesellschaft, Baden-Baden 2016, pp. 299 et seq. para. 570 et seq.

89 E. Castellanos Ruiz, above n. 88, Article 23 SR para. 11.

90 LG Hamburg 12.02.1991, *IPRspr.* 1991, No. 142, pp. 264, 272 et seq.; H. Dörner, above n. 13, Preliminary statement to Article 25 et seq. EGBGB para. 151. With respect to the German-Turkish Agreement on Succession Matters and the German-Soviet Consular Treaty, a choice of law pursuant to Article 25 (2) EGBGB (old version) was not considered because

this was largely rejected.[91] The latter view must be accepted. The admission of a choice of law would be a serious interference with the concept of the German-Iranian Treaty on Establishment and should only be achieved by amending the Treaty. Therefore, within the scope of the bilateral treaties between Germany and third States, Article 22 SR is not applicable.[92] In any event, the law that can be chosen under Article 22 SR largely corresponds with the objective connection of succession matters under Article 8(3) of the German-Iranian Treaty on Establishment. The need for the admission of a choice-of-law rule would be more likely with regard to the law of the State where the deceased had his habitual residence at the time of death. Against this background, it becomes clear that a critical function of the choice-of-law option in Article 22 SR is the reduction of tensions between the principle of residence and the principle of nationality.

3.3. APPLICATION OF THE BILATERAL TREATIES BETWEEN GERMANY AND THE THIRD STATES AT ISSUE

Until recently, German courts have applied the bilateral treaties regarding matters of succession between Germany and the third States at issue.[93] However, since the entry into force of the European Succession Regulation, no relevant decision has yet been published. Therefore, at the present time it is not possible to say whether the German Courts will try to interpret the provisions of the Treaties narrowly to avoid frictions with the European Succession Regulation. But, even before the entry into force of the European Succession Regulation, there was a tendency to interpret the Treaties narrowly. As indicated above, the German courts mostly do not apply the bilateral treaties to dual nationals who have German nationality and the nationality of the other Contracting State. The Treaties will be applied to dual nationals who have the nationality of a third State besides the nationality of the other Contracting State only if they are most closely connected to the Contracting State. Consistent with the prevailing opinion, estate assets that are located in a third country are not covered.

---

the succession to immovables is in any event governed by the law of the State where they are located.

91 A. Dutta, above n. 4, Article 75 EuErbVO para. 12; S. Lorenz, above n. 15, Article 25 EGBGB para. 11; I. Ludwig, above n. 27, Article 25, 26 EGBGB para. 32; G. Hohloch, above n. 79, Article 75 EuErbVO para. 3; C. v. Bar, above n. 20, para. 354.

92 A. Dutta, above n. 4, Article 75 EuErbVO para. 12.

93 BGH 21.10.2015, *ZEV* 2016, 150; LG Karlsruhe 17.12.2014, *ZEV* 2015, 588 (previous instance); OLG Hamburg 04.12.2014, *FamRZ* 2015, 1232 = *MittBayNot* 2016, 261; OLG München 01.02.2010, *ZEV* 2010, 255; AG Hamburg St. Georg 13.04.2015, *ZEV* 2015, 580.

The attitude of the German courts towards the territorial scope of application can be illustrated by a decision of the Local Court of Hamburg St. Georg.[94] The deceased, born in Tehran, died in Hamburg. At the time of his death he had both Iranian and Canadian nationality. Among other things, property in Ontario, Canada, was part of the estate. The Local Court of Hamburg St. Georg assumed that the German-Iranian Treaty on Establishment (**Treaty 17**) was in principle applicable. It proceeded on the basis that the deceased had his closest connection to Iran. Therefore, Iranian law was applicable. The Local Court, however, did not apply Iranian law to the immovable property in Ontario. On the one hand, the Local Court referred to Article 3a(2) EGBGB (old version). On the other hand, it argued that the German-Iranian Treaty on Establishment is a bilateral agreement which should only regulate the relations between the two Contracting States. The latter argument remains relevant in the field of succession law even after the repeal of Article 3a(2) of the EGBGB in the area of international succession law. Therefore, in accordance with current law, the conflict-of-laws rules of the European Succession Regulation are decisive for German courts.[95]

3.4. PRACTICAL SIGNIFICANCE OF THE TREATIES

The German-Turkish Consular Treaty (**Treaty 19**) has the greatest practical importance among the bilateral agreements between the Federal Republic of Germany and third States. This is mainly due to the large number of Turkish nationals having habitual residence in Germany. More than 1,500,000 Turkish nationals live in Germany. In addition, approximately 530,000 people living in Germany possess German and Turkish nationality. About 800,000 people of Turkish origin have only German nationality.[96] For the practical significance of the German-Turkish Consular Treaty, the latter group is of high interest, too, because these individuals often bequeath immovable property in Turkey. Conversely, there are many Turks who, after working in Germany, have returned to Turkey but still have immovable property in Germany.[97]

The German-Iranian Consular Treaty (**Treaty 17**) is of much less practical significance.[98] Nevertheless, about 153,000 people with an Iranian migration

94 AG Hamburg St. Georg 13 04.2015, *ZEV* 2015, 580. For further details see section 2.2.2.2.

95 Note on the decision of the AG Hamburg St. Georg 13.04.2015, *DNotI-Report* 2015, 120.

96 2011 census numbers, reported in: C. Sydow, 'Debatte über den Doppelpass – das sind die Fakten' [2016] *Spiegel ONLINE*, <http://www.spiegel.de/politik/deutschland/deutschtuerken-doppelte-staatsbuergerschaft-das-sind-die-fakten-a-1106363.html> accessed 02.04.2019.

97 C. F. Majer, above n. 4, 182.

98 D. Lehmann, above n. 3, 232, 234.

background live in Germany.[99] Approximately 72,500 of them have Iranian nationality.[100] Since Iran generally does not release its nationals from Iranian nationality, the naturalization of Iranians usually leads to dual nationality. More than 80,000 Germans also have Iranian nationality.[101]

The practical significance of the German-Soviet Consular Treaty (**Treaty 18**) is limited in so far as only the succession to immovables is covered by the Treaty. On the other hand, about 230,000 nationals of the Russian Federation live in Germany.[102] Another important group, with about 134,000 people, are the nationals of Ukraine. The late emigrants (*Spätaussiedler*) from the former Soviet Union who have German ancestry can also be relevant since they might have immovable property in the successor States of the Soviet Union.

4. PROCEDURAL ISSUES

4.1. JURISDICTION

Procedural issues are scarcely covered by the bilateral treaties. In fact, only the German-Turkish Agreement on Succession Matters (**Treaty 19**) contains rules on jurisdiction in succession matters. The relevant provision of Section 15 of the Agreement merely governs claims for a declaratory judgment on the entitlement to an estate, claims to an inheritance, claims arising from a legacy or claims to a reserved share of an estate. Only disputes between persons potentially entitled to the inheritance in regards to either their status as heir or their entitlement to the estate are covered by the provision.[103] The German Federal Court of Justice has recently emphasized that Section 15 of the Agreement lists the claims concerned exhaustively. The common basic idea is that the legal dispute must refer to the status as heir or to the entitlement to the inheritance as such. Therefore, the Section definitely does not cover all disputes between heirs. The dispute must have a particularly close link to the succession. A controversy over the amount of a co-heir's share to the proceeds, which were obtained by the sale

---

99 See the Results of the Micro Census 2015 by the Federal Statistical Office: Statistisches Bundesamt, *Bevölkerung und Erwerbstätigkeit, Bevölkerung mit Migrationshintergrund – Ergebnisse des Mikrozensus 2015*, Statistisches Bundesamt, Wiesbaden 2015, p. 66.

100 Central Register of Foreign Nationals compiled by the Federal Statistical Office: Statistisches Bundesamt, *Bevölkerung und Erwerbstätigkeit, Ausländische Bevölkerung* (reporting date: 31.12.2015), Statistisches Bundesamt, Wiesbaden 2015, p. 153.

101 N. Frumkina, 'Deutsche Doppelstaatler – "Vereinbaren Sie keinen Termin"' [2017] *Tagesschau.de* <https://www.tagesschau.de/inland/useinreiseverbot-deutsche-101.html> accessed 02.04.2019.

102 Statistisches Bundesamt, above n. 100, p. 146.

103 BGH 21.10.2015, *ZEV* 2016, 150, 151; H. Dörner, above n. 13, Preliminary statement to Articles 25 et seq. EGBGB para. 181.

of estate property to a third party, is therefore not covered.[104] The same applies to the assertion of succession claims against third parties.[105] Pursuant to Section 8 of the Agreement, disputes arising from claims against the estate are to be asserted before and decided by the competent authorities of the State in which they are located. This is an exclusive jurisdiction.[106]

With respect to jurisdiction, Section 15 of the Agreement, following the system of scission in conflict of laws, distinguishes between movables and immovables. As far as movables are concerned, the courts of the State of which the deceased was a national at the time of his death have jurisdiction. In the case of immovables, the courts of the State in which they are located have jurisdiction. These jurisdictions are exclusive too.[107] In consequence, if a Turkish national who had his last habitual residence in Germany dies, the Turkish courts are exclusively competent with regard to movable property. This is in stark contrast to Article 4 SR, under which the courts of the Member State in which the deceased had his last habitual residence are competent to make decisions regarding matters of succession. For many Turks in Germany, the exclusive competence of the Turkish courts with regard to the movable part of the estate may cause serious practical problems.

Section 15 of the German-Turkish Agreement on Succession Matters only concerns jurisdiction in adversarial proceedings.[108] The competence to issue certificates of succession is not regulated in the Agreement.[109] The European Court of Justice recently rejected the prevailing opinion in Germany that the rules of the European Succession Regulation on international jurisdiction are not applicable to the jurisdiction for issuing a national certificate of succession.[110] Hence, in the event of the death of a Turkish national who had his last habitual residence in Germany, the international jurisdiction of the

---

104 BGH 21.10.2015, *ZEV* 2016, 150, 151; contra LG Karlsruhe 17.12.2014, *ZEV* 2015, 588, 589 (previous instance).

105 H. Dörner, above n. 13, Preliminary statement to Article 25 et seq. EGBGB para. 181.

106 B. Hoffmann and K. Thorn, *Internationales Privatrecht*, 9th ed., C. H. Beck, München 2007, §3 para. 60.

107 LG München I 26.09.2006, *ZEV* 2007, 436; R. Sieghörtner, in: M. Hahne and J. Munzig (eds.), *Beck'scher Online Kommentar FamFG*, 28th ed., date: 01.01.2019, C. H. Beck, München, §105 para. 19; B. v. Hoffmann and K. Thorn, above n. 106, §3 para. 60; F. Odersky, above n. 21, §15 para. 350; more restrictive H. Dörner, above n. 13, Preliminary statement to Articles 25 et seq. EGBGB para 182.

108 LG München I 26.09.2006, *ZEV* 2007, 436; H. Dörner, above n. 13, Preliminary statement to Article 25 et seq. para. 181 et seq.; R. Sieghörtner, above n. 107, §105 para. 19; C. Bachmayer, 'Ausgewählte Problemfelder bei Nachlasssachen mit Auslandsberührung' [2010] *BWNotZ* 146, 149

109 LG Braunschweig 18.05.2009, *IPRax* 2010, 255; F. Odersky, above n. 21, §15 para. 350; P. Sticherling, 'Türkisches Erbrecht und deutscher Erbschein' [2010] *IPRax* 234, 236.

110 ECJ 21.06.2018 – C-20/17, *NJW* 2018, 2309 (Oberle); cf. A. Dutta, above n. 4, Preliminary statement to Article 4 EuErbVO para. 4.

German courts for issuing a certificate of succession follows from Article 4 SR. For immovable property, however, reference is partly made to Section 12(1) of the German-Turkish Agreement on Succession Matters,[111] but it is clear from the systematic position of the provision that Section 12(1) and (2) is only concerned with distinguishing the powers of the consul from those of the competent authority at the place where the immovable property is located.

4.2. RECOGNITION OF DECISIONS

The German-Turkish Agreement on Succession Matters (**Treaty 19**) also contains rules on the recognition of decisions. Pursuant to Section 15, decisions of the courts of a Contracting State regarding claims for a declaratory judgment on the entitlement to an estate, claims to an inheritance, claims arising from a legacy or claims to a reserved portion of an estate are to be recognized in the other Contracting State.

Furthermore, as far as the succession to movables is in question, under Section 17 a certificate of succession issued by the competent authority of the deceased's home State is also sufficient for the proof of the succession in the other Contracting State.[112] The same applies to certificates of executorship. Nevertheless, it is problematic that under Turkish law the certificate of succession has much weaker effects than under German law.[113] However, the recognition cannot entail that a foreign certificate of succession has a wider effect than in the decision-rendering State.[114] Since Section 17 relates only to the succession to movables, a domestic certificate of succession is required for the proof of succession to domestic immovables pursuant to Section 35 of the German Real Estate Registry Act (GBO).[115] Hence, despite the existence of a Turkish certificate of succession, there may be a need for the issue of a domestic certificate of succession. The possibility of recognizing Turkish certificates of succession pursuant to Section 17 does not, therefore, exclude the jurisdiction of the domestic probate courts for the issuance of a German certificate of succession.[116]

---

111 Z. Kaya, above n. 51, 208, 212; C. Bachmayer, above n. 108, 146, 149.

112 LG München I 25.10.2011, *ZEV* 2012, 596; R. Sieghörtner, above n. 107, §108 para. 42.

113 H. Dörner, above n. 47, 90, 96.

114 A. Dutta, above n. 4, Article 75 EuErbVO para. 25; U. Haas and R. Sieghörtner, in: M. Bengel and W. Reimann (eds.), *Handbuch der Testamentsvollstreckung*, 5th ed., C. H. Beck, München 2013, Ch. 9 para. 456.

115 KG Berlin 25.03.1997, *NJW-RR* 1997, 1094.

116 H. Dörner, above n. 13, Preliminary statement to Article 25 et seq. EGBGB para. 190; G. Hohloch, above n. 79, Article 75 EuErbVO para. 12; *DNotI-Report*, above n. 44, 103, 105.

4.3. JURISDICTION AND CONSULAR RIGHTS

The German-Turkish Agreement on Succession Matters (**Treaty 19**) and the German-Soviet Consular Treaty (**Treaty 18**) provide the consular staff of the foreign Contracting State with special powers concerning the administration of the estate. Particularly extensive powers for the consular staff are granted by the German-Turkish Agreement on Succession Matters. This raises the question of the relationship between the powers of the consular staff and the jurisdiction of the probate court. The powers of the consular staff are primarily intended to secure the estate in the event of a local absence of the heirs. Section 13 of the German-Turkish Agreement on Succession Matters expresses this idea by depriving the consular staff of the power of representation if all persons entitled are present or represented.[117] In general, it can be said that the powers of the consular staff do not exclude the jurisdiction of the domestic probate courts. It should rather be left to the beneficiaries present whether they avail themselves of the assistance of the consular staff in the administration of the estate or settle the estate by themselves with the involvement of the probate court.[118]

4.4. ISSUING OF A EUROPEAN CERTIFICATE OF SUCCESSION WITHIN THE SCOPE OF THE BILATERAL TREATIES

It is not yet possible to foresee whether the German probate courts will issue a European Certificate of Succession if the applicable law is determined by a bilateral treaty with a third country. The German legislature did not follow the proposal[119] to regulate the problem in the Accompanying Act to the European Succession Regulation. Under current law, a proper solution could be to restrict the European Certificate of Succession to the part of the estate which is located in other Member States and is therefore not to be assessed under the conflict-of-laws rules of the bilateral treaty, but according to the European Succession Regulation. With regard to the part of the estate which is located in Germany, a German certificate of succession limited to the domestic estate pursuant to Section 352c of the Act on Court Procedure in Family Matters and Non-litigious Matters (FamFG) would have to be issued pursuant to the relevant

---

117 D. Damar, 'Deutsch-türkisches Nachlassabkommen: zivilprozess- und kollisionsrechtliche Aspekte' [2012] *IPRax* 278, 279.

118 LG Braunschweig 18.05.2009, *IPRax* 2010, 255; H. Dörner, above n. 13, Preliminary statement to Articles 25 et seq. EGBGB para. 190; F. Bauer, above n. 52, 1252 et seq.; D. Damar, above n. 117, 278, 279.

119 D. Lehmann, above n. 3, 232 et seq.

bilateral treaty.[120] This approach has the advantage that a European Certificate of Succession would be issued only in so far as there is conformity with the assessment of succession in other Member States. Admittedly, the unfavourable consequence of the approach is that the heirs, legatees, executors of wills and administrators of the estate cannot demonstrate their legal status, rights and powers in all Member States with the European Certificate of Succession,[121] but they at least have the opportunity to use the European Certificate of Succession in other Member States.

A further problem is that the courts of other Member States are not bound by the bilateral treaties and therefore will assess the succession in accordance with the European Succession Regulation even in regards to property located in Germany.[122] In the academic literature it is pointed out that in such cases international law might prevent German courts from recognizing the effects of a European Certificate of Succession issued in another Member State.[123] In this context, it must be taken into account that according to Article 69(1) SR, the European Certificate of Succession produces its effects in all Member States *ipso iure*.[124] A special recognition procedure is not required. However, it is questionable whether in such cases a German Land Registry is – pursuant to Section 35 of the German Real Estate Registry Act (GBO) – entitled or obliged to refuse the registration of an heir on the basis of a European Certificate of Succession issued in another Member State.[125] Such a right or duty of the Land Registry could be supported by the argument that the presumptions under Article 69(2) SR are rebuttable.[126]

On the other hand, under German Law a Land Registry is generally not entitled or obliged to verify whether the information contained in a Certificate of Succession is in concordance with the substantive legal situation.[127]

---

[120] R. Süß, above n. 4, 181 et seq. para. 24; contra Hohloch, above n. 79, Article 75 EuErbVO para. 13: unrestricted application of Art. 62 et seq. in cases with connection to other member states.

[121] Crit. A. Dutta, above n. 4, Article 75 EuErbVO para. 5.

[122] D. Lehmann, above n. 3, 232, 234.

[123] R. Magnus, in: B. Dauner-Lieb, T. Heidel and G. Ring (eds.), *NomosKommentar BGB*, Vol. 6, 3rd ed., Nomos-Verlagsgesellschaft, Baden-Baden 2019, Article 75 EuErbVO para. 11; D. Lehmann, above n. 3, 232, 234.

[124] C. Budzikiewicz, in: A.-L. Calvo Caravaca, Angelo Davì and H.-P. Mansel (eds.), *The EU Succession Regulation*, Cambridge University Press, Cambridge 2016, No. 2; C. F. Nordmeier, in: B. Dauner-Lieb, T. Heidel and G. Ring (eds.), *NomosKommentar BGB*, Vol. 6, 3rd ed., Nomos-Verlagsgesellschaft, Baden-Baden 2019, Article 69 EuErbVO para. 4.

[125] In this sense, see D. Lehmann, above n. 3, 232, 234.

[126] Cf. C. Budzikiewicz, above n. 124, Article 69 SR No. 9; A. Dutta, above n. 4, Article 69 EuErbVO para. 11; C. F. Nordmeier, above n. 128, Article 69 EuErbVO para. 13.

[127] OLG München 21.12.2015 *RNotZ* 2016, 185, 187; H. Wilsch, in: S. Hügel (ed.), *Beck´scher Online-Kommentar GBO*, 34th ed., date: 01.12.2018, C. H. Beck, München, §35 GBO para. 51.

Consequently, the Land Registry also cannot be considered entitled to validate the content of a European Certificate of Succession in terms of conformity with bilateral treaties.[128] The opposite view cannot be based on the primacy of the treaties under Article 75(1) SR because the international obligations of Germany established by the bilateral treaties do not go so far as to limit the effects of a European Certificate of Succession issued by the competent authority of another Member State.

5. THE FUTURE OF THE EXISTING TREATIES WITH THIRD STATES

In the run-up to the entry into force of the European Succession Regulation, it had been proposed to either terminate or renegotiate the bilateral treaties.[129] In this context, the State of North Rhine-Westphalia in 2013 strongly urged renegotiation of the Agreement with Turkey (**Treaty 19**).[130] However, the German Federal Government has not yet adopted this idea.

The vast majority of authors in German academic literature are very critical of the continuing applicability of the existing bilateral treaties with third States.[131] In particular, it is pointed out that the connection criteria of the agreements are not in line with the modern approaches in private international law and that the application of the agreements is contrary to the objective of legal unification pursued by the European Succession Regulation. However, especially in view of the German-Turkish Agreement on Succession Matters (**Treaty 19**), it has to be considered that the majority of German-Turkish successions do not have any connection with other Member States; accordingly, in these cases the harmonization of decisions with Turkey should be valued more highly than the harmonization of decisions with other Member States.[132] This argument applies to German-Iranian and German-Russian succession cases as well.

128 In this sense, see H. Wilsch, above n. 127, §35 GBO para. 41.

129 Deutscher Notarverein, 'Entwurf eines Gesetzes zum internationalen Erbrecht und zur Änderung von Vorschriften zum Erbschein – Stellungnahme des Deutschen Notarvereins' [2014] pp. 14 et seq. <http://www.dnotv.de/_files/Dokumente/Stellungnahmen/2014-06-04_Stellungnahme-DNotV_IntErbG.pdf> accessed 02.04.2019.

130 LTO-Redaktion, 'NRW fordert neues Abkommen mit der Türkei' [2013] *Legal Tribune Online*, <http://www.lto.de/recht/nachrichten/n/erbrecht-familienrecht-neuregelung-abkommen-tuerkei-migranten-nrw-justizminister-kutschaty> accessed 15.04.2019.

131 D. Looschelders, above n. 4, Preliminary statement to Article 1 EuErbVO para. 26; R. Magnus, above n. 123, Article 75 EuErbVO para. 13; A. Dutta, above n. 4, Article 75 EuErbVO para. 4; S. Lorenz, 'Erbrecht in Europa – Auf dem Weg zu kollisionsrechtlicher Rechtseinheit' [2012] *ErbR* 39, 49; P. Mankowski, above n. 3, 529, 530, 534; C. F. Majer, above n. 4, 182 et seq.; K. Siehr, 'Ausländischer Erbschein für Nachlass in Deutschland?' [2013] *IPRax* 241, 244; R. Süß, above n. 4, 181 et seq. para. 14; M. Gebauer, above n. 4, 345, 351.

132 R. Süß, above n. 4, 181 et seq. para. 57.

A consensual modification of the Agreements seems difficult to achieve. It should be noted that Iranian and Turkish private international law with regard to personal-statute-related issues are based on the principle of nationality. The introduction of the residence principle would be an unknown factor for international successions in the countries concerned. Furthermore, it is an important objective of the bilateral treaties to make sure that the nationals of a Contracting State in the territory of the other Contracting State are not subject to the local law of the latter State. At best, a choice-of-law option in favour of the law of residence could be considered. There is, however, the problem that the Iranian and Turkish conflict-of-laws rules have no familiarity with party autonomy in matters of succession law. In terms of succession to immovables, the reference to the *lex rei sitae* has a long tradition in Turkey and Russia, too. Here as well, an abandonment seems unlikely. Therefore, an amendment of the German-Turkish Agreement on Succession Matters (**Treaty 19**) is realistic only to the extent that disputes concerning the movable part of the estate would no longer be heard exclusively by the courts of the home State but instead could alternatively be brought before the courts at the habitual residence of the deceased. For many Turks living in Germany this would mean a considerable improvement.

6. CONCLUSION

The bilateral treaties of the Federal Republic of Germany with Iran, Turkey, Russia and most of the other successor States of the Soviet Union are in practice very important in cross-border disputes regarding succession. This is particularly true with regard to the German-Turkish Consular Treaty (**Treaty 19**). The conflict-of-laws rules of the treaties are based on antiquated and inflexible connecting factors and can therefore lead to substantial deviations from the judgment of succession matters under the European Succession Regulation. In some cases this may produce considerable difficulties for the issuance of a European Certificate of Succession. However, the harmonization of decisions between Germany and the concerned third States is important, too. In practice, the tensions with the European Succession Regulation are widely alleviated by the fact that most of the succession cases in question have no relevant connection with another Member State. The remaining deviations can be reduced by not applying the bilateral treaties to property which is not located in any Contracting State.

THE EXTERNAL RELATIONS OF ITALY

Pietro FRANZINA

1. INTRODUCTION

1.1. OBJECT AND SCOPE OF THE REPORT

This report gives an account of the international conventions relating to succession which are currently in force between Italy, on the one hand, and non-Member States of the European Union, on the other. Specifically, the report examines the conventions that deal with matters covered by Regulation (EU) No. 650/2012 of 4 July 2012 on successions (hereinafter the European Succession Regulation, or the Regulation),[1] to the extent to which they benefit from the subordination clause in Article 75 of the Regulation.[2]

1.2. THE CONVENTIONS ON SUCCESSIONS: AN OVERVIEW

1.2.1. Multilateral Conventions

Neither the Convention of 5 October 1961 on the Conflicts of Laws Relating to the Form of Testamentary Dispositions nor the Convention of 2 October 1973 Concerning the International Administration of the Estates of Deceased Persons, both adopted at the Hague Conference on Private International Law,[3] are in force for Italy. Italy signed them, but ratification never followed.

Italy is a party to the UNIDROIT Convention Providing a Uniform Law on the Form of an International Will, concluded in Washington on

1 [2012] OJ L201/107.

2 Pursuant to Art. 75(1), the Regulation 'shall not affect the application of international conventions to which one or more Member States are party at the time of adoption of this Regulation and which concern matters covered by this Regulation'.

3 <http://www.hcch.net> accessed 04.04.2019.

26 October 1973,[4] and the Council of Europe Convention on the Establishment of a Scheme of Registration of Wills, signed in Basel on 16 May 1972.[5] The two instruments, however, are concerned with the substantive aspects of successions and do not include provisions that affect the operation of the European Succession Regulation.[6]

1.2.2. *Bilateral Conventions*

Italy is a party to several bilateral conventions which lay down rules relating to cross-border successions. These include treaties of friendship, commerce and navigation, and consular and establishment conventions.

The vast majority of these rules have no bearing on the operation of the European Succession Regulation. They will not be considered in this report.

They concern, for example, rules on the taxation of estates, a matter which falls plainly outside the scope of the Regulation pursuant to Article 1(1),[7] and rules regarding the measures that the consular authorities of each Contracting State may take, along the lines of the customary rule in Article 5(g) of the Vienna Convention on Consular Relations of 24 April 1963, whenever a national of that State dies on the territory of the other.[8] These measures do not prevent the courts of the former country – Italy, for present purposes – from exercising their jurisdiction, if any, under the Regulation.[9]

---

4 <http://unidroit.org> accessed 04.04.2019.

5 <http://coe.int> accessed 04.04.2019.

6 A. Bonomi and P. Wautelet, *Le droit européen des successions*, 2nd ed., Bruylant, Bruxelles 2016, p. 938.

7 That is the case in, among others, the Treaty of Commerce and Navigation between Italy and the United Kingdoms of Sweden and Norway, of 14.06.1862: *Gazzetta ufficiale del Regno d'Italia*, No. 266 of 10.11.1862. The treaty is still in force in the relations between Italy and Norway. Art. 13 provides that the heirs of a national of a contracting party having died on the territory of the other will be subject to taxation, in the latter country, under the same conditions as the nationals of the territorial State. Rules prohibiting discriminatory taxation in matters of succession appear in several other conventions: see, for example, Art. 7(3) of the Treaty of Friendship, Commerce and Navigation between Italy and the United States of America, of 2.02.1948: *United Nations Treaty Series*, vol. 79, 171.

8 See in this regard, among others, Art. 16 of the Consular Convention between Italy and the United States of America of 18.09.1878: *Gazzetta ufficiale del Regno d'Italia*, No. 247 of 19.10.1878. Substantially similar provisions can be found in the agreement between Italy and the United Kingdom regarding the disposal of the estates of deceased seamen, concluded in London on 17.04.1877 and presently in force for Italy in its relations with New Zealand and Sri Lanka: *United Nations Treaty Series*, vol. 104, 70.

9 The prerogatives granted to the consular authorities of the deceased's State of nationality often include the power to administer and liquidate the deceased's assets. Some conventions stress that these powers can be exercised without the intervention of local authorities being required. See, for example, Art. 14(6) of the Treaty of Friendship, Commerce and Navigation between Italy and Nicaragua, concluded in Managua on 25.01.1906: *Gazzetta ufficiale del Regno d'Italia*, No. 267 of 16.11.1906. This does not amount, however, to a limitation of

Equally disregarded in this report are the rules included in consular and establishment conventions whereby, in each Contracting State, the nationals of the other Contracting State are recognized as having the capacity to inherit and to make a disposition of property upon death under the same conditions as the nationals of the former State.[10] The purpose of these rules is to avoid the risk that the nationals of the parties suffer from discrimination based on nationality. These provisions do not require that the issue of capacity be submitted systematically to the law of the forum, or any other law. In fact, the operation of bilateral conflict-of-laws rules, including those using nationality as a connecting factor, does not result as such in prohibited discrimination. Accordingly, nothing in these conventions seems to affect the ability of the conflict-of-laws provisions of the European Succession Regulation to determine the law applicable to the capacity to inherit and to make a disposition of property upon death.[11]

Finally, no account is given in this report of the rules that govern the recognition and enforceability of judgments in succession matters as may be found in several bilateral conventions concluded by Italy, be they consular conventions[12] or conventions relating, generally, to judicial assistance or the authority of foreign judgments.[13] In fact, the European Succession Regulation is

---

the jurisdiction of local courts, as understood by the European Succession Regulation. In fact, the relevant conventions specify that, should a claim as to the succession be raised by a citizen of the territorial State or of a third country, the consular authorities cannot rule on the matter. All difficulties should rather be settled by the competent courts. See, in this vein, Art. 21(3) of the Treaty of Commerce and Navigation between Italy and Venezuela, concluded on 19.06.1861: *Gazzetta ufficiale del Regno d'Italia*, No. 266 of 10.11.1862. More recent conventions employ, in this respect, clearer and stricter language. For instance, Art. 50(3) of the Consular Convention between Italy and Georgia of 12.07.2002: *Gazzetta ufficiale della Repubblica italiana – Supplemento ordinario*, No. 186 of 10.08.2004 provides that consular officers can *request* local courts to grant provisional measures for the protection of the assets of the deceased. On the evolution of the consular conventions of Italy in this regard, see E. Vitta, *Diritto internazionale privato*, Utet, Turin 1975, p. 201.

10 See, for instance, Art. 12 of the Treaty of Commerce and Navigation between Italy and Denmark, of 01.05.1864, and Art. 16 of the Treaty of Commerce and Navigation between Italy and Peru of 23.12.1874: *Gazzetta ufficiale del Regno d'Italia*, No. 292 of 10.11.1864 and No. 14 of 18.01.1879, respectively.

11 See Art. 23(2)(c) and Art. 26 of the Regulation.

12 One such convention is the Consular Convention between Italy and Turkey of 09.09.1929 (**Treaty 21**), other provisions of which are analyzed below, section 2.2: *Gazzetta ufficiale del Regno d'Italia*, No. 265 of 14.11.1930. Art. 21(11) sets forth in its last sentence the principle whereby, as regards the succession of Turks who died in Italy and Italians who died in Turkey, judgments rendered by the authorities of the State of nationality of the deceased qualify for recognition in the other.

13 Italy is a party to several conventions providing, *inter alia*, for the mutual recognition of judicial decisions. See, for example, the convention between Italy and Tunisia, concluded in Rome on 15.11.1967: *Gazzetta ufficiale della Repubblica italiana*, No. 128 of 21.05.1971, or the treaty between Italy and the People's Republic of China, concluded in Beijing on 20.05.1991: *Gazzetta ufficiale della Repubblica italiana – Supplemento ordinario*, No. 71 of 26.04.1994. These conventions govern the recognition of civil judgments generally and apply, as such, also to judgments in matters relating to succession.

solely concerned with the recognition and enforcement of judgments rendered in a Member State, and it simply fails to come into play where recognition or enforcement is sought, in a Member State, of a judgment given in a third country.

In the end, only two conventions include provisions on cross-border successions that interfere with the Regulation and accordingly call Article 75 into question. These are the Consular and Establishment Convention between Italy and Switzerland of 1868 (**Treaty 20**), and the Consular Convention between Italy and Turkey of 1929 (**Treaty 21**).

2. CONVENTIONS TAKING PRECEDENCE OVER THE EUROPEAN SUCCESSION REGULATION

2.1. THE CONSULAR AND ESTABLISHMENT CONVENTION OF 1868 BETWEEN ITALY AND SWITZERLAND

2.1.1. The Convention in a Nutshell

The Consular and Establishment Convention between Italy and Switzerland (**Treaty 20**), concluded on 22 July 1868 in Berne,[14] entered into force internationally on 1 May 1869. On the latter date, the parties concluded a protocol regarding certain provisions in the Convention. The protocol entered into force immediately upon its conclusion.[15]

Declarations issued by the governments of the two countries in 1879, 1920 and 1948 confirmed the ongoing applicability of the convention, in spite of supervening circumstances which would normally have resulted in its termination.[16]

The Convention has granted Italian citizens the right to enter Swiss territory and carry out a professional or remunerated activity there, and it has accorded Swiss citizens the right to do the same in Italy.[17]

The provisions in the convention cover a variety of subjects, ranging from taxation to access to justice and from insolvency to letters rogatory.

---

14 *Gazzetta ufficiale del Regno d'Italia*, 29.05.1869, No. 145. The Convention, which was drawn up in French only, has been amended under a bilateral agreement concluded in 2007. The amendments, however, do not concern the provisions that form the object of this paper.

15 *Gazzetta ufficiale del Regno d'Italia*, 29.05.1869, No. 145.

16 ATRIO – Archivio dei trattati internazionali online <http://itra.esteri.it> accessed 04.04.2019; Banque de données des traités internationaux <http://www.eda.admin.ch> accessed 04.04.2019.

17 'Les Italiens seront reçus et traités dans chaque Canton de la Confédération suisse, relativement à leurs personnes et à leurs propriétés, sur le même pied et de la même manière que le sont ou pourront l'être à l'avenir les ressortissants des autres Cantons. Réciproquement, les

2.1.2. *Background*

When the Consular Convention was concluded, thousands of Italians had already crossed the Swiss border looking for work there. Many would follow in the subsequent decades, making Switzerland one of the preferred destinations of Italian migrants.

Between 1860 and 1980, more than four million Italians moved to Switzerland. Less than half of them eventually returned to Italy. In 2018, the number of Italians permanently residing in Switzerland totalled 322,127.[18]

By contrast, the presence of Swiss nationals in Italy has always been numerically negligible. In 2018, only 7,914 Swiss were registered as permanently residing in Italy.[19]

The issues raised by the flow of Italian economic migrants towards Switzerland was one of the main concerns underlying the negotiation of the Convention. During the second half of the 19th century, the Swiss economy became increasingly industrial, and Italian migrants provided a significant share of the workforce required to support that development. Switzerland, then a country of emigration, rapidly turned into a target of immigration.[20] Concurrently, mobility grew into a sensitive topic in Italian internal and foreign politics. Measures had been taken since the 1860s by Italian authorities with the aim of providing migrants with the assistance they needed, both when leaving the country and, through the consular network, upon their arrival in the place of destination and during their stay there.[21]

2.1.3. *The Rules Relating to Succession: An Overview*

One provision in the Convention, Article 17, deals specifically with successions. Pursuant to Article 17(1) and (2), the authorities of the Contracting State on the territory of which a national of the other State has died must give notice of the death to the legation or the consular officer of the latter State. Paragraphs (3) and (4), the only provisions in Article 17 that are relevant to Article 75 of the Succession Regulation, concern disputes relating to the

Suisses seront reçus et traités en Italie, relativement à leurs personnes et à leurs propriétés, sur le même pied et de la même manière que les nationaux' (Art. 1(1) and (2)).

18 The State Secretariat for Migration of Switzerland: <http://www.sem.admin.ch> accessed 04.04.2019.

19 The Italian Institute of Statistics: <http://istat.it> accessed 04.04.2019.

20 See generally on the whole topic M. Vuilleumier, *Immigrés et refugiés en Suisse – Aperçu historique*, Pro Helvetia, Zurich 1987.

21 For an overview, see A. Golini and F. Amato, 'Uno sguardo a un secolo e mezzo di emigrazione italiana', in: P. Bevilacqua, A. De Clementi and E. Franzina (eds.), *Storia dell'emigrazione italiana, Partenze*, Donzelli, Roma 2001, 45, and M.R. Ostuni, 'Leggi e politiche di governo nell'Italia liberale e fascista', ibidem, 309.

succession of a national of a Contracting State who died on the territory of the other.

Specifically, Article 17(3) provides that disputes between the heirs of an Italian who died in Switzerland, and relating to his or her succession, be brought before the courts for the place where the deceased had his or her last domicile in Italy.[22] Reciprocity applies, under Article 17(4), to such disputes as may arise between the heirs of a Swiss national having died in Italy.[23]

The purpose of Article 17(3) and (4) is to regulate adjudicatory jurisdiction.[24] The wording of the two provisions, however, indicates that they go on to regulate venue as well, since they identify – within Italy and Switzerland, respectively – the particular district whose courts are entitled to hear the case.

The meaning of Article 17(4) has been clarified in the above-mentioned protocol of 1869. Pursuant to Article IV of the protocol, proceedings involving the heirs of a Swiss citizen who died in Italy are to be brought before the courts of the 'place of origin' of the deceased.[25] The clarification alludes to the distinction, known to Swiss law, between the domicile of a natural person and his or her 'lieu d'origine', or 'Heimatort'.

Domicile, as stated in Article 23 of the Swiss Civil Code of 1907 (and, previously, in Article 2 of the Federal Law of 1891 on the Civil Law Relationships of Settled or Resident Citizens, which in turn reflected pre-existing law), is the place where a person resides with the intention of settling. The origin of a person, by contrast, reflects that person's 'droit de cité', i.e. the special kind of citizenship which links Swiss nationals to a particular city ('commune') under public law.[26]

2.1.4. Scope of Application of the Rules on Successions

As stated above, Article 17(3) and (4) apply to disputes ('contestations') between heirs ('entre les héritiers') concerning the succession ('au sujet de [la] succession') of a national of a contracting party who died on the territory of the other.

---

22 'Les contestations qui pourraient s'élever entre les héritiers d'un Italien mort en Suisse, au sujet de sa succession, seront portées devant le juge du dernier domicile que l'Italien avait en Italie.'

23 'La réciprocité aura lieu à l'égard des contestations qui pourraient s'élever entre les héritiers d'un Suisse mort en Italie.'

24 See, however, below, section 2.1.7, where the opinion is discussed according to which Art. 17 also includes an implicit rule on the law applicable to succession.

25 'Le Gouvernement royal admet que, d'après la réserve faite par l'Assemblée fédérale, au sujet du dernier alinéa de l'article 17 de la Convention susdite, les contestations qui pourraient s'élever entre les héritiers au sujet de la succession d'un Suisse mort en Italie, devront être déférées au juge du lieu d'origine du défunt.'

26 Regarding the notion of 'origin', see further, in recent literature, B. Müller, 'Das Schweizer Bürgerrecht und die Einbürgerung' in: J. Steffen (ed.), *Die Wohnsitzverlegung in die Schweiz*, 2nd ed., Springer Gabler, Wiesbaden 2012, p. 207.

The Convention fails to distinguish between testamentary and intestate succession, or between succession to movable and immovable property. Its broad language indicates that it covers all such scenarios.

Italian courts have generally expressed the view that the Convention applies to *any* dispute whose subject matter is succession. Its operation is not restricted – as the wording of Article 17 would appear to suggest – to proceedings opposing two or more heirs, or alleged heirs. In 1967, the *Corte di Cassazione* referred to the Convention in a case involving the heirs, the legatees and the executor of a Swiss national who was living in Italy at the time of his death.[27] In a judgment of 1992, the Court reiterated that the Convention is applicable to any succession dispute.[28] The District Court of Brescia, based on these precedents, relied on Article 17(3) to assert its jurisdiction over a dispute between the heirs of an Italian national who had died in Switzerland, on the one hand, and the administrator of the latter's estate, appointed by the Swiss authorities, on the other.[29]

The Federal Tribunal of Switzerland opted for a similarly broad reading of the Convention in a judgment of 1932, relating to a claim by the legatee of an Italian who had died in Switzerland against the heirs of the latter.[30] The Tribunal held that excluding this kind of claim from the scope of the Convention would frustrate the goal of Article 17(3) and (4), namely unity of succession. Different claims relating to one and the same succession would in fact risk being litigated in the two countries and eventually decided under different substantive rules.

In a ruling of 1965, the Federal Tribunal expressed doubts as to the relevance of the Consular Convention to proceedings brought against the heirs of an Italian national by a creditor of one such heir, in a situation where the enforcement of the claim implied the sharing out of the estate.[31] The Court, however, stated that it was unnecessary, for the purposes of that dispute, to take a stance on the matter and left the question unanswered.[32]

In 1972, the Tribunal found that the Convention was applicable to a dispute between the daughters of an Italian who had died in Switzerland – his heirs – and the widow of the deceased and regarding the usufruct of part of the estate.[33]

---

27 Cass. 31.07.1967, No. 2038, 4, *RDIPP* (1968), 174.

28 Cass. 1.07.1992, No. 8081, 29, *RDIPP* (1993), 406.

29 Trib. Brescia, 25.11.1999, 36 *RDIPP* (1993), 1041.

30 BGer., 16.12.1932, 58 *BGE*, I, 319.

31 BGer., 25.03.1965, 91 *BGE*, III, 19.

32 The prevailing view among scholars is that the Convention does not apply to disputes between one or more heirs, on the one hand, and their creditors, on the other. See, *inter alia*, A. Bucher, 'Chapitre 6: Successions', in A. Bucher (ed.), *Loi sur le droit international privé – Convention de Lugano*, Helbing & Lichtenhahn, Bâle 2011, 779, at 782.

33 BGer., 27.01.1972, 98 *BGE*, II, 88.

On a different note, the opinion has been advanced, in particular by the Swiss Federal Ministry of Justice, that the Convention does not apply when the deceased leaves no heirs.[34] The existence of heirs may itself be disputed, in which case nothing should prevent the Consular Convention from applying.[35]

The language of Article 17 seems to suggest, in any case, that the Convention solely concerns jurisdiction to rule on the merits of a disputed succession. By contrast, the powers of Italian and Swiss authorities to grant provisional measures, or to entertain non-contentious proceedings regarding the administration of the estate (as may concern, for example, the appointment of an administrator or the inventory of the deceased's assets), do not rest on the Convention and are not affected by the latter.[36]

A judgment rendered by the Italian *Corte di Cassazione* in 2018 appears, however, to depart from the latter finding.[37] The case concerned an Italian who had died in Switzerland. A creditor of the deceased had brought proceedings in Italy against the children of the deceased. She wanted to prevent the assets of the deceased from merging with those of her heirs, for a merger would have undermined the prospect of enforcing her claims. The Supreme Court took the view that proceedings for the separation of the deceased's assets, as contemplated under Article 512 of the Italian Civil Code, come within the scope of Article 17 of the Convention, as the matter 'concerned' a succession. The fact is that the case was not about the children's entitlement to the estate of the deceased – that right was not disputed. Rather, the crux was the creditor's ability to enforce her claim, and the Italian authorities had been asked to tag the assets of the deceased as being primarily available for the satisfaction of the creditor's claim. The proceedings, the *Corte* observed, were accordingly non-contentious in nature.

2.1.5. *Conditions of Applicability*

2.1.5.1. Nationality

The jurisdictional rules in Article 17 apply, in Switzerland, to the succession of persons of Italian nationality and, in Italy, to the succession of Swiss nationals.

---

34 See the opinion of the Ministry, dated 30.09.1997, referred to by G. Broggini, 'Le successioni nei rapporti italo-svizzeri: competenza di autorità svizzere e italiane per la pubblicazione di testament e per emanare provvedimenti conservative', in D. Accoccella et al., *Temi scelti di diritto ereditario – Atti della giornata di studio del 16 ottobre 2000*, Helbing & Lichtenhahn, Basel 2002, p. 143, at 154.

35 T. Ballarino and I. Pretelli, 'Una disciplina ultracentenaria delle successioni' [2014] *Rivista ticinese di diritto*, 889, at 907.

36 See in this connection BGer., 17.05.1973, 99 *BGE*, II, 246.

37 Cass. 15.05.2018, No. 11849, 54, *RDIPP* (2018), 1053.

The common view among scholars is that Article 17(3) and (4) do not apply where the deceased possessed both Italian and Swiss nationality.[38]

Swiss courts have explicitly endorsed this finding with reference to the rule on jurisdiction featured in the (no longer in force) Convention of 15 June 1869 between Switzerland and France on jurisdiction and the recognition of judgments in civil matters, which is similar to the rule in Article 17(3) and (4) of the Convention between Italy and Switzerland.[39]

The reading could be justified by the fact that the Consular Convention, by failing to prescribe a solution for positive conflicts of nationality, enables the courts in the two countries to rely, for this purpose, on the domestic rules of the forum, which in fact provide in the two countries for the primacy of the nationality of the forum State.[40] The obvious corollary of this state of affairs is the risk of positive conflicts of jurisdiction.[41]

The Convention is silent as to whether Article 17(3) and (4) should still apply in each Contracting State where the deceased possessed, in addition to the nationality of the other Contracting State, the nationality of a third country, as would occur, for example, if a dispute was brought in Switzerland concerning the succession of an Italian who is also, say, a national of Argentina.

One possible answer consists in submitting this occurrence to the rules of the forum that deal with dual and multiple nationality for private international law purposes, based on the assumption, mentioned above, that, absent a clear indication to the contrary, the issues that the Convention fails to address

---

38 See, among others, B. Dutoit et al., *Répertoire de droit international privé suisse*, vol. III – *Les principales conventions d'établissement touchant le droit international privé*, Staempfli, Bern 1986, 125, and F.-H. Hool, *Les effets de la double nationalité en droit Suisse*, Editions du Griffon, Neuchâtel 1949, 63 and 83. See, however, more restrictively, G. Pesce, *Svizzera & Italia – Questioni di diritto*, Stamperia Nazionale, Roma 2011, 184, suggesting that the Convention does not prevent Italian courts from regarding a bi-national deceased as one merely possessing Italian nationality whenever the deceased's last domicile was in Italy (and, reciprocally, for Swiss courts, where the deceased's last domicile was in Switzerland).

39 BGer., 15.10.1955, 81 *BGE*, II, 495, referring to Art. 5 of the convention between France and Switzerland. In the relevant passage, the latter provision reads as follows: 'Toute action relative à la liquidation et au partage d'une succession testamentaire ou ab intestat ou aux comptes à faire entre les héritiers ou légataires sera portée devant le tribunal de l'ouverture de la succession, c'est-à-dire, s'il s'agit d'un Français mort en Suisse, devant le tribunal de son dernier domicile en France, et s'il s'agit d'un Suisse décédé en France, devant le tribunal de son lieu d'origine en Suisse'.

40 See, today, Art. 23(1) of the Swiss Federal Statute on Private International Law, and Art. 19(2) of the Italian Statute on Private International Law (Law No. 218 of 31.05.1995).

41 A. Bucher, n. 32, p. 782. The Convention fails to address this risk. However, nothing in the Convention seems to prevent the courts of the Contracting States from resorting to the domestic rules that regulate international parallel litigation. Thus, for example, if proceedings happen to be pending at the same time in Switzerland and Italy concerning the succession of a dual Swiss and Italian national, the second-seized Italian court will be able to rely on Art. 7 of the Italian Statute on Private International Law to stay the proceedings before it on grounds of *lis pendens*.

must be decided in each Contracting State in accordance with the pertinent local rules. Both Switzerland and Italy follow the principle whereby dual and multiple nationals must be deemed to possess the nationality of the country with which they are most closely connected. This approach is enshrined in provisions which are meant to complement conflict-of-laws rules rather than rules on jurisdiction,[42] but the underlying approach is apparently a general one in the two countries and is suited, in principle, to fill the gap in the Consular Convention. Thus, in the example above, the deceased would be treated as possessing solely Argentinean nationality if his or her ties with Italy are less meaningful and intense than the connections with Argentina. Swiss courts would ultimately be able to rely on Article 86(1) of the Federal Statute on Private International Law to assert their jurisdiction over disputes relating to the succession of the deceased, based on the fact that the last domicile of the latter was in Switzerland.

A different approach to conflicts of nationalities consists of the courts of each Contracting State systematically granting the primacy of the nationality of the other Contracting State. Thus, in the example considered earlier, the deceased would always need to be treated in Switzerland as a national of Italy, regardless of the nature and quality of his or her connections with Argentina. Should a Swiss court be seized of the matter, the dispute would then be considered as belonging to the jurisdiction of Italian courts in accordance with the Convention. Reciprocally, Italian courts should refrain from ruling on the succession of a Swiss national having died in Italy, under the Convention, without having to wonder whether the deceased possessed another nationality (other than the Italian nationality) and whether such other nationality is more effective than the Swiss one.

The second understanding, it is contended, ought to be preferred, as it better suits the purposes of the Convention. The latter aims to ensure, in each Contracting State, the protection of the nationals of the other (as distinct from the nationals of any other State), and it does so by referring disputes relating to their succession to the courts of their country of nationality.

2.1.5.2. Place of Death and Domicile

Article 17(3) and (4) of the Convention concern, literally, the succession of Italians who 'died' in Switzerland and the succession of Swiss nationals who 'died' in Italy ('un Italien mort en Suisse', 'un Suisse mort en Italie').

The provisions have mostly been interpreted, however, as referring to the succession of Italians and Swiss who had their *domicile* in Switzerland and

---

42 Art. 23(2) of the Swiss Federal Statute on Private International Law; Art. 19(2) of the Italian Statute on Private International Law.

in Italy, respectively, at the time of their death.[43] In other words, Article 17(3) and (4) only apply to those disputes as concern the succession of a Swiss national whose last domicile was in Italy and, reciprocally, the succession of an Italian whose last domicile was in Switzerland, regardless of the place where they actually passed away.

This reading conforms with the object and purpose of the Consular Convention, considered as a whole. As noted above, the Convention was originally meant to address, in particular, the issues arising from migratory movement and, more generally, economic mobility. Its rules are essentially concerned with the nationals of one country who decide to settle in the territory of the other, or who are otherwise bound to the latter country by economic and social ties which are stable in nature. Against this background, the mere fact that a Swiss national died in Italy is not enough to justify the application of Article 17(3) and (4) if the deceased had not availed himself or herself of the freedom of movement and establishment enshrined in the Convention. Thus, for example, the succession of a Swiss national who accidentally died in Italy (e.g., while on holiday there) does not come with the scope of the Convention. By contrast, the Convention applies to the succession of a Swiss national who had settled in Italy, e.g. to carry out work, no matter whether his or her death occurred elsewhere.

It is unclear how the word 'domicile' should be construed for the purposes of Article 17. The Convention fails to provide a uniform definition of this concept, and no judgment could be retrieved that discusses the issue in some detail. Actually, the courts in the two countries seem to rely on the notion of domicile shaped by their respective domestic rules.

This approach is likely to result, in some circumstances, in positive or negative conflicts of jurisdiction. There is no evidence, however, that these conflicts have actually arisen in practice. This is plausibly due to the fact the concept of domicile, though defined somehow differently in the two legal systems, often leads in fact to the same practical results. Under Swiss law, as has already been observed, a person is domiciled where he or she resides with the intention of settling. For its part, Article 43 of the Italian Civil Code considers that the domicile of a person corresponds to the centre of his or her personal and financial interests. Both the Italian and the Swiss Civil Codes (Article 45(2) and (3), and Articles 25 and 26, respectively) include special provisions regarding the domicile of children and adults who benefit from a measure of protection, but these rules, too, tend to give rise, in practice, to the same outcome.

On a different note, since Article 17(3) and (4) confer jurisdiction on the courts of the place where the deceased was last domiciled within his or her State

43 See, among others, Cass. 31.07.1967, No. 2038, 4 *RDIPP* (1968), 174, and BGer., 17.05.1973, 99 *BGE*, II, 246. Doubts as to the relevance of the last domicile of the deceased have been expressed by BGer., 27.01.1972, 98 *BGE*, II, 88.

of nationality (or had his or her 'place of origin', in the case of a Swiss national), the jurisdictional rules in the Convention do not apply to those Swiss nationals or Italians who have never been domiciled in their country of nationality.[44] In practice, where a dispute arises between the heirs of a Swiss national whose last domicile was in Italy, but it is established that the deceased has always been living in Italy or in a third country, the Italian courts seized of the matter will not be required to resort to the Consular Convention to rule on their jurisdiction. This interpretation, too, appears to be consistent with the object and purpose of the Convention in general.

2.1.6. Relationship with Domestic Rules of Jurisdiction

Different views have been expressed as to whether, in proceedings falling within the scope of application of the Convention of 1868, jurisdiction could still be asserted in the two Contracting States on the basis of domestic rules.

Ever since a ruling rendered by the *Corte di Cassazione* in 1934, Italian courts have generally taken the view that, where the Convention is applicable, no room is left for the jurisdictional rules of the forum.[45] In practice, if a dispute is brought in Italy in a situation where jurisdiction cannot be asserted on the basis of the Convention, the claim should be dismissed for lack of jurisdiction no matter whether the case is one that Italian courts would normally be entitled to hear in accordance with national rules, including those on tacit submission. The opinion has met with the approval of Italian scholars.[46]

By contrast, well-settled case law exists in Switzerland indicating that nothing in the Consular Convention prevents Swiss courts from hearing a claim for which the defendant has explicitly accepted – or has failed to challenge, as the case may be – the jurisdiction of Swiss courts seized by the plaintiff.[47]

The author of this contribution is not aware of any protest raised by the Italian government as regards the described Swiss practice.

In fact, the Swiss reading seems to rest on two plausible assumptions and deserves approval.

First, the Convention achieves its goals by simply enabling, as opposed to requiring, the courts of the State of nationality of the deceased to hear disputes relating to the latter's succession. The purpose of Article 17(3) and (4) is

---

44 T. Ballarino and I. Pretelli, n. 35, pp. 897 et seq.

45 Cass. 23.05.1934, [1935] 30 *Rivista di diritto internazionale* 162.

46 G. Morelli, *Diritto processuale civile internazionale*, 2nd ed., CEDAM, Padova 1954, p. 236.

47 BGer., 12.07.1939, 65 *BGE*, I, 125; BGer., 19.11.1954, 80 *BGE*, II, 362; BGer., 25.03.1965, 91 *BGE*, III, 19; BGer., 26.07.2010, 136 *BGE*, III, 461; BGer., 23.09.2011, 5A_87/2011, available through <http://www.servat.unibe.ch> accessed 04.04.2019. According to T. Wüstemann and L. Martínez Marolda, 'Der schweizerisch-italienische Erbfall' [2011] 5 *Successio* 62, 66, the Convention should further be understood as not preventing the enforcement of a choice of court made by the *de cuius*.

basically to allow litigation to take place in the country of origin of the deceased where, presumably, most of his or her family members live and most of his or her interests are located. That said, if the litigants have a different opinion, and actually prefer to have the matter adjudicated in another country (whose courts are ready to hear the case), it is hard to see why the Convention should prevent them from doing so.

Second, the finding whereby the courts of the State of domicile should systematically be barred from dealing with the succession of a national of the other country, no matter whether their jurisdiction has been accepted by the litigants, amounts to a significant limitation of the sovereignty of that State, something which cannot be lightly presumed and something which lacks a clear indication in the Convention.

2.1.7. The Opinion According to which the Convention also Implicitly Identifies the Law Applicable to Successions

The opinion has been advanced, and actually endorsed by Swiss courts in some decisions, that Article 17(3) and (4), while explicitly addressing the jurisdiction of courts, equally identifies, by implication, the law applicable to the substance of the succession.[48] According to this view, a Swiss court seized of a dispute relating to the succession of an Italian who died in Switzerland should rule on the substance of the matter (if indeed it can assert its jurisdiction) in accordance with Italian law, in spite of the fact that, under the domestic conflict-of-laws rules of Switzerland, the case would be submitted, absent a *professio iuris*, to Swiss law.[49]

---

48 BGer., 16.12.1965, 91 *BGE*, II, 457; BGer., 25.03.1965, 91 *BGE*, III, 19; BGer., 27.01.1972, 98 *BGE*, II, 88; BGer., 17.05.1973, 99 *BGE*, II, 246. See generally, and among various authors, H. Chenevard, *Le régime civil des successions dans les rapports italo-suisses*, Payot, Lausanne 1985, pp. 28 et seqq.; B. Dutoit et al., *Répertoire de droit international privé suisse*, vol. III – *Les principales conventions d'établissement touchant le droit international privé*, Staempfli, Bern 1986, p. 129. In Italian literature, the opinion has been espoused in particular by E. Vitta, n. 9, p. 116. To corroborate the view whereby Art. 17(3) and (4) provide for an implicit conflict-of-law rule, some have resorted to an argument *a simili*, pointing out that Art. 5 of the previously mentioned Consular Convention between France and Switzerland of 1869, while essentially equally concerned with jurisdiction, includes a reference to the applicable law. The sharing out of immovable property and other issues, in accordance with the latter provision, are *nevertheless* ('toutefois') governed by the *lex rei sitae*: an indirect indication that, for the rest, the law of nationality should apply. See generally on this provision A. Aujay, *Études sur le Traité Franco-Suisse du 15 Juin 1869*, Pedone, Paris 1903, pp. 195 et seq., and A. Pillet, *Les Conventions internationals relatives à la compétence judiciaire et à l'exécution des jugements*, Librairie de la Société du Recueil Sirey, Paris 1913, pp. 147 et seqq.

49 Pursuant to Art. 90(1) of the Federal Statute on Private International Law, the succession of a person who had his or her last domicile in Switzerland is governed by Swiss law, except where the *de cuius* (of foreign nationality) had entered into a *professio iuris* designating the law of his or her *lex patriae*, in conformity with Art. 90(2).

The reading has since been mitigated in its practical implications by both scholars and tribunals. One factor prompting this reconsideration was the adoption, in 1995, of the reformed Italian Statute on Private Law. While confirming that the law applicable to succession is in principle the *lex patriae* of the deceased, the reform enabled the *de cuius* to submit the whole of the succession to the law of the country where he or she resided, provided that this was his or her last residence.[50] Some have contended that the implicit conflict-of-laws rules in the Consular Convention ought to be construed as contemplating the possibility of *renvoi* – with the consequence that the Swiss court seized of the succession of an Italian should apply Swiss law, without really departing from the Convention – each time it is established that the deceased had availed him or herself of the possibility of choosing the law of Switzerland in accordance with the Italian Statute.[51] Others have noticed that it would be curious if the two countries, once their respective conflict-of-laws rules happen to follow the same approach as to the admissibility of a *professio iuris*, were restricted from taking advantage of such a convergence out of respect for a Convention which is more than a century old.[52]

The Federal Tribunal eventually conceded in a ruling of 2010 that, if the Italian deceased entered into a *professio* in favour of Swiss law, Swiss courts should in principle follow that choice.[53] The Tribunal did not, however, consider it necessary to take a stance on the existence of an implicit conflict-of-laws rule in the Convention or to address the questions of its operation or (dipositive) nature.

One scholar observed that, at the time when the Consular Convention was concluded, the parallelism of *forum* and *ius* merely reflected the current state of the rules of private international law in the two countries, i.e. the fact that the relevant rules, as they existed then, led in principle to the application of the law of nationality of the deceased.[54] The same author argued that, as a result of the changes in both Italian and Swiss conflict-of-laws rules relating to successions,

---

50 Art. 46 of the Italian Statute on Private International Law.

51 B. Dutoit, *Commentaire de la loi fédérale du 18 décembre 1987*, 4th ed., Helbing & Lichtenhahn, Zurich 2005, 301.

52 A. Bonomi, 'La loi applicable aux successions dans le nouveau droit international privé italien et ses implications dans les relations italo-suisses', [1996] 4 *Schweizerische Zeitschrift für internationales und europäisches Recht* 479, 503.

53 BGer., 26.07.2010, 136 *BGE*, III, 461. Several scholarly contributions had paved the way to the conclusion reached in the ruling. See, in particular, in addition to the works referred to in nn. 51 and 52, A. Bonomi, 'Autonomie des parties en droit patrimonial de la famille et intérêt des entrepreneurs: aspects de droit matériel et de droit international privé' [2004] 14 *Schweizerische Zeitschrift für internationales und europäisches Recht* 459, 478, and B. Dutoit, 'Le droit international privé suisse de la famille et des successions à l'épreuve du temps: dix ans de LDIP' [2000] 10 *Schweizerische Zeitschrift für internationales und europäisches Recht* 279, 295.

54 A. Bucher, n. 32, p. 782.

the understanding on which the Convention was originally built has become obsolete, thereby suggesting that the Convention can no longer be understood as laying down, alongside the rules on jurisdiction, an implicit rule on the applicable law.

This reading provides a convincing interpretation of the reasons why the Convention has been seen as including a hidden conflict-of-laws rule. However, in the opinion of the present author, the changes which affected the domestic rules of private international law in Italy and Switzerland can hardly serve as a justification for a change in the substance of the Convention or in its interpretation. Under the customary rules on the law of treaties, as codified in the Vienna Convention of 23 May 1969, a mere change in the domestic legislation of the contracting parties cannot entail, as such, an amendment to an international treaty, and is not enough to trigger in itself a change in the interpretation of a treaty's provisions. Rather, the former outcome requires an 'agreement' between the parties, while the latter presupposes, at least, a 'subsequent practice in the application of the treaty' reflecting 'the agreement of the parties regarding its interpretation'. None of these conditions, no matter how liberally interpreted, has apparently been met.

The Convention, it is contended, has never required, as such, that the successions of Italians who died in Switzerland be decided by Swiss courts in accordance with Italian law. This was, simply, the outcome that the negotiators of the Convention regarded as 'normal' based on the then existing rules of private international law in the two countries.

This is confirmed by the judicial practice of Italy. Italian courts, too, have traditionally adjudicated disputes falling within the scope of Article 17(3) of the Consular Convention in accordance with Italian substantive law, but – apart from an *obiter dictum* in an isolated judgment of the Court of Cassation[55] – they have always reached this conclusion on the basis of the relevant Italian conflict-of-laws rules, pursuant to which, as noted earlier, successions are normally governed by the law of the State of nationality of the deceased.

2.2. THE CONSULAR CONVENTION OF 1929 BETWEEN ITALY AND TURKEY

2.2.1. *The Convention in a Nutshell*

The Consular Convention between Italy and Turkey (**Treaty 21**) was concluded in Rome on 9 September 1929. It provides for the creation of consulates and

55 Cass. 31.07.1967, No. 2038, 4 *RDIPP* (1968), 174, observing that the ultimate goal of the Consular Convention is to ensure the convergence of *forum* and *ius*.

consular offices of each contracting party on the territory of the other, and it specifies the powers of the respective consular authorities in a broad range of areas, such as guardianship, succession and navigation.[56]

The Convention entered into force internationally on 13 April 1932.

2.2.2. Background

Concluded in the aftermath of the abolition of capitulations, as brought about by the Treaty of Lausanne of 24 July 1923 respecting conditions of residence and business and jurisdiction,[57] the Consular Convention of 1929 marked the beginning of a period of 'warmth' in the relations between Italy and Turkey. This new stage had been preceded by decades of tensions (fuelled by the expansionism of Italy, with Turkey being regarded as a potential colony, especially easy to reach from the Dodecanese Isles, then under Italian sovereignty), and it was followed, as early as 1932, by a new frost.[58]

Around 1927, Turkey began to appear to Italy more as a regional actor than just as a possible target of expansionism. Ankara, for its part, wished to take advantage of Mussolini's diplomatic activism to strengthen its international position with respect to its relations with Greece (whose normalization would later benefit from Italian efforts) and France (a common problem for Italy and Turkey).[59] The diplomatic exchanges between Ankara and Rome turned particularly intense and culminated in the stipulation of a Treaty of Neutrality and Conciliation on 30 May 1928.

The restoration of political trust between the two countries resulted in accrued economic cooperation and fuelled an already flourishing commercial intercourse.[60] The Italian community in Istanbul – not especially numerous, but socially active and economically influential[61] – was set to attract new members, and it was intended to play an important role in forging political relations between the two countries in the coming years.

---

56 *Gazzetta ufficiale del Regno d'Italia*, No. 265 of 14.11.1930. The Convention was drawn up in French only.

57 [1924] 18 *American Journal of International Law – Supplement* 67.

58 Regarding this stage of the relations between the two countries, see, in general, D. Barlas, 'Friends or Foes? Diplomatic Relations Between Italy and Turkey, 1923–36' [2004] 36 *International Journal of Middle East Studies*, 231.

59 D. Barlas, n. 58, pp. 237 et seq.

60 F. Pongiluppi, 'La Colonia Italiana di Costantinopoli attraverso gli articoli de La Rassegna Italiana – Organo degl'interessi italiani in Oriente', in: G. Conte et al. (eds.), *Imperia. Lo spazio mediterraneo dal mondo antico all'età contemporanea*, New Digital Frontiers, Palermo 2016, p. 219, at 233 et seqq.

61 For a portrait, see the essays collected in A. De Gasperi and R. Ferrazza (eds.), *Italiani di Istanbul: figure, comunità e istituzioni dalle Riforme alla Repubblica 1839–1923*, Fondazione Giovanni Agnelli, Torino 2007.

The Consular Convention of 1929 was an element of the measures through which Italy and Turkey attempted to consolidate the new stage of their relationship. The short time needed for its negotiation and entry into force permitted the Convention to survive the subsequent deterioration of relations between the countries.

Today, the practical relevance of the Convention is apparently very limited. This plausibly reflects the rather small number of Turks living in Italy (they were 19,509 in 2018),[62] as well as the even smaller size of the Italian community in Turkey.

2.2.3. The Rules Relating to Succession: An Overview

Succession upon death specifically forms the object of Article 21 of the Convention. Article 21(1) to (10), and also (12) to (14), deal with the tasks that the consular authorities of the State of nationality of the deceased are permitted to discharge on the territory of the other Contracting State, in particular as regards the protection and the administration of the assets of the deceased.[63] These provisions will not be examined here – save for a passage of Article 21(8), which is meant to complement Article 21(11) – since they do not serve a private international law function.

Article 21(11) and (15), the only provisions that affect the operation of the European Succession Regulation, lay down rules on jurisdiction and the applicable law concerning, respectively, succession to movable and immovable property. They will be analyzed below in some detail.

Article 21(11) is also concerned with the recognition of judgments relating to succession to movable property rendered by the courts of the Contracting State of nationality of the deceased (although the provision in fact merely states that those judgments enjoy recognition, without more). Article 21(15) does not include a corresponding rule on recognition. As indicated above, the rules on the recognition of judgments included in conventions between a Member State and a third country do not have, as such, a bearing on the Regulation. Accordingly, that part of Article 21(15) will not be considered in this report.

Finally, Article 21(16) clarifies the scope of application of the above provisions.

No published judgments could be retrieved in Italian databases which mention, let alone discuss, the private international law rules in the Convention of 1929. Similarly, no documented evidence exists as to the practice of Italian notaries regarding the above provisions. The practice of the Italian consular offices in Turkey is likewise undocumented. Contributions by Italian scholars

62 <http://istat.it> accessed 04.04.2019.

63 Under Art. 21(7), consular authorities are permitted, *inter alia*, to issue certificates to be used by the heirs: 'délivrer des certificats aux héritiers en vue de leur légitimation'.

are also virtually non-existent: the Convention has been the object of a limited number of short works, most of which hardly go beyond a mere restatement of its main provisions.[64]

2.2.4. Scope of Application of the Rules on Successions

Article 21 of the Convention explicitly states that it regulates succession to movable and immovable property. Consistent with the broad language employed, the provision must be deemed to cover testamentary and intestate successions alike.[65]

It is not immediately clear, based on their rather imprecise wording, whether the provisions in Article 21(11) and (15) are meant to apply to any proceedings whose subject matter is the succession of a national of the two States and to any issue as may arise in connection therewith.

Concerning movables, the conflict-of-laws rule in Article 21(11) speaks, broadly, of 'droit successoral' (a general formula which could be translated as 'the law of succession' or the 'right to inherit'). It adds, however, a definitely more specific reference to the sharing out of the estate ('partage'). The jurisdictional rule in the same provision contemplates the questions which may arise regarding the title to an inheritance or legacy ('questions reposant sur le titre d'hérédité ou des legs'), as well as the questions affecting the right to benefit from the succession and the sharing out of the estate ('le droit à ladite succession ou à son partage').

As to immovable property, Article 21(15) begins by laying down a conflict-of-laws rule which applies – the language is the same as the jurisdictional rule for movables – to the title to an inheritance or legacy, the right to benefit from the succession and the sharing out of the estate. Jurisdiction is governed by the same provision under a particularly broad wording, encompassing any claim or dispute relating to the succession to immovable property ('toutes demandes ou contestations concernant les successions immobilières'). This language suggests that Article 21(11) and (15) cover, as regards the applicable law, all issues relating to the substance of succession (the determination of the beneficiaries and their respective shares, forced heirship, disinheritance, the validity of dispositions of property upon death, etc.), and confer jurisdiction

---

64 A short analysis of the text of the Convention, authored by T. Perassi, appeared in [1932] 24 *Rivista di diritto internazionale*, 260. Later literature on the Convention almost exclusively consists of general works on (cross-border) successions, mentioning the Convention of 1929 among the relevant sources and providing a brief account of the principles on which Art. 21(11) and (15) are based. See, for instance, F. Trombetta Panigadi, 'La successione nel diritto internazionale privato' in: G. Bonilini (ed.), *Trattato di diritto delle successioni e donazioni*, Giuffrè, Milano 2009, vol. V, p. 211, at 216.

65 E. Vitta, n. 9, p. 116.

over any dispute in matters of succession. Only contentious cases, it is submitted, are contemplated by the jurisdictional rules in Article 21(11) and (15): the words 'demandes', 'contestations' and 'questions', albeit not unequivocally, seem to imply – taken together – a reference to litigation. Non-contentious proceedings and proceedings otherwise unable to affect the outcome of disputes (including proceedings to obtain an order for provisional or protective measures) should accordingly be regarded, it is argued, as falling outside the scope of the above provisions.

On a different note, the Convention solely applies to such movable and immovable property belonging to a national of one Contracting State as may be found on the territory of the other. Here, too, the language of the relevant provisions lacks the desired degree of clarity. The proposed interpretation rests, however, on the following findings.

First, Article 21(1), which apparently shapes the scope of application of the subsequent parts of the provision, speaks of the succession to movable property belonging to a national of a High Contracting Party *on the territory of the other* ('les successions mobilières des sujets de l'une des Hautes Parties Contractantes sur le territoire de l'autre').

Second, Article 21(11) submits the succession to immovable property to the *lex rei sitae* and confers jurisdiction over matters relating to that property on the courts of the Contracting State where the assets are situated. This part of the provision clearly fails to consider the fate of property located elsewhere.

Third, Article 21(16) clarifies, as will be seen below in more detail, that the Convention can be resorted to also where a national of a Contracting State dies outside the territory of the other. Still, in the latter event, the regime laid down in the Convention will apply – it is stated – only to such movable and immovable property as is located on the territory of a Contracting State ('biens meubles et immeubles qui se trouvent sur le territoire de l'une des Parties').

2.2.5. Conditions of Applicability

2.2.5.1. Nationality

The applicability of Article 21 is confined, in each Contracting State, to the succession of persons who hold the nationality of the other Contracting State.

No provision can be found in the Convention clarifying how dual and multiple nationals should be treated for the purposes of the rules on succession. In the absence of documented practice, the gap must be filled based on the object and purpose of the Convention.

The Convention, it is contended, should be deemed to be inoperative whenever the deceased held both Turkish and Italian nationality. Like the Consular Convention between Italy and Switzerland of 1868 (**Treaty 20**), examined above, the Convention between Italy and Turkey is, plausibly, only concerned with the protection, on the territory of each Contracting State, of those individuals who would otherwise suffer from the lack of protection by the authorities of the country of nationality. The Convention, in other words, deals with the assets left by a Turkish national in Italy or an Italian in Turkey, on the assumption that it could be difficult or impossible for the authorities of the country of nationality – absent a convention – to effectively protect and administer those assets. That said, if the deceased happens to be also a national of the territorial State, capable as such of soliciting the intervention of local authorities, the above concern simply ceases to exist.

By contrast, nothing prevents the Convention from applying, in a Contracting State, where the deceased concurrently held the nationality of the other Contracting State along with the nationality of one or more third countries. For reasons similar to those illustrated above with reference to the Convention between Italy and Switzerland, it is believed that the authorities of each Contracting State should resort to the Convention on the mere ground that the deceased possessed the nationality of the other Contracting State, no matter whether his or her ties with the other country of which he is a national appear to be stronger and more significant.[66]

---

66 Arguably, the applicability of the Convention merely rests, in a Contracting State, on the fact that the deceased possessed the nationality of the other Contracting State, no matter how effective that bond may be. If a different reading were espoused, the Convention would turn out to be inapplicable to, say, the succession of a Turkish-French national who died in Italy, where, in the view of the competent Italian court, the ties of the *de cuius* with France had been stronger than his or her ties with Turkey. A similar conclusion, it is believed, would hardly be compatible with the object and purpose of the Consular Convention. By virtue of the Convention, Italy undertook to protect Turkish nationals by dealing with their estates in the manner stipulated by the Convention itself. Turkey is thus entitled to expect that Italian authorities will conform to Art. 21 of the Convention each time the succession of a Turkish national is at issue. Would the 'more effective' French nationality of the deceased provide Italy with a sufficient excuse for not meeting such expectations in the example above? The question must arguably be answered in the negative. True enough, effectiveness as a means to address the problem raised by dual and multiple nationals has gained importance in domestic systems of private international law. This approach, however, does not seem to be required – when it comes to conflicts of laws or conflicts of jurisdiction – by any rule of public international law (admittedly, the principle of effectiveness plays a role in the rules of public international law regarding diplomatic protection, yet nothing indicates that the treatment of dual nationals for private international law purposes should necessarily follow the same rules that govern the treatment of dual nations for the purposes of diplomatic protection). In these circumstances, if the Italian court seized of the succession of the dual Turkish-French national of the example above were to rule out the applicability of the Convention based on the non-effectiveness of the Turkish nationality, the failure of Italy to adhere to its international obligations under the Consular Convention could not be justified for reasons admitted by the law of treaties or the law of the responsibility of States for international wrongful acts. Readers are warned that the above interpretation does not coincide with that suggested by B. S. Güneş in her contribution to this volume.

2.2.5.2. Place of Death and Domicile

It is unclear whether the applicability of the Convention in a Contracting State rests on the fact that the *de cuius* died on the territory of that State or was domiciled there when he or she passed away. Article 21(2) includes a reference to the place of death, but it does so for the mere purpose of providing that the authorities of the Contracting State where a national of the other State has died must inform the consular authorities of the latter country.

The applicability of the remaining provisions in Article 21, including those on jurisdiction and the applicable law that appear in paragraphs (11) and (15), does not seem to depend, contrary to their wording, on either the place of death or the last domicile of the *de cuius*. One must also consider, however, Article 21(16) of the Convention. This clarifies that the provisions in Article 21 apply 'by analogy' ('par analogie') to such movable and immovable property as is located on the territory of one contracting party, insofar as it belongs to the estate of a national of the other contracting party who died outside such territory.

This indicates, albeit with some linguistic contortion, that the applicability of Article 21(11) and (15) in a Contracting State is indeed contingent, as a matter of principle, on the place of death being situated on the territory of that State, but that – failing that condition – the above provisions will nevertheless apply by means of analogy, provided that property belonging to a national of the other Contracting State is situated on that territory.

2.2.6. The Scissionist Approach

The Consular Convention with Turkey is noteworthy in that it follows a scissionist approach. Succession to movable property and succession to immovable property are governed by distinct rules which designate, respectively, the State of nationality (the courts therein, the law thereof), and the State where the property is situated.

The option taken by the authors of the Convention departs from the solution followed by the Italian rules of private international law of that time,[67] which enshrined the principle of unity, and rather reflects the approach underlying the rules in force in Turkey.

No evidence exists to suggest that Italy might have insisted, in the negotiations, on the adoption of a monist approach. On the contrary, Italy had already showed its readiness to depart from monism in other bilateral conventions of that time (now abrogated), such as the Treaty of Commerce and Navigation with the Soviet

---

67 Art. 8 of the introductory provisions to the Civil Code of 1865.

Union of 7 February 1924 (Article 11(1))[68] and the Consular and Establishment Convention with Yugoslavia of 21 August 1924 (Article 4(2)).[69]

The Convention fails to clarify what exactly makes property movable or immovable for the purposes of Article 21. Due to the lack of published case law and notarial or consular practice, one can only speculate about the way in which the courts or other authorities in the two States would characterize a particular item of property as being movable or immovable for the application of the above provisions. The courts of each State might be inclined to rely on the definitions provided under their domestic law. To the extent to which these definitions do not coincide, such an inward-looking approach may lead to either negative or positive conflicts of jurisdiction, and eventually frustrate the harmony of solutions that the Convention plausibly seeks to ensure by laying down uniform conflict-of-laws rules. Efforts, it is submitted, should be deployed to ground the characterization of property for the purposes of the Convention on an understanding of the above notions common to the two countries, thereby avoiding the risks of parochial readings. Admittedly, such a common ground may in some instances be difficult to substantiate.

2.2.7. Succession to Movable Property

Article 21(11) of the Convention submits succession to movable property to the *lex patriae* of the deceased. It also confers jurisdiction on issues relating to succession to the courts of the country of which the deceased was a national.

2.2.7.1. Jurisdiction

It is not specified whether the jurisdiction conferred under Article 21(11) is exclusive in nature or can be derogated from by means of an express agreement between the litigants or by means of tacit submission. Article 21(15), by contrast, explicitly states that jurisdiction to rule on matters regarding succession to immovable property lies exclusively ('exclusivement') with the courts of the Contracting State where such property is situated.

The difference in language between one provision and the other, and the legal background against which they have been elaborated, suggests that, when it comes to movable property as opposed to immovables, the Convention can in fact be derogated from by agreement or submission.

The roots of the provisions on jurisdiction in Article 21 can be traced back to Article 16 of the Treaty of Lausanne, mentioned above. This granted exclusive

[68] *Gazzetta ufficiale del Regno d'Italia*, No. 68 of 20.03.1924.
[69] *Gazzetta ufficiale del Regno d'Italia*, No. 234 of 08.10.1928.

jurisdiction in matters relating to the succession of non-Muslim nationals of the other contracting powers in Turkey to the courts of the State of nationality of the deceased, adding that the latter rule could nonetheless be departed from by submission to the jurisdiction of Turkish courts.[70]

The Consular Convention of 1929, though not explicitly providing for an exception in the event of submission, turned the rule in the Lausanne convention into a perfectly bilateral provision (thereby displaying the will of the parties to put an end to the asymmetry that used to characterize the relationship between western countries and Turkey), split its scope in two so as to distinguish the fate of movables from that of immovables, and limited the conferral of exclusive jurisdiction to disputes regarding the latter.

Read against this background, Article 21(11) of the Convention with Turkey should be interpreted, it is argued, as vesting the courts of the State of nationality with non-exclusive jurisdiction over disputes concerning succession to movables.[71] This means that Italian courts would not infringe the Convention by ruling on a claim regarding the succession to the movable property of a Turkish national in Italy whenever the parties to the litigation had agreed on, or otherwise submitted to, the jurisdiction of Italian courts.

Be that as it may, the jurisdiction of the courts of the State of nationality of the deceased suffers from a limitation resulting from Article 21(8). The courts of the Contracting State where the property is situated retain for three months after the opening of the succession was made public (or for four months after the *de cuius* died, whichever delay runs first) the power to rule on any dispute relating to the estate, other than disputes over title to an inheritance or legacy.

The rule complements the provision in Article 21(6), pursuant to which the consular authorities of the State of the deceased must, during the said period, preserve the movable assets of the *de cuius*, the proceeds of their sale, if any, and also any sum recovered in the interest of the estate. The jurisdiction of local courts exists for such claims as may arise when these tasks are discharged by the consular authorities.

---

70 Art. 16(1): 'In matters of personal status, i.e., [...] in matters relating to succession to personality, whether by will or on intestacy, and the distribution and winding up of estates ... it is agreed between Turkey and the other contracting Powers that, as regards non-Moslem nationals of such Powers in Turkey, the national tribunals or other competent national authorities established in the country of which the party whose personal status is in question will alone have jurisdiction.' Art. 16(3): 'By way of exception to the first paragraph of this Article, the Turkish courts will also have jurisdiction in the matters referred to therein, if all the parties to the case submit in writing to the jurisdiction of the said courts. In such case the Turkish courts will apply the national law of the parties.'

71 The finding, readers should be aware, does not correspond with the conclusions reached on the same issue by B. S. Güneş in her contribution to this volume.

2.2.7.2. Applicable Law

As regards conflicts of laws, Article 21(5) limits itself to submitting the succession to movables to the *lex patriae* of the deceased. No further details are provided by the Convention concerning the operation of the rule.

The Convention is silent as regards the possibility, for the *de cuius*, to depart from the above rule by means of a choice of law. This silence, it is submitted, implies that no departure from the *lex patriae* is permitted under the Convention. The conflict-of-laws rule in Article 21(11), considered in light of the options generally followed by the private international law legislation at the time when the Convention was made, is to be understood as mandatory in nature.

It may be questioned, on a different note, whether the issue of the applicable law should be treated, under the Convention, as independent from the issue of jurisdiction. Clearly enough, Article 21 rests on the idea that the *forum* and *ius* should normally converge: the same connecting factor is employed for both jurisdiction and applicable law, as regards movables as well as immovables (as will be seen below). That said, since the rule on jurisdiction over movables in Article 12(11) can be derogated from by agreement or tacit submission, the problem arises of whether the courts of the Contracting State that would normally lack jurisdiction, but for the agreement or the submission, should still comply with the relevant conflict-of-laws rule in the Convention. In other words, whether the Turkish court seized by agreement of a dispute regarding succession to the movables left in Turkey by an Italian deceased should still apply Italian law.

The question, it is believed, should be answered in the affirmative. Within Article 21(11), different subparagraphs address the jurisdictional and conflict-of-laws issues. Clearly, a link exists between the various rules which make up the provision as a whole, but nothing seems to indicate that the link is such that the different parts must either stand together, or fall together.

It is worth adding that, while the jurisdictional rule in Article 21(11) merely applies, as suggested above, to contentious proceedings, the conflict-of-laws rule in the same provision is likely to come into consideration in settings other than litigation. Thus, if the substance of the succession of a Turkish national is to be assessed in the framework of non-contentious proceedings in Italy, the seized court will still be required to avail itself of the conflict-of-laws rule in Article 21(11).

2.2.8. Succession to Immovable Property

Pursuant to Article 21(15), succession to immovable property is governed by the law of the Contracting State where that property is situated, and jurisdiction lies *exclusively* with the courts or other competent authorities of that country.

Here, too, as with movables, the Convention follows as a matter of principle the formula *lex propria in foro proprio*. However, the question whether the issue of jurisdiction and the issue of the applicable law can be dealt with separately presents itself under a different light, since the courts of the country of nationality appear to be barred from extending their jurisdiction over the immovable property of the deceased, regardless of the agreement of the parties.

3. THE IMPACT OF THE CONVENTIONS CONCERNED ON THE OPERATION OF THE EUROPEAN SUCCESSION REGULATION IN ITALY

Under Article 75 of the European Succession Regulation, Italy is not required to conform with the provisions in the Regulation itself whenever doing so would result in the infringement of its international obligations vis-à-vis Switzerland or Turkey, as they result from the conventions examined above (**Treaties 20 and 21**).

This means that, while the Regulation remains applicable as a matter of principle to the situations covered by the two conventions, the provisions of the latter must be displaced to the extent to which their application would amount to a breach of those conventions. Actually, the problem with Article 75 is not one of delimitation and mutual exclusion of EU and conventional regimes, but rather one of coordination. Otherwise stated, the question is not (or is not only) whether a given case falls under a certain convention and is accordingly governed by the provisions therein instead of the Regulation. Rather, where the case is one to which a convention is applicable, the question is the manner in which the Regulation and the convention interact.

The following sections illustrate by means of examples the relationship and possible interaction of the conventions and the Regulation in light of Article 75.

3.1. THE IMPACT OF THE CONVENTION WITH SWITZERLAND

3.1.1. Case No. 1

The scenario – A dispute arises regarding the succession of a Swiss national who had moved from Switzerland to Italy and whose last habitual residence was in Italy.

In accordance with the Regulation, namely Article 4 thereof, Italian courts would normally be entitled to rule on the case. They will, however, be barred from doing so out of respect for the Consular Convention between Italy and Switzerland (**Treaty 20**), since – pursuant to Article 17(4) of the Convention – jurisdiction over the dispute lies instead with the court in Switzerland as the place of origin of the deceased.

That said, since the jurisdictional regime of the Convention should not be regarded as exclusive, the courts of Italy would not infringe the Convention by asserting jurisdiction over the matter if the litigants agreed on having the case tried in Italy, or tacitly submitted to the jurisdiction of Italian courts.

The will of the litigants, in the above scenario, does not entail as such a conferral of jurisdiction (as would be the case of the will expressed through a choice-of-court agreement pursuant to Article 5 of the Regulation). Its legal effect is merely to suppress an obstacle that would otherwise restrict the operation of the Regulation, i.e., the deference Italian courts owe to the jurisdiction of Swiss courts. As soon as the parties to the dispute agree that they do not wish to avail themselves of the rules in the Convention, Italian courts are free to rely on the Regulation to assert their jurisdiction as they no longer run the risk of breaching the international obligations of Italy in regard to Switzerland.

3.1.2. Case No. 2

The scenario – The same as in Case No. 1, save for one variation, namely that no dispute exists regarding the succession. Rather, the widow of the deceased simply wishes to exercise her rights as heir in respect of the estate, which comprises assets situated on the territory of several Member States.

For this, she would normally seek a European Certificate of Succession. Pursuant to Article 64 of the European Succession Regulation, the power to issue such a Certificate lies with the competent authorities of 'the Member State whose courts have jurisdiction under Article 4, Article 7, Article 10 or Article 11' of the Regulation itself, that is, in these circumstances, the authorities of Italy.

It is believed that nothing in the Consular and Establishment Convention between Italy and Switzerland (**Treaty 20**) prevents the Italian authorities – specifically, the notaries – from issuing a European Certificate of Succession in the scenario described. Article 17(3) and (4) of the Convention are solely concerned with the power to adjudicate disputes relating to succession. They do not affect the ability of the courts and other authorities of a Contracting State to discharge functions other than adjudication, such as certification powers.

True enough, the Certificate will then reflect the rights relating to the estate as they appear to exist under the law applicable to the succession pursuant to the Regulation. Should the rights attested in the certificate become the object of a dispute, the jurisdiction to hear the case will, as a rule, belong to Swiss courts. This change of perspective might, in principle, change the whole picture: the above courts will look at the matter through the lens of Swiss conflict-of-laws rules and might be instructed by the law designated thereunder to enforce succession rights that differ to some extent from those attested in the Certificate.

A risk of this kind, however, is mitigated, if not averted in its entirety, under Article 91(1) of the Swiss Federal Statute on Private International Law, i.e. the conflict-of-laws rule that a Swiss court would rely upon if seized of a dispute concerning the succession of a Swiss national having lived in Italy (assuming, for the reasons illustrated earlier, that the 1868 Convention is not concerned, as such, with the determination of the law applicable to the succession). Under Article 91(1), the law governing the succession of those who died while domiciled abroad is the law designated under the conflict-of-laws rules in force in the country of domicile, i.e. in these circumstances, the rules in the Regulation.

3.2. THE IMPACT OF THE CONVENTION WITH TURKEY

3.2.1. Case No. 1

The scenario – A Turkish national dies while habitually residing in Italy. He leaves an estate consisting of movable and immovable property located in Italy and in other Member States.

Should a dispute arise relating to the succession, Italian courts will not be able to rule on the whole of the succession, although they normally would on the ground of Article 4 of the Regulation. Specifically, they will not be entitled to hear the matter insofar as it concerns the succession to movable property situated on Italian territory. A ruling given on the latter issue would amount to an infringement of Article 21(11) of the Convention (**Treaty 21**) since, according to that provision, the matter should under the circumstances be decided by Turkish courts, unless the parties agree otherwise.

Measures aimed at protecting the estate on a provisional basis may still be granted in Italy, since – according to the preferred reading – the Convention, as far as jurisdiction is concerned, relates only to contentious proceedings.

3.2.2. Case No. 2

The scenario – The *de cuius*, a national of Turkey, dies while habitually residing in Belgium. His estate includes immovable property located in Italy. A dispute arises regarding the succession.

In a case like this, Italian courts would normally be required by the Regulation to decline their jurisdiction: it is for Belgian courts, as a rule, to deal with the case. However, since Article 21(15) of the Convention (**Treaty 21**) (in combination with Article 21(16)) grants jurisdiction over immovables to the courts of the State of the situs, one would argue that Italian courts can nevertheless, via Article 75, rule on the succession to the immovable property situated in Italy.

The latter finding cannot be endorsed without further qualifications. The crucial point is whether, in these circumstances, the Consular Convention between Italy and Turkey *requires* Italy to assume jurisdiction, instead of simply *allowing* Italian courts to do so.

The relevance of the distinction lies in the fact that Article 351 TFEU, the provision embodying the general principle on which Article 75 of the Regulation is built, is understood to preserve the pre-existing international obligations of the Member States, as opposed to their rights. This means that when an international agreement allows a Member State to adopt a measure which appears to be contrary to EU law, the Member State in question must refrain from adopting such a measure.[72] Subordination clauses – Article 75 of the European Succession Regulation no less than Article 351 TFEU – simply do not permit a Member State to rely on an international convention in order to do more than the latter demands.

It is hard to say, given the lack of authority and relevant practice, whether the exercise of jurisdiction under Article 21(16) is compulsory rather than optional. The most persuasive reading is that Italian courts, in the case under examination, cannot abstain from ruling on the matter. If they did abstain, they would infringe the Convention. This is because the jurisdiction conferred on the *forum rei sitae* is exclusive in nature. The courts of Turkey are in fact barred from taking up the case, and if the courts in both countries were to decline their jurisdiction, the claimant would be at risk of suffering from a denial of justice. The Convention can hardly be interpreted as making room for a similar outcome (the fact that the courts of Belgium would indeed be available to hear the case does not really change the picture). Turkish authorities cannot, as a matter of international law, rely on this availability: they are entitled to expect that Italian courts will entertain the case.

That said, it is believed that the Italian court seized of the matter would not infringe the obligations of Italy towards Turkey by staying the proceedings before it, under Article 17 of the Regulation, whenever proceedings involving the same cause of action and between the same parties have been brought in Belgium prior to the case being brought in Italy. While requiring the courts of the situs to assume jurisdiction, the Consular Convention, it is contended, does not go as far as to determine the way in which proceedings should be conducted, especially when the need arises to address the problem of parallel litigation.

3.2.3. Case No. 3

The scenario – Two spouses, both of Turkish nationality, move to Italy with their children. The mother dies there. Her estate consists of movable property, all of which is located in Italy. A dispute arises between the surviving husband,

---

[72] Case C-324/93, *The Queen v. Secretary of State for Home Department, ex parte Evans Medical Ltd and Macfarlan Smith Ltd*, ECLI:EU:C:1995:84, para. 32.

on the one hand, and the children, on the other. All submit to the jurisdiction of Italian courts.

The Italian court seized of the matter would normally rule on the merits of the case in conformity with Italian law, under Article 21(1) of the European Succession Regulation, Italy being the State where the deceased had her last habitual residence.

The Consular Convention (**Treaty 21**) requires otherwise. Pursuant to the conflict-of-laws rule in Article 21(11), the matter is to be decided in accordance with Turkish law.

What if Turkish law, as applicable in the circumstances, proved irretrievably at odds with a fundamental principle of the Italian legal system? The Consular Convention does not contemplate, at least not explicitly, a public policy exception.

Does this mean that the Convention requires the application of the law specified thereunder in each and every case, no matter how serious the reasons may be for not doing so in particular circumstances? The answer is plausibly no: the Convention was not meant to be so strict. The customary rules governing the international responsibility of States, as they stood at the time of the Convention's conclusion, allowed States, 'in extreme cases of necessity', to 'commit what would ordinarily be an infraction of the Law of Nations'.[73] Necessity served, then, as an excuse for an internationally wrongful conduct pursuant to conditions that were far more liberal than those codified presently in Article 25 of the Draft Articles on the Responsibility of States as adopted in 2001 by the International Law Commission.[74]

All in all, this suggests that, back in 1929, the negotiators of the Consular Convention between Italy and Turkey probably believed that an express provision on public policy (a rare occurrence in the private international law conventions of the time) was unnecessary, as it would have simply stated the obvious.[75]

3.3. ASSESSMENT

The Consular and Establishment Convention between Italy and Switzerland (**Treaty 20**) and the Consular Convention between Italy and Turkey (**Treaty 21**) bring about a rather limited, but not at all negligible, interference with the European Succession Regulation.

73 A. S. Hershey, *The Essentials of International Public Law and Organization*, 2nd ed., Macmillan, New York 1927, pp. 231 et seq.

74 <http://legal.un.org/ilc> accessed 04.04.2019.

75 According to D. Anzilotti, *Corso di diritto internazionale*, 3rd ed., Athenaeum, Roma 1928, p. 457, the authority of international law finds its logical limitation in the States' right to self-preservation ('limite logico dell'obbligatorietà del diritto internazionale').

The two conventions presumably call for their consideration in a small number of cases. In these cases, however, they have the ability to alter rather distinctively the ordinary operation of the European regime.

Admittedly, there may be excellent political reasons for keeping the two agreements unchanged. That said, the 'quality' of the private international law provisions therein is far from satisfactory.

Both texts fall short, quite obviously, in terms of technical refinement. Cross-border successions give rise to a broad range of inter-connected issues, which call in turn for a sufficiently rich set of well-crafted and sensible solutions.

Generally speaking, the conventions examined suffer from two (largely interrelated) technical shortcomings.

First, they fail to grasp the complexity of the phenomenon of succession as resulting – today – from the variety of policies underlying this area of law (from legal certainty to the self-determination of the *de cuius*, from the protection of weaker family members to the preservation of the ability of States to govern the use of strategic or socially sensitive assets) and from the variety of the issues that surround a transfer of ownership as well as other rights upon death (a challenge to which modern private international law tends to respond by increasing the degree of specialization in its rules). The tools provided by the two conventions are clearly insufficient. This is particularly evident with estate planning. Efficient and reliable planning, a crucial concern, requires dedicated rules of private international law, capable of enhancing certainty while discouraging fraudulent or abusive practices. Nothing of the kind can be found in the conventions with Switzerland and Turkey.

Second, they lack a sufficient degree of flexibility. They were conceived at a time when the mobility of individuals and assets across borders was simply a fraction of what it is today and when it had clearly not reached the rapidity which is typical of contemporary 'liquid' societies. The scenarios that the drafters of the 1868 and 1929 conventions presumably considered as typical were centred on persons who left their country of origin on an almost definitive basis (whereas today's mobility is often peripatetic and circular) and on financial interests which were always easy to situate in space (whereas a growing share of a person's assets today consists of immaterial goods or assets that can change their locality swiftly and seamlessly).

3.4. PROSPECTS

The above findings suggest that the cases that fall with the scope of the two conventions would be dealt with more satisfactorily in Italy if, instead, either the European Succession Regulation were applied or if the pertinent provisions in the conventions were – at least – amended or clarified by means of (authentic) interpretation.

It is not the purpose of this contribution to discuss in which manner and subject to which limitations individual Member States are entitled (if not indeed required) to act internationally in respect of those conventions covering topics subsequently covered by EU legislation.

Suffice it to note that, apparently, no initiative of this kind has been taken by the Italian government regarding the Consular Convention with Turkey (**Treaty 21**). As regards the Consular and Establishment Convention with Switzerland (**Treaty 20**), various scholars in the two countries have called for the revision of the relevant private international law rules.[76] However, no official steps have been taken so far by the two governments in that direction.

76 See, among others, G. Broggini, 'La nouvelle loi italienne de droit international privé' [1996] 4 *Schweizerische Zeitschrift für internationales und europäisches Recht* 25.

PART II

THE PERSPECTIVE OF THIRD STATES

THE RELATIONS OF BOSNIA AND HERZEGOVINA, SERBIA, NORTH MACEDONIA AND MONTENEGRO WITH EU MEMBER STATES

Slavko Đorđević and Zlatan Meškić

1. INTRODUCTION

In the 1950s and 1960s, former Yugoslavia entered into bilateral treaties on legal assistance with Austria (**Treaty 3**), Bulgaria (**Treaty 22**), Czechoslovakia (**Treaty 13**), Hungary (**Treaty 25**), Poland (**Treaty 26**) and Romania (**Treaty 27**). Today these treaties are in force between the four successor countries of Yugoslavia – i.e. Serbia, Bosnia and Herzegovina (henceforth: B&H), North Macedonia (henceforth: Macedonia) and Montenegro – and all the above-mentioned European countries, which in the meantime have become EU Member States (in the case of Czechoslovakia, the Czech Republic and Slovakia as its successors). Each of these bilateral treaties contains the conflict-of-laws rules and procedural rules on succession that take precedence over, respectively, the rules of the Succession Regulation (Article 75(1)) in the contracting parties that are now EU Member States and the national private international law (PIL) rules in the four successor countries of former Yugoslavia that are not EU members. As these rules are based on the principle of nationality and the principle of the location of the estate, they are completely incompatible with the rules of the Succession Regulation and are, therefore, undesirable in the EU Member States. From the perspective of the successor countries of former Yugoslavia, a general assessment of the rules on succession contained in bilateral treaties cannot be given, mainly because international succession law is not consistently regulated in the successor countries: the rules of Serbian, B&H and Macedonian international succession law are based on traditional principles that correspond to those of the bilateral treaties, while the rules of Montenegrin international succession law follow the principles contained in the Succession Regulation. In order to make a proper assessment, it is first necessary to make a few remarks on the conflict-of-laws and procedural rules on succession in Serbia, B&H, Macedonia and Montenegro and then to look into the conflict-of-laws regimes and the procedural rules of the bilateral treaties in detail.

2. A FEW REMARKS ON NATIONAL PRIVATE INTERNATIONAL LAW RULES IN SUCCESSION MATTERS

2.1. SERBIA AND BOSNIA AND HERZEGOVINA

The main legal source of private international law in Serbia and B&H is the Act on Resolution of Conflict of Laws with Regulations of Other Countries[1]

---

1 Zakon o rešavanju sukoba zakona sa propisima drugih zemalja, Official Gazette of SFRY, No. 43/82 and 72/82.

(henceforth: PIL Act), which was enacted in 1982 in the former Socialist Federal Republic of Yugoslavia (henceforth: SFRY) and is, with minor amendments, still in force today in both countries.[2] With regard to succession matters, the PIL Act contains conflict-of-laws rules and jurisdiction rules which will be presented briefly in this contribution. In addition, the law of B&H recognizes special procedural rules on handing over and retaining movable property in succession cases with a foreign element – which deserve our attention, too, considering that almost all bilateral agreements discussed in this contribution regulate these procedural issues.

2.1.1. Conflict-of-Laws Rules

Article 30(1) PIL Act contains the general conflict-of-laws rule on succession that adopts the nationality of the deceased as the sole connecting factor and that follows the so-called principle of unity of succession. Pursuant to this rule, the succession as a whole is to be governed by the law of the State whose nationality the deceased had at the time of his/her death. The national law of the deceased applies to all substantive issues of intestate and testamentary succession, except the capacity to make a will, which is, pursuant to the special conflict-of-laws rule of Article 30(2) PIL Act, governed by the law of the State whose nationality the testator had at the time of making the will.[3] It is obvious that these conflict-of-laws rules have almost nothing in common with those of the Succession Regulation, which are based on completely different principles.

In the case of multiple nationalities of the deceased (or the testator), the conflict-of-laws rules of Article 30 PIL Act are to be complemented by the interpretative rules of Article 11 PIL Act. If the deceased (or the testator) possessed Serbian/Bosnian (domestic) nationality and the nationality of

---

2 For Serbia see: Zakon o rešavanju sukoba zakona sa propisima drugih zemalja, Official Gazette of SFRY, No. 43/82 and 72/82, Official Gazette of the Federal Republic of Yugoslavia (FRY), No. 46/96 and Official Gazette of Republic of Serbia, No. 46/2006 – other laws; for Bosnia and Herzegovina see: Zakon o rešavanju sukoba zakona sa propisima drugih zemalja, Official Gazette of SFRY, Nos. 43/82 and 72/82 and Official Gazette of Republic of Bosnia and Herzegovina No. 2/1992.

3 On Art. 30(1) and (2) PIL Act see in detail S. Đorđević, 'Länderbericht Serbien' in W. Burandt, D. Rojahn (ed.), *Erbrecht*, 2nd ed., C.H. Beck, Munich 2014, pp. 1622–1623; M. Stanivuković and M. Živković, 'Serbia' in Bea Verschraegen (ed.), *International Encyclopedia of Laws*, vol. 2, Private International Law, supp. 21, Kluwer Law International, Alphen aan den Rijn 2009, pp. 216 et seqq.; Z. Meškić and S. Đorđević, 'Bosnia nad Herzegovina' in B. Verschraegen (ed.), *International Encyclopedia of Laws*, Private International Law, supp. 56 (Kluwer Law International, Alphen aan den Rijin 2018), pp. 132 et seqq.; M. Dika, G. Knežević and S. Stojanović, *Komentar Zakona o medđunarodnom privatnom i procesnom pravu*, Nomos, Belgrade 1991, pp. 101–108; T. Varady, B. Bordaš, G. Knežević and V. Pavić, *Međunarodno privatno pravo*, JP 'Službebni glasnik', Belgrade 2007, pp. 343–347; M. Stanivuković and P. Đundić, *Međunarodno privatno pravo – posebni deo*, 1st ed, Univerzitet u Novom Sadu, Pravni fakultet – Centar za izdavačku delatnost, Novi Sad 2008, pp. 198–199.

other States at the time of death (or at the time of making the will), he/she will be considered to have solely Serbian/Bosnian nationality (Article 11(1)). If he/she had two or more foreign nationalities (none of which is Serbian/Bosnian), the nationality of the State in which he/she had a domicile prevails (Article 11(2)). Finally, if a deceased who possessed multiple foreign nationalities was not domiciled in any of the States of which he/she was a national, he/she will be considered to be a national of one of these States, specifically the one with which he/she had the closest connection (Article 11(3) – effective nationality).[4]

The law applicable to the formal validity of a will is to be determined by the rules of the Hague Testamentary Disposition Convention of 1961, which are implemented in Article 31 PIL Act.[5] It is important to mention that the rules of this Convention apply only to wills and joint wills (which are autonomously defined in Article 4), but not to other dispositions of property upon death, such as agreements as to succession (inheritance contracts), because the Serbian/Bosnian legislature failed to extend the application of this Convention to other dispositions upon death.

2.1.2. *Jurisdiction Rules*

The rules on jurisdiction of the Serbian/Bosnian courts in succession matters are contained in the provisions of Articles 71–73 PIL Act, which apply to the distribution (liquidation) of an estate in non-litigious proceedings as well as to disputes concerning all inheritance claims and creditor claims towards estates in litigious proceedings. They are based on the criteria of distinction between movable and immovable property and the nationality of the deceased, which means that they have hardly anything in common with jurisdiction rules of the Succession Regulation.

The Serbian/B&H courts have exclusive jurisdiction to rule on immovable property which is situated in Serbia/B&H, irrespective of the nationality of the deceased (Articles 71(1), 72(1) and 73(1)). It means, *argumentum a contrario*, that the jurisdiction of Serbian/B&H courts is excluded for immovable property situated abroad.[6] Serbia/B&H is not interested in the succession of immovable

---

4 On Art. 11 PIL Act see M. Dika, G. Knežević and S. Stojanović, above n. 3, pp. 46–48.

5 Namely, Art. 31 PIL Act only repeats the rules of Arts. 1(1) and 2(1) of the Hague Convention of 1961 and introduces one more alternative conflict-of-laws rule (application of *lex fori*) in accordance with the principle of *in favorem testamenti* contained in Art. 3 of the Hague Convention. This means that the formal validity of testamentary dispositions is governed by the rules of the Hague Testamentary Disposition Convention, which are complemented by Art. 31 PIL Act. See in detail M. Stanivuković and M. Živković, above n. 3, p. 219; M. Dika, G. Knežević and S. Stojanović, above n. 3, pp. 108–112.

6 M. Dika, G. Knežević and S. Stojanović, above n. 3, pp. 233–234, 239 and 241; M. Stanivuković and P. Đundić, above n. 3., pp. 195–196; S. Đorđević, 'O problemima

property situated abroad. From their point of view, it is the concern of the foreign State or States in which that immovable property is located, which leads to the conclusion that the unity principle is broken by Serbian/B&H jurisdiction rules.[7] The unity principle may be achieved only if all (immovable and movable) property of the deceased is located in Serbia/B&H.

With regard to movable property, the jurisdiction of Serbian/B&H courts depends on both criteria, i.e. the location of the movable property and the nationality of the deceased. If the deceased was a national of Serbia/B&H, the Serbian/B&H courts have elective jurisdiction to rule on movable property which is situated in Serbia/Bosnia and on movable property which is situated abroad, but in the latter case only if a foreign authority of the State in which movable property is situated has no jurisdiction pursuant to its own law or declines jurisdiction to rule on that property (Article 71(2)). Where the deceased was a foreign national, the courts of Serbia/B&H have jurisdiction to rule on the deceased's movable property situated in Serbia/B&H, unless the court of the deceased's home State has no jurisdiction to rule on the movable property of a Serbian/B&H national (Article 72(2)). It means that domestic courts have no jurisdiction at all to rule on the movable property of a foreign national which is situated abroad, but they may have jurisdiction to rule on his/her movable property situated in Serbia/B&H, if the court of the deceased's home State in analogous situations declares its jurisdiction to rule on movable property of a Serbian/B&H citizen.[8] Finally, where the deceased was stateless or a refugee, the courts of Serbia/B&H have jurisdiction to rule on his/her movable property if the movable property is situated in Serbia/B&H and the deceased was domiciled in Serbia/B&H (Article 73(2)).[9] However, if a stateless deceased was domiciled abroad, the jurisdiction of domestic courts is to be determined in accordance with the provisions on establishing jurisdiction with respect to a deceased who was a foreign national (Article 73(3)).

It should be mentioned that the Act on non-litigious procedure of the Republic of Srpska[10] (henceforth: ANPRS), which is one of the entities of B&H

nekoordiniranog raspravljanja zaostavstine jednog lica u razlicitim pravnim porecima' in S. Bejatovic (ed.), *Pravni sistem Srbije i standardi Evropske unije i Saveta Evrope*, Pravni fakultet u Kragujevcu, Kragujevac 2010, pp. 377–399.

7 However, the Serbian/B&H courts have jurisdiction to rule on immovable property situated abroad only if the deceased was a national of Serbia/B&H and the courts or other authorities of the State where the immovable property is situated have no jurisdiction to rule on that property pursuant to its own law (Art. 71(2) PIL Act). See S. Đorđević, above n. 6, pp. 378–379; S. Đorđević, above n. 3, pp. 1623–1624.

8 See in detail M. Stanivuković and P. Đundić, above n. 3, pp. 197–198.

9 See the interpretation of this provision in M. Dika, G. Knežević and S. Stojanović, above n. 3, p. 241.

10 Official Gazette of Republic Srpska, Nos. 36/2009 and 91/2016.

(B&H is a State with more than one legal order),[11] contains a special and 'a little bit' strange rule on establishing the jurisdiction of domestic courts in succession matters which derogates from the rule of Article 72(2) PIL Act. Pursuant to Article 144(1) ANPRS, although the foreign authority has jurisdiction to rule on movable property of a deceased who was a foreign national, the court of the Republic of Srpska may establish jurisdiction to rule on such property if all heirs who reside in the Republic of Srpska apply for it and all heirs and legatees who reside abroad do not object to it within six months of the court's sending them an invitation or publishing notice in an official journal. Considering that in most cases it is hard to find or reach heirs and legatees who live abroad, it could be concluded that 'domestic' heirs may have a strong influence on establishing the jurisdiction of the home court. However, it seems that this jurisdiction rule has been completely forgotten because no example could be found in the judicial practice of the Republic of Srpska which could confirm that the court of the Republic of Srpska has established its jurisdiction in accordance with Article 144 ANPRS; nor could any comment on this rule be found in B&H private international law literature.

Finally, it should also be mentioned that a choice of court agreement in succession matters is possible, although it is never used in practice. The provisions of Article 49 PIL Act, which contain general rules on prorogation of domestic and foreign courts, also allow for the conclusion of prorogation agreements in succession matters.[12] The parties to such an agreement can be heirs and other beneficiaries. If they intend to agree that the domestic court (i.e. the court of Serbia/B&H) is to have jurisdiction to rule on any succession matter, at least one of them must be a national of Serbia/B&H. If they intend to prorogate the jurisdiction of a foreign court, at least one of them must be of foreign nationality and the dispute in question must not fall under exclusive jurisdiction of Serbian/B&H courts. Therefore, it is clear that the prorogation of jurisdiction of a foreign court is ineffective in respect of immovable property situated in Serbia.

2.1.3. Rules on Handing Over and Retaining Movable Property

The law of both entities of B&H, titled the Federation of B&H (henceforth: FB&H) and the Republic of Srpska, regulate two closely connected procedural issues which may arise in situations in which a foreign court has jurisdiction to rule on movable property of a deceased who was a foreign national. The first one is handing over the movable property of a foreign national which is located

---

11 See Z. Meškić, A. Duraković and J. Alihodžić, 'Bosnien und Herzegowina als ein Mehrrechtsstaat', [2018] *IPRax* 633.

12 See M. Dika, G. Knežević and S. Stojanović, above n. 3, pp. 178–191.

in the home State to the foreign competent authority, and the second one is retaining that movable property in the home State until the foreign competent court finally decides on succession matters. The rules on these issues have been formulated in detail for the first time in the Yugoslav Succession Law Act of 1955, with the aim to protect heirs, legatees and creditors who are nationals of or domiciled or reside in the home State.[13]

Pursuant to Article 255(1) of the Succession Act of FB&H[14] (henceforth: SAFBH) and Article 142(1) ANPRS, if the foreign authority has jurisdiction to conduct succession proceedings, the court in B&H on whose territory the deceased died is to hand over the movable property located in B&H to the competent foreign authority. However, before the court of B&H does that, it is to inform by public notice all heirs, legatees and creditors who reside in B&H to register their claims toward the property within a term which cannot be shorter than 30 days nor longer than six months. If they register the claims, the court in B&H is to retain that movable property or a sufficient part of it until the foreign authority finally decides on such claims (Article 256 SAFBH and Article 143 ANPRS).

It is obvious that handing over movable property to the foreign authority and retaining the same movable property in the home country are essentially acts connected between themselves and, at the same time, with the jurisdiction rules on movable property. It means that courts of B&H can hand over the movable property of a foreign national located in B&H to the foreign competent authority in cases in which it has no jurisdiction to rule on such movable property. Pursuant to (the above-discussed) Article 72(2) PIL Act, it may happen only if the court of the deceased's home State has no jurisdiction to rule on the movable property of a B&H national located in that State at the same time. However, B&H courts may decide to retain the movable property until the decision of a foreign court becomes final, if heirs, legatees or creditors who reside in B&H simply apply for it. The aim of these provisions is to protect the 'domestic' heirs and legatees in order to enable them to obtain their share from movable property located in B&H.[15]

It should be emphasized that the provisions on handing over and retaining movable property do not in practice apply for a long time. The main reason for that is that foreign courts do not request the handing over movable property from the courts of B&H, mainly because their own laws do not recognize such requests. If no one submits a request for handing over movable property located in B&H, there is nothing to retain. Therefore, these provisions may be considered as useless and outdated.

---

13 See O. Antić, *Nasledno pravo*, Narodna knjiga, Belgrade 1994, pp. 310–311; M. Stanivuković and P. Đundić, above n. 3, p. 200.

14 Official Gazette of FB&H, No. 80/2014.

15 See O. Antić, above n. 13, p. 311.

2.2. MACEDONIA

The main legal source of private international law in Macedonia is the Private International Law Act of 2010[16] (henceforth: Mac. PIL Act), which contains in Articles 35–37 and Articles 84–86 the same conflict-of-laws and jurisdiction rules in succession matters as those of Articles 30–31 and Articles 71–73 of the Serbian/B&H PIL Act. What has been previously said with respect to these rules applies here too. Macedonia is also party to the Hague Testamentary Disposition Convention of 1961, whose rules apply to the formal validity of a will.

With regard to handing over and retaining movable property, the Macedonian Act on non-litigious procedure[17] (Articles 189–190) contains the same rules on these issues as the corresponding acts of FB&H and the Republic of Srpska. The observations and criticisms given on these issues in previous sub-sections apply here too.

It should be mentioned that a draft for a new Private International Law Act of Macedonia was authored in 2015 and currently awaits enactment by the Macedonian Parliament.[18] This draft contains conflict-of-laws and jurisdiction rules on succession that are in line with those of the Succession Regulation.

2.3. MONTENEGRO

The main legal source of private international law in Montenegro is the Private International Law Act of 2014[19] (henceforth: Mon. PIL Act), which entirely replaced the Yugoslav PIL Act of 1982. The Mon. PIL Act contains conflict-of-laws and jurisdiction rules in succession matters that are based on the same or similar criteria as those of the Succession Regulation.[20] It means that the Mon. PIL Act also strives to implement the principle of unity of succession on both levels, i.e. the conflict-of-laws level and the jurisdiction level, as has already been done in the Succession Regulation. The habitual residence of the deceased at the time of his/her death is a general connecting factor for determining both the jurisdiction of domestic courts and the applicable law.[21]

---

16 Official Gazette of the Republic of Macedonia, No. 87/2007 and 156/2010.

17 Official Gazette of the Republic of Macedonia, No. 9/2008.

18 See C. Jessel-Holst, 'Makedonija na putu kao modernom međunarodnom privatnom pravu' [2016] *Nova pravna revija – časops za domaće, njemačko i evropsko pravo* 12, pp. 7–14.

19 Official Gazette of the Republic of Montenegro, Nos. 1/2014, 6/2014, 11/2014, 14/2014 and 47/2015.

20 The Mon. PIL Act has borrowed the rules on jurisdiction and the rules for determining the applicable law in succession matters from the Proposal for a Succession Regulation of 2009 and from the MPI Comments on this Proposal (see below n. 23).

21 On the new Montenegrin international succession law see M. Kostić-Mandić, *Međunarodno privatno pravo*, Pravni fakultet Univerziteta Crne Gore, Podgorica 2017, pp. 366–372. See also

2.3.1. *Conflict-of-Laws Rules*

The general conflict-of-laws rule is the same as that of Article 21 Succession Regulation – the law governing the succession as a whole is the law of the State in which the deceased had his/her habitual residence at the time of death (Article 71 Mon. PIL Act).

The Mon. PIL Act contains rules on choice of law which differ from those of Article 22 Succession Regulation. Pursuant to Article 72(1) Mon. PIL Act, a person may choose the law of the State whose nationality he/she possesses or the law of the State in which he/she has habitual residence, both at the time of making the choice or at the time of death. A person may also choose *lex rei sitae* to govern the succession to his/her immovable property (Article 72(2) Mon. PIL Act), which means that the principle of unity may be broken by a testator's will, leading to the application of two or more national laws on succession.[22]

The conflict-of-laws rules for substantive issues regarding the disposition of property upon death (Article 74 Mon. PIL Act) are very similar to those of the Succession Regulation (Articles 24 and 25). The law applicable to the formal validity of dispositions upon death is to be determined by the Hague Testamentary Disposition Convention of 1961.

2.3.2. *Jurisdiction Rules*

The general jurisdiction rule in succession matters of the Mon. PIL Act completely corresponds to that contained in Article 4 of the Succession Regulation – the Montenegrin court has jurisdiction to rule on the succession as a whole if the deceased had his/her habitual residence in Montenegro at the time of death (Article 127 Mon. PIL Act). There are no rules on exclusive jurisdiction.

The Mon. PIL Act contains rules on subsidiary jurisdiction similar to those of Article 10 of the Succession Regulation. The Montenegrin court has jurisdiction to rule on the succession as whole if the assets of the estate are located in Montenegro and if: (a) the law of Montenegro is chosen as the governing law (this rule does not exist in the Succession Regulation); or (b) the deceased had Montenegrin nationality at the time of his/her death. Failing that, the Montenegrin court will have jurisdiction to rule only on those assets which are located in Montenegro.

Finally, the Mon. PIL Act does not contain rules on a choice of court agreement, but rather a special rule on choice of court, which enables a testator to choose the competent court. Namely, under Article 129 Mon. PIL Act,

---

S. Đorđević, 'Länderbericht Montenegro' in W. Burandt, D. Rojahn (eds.), *Erbrecht*, 2nd ed., C.H. Beck, Munich 2014, pp. 1547–1548.

22 On Art. 72 see M. Kostić-Mandić, above n. 21, pp. 369–370.

the testator may indicate that the Montenegrin court has exclusive jurisdiction to rule on his/her whole estate or part of it if he/she has at the same time chosen Montenegrin law to govern his/her succession. This rule does not exist in the Succession Regulation but rather comes from the Max Planck Institute (MPI) Comments on the Proposal for a Succession Regulation 2009.[23]

2.3.3. Rules on Handing Over and Retaining Movable Property

The Act on Non-litigious Procedure of Montenegro[24] (henceforth: ANP Mon.) contains the same rules on handing over and retaining movable property as the corresponding acts of B&H. However, unlike in the B&H legal system, in which these rules complement the jurisdiction rules of the PIL Act B&H, the rules of the ANP Mon. are totally incompatible with the jurisdiction rules of the Mon. PIL Act. In other words, they cannot be applied because they presume that jurisdiction rules are based on the criteria of the deceased's nationality and the distinction of movable and immovable property, which is no longer the case (since enacting the PIL Act in 2014). Therefore, it should be expected that the Montenegrin legislature will terminate these obsolete rules.

3. BILATERAL TREATIES

3.1. OVERVIEW

Yugoslavia concluded six bilateral treaties between 1954 and 1968 with now seven different EU Member States that concern matters governed by the EU Succession Regulation:

- Agreement with Austria on Mutual Legal Assistance of 1954[25] (henceforth: Agreement with Austria **Treaty 3**);
- Agreement with Bulgaria on Mutual Legal Assistance of 1956[26] (henceforth: Agreement with Bulgaria **Treaty 22**);

---

23 Max Planck Institute for Comparative and International Private Law, 'Comments on the European Commission's Proposal for a Regulation of the European Parliament and of the Council on jurisdiction, applicable law, recognition and enforcement of decisions and authentic instruments in matters of succession and the creation of a European Certificate of Succession', [2010] 3 *RabelsZ* 522, also available on <http://www.europarl.europa.eu/document/activities/cont/201005/20100526ATT75035/20100526ATT75035EN.pdf> accessed 04.04.2019.

24 Official Gazette of the Republic of Montenegro, Nos. 27/2006 and 20/2015.

25 Official Gazette of the Federal People's Republic of Yugoslavia – Supplement: International treaties and other agreements, No. 8/55 and OJ of the SFRY, No. 2/83 – other laws.

26 Official Gazette of the Federal People's Republic of Yugoslavia – Supplement: International treaties and other agreements, No. 1/57.

- Agreement with Poland on Mutual Legal Assistance of 1960[27] (henceforth: Agreement with Poland **Treaty 26**);
- Agreement with Romania on Mutual Legal Assistance of 1960[28] (henceforth: Agreement with Romania **Treaty 27**);
- Agreement with Czechoslovakia on Mutual Legal Assistance of 1964[29] (henceforth: Agreement with Czechoslovakia **Treaty 13**);
- Agreement with Hungary on Mutual Legal Assistance of 1968[30] (henceforth Agreement with Hungary **Treaty 25**).

The bilateral agreement with Czechoslovakia is by virtue of succession binding for both the Czech Republic[31] and Slovakia.[32]

Four ex-Yugoslavian republics – and now independent States – which are not yet Member States of the EU are still bound by the above-cited treaties: Bosnia and Herzegovina (B&H); Macedonia; Montenegro; and Serbia. Yugoslavia entered into the treaties under the name of the Federal People's Republic of Yugoslavia and the Socialist Federal Republic of Yugoslavia. B&H,[33] Macedonia,[34] Montenegro[35] and Serbia[36] have gone through changes of State form as well as

27 Official Gazette of the SFRY – Supplement: International treaties and other agreements, No. 5/1963.

28 Official Gazette of the Federal People's Republic of Yugoslavia – Supplement: International treaties and other agreements, No. 8/1961, with the Additional Protocol, Official Gazette of the SFRY – Supplement No. 4/1973.

29 Official Gazette of the SFRY – Supplement: International treaties and other agreements, No. 13/1964.

30 Official Gazette of the SFRY – Supplement: International treaties and other agreements, No. 3/1968; Official Gazette of the SFRY – International agreements No. 1/198.

31 See also the report on the Czech Republic by Magdalena Pfeiffer in this edition.

32 It needs to be taken into account that Montenegro has signed a new Protocol to the Agreement on Mutual Legal Assistance with Slovakia in 2014 that confirms the application of the Agreement with Czechoslovakia between Montenegro and Slovakia, but that also sets aside the most important provisions on succession matters in this Agreement. See more in the heading on the Agreement with Czechoslovakia.

33 For B&H see the website of the Ministry of Justice of B&H: <http://www.mpr.gov.ba/organizacija_nadleznosti/medj_pravna_pomoc/bilateralni_ugovori/default.aspx?id=939&langTag=en -US> accessed 04.04.2019; See also E. Muminović, *Međunarodno privatno pravo*, Law Faculty Sarajevo, Sarajevo 2008, p. 29.

34 Macedonia did conclude its own new agreements on mutual legal assistance with Bulgaria in 2002 (OJ of the Republic of Macedonia, No. 13/02) and with Romania in 2004 (OJ of the Republic of Macedonia, No. 41/04) – which do not regulate succession matters – but they did not set aside the previous Agreements taken over by succession that will be analyzed in this report; see the website of the Ministry of Justice of Macedonia: <http://www.pravda.gov.mk/mpd-bilaterala5> accessed 04.04.2019.

35 See the website of the Ministry of Justice of Montenegro: <http://www.pravda.gov.me/rubrike/medjunarodni_ugovori/drzave> accessed 04.04.2019; see also M. Kostić-Mandić, above n. 21, p. 43.

36 See the website of the Ministry of Justice of Serbia: <https://www.mpravde.gov.rs/tekst/873/bilateralni-ugovori.php> accessed 04.04.2019; see also S. Đurđević, 'O potrebi izmene

name changes, but they have remained bound by the bilateral treaties by virtue of succession.

The six bilateral treaties concluded by Yugoslavia show great similarities and contain almost identical provisions for many of the situations covered. In case of ambiguity in any of the provisions, it is recommended to read the treaties together. The analysis of the treaties in this contribution will follow this approach and, in order to adhere to the limited number of pages, where it is appropriate simply refer to explanations already given with regards to the identical provisions in one of the six agreements. Finally, it should be mentioned that these treaties have limited practical relevance in Serbia, B&H, Montenegro and Macedonia, especially with regard to their provisions on succession matters.[37] This is mainly because only a very small number of nationals of the other contracting parties (i.e. Austria, Bulgaria, Czech Republic, Hungary, Poland, Romania and Slovakia) are domiciled or reside in Serbia, B&H, Montenegro and Macedonia.

3.2. SCOPE OF APPLICATION

3.2.1. Agreement with Austria

None of the six bilateral agreements concluded by Yugoslavia contain specific provisions on the scope of application, let alone as to the scope of application in respect of succession matters. The bilateral agreement with Austria (**Treaty 3**) only indicates the scope of application in the heading of the first part regulating legal assistance 'in civil matters', whereas the heading of the third part which is relevant for the analysis in this contribution is simply titled 'succession'.

The lack of clear provisions on the scope of application makes it difficult to determine the exact personal or substantive scope of application. There is great risk in determining the scope of application based on the provisions of the Agreement providing solutions for specific persons or subject matters, because they do not answer the question of how to fill legal gaps. In the event of a legal gap, it seems questionable to immediately deduce the answer from the application of a different legal source (EU Regulation, another international

dvostranih ugovora o pravnoj pomoći u građanskim stvarima na snazi između Republike Srbije i država članica Evropske unije', [2016] *Zbornik radova Pravnog fakulteta u Nišu* 269.

37 There are court decisions in which the provisions of these treaties on legal assistance (delivery of court documents, taking of evidence, etc.) or on recognition and enforcement of court decisions have been applied (see for example Serbian Commercial Court of Appeal, 24.11.2010, Iž 3127/2010, Serbian Commercial Court of Appeal, 23.2.2011, PŽ14462/2010, both available at <https://www.paragraf.rs> accessed 04.04.2019). However, in last two decades there has not been a court decision in which provisions on succession have been applied.

treaty or national law). The present authors believe that a legal gap should be filled by analogous application of the rules of the Agreement or the general principles thereof.[38] Only if such filling of gaps is unsuccessful should the conclusion be made that the question is not within the scope of application and that the next legal source should be applied.

The personal scope of application is restricted to deceased who were nationals of one of the Contracting States. Where the deceased was a national of the other Contracting State, the personal scope of application is fulfilled. A more difficult question arises as to what kind of connection there needs to be to the other Contracting State in addition to the domestic nationality of the deceased. The Austrian agreement has in its focus the case where the deceased of one Contracting State has movable assets in the territory of the other Contracting State. But even if there are immovable assets of the deceased in the territory of the other Contracting State, the Austrian agreement applies and provides for exclusive jurisdiction for immovable assets (Article 30 of the Austrian Agreement). Other situations that are regulated include the death or the last domicile of the deceased on the territory of the other Contracting State. But also the nationality of the heirs of the other Contracting State triggers the personal scope of application (Article 29(2) of the Austrian Agreement).

None of the Yugoslavian bilateral agreements regulate the case of dual nationals, neither where the deceased possessed a nationality of both Contracting States nor where he/she is a national of one of the Contracting States and a third State. The legal theory in ex-Yugoslav States is based on Article 11(1) of the Yugoslav PIL Act, which is still in force in B&H and Serbia and which has been carried over in the new PIL Codes of Montenegro and Macedonia. It provides that in cases of dual nationality where one of them is domestic, only the domestic nationality will apply.[39] Pursuant to Article 11(3) of the Yugoslavian PIL Act, the principle of effective nationality applies only when none of the nationalities is a domestic one and the person has no domicile in one of the States of which he/she is a national.[40] It is true that the application of many provisions in the bilateral agreements would be without practical importance in cases of a dual nationality of both Contracting States, especially provisions on diplomatic and consular powers, securing measures, provisions which

---

38 M. Shaw, *International Law*, 6th ed., Cambridge University Press, Cambridge 2008, p. 99; P. Malanczuk, *Akehurst's Modern Introduction to International Law*, Routledge, London and New York 1997.

39 See M. Dika, G. Knežević and S. Stojanović, above n. 3, p. 47. The same rule still applies under Art. 11(2) of the PIL Act of Montenegro and Art. 11(1) of the PIL Act of Macedonia.

40 The provision remained the same in the Macedonian PIL Act, and even in the new draft code of Macedonia only domicile would be replaced by habitual residence. In Art. 11(3) of the PIL Code of Montenegro this rule has changed slightly, as the principle of effective nationality applies as soon as neither of the two nationalities in question is of Montenegro and habitual residence is taken into account only when determining effecting nationality.

require the nationality of the other Contracting State, etc.[41] However, there are also provisions that guarantee rights to heirs who are nationals of the other Contracting State (Article 29(2) or 36(1) of the Austrian Agreement), and these individuals should not be deprived of their rights just because the deceased was a national of both Contracting States. The purpose of the Agreement is not just to provide nationality treatment for the deceased, but also for the heirs. Additionally, from the perspective of B&H, Serbia and Macedonia, there is no meaningful reason to try to interpret one's way out of the application of the Agreement as the national PIL Acts contain very similar rules. Such motive does, however, exist in Montenegro, whose rules on international succession are almost identical to those of the Succession Regulation. Bearing in mind that the bilateral agreement has tried to ensure succession rights for the citizens of the two Contracting States, it seems contradictory to say that it will not apply in cases where possibly the strongest connection to both Contracting States exists – and that is when the deceased had the nationality of these two States. Consequently, it is also contradictory if we conclude that the Agreement should be applied to deceased who were dual nationals of one Contracting State and a third State, but not to those who were nationals of both Contracting States. Therefore, we consider the problem of dual nationality not to be a problem regarding the scope of application of the Agreement; instead, it is a problem once we apply it, because it also needs to be solved with regards to heirs as well as to the deceased.

The substantive scope of application encompasses statutory succession (including reserved shares), testaments and legacies, which means it applies to both intestate and testamentary succession matters. The Agreement with Austria also includes a rule on the right of nationals of both Contracting States to conclude donations *mortis causa*, which may be a ground for disposition and acquisition of property under the equality principle (Article 29 of the Austrian Agreement). However, under the national succession and obligation laws of B&H, Serbia, Montenegro and Macedonia, a donation *mortis causa* is not regulated and is therefore intensively discussed with regards to its effects. The prevailing view is that both donation *mortis causa* and donation *ad mortem* are possible, but with their conclusion being done in accordance with the Obligation Law Act[42] and not under the rules of substantive succession laws.[43]

---

41 See also in this regard the report of Claudia Rudolf in this edition.

42 Official Gazette of SFRY, Nos. 29/78, 39/85, 46/85, 45/89, 57/89; Official Gazette of the Republic Srpska, Nos. 17/93, 57/98, 39/03, 74/04; Official Gazette of the Republic of Bosnia and Herzegovina, Nos. 2/29, 13/93, 13/94 and Official Gazette of the Federation of Bosnia and Herzegovina, Nos. 29/03 and 42/2011; Official Gazette of FRY, No. 31/93 and Official Gazette of Serbia and Montenegro, No. 1/2003.

43 M. Đurđević, 'Ugovor o poklonu za slučaj smrti' [2011] *Zbornik radova Pravnog fakulteta u Novom Sadu* 241; E. Bikić and S. Suljević, *Nasljedno pravo*, Planjax, Tešanj 2014, p. 165.

The same understanding can now be found in Austrian succession law.[44] This means that although there is a provision on the equality principle with regards to a donation *mortis causa* in the Agreement with Austria's chapter on succession, none of the Contracting States would classify donation *mortis causa* under the succession rules. Under the national PIL of B&H, Serbia, Macedonia and Montenegro, the conflict-of-laws rules for contracts apply to contractual issues while conflict-of-laws rules for succession apply to the succession law effects of these contracts.[45]

Therefore, it is of significance that the equality principle of Article 29 of the Austrian Agreement explicitly applies to last wills, donation *mortis causa* and intestate succession, but it does not cover agreements as to succession, although they were allowed in Austria (and null and void in Yugoslavia) at the time of the conclusion of the Agreement. The formulation of the other provisions of the Agreement as well as the chosen connecting factors also indicate that there was no intention of the Contracting States to include agreements as to succession under its scope of application. The situation is unchanged in Macedonia, Serbia and Montenegro because their national succession laws still consider the agreements as to succession null and void. However, in the national law of Bosnia and Herzegovina or, to be precise, in the entity of the Federation of Bosnia and Herzegovina as well as in the Brčko District, agreements as to succession are allowed, while in the Republic of Srpska they are still null and void.[46] From the perspective of (the most parts of) B&H and Austria – that now both allow agreements as to succession – it would make sense to apply the Austrian Agreement to agreements as to succession at least with regards to the recognition and enforcement of judgments under Article 31(2) of this Agreement. Such interpretation is possible because agreements as to succession are nowhere explicitly excluded and the provision in question simply refers to 'decisions on succession'.

The territorial scope of application is, again, not expressly determined. Considering that the courts of the State of which the deceased was a national are to have jurisdiction to rule on all movable assets without restriction, it means that movable assets located in third States are not excluded from the territorial scope of application of the Agreement. However, in many cases only the jurisdiction with regards to assets located on domestic territory will be established (e.g. Article 30 or Article 36 of the Austrian Agreement).[47]

---

44 See the new formulation in §603 ABGB after the Act on the Amendment of the Succession Act of 2015, BGBl. I 2015/87.

45 S. Đorđević, 'Private International Law Regime of Inter Vivos Contracts whose Effects are Postponed to the Death of the Contracting Party Disposing of the Property – de lege lata and de lege ferenda' [2015] 2–3 *Revija za evropsko pravo*, 59.

46 Bosnia is a State with more than one legal order. See Z. Meškić, A. Duraković and J. Alihodžić, above n. 11.

47 See also in this regard the report of Claudia Rudolf in this edition.

3.2.2. *Agreement with Bulgaria*

The bilateral agreement with Bulgaria (**Treaty 22**) also does not contain specific provisions on its scope of application. Only in the title of the first part of the Agreement is it specified that mutual legal assistance is to be established in 'civil matters', and one of its subheadings is titled 'succession'.[48]

The personal scope is fulfilled whenever the deceased was a national of the other Contracting State. If the deceased possessed domestic nationality, there needs to be a connecting factor within the other Contracting State, such as the death or the last domicile of the deceased, the location of movable or immovable assets of the deceased, the location of the last will, domicile of the heirs, etc.

The substantive scope of application encompasses intestate succession and testamentary succession (testaments and legacy). The conflict-of-laws rules and jurisdiction rules are very comprehensive, and therefore the solutions for not expressly regulated situations are to be looked for within the Agreement. However, the formulation of the provisions indicates that there was no intention of the Contracting States to encompass agreements as to succession.[49] Therefore, the Succession Regulation in Bulgaria and the national PIL of B&H, Serbia, Montenegro and Macedonia will apply to succession agreements. In addition, the Agreement with Bulgaria contains, among others, the conflict-of-laws rules for adoption (Article 40), guardianship (*tutela* and *curatela*) (Articles 35–36), legal capacity (Article 37), determination of paternity/maternity (Articles 38–39) and declaration of death (Article 41), all based on the nationality principle. It also contains the rules on recognition and enforcement (Articles 42–48), which are even more comprehensive, as they also encompass matrimonial matters and they are written in a way to cover all civil matters.

The territorial scope of application is not expressly determined. As discussed with respect to the Agreement with Austria (**Treaty 3**), movable property located in third States should also be included in the scope of application of the Agreement with Bulgaria (see jurisdiction rule on movable property in Article 24(1)). However, in many cases jurisdiction only with regards to assets on domestic territory may be established (e.g. Article 23 or Article 30 of the Agreement with Bulgaria).

3.2.3. *Agreement with Czechoslovakia*

As with previous agreements, the Agreement with Czechoslovakia (**Treaty 13**) contains no specific provisions on its scope of application. The preamble of

48 For more detailed observations on the scope of application see the explanations with regards to the very similar Agreement with Austria.

49 For more detailed observations see the arguments on the scope of application of the Austrian Agreement.

the Agreement observes that the Contracting States 'in the spirit of common friendship and cooperation' wish to make legal relations between them easier. The title of the Agreement refers to 'civil, family and criminal' matters, whereas the heading of the fourth chapter of this Agreement is simply titled 'succession'.[50]

The personal scope of application and the problem with a dual nationality of the deceased should be understood in the same manner as has been explained in the above sub-sections dedicated to the Agreements with Austria (**Treaty 3**) and Bulgaria (**Treaty 22**). However, the Agreement with Czechoslovakia adds new arguments in favour of its application to persons with dual nationality (persons who are nationals of both Contracting States). The provision on matrimonial property in Article 24(2) of this Agreement determines that where the spouses are nationals of two different Contracting States, the law governing personal relations and the statutory property regime of spouses is the law of the State of their last common nationality. The case regulated here is when one of the spouses acquires the nationality of the other Contracting State and the other spouse does not, this without restriction to persons who give up their previous nationality. Again, as already argued with regards to the Agreement with Austria, the dual nationality needs to be solved only in the context of determining the applicable law. Dual nationality will not exclude dual nationals of both Contracting States, i.e. persons who have the closest possible relation to the Agreement, from its scope of application.

The substantive scope of application of this Agreement with regards to succession matters encompasses intestate succession (including reserved shares) and testamentary succession (testaments and legacy), which means it fully corresponds to the substantive scope of application of the Agreement with Bulgaria. The same arguments with regard to putting agreements as to succession under the substantive scope of application, which are cited above, also apply to this Agreement. In addition, it should be mentioned that the Agreement with Czechoslovakia contains, among others, the conflict-of-laws rules for legal capacity (Article 18), declaration of death (Article 19), marriage (Articles 23 and 25), divorce (Article 26), matrimonial property regime (Articles 24–25), relations between parents and children (Article 28(3) and (4)), determination of paternity/maternity (Article 28(1), (2) and (4)) and adoption (Article 29), which are based on the nationality principle – and in some cases, when the nationality of a Contracting State is not given, the domicile principle is followed.[51] It also

---

50 For more detailed observations on the scope of application see the explanations with regards to the very similar Agreement with Austria (**Treaty 3**), with the remark that the substantive scope of application of the Austrian Agreement is much narrower with regards to matters other than succession matters.

51 See A. Duraković, *Međunarodno privatno pravo razvoda braka u Europskoj uniji i Bosni i Hercegovini*, Mostar 2016, p. 222.

contains the rules on recognition and enforcement of decisions, which are very comprehensive and written in a way to cover all civil matters.

With regards to relations between Montenegro and Slovakia, it needs to be taken into account that in 2014 these two States signed an additional Protocol to this Agreement that sets aside the most important provisions of the Agreement with regards to succession relations, namely Articles 35–39 and 44.[52] This means that the rules on jurisdiction and conflict of laws in succession matters are basically inapplicable between Slovakia and Montenegro.

The territorial scope of application is again not expressly determined. As was the case with two previous bilateral agreements, the same view should be taken here in respect of movable property located in a third State. This property should be also covered by the scope of application of the Agreement with Czechoslovakia, considering that the general conflict-of-laws rule of Article 36 (that follows a monistic approach) and the general jurisdiction rule on movable property of Article 39(1) do not restrict their application to movable property located in the Contracting States.

3.2.4. *Agreement with Hungary*

The Agreement with Hungary (**Treaty 25**) also does not contain specific provisions on its scope of application. The title of the Agreement refers to 'civil, family and criminal' matters, whereas the title of the fourth heading of this Agreement is simply 'succession'.[53]

The personal scope of application and the problem with dual nationality should be understood in the same manner as was explained in the context of previously discussed bilateral agreements.

The substantive scope of application with regards to succession matters also encompasses issues of intestate and testamentary succession. With regard to agreements as to succession, what was cited in the previous sub-sections on other bilateral agreements applies here too. In addition, it should be mentioned that the Agreement with Hungary contains conflict-of-laws rules for legal capacity (Article 23), declaration of death (Article 38), marriage (Article 26), divorce (Article 29), matrimonial property regime (Article 27), relations between parents and children (Article 32), maintenance (Article 34), determination of

---

52 Art. 5(b) of the new Protocol to the Agreement between the Social Federal Republic of Yugoslavia and the Czechoslovak Socialist Republic on the Regulation of Legal Relations in Civil, Family and Criminal Matters signed on 29.05.2014; available at the website of the Ministry of Justice of Montenegro: <http://www.mpa.gov.me/rubrike/Bilateralni-ugovori/156296/Protokol-izmedu-Crne-Gore-i-Republike-Slovacke.html> accessed 04.04.2019.

53 For more detailed observations on the scope of application see the explanations with regards to the very similar Agreement with Austria (**Treaty 3**), with the remark that the substantive scope of application of the Austrian Agreement in respect of matters other than succession matters is much narrower.

paternity/maternity (Article 32) and adoption (Article 36). These are based on the nationality principle and in some cases, when the nationality of a Contracting State is not given, on the domicile principle. It also contains a conflict-of-laws rule for rights *in rem* in immovables (Article 39) as well as for the formal validity of acts (Article 38). The recognition and enforcement of court decisions is regulated by the provisions of Articles 56–57, which intend to cover all civil matters.

The territorial scope of application, which is not expressly determined, should be understood in the same manner as was explained with regard to previously discussed bilateral agreements. It means it encompasses not only immovable and movable property located in the Contracting States, but also movable property which is located in third States (see and compare Articles 41 and 45(1)).

In general, the scope of application in civil matters is so broad that the Agreement contains qualities of a statute rather than just an agreement on legal assistance. Out of the agreements concluded with Yugoslavia, the Hungarian Agreement is the most advanced with regards to the quality of its provisions.

3.2.5. Agreement with Poland

The bilateral Agreement with Poland (**Treaty 26**) does not contain specific provisions on its scope of application. The preamble of the Agreement observes that the Contracting States 'in the spirit of common friendship and cooperation' aim to make legal relations between them easier. The title of the Agreement refers to 'civil and criminal' matters and the name of the first part of the Agreement specifies that mutual legal assistance is to be established in 'civil matters', and one of its subheadings is titled 'succession'.[54]

The personal scope of application and the problem with dual nationality should be understood in the same manner as was explained in the previously discussed bilateral agreements.

The substantive scope of application with regards to succession matters is the same as that of the previously discussed agreements (except that of the Agreement with Austria (**Treaty 3**), which adds donation *mortis causa* to its scope of application). This means it encompasses all issues that belong to intestate and testamentary succession. With regard to agreements as to succession, what was said in the previous sub-sections on other bilateral agreements applies here too. Also, the Agreement with Poland contains conflict-of-laws rules for status and family matters, such as legal capacity (Article 20), declaration of death (Article 31), marriage (Article 25), divorce (Article 27), matrimonial property

---

[54] For more detailed observations regarding the scope of application see the explanations with regards to the very similar Agreement with Austria (**Treaty 3**), with the remark that the substantive scope of application of the Austrian Agreement with regards to matters other than succession matters is much narrower.

regime (Article 26), relations between parents and children (Article 28), determination of paternity/maternity and adoption (Article 30), which are mostly based on the nationality principle. Also found are conflict-of-laws rules for contracts (Article 34), the formal validity of acts (Article 32), rights *in rem* on immovables (Article 33) and the rules on recognition and enforcement in civil matters. In general, the substantive scope of application in civil matters is so broad and regulated in such detail that this Agreement possesses qualities of a statute rather than just an agreement on legal assistance.

Here again, the territorial scope of application is not expressly determined by the Agreement. As it has been already said with respect to previous agreements, the scope of application of the Agreement with Poland should also cover movable property located in third States (see general conflict-of-laws rule in Article 36 and general jurisdiction rule on movable property in Article 43(1)).

3.2.6. Agreement with Romania

There are no specific provisions on the scope of application of this agreement (**Treaty 27**) either. The title of the Agreement with Romania refers to 'civil, family and criminal' matters. The second part of the Agreement is dedicated to legal assistance in civil and family matters, whereas its fourth heading is simply titled 'succession'.[55]

In terms of this Agreement, everything that was said about the personal scope of application and problems with dual nationality in respect of previously discussed bilateral agreements applies here too.

The same is to be said for the substantive scope of application. The Agreement with Romania applies to both intestate and testamentary succession, whereas agreements as to succession should be taken into account only in the context of application of the rules on recognition and enforcement of court decisions.

The determination of territorial scope of application is to be understood in the same manner as has been explained in respect of other bilateral agreements.

4. PRIVATE INTERNATIONAL LAW: CONFLICT-OF-LAWS RULES OF THE TREATIES

4.1. AGREEMENT WITH AUSTRIA

The Austrian Agreement (**Treaty 3**) lacks a general conflict-of-laws rule. Basically, it does not regulate the conflict of laws. Therefore, as a rule, with regards

[55] For more detailed observations on the scope of application see the explanations on the very similar Agreement with Austria (**Treaty 3**), with the remark that the substantive scope of application of the Austrian Agreement with regards to matters other than succession matters is much narrower.

to questions regarding the applicable law, the Succession Regulation applies in Austria and the national PIL in B&H, Serbia, Montenegro and Macedonia. The Agreement contains only a very special rule that is almost without any practical significance. Namely, a special conflict-of-laws rule is construed for the situation when a deceased who was a national of one Contracting State had his/her last domicile in the territory of another Contracting State; here the heirs that live in the territory of that second State may request within a certain timeframe (three to six months pursuant to Article 35(1)) that the court of that State conduct the proceedings on movable property that is located in the same State (Article 36(1)). For these cases a special conflict-of-laws rule provides that the law of the State of which the deceased was a national will be applicable to the succession proceedings, contentious inheritance claims, reserved shares and legacies (Article 36(2) of the Austrian Agreement). This conflict-of-laws rule is based on the nationality principle and therefore very much differs from the Succession Regulation and the Mon. PIL Act, but it is the same as in B&H, Serbian and Macedonian private international law. At the same time, it only applies to specific requests pursuant to Article 36(1); yet it is very unusual to have a conflict-of-laws rule only for one specific case and not for all of the other cases. In most other bilateral agreements concluded by Yugoslavia, there is a general conflict-of-laws rule based on the nationality principle (the Agreements with Austria and Romania (**Treaty 27**) are the exceptions), but in those instances it is found alongside the same special conflict-of-laws rule formulated here in Article 36(2) of the Agreement with Austria.

Apart from the conflict-of-laws rule having a very narrow scope of application, there is a rule which from the perspective of Yugoslavian theory belongs to the field of law regarding the rights of foreigners ('Fremdenrecht').[56] Nationals of one Contracting State may, in accordance with the law of that State or the law of the other Contracting State, dispose of all their property which is located on the territory of the other Contracting State through a last will or donation *mortis causa* (Article 29(1)), and in accordance with statutory succession rules or mandatory succession rules or under a will or donation *mortis causa*, they may acquire property rights in the other Contracting State under the same conditions and in the same scope as nationals of that State (Article 29(2)). In the opinion of the present authors, this rule simply aims to ensure the application of the equal treatment principle in order to guarantee

56 According to the prevailing opinion in the ex-Yugoslav States, the law on the rights of foreigners is a part of PIL; P. Gavrovska and T. Deskoski, *Меѓународно приватно право*, Law Faculty 'Iustinianus Primus' Skopje, Skopje 2011, p. 165; M. Stanivuković and M. Živković, *Međunarodno privatno pravo – opšti deo*, 3rd ed, Službeni glasnik, Belgrade 2008, p. 15; E. Muminović, above n. 33, p. 19; M. Kostić-Mandić, above n. 21, pp. 161, 231; for the only opposite view Z. Meškić and S. Đorđević, *Međunarodno privatno pravo – opći dio*, Privredna štampa, Sarajevo 2016, p. 16.

dispositions upon death as well as inheritance rights for the nationals of both Contracting States on the territory of both Contracting States. This is also supported by the fact that Article 35 of the Agreement with Czechoslovakia (**Treaty 13**) contains the same provision under the 'principle of equality'. It is questionable whether this rule aimed at anything more than simply making any succession law barriers imposed on non-nationals inapplicable to nationals of the other Contracting State, which is a typical purpose of a law on the rights of foreigners.[57] Discussions on a hidden conflict-of-laws rule effect are the result of a lack of a general rule on conflict of laws in this agreement. However, a comparative look at the other agreements analyzed here shows that the same rule is contained in other agreements that do contain a general rule on conflict of laws, so that a conflict-of-laws content was not the intention of the creators of the Agreement with Austria. Further, the Hague Convention on the Conflicts of Laws Relating to the Form of Testamentary Dispositions, ratified a few years later, applies to the formal validity of wills.

In Article 39 of the Austrian Agreement there is a classification rule for immovable and movable property. Whether the property is to be considered movable or immovable is to be determined by the law of the State in which the property is located. It is interesting that all six bilateral agreements contain the same rule and the much later adopted Yugoslav PIL Act does not, although it is a firm part of Yugoslav theory as well as the theory of B&H, Serbia, Montenegro and Macedonia.[58]

4.2. AGREEMENT WITH BULGARIA

The Agreement with Bulgaria (**Treaty 22**) contains a general conflict-of-laws rule providing for the law of the Contracting State of which the deceased was a national at the time of death as the law applicable to the succession as a whole, i.e. to both movable and immovable property (Article 20). The provision is very comprehensive and applies also to movable assets in the other Contracting State and in a third State, when jurisdiction is based on the nationality of the deceased (see Article 24 of the Agreement with Bulgaria). Consequently, the conflict-of-laws rules of the Succession Regulation in Bulgaria and the PIL Act of Montenegro, which are based on habitual residence, will not be applicable within the scope of application of this agreement. For B&H, Serbia and Macedonia, the provisions in the national PIL Act are also based on the nationality principle and are very similar to those of the Agreement with Bulgaria.

---

57 E. Muminović, *Procesno međunarodno privatno pravo*, Law Faculty Sarajevo, Sarajevo 2008, p. 161.

58 M. Stanivuković and M. Živković, above n. 56, p. 256.

There are four special conflict-of-laws rules. The conflict-of-laws rule on the capacity to make or revoke a testament and on the absence of intent (fraudulent misrepresentation, fault, etc.) follows the nationality principle at the time the testament was made or revoked (Article 21). The second special conflict-of-laws rule relates to the form of the testament and raises more difficult questions. Bulgaria is not a party to the Hague Convention on the Conflicts of Laws Relating to the Form of Testamentary Dispositions, which means that Article 22 of this Agreement is applicable in respect to Bulgaria. It offers only two alternatives for determining the applicable law for the form of the testament: the nationality of the deceased at the time the testament was made (or revoked); or the place where the testament was made or revoked. Even more problematic, it restricts the applicable law in both alternatives to the law of the Contracting State. Namely, in cases where the testament does not meet the formal requirements of the State of which the deceased was a national and where it was not made in any of the Contracting States, it will, pursuant to the Agreement, be invalid. This provision is clearly less favourable than Article 27 of the Succession Regulation, which provides five different connecting factors combined with different times of assessment (time of disposition and time of death) and may lead to a great number of different applicable laws following the principle *favorem testamenti*. B&H, Serbia, Montenegro and Macedonia are Contracting States of the Hague Convention of 1961, which has universal application irrespective of the fact that Bulgaria is not a Contracting State (Article 6(1) of the Hague Convention). The Hague Convention of 1961 does not regulate its relation to bilateral treaties, but it does clearly state that other legal sources may be applicable only if they allow further forms of a will (Article 3 of the Hague Convention 1961). As the Hague Convention of 1961 is in this case *lex posterior* and *lex specialis*, it remains applicable as to the form of wills in B&H, Serbia, Macedonia and Montenegro.[59] Agreements as to succession do not fall under the scope of application of the Hague Convention of 1961 (Article 4 of the Hague Convention 1961).[60]

The third special conflict-of-laws rule, similar to the Agreement with Austria (**Treaty 3**), provides that the nationality principle also applies to requests of heirs living in the Contracting State in which the movable assets and the domicile of the deceased are located, if the deceased was a national of the other Contracting State (Article 30(2) of the Agreement with Bulgaria). The provision is redundant because the general rule already calls for the application of the nationality principle (Article 20(1)).

---

59 M. Stanivuković and P. Đundić, above n. 3, p. 199; Z. Meškić and S. Đorđević, above n. 56, p. 31.

60 A. Dutta, 'Art. 27 EuErbVO' in F.J. Säcker et al. (eds.), *Münchener Kommentar zum BGB*, C.H. Beck, Munich 2015, para. 6; A. Köhler in W. Gierl, A. Köhler, L. Kroiß and H. Wilsch, *Internationales Erbrecht*, Nomos/Manz, Baden-Baden/Vienna 2015, p. 125.

The fourth special conflict-of-laws rule relates to the situation in which there are no living successors (vacant estate). In such a situation the Agreement diverges from the monist approach provided for in the general conflict-of-laws rule. Namely, for immovable property Article 20(2) provides for the application of the law of Contracting State in which it is located and for movable property it provides for the application of the law of the Contracting State of which the deceased was a national regardless of whether it is located in a Contracting State or in a third State.

Article 33 contains a classification rule covering whether property is to be considered movable or immovable, stipulating that it is to be determined by the law of the State in which the property is located.

Finally, the Agreement with Bulgaria also contains a provision on the rights of foreigners ('Fremdenrecht'). Nationals of one Contracting State may dispose of their property and inherit under the same conditions as the nationals of the other Contracting State (Article 19(1) and (2) of the Bulgarian Agreement). The only difference to the Agreement with Austria (**Treaty 3**) is that donation *mortis causa* is not mentioned.

The Agreement with Bulgaria, like all of the other agreements analyzed in this contribution, lacks rules on the general part of private international law. However, in the procedural rules and the rules on recognition and enforcement, it does refer several times to the *ordre public* (Articles 24(2), 26(2), 46(v)), leading to the conclusion that it is one of the general principles of the Agreement.

4.3. AGREEMENT WITH CZECHOSLOVAKIA

The Agreement with Czechoslovakia (**Treaty 13**) contains the same general conflict-of-laws rule as that of the Agreement with Bulgaria (**Treaty 22**). It provides that the law of the Contracting State of which the deceased was a national at the time of death is applicable to the succession as a whole, including both movable and immovable assets (Article 36). The provision is very comprehensive and applies not only to movable assets located in the other Contracting State, but also to those located in a third State, when the jurisdiction is based on the nationality of the deceased (Article 39). Consequently, the principle of habitual residence, followed by the conflict-of-laws rules of the Succession Regulation in the Czech Republic and Slovakia and the national PIL Act of Montenegro, will not be applicable within the scope of application of the Agreement. However, the Succession Regulation will remain applicable in relation to Montenegro, along with the PIL Act of Montenegro in relation to Slovakia, because of the additional Protocol signed between these two States in 2014 that excludes the application of Articles 35–39 and Article 44 of the Agreement. For B&H, Serbia and Macedonia, the provisions in national PIL are based on the nationality principle, as in the Agreement.

There are two special conflict-of-laws rules in the Agreement with Czechoslovakia (**Treaty 13**), both related to last wills. The conflict-of-laws rule on the capacity to make or revoke the testament and on the absence of intent follows the nationality principle at the time the testament was made or revoked (Article 38(1)). The second special conflict-of-laws rule relates to the form of the testament. Both the Czech Republic and Slovakia are not parties to the Hague Convention on the Conflicts of Laws Relating to the Form of Testamentary Dispositions. Without doubt Article 38(2) of the Agreement with Czechoslovakia is applicable in the Czech Republic and Slovakia (except for relations between Slovakia and Montenegro because of the additional Protocol signed between these two States), and it offers only two alternatives for determining the law applicable to form: the nationality of the deceased at the time the will was made (or revoked); or the law of the Contracting State where the will was made or revoked. Therefore, everything that was already said for the Agreement with Bulgaria (**Treaty 22**) on the formal validity of the testament applies here too, and for more details we refer to the observations on the Bulgarian Agreement. The Hague Convention of 1961 applies as to the form of wills in B&H, Serbia, Macedonia and Montenegro as *lex posterior* and *lex specialis*.[61]

Contrary to the Agreement with Bulgaria, there is no special conflict-of-laws rule for a vacant property. However, there is a substantive rule in Article 37 providing that in accordance with the applicable law, movable property is to be handed over to the Contracting State of which the deceased was a national at the time of his/her death and immovable property to the Contracting State on whose territory this property is located.

Article 39(5) of the Agreement with Czechoslovakia contains a similar rule on classification of the property as movable or immovable, stipulating that it is to be determined by the law of the State in which property is located.

Finally, the Czechoslovakian Agreement contains a provision on the rights of foreigners ('Fremdenrecht'), which is the same as that of two previously discussed bilateral agreements: nationals of one Contracting State may dispose of their property with their last will and inherit based on statutory or testamentary succession under the same conditions and in the same scope as the nationals of the other Contracting State (Article 35(1) and (2) of the Agreement with Czechoslovakia). The heading of this provision, 'principle of equality', shows that Article 35 of the Agreement with Czechoslovakia is merely a provision on non-discrimination based on nationality.

There are no rules on the general part of private international law in this Agreement. However, the rules on legal assistance (Article 13) as well as the

---

61 M. Stanivuković and P. Đundić, above n. 3, p. 199; Z. Meškić and S. Đorđević, above n. 56, p. 31.

rules on recognition and enforcement of decisions (Article 51) make reference to the *ordre public*, allowing the conclusion that it is one of the general principles of the Agreement.

4.4. AGREEMENT WITH HUNGARY

The Hungarian Agreement (**Treaty 25**) contains the same general conflict-of-laws rule as previously discussed bilateral agreements, and it provides for the law of the Contracting State of which the deceased was a national at the time of death as the law applicable to both movable and immovable property (Article 41 of the Hungarian Agreement). This rule applies not only to immovable and movable property located in the Contracting States, but also to movable property that is located in a third State, when jurisdiction is based on the nationality of the deceased (Article 45(1) of the Agreement with Hungary). Consequently, the Agreement is dominated by the nationality principle as opposed to the habitual residence principle followed by the conflict-of-laws rules of the Succession Regulation in Hungary and the national PIL Act of Montenegro. For B&H, Serbia and Macedonia, the provisions in national PIL are based on the nationality principle as in the Agreement.

There are four special conflict-of-laws rules. Three of them – the conflict-of-laws rule on the capacity to make or revoke a testament and on the absence of intent, following the nationality principle at the time the testament was made (Article 41(1)); the conflict-of-laws rule regarding requests of the heirs living in the State where the movable assets and the domicile of the deceased are located, when the deceased was a national of the other Contracting State, following the nationality principle (Article 51(2)); and the conflict-of-laws rule for vacant property, which follows a dual regime with the nationality principle for movables and *lex rei sitae* for immovables (Article 42 of the Hungarian Agreement) – are identical to those contained in the Agreement with Bulgaria (**Treaty 22**), and therefore we refer to the observations there.

The conflict-of-laws rule on the form of a testament in Article 43(2) of the Hungarian Agreement is much more advanced than in the other bilateral agreements and clearly inspired by the Hague Convention on the Conflicts of Laws Relating to the Form of Testamentary Dispositions. Hungary is not a party to this Convention, whereas Yugoslavia was a party from 1964 and all of the later independent States became parties by succession. Article 43(2) of the Agreement with Hungary offers five alternatives for determining law applicable to the form of a testament, some of which also incorporate the time of assessment: the nationality, domicile or residence of the deceased at the time the testament was made (or revoked) or at the time of death; the place where the testament was made and the law of the State in which immovable property is located. The only difference between the Agreement with Hungary and the Hague Convention of 1961 is that *habitual residence* as found in the Convention was, likely due to an inaccurate translation,[62] carried over as *residence* in the Agreement. Substantially, the Agreement is even more favourable to the testament than the Convention because the connecting factor *residence* in Article 43(2)(b) is – as compared to domicile – more likely to lead to a different alternative legal order than will occur under the *habitual residence* of Article 1(d) of the Hague Convention of 1961. For B&H, Serbia, Macedonia and Montenegro, the Hague Convention of 1961 is applicable as *lex specialis* and *lex posterior*.[63]

In the Hungarian Agreement there are two rules on classification. The first one in Article 43(3) stipulates that the question whether the deceased resided or was domiciled in a certain place is to be determined by the law of that place. The second one is similar to all of the other bilateral agreements, providing in Article 54 that whether the property is to be considered immovable or movable is to be determined by the law of the State in which the property is located.

Additionally, the Hungarian Agreement contains the same provision on the rights of foreigners ('Fremdenrecht') as previously discussed bilateral agreements (see Article 40(1) and (2) of the Agreement with Hungary).

Finally, the provision on *ordre public* (Article 15(2) of the Hungarian Agreement) is found among the provisions on legal assistance as well as among provisions on recognition and enforcement (Article 57(c) of the Hungarian Agreement), which leads to the conclusion that it is one of the general principles of the Agreement.

4.5. AGREEMENT WITH POLAND

As is the case in previously discussed agreements, the general conflict-of-laws rule in succession matters contained in the Agreement with Poland (**Treaty 26**) also follows the nationality principle – the law of the Contracting State of which the deceased was a national at the time of death is applicable to both movable and immovable property (Article 36 of the Polish Agreement). Everything that was said about this rule previously applies here too.

In addition to the general rule, the Agreement with Poland contains three special conflict-of-laws rules. Two of them – the conflict-of-laws rule on the capacity to make or revoke a testament and on the absence of intent, following

62 The same translation error was later made in the Yugoslav PIL Act, see Art. 31 of the Yugoslav PIL Act; M. Dika, G. Knežević and S. Stojanović, above n. 3, p. 110.

63 M. Stanivuković and P. Đundić, above n. 3, p. 199. Although Yugoslavia had originally already become a member of the Hague Convention of 1961 in 1964, and therefore before the bilateral agreement with Hungary was concluded, the successor States all became members only in 1990s on the grounds of succession.

the nationality principle at the time the testament was made (Article 37); and the conflict-of-laws rule regarding requests of the heirs living in the State where the movable assets and the domicile of the deceased are located, if the deceased was a national of the other Contracting State, following the nationality principle (Article 43(4)) – are identical to those of the Agreement with Bulgaria (**Treaty 22**), and therefore the reader is referred to the observations which were made there. Unlike the Agreement with Bulgaria, there is no special conflict-of-laws rule for a vacant estate.

The third special conflict-of-laws rule is on the form of a testament, as contained in Article 38 of the Agreement with Poland. It offers only two alternatives for determining the applicable law for testament form: the nationality of the deceased at the time the testament was made (or revoked); or the place where the testament was made or revoked. Even more problematic, it restricts the determination of the applicable law in both alternatives to the law of the Contracting State. Namely, in cases where the testament does not fulfil the formal requirements of the State of which the deceased was a national, and where it also was not made in any of the Contracting States, the testament would, pursuant to Article 38, be invalid. Luckily, this provision applies neither to Poland, nor to B&H, Serbia, Macedonia or Montenegro, because they are all parties to the Hague Convention of 1961. The Hague Convention of 1961 is applicable to the formal validity of a testament as *lex specialis* and *lex posterior*.[64]

The Agreement with Poland also contains the same rule on classification of movable and immovable property (Article 48) as other bilateral agreements.

Finally, this agreement provides the same provision on the rights of foreigners ('Fremdenrecht') as in previously discussed bilateral agreements (see Article 35(1) and (2)), and it makes a reference to *ordre public* in the rules on legal assistance (Article 14(1)) as well as in the rules on recognition and enforcement of decisions (Article 50).

4.6. AGREEMENT WITH ROMANIA

The Romanian Agreement (**Treaty 27**) lacks a general conflict-of-laws rule on succession matters. This is quite extraordinary because it is, together with the Austrian Agreement (**Treaty 3**), the only one without a general conflict-of-laws rule on succession matters. This is even more surprising because the Romanian Agreement contains conflict-of-laws rules for the whole area of family law and also comprehensive jurisdiction rules for succession matters, but for some reason a general conflict-of-laws rule on succession matters was, obviously, intentionally left out.

64 M. Stanivuković and P. Đundić, above n. 3, p. 199.

Consequently, apart from two special conflict-of-laws rules on the capacity of making the testament and on the formal validity of the testament, the conflict-of-laws rules of the Succession Regulation apply in Romania and the national PIL applies in B&H, Serbia, Macedonia and Montenegro. The conflict-of-laws rule on the capacity to make or revoke a testament and on the absence of intent follows the nationality principle at the time the testament was made or revoked (Article 35(1) of the Agreement with Romania).

The conflict-of-laws rule on the form of a testament in Article 35(2) of the Agreement with Romania offers only two alternatives for the applicable law governing form: the nationality of the deceased at the time the will was made (or revoked); or the place where the will was made or revoked. Both alternatives are restricted to the laws of the Contracting States. Thus, in cases where the testament does not fulfil the formal requirements of the law of the State of which the deceased was a national and where it also was not made in any of the Contracting States, it will, pursuant to Article 35(2), be invalid. This rule applies in Romania because Romania is not a contracting party to the Hague Convention of 1961. In B&H, Serbia, Montenegro and Macedonia, the Hague Convention of 1961 applies as *lex posterior* and *lex specialis*.[65]

The Agreement with Romania also contains the rule on classification of property as movable or immovable (see Article 38 of the Agreement with Romania) which is the same as that of previously discussed agreements. Also, the provisions on the rights of foreigners contained in Article 34(1) and (2) ('Fremdenrecht') and provisions on *ordre public* (Articles 13 and 51(1)(c)) are completely consistent with corresponding provisions of previously discussed agreements.

5. PROCEDURAL RULES

5.1. AGREEMENT WITH AUSTRIA

5.1.1. Jurisdiction in Succession Matters

In the Agreement with Austria (**Treaty 3**), as well as in all other bilateral treaties, the jurisdiction rules in succession matters are based on the criterion of a distinction between movable and immovable property. It means there are two sets of jurisdiction rules (one for immovable property and the other for movable property), which establish the so-called scission system (on a

[65] M. Stanivuković and P. Đundić, above n. 3, p. 199; Yugoslavia became a member of the Hague Convention of 1961 in 1964, and the successor States all became members only in 1990s on the grounds of succession. See <https://www.hcch.net/en/instruments/conventions/status-table/?cid=40> accessed 04.04.2019.

jurisdictional level). As will be seen below, these rules are similar to the jurisdiction rules in succession matters under the Serbian, B&H and Macedonian PIL Acts,[66] but they are completely different from the rules of the Montenegrin PIL Act that follow the jurisdiction principles which are the same as or similar to those of the Succession Regulation.[67]

Jurisdiction in respect of immovable property is regulated by Article 30 of the Agreement with Austria, which provides for the exclusive jurisdiction of the courts of the Contracting State in which immovable property is located. This rule applies to non-litigious succession proceedings for the distribution (liquidation) of an estate and to litigious proceedings undertaken to resolve disputes concerning inheritance claims, reserved shares and legacies. Although it is not expressly cited, claims arising from donation *mortis causa* are also covered by this jurisdiction rule, considering that such dispositions fall under the general substantive scope of application of this agreement.[68]

Succession matters related to movable property fall under the jurisdiction of the courts of the Contracting State of which the deceased was a national, notwithstanding its being located in this or another Contracting State or in both Contracting States or in a third State (Article 31(1) first sentence). As was the case with the jurisdiction rule on immovable property, this jurisdiction rule also applies to the above-mentioned non-litigious and litigious proceedings which concern not only inheritance and legacy claims but also the claims that arise from a donation *mortis causa*. In addition, in our opinion this rule should cover the claims of the deceased's creditors too. The argument for this view may be found in the provision of Article 34(2) on retaining movable property, which explicitly mentions that creditors of the deceased may, under certain conditions, request the retention of movable property. Considering that these provisions are closely connected to the jurisdiction rule on movable property (see section 5.1.2), it may be concluded that creditor claims have to be included into the scope of application of this rule. Bearing in mind that it could be seen as logically inconsequential that the jurisdiction rule on movable property applies to creditor claims, whereas the jurisdiction rule on immovable property does not, we find that the latter should apply to such claims too.

The aforementioned jurisdiction rule on movable property (first sentence of Article 31(1)) represents a general rule which should apply in all succession cases related to movable property. However, the Agreement provides two exceptions from this rule which could be marked as special jurisdiction rules on movable property. The first is regulated by the second sentence of Article 31(1), and it gives the courts of a Contracting State of which the deceased was not

---

66 See sections 2.1 and 2.2 in this contribution.

67 See section 2.3 in this contribution.

68 See section 3.2.1 in this contribution. On donation *mortis causa* in Serbian law see M. Đurđević, above n. 43, p. 241; S. Đorđević, above n. 45, p. 59.

a national jurisdiction to rule on movable property located in that State if the decision of the Contracting State of the deceased's nationality cannot be enforced there. In our opinion, this means that the court of this Contracting State is to establish jurisdiction not only in cases in which recognition and enforcement of a decision of the Contracting State of the deceased's nationality has already been refused, but also in cases in which it may be expected that such a decision will not be recognized and enforced. The provisions of Article 31(2) stipulate that the Contracting State in which movable property is located commits itself to recognize and enforce decisions related to movable property that have been given by the courts of the Contracting State of the deceased's nationality. However, these decisions will not be recognized if they are contrary to the *ordre public* of the Contracting State in which the movable property is located (i.e. 'contrary to the basic principles of legislation' of that State) or if other provisions of the Agreement so provide.

The second exception that is regulated by Article 36(1) of the Agreement deals with the situation in which the deceased, a national of one Contracting State, had his/her last domicile in the other Contracting State. In such a situation the heirs and mandatory heirs who reside in the Contracting State of the deceased's last domicile may make application, within a term of three to six months, requesting that the courts of that State establish jurisdiction to conduct the succession proceedings for distribution of movable property located in the same State (Article 36(1) first sentence). This application is to be accepted by the court of the Contracting State of the deceased's last domicile only if an heir, mandatory heir or legatee does not object to it within the term of one to three months as set by the court (Article 36(1) second sentence).

It should be emphasized that establishing jurisdiction in accordance with the rules of Article 36(1) is possible only to conduct succession proceedings – for distribution of movable property – which is of a non-litigious nature in both Contracting States (i.e. Serbia/Bosnia/Montenegro/Macedonia and Austria). In accordance with the wording of Article 36(1), these rules cannot be applied to litigious proceedings. Also, it is interesting to note that, pursuant to the first sentence of Article 36(1), the application to conduct the proceedings in the Contracting State of the deceased's last domicile may be filed by heirs and mandatory heirs, but not by a legatee, this despite the courts of this State having jurisdiction to rule on legacies as well. In the opinion of the present authors, this is an accidental omission made by the drafters of this agreement, which becomes obvious after the reading of the second sentence of Article 36(1) entitling legatees (alongside heirs and mandatory heirs) to oppose the application. If a legatee may object to establishing the jurisdiction of the courts of the Contracting State of the deceased's last domicile, there are no meaningful reasons to prevent him/her from applying for it. Therefore, the legatee should also be entitled to apply for establishing the jurisdiction of the courts of this Contracting State.

5.1.2. *Handing Over and Retaining Movable Property*

The rules on handing over movable property are contained in Article 31(4), and the rules on retaining movable property are found in Article 34 of the Agreement.[69] These rules complement the jurisdiction rule on movable property set out in Article 31(1).

The rules on handing over movable property come into play when movable property is not located in the Contracting State of the deceased's nationality whose courts, pursuant to Article 31(1), have jurisdiction to rule on that property. In such a situation, the courts of the Contracting State in which the movable property is located must, upon request of the competent authorities of the Contracting State of the deceased's nationality, hand over that movable property for the purpose of conducting the succession proceedings in this State (Article 31(4)). However, the handing over of movable property is to be refused if its transfer conflicts with the provisions on export bans or provisions on foreign currency or with some other provision of the Agreement.

The provisions on retaining movable property in the Contracting State in which it is located represent exactly those provisions which conflict with the provisions on handing over movable property and may supersede them if the requirements for their application have been fulfilled in a concrete case. Therefore, despite the request of the Contracting State of the deceased's nationality for handing over movable property, this property may be retained by the court of the Contracting State in which it is located, provided the heirs, mandatory heirs or legatees who are nationals of or reside in that Contracting State simply apply for its retention.[70] The retention lasts until the competent court of the Contracting State of the deceased's nationality finally decides on inheritance claims, reserved shares or legacies (Article 34(1)). The same applies when an application to retain movable property is filed by creditors of the deceased who are nationals of or reside in the Contracting State in which the movable property is located, provided they have registered their claims and, if needed, initiate the proceedings for their recognition (Article 34(2)).

5.1.3. *Undertaking Measures for the Securing and Administration of the Estate*

The rules on taking measures necessary for securing and administrating movable property are contained in Article 33(1) and (2). Pursuant to these rules, the court or another competent authority of the Contracting State in which the movable property of a national of the other Contracting State is located is to, upon request or on its own motion, undertake the measures necessary for the securing and the administration of the property as well as damage prevention

---

69 On retaining movable assets see M. Stanivuković and P. Đundić, above n. 3, p. 200.

70 See more ibid.

measures. In these cases, the court or other competent authority of the Contracting State in which the movable property is located has, in accordance with its own law, to make a list of all movable assets belonging to the estate and, depending on the circumstances of the case, put these assets under seal or in a safe place or appoint a confident person as a custodian of these assets. Upon request of the other Contracting State, these measures may be taken in some special form, provided it is not contrary to the *ordre public* of the requested Contracting State (i.e. contrary 'to the basic principles of the legislation of the requested Contracting State').

5.2. AGREEMENT WITH BULGARIA

5.2.1. Jurisdiction in Succession Matters

The rules on jurisdiction in succession matters in the Agreement with Bulgaria (**Treaty 22**) are based on the same criteria as those of the Agreement with Austria (**Treaty 3**) and, consequently, are structured in the same manner. Immovable property falls under the exclusive jurisdiction of the courts of the Contracting State in which this property is located (Article 23), and movable property under the jurisdiction of the Contracting State of the deceased's nationality (Article 24(1) first sentence). However, the material scope of application of these rules is a little bit different. They cover the distribution (liquidation) of the property in non-litigious proceedings and the resolution of disputes concerning inheritance claims, reserved shares and legacies in litigious proceedings, if these issues arise out of intestate and testamentary succession. Donation *mortis causa*, which is encompassed by the Agreement with Austria, is not expressly mentioned in the Agreement with Bulgaria and, therefore, should be considered as excluded from material scope of application.

The Agreement with Bulgaria also provides two exceptions from the general jurisdiction rule on movable property that are contained in provisions of the second sentence of Articles 24(1) and 30(1) and which fully correspond to the provisions of the second sentence of Articles 31(1) and 36(1) of the Agreement with Austria. Considering that these provisions are between themselves almost identical, everything that was said in respect of the interpretation and application of these exceptions in the Agreement with Austria applies here too.

5.2.2. Handing Over and Retaining Movable Property

The provisions of Articles 24(4) and 28 of the Agreement with Bulgaria which regulate handing over and retaining movable property are identical to those of Articles 31(4) and 34 of the Agreement with Austria (**Treaty 3**).

5.2.3. *Opening of a Will*

Contrary to the Agreement with Austria, the Agreement with Bulgaria contains special provisions on the opening of a will in Article 27. Pursuant to the first sentence of Article 27, the opening of a will is to be conducted by the court (authority) of the Contracting State in which the testament is located. As soon as this court opens the testament, it is to deliver a certified copy, the protocol (court record) on its condition and content and, depending on the circumstances of the case, the protocol (court record) on its opening to the court of the Contracting State of the deceased's nationality which has jurisdiction to conduct the succession proceedings (Article 27 second sentence). In addition, the court of the Contracting State of the deceased's nationality may request delivery of the original testament (Article 27 third sentence) if it finds it is needed for succession proceedings. However, the cited documents are not to be delivered if the court of the Contracting State in which testament has been opened has jurisdiction for conducting the succession proceedings under the jurisdiction rules of this Agreement (Articles 23, 24(1) and Article 30(1)).

5.2.4. *Undertaking Measures for the Securing and Administration of the Estate*

The rules on undertaking measures necessary to secure and administrate movable property are contained in Article 26(1) and (2), and they are the same as those contained in the Agreement with Austria (**Treaty 3**).

5.3. AGREEMENT WITH CZECHOSLOVAKIA

Before outlining the procedural rules of the Agreement with Czechoslovakia (**Treaty 13**), it should be mentioned again that Montenegro and Slovakia signed an additional Protocol to this Agreement in 2014, which set aside the provisions on succession matters contained in Articles 35–39 and 44 of this Agreement.[71] This means that the jurisdiction rules of Article 39 and the rules on opening of the will of Article 44 are inapplicable between Montenegro and Slovakia, while the rules on undertaking the measures of Article 40 and the rules on handing over the estate to the heirs as found in Article 45 are still in force. With regard to other countries (respective Contracting States) nothing has changed.

---

[71] Art. 5(b) of the new Protocol to the Agreement between the Social Federal Republic of Yugoslavia and the Czechoslovak Socialist Republic on the Regulation of Legal Relations in Civil, Family and Criminal Matters signed on 29.05.2014; available on the website of the Ministry of Justice of Montenegro: <http://www.mpa.gov.me/rubrike/Bilateralni-ugovori/156296/Protokol-izmedu-Crne-Gore-i-Republike-Slovacke.html> accessed 04.04.2019.

5.3.1. *Jurisdiction in Succession Matters*

As is the case with the two previously discussed agreements, the Agreement with Czechoslovakia provides that succession matters concerning movable property fall under the jurisdiction of the courts of the Contracting State of the deceased's nationality (Article 39(1)), and succession matters concerning immovable property fall under the exclusive jurisdiction of the Contracting State in which it is located (Article 39(2)). The Agreement also expressly specifies that these rules apply not only to distribution of the estate in non-litigious succession proceedings, but also to resolving all disputes concerning intestate and testamentary succession in litigious proceedings (Article 39(3)). Contrary to the Agreements with Austria (**Treaty** 3) and Bulgaria (**Treaty** 22), this Agreement prescribes only one exception from the general jurisdiction rule on movable property. Specifically, the exception relates to establishing jurisdiction of the courts of the Contracting State of which the deceased was not a national for ruling on distribution of movable property located on its territory, if the deceased had his/her last domicile in this State and the heirs who are domiciled or reside in the same State apply for it within six months of the death of deceased (Article 39(5)).

5.3.2. *Opening of a Will*

The authority of the Contracting State in which the testament is located has jurisdiction to open the will. A certified copy of the testament, the protocol (court record) on its opening and, upon request, the original testament are to be delivered to the court which has jurisdiction to conduct the succession proceedings (Article 44).

5.3.3. *Undertaking Measures for the Securing and Administration of the Estate*

The undertaking of measures for securing and administrating an estate is regulated by Article 40. The competent authority of the Contracting State in which the estate of the deceased, who was a national of the other Contracting State, is located is, in accordance with its own law, to undertake measures for the securing and administration of the estate that are highly necessary (Article 40(1)). The diplomatic or consular office of the Contracting State of the deceased's nationality is to be informed about any measures that are undertaken, and it may directly or through its representative participate in the implementation of such measures (Article 40(2)).

5.3.4. *Handing Over Movable Property to the Heirs*

The Agreement with Czechoslovakia contains neither rules on handing over movable property so as to allow the court of the Contracting State of which the deceased was a national to receive all movable assets with the purpose of conducting succession proceedings, nor rules on retaining movable property in the Contracting State in which it is located. It rather regulates in Article 45 the handing over of movable property or an equivalent value received from the sale of movable or immovable property to the heirs on the basis of the final decision given in the succession proceedings. If the movable property or an equivalent value is, in accordance with the final decision on succession, to be handed over to heirs who are domiciled or reside in the other Contracting State, the handing over is to be performed directly to the heir or to his/her representative. However, if direct handing over is not possible, the competent authority is to hand over the movable property (or its equivalent value) to the diplomatic or consular office of the cited Contracting State (Article 45(1)). The handing over of movable property or its equivalent value can be performed only if creditor claims and succession fees have been paid or secured in the Contracting State in which such property is located and only if the competent authority of this State has approved the transfer (export) of the assets or money (Article 45(2)).

5.4. AGREEMENT WITH HUNGARY

5.4.1. Jurisdiction in Succession Matters

The jurisdiction rules in succession matters contained in this agreement (**Treaty 25**) also follow the scission system providing for the courts of the Contracting State to have exclusive jurisdiction to rule on immovable property which is located in that State (Article 44) and for the courts of the Contracting State of which the deceased was a national to have jurisdiction to rule on movable property (Article 45(1)). These rules are fully consistent with those contained in the Agreements with Bulgaria (**Treaty 22**) and Czechoslovakia (**Treaty 13**) and what was said above applies here too.

The Agreement with Hungary also provides two exceptions from the general jurisdiction rule on movable property. The first provides for establishing jurisdiction of the courts of the Contracting State of which the deceased was not a national, but where he/she was last domiciled, for distribution of movable property located in its territory, if the heirs who reside in the same State apply for it (Article 51(1)). This rule is the same as that provided by previously mentioned bilateral agreements and has been already adequately discussed.

However, the second exception is characteristic of the Agreement with Hungary and is completely unknown to the other bilateral agreements. It provides for the prorogation of jurisdiction of the court of the Contracting State in which the movable property is located: if all movable assets of the deceased are located in one of the Contracting States, the court (authority) of that Contracting

State may have jurisdiction to conduct succession proceedings for distribution of these movable assets, provided one of the heirs or legatees applies for it and all other known heirs and legatees give their consent to it (Article 51(2)), this notwithstanding whether the deceased was a national of this Contracting State. The form in which the consent of the heirs and legatees has to be given is not regulated. In our view, the national procedural rules of the Contracting States that apply to prorogation agreements as well as to statements given by the parties in civil proceedings should be applied. From the perspective of Serbian/Bosnian/Montenegrin/Macedonian law, consent has to be expressed in writing, dated and signed by an heir or legatee, or given orally before the court at the beginning of non-litigious succession proceedings (in which case oral consent is to be recorded in the court minutes of the proceedings).

5.4.2. *Handing Over and Retaining Movable Property*

The rules on handing over movable property (Article 45(2)) and on its retention (Article 49) are identical to those of Agreements with Austria (**Treaty 3**) and Bulgaria (**Treaty 22**) and should be applied in the same manner as was explained in the respective sub-sections (see sections 5.1.2 and 5.2.2).

5.4.3. *Undertaking Measures for the Securing and Administration of the Estate*

The undertaking of measures for securing and administrating movable property is regulated by Article 47(1) and (2), provisions which are fully consistent with the corresponding provisions of the Agreements with Austria (**Treaty 3**) and Bulgaria (**Treaty 22**) that have been discussed above.

5.5. AGREEMENT WITH POLAND

5.5.1. *Jurisdiction in Succession Matters*

The Agreement with Poland (**Treaty 26**) provides the same jurisdiction rules in succession matters as those contained in previously discussed agreements: the court of the Contracting State in which the immovable property is located has exclusive jurisdiction to rule on succession matters related to that property (Article 42), and the court of the Contracting State of which the deceased was a national has jurisdiction to rule on movable property (Article 43(1)). These apply to non-litigious succession proceedings as well as to litigious proceedings for resolving disputes arising from intestate and testamentary succession.

The Agreement with Poland provides in Article 43(2) and (3) two exceptions from the general jurisdiction rule on movable property which are similar to those provided by the Agreement with Austria (**Treaty 3**). The first one is related to the situation in which the deceased, who was a national of one Contracting State, had his/her last domicile in the other Contracting State. In such a situation, the court of the Contracting State of the deceased's last domicile may have jurisdiction to conduct the succession proceedings for distribution of movable property located in this State, if heirs, mandatory heirs or legatees who reside in the Contracting State of the deceased's last domicile apply for it (Article 43(2) first sentence), unless any of the heirs or legatees, notwithstanding where they reside, object to it (Article 43(2) second sentence). The second exception provides the courts of a Contracting State in which movable property is located and of which the deceased was not a national with jurisdiction to rule on that movable property if the decision of the court of Contracting State of which the deceased was a national cannot be enforced (Article 43).

5.5.2. Handing Over and Retaining Movable Property

The rules on handing over (Article 43(4)) and retaining movable property (Article 45) are fully consistent with those of previously discussed agreements, and what was said there applies here too.

5.5.3. Opening of a Will

The opening of a will is regulated by the provisions of Article 40. These are identical to the provisions on the opening of wills contained in Article 27 of the Agreement with Bulgaria (**Treaty 22**), which have been already discussed above (see section 5.2.3).

5.5.4. Undertaking Measures for the Securing and Administration of the Estate

The provisions on undertaking measures for the securing and administration of the succession estate (Article 39) are the same as the corresponding provisions in previously discussed agreements.

5.6. AGREEMENT WITH ROMANIA

5.6.1. Jurisdiction in Succession Matters

As was the case in previously discussed bilateral agreements, the Agreement with Romania (**Treaty 27**) provides two sets of jurisdiction rules in succession matters, one for immovable property and another for movable property. Immovable property falls under the exclusive jurisdiction of the courts of the Contracting State in which immovable property is located (Article 36(2)). With respect to movable property the courts of the Contracting State of which the deceased was a national have jurisdiction to rule on such property (Article 36(1)). However, this agreement provides one exception from this general jurisdiction rule on movable property. Instead of the courts of the Contracting State of the deceased's nationality, the courts of the other Contracting State may have jurisdiction to conduct succession proceedings for distribution of movable property which is located in this State, provided the deceased was last domiciled in this State and provided the heirs apply for it within six months of the death of deceased (Article 37 first sentence) and none of the heirs or legatees objects to it (Article 37 third sentence). This exception is the same as that contained in Article 36(1) of the Agreement with Austria (**Treaty 3**), which has been adequately discussed above. What was said there applies here too.

5.6.2. *Handing Over Movable Property to the Heirs*

The provisions of Article 42 of the Agreement with Romania regulate handing over movable property to the heirs on the basis of a final decision on succession. It should be clearly distinguished from handing over movable property located in one Contracting State for the purpose of conducting the succession proceedings in the other Contracting State (i.e. the Contracting State of the deceased's nationality), a topic which is not regulated by this Agreement.

The provisions of Article 42 are similar to those of Article 45 of the Agreement with Czechoslovakia (**Treaty 13**). Pursuant to Article 42(1), if a court of Contracting State which adopts a final decision in succession proceedings has to hand over movable property to heirs who are domiciled or have a residence in the other Contracting State, the court is to hand it over to a diplomatic or consular office of that State. The handing over of movable property may be performed only if creditor claims have been paid in accordance with the below-discussed provisions of Article 43 and if the competent authority has approved the transfer (export) of assets in those cases in which such transfer is forbidden.

5.6.3. *Retaining Movable Property Upon Request of Creditors*

The provisions on retaining movable property are contained in Article 43 of this agreement. Unlike corresponding provisions of the Agreements with Austria (**Treaty 3**), Bulgaria (**Treaty 22**), Hungary (**Treaty 25**) and Poland (**Treaty 26**), which entitle all beneficiaries (heirs, legatees and creditors) to apply for retention of movable property, these provisions empower only creditors to apply for such a measure.

Upon application of creditors who are domiciled or have residence in the Contracting State in which movable property is located, the competent authority of this Contracting State may retain the whole movable property or a sufficient part of it until a competent court or authority of the other Contracting State finally decides on the creditor claims (Article 43(1)). In order to enable the creditors to submit such an application, the competent authority of the Contracting State in which movable property is located is to inform creditors via public notice that they have to register their claims and, if needed, initiate proceedings for their recognition within certain period of time, which is not to be shorter than 30 days nor longer than six months (Article 43(2) first sentence). If they fail to do so, the competent authority cannot refuse to hand over movable property to the heirs in accordance with Article 42 on the grounds that creditor claims have not been paid or secured.

5.6.4. *Opening of a Will and Undertaking Measures for the Securing and Administration of the Estate*

The provisions on opening a will (Article 44) are the same as those in the Agreements with Bulgaria (**Treaty 22**) and Poland (**Treaty 26**). There is no need to discuss them again. The same can be said for provisions on undertaking measures for the securing and administration of the estate, which fully correspond to the respective provisions of previously discussed agreements.

6. THE FUTURE OF EXISTING BILATERAL AGREEMENTS

6.1. THE ASSESSMENT WITH RESPECT TO SERBIA, BOSNIA AND HERZEGOVINA AND MACEDONIA

From the Serbian, B&H and Macedonian point of view, the above-discussed bilateral agreements should remain in force, but they have to be revised.

The conflict-of-laws rules and jurisdiction rules of bilateral agreements are in line with those contained in the national private international law acts of Serbia, B&H and Macedonia, although one may say that the national rules are better composed. It leads to the conclusion that the status quo in respect of these rules should be retained. However, the rules on handing over and retaining movable property are outdated and ignored by the courts. There is no court decision in which these rules have been applied. Therefore, they should be removed from the agreements. Additionally, the conflict-of-laws rules on the formal validity of testaments contained in the Agreements with Bulgaria[72] (**Treaty 22**), Czechoslovakia[73] (Czech Republic and Slovakia **Treaty 13**)

[72] See section 4.2.
[73] See section 4.3.

and Romania[74] (**Treaty 27**) should be renegotiated and revised too, considering that they are very restrictive and may result in the formal invalidity of testament. The revision may be performed so as either to eliminate these rules from the Agreements, in which case the national conflict-of-laws rules on the formal validity of testaments would find application, or to create new conflict-of-laws rules based on the same principles as those of the Hague Testamentary Convention of 1961.

In addition, it should be stressed that all bilateral agreements contain rules on recognition and enforcement of court decisions, which is an additional reason for supporting the view that these agreements should remain in force. Particularly, the Agreement with Austria (**Treaty 3**) is very important, because Austrian law requires diplomatic reciprocity for recognition and enforcement of foreign decisions. This agreement meets this requirement because it stipulates in Article 31(2) that the courts of both Contracting States commit themselves to recognize and enforce the decisions of the other Contracting State, provided it is not contrary to the State's basic principles of legislation (i.e. *ordre public*) or to other provisions of the Agreement.

Finally, it should be mentioned that Macedonia expects to enact a new PIL Act whose conflict-of-laws and jurisdiction rules on succession will be completely consistent with those of the Succession Regulation. When that happens, the approach to these bilateral agreements should be the same as that with regard to Montenegro (see below, section 6.2).

6.2. THE ASSESSMENT WITH RESPECT TO MONTENEGRO

The Mon. PIL Act contains conflict-of-laws and jurisdiction rules in succession matters which are compatible with those of the Succession Regulation. It means that the rules of the above-discussed bilateral agreements clash with the new system of rules set up by the Mon. PIL Act, which are harmonized with the Succession Regulation. Therefore, the government of Montenegro should propose to other Contracting States the termination of the rules on succession matters contained in these agreements. It has already made such move and has renegotiated the Agreement with Slovakia (**Treaty 13**) by concluding the additional Protocol to this Agreement in 2014, which set aside most provisions on succession matters. The same should be done with regard to other agreements.

However, termination of the rules on succession matters does not mean that these agreements should be terminated entirely. As it has been said with regard to Serbia, B&H and Macedonia, these agreements contain rules on

[74] See section 4.6.

recognition and enforcement in civil matters which enable an easier movement of court decisions between Montenegro and the other Contracting States. This constitutes a reason why these agreements should remain in force in respect of civil matters other than succession matters.

Finally, it should be stressed that the European Certificate of Succession issued in EU Member States can produce its effects in Montenegro. Pursuant to the Montenegrin Act on the State Surveying and Cadastre of Immovable Property[75] (Article 89 point 4), the valid document for entering rights *in rem* into the public register may be, among others, a foreign authentic instrument. Considering that Montenegrin courts, pursuant to Mon. PIL Act, do not have exclusive jurisdiction to rule on immovable property located in Montenegro, it is quite possible that foreign public instruments – including the European Certificate of Succession – which deal with immovable property located in Montenegro will be recognized and enforced by Montenegrin authorities and also serve as a legal title for entering rights *in rem* in the public registry of immovable assets. However, this is not possible where a European Certificate of Succession has been issued by EU Member States which are contracting parties to the above-discussed bilateral agreements because the rules of the agreements take precedence over national rules. Therefore, by removing succession matters from the scope of application of these agreements, it should become possible to recognize and enforce in Montenegro a European Certificate of Succession issued by Contracting States to these agreements.

---

75 Official Gazette of the Republic of Montenegro, Nos. 29/2007, 32/2011 and 43/2015.

THE RELATIONS OF IRAN WITH EU MEMBER STATES

Nadjma Yassari

1. INTRODUCTION

This contribution intends to evaluate the impact of bilateral treaties concluded between certain European countries and Iran from the perspective of Iranian law. In the late 1920s and early 1930s, Iran concluded a series of such treaties with different countries, including Poland, Germany, Belgium and Luxembourg, Greece, France, Switzerland, Austria and Czechoslovakia. Some of these treaties were concluded on a provisional basis and were not extended after their initial period of validity; some of them have been extended and renewed and are still in force today.

The question of whether and how these treaties are dealt with in Iranian legal writing and interpreted by Iranian courts is difficult to answer for mainly three reasons. The first is that Iranian legal writing does not discuss the treaties in any depth. Where reference is made to any of these treaties, they figure as abstract examples of treaties concluded by Iran that take priority over the domestic conflict-of-laws rules, without any detailed analyzes of their structure, purpose or interpretation. This relates also to a second blank spot, which is the lack of case law on the application of the treaties. In fact, until very recently court decisions were not published at all by any official State-run institution. For a long time case law could only be retrieved from two sources: the compilation of the legal opinions of the plenary session of the Iranian Supreme Court, published by the court itself (since 1995), and private compilations of cases collected by lawyers, law professors or researchers. Both sources, however, are selective, and none of the reported cases relates to the application of the treaties. In an endeavour to bring about more transparency, in 2011 the Law on the five-year development scheme of the Islamic Republic of Iran incorporated a regulation according to which the judiciary became obliged to publish important court decisions. Although some compilations have been published, here again no mention is made of the application or the interpretation of these treaties.

This brings us to the last point, which is a factual one: the lack of academic interest in the treaties as well as of case law may be accounted for by the very few numbers of European nationals having an Iranian domicile or habitual residence. In fact, their number can be assessed only vaguely. The Statistical Centre of Iran that conducts censuses on a five-year basis[1] publishes its findings regularly online. Whereas the most recent census of 2016 does not include any data on the numbers and nationalities of foreigners living in Iran, the reports for the 2006 and 2011 censuses include such figures. According to the official data, the population living in Iran in 2006 consisted of 68,901,154 Iranians, 1,211,171 Afghans or vice versa, 44,094 Iraqis, 15,455 Pakistanis and 886 Turks. Additionally, a total number of 32,410 were categorized as 'others' without precise identification of their nationality. This last figure diminished in 2011 to 24,290.[2] This number similarly accounts for the number of all other foreigners, including Europeans, without pointing specifically to definite nationalities.

Thus, in order to bring some fruitful thoughts into the present research question, namely what impact the treaties with third States may have on the Europeanization of private international law, the political and legal situation surrounding the enactment of the treaties will be the focus of this contribution. With this approach, it is intended to shed some light on the question of such treaties' legal relevance and the significance that Iran attaches to them.

---

1 See its website in English at <https://www.amar.org.ir/english/Population-and-Housing-Censuses> accessed 05.04.2019.

2 See Statistical Centre of Iran, 'Table 4: Population by citizenship: 2006 and 2011' [2012] *Selected Findings of National Population and Housing Census, 2011* <https://www.amar.org.ir/Portals/1/Iran/90.pdf> accessed 05.04.2019.

2. HISTORICAL SETTING OF THE ENACTMENT OF THE TREATIES

The background against which most of the treaties were concluded was a particularly difficult political situation in Iran. Since the beginning of the 19th century, Iran had been under the de facto domination of the British and the Russians, although never colonized officially. In 1905 a nationalist uprising against the then ruling Qajar dynasty and the subsequent establishment of a limited constitutional monarchy in 1906 marked the beginning of modern Iranian private law.[3] In 1921, Reza Khan, an Iranian officer of the Persian Cossack Brigade, seized control of the government with the help of the British and, having ousted the last Qajar king in 1925, became the Shah of Iran, establishing the Pahlavi dynasty as of 25 April 1926.

In May 1927, the Iranian Ministry of Foreign Affairs issued an announcement on the revocation of the so-called 'Capitulation Regimes' in Iran. Observed initially as unwritten law geared towards European merchants and nationals, the capitulation regime was enforced as law subsequent to the Russo-Iran Wars (early 1820s) and the Treaty of Turkmenchay signed on 10 February 1828.[4] According to these regimes, foreigners of particular nations did not fall under Iranian jurisdiction but were instead subject to the adjudication of foreign consular 'courts' of their own States.[5] In addition, some foreigners, at first Russians, were granted preferential treatment in commercial matters. These privileges were later extended to other European nationals by subsequent contracts, which included most-favoured-nation clauses.[6] By the early 1920s, however, these kinds of arrangements weighed heavily on non-Western countries, as they subjected them to foreign domination.[7] In 1914, the Ottoman

---

3 See for a thorough account, S. Marin, 'The Ancients and the Moderns? The Ideal of Justice and Constitutional Revolution in Iran (1905–1911)' (2006) 52 *Droit et cultures*, 139–167.

4 See for its *Farsi* version: S. Jalāl al-Din Madanī, *Ḥuqūq-i Bayn al-Milal-i Khuṣūṣī [Private International Law]*, Intishārāt-i Pāydār, Tehran 2009–2010, pp. 330–335.

5 S. Hassan Amin, *Middle East Legal Systems*, Royston Limited, Glasgow 1985, p. 55 et seq.; M. Zirinsky, 'Riza Shah's Abrogation of Capitulations, 1927–1928' in S. Cronin (ed.), *The Making of Modern Iran: State and Society under Riza Shah*, 1921–1941, *Routledge/BIPS Persian Studies Series*, Routledge, London 2003, pp. 81 et seq.

6 See, for example, the Prussian-Persian Treaty on Friendship and Commerce of 25.06.1857 as well as its successor, the German-Persian Treaty on Friendship, Commerce and Navigation of 11.06.1873, that completely excluded all German nationals from Iranian jurisdiction, see H. Krüger, 'Kollision von Staatsverträgen' (1973) *FamRZ*, 8; M. Gorges, *Business-Knigge Iran*, 3rd ed., Gabler Verlag, Wiesbaden 2016, pp. 34–36.

7 For an account of the different regimes governing the relations between Iranians and foreigners and between foreigners in Iran see Z. Bālāzādih, *Ḥuqūq-i Bayn al-Milal-i Khuṣūṣī va Muqarrarāt-i Īrān dar Zamīnih-i Tābiʿiyat, Iqāmatgāh va Vażʿiyat-i Bīgānigān [Private International Law & Iran's Regulations on Nationality, Residency and Situation of Foreigners]*, Nashr-i Mardum-i Sālārī, Tehran 2004, p. 133 et seq.

government denounced the Ottoman Capitulation and it was subsequently abolished pursuant to the Peace Settlement of Lausanne of 24 July 1923.[8] As the political strength of the succession States to the great European powers of the 19th century, in particular Germany and Austria-Hungary, had diminished after World War I, extra-territorial jurisdiction could hardly be upheld to the same extent. Also, the renunciation of capitulary powers by the Soviet government sparked momentum for non-Western countries to do away with all treaties undermining their juridical and ultimately political authority.[9]

In Iran, the abolition of the capitulation regimes was anticipated by a radical reorganization of juridical structures and the restructuring of the court system. In April 1927 a new law regulating the judiciary, a new Code on the Organization of the Judiciary and a new Civil Procedure Code were enacted, abolishing religious courts and introducing a State court system with civil servants as judges.[10] Shortly thereafter, in May 1927 Reza Shah formally notified the foreign powers enjoying capitulation privileges in Iran of the abolition of all of them as of 28 May 1928.[11] In effect, a year after that announcement all treaties and agreements concluded by the previous Qajar dynasty were revoked.

The Western powers reacted to the announcement with an enhancement of bilateral diplomatic communications. The Iranian government signalled its willingness to negotiate the details of possible bilateral treaties if the question of abolition was principally accepted and settled as Iran wished. The new regulation for the courts provided leeway by providing that lawsuits between Iranians and foreigners could be transferred to arbitration proceedings if so desired by the parties.[12] France was the first country to react: accepting the abolition of the capitulation regime, the French government expressed its readiness to enter into bilateral negotiations as long as French nationals would enjoy most-favoured-nation treatment under a potential new regime. On 11 May 1928, Iran and France signed a provisional agreement for one year[13] to be subsequently followed by a Convention of Friendship addressing questions regarding customs, consular and commercial matters as well as the establishment and settlement of foreign nationals in each country. The agreement foresaw complete reciprocity and equal treatment of nationals on the territory of the other in conformity with the rules of international law. It also contained

8 A. J. Toynbee, *Survey of International Affairs 1928*, Oxford University Press, London 1929, p. 349; see B. S. Güneş, in this volume p. 290.

9 A. J. Toynbee, above n. 8, p. 349.

10 See for more details: S. Marin 'The lukewarm reception of Napoleonic codes in Iran (1911–1935)' (2004) 48 *Droit et cultures* [online since March 2010], margin notes 41–43 <http://journals.openedition.org/droitcultures/1723> accessed 05.04.2019.

11 A. J. Toynbee, above n. 8, p. 350; Z. Bālāzādih, above n. 7, p. 134.

12 A. J. Toynbee, above n. 8, p. 351.

13 The *Farsi* version of this provisional treaty is available on the website of the Iranian Parliament <http://rc.majlis.ir/fa/law/show/91960> accessed 05.04.2019.

provisions on private international law, according to which in matters of personal status each national remained subject to his/her own national law on the territory of the other country. On 15 May 1928 a similar provisional agreement was signed with Belgium.[14] Iran also reached out to Germany[15] and the United States, offering them analogous treaties. Subsequently Iran concluded provisional treaties with, *inter alia*, Sweden[16] (27 May 1929), Italy[17] (5 September 1929) and the Netherlands[18] (12 March 1930).[19]

Another interesting step that Iran took in 1928 was to sort out the status of Iranians with potentially dual or multiple nationalities. The Ministry of Foreign Affairs initiated an investigation on the status of Iranians residing abroad and inside Iran who claimed to hold a foreign nationality in addition to that of Iran.[20] According to a draft brought to Parliament early in 1928, Iranians living abroad were to be barred from re-entering Iran unless they could prove that they had formally and legally acquired a foreign nationality – and thus given up Iranian nationality – or produce evidence that they were holding an Iranian passport issued by an Iranian consulate abroad. Subsequently, the provisions on nationality incorporated in the Iranian Civil Code (CC) of 1935 generally adopted this position. According to Article 989 CC, any person who acquired a foreign citizenship after the Iranian solar year 1280 (21.3.1901–28.2.1902) without observing the legal requirements would have his/her foreign nationality declared null and void and would be regarded as an Iranian national only.

Further, the revocation of the capitulation system had to be met with the promise of Reza Shah to provide for a stable and reliable private law legal system, the lack of which having been the main reason put forward by the European powers for installing the capitulation systems in the first place.[21]

---

14 The *Farsi* version of this provisional treaty is available on the website of the Iranian Parliament <http://rc.majlis.ir/fa/law/show/91968> accessed 05.04.2019.

15 On German–Iranian relations in the late 1920s and the 1930s see F. Kochwasser, *Iran und wir: Geschichte der deutsch-iranischen Handels- und Wirtschaftsbeziehungen*, H. Erdmann Verlag, Freiburg 1961. Alongside the treaty of Establishment, Iran concluded the Convention on Commerce, Customs and Navigation (17.02.1929) and the Convention on reciprocal protection of patents on inventions, marks and trade names and marks and designs as well as the protection of literary and artistic works (27.07.1930).

16 *Farsi* version available online <http://rc.majlis.ir/fa/law/show/91984> accessed 05.04.2019.

17 *Farsi* version available online <http://rc.majlis.ir/fa/law/show/91992> accessed 05.04.2019.

18 *Farsi* version available online <http://rc.majlis.ir/fa/law/show/91990> accessed 05.04.2019.

19 Provisional treaties were also signed with, *inter alia*, Greece (09.01.1931) <http://rc.majlis.ir/fa/law/show/92405> accessed 05.04.2019, the former Czechoslovakia (17.06.1928) <http://rc.majlis.ir/fa/law/show/91956> accessed 05.04.2019, and Denmark (20.02.1934) <http://rc.majlis.ir/fa/law/show/92866> accessed 05.04.2019; for a list of the international treaties concluded between Iran and other States see the website of the Iranian Foreign Ministry <http://de.frankfurt.mfa.ir/uploads/majmoe_93758.pdf> accessed 05.04.2019.

20 A. J. Toynbee, above n. 8, p. 357.

21 S. Marin, 'Ostad Elahi et les droits de l'homme: éthique et modernité' in J.-L. Chabot, P. Didier and J. Ferrand (eds.), *Le code civil et les droits de l'homme*, L. Harmattan, Grenoble 2005, p. 423.

In fact, alongside the reorganization of the judiciary, the codification of substantive private law had been on the agenda of the Iranian government since the 1910s. Here, the Iranians took special interest in French law. The French Civil Code had been translated into *Farsi* in the second half of the 19th century, and in 1919 a first school of law, staffed mainly with French professors of law, was installed to train judges and civil servants.[22] As of 1915, preparatory works on the codification of an Iranian Civil Code had been taken up, but it was only in 1928 that the Civil Code was voted on in Parliament.[23] The drafters of the Code were Iranian jurists (trained partly in Europe), Shiite clerics and civil servant of the Ministry of Justice. The first part of an Iranian Civil Code comprising 975 articles, including regulations on succession law and private international law, was promulgated in 1928. In 1935 the second part of the Code (Articles 976–1335), with regulations on nationality and family law, followed. The Code has been in force since and has been subject to (very) minimal reform.

The bilateral treaties that are still in force today are essentially the Treaty of Establishment between the German Empire and the Persian Empire of 17 February 1929 (**Treaty 17**), the Treaty of Friendship between the Swiss Confederation and the Persian Empire of 25 April 1934, the Treaty of Friendship and Establishment between the Republic of Austria and the Persian Empire of 9 September 1959 (**Treaty 1**) and the Convention on Establishment and Navigation between France and Iran of 24 June 1964.

3. THE TREATIES

3.1. GENERAL REMARKS

The initiative to enact new bilateral treaties with European countries was not met with unanimous acceptance in Iran in the late 1920s. Critics saw those treaties as a backdoor for re-opening special jurisdictions for foreigners. This risk was, however, limited in scope. First, the treaties foresee the application of foreign law only in matters related to personal status, whereas the capitulation system had an all-embracing scope encompassing all legal fields, including penal and administrative matters. Second, the treaties apply on a reciprocal basis, safeguarding that Iranian nationals are given the same privileges of law in the other Contracting State as received by nationals of the latter in Iran, and ensuring equal access to justice and rights of settlement for the respective nationals in

22 S. Marin, above n. 10, margin note 30 <http://journals.openedition.org/droitcultures/1723> accessed 05.04.2019.

23 S. Marin, above n. 21, p. 423.

the other country. One important provision that deserves to be highlighted is the right of nationals of the Contracting State to own immovable property in Iran for private and professional reasons. This right is important as generally non-Iranians are barred from owning any immovables on Iranian soil.[24] The bulk of provisions in the treaties thus relates to establishing free movement and businesses in and between the respective Contracting States so as to spark economic growth and the transfer of technology.

3.2. PRIORITY OF THE TREATIES OVER DOMESTIC RULES

As mentioned above, Iranian private international law is regulated in the Iranian Civil Code (Articles 1–10 and 962–974 CC). Article 9 CC provides that provisions in treaties concluded between Iran and other States in accordance with the Iranian Constitution are to have the force of law. Principles 77 and 125 of the Iranian Constitution demand that those treaties be ratified by the Parliament and officially published to enter into force. Further, Article 974 CC stipulates that the domestic provisions on private international law are applicable only where they do not contradict international treaties. From this, it can be inferred that international treaties that have observed the legal proceedings take precedence over domestic rules.[25]

3.3. GENERAL STRUCTURE OF THE TREATIES

The Swiss-Iranian treaty is composed of three parts. The first part, entitled 'Friendship Agreement between the Swiss Confederation and the Persian Empire', consists of five articles and enunciates the intent of the Contracting States to strengthen their diplomatic and consular relations and to establish a framework for the settlement of the nationals of each country in the other country. The second part, entitled the 'Convention of Settlement between the Swiss Confederation and the Persian Empire', encompasses ten articles mainly dealing with private international law; and finally, its third part deals with legal aid (*Armenrecht*).

---

24 See e.g. Art. 6 of the German-Iranian Treaty; M. Suhrābī, *Ḥuqūq-i Bayn al-Milal-i Khuṣūṣī [Private International Law]*, Kitāb-Khānih-i Ganj-i Dānish, Tehran 2006, p. 100; B. Arfa^c Niyā, *Ḥuqūq-i Bayn al-Milal-i Khuṣūṣī: Tābi^ciyat, Iqāmatgāh, Vaż^c-i Bīgānigān [Private International Law: Nationality, Domicile and Position of Foreign Nationals]*, vol. 1, 5th ed., Intishārāt-i Bihtāb, Tehran 2003, p. 238.

25 B. Arfa^c Niyā, above n. 24, p. 30; M. Saljūqī, *Ḥuqūq-i Bayn al-Milal-i Khuṣūṣī [Private International Law]*, vol. 2, 2nd ed., Nashr-i Dādgustar, Tehran 1998, p. 221.

The German-Iranian Treaty (**Treaty 17**) comprises two parts: the Treaty on Establishment; and its final Protocol. Here again, both themes, i.e. the relations between the Contracting States and private international law, are addressed.

The Agreement with Austria (**Treaty 1**) is articulated in one document. It announces its aim to foster friendship between the Contracting States and to enhance economic and technological exchange. As with the other treaties, it also incorporates rules on the applicable law in family and succession law matters.

Finally, the French-Iranian treaty has a slightly different connotation as it only very briefly touches upon matters of private international law, with the bulk of its provisions being concerned with navigation and the corresponding rights and duties of the Contracting States.

3.4. CONFLICT-OF-LAWS RULES

3.4.1. Scope of Application

3.4.1.1. Subject Matter

The wording of the provisions in the German-Iranian Treaty (**Treaty 17**) and the Swiss-Iranian Treaty regarding the regulated subject matter are identical. Article 8(3) and its explanatory note in the final Protocol of the German-Iranian Agreement as well as Article 8(3) and (4) of the Swiss-Iranian Agreement refer explicitly to the following matters: the law of persons ('*masā'il-i marbūṭih bi-ḥuqūq-i shakhṣī*'); family law ('*ḥuqūq-i khānivādigī*'); and succession law ('*irs̱*'). Further the relevant legal fields are enumerated as follows: marriage ('*izdivāj*'); matrimonial property regime ('*tartīb-i amvāl bayn-i zawjayn*'); divorce ('*ṭalāq*'); separation ('*iftirāq*'); dowry ('*jahīz*'); paternity ('*ubuvvat*'); filiation ('*nasab*'); adoption ('*qabūlī-i farzandī*'); legal capacity ('*ahliyyat-i ḥuqūqī*'); majority (lit. puberty) ('*bulūgh*'); legal and nominated guardianship ('*vilāyat va qaymūmat*'); deprivation of legal capacity ('*ḥajr*'); wills and intestate succession ('*ḥaqq-i vurās̱at*'); the settlement and division of the estate ('*taṣfiyih va taqsīm-i mā tarak va yā amvāl*'); and all further matters relating to family law and personal status ('*masā'il-i marbūṭih bi-ḥuqūq-i khānivādigī va … aḥvāl-i shakhṣiyyih*').

The term 'personal status' ('*aḥvāl-i shakhṣiyyih*') is used in both treaties as a generic term encompassing all matters not enumerated in the explicit list and is meant to include any matter regarding the law of persons, family law and succession law.

The Austrian-Iranian Agreement (**Treaty 1**) sets out a similar, only slightly differing enumeration, but one not using the term 'personal status' at all. According to Article 10(3), the following matters fall under the treaty: marriage ('*izdivāj*'); matrimonial property regimes ('*ravārtīb-i mālī bayn-i zan va shūhar*'); divorce ('*ṭalāq*') and legal separation ('*matārikih*'); dowry ('*jahīziyih*');

paternity (*'ubuvvat'*); filiation (*'bunuvvat'*); adoption (*'farzand-khāndigī'*); legal capacity (*'ahliyyat'*); majority (*'rushd-i qānūnī'*); nominated guardianship (*'qaymūmat'*); and intestate and testate succession (*'irs̱ va vaṣiyyat'*). The French-Iranian Treaty, on the other hand, only refers to the 'statut personnel' (Article 2) without enumerating any concrete subject matter.

For the interpretation and delimitation of the scope of application of the treaties, relating in particular to the term 'personal status', one must consider the binding languages of the treaties. The German-Iranian and the Austrian-Iranian treaties were written and published in Farsi, German and French. According to Article 10 of the German-Iranian Treaty and Article 16 of the Austrian-Iranian Treaty, in the event of a disagreement on the interpretation of the treaties, the French version is binding. The original version of the Swiss-Iranian Treaty was written and published in French and German in Switzerland. Its binding language is also French. Unfortunately, in the Archives of the Iranian Parliament only a *Farsi* version of the Swiss-Iranian Treaty could be found.

The French-Iranian Treaty, on the other hand, was available only in its French version. The archives of the Iranian Parliament held the *Farsi* version of the preliminary French-Iranian treaty of 1928 that was not subsequently ratified in its original version. Rather, the treaty between France and Iran came into force in 1964 in the context of a wider agreement related in particular to navigation. According to Article 15 of the French-Iranian Treaty of 1964, both languages (French and Farsi) are authoritative.

To delimitate the scope of application of the treaties, the term 'personal status' (*'aḥvāl-i shakhṣiyyih'*) must be evaluated. Iranian legal texts use the term *'aḥvāl-i shakhṣiyyih'* without explicitly defining it. There are some debates about the scope of application and the definition of the term.[26] The use of the term in the legislation is not always consistent. In some provisions, one can find a specific description of what the term addresses: Article 6 CC, for example, states that matters of personal status encompass, *inter alia*, the conclusion of marriage, divorce, legal capacity and succession law. Similarly, Principle 12 of the Iranian Constitution specifies matters of personal status as those regarding marriage, divorce, succession law and last wills. Article 7 CC, however, separates the area of personal status from succession law. Nevertheless, the majority view holds that the term personal status in Iranian legal terminology encompasses all matters regarding capacity, family law and succession law.[27] Yet in French legal terminology, as is shown by the French report,[28] the term 'statut personnel' refers – for the sake of private international law – only to family law.

---

26 See the discussion in S. Fadavī, *Taʿāruż-i Qavānīn dar Ḥuqūq-i Īrān bā Tākīd bar Aḥvāl-i Shakhṣiyyih [The Conflict of Laws in the Iranian Legal Rulings]*, Intishārāt-i Ṭarḥ-i Nuvīn-i Andīshih, Tehran 2006, pp. 251 et seq.

27 Ibid., p. 253.

28 See Fulli-Lemaire, in this volume p. 146.

This discrepancy has, however, no effect on the substantive reach of the German-, Austrian- and Swiss-Iranian treaties. Although their authoritative language is French, the wording of the treaties explicitly extends to succession law.[29] Thus, as far as these treaties are concerned, succession law falls within their scope. As the provisions of the treaties take priority over the Iranian domestic conflict-of-laws rules, the applicable law in all matters of succession must be determined according to the provisions of these treaties. This includes intestate succession, succession by testamentary disposition, forced heirship, testamentary executors, administration and *in eventu* special succession regimes for certain assets.

As far as the French-Iranian treaty is concerned, both Farsi and French are authoritative. This would potentially mean that – from the Iranian perspective – succession law would be included in its scope of application, whereas from the perspective of French law, the French-Iranian treaty is limited to matters of family law. How this issue is managed in the courts must, however, remain a puzzle, as there are neither Iranian nor French court decisions on this matter.[30]

3.4.1.2. Formalities

Except for the Austrian-Iranian Treaty (**Treaty 1**), none of the other treaties deals with formalities. The scope of application of foreign law in the German-, Swiss- and French-Iranian treaties is thus limited to substantive law and does not extend to matters of form, and in particular not to the law applicable on the formal validity of a last will. This law must therefore be determined by the general rules of Iranian private international law. As Iran has not ratified the Hague Convention on the Form of Testamentary Dispositions, the form of a last will is to be governed by the domestic Iranian rule, i.e. Article 969 CC, that adheres to the rule of *lex loci actus*.[31]

The Austrian-Iranian treaty on the other hand addresses matters of form. Article 10(4)(2) states that the fact that a last will has been established according to the law of the place of its making, and not according to the law of the nationality of the deceased, does not jeopardize the validity of the instrument. It follows from an Iranian perspective that the formal validity of a will may be established if the will concurs with the rules of Austrian law (law of nationality of the deceased) or with the law of the place where the will has been made. A last will drafted in Iran that is formally invalid under Austrian law may still be valid

29 For an interpretation of the French term 'testament' in the Austrian-Iranian treaty, see Rudolf, in this volume, p. 19.
30 See Fulli-Lemaire, in this volume p. 147.
31 B. Arfac Niyā, above n. 24, p. 312.

if conforming with the formal requirements of Iranian law, as regulated in the Code of Non-Contentious Proceedings of 1940.[32]

3.4.1.3. Location of the Assets

No treaty differentiates as to the location of estate assets. As the focus of the treaties is the individual person and the application of his/her national law on the territory of the other State, it can be argued that the treaties are directed towards assets situated in the respective other country.[33] From an Iranian perspective, this would mean that the treaties only cover assets located in Iran. This is supported by the systematics of Iranian private international law. According to Article 967 CC, movable and immovable assets of a deceased foreigner that are located in Iran are subject to the substantive law[34] of the deceased's nationality. The restriction of the scope of application of foreign law to assets located in Iran is an indication that as a general rule Iranian international succession law is primarily concerned with assets in Iran.[35] There is thus the possibility of dépeçage if the deceased has assets in different countries.

3.4.2. Choice of Law

None of the treaties allows the parties to choose the applicable law. Rather, the relevant articles refer to the law of the nationality of the concerned party, without mentioning the possibility of a choice of law. This corresponds also with Iranian international succession law, which does not foresee an *optio juris* in succession matters. In fact, there is only a very restricted space for choice of law in Iranian private international law, its being strictly limited to international contracts.[36]

3.4.3. Connecting Factor

The connecting factor in all treaties is nationality. In succession law cases the decisive nationality is the nationality of the deceased, whereas the nationality of

---

32 For the formal requirements of a last will under Iranian law see N. Yassari, 'Testamentary Formalities in Islamic Law and their Reception in the Modern Laws of Islamic Countries' in K. G. C. Reid, M. J. de Waal and R. Zimmermann (eds.), *Comparative Succession Law, vol. 1: Testamentary Formalities*, Oxford University Press, Oxford 2011, pp. 282–304.

33 See for a similar understanding of this issue from the perspective of German law, Looschelders in this volume, p. 153.

34 Substantive law in this context refers to the determination of the heirs, their respective shares in the estate and the portion of the estate that can be disposed of by virtue of a testamentary disposition.

35 Similarly, B. Arfaᶜ Niyā, above n. 24, p. 254.

36 See N. Yassari, 'Das Internationale Vertragsrecht des Irans' (2009) *IPRax*, 451–456.

the heirs is not taken into consideration.[37] Thus, if the succession to the estate of a German, an Austrian or a Swiss national and most probably a French national is dealt with in an Iranian court, the substantive law of the deceased's nationality must be applied.

The treaties do not touch upon the question of dual or multiple nationalities. It must also be remembered – as mentioned above – that the Iranian government endeavoured in 1928 to extinguish the possibility of Iranians having multiple nationalities. The conclusion of the treaties was mainly directed towards securing the rights and the status of Iranians abroad by granting the same rights to the nationals of the other States. The starting point from an Iranian perspective was thus the single nationality that the deceased possessed. This is also supported by the provisions on nationality law that were codified in the Iranian Civil Code in 1935. Accordingly, only in very specifically regulated cases may a person have more than one nationality, in particular through marriage to an Iranian citizen. Thus, according to Iranian nationality law,[38] a foreign woman marrying an Iranian man will automatically be awarded Iranian nationality and be treated as Iranian in Iran (Article 976 no. 6 CC);[39] she will not, however, lose her former nationality as this does not fall under the competence of Iranian authorities.[40] It follows, however, that for the sake of the applicability of the treaties, she will be considered Iranian only and thus fall outside their scope of application.

Conversely, foreign men marrying Iranian women may be granted Iranian citizenship solely by application and only if they have common children with the Iranian mother (Article 979 CC).

It is also important to note that an Iranian by birth may not revoke his nationality unless Parliament agrees to denaturalize this person (Article 988 CC).[41] If a person acquires a foreign nationality without going through the process of denaturalization, he/she will still be considered an Iranian citizen (Article 989 CC).[42] Thus the question of how to proceed in cases of dual or multiple nationalities will arise only where the deceased had one of the relevant European nationalities as well as another non-Iranian nationality. No provision – other than the ones mentioned above – addresses this issue, and Iranian legal writing treats of it

---

37 M. Saljūqī, above n. 25, p. 300.

38 Nationality law is regulated in the Iranian Civil Code (Art. 976–991 CC) as well as in a special 2006 Act regarding the transfer of citizenship from an Iranian woman to her children in cases where she is married to a non-Iranian husband.

39 Ḥ. Āl-i Kajbāf, *Tābiʿiyat dar Īrān va Sāyir-i Kishvarhā [Nationality in Iran and other Countries]*, Intishārāt-i Jangal, Tehran 2010, p. 44.

40 Ibid., p. 75.

41 Denaturalization entails a very lengthy and burdensome process in which the reasons for this must be declared officially and evaluated; for an account of the procedure see Ḥ. Āl-i Kajbāf, above n. 39, pp. 62 et seq.

42 S. Jalāl al-Din Madanī, above n. 4, p. 80.

rather hypothetically. One must therefore turn to the general rules and doctrines of Iranian private international law. There the principle of effective nationality is generally accepted.[43] Accordingly, the nationality of the country to which the party has the closest connection will prevail. According to literature this close connection must be determined by the court with due consideration of, for instance, the place of residence/domicile, the first language and other personal factors that connect the party to a particular country as the centre of his/her life.[44] The actual assessment of an effective nationality by Iranian courts remains, however, largely hypothetical as no case law could be retrieved dealing with this issue.

3.5. *ORDRE PUBLIC*

All the Agreements contain a rule according to which the application of the substantive law of any of the two Contracting States can only exceptionally be restricted or excluded, and only insofar as such restrictions or exclusions are valid against all foreign States. This means that the non-application of a foreign (European) rule can be justified only if its application would be equally unacceptable from an Iranian perspective if it had resulted from the application of any other than the European one in question.

4. CONCLUSION

Where does this leave us? One can firstly state that the treaties seem not to have any relevance in practice. Besides the fact that very few Germans, Austrians, Swiss or French live (and prospectively die) in Iran, thus meaning few if any cases where the application of these treaties arises in court, there is also another reason for the insignificance of the treaties in practice. Assuming that judges were aware of the treaties, the connecting factor under Iranian international succession law would nevertheless correspond with the connecting factor in the treaties. Therefore, the result from the application of the treaties coincides with the result from the application of the domestic rules on international succession law. In interviews conducted in Iran in October 2017, the present author was told that the treaties would not really matter anyway as Iranian judges would resort to nationality as the connecting factor in succession law in all cases involving foreigners.

Does this give way for an argument to withdraw or terminate the treaties? Or does the significance of the treaties lie elsewhere? From an Iranian

---

43 Ibid., pp. 81–83.

44 Ibid., p. 83.

perspective, nationality is the decisive connecting factor in international family and succession law. It is nationality that transcends the closest connection of a person in family and succession matters. Integrative policies aiming to gradually switch from nationality to habitual residence – as a stronger factor exemplifying the closest connection of a person to a State and its laws – have not taken root and are not being discussed in Iran at all. The policy of the Iranian government is geared towards securing the application of Iranian law in all matters of family and succession law in respect of Iranians abroad. From an Iranian perspective one can anticipate strong resistance to any attempt to alter the connecting factor in succession matters.

THE RELATIONS OF SWITZERLAND WITH EU MEMBER STATES

Andrea Bonomi

1. INTRODUCTION

Since the 19th century, Switzerland has established a net of bilateral treaties dealing with a number of private international law issues, with both European and non-European countries. Several of these instruments also cover international succession matters.

To begin with, a number of Swiss bilateral treaties regulate the reciprocal recognition and enforcement of decisions among the Contracting States. While an 1869 treaty with France was denounced in 1992 after the ratification of the 1988 Lugano Convention,[1] similar instruments are still applicable in the relationships with several other Member States of the EU.[2] Although these

[1] Convention of 15.06.1869, Recueil systématique du droit fédéral [Systematic Collection of Swiss Federal Law (henceforth referred to as 'RS')] 1848–1947, vol. 12, p. 315.

[2] Austria (Convention of 16.12.1960, RS 0.276.191.632); Belgium (Convention of 29.04.1959, RS 0.276.191.721); Germany (Convention of 02.11.1929, RS 0.276.191.361); Italy (Convention

treaties also cover decisions rendered in succession matters, they do not interfere with the European Succession Regulation (SR),[3] which governs only the mutual recognition and enforcement of decisions among the Member States.

Another group of bilateral instruments impose only some limited cooperation duties on a Contracting State's authorities whenever a citizen of the other Contracting State dies within their territory, such as the duties to inform the authorities of the national State[4] or to take conservation measures to protect the estate's assets.[5] As in the previous case, the European Regulation is not affected by these narrow cooperation mechanisms.

The only bilateral conventions that do interfere with the Succession Regulation are those that contain common rules on jurisdiction and/or the applicable law. While two treaties within this category are in force with third States (Iran and the United States of America),[6] two of them are applicable in relationships with Member States of the EU bound by the Succession Regulation, i.e. Greece (**Treaty 23**) and Italy (**Treaty 20**).

First in time and practical importance, the Convention between Italy and Switzerland of 22 July 1868[7] includes in its Article 17 rules specifically regulating the jurisdiction over disputes concerning the estate of a citizen of one Contracting State with a last domicile in the other Contracting State. These jurisdictional rules, based on the nationality of the deceased, have been interpreted by the courts of both countries as also implicitly including a choice-of-law rule.

By contrast, Article 10(3) of the Convention between Greece and Switzerland of 1 December 1927[8] contains only a choice-of-law rule, also based on the last nationality of the deceased.

---

of 03.01.1933, RS 0.276.194.541); and Spain (Convention of 19.11.1896, RS 0.276.193.321). Switzerland is also bound by a treaty with Liechtenstein (RS 0.276.195.141). The texts of all these treaties are available at <https://www.admin.ch/gov/fr/accueil/droit-federal/recueil-systematique.html> accessed 08.04.2019, by entering the respective reference number.

3 Regulation (EU) No. 650/2012 of the European Parliament and of the Council of 04.07.2012 on jurisdiction, applicable law, recognition and enforcement of decisions and acceptance and enforcement of authentic instruments in matters of succession and on the creation of a European Certificate of Succession [2012] OJ L201/107.

4 See the treaties with Austria (1875, Art. 8, RS 0.142.111.631), Greece (1927, RS 0.142.113.721), Italy (1868, Art. 17(1) and (2), RS 0.142.114.541), Portugal (1883, Art. VIII, RS 0.191.116.541), and Romania (1880, Art. VIII, RS 0.191.116.631).

5 See the treaties with Japan (1911, Art. 5, RS 0.142.114.631), Portugal (1883, Art. VIII, RS 0.191.116.541) and Romania (1880, Art. VIII, RS 0.191.116.631).

6 Treaty between Switzerland and the United States of America of 25.11.1855 (Art. VI, RS 0.142.113.361); Treaty between Switzerland and the Persian Empire of 25.04.1934 (Art. 8, RS 0.142.114.362).

7 *Convention d'établissement et consulaire entre la Suisse et l'Italie* (Establishment and Consular Treaty between Switzerland and Italy), 22.07.1868, RS 0.142.114.541.

8 *Convention d'établissement et de protection juridique entre la Suisse et la Grèce* (Treaty on Establishment and Legal Protection between Switzerland and Greece), 01.12.1927, RS 0.142.113.721.

In both cases, the treaty provisions interfere with the provisions of the European Regulation and, since they involve a third State, they take precedence over the uniform rules, as stated under Article 75(1) SR.

In the first part of this contribution, the focus will be mainly on the treaty with Italy, which has given rise to a rich and interesting body of case law (section 2). The last part will include some brief remarks on the treaty with Greece, which raises partly similar issues but whose practical impact has been so far much less significant (section 3).

2. ARTICLE 17 OF THE 1868 TREATY BETWEEN ITALY AND SWITZERLAND

2.1. ARTICLE 17 AS A FORERUNNER OF INTERNATIONAL COOPERATION IN CIVIL MATTERS

2.1.1. An Original Jurisdictional Provision

Article 17 of the 1868 Convention between Italy and Switzerland of 22 July 1868 (**Treaty 20**)[9] is a notable attempt to coordinate the exercise of judicial power in inheritance disputes between the two Contracting States. Conferring jurisdiction to the courts of the deceased's national country, it prevents in an effective way positive conflicts and parallel proceedings.

This provision is even more remarkable when one considers that it was established at a time when legislation in the area of private international law was taking its very first steps.[10] A set of codified conflict-of-laws rules had been included only three years before in the first Italian Civil Code of 1865:[11] seen from a comparative perspective, this was one of the very first examples of codification in this area of law. In Switzerland, the first legislative act in this field would be adopted only in 1891; it was initially designed to govern inter-cantonal relationships and was made applicable to international situations only by analogy.[12]

---

9 In this contribution, the content of Art. 17 of the 1868 Convention will not be described in detail: see instead the very accurate presentation in the Italian contribution to this book drafted by P. Franzina p. 176 et seq. The purpose here is mainly to discuss, from a Swiss perspective, the present utility of that provision and to propose possible ways forward.

10 See also T. Ballarino and I. Pretelli, 'Una disciplina ultracentenaria delle successioni' [2014] *Rivista ticinese di diritto* 889, 893 et seq.

11 *Codice civile del Regno d'Italia*, of 02.04.1865, *Disposizioni sulla pubblicazione, interpretazione ed applicazione delle leggi in generale*, Art. 6 to 12. This first codification would then be replaced by that included in the preliminary provisions of the Civil Code of 1942 and then by the Private International Law Act of 31.05.1995.

12 *Bundesgesetz vom 25. Juni 1891 betreffend die zivilrechtlichen Verhältnisse der Niedergelassenen und Aufenthalter*, BS 2 737. According to its Art. 32, the provisions of this act were also

International cooperation in civil matters was even less developed. The Hague Conference would only be created 25 years later, in 1893, on the initiative of the well-known jurisconsult T. M. C. Asser. The first multilateral treaty devoted to issues of international succession would be elaborated, under the auspices of the Conference, only in 1961.[13]

The approach taken by Article 17 is also original. Contrary to the rules on international succession that can be found in some other bilateral treaties signed by Switzerland,[14] Article 17 is drafted as a jurisdictional provision, without any express reference to the law applicable to succession. This is noteworthy, when one considers that none of the multilateral treaties elaborated by the Hague Conference in the area of succession ever included jurisdictional rules on inheritance disputes.[15] The European Regulation was the first multilateral instrument aiming to achieve the unification of jurisdictional rules in the field of succession.

The jurisdictional criterion used in Article 17 is the last nationality of the deceased. This solution clearly reflects the basic philosophy that was then prevailing in Italy. The Italian choice-of-law codification of 1865, as that of 1942, was largely influenced by the nationality principle, as propounded by Pasquale Stanislao Mancini. According to Article 8 of the preliminary provisions of the 1865 Civil Code, succession upon death was governed by the national law of the deceased at the time of death, whatever the nature and the location of the assets.[16]

Besides its theoretical underpinnings, the nationality principle reflected important policy goals. In a period of massive emigration of Italians towards both European and extra-European countries, the use of nationality as a connecting factor – for both jurisdiction and choice of law – ensured access to Italian courts as well as the application of Italian law. In the area of succession, it allowed the heirs of Italian emigrants, in particular those who had remained in Italy, to have

applicable by analogy to foreigners having their residence in Switzerland. This act would later be replaced by the Private International Law Act of 18.12.1987, RS 291.

13 Hague Convention of 05.10.1961 on the Conflicts of Laws Relating to the Form of Testamentary Dispositions.

14 Art. VI of the Convention between Switzerland and the United States of America and Art. 8 of the Convention between Switzerland and the Persian Empire, above n. 6; Art. 10 of the Treaty between Switzerland and Greece, below section 3. Art. 5 of the Convention between Switzerland and France of 15.06.1869, denounced in 1992, above n. 1, did follow a jurisdictional approach like the 1868 Treaty; however, it imposed the application of the *lex situs* for immovable property.

15 Besides the 1961 Convention, above n. 13, we refer to the Hague Convention of 02.10.1973 concerning the International Administration of the Estates of Deceased Persons and the Hague Convention of 01.08.1989 on the Law Applicable to the Succession of Deceased Persons.

16 The applicability of the national law of the deceased was then reaffirmed in Art. 23 of the preliminary provisions to the 1942 Civil Code and, subject to a choice of law by the deceased, in Art. 46(1) of the Italian PIL Act of 1995.

access to Italian courts and, indirectly, to benefit from the application of Italian law on succession.

It is an easy guess that Article 17(3) of the Convention reflected the wishes of the Italian government. However, the provisions of the treaty are based on reciprocity (see Article 17(4)), which means that Swiss courts also have jurisdiction over inheritance disputes concerning the succession of a Swiss citizen who died with their last domicile in Italy.

2.1.2. An Unwritten Choice-of-Law Rule?

Although conceived as a jurisdictional rule, Article 17 of the Convention has come, over the years, to be interpreted as including an implicit choice-of-law rule, also based on the last nationality of the deceased.

This interpretation *praeter legem* was developed by the Swiss courts in a long series of decisions.[17] Although the reasons behind this solution are not clearly stated in the relevant rulings, they are understandable. Under Article 17(4) of the Convention, Swiss courts have jurisdiction to rule over the succession of a Swiss citizen with last domicile in Italy. In this case, Swiss choice-of-law rules would generally lead to the application of the law of the country of the last domicile. However, Swiss courts would take into account a *renvoi* ('*Rückverweisung*') resulting from the foreign choice-of-law rules.[18] This used to be the case, at the time of the relevant decisions, in the relationship with Italy. Indeed, under the then applicable Italian rules of private international law, the succession was governed by the national law of the deceased.[19] Swiss courts would accept this reference back and therefore finally apply Swiss law to the succession of a Swiss citizen domiciled in Italy. Dispensing with this complex reasoning, Swiss courts simply held that Article 17 of the Convention included an unwritten choice-of-law rule providing for the application of Swiss law as the last national law of the deceased.

For Italian courts, the question was, for a long time, devoid of practical importance. Certainly, the application of Italian law to the estate of Italian

---

17 ATF 43 II 213, pp. 218–219; ATF 91 II 457, pp. 460–461; ATF 91 III 19, p. 24; ATF 98 II 88, p. 92; ATF 99 II 246, p. 252; ATF 136 III 461, p. 464; ATF 138 III 354, p. 356. See also H. Chenevard, *Le régime civil des successions dans les rapports italo-suisses*, Payot, Lausanne 1985, p. 28 et seq.; A. Bucher, in A. Bucher (ed.) *Commentaire Romand - LDIP/CL*, Helbing Lichtenhahn, Basel 2011, Art. 86–96 No. 12; T. Wüstemann and L. Marolda Martinez, 'Der schweizerisch-italienische Erbfall' [2011] *successio* 62, 66; T. Ballarino and I. Pretelli, above n. 10, 901 et seq.

18 This was already the case under Art. 28(2) of the 1891 Act (see above n. 12): see A. F. Schnitzer, *Handbuch des Internationalen Privatrechts*, vol. II, 3rd ed., Verlag für Recht und Gesellschaft, Basel 1950, p. 460 et seq. The same solution results now, even more clearly, from Art. 91(1) of the 1987 Swiss PIL Act.

19 See above n. 16.

citizens was one of the reasons why Italy insisted on conferring jurisdiction to the Italian courts.[20] However, this result was granted in any event by the Italian choice-of-law rules.[21] Therefore, it was not necessary to read a choice-of-law rule into the Convention.

2.2. ARTICLE 17 AS AN OUTDATED PROVISION

Notwithstanding its initial merits, Article 17 of the 1868 Convention (**Treaty 20**) has grown outdated over the years. Several reasons can be named for this ageing process.

2.2.1. Sociological Factors

It should be first noted that, although the number of Italians living in Switzerland continues to grow,[22] the sociological reality of the Italian community has evolved.

On one hand, an important segment of the Italians living in Switzerland (probably around one-fifth of them) is now constituted by descendants of emigrants of the second or third generation (called in Switzerland '*secondos*'). These individuals were born and grew up in Switzerland, and, for the majority of them, never had a domicile in Italy. This component of the Italian community in Switzerland will, for natural reasons, become increasingly important in the future.

On the other hand, a significant number of Italians with domicile in Switzerland acquire Swiss nationality. Thanks to another agreement with Italy,[23] they can do so without renouncing their Italian nationality. The tendency towards naturalization will probably grow, following recent legislative reforms facilitating the acquisition of Swiss nationality by descendants of immigrants of the third generation.[24]

In this context, Article 17(3) of the Convention appears outdated for several reasons.

---

[20] In one of its rare rulings on the 1868 Convention, the Italian *Corte di cassazione* noted, in a *dictum*, that a parallel between jurisdiction and applicable law was the goal of the Convention: Cass., 31.07.1867, No. 2038, *Riv. dir. int. priv. proc.* 1968, p. 174.

[21] See above n. 16.

[22] See, for instance, L. Monnat, 'Les Italiens reviennent s'installer en Suisse', in the newspaper *24Heures* of 17.05.2016, available at <https://www.24heures.ch/suisse/italiens-reviennent-s-installer-suisse/story/30217834> accessed 08.04.2019.

[23] *Notenaustausch vom 24. April/1. Mai 1998 zwischen der Schweiz und Italien zur Erleichterung des Erwerbs des Doppelbürgerrechts*, RS 0.141.145.4.

[24] *Bundesbeschluss über die erleichterte Einbürgerung von Personen der dritten Ausländergeneration of 30 June 2016*, BBl. [*Bundesblatt*] 2016 7581. The Swiss voters accepted this text in a referendum on 12.02.2017 with a majority of more than 60%.

According to a widely held opinion, the treaty provision is not applicable when the deceased held both Italian and Swiss nationality.[25] This conclusion corresponds to the judicial interpretation of an analogous provision included in the 1869 Consular Convention between Switzerland and France.[26] In the case of dual nationality, a plain application of Article 17 would confer jurisdiction to both Italian and Swiss courts, thus failing to meet its purpose. In the alternative, it would be necessary to establish which nationality is more effective, but the treaty fails to provide any indication in that respect.

Although this is not entirely clear yet, Article 17(3) is probably also inapplicable to the succession of an Italian who never had his/her domicile in Italy.[27] A literal reading seems to exclude its application in this case because that provision confers jurisdiction to the court of the place where the deceased had his/her last domicile in Italy before leaving the country. Considerations based on proximity and predictability support this interpretation: not only are Italian courts very poorly placed to rule on the succession of a person who never had his/her domicile in Italy, but their jurisdiction would probably be, in such a case, very surprising for the parties concerned.

As a result of these limitations, the succession of both dual nationals and descendants of immigrants normally fall outside the scope of the treaty provision. Accordingly, these cases must be dealt with under the private international law rules applicable in Italy and Switzerland. This not only reduces the practical importance of Article 17, but also leads to uncertainty and inconsistencies in the treatment of Italian citizens living in Switzerland.

Certainly, Article 17(3) continues to apply to the succession of Italians who immigrated to Switzerland from Italy (or after having lived a part of their life in Italy), provided that they did not acquire Swiss nationality. However, even in such cases, the application of the treaty provision produces unconvincing results when the close family members of the deceased were born in Switzerland ('*secondos*') and/or had acquired Swiss nationality. Why should the heirs of a person domiciled in Switzerland be denied access to Swiss courts despite their also being (and always having been) Swiss residents and even where they hold Swiss nationality? Of course, this question is even more legitimate where the assets (or the most important part of them, usually savings and the family home) are located in Switzerland and were acquired with the income of a Swiss professional activity.

---

25 See B. Dutoit et al., *Répertoire de droit international privé suisse*, vol. III, Helbing Lichtenhahn, Bern 1986, p. 125; F.-H. Hool, *Les effets de la double nationalité en droit suisse*, Editions du Griffon, Neuchâtel 1949, pp. 63 and 83; H. Chenevard, above n. 17, p. 40 et seq. For a more detailed analysis, see the report by P. Franzina, in this book, above n. 9.

26 ATF 81 II 495, p. 499.

27 T. Ballarino and I. Pretelli, above n. 10, p. 897 et seq.

In these scenarios, the exclusive jurisdiction of Italian courts and the application of Italian law are surprising and, normally, rather inconvenient for the parties.

2.2.2. *Radical Changes in the Private International Law Rules on International Succession Applicable in Italy*

A second, even more significant reason for the obsolescence of Article 17 is the spectacular changes that the rules on international succession have gone through in Italy, first with the Private International Law (PIL) Act of 1995 and, more recently, with the European Succession Regulation.

The 1995 PIL Act was still largely based on the nationality principle. Thus, in matters of succession, the law applicable was, in principle, that of the deceased's last nationality (Article 46(1)). At the same time, the Act also introduced, for the first time, the right of the testator to opt for submitting the succession to the law of his/her habitual residence (Article 46(2)). By admitting a choice of law in the field of succession ('*professio iuris*'), Italian law was, historically, one of the first European legislations to join the traditional Swiss approach favouring party autonomy.[28] However, party autonomy was still restricted in Italy because the choice of a foreign law could in no case deprive the heirs of an Italian testator of the reserved share granted to them by Italian law, provided that they had their residence in Italy at the moment of death (Article 46(2)).

Following this legislative reform, Swiss courts were confronted with the question of whether an Italian citizen having his/her habitual residence in Switzerland could submit the succession to Swiss law. The Swiss Federal Court was thus forced to adapt its interpretation of the 1868 Convention. In a first ruling in 2010,[29] it held that it would be regrettable if 'a more than one century-old treaty' prevented the choice of the law applicable to the succession, while both the Swiss and the Italian private international law system allowed it.[30] Therefore, party autonomy had to prevail over the 1868 Convention, and the succession had to be governed, in the particular case, by the Swiss law chosen by the deceased.

It was not clear, from this first decision, whether the application of Swiss law was based on the admission of a 'reference back' ('*renvoi*', '*Rückverweisung*')

---

28 The *professio iuris* is traditionally permitted in Switzerland. It was already provided for by Art. 22(2) of the 1891 Act (see above n. 12) and is now regulated in Arts. 87(2) and 90(2) of the 1987 PIL Act.

29 ATF 136 III 461, p. 465.

30 *Ibid.*, p. 465: '*[s]arebbe [...] insoddisfacente che, in un caso come quello in esame, la legge applicabile secondo il diritto internazionale privato vigente sia in Italia che in Svizzera [...] venga accantonata in forza di un trattato ultra-centenario*'. With similar language, see A. Bonomi, 'La loi applicable aux successions dans le nouveau droit international privé italien et ses implications dans les relations italo-suisses' [1996] *RSDIE/SZIER* 503.

resulting from Article 46(2) of the Italian PIL Act[31] or on an autonomous rule. However, this was clarified in a second ruling in 2012,[32] where the Federal Court held that the validity and effects of the choice of law did not depend on Article 46(2) of the Italian Act but should be recognized irrespective of that provision. It follows that the choice of Swiss law is not subject to the limits provided for under the Italian Act to protect forced heirs.

This approach is remarkable because it implies a clear departure from the traditional reading of Article 17. While the admission of *renvoi* would have been a sort of compromise between the application of Italian law based on the 1868 Convention and the fact that the *professio iuris* had become possible in Italy after the 1995 law reform, the second ruling of the Federal Court clearly invites lower courts to allow an exception from the unwritten choice-of-law rule it used to read into the Convention. Implicitly, this means that the treaty does not necessarily impose the application of the national law of the deceased.

As shown by these decisions of the Swiss Federal Court, the Italian Act of 1995 had a not negligible impact on the interpretation of the 1868 Convention. This might be difficult to justify, in theory, under the rules on treaty interpretation.[33] Nevertheless, the new case law of the Swiss Federal Court should be approved because it is well adapted to the new legislative framework. *A fortiori*, courts should now take into account the entry into force of the European Regulation, which produces much more significant changes in the Italian legal system than the 1995 law reform.

On one hand, the Regulation not only allows for party autonomy in a much more liberal way than the 1995 Italian Act (i.e. without any specific protection for forced heirs, Article 22 SR), but also brings about a 'Copernican revolution' with respect to the traditional Italian approach: nationality as the main connecting factor has now been replaced by the last habitual residence of the deceased (Article 21(1) SR).

On the other hand, the Regulation not only determines the law applicable to the succession but also regulates the jurisdiction of the courts. Here also, the last habitual residence becomes the main criterion, while nationality can only be relevant on a subsidiary basis.

These changes are particularly relevant in the relationships between Italy and Switzerland. As a matter of fact, the solutions provided for in the Regulation are very similar to those that are traditionally followed in Switzerland: under

31 In other terms, Italian law – applicable by virtue of the unwritten choice-of-law rules of the 1868 Convention – would 'refer back' to Swiss law by admitting the deceased's choice of the law of the habitual residence.

32 ATF 138 III 354, p. 356.

33 See P. Franzina, in his contribution on Italy, in this book, rightly pointing out that 'the changes in the private international law legislation of Italy and Switzerland can hardly be regarded as a justification for a change in substance of the Convention'.

the Swiss PIL Act, both jurisdiction and applicable law essentially depend on the last domicile of the deceased,[34] a criterion that is very close to the last habitual residence.[35]

Accordingly, if the 1868 Convention were not in force, the European Regulation, on one hand, and the Swiss PIL rules, on the other, would now lead to converging results. In the case of an Italian with last habitual residence and last domicile in Switzerland, Swiss courts would have jurisdiction and would normally apply Swiss law (Articles 86(1) and 90(1) of the PIL Act). In this case, Italian courts would have jurisdiction only if assets were situated in Italy (Article 10 SR), but, even then, they would also apply Swiss law (Article 21(1) SR). Italian law would become applicable, under both systems, only if the deceased had opted for it (Article 90(2) Swiss PIL Act, Article 22 SR). The situation is similar (although reversed) in the case of a Swiss citizen domiciled in Italy.

However, the newly created convergence between the two systems is disturbed by Article 17 of the Convention, which is still based on the nationality principle and therefore leads to opposite results.[36]

While this runs counter to the policy choices made in the two countries involved, it can also be quite confusing for the individuals involved. Thus, if an Italian with last domicile in Switzerland intends to draft his/her dispositions upon death, he/she might mistakenly assume, based on both the PIL Act and the European Regulation, that the succession will be regulated by Swiss law. If the testator is not informed of the existence of the 1868 Convention (and of its interpretation by the courts), he/she will neither anticipate that Italian law is applicable nor that this might be changed through a *professio iuris* in favour of Swiss law. This might lead to unexpected and unfortunate results: the dispositions upon death might prove invalid in whole or in part or be subject to claw back because of a violation of forced heirship rights.

While this is more likely to happen to laymen when they draft a holographic testament without a lawyer's assistance, legal practice shows that even professionals sometimes ignore the existence and the effects of the 1868 Convention.

It should also be stressed that the solutions enshrined by Swiss law and by the European Regulation, based on the last domicile and habitual residence, are more convincing than those of the 1868 Convention, in particular in the cases we have discussed above.[37]

---

34 See Arts. 86(1) and 90(1) of the Swiss PIL Act.

35 See A. Bonomi, 'Le Règlement européen sur les successions et son impact pour la Suisse' [2014] II *Semaine judiciaire* 391, 403 et seq.

36 See also T. Ballarino and I. Pretelli, above n. 10, p. 918.

37 See above section 2.1.

2.2.3. *No Compelling Reasons to Ensure the Application of National Law*

There is also a third reason why Article 17 of the Convention is now outdated. As mentioned above, the nationality principle was traditionally perceived in Italy as a tool for the protection of Italian citizens living abroad. This concern was linked to the traditional conviction that the succession of Italian citizens should mandatorily be submitted to certain specific rules of Italian succession law, such as those prohibiting agreements as to succession ('*patti successori*'), mutual wills ('*testamenti congiuntivi*') and succession by substitution ('*sostituzione fideicommissaria*') and also those protecting forced heirs ('*legittima*').

However, the application of these rules in cases involving an international succession is no longer regarded as so crucial as it used to be.

With the entry into force of the Succession Regulation, it is now clear that an agreement as to succession concluded by an Italian citizen in conformity with the law of his/her habitual residence at the time of the execution of the agreement must be recognized in Italy, notwithstanding the prohibition of '*patti successori*' under Italian law (Article 25 SR). The same is also true for mutual wills based on an agreement between the testators (Article 3(1)(b) SR). The prohibition of 'succession by substitution' is also obsolete, at least since the entry into force in Italy of the Hague Trust Convention of 1985, and it can certainly no longer be considered as belonging to Italian public policy. As for the rules on forced heirship, while they were still protected against the choice of a foreign law by Article 46(2) of the 1995 Act, an Italian testator can now easily circumvent these rules by moving his/her habitual residence abroad; indeed, the Italian *Corte di cassazione* has ruled that they do not belong to Italian public policy.[38] In any case, the application of Swiss law is not problematic in this respect because it ensures a broad protection to the spouse and the children of the deceased.

In this context, there clearly is no need to ensure the application of Italian law to Italian citizens domiciled in Switzerland. That being so, there is also no compelling reason to impose on them the jurisdiction of Italian courts.

Of course, this is also true from a Swiss perspective. Under the Swiss PIL Act, subject to a *professio iuris* (Article 87(2)), Swiss courts normally do not have jurisdiction to rule on the estate of Swiss citizens domiciled abroad, unless the foreign authorities do not deal with such estate (Article 87(1)). It follows that even under the national private international law rules, the application of Swiss law is not granted in such situations.

---

38 Cass., 24.06.1996, No. 5832, *Riv. dir. int. priv. proc.* 2000, 784.

2.3. WHAT IS NEXT?

In the light of the previous considerations, what is the future of Article 17 of the 1868 Convention (**Treaty 20**)?

A first immediate consequence of the developments mentioned above should be a change in the current judicial interpretation of Article 17 so as to include an implicit conflict rule. The time has come for the courts to clearly recognize that the Convention does not cover choice-of-law issues and does not impose any obligation as to the law applicable to the succession. This already follows from the literal wording of that provision, and it was also implicitly confirmed by the 2010 and 2012 rulings of the Swiss Federal Court.[39] When Italy introduced a limited party autonomy in international succession, the Swiss highest court had no hesitation in recognizing the *professio iuris* notwithstanding the silence of the treaty rule. Now that the old Italian rules on international succession have been entirely replaced by the European Regulation, courts should accept all the consequences and recognize that the traditional reading of the Convention cannot be maintained. This also corresponds to the opinion expressed by other Swiss authors.[40]

However, one also has to recognize that this more literal interpretation of Article 17, although certainly better than the one presently followed, also entails some problems.

On one hand, this reading of the treaty provisions will end the parallel between jurisdiction and applicable law. Accordingly, Italian courts, having jurisdiction over the succession of an Italian citizen domiciled in Switzerland under Article 17(3) of the Convention, will from now on have to apply the law of the last habitual residence as prescribed by Article 21(1) of the Succession Regulation: as a rule, and in the absence of a choice of Italian law, they will thus have to apply Swiss succession law. Reciprocally, Swiss courts will have to apply Italian law to the succession of a Swiss citizen domiciled in Italy, as prescribed by Article 91(1) of the Swiss PIL Act. This can be cumbersome in terms of time and cost.

On the other hand, Article 17 will continue to confer jurisdiction to the courts of the national country of the deceased, a result which is often at odds with the needs for proximity and predictability for the parties involved.

---

39 See above n. 29 and 32.

40 See already A. Bucher, above n. 17, Art. 86–96 No. 12: '... *il semble légitime de déduire des réformes législatives survenues en Suisse et en Italie qu'il n'y a plus d'entente en matière de droit applicable, si bien que l'art. 17 al. 3 et 4 doit être confiné dorénavant à son texte, limité à la compétence*'. *Contra*: T. Ballarino and I. Pretelli, above n. 10, p. 919, who consider that the traditional solution should be maintained for the sake of uniformity: however, as mentioned before, uniformity can also be achieved today (and in a more consistent and satisfactory way) by applying the converging solutions provided now by the national systems of the two States concerned.

These shortcomings directly follow from the provision of Article 17 itself and cannot be adjusted by way of interpretation. Instead, they call for a modification of, or the withdrawal from, the treaty.

A Swiss or Italian withdrawal from the treaty could be envisaged as a solution of last resort, but it is certainly not the best way forward. On one hand, while Article 17 is outdated, there probably is an interest in preserving some of the other provisions of the 1868 Convention. On the other hand, even Article 17 still has some value since – as mentioned at the very beginning of this contribution – it prevents positive conflicts and parallel proceedings.

While the proximity between the European Regulation and Swiss PIL very much reduces, with respect to the applicable law, the risk of positive conflicts between Italy and Switzerland, these could still arise, notably, when Swiss authorities hold that the deceased's last domicile was in Switzerland, whereas Italian courts consider that the last habitual residence was in Italy. In such a case, the courts of both countries would entertain jurisdiction and they would both apply their own national law on the merits.

The probability of parallel proceedings is higher still because of the rules of subsidiary jurisdiction included in Article 10 of the European Regulation. When the deceased had his/her last domicile in a non-Member State, and if the estate includes assets located in the national State of the deceased, Article 10(1)(a) SR confers general (all-inclusive) jurisdiction to the latter State's courts. This very broad jurisdictional grant gives way to parallel proceedings in the third State of the last domicile and in the Member State of the deceased's nationality.

Parallel proceedings are always a waste of time and money; they are also a source of uncertainty and can create obstacles to the recognition and enforcement of decisions. This is true even when the courts of the two countries concerned will, in the end, apply the same law on the merits, as would frequently be the case in Switzerland and Italy under the ordinary choice-of-law rules of, respectively, the Swiss PIL Act and the European Regulation.

One should consider that, in both scenarios that we have just described, the rules on *lis pendens* and related actions included in the Regulation (Articles 17 and 18) are of no assistance because they are applicable only between Member States bound by the Regulation. As for the *lis pendens* rules included in the 1933 Convention between Italy and Switzerland, they will provide relief only under specific circumstances.[41]

The renegotiation of Article 17 can be the opportunity to tackle these problems and thus ensure a better coordination between Italian and Swiss courts. A revised treaty provision should ideally be based on the priority

---

41 Art. 7 of the Convention of 03.01.1933 (see above n. 2) is subject to the condition that the court first seized has jurisdiction under Art. 2 of the same treaty. This will not always be the case in the scenarios we have sketched.

of the courts of the deceased's last habitual residence (or last domicile), and these courts should apply their own law, subject to a *professio iuris*. This would reflect the already prevailing solutions under both the Swiss PIL Act and the European Regulation. Moreover, in order to prevent parallel proceedings, Italy should be willing to restrict the application of Article 10 SR only to exceptional cases (e.g. when the Swiss authorities at the place of the last habitual residence of the deceased do not take the necessary measures).[42] Finally, a *lis pendens* rule should be added to the agreement in order to reduce the risk of positive conflicts and parallel proceedings.

Such a new treaty scheme would promote legal certainty for both Italian citizens living in Switzerland and Swiss citizens living in Italy, while respecting the fundamental policy choices now reflected in the national private international law systems of the States concerned.

Of course, to renegotiate the 1868 Convention, Italy would have to be authorized by the European Union, which is now exclusively competent to negotiate and enter into treaty relations with third States in the areas covered by the Succession Regulation.

3. ARTICLE 10 OF THE 1927 TREATY BETWEEN GREECE AND SWITZERLAND

Contrary to the treaty with Italy, the 1927 Convention between Greece and Switzerland (**Treaty 23**) includes an express choice-of-law rule. Under Article 10(3) of this treaty, when a Greek or Swiss citizen dies having his/her last domicile in the other Contracting State, the law of the country of his/her nationality is applicable to the whole of the estate, but only in so far as it concerns the determination of legal heirs and their portions or forced heirship rights ('*réserve*').[43]

At the time when it was negotiated, this provision was a compromise between Swiss PIL (which was based on domicile) and Greek PIL (which followed the national law but had not yet adopted, at that time, the unitary approach).[44]

The reference to national law is limited to the specific issues expressly mentioned in Article 10(3) (legal heirs and forced heirship).[45] All other aspects

---

42 This corresponds to what is provided in Switzerland: under Art. 87(1) of the PIL Act, Swiss authorities only have jurisdiction to rule on the estate of a Swiss citizen domiciled abroad 'to the extent that the foreign authorities do not deal with such estate'.

43 On this provision see: B. Dutoit et al., above n. 25, p. 152 et seq.; A. Bucher, above n. 17, Art. 86–96, No. 15; O. Gaillard, 'Les relations entre la Grèce et la Suisse en matière successorale: la Convention d'établissement et de protection juridique du 1er décembre 1927' [2016] *RSDIE/SZIER* 53.

44 B. Dutoit et al. (see above n. 25), p. 152 et seq.; O. Gaillard, above n. 43, 59.

45 ATF 94 II 5, p. 11.

of the succession (e.g. the validity of wills[46] and succession agreements) are governed by the law designated by the ordinary choice-of-law rules of the two countries, i.e. in Switzerland by the law of the last domicile (Article 90(1) of the Swiss PIL Act) and in Greece by the law of the last habitual residence (Article 21(1) of the European Regulation). This will normally lead to a 'functional scission', i.e. to two different laws being applied to distinct aspects of the succession.[47]

However, the deceased can prevent the split by submitting the whole of the estate to his/her national law. In the past, the admissibility of the *professio juris* in a case governed by the treaty was recognized (in an *obiter dictum*) by the Swiss Federal Court.[48] This must be true *a fortiori* today as the *professio juris* is also possible now from a Greek perspective under Article 22 of the Succession Regulation. However, the Swiss Federal Court did not have the opportunity to clarify whether a Greek citizen domiciled in Switzerland can submit his/her succession to Swiss law by a *professio juris* and thus derogate from the treaty provision.[49]

Since the entry into force of the European Regulation, the treaty provision is outdated for the same reasons that we have stated with respect to Article 17 of the Convention between Italy and Switzerland (**Treaty 20**). In particular, in the absence of a *professio juris*, the connecting factor of the last nationality has now been given up in Greece as in the other Member States of the European Union. We see no reason why certain aspects of the succession of a Greek citizen domiciled in Switzerland and of a Swiss citizen domiciled in Greece should still be governed by the national law of the deceased, in derogation from the general choice-of-law rules applicable to all other international succession.

The reference to the deceased's national law is also an unnecessary source of complexity for the authorities in charge of the administration of the estate or as regards disputes between heirs. Indeed, contrary to the 1868 Convention between Italy and Switzerland (**Treaty 20**), the treaty with Greece (**Treaty 23**) does not affect jurisdiction, which continues to be governed by the ordinary rules in force in the two countries. As a consequence, the authorities of the deceased's last domicile or habitual residence, which are normally competent in Switzerland under Article 86 of the Swiss PIL Act and in Greece under Article 4 of the European Regulation, have to apply a foreign law (that of the nationality) to several important aspects of the succession. Besides the practical difficulties, this might even lead, in certain cases, to the application of foreign rules based on Muslim law, which may well be incompatible with Swiss public policy.[50]

---

46 Ibid.

47 O. Gaillard, above n. 43, 61 et seq.

48 Ibid.

49 For a more detailed analysis of this question, see O. Gaillard, above n. 43, p. 75 et seq.

50 Muslim law is still applied in family and succession law in certain areas of Greece (Thrace) to members of the Turkish minority: see O. Gaillard, 'Les droits successions musulmans et leur

For all of these reasons, we think that Article 10 of the 1927 Convention should instead be deleted.[51] However, as mentioned in relation to the treaty with Italy, the renegotiation of the Convention between Switzerland and Greece might help in developing more innovative solutions.

4. CONCLUSION

As the previous analysis has shown, the solutions provided in the bilateral treaties concluded by Switzerland with both Italy (**Treaty 20**) and Greece (**Treaty 23**) are now outdated, in particular since the entry into force of the European Succession Regulation.

Although denunciation of these treaties could offer an easier solution, renegotiation would probably represent a more interesting option in order to improve the coordination between the legal systems of the countries involved and enhance legal certainty for individuals.

Another more ambitious approach would be to try to develop a broader treaty scheme also involving all other Member States bound by the Regulation, and possibly other third States. Indeed, the same risks of positive conflicts and parallel proceedings that have been noted between Italy and Switzerland also arise on a broader scale. Therefore, the treaty regulation tentatively sketched in this contribution[52] could also be suited to the relationships between Member States and third States at large. Of course, if such a broad approach is envisaged, it would have to be negotiated by the European Union itself, ideally under the auspices of the Hague Conference of Private International Law.

application par le juge suisse', in F. Bernard, E. Mcgregor and D. Vallée-Grisel (eds.), *Etudes en l'honneur de Tristan Zimmermann*, Schulthess, Geneva/Zurich 2017, p. 86. On the incompatibility of certain Muslim succession law rules with Swiss public policy based on discrimination, see ATF 143 III 51.

51 The same conclusion is reached by O. Gaillard, above n. 43, p. 77.

52 See above section 2.3.

THE RELATIONS OF TURKEY WITH EU MEMBER STATES

Biset Sena GÜNEŞ

1. INTRODUCTION

Among the third-State cases, the cases related to Turkey are of paramount importance for European private international law by virtue of the substantial number of Turkish nationals resident in the Union. According to the numbers provided by the official statistical office of the European Union (Eurostat) in 2011, Turkish citizens constitute the second largest group of third-country nationals living in the Union, with approximately 2.1 million citizens.[1] It seems that this number has not changed much in recent years.[2] The practical significance of the Turkey-related cases is even bigger for the European Succession Regulation[3] (hereinafter 'the Regulation'), in which treaties between Member States and Turkey covering issues of succession enjoy priority of application as a consequence of the so-called 'Achilles' heel'[4] of the Regulation (Article 75). Turkey has such treaties[5] with Germany (Turkish-German Consular Treaty of 1929 **Treaty 19**),[6] Italy (Turkish-Italian Consular Treaty of 1929 **Treaty 21**)[7] and Hungary (Turkish-Hungarian Consular Treaty of 1938 **Treaty 24**).[8] Whereas the numbers of Turkish nationals residing in Italy[9]

---

1 Eurostat, *People in the EU – Who Are We and How Do We Live?*, Publications Office of the European Union, Luxembourg 2015, p. 90, Table 1 <https://ec.europa.eu/eurostat/statistics-explained/index.php/People_in_the_EU_-_who_are_we_and_how_do_we_live%3F> accessed 21.04.2019. The Turkish Ministry of Foreign Affairs, on the other hand, reports the number of Turkish citizens living in the EU Member States as approximately four million which includes two million Turkish nationals in Germany. See <https://www2.tbmm.gov.tr/d27/7/7-2838sgc.pdf> accessed 21.04.2019.

2 For an approximate number provided more recently on a Member State basis (reporting Member States only), see Eurostat, *Population on 1 January by age group, sex and country of birth (migr_pop3ctb) with the bookmark 'Turkey'* <http://ec.europa.eu/eurostat/web/population-demography-migration-projections/population-data/database> accessed 21.04.2019.

3 Regulation (EU) No. 650/2012 of the European Parliament and of the Council of 04.07.2012 on jurisdiction, applicable law, recognition and enforcement of decisions and acceptance and enforcement of authentic instruments in matters of succession and on the creation of a European Certificate of Succession [2012] OJ L201/107.

4 A. Dutta, 'Das neue internationale Erbrecht der Europäischen Union Eine erste Lektüre der Erbrechtsverordnung' (2013) *FamRZ* 4, 15.

5 Turkey signed other similar consular treaties having conflict and jurisdictional rules in the 1920s with Armenian, Azerbaijan and Georgian Soviet Socialist Republics (*Düstur*, Tertip III, Cilt VI, 257 (152)), Poland (*Düstur*, Tertip III, Cilt VIII, 1258 (583); Protocol of 19.01.1938 amending the Treaty: *Düstur*, Tertip III, Cilt XIX, 1340 (553)), and Albania (*Düstur*, Tertip III, Cilt IX, 306 (159)). However, these treaties never entered into force since the instruments of ratification were not exchanged: H. Yaşar, 'Konsoloslara İlişkin Adli Ayrıcalıklar ve Bağışıklıklar (I)' (1982) 8 *Yargıtay Dergisi* 37, 42.

6 *Resmi Gazete* of 08.06.1930, No. 1514.

7 *Resmi Gazete* of 07.04.1931, No. 1768.

8 *Resmi Gazete* of 27.12.1939, No. 4395.

9 The Italian National Institute of Statistics (Istat) reported on 01.01.2019 that there were 19,509 Turkish nationals living in Italy in 2018. See Istat, *Resident foreigners on*

and in Hungary[10] are not very high, roughly 1.5 million Turkish nationals are resident in Germany.[11] This means that a significant number of the third-country-related succession cases would fall outside the system provided by the Regulation. These treaties were signed almost a century ago and, hence, reflect the legal and political atmosphere of those times. In this sense, they are incompatible with the rules of the Regulation and thus vitiate the desired harmonization through it.[12]

Their impact on Turkish practice, however, does not seem to be as considerable as in the European Union. In the first place, the potential number of cases they might be applicable to is not many. According to the statistics provided by Turkish Statistical Institute (TurkStat), there were only around 75,000 German and 3,000 Italian residents in Turkey in the year 2016. The number of Hungarian residents was not even presented in the statistics, probably because of the fact that it is under 500.[13] Furthermore, treaties seem to have been forgotten by the Turkish courts in many cases,[14] unlike the courts of contracting Member States

1st January – Citizenship <http://dati.istat.it/Index.aspx?QueryId=19675&lang=en> accessed 21.04.2019.

10 According to the numbers provided by Eurostat, only 2,825 Turkish nationals are resident in Hungary. See the statistics of Eurostat, above n. 2.

11 Statistisches Bundesamt (Destatis), *Bevölkerung und Erwerbstätigkeit: Ausländische Bevölkerung Ergebnisse des Ausländerzentralregisters 2018 (Fachserie 1, Reihe 2)*, Statistisches Bundesamt (Destatis), Wiesbaden 2019, p. 27 <https://www.destatis.de/DE/Themen/Gesellschaft-Umwelt/Bevoelkerung/Migration-Integration/Publikationen/Downloads-Migration/auslaend-bevoelkerung-2010200187004.pdf?__blob=publicationFile&v=3> accessed 21.04.2019. There was also no significant change in this number between 2011 and 2018: ibid., pp. 24–27.

12 Max Planck Institute for Comparative and International Private Law, 'Comments on the European Commission's Proposal for a Regulation of the European Parliament and of the Council on Jurisdiction, Applicable Law, Recognition and Enforcement of Decisions and Authentic Instruments in Matters of Succession and the Creation of a European Certificate of Succession' (2010) 74 *RabelsZ* 522, 532–533 (hereinafter 'Max Planck Report').

13 The statistic was prepared on the Address-Based Population Registration System on 31.12.2016 and sent to the author via E-mail upon request. For more information, please refer to info@tuik.gov.tr.

14 There seems to be only one case in which the Turkish Court of Cassation (*Yargıtay*) applied the Turkish-German Treaty: Yargıtay 2. Hukuk Dairesi, T. 27.1.1977, E. 401, K. 665 commented in E. Nomer, 'Ehliyetsizlik Sebebi İle Almanya'daki Gayrimenkul Mallar İçin Vasiyetin İptali' (1981), 1 *MHB* 61. On the other hand, a number of examples could be given here where the treaties were not applied or were not referred to by the Turkish Court of Cassation (*Yargıtay*). See, for instance, Temyiz Mahkemesi 2. Hukuk Dairesi, T. 17.11.1939, E. 1377, K. 3687 commented in O.F. Berki, 10 *AÜHFD* 1953, 792 (succession claim on the estate of an Italian deceased in Turkey); Temyiz Mahkemesi 2. Hukuk Dairesi, T. 09.11.1951, E. 6788, K. 7012 commented in O.F. Berki and H. Ergüney, *Yabancılar Hukuku ve Kanun İhtilafları ile İlgili Yargıtay Kararlarının Tahlil ve İzahları*, Banka ve Ticaret Hukuku Araştırma Enstitüsü, Ankara 1963, pp. 121–122 (succession claim of an Italian national); Yargıtay 2. Hukuk Dairesi, T. 21.12.2005, E. 2006/4387 K. 2006/11476 <http://www.kazanci.com> accessed 21.04.2019 (succession case regarding a German deceased); Yargıtay 7. Hukuk Dairesi, T. 17.07.2008, E. 2008/3686, K. 2008/3210 published in A.C. Ruhi, *Milletlerarası*

actually applying them.[15] There also appears to be no documented notarial[16] or consular practice regarding the treaties' private international law rules. Despite their limited impact on Turkish practice, the treaties are still crucial for Turkey, particularly from the perspective of Turkish nationals living for many years in the countervailing countries. Therefore, this report aims to analyze the scope of application of the treaties and the issues regarding private international and procedural law in them in the aftermath of the Regulation's entry into force. In the light of this, this contribution examines the background of the treaties, the scope of the treaties, the private international law of treaty regimes and the associated procedural issues, looking comparatively at the Regulation as well as at the Turkish Private International Act.[17] Finally, the future of the treaties is addressed.

It is important to clarify here at the outset that Turkey is a party to the Hague Convention of 5 October 1961 on the Conflict of Laws Relating to the Form

---

Özel Hukuk ve Usul Hukuku Hakkında Kanun - Gerekçeli, Açıklamalı, Yargıtay İçtihadlı, 3rd ed., Seçkin, Ankara 2009, pp. 189–190 (succession claims on the immovable property of a German deceased in Turkey); Yargıtay 8. Hukuk Dairesi, T. 20.06.2014, E. 2013/13351, K. 2014/13084 <http://www.kazanci.com> accessed 21.04.2019 (succession case regarding an Italian deceased).

However, it should be noted that it is often not clear from the facts of the cases summarized in the judgments whether the case entirely falls within the scope of the treaties. Additionally, there might be other cases regarding the treaties which cannot be accessed due to the limited public availability of the judgments.

15 The case examples in which the provisions of the Treaty were discussed could at least be provided for Germany. See, for instance, LG Munich I 26.09.2006, *FamRZ* 2007, 1250, commented in F. Bauer, 'Anmerkung zur Entscheidung LG Munich 26.09.2006 – 6 O 15963/05' (2007) *FamRZ* 1252; LG Braunschweig 18.05.2009, *IPRax* 2010, 255; LG Munich I 25.10.2011, *ZEV* 2012, 596; LG Karlsruhe 17.12.2014, *ZEV* 2015, 588, commented in C.F. Majer, (2015) *ZEV* 588; OLG Karlsruhe 21.04.2015, *BWNotZ* 2015, 81; BGH 21.10.2015, *FamRZ* 2016, 122, commented in P. Gottwald, (2016) *FamRZ* 122.

16 The practice of notaries in the field of succession law in Turkey, in accordance with their powers, is mostly limited to the drawing up of dispositions of property upon death and agreements between heirs regarding the sharing out of the estate. The authority of notaries to issue succession certificates might have increased the number of cases where the conflict-of-laws rules of the treaties applied. Nevertheless, notaries cannot issue succession certificates when either foreign nationals ask for such certificates (Art. 71(B) (3) of the Law on Notaries ('*Noterlik Kanunu*' – *Resmi Gazete* of 05.02.1972, No. 14090), Art. 37 of the Land Registry Law ('*Tapu Kanunu*' – *Resmi Gazete* of 29.12.1934, No. 2892)) or the dispute involves a foreign element (Art. 5 of the By-law on the Issuance of Succession Certificates by Notaries ('*Mirasçılık Belgesi Verilmesi ve Terk Eden Eşin Ortak Konuta Davet Edilmesi İşlemlerinin Noterler Tarafından Yapılmasına İlişkin Usul ve Esaslar Hakkında Yönetmelik*' – *Resmi Gazete* of 04.10.2011, No. 28074)).

17 *Resmi Gazete* of 12.12.2007, No. 26728 ('*Milletlerarası Özel Hukuk ve Usul Hukuku Hakkında Kanun*', hereinafter 'the Turkish PILA' in footnotes). For an English translation of the Act, see N.A. Odman Boztosun, 'The 2007 Turkish Code on Private International Law and International Civil Procedure' (2007) IX *YbPIL* 583. For a review on the rules of the Turkish PILA regarding succession, see C. Süral, 'Matters of Succession under Turkish Private International Law' (2016/2017) XIII *YbPIL* 371.

of Testamentary Dispositions,[18] which is also primarily applicable between Turkey and the contracting Member States under Article 75 of the Regulation. This Convention, however, will not be analyzed here; rather, reference will be made where needed. As to other relevant multilateral conventions,[19] Turkey is a party to the Basel Convention of 16 May 1972 on the Establishment of a Scheme of Registration of Wills[20] and a signatory of the Hague Convention of 2 October 1973 Concerning the International Administration of the Estates of Deceased Persons.[21] Both conventions aim to establish uniform substantive rules on the relevant aspects of succession and thus do not fall within the scope of either the Regulation[22] or this contribution.

In addition, Turkey is party to other bilateral consular treaties and treaties on mutual legal assistance and recognition and enforcement of decisions with EU Member States. Consular treaties including provisions on succession exist with Belgium (Articles 43–45),[23] Bulgaria (Articles 31–37),[24] Croatia (as a successor of the Socialist Federal Republic of Yugoslavia, Articles 35–38),[25] Czech Republic and Slovakia (as former Czechoslovakia, Articles 35–37),[26] Lithuania (Article 46),[27] Poland (Article 45)[28] and Romania (Article 19).[29] These treaties often have rules on the duties of the local authorities and consular staff in the event of the death of a national of the other State; they also address the right of consular staff, if applicable, to take appropriate measures for the preservation

18 For the full text of the Convention, see <https://www.hcch.net/en/instruments/conventions/full-text/?cid=40> accessed 21.04.2019. The Convention entered into force in Turkey on 22.10.1983. See, in this regard, <https://www.hcch.net/en/instruments/conventions/status-table/?cid=40> accessed 21.04.2019. For Turkey, see *Resmi Gazete* of 17.01.1983, No. 17931.

19 A. Bonomi, 'Art. 75' in A. Bonomi and P. Wautelet (eds.), *Le droit européen des successions- Commentaire du Règlement n°650/2012 du 4 juillet 2012*, 2nd ed., Bruylant, Brussels 2016, para. 3; F. Bauer, 'EuErbVO Art. 75' in A. Dutta and J. Weber (eds.), *Internationales Erbrecht*, C.H. Beck, Munich 2016, paras. 15–16; G. Tekinalp and A. Uyanik, *Milletlerarası Özel Hukuk Bağlama Kuralları*, 12th ed., Beta, İstanbul 2016, p. 247; A. Zanobetti, 'Article 75' in A.L. Calvo Caravaca, A. Davì and H.-P. Mansel (eds.), *The EU Succession Regulation – A Commentary*, Cambridge University Press, Cambridge 2016, pp. 833–34; J. Schmidt, 'EuErbVO Art. 75' in B. Gsell et al. (eds.), *BeckOGK*, C.H. Beck Munich 2017, paras. 18–21.

20 For the full text of the Convention, see <https://www.coe.int/en/web/conventions/full-list> accessed 21.04.2019. For Turkey, see *Resmi Gazete* of 07.08.1975, No. 15319.

21 For the full text of the Convention see <https://www.hcch.net/en/instruments/conventions/full-text/?cid=83> accessed 21.04.2019. Turkey signed the Treaty on 01.11.1983 but never ratified it.

22 A. Bonomi, above n. 19, para. 3.

23 *Resmi Gazete* of 23.9.1975, No. 15365.

24 *Resmi Gazete* of 16.07.1973, No. 14596.

25 *Resmi Gazete* of 14.8.1971, No. 13926. For the protocol on the succession of Croatia to the Treaty, see *Resmi Gazete* of 02.09.1997, No. 23098.

26 *Resmi Gazete* of 15.01.1979, No. 16520.

27 *Resmi Gazete* of 22.08.1997, No. 23088 (mükerrer).

28 *Resmi Gazete* of 24.12.1988, No. 20029.

29 *Resmi Gazete* of 25.07.1973, No. 14605.

of movable estate assets and the right of the consular staff to receive the movable property of the deceased. They do not, however, provide jurisdictional or conflict-of-laws rules on succession, and thus they do not conflict with the Regulation.[30]

Treaties on mutual legal assistance and the recognition and enforcement of judgments exist, in respect of European Union Member States, with Austria,[31] Croatia (Articles 17–21),[32] Italy (Article 19),[33] Lithuania (Articles 19–23),[34] Poland (Articles 18–25),[35] Romania (Articles 16–23)[36] and Slovakia (Articles 18–22).[37] The treaties provide for the recognition and/or enforcement of civil judgments, which also includes judgments on succession. These treaties are not in the scope of the Regulation as the Regulation only provides rules on recognition and enforcement of judgments between Member State courts.[38] Therefore, neither of these two types of treaties will be analyzed here.

2. BACKGROUND OF THE TREATIES

There is no doubt that consuls have always played an important role in the relations of States throughout history.[39] This was the case also in the Ottoman Empire. Alongside their diplomatic duties, these consuls acted as judges in legal conflicts of a private law nature between the nationals of their States and dealt with the administration of estates of these nationals by applying their own laws.[40] In the last days of the Ottoman Empire, featuring capitulations,[41] the competence of the consuls had increased even more, to the extent that consular

---

30 N. Ekşi, *Yargıtay Kararları Işığında Milletlerarası Miras Hukuku*, Beta, İstanbul 2013, pp. 26–27. Such consular treaties also exist with some other third States. See, for the collection of Turkey's consular treaties, A. Çelikel et al., *Milletlerarası Özel Hukuk Sözleşmeleri*, vol. II, Beta, İstanbul 2005.

31 *Resmi Gazete* of 23.09.1991, No. 21000. The Treaty is entirely on the recognition and enforcement of judgments in civil and commercial matters. Arts. 8 and 9 of the Treaty have jurisdictional rules on succession matters for the purposes of recognition and enforcement.

32 *Resmi Gazete* of 24.05.2000, No. 24058.

33 *Resmi Gazete* of 03.03.1929, No. 1133.

34 *Resmi Gazete* of 20.04.2004, No. 25439.

35 *Resmi Gazete* of 25.07.1990, No. 20583.

36 *Resmi Gazete* of 10.02.2008, No. 26783.

37 *Resmi Gazete* of 07.12.2007, No. 26723.

38 A. Zanobetti, above n. 19, p. 833.

39 R. Aybay, *Tarih ve Hukuk Açısından Konsolosluk*, Türkiye İş Bankası Kültür Yayınları, Ankara 2009, p. 11.

40 See, with regards to the capitulations granted to the Genoese, ibid., pp. 17–18.

41 See, for more information on the capitulations in the Ottoman Empire, H. İnalcık, 'Imtiyâzât: The Ottoman Empire' in B. Lewis et al. (eds.), *The Encyclopaedia of Islam*, vol. III H-Iram, 2nd ed., J. Brill, Leiden & Luzac & Co., London 1986, pp. 1179 et seq.

courts were the only competent authorities for most of the legal matters between their nationals. They even started asserting their competence over the nationals of other States.[42]

The role of consuls in this era could be better explained with the example of Turkish-German relationships. Pursuant to the capitulations, German consular courts had jurisdiction over legal issues in connection with German nationals and other individuals under the protection of German Empire.[43] Since succession issues of foreign nationals, especially of merchants,[44] were one of the most important issues for States at the time, it was always addressed separately within the capitulary system between the German and the Ottoman Empire. Consuls were competent over the succession issues of German nationals regarding their movable property without the interference of local Ottoman authorities. Only legal matters regarding the immovable property of the deceased were subject to the jurisdiction of Ottoman courts.[45]

The same rights and privileges, nonetheless, were not granted in favour of the Ottoman Empire by other States already enjoying them within territories of the Empire. This was obviously contrary to the principle of sovereign equality of States, but it nevertheless continued until the last years of the Ottoman Empire.[46] The Ottoman Empire, therefore, aimed to abolish this burdensome regime counter to its national dignity and independence, and to replace it with a new international regime which was consistent with the principles of international law during and in the years following the First World War.[47]

---

42 M.R. Seviğ and V.R. Seviğ, *Devletler Hususi Hukuku (Giriş-Vatandaşlık)*, 4th ed., İstanbul Üniversitesi Hukuk Fakültesi Yayınları, İstanbul 1983, p. 65.

43 These were either the nationals of third States or the non-Muslim Ottomans (*protégés*) who were granted the protection of the German consuls. For further information on the system of *protégés* in the capitulary system, see B. Konan, 'Osmanlı Devletinde Protégé (Koruma) Sistemi' (2009) 58 *AÜHFD* 169.

44 There were always rules ensuring that the estates of merchants who died in the territory of the Ottoman Empire should be given to their heirs. See, in this regard, *Başbakanlık Arşivi, Muhtelif ve Mütevenni Defteri*, No. 65, p. 8 cited in A.İ. Bağış, *Osmanlı Ticaretinde Gayri Müslimler: Kapitülasyonlar-Beratlı Tüccarlar-Hayriye Tüccarları (1750–1839)*, Turhan Kitabevi, Ankara 1983, p. 65, n. 89.

45 See, for example, Art. 6 of the Amity and Commerce Treaty of 22.03.1761 between the Kingdom of Prussia and the Ottoman Empire. This Treaty was extended for fifty years in 1790 and later replaced with a new agreement based on the same rules on behalf of the *Zollverein* on 10. and 20.10.1840. The rules of the Treaty remained applicable also in the relationships with the German Empire. See, in this regard, *Denkschrift zu dem Konsularvertrag von 1917*, Reichstagsdrucksache No. 755, 13. Legislaturperiode, 11th Session (1914–1918) 171 (hereinafter 'Denkschrift 1917'). For an edited version of the text of the article, see N. Kurdakul, *Osmanlı Devleti'nde Ticaret Anlaşmaları ve Kapitülasyonlar*, Döler Neşriyat, İstanbul 1981, p. 155.

46 H. Krüger, 'Studien über Probleme des türkischen Internationalen Erbrechts' in S. Arkan and A. Yongalik (eds.), *Festschrift Liber Amicorum Tuğrul Ansay – Zum 75. Geburtstag/in Honour of his 75th Birthday*, Kluwer Law International, Alphen aan den Rijn 2006, p. 144.

47 Denkschrift 1917, above n. 45.

To this end, the Ottoman Empire abolished the capitulations[48] and adopted legislative acts[49] in order to regulate the rights of foreign nationals consistent with the principles of international law.[50] In addition to these acts, it was also desirable for the Ottoman Empire to enter into international agreements based on the principle of sovereign equality of States. By virtue of the war, however, this proved possible only with the allies of the Empire.[51]

Conversely, the acts of the Ottoman Empire regarding foreign nationals were not satisfactory for other States, as they had always mistrusted Ottoman law, which was based on the rules of Islamic law. A system without capitulations could obviously have been disadvantageous for their nationals residing in the Ottoman Empire.[52] Hence, an order based on international agreements that replaced the capitulary regime would also be a reasonable solution for these States.[53] These two-sided circumstances of the time thus paved the way for the consular treaties between the States. To this end, the Consular Treaty between the German and the Ottoman Empires of 1917 was made,[54] which also included as an annex an Agreement on Succession. This Treaty replaced the extraterritorial status of consuls in the capitulary regime with a reciprocal status under which Ottoman consuls were vested with the same rights and privileges in the German Empire.[55] A consular treaty between the then Austro-Hungarian

---

48 The Ottoman Empire unilaterally abolished capitulations with an imperial decree in 1914 ('*İmtiyazat-ı Ecnebiyenin (Kapitülasyon) İlgası Hakkında İrade-i Seniyye*,' *Takvim-i Vekayi* of 17.09.1914, No. 1938) and announced the abolition to the relevant States through diplomatic notes (*Düstur*, Tertip II, Cilt VI, 1273). There were, however, protests by the other States because mutually agreed capitulations were not capable of unilateral abolition. Therefore, the final abolition of capitulations was possible only with the Treaty of Lausanne of 1923. For the text of the Treaty, see <http://treaties.fco.gov.uk/docs/pdf/1923/ts0016-1.pdf> accessed 21.04.2019. See also, in general on the abolition of capitulations, T. Taner, *Kapitülasyonlar Nasıl İlga Edildi?*, İsmail Akgün Matbaası, İstanbul 1956.

49 These are the Temporary Act Regarding the Abolition of the Provisions of Former Arrangements of 15.10.1914 ('*Kavanin-i Mevcudede Uhud-u Atikaya Müstenid Ahkamın Lağvı Hakkında Kanun-u Muvakkat*' – *Düstur*, Tertip II, Cilt VI, 1336) and the Temporary Act on Rights and Duties of Foreigners in Ottoman Lands of 23.02.1915 ('*Memaliki Osmaniyede Mukim Tebaayı Ecnebiyenin Hukuk ve Vezaifine Müteallik* 23 *Şubat* 1330 *Tarihli Kanun-u Muvakkat*' – *Düstur*, Tertip II, Cilt VII, 458 (hereinafter 'the Temporary Act')).

50 Z. Toprak, 'Almanya'ya İlk İşçi ve Öğrenci Göçü 1916–1918' [1981] *Bilim ve Sanat* 26; Y. Saner Gönen, 'Osmanlı Konsolosluk Sözleşmeleri – II' [1999] *Toplumsal Tarih* 36.

51 Z. Toprak, above n. 50; Y. Saner Gönen, above n. 50, 36; N. Bilgi, 'Osmanlı Devleti'nin 1917 Yılı Yabancı Nüfusu' (2010) XXV *Tarih İncelemeleri Dergisi* 101, 104–105.

52 In 1917, there were 6,996 Italian, 6,744 Austro-Hungarian and 3,024 German residents in the Ottoman Empire. See, in this regard, *BOA, DH. EUM. ECB.*, 17/39, lef 3. cited in N. Bilgi, above n. 51, 115.

53 Denkschrift 1917, above n. 45, 171. See also E. Nomer, 'Yabancıların "Ahkamı Şahsiyesi" (Statut Personnel) ve Terekesi ile İlgili İhtilaflarda Türk Kanunlar İhtilafı Sisteminin Gelişimi' in İstanbul Üniversitesi Hukuk Fakültesi (ed.), *50. Yıl Armağanı: Cumhuriyet Döneminde Hukuk*, İstanbul Üniversitesi Hukuk Fakültesi Yayınları, İstanbul 1973, pp. 500–501.

54 *Düstur*, Tertip II, Cilt IX, 467–486. The treaty became effective on 10.07.1918 in accordance with Art. 29.

55 Denkschrift 1917, above n. 45.

Empire and the Ottoman Empire was also signed on 12 March 1918 in Vienna, among other treaties; however, the treaty could not be published in the official gazette due to translation issues.[56]

This reconstituted system between the States was not able to remain in force for very long due to the conditions of war. Yet the newly founded Turkish Republic that came afterwards was also decisive in establishing international relationships based on the principle of sovereign equality of the States, unlike the earlier times of the Ottoman Empire.[57] In the scheme of this policy, Turkey signed consular treaties in order to regulate the rights and privileges – including the freedom of residence and travel – of Turkish nationals in the States with whom Turkey had political ties.[58]

The first treaty in this sense was the Consular Treaty between the Republic of Turkey and Germany of 1929 (**Treaty 19**), signed on 28 May 1929 in Ankara. Whilst the application of the Treaty was suspended following Turkey's declaration of war against Germany during the Second World War in 1945,[59] it was put into force again after the war on 1 March 1952 and is still applicable in both States.[60] Article 20 of the Treaty and its attached annex ('*Terekeye Ait Ahkâm*' or Agreement on Succession) lay out detailed rules on succession issues of nationals of the Contracting States and define the role of the consular staff over the movable property of the deceased.

Similar to the Turkish-German Treaty, the Consular Treaty between the Republic of Turkey and the Kingdom of Italy of 1929 (**Treaty 21**) was signed on 9 September 1929 in Rome. Article 21 of the Treaty, which consists of sixteen paragraphs, deals with succession issues and includes detailed rules on the rights of consular staff regarding the movable property of their nationals in accord with the circumstances of the time in which the powers of consular staff played an important role in the relations between States.[61]

---

56 *Düstur*, Tertip II, Cilt X, 455 cited in Y. Saner Gönen, above n. 50, 37.

57 This is also evident from the speech in the parliament given by the Turkish Minister of Foreign Affairs at the time after signing the Treaty with Germany. See, in this regard, '*Meclis-i Mebusan Zabıt Ceridesi*, Cilt I [1916 – Devre: 3 İçtima Senesi: 3]' pp. 362–364 <https://www.tbmm.gov.tr/tutanaklar/TUTANAK/MECMEB/mmbd03ic03c001/mmbd03ic03c001ink025.pdf> accessed 21.04.2017. See, also, the preamble of the Treaty <https://www.tbmm.gov.tr/tutanaklar/TUTANAK/TBMM/d03/c019/tbmm03019062ss0163.pdf> accessed 21.04.2019. See, also, the preamble of the Turkish-Italian Consular Treaty <https://www.tbmm.gov.tr/tutanaklar/TUTANAK/TBMM/d03/c026/tbmm03026039ss0109.pdf> accessed 21.04.2019.

58 See, for example, the preamble of the Turkish-Hungarian Treaty, <https://www.tbmm.gov.tr/tutanaklar/TUTANAK/TBMM/d06/c007/tbmm06007012ss0012.pdf> accessed 21.04.2019.

59 See, in this regard, Decision of the Grand National Assembly of Turkey of 23.02.1945, *Resmi Gazete* of 24.02.1945, No. 5940.

60 See Decree of the Cabinet of Ministers of 29.05.1952, No. 3/14511, *Resmi Gazete* of 03.05.1952, No. 8100.

61 For an analysis of the powers of consular staff, see A.K. Yörük, *Nazari ve Ameli Devletler Hususi Hukuku*, 2nd ed., İsmail Akgün Matbaası, İstanbul 1950, pp. 439 et seq.

Lastly, the Consular Treaty between the Republic of Turkey and the Kingdom of Hungary of 1938 (**Treaty 24**) was signed on 18 June 1938 in Ankara. Article 18 of the Treaty with its seven paragraphs specifies the rights of consular staff regarding the movable property of the deceased from one of the Contracting States and encompasses conflict-of-laws and jurisdictional rules for the issue of succession.

3. SCOPE OF APPLICATION OF THE TREATIES

3.1. TURKISH-GERMAN CONSULAR TREATY OF 1929

3.1.1. Ratione Materiae

The Treaty (**Treaty 19**) has rules on both intestate and testamentary succession. The rule provided under Article 20(14) of the Treaty uses a very broad formulation and submits the issues related to succession ('*hakkı verasete müteallik/müteferri mesail*') regarding movable property to the national law of the deceased and regarding immovable property to the *lex rei sitae*. This was in accordance with the rule under Article 4 of the then-current Turkish Private International Law Act (the Temporary Act).[62] The meaning of the term 'issues related to succession', however, is not clear.[63] The German preamble to the Treaty specifies that this should be understood as all the issues connected with succession, and hence, it covers not only the issues regarding the order of succession or the right of succession but also the liability of the heirs for the deceased's debts and obligations.[64]

A broad interpretation of the term would suggest that other areas of civil law connected to succession, such as matrimonial property regimes or family status, also fall within the ambit of the Treaty. However, legal texts reflect the circumstances of the time when they are made and thus should be considered against their historical background.[65] Whereas matrimonial property regimes are

---

62 Art. 4 of the Temporary Act also regulated both testamentary and intestate succession: M.R. Seviğ, *Türkiye Cumhuriyeti Kanunlar İhtilafı Kaidelerinin Sentezi*, Kenan Basımevi ve Klişe Fabrikası, İstanbul 1941, p. 38; M.R. Seviğ and V.R. Seviğ, *Devletler Hususi Hukuku*, 3rd ed., İsmail Akgün Matbaası, İstanbul 1962, p. 507.

63 See, in this regard, H. Dörner, 'Das deutsch-türkische Nachlassabkommen' (1996) *ZEV* 90, 91; H. Krüger, above n. 46, p. 149.

64 Denkschrift zu dem Konsularvertrag von 1929, *Verhandlungen des Reichstags Band 439*, 4. Wahlperiode (1928), Anlage No. 1584 29. At the time when the Treaty was drafted, the issue of the law applicable to the liability of heirs for a deceased's debts and obligations was one of the challenging questions of private international law: V.R. Seviğ, *Mirasla İlgili Devletler Hususi Hukuku Kaideleri*, Sulhi Garan Matbaası, İstanbul 1963, pp. 131 et seq.

65 H. Krüger, above n. 46, p. 149.

closely connected to succession, it cannot be argued that the drafters intended to include these matters in the Treaty at the time.[66] Other succession-related areas of law, such as family status or the validity of the adoption of a child, are issues on the status of natural persons[67] and fall outside the scope of the Treaty.

Notwithstanding this, the wording of the article does not restrict succession issues from falling within the ambit of the Treaty. Due to the absence of court practice in respect of the Treaty, some guidance can be taken only from the scope of *lex successionis* under the Turkish Private International Law Act at the time (the Temporary Act) so as to exemplify the issues which are covered by the Treaty. Hence, encompassed issues are: determining the legal heirs and their shares; forced heirship; succession rights of the surviving spouse; the liability of the heirs for the deceased's debts and obligations; disinheritance or disqualification by conduct; succession issues in cases of *commorientes*; the causes, place and time of the opening of succession; the transfer and the sharing out of an estate; the succession rights of the State on an heirless estate; issues regarding the administration of the estate; and issues regarding the testamentary executors.[68]

3.1.2. Ratione Loci

Another problematic issue on the scope of the Treaty is whether it solely covers assets located in the Contracting States or also assets located in other States. The controversy here arises from the divergent use of terms in different provisions of the Treaty. The first rule is Article 20 of the Treaty as the main source of succession rules. This prescribes that consular staff are to have the rights provided in the Treaty over the estate found in one of the Contracting States. Furthermore, Article 20(1) stipulates that consular staff and the local authorities are under a duty to inform each other, 'in the event of the death of a national of one of the Contracting States in the territory of the other Contracting State'. This means that the Treaty is applicable only if the deceased has died in one of the Contracting States. Nonetheless, the Treaty itself expands

---

66 Ibid., p. 148. With regards to matrimonial property regimes, see also M. Kılıç, 'Türkei' in R. Süß (ed.), *Erbrecht in Europa*, 3rd ed., Zerb Verlag, Angelbachtal 2015, paras. 12–14, M. Gebauer, 'Erbrechtliche Fragen im deutsch-türkischen Rechtsverkehr' (2018) 27 *Informationsbrief der DTJV* 18, 21ff.

67 E. Nomer, above n. 53, p. 507.

68 O.F. Berki, *Kanuni Miras ve Ölüme Bağlı Tasarruflardan Doğan Kanun İhtilafları*, Güzel Sanatlar Matbaası, Ankara 1960, pp. 30 et seq.; V.R. Seviğ, above n. 64, pp. 86 et seq.; N. Uluocak, *Kanunlar İhtilafı (Yasama Yetkisi Kuralları)*, Fakülteler Matbaası, İstanbul 1971, pp. 91–99; E. Göğer, *Devletler Hususi Hukuku (Kanunlar İhtilafı)*, 4th ed., Sevinç Matbaası, Ankara 1977, pp. 260 et seq.; F.B. Tanrıbilir, *Kanuni Mirasçılıktan Doğan Kanunlar İhtilafı*, Gazi Üniversitesi İletişim Fakültesi Basımevi, Ankara 2000, p. 122; F. Sütçü, 'Deutsch-türkische Erbrechtsfälle in der Anwaltspraxis' (2015) *ZErb* 42, 45.

its scope in Article 20(18), where it specifies that Article 20(1) to (17) of the Treaty will be applicable by analogy if the deceased dies in a third State.[69]

In contrast to the references to the 'Contracting States' in these provisions, Article 20(14) (2) of the Treaty requires that succession issues regarding immovable property be settled in accordance with the law of the State where such property is located (*lex rei sitae*), and as if the deceased had been a national of the *forum* State. The reference to 'States' rather than 'Contracting States' in this provision creates a controversy over the territorial scope of the Treaty.[70]

It has, therefore, been posited that the Treaty also covers the estate located outside the territories of Contracting States.[71] Nonetheless, it appears that such a consequence cannot be reached by virtue of the different use of terms, and only the estate located in the Contracting States falls within the scope of the Treaty.[72] This is firstly because a contrary interpretation would contradict the rationale of a bilateral consular treaty. A bilateral treaty between the States is, almost without exception, drafted to resolve legal conflicts between the Contracting States. Legal issues outside these States are of no interest to the contracting parties.[73] In addition, the Treaty was drafted to protect succession rights of the nationals of the Contracting States in each other's territory and, hence, gives broad powers to the consular staff regarding these issues. A broad interpretation of the Treaty including assets in third States would run counter

69 F. Bauer, 'EuErbVO Art. 75 Anhang II-deutsch-türkisches NA' in A. Dutta and J. Weber (eds.), *Internationales Erbrecht*, C.H. Beck, Munich 2016, para. 4.

70 A. Dutta, 'EuErbVO' in F.J. Säcker et al. (eds.), *Münchener Kommentar zum Bürgerlichen Gesetzbuch*, vol. 11, 7th ed., C.H. Beck, Munich 2018, Art. 75, para. 20.

71 H. Krüger, above n. 46, p. 150; J. Fetsch, 'Auslandsvermögen im Internationalen Erbrecht – Testamente und Erbverträge, Erbschein und Ausschlagung bei Auslandsvermögen –' (2006) *RNotZ* 77, 114; A. Dutta, above n. 70, Art. 75, para. 20; cf. F. Bauer, above n. 69, para. 4.

72 H. Dörner, above n. 63, 94; G. Schotten and C. Schmellenkamp, *Das Internationale Privatrecht in der notariellen Praxis*, 2nd ed., C.H. Beck, Munich 2007, para. 264; C.F. Majer, 'Das deutsch-türkische Nachlassabkommen: ein Anachronismus' (2012) *ZEV* 182, 184; R. Süß, 'Der Vorbehalt zugunsten bilateraler Abkommen mit Drittstaaten' in A. Dutta and S. Herrler (eds.), *Die Europäische Erbrechtsverordnung, 20 Jahre DNotI 1993–2013*, C.H. Beck, Munich 2014, pp. 187 et seq.; K. Lechner, 'EU Regulation 650/2012 on successions and the creation of a European Certificate of Succession' in European Parliament, Directorate General for Internal Policies, Policy Department C: Citizens' Rights and Constitutional Affairs – Legal Affairs (ed.), *Cross-border activities in the EU Making life easier for citizens – Workshop for the JURI Committee – PE 510.003* (2015) p. 144 <http://www.europarl.europa.eu/RegData/etudes/STUD/2015/510003/IPOL_STU(2015)510003_EN.pdf> accessed 21.04.2019. S. Lorenz, 'EGBGB Art. 25', in H.G. Bamberger et al. (eds.), *BeckOK BGB*, 41st ed. (01.11.2015), para. 6; K. Lechner, 'Die Europäische Erbrechtsverordnung' [2016] *DNotZ-Sonderheft* 102, 113; 'Türkei: Gesetzliche Erbfolge nach einem türkischen Staatsangehörigen Deutsch-türkisches Nachlassabkommen; EuErbVO' [2016] *DNotI-Report* 103, 104. See also V.R. Seviğ, *Ahkâmı Şahsiye Davalarında Türk Mahkemesinin Yetkisi*, Sermet Matbaası, İstanbul 1964, pp. 15–16.

73 C.F. Majer, above n. 72, 184.

to the rationale of vesting consular staff with such powers.[74] Last but not least, disregarding the national conflict rule and giving priority to a third State law even without an explicit *ordre public* exception would go beyond the intention of the drafters. Therefore, the mere reference to the 'State' rather than the 'Contracting States' in Article 20(14) (2) should not be interpreted in such a way. This is also evident from the term 'Contracting States' used in Article 20 of the Consular Treaty as it is the main source of the succession rules.[75]

3.1.3. Ratione Personae

As already explained above, the Treaty applies to succession issues arising from the death of a national of one of the Contracting States in the territory of the other contracting party (Article 20 of the Consular Treaty and also under paragraph (1)). This means that succession cases of German nationals who died in Turkey and Turkish nationals who died in Germany should be handled in accordance with the rules of the Treaty.[76]

A crucial question arising here is whether the Treaty also governs succession issues of deceased who have dual and/or multiple nationalities, i.e. instances where the deceased is a national of both Contracting States or is a national of a Contracting State and another State. The views on the issue are divergent.

First and foremost, it has been contended that the Treaty is not applicable in this case, hence national rules of the Contracting States should be applied. The Treaty was concluded in order to replace the former capitulary regime (that was based on the inequality of the States) with the principle of equality and with the underlying aim that nationals of the Contracting States would not be discriminated against in each other's territory. There is, however, no risk of discrimination for individuals holding citizenship of both Contracting States as they would not be treated as foreign in either of the Contracting States.[77] Thus, such situations do not fall within the scope of the Treaty, and domestic conflict-of-laws rules of the States regarding succession would be applicable instead.[78]

The second view, by contrast, argues that the gap in the Treaty with regards to multiple nationalities could be filled with a reference to the domestic conflict-of-laws rules of the States determining the law applicable in the event

74 R. Süß, above n. 72, p. 187.
75 H. Dörner, above n. 63, 94; R. Süß, above n. 72, p. 187.
76 H. Krüger, above n. 46, p. 149.
77 G. Kegel, 'EGBGB Art. 25' in W. Siebert (ed.), *Soergel BGB*, vol. 10 (Einführungsgesetz), 12th ed., Kohlhammer, Stuttgart 1996, para. 108; H. Krüger, above n. 46, pp. 150 et seq.; F. Bauer, above n. 15, 1255; C.F. Majer, above n. 72, 183–184; A. Dutta, above n. 70, Art. 75, para. 19; cf. F. Bauer, above n. 69, para. 3: The Treaty is only applicable if the deceased holds solely the nationality of Turkey.
78 F.B. Tanribilir, above n. 68, p. 193.

of dual and/or multiple citizenships.[79] When this is the case, in accordance with Article 4(b) and (c) of the Turkish Private International Law Act, Turkish nationality prevails for a person who holds a passport from both Turkey and Germany; for a person who holds a passport from Germany and another State, the test of effective nationality applies. Thus, the Treaty can be applied by the Turkish courts only in cases where the deceased is a national of Germany and another State, and here his/her German nationality is effective.

Last but not least, some scholars hold the opinion that gaps in international agreements cannot be filled with the help of national rules, and thus the correct solution should be the use of the effective nationality test in this context.[80] This is because using national rules would impair the harmony of decisions desired by the Treaty[81] since each Contracting State would give priority to the nationality of the *forum* and apply the effective nationality test only in other situations.[82] Furthermore, it would also undermine the reciprocal recognition of decisions as well as, in this case, certificates of succession.[83]

From these perspectives, the use of the effective nationality test would undoubtedly serve the interests of the parties[84] and the desired harmonization

79 H.P. Schömmer and N. Kesen, *Internationales Erbrecht Türkei*, C.H. Beck, Munich 2004, para. 242; G. Schotten and C. Schmellenkamp, above n. 72, para. 264; Ş. Akipek, 'Länderbericht Türkei', in L. Kroiß, C. Ann and J. Mayer (eds.), *NK-BGB Erbrecht*, vol. 5, 4th ed., Nomos, Baden-Baden 2014, paras. 125–127; S. Lorenz, above n. 72, para. 6;. See A. Dutta, above n. 70, Art. 75, para. 19: Reference to national rules is possible only for dual/multiple nationals who hold a passport from a Contracting State as well from a non-Contracting State.
A Turkish-Dutch citizen was considered as a Dutch national by a German court on the grounds that the Dutch nationality of the individual was effective, and the court applied Dutch law in accordance with Art. 24 of the German PILA at the time: AG Bad Homburg 13.7.1977, *IPRspr* 1977 No. 103.

80 H. Dörner, above n. 63, 92; J. Fetsch, above n. 71, 115.

81 H. Dörner, above n. 63, 92; J. Fetsch, above n. 71, 115; cf. H. Krüger, above n. 46, p. 151. See, generally on this issue, J. Kropholler, *Internationales Einheitsrecht*, Mohr Siebeck, Tübingen 1975, pp. 292 et seq.

82 H.-P. Mansel, *Personalstatut, Staatsangehörigkeit und Effektivität*, C.H. Beck, Munich 1988, paras. 480 et seq.; H.J. Sonnenberger, 'Anerkennung der Staatsangehörigkeit und effektive Staatsangehörigkeit natürlicher Personen im Völkerrecht und im Internationalen Privatrecht' (1988) 29 *BerGesVR* 9, 21–22; W. Meyer-Sparenberg, *Staatsvertragliche Kollisionsnormeni*, Duncker & Humblot, Berlin 1990, pp. 135 et seq.; İ. Ataman Figanmeşe, 'Çifte Vatandaşlık Halinde MÖHUK'un 4. Maddesinin b ve c Bentlerinin Uygulama Alanı' (2000) 19–20 *MHB* 95, 101–102. See also K. Siehr, 'Multilaterale Staatsverträge erga omnes und deren Inkorporation in nationale IPR-Kodifikationen – Vor- und Nachteile einer solchen Rezeption' (1986) 27 *BerGesVR* 129.

83 J. Fetsch, above n. 71, 115.

84 See, in this regard, G. Bayraktaroğlu Özçelik, 'Kanunlar İhtilafı Hukukunda Olumlu Vatandaşlık İhtilaflarının Çözümü ve MÖHUK m. 4(1) (b) ve (c) Hükümlerinin Değerlendirilmesi' (2015) 19 *GÜHFD* 111, 125–126; V. Doğan, *Milletlerarası Özel Hukuk*, 5th ed., Savaş Yayınevi, Ankara 2019, pp. 207–208; C. Şanlı, E. Esen and İ. Ataman Figanmeşe, *Milletlerarası Özel Hukuk*, 6th ed., Vedat Kitapçılık, İstanbul 2018, p. 32, n. 62.

within the treaties.[85] Nevertheless, its applicability to dual and/or multiple nationality citizens who are also Turkish nationals does not seem realistic under Turkish law. This is because it has been contended that the sovereignty of the State requires that Turkish citizens be subject to Turkish law.[86] This would be applicable even in situations where there is no provision, providing that the nationality of the *forum* State is to prevail.[87] In addition, it is the general policy of States to apply their own law to their citizens in order to protect them from the effects of foreign law, particularly in the field of family law.[88] Therefore, the Turkish citizenship of a Turkish-German national will prevail before the Turkish courts and the Treaty will not be applicable to them.[89] This is also consistent with the circumstances existing at the time in which the treaties were concluded. As underlined by the proponents of the first view, the aim of the parties when drafting the Treaty was to prevent discrimination against their nationals in each other's State. Therefore, it would seem that the parties did not intend the application of the Treaty to dual and/or multiple nationals who hold the nationality of the *forum* State. The application of the treaty to dual/and or multiple nationals who hold the nationality of the other Contracting State and also a non-Contracting State, e.g. a German-French deceased who left an amount of money in a Turkish bank remains possible based on the effective nationality.

---

85 İ. Ataman Figanmeşe, above n. 82, 105; M. Gebauer, above n. 66, 23.

86 E. Göğer, 'Çifte Vatandaşlık' (1995) *AÜHFD* 132, 163; G. Güngör, *Tâabiyet Hukuku: Gerçek Kişiler - Tüzel Kişiler - Şeyler*, 6th ed., Yetkin, Ankara 2018, p. 30; E. Nomer, *Türk Vatandaşlık Hukuku*, 25th ed., Filiz Kitabevi, İstanbul 2018, pp. 37 et seq. In the same direction, at the time of the Temporary Act, O.F. Berki, above n. 68, p. 20; V.R. Seviğ, above n. 64, p. 91.

87 G. Güngör, above n. 86, p. 30.

88 E. Nomer, 'Türk Devletler Özel Hukukunda Çifte Vatandaşlık' (1994) 14 *MHB* 55, 58. See also A. Çelikel and B. Erdem, *Milletlerarası Özel Hukuk*, 15th ed., Beta, İstanbul 2017, p. 68.

89 It is also noteworthy to mention the practice of the Turkish Court of Cassation ('*Yargıtay*') in certain divorce cases. Art. 14(1) of the Turkish PILA provides that the law applicable to divorce and separation is the common nationality of the parties. If parties have different nationalities, the law of the State in which the parties have their common habitual residence applies. Where this does not exist, Turkish law applies. In a divorce case where one of the spouses was, for instance, a Turkish-French national and the other a French national, application of this provision would seemingly require that French law be applicable, as it is the common nationality of the parties. *Yargıtay*, however, has held in a couple of cases that the Turkish nationality will prevail for the spouse holding a Turkish passport as a result of the mandatory nature of Art. 4 of the Turkish PILA and consequently the spouses have no common nationality, thereby requiring the application of the common habitual residence of the parties to the divorce. See, in this regard, Yargıtay 2. Hukuk Dairesi, T. 12.10.2004, E. 2004/9208, K. 2004/11702; Yargıtay 2. Hukuk Dairesi, T. 13.02.2008, E. 2007/4214, K. 2008/1476 published in N. Ekşi, *5718 Sayılı Milletlerarası Özel Hukuk ve Usul Hukuku Hakkında Kanuna İlişkin Yargıtay Kararları*, Beta, İstanbul 2010, pp. 3 et seq. See, for different views on this issue under Turkish law, B. Tiryakioğlu, 'Multiple Citizenship and its Consequences in Turkish Law' (2006) 3 *Ankara L. Rev.* 1, 14; A. Uyanik Çavuşoğlu, *Türk Milletlerarası Özel Hukukunda Boşanma*, Beta, İstanbul 2006, p. 46; G. Bayraktaroğlu Özçelik, above n. 84, 138; C. Şanlı, E. Esen and İ. Ataman Figanmeşe, above n. 84, p. 135, n. 74.

3.2. TURKISH-ITALIAN CONSULAR TREATY OF 1929

3.2.1. Ratione Materiae

Article 21(11) (**Treaty 21**) provides that in respect of movable property, all issues based on the title to inheritance and legacy and pertaining to the right or the sharing out of succession are governed by the national law of the deceased. In the same vein, similar legal issues on immovable property are governed by the *lex rei sitae* (Article 21(15)). Here again, other areas of law such as the matrimonial property regimes or family status are not governed by the Treaty. Notwithstanding the variant phrasing, subjects falling within the scope of the Treaty, as in the Turkish-German Treaty (**Treaty 19**), are mainly issues regarding succession rights and the sharing out of an estate.[90] Also here, legal matters such as the determination of the legal heirs and their respective shares, the reserved portion and disqualification are encompassed by the rules.

3.2.2. Ratione Loci

The same conclusion regarding assets in third States under the Turkish-German Treaty (**Treaty 19**) is also applicable here. Article 21 of the Treaty, as the main source of the rules on succession, vests consular staff with powers regarding the movable property belonging to nationals of the contracting parties in the territory of the other State. The first paragraph of the article deals with the duty of the consular staff and the local authorities to inform each other when a national of a Contracting State dies in the other Contracting State. Paragraph (16) of the article extends the ambit of the Treaty to situations where the deceased died in a third State. It clarifies, nonetheless, that the estate must be in one of the Contracting States. In all these provisions, reference is made to the 'Contracting States'. Paragraph (15), by contrast, refers to the 'State' where the estate is located for the law applicable to immovable property. This, nevertheless, does not mean that the Treaty is applicable on assets found in third States.

3.2.3. Ratione Personae

The Treaty is applicable for nationals of the Sending State who have died in the territory of the Receiving State or in a third State. The Treaty has no rule on dual and/or multiple nationals. The same conclusion regarding the Turkish-German Treaty (**Treaty 19**) should apply here, that the Treaty is not applicable to dual and/or multiple nationals who hold the nationality of both Contracting States. Neither the text nor the drafting history of the Treaty espouses a contrary

---

[90] The preamble of the Treaty, above n. 57.

interpretation. The Treaty may, however, still be applicable to dual and/or multiple nationals holding passports from the other Contracting State as well as from a non-Contracting State based on the effective nationality.[91]

3.3. TURKISH-HUNGARIAN CONSULAR TREATY OF 1938

3.3.1. Ratione Materiae

Article 20(3) of the Treaty (**Treaty 24**) provides that all legal conflicts regarding succession and dispositions of property upon death in respect of movable property are subject to the national law of the deceased; as to immovable property the *lex rei sitae* is applicable. The Treaty, therefore, covers both testamentary and intestate succession in a manner analogous to the other two treaties. The material scope of the Treaty again broadly covers all issues concerning the substance of a succession or a legacy.

3.3.2. Ratione Loci

In accordance with the Turkish-German (**Treaty 19**) and the Turkish-Italian Treaties (**Treaty 21**), the Turkish-Hungarian Treaty is not applicable to assets located in non-Contracting States. Article 18 of the Treaty on succession specifies that consular staff has authority over movable property of the deceased found in the relevant Contracting State. The first paragraph of the article is on the duty of the consular staff and the local authorities to inform each other as to the death of a national of one of the Contracting States. Both of these provisions refer to the 'Contracting States'. Unlike the other two treaties, the Treaty does not have a specific provision extending its scope to situations where the nationals of the contracting parties die in a third State. Article 18(3) states that the immovable property is to be governed by the law of the 'State' where the asset is located. Although use of the term 'State' rather than 'Contracting State' creates an impression that the Treaty covers assets in third States, the bilateral and consular nature of the Treaty as well as the lack of an explicit *ordre public* exception requires that the Treaty not be applied to assets found outside the Contracting States.

3.3.3. Ratione Personae

The Treaty is applicable in cases where a national of one contracting party dies in the other side's territory. Thus, it is only applicable to the succession issues of

---

91 See, however, P. Franzina, section 2.2.5.1, n. 66 of the Italian report in this volume.

nationals of the Contracting States. The Treaty is silent on the law applicable to instances where a person holds either passports of both Contracting States or the passport of a Contracting State in addition to the passport of a non-Contracting State. It must once more be accepted that the Treaty is not applicable in cases where the deceased is a national of both Contracting States. Nevertheless, if a person is a Hungarian national and a national of another State, the Treaty may still be applicable if the Hungarian nationality is the effective one.

4. PRIVATE INTERNATIONAL LAW OF THE TREATY REGIMES

4.1. DUALIST APPROACH

Regarding movable property, the law applicable to succession issues under the treaties is the national law of the deceased at the time of death (Article 20(14) (1) of the Turkish-German Treaty (**Treaty 19**), Article 21(11) of the Turkish-Italian Treaty (**Treaty 21**), Article 18(3) (1) of the Turkish-Hungarian Treaty (**Treaty 24**)). Succession issues with regards to immovable property, on the other hand, are governed by the law of the State where the property is located (Article 20(14) (2) of the Turkish-German Treaty, Article 21(15) (3) of the Turkish-Italian Treaty, Article 18(3) (3) of the Turkish-Hungarian Treaty). By doing so, the treaties adopt a dualist approach with respect to movables and immovables that is consistent with the Turkish private international law on succession at the time of the treaties' adoption.[92] The general rule provided under the current Turkish Private International Law Act is, to some extent, different from the rules in the treaties. Article 20(1) of this Act clarifies that the law applicable to the succession as a whole is the national law of the deceased. However, the second sentence of the provision provides an exception and states that immovables located in Turkey are to be governed by Turkish law.[93]

---

92 Art. 4 of the Temporary Act.

93 As a consequence of this provision, the nature of the system adopted in the Turkish PILA, i.e. whether it is a unitary, scission or hybrid system, has been a matter of discussion among scholars. See, for different views on the issue, *Milletlerarası Özel Hukuk ve Milletlerarası Usul Hukuku Kanunu Öntasarı Sempozyumu, 22–24 Kasım 1976*, Fakülteler Matbaası, İstanbul 1978, pp. 138 et seq.; G. Tekinalp, 'Türk "Milletlerarası Özel Hukuk ve Milletlerarası Usul Hukuku Tasarısı"' (1978) 44 *İÜHFM* 91, 110 et seq.; N. Uluocak, *Milletlerarası Özel Hukuk Dersleri (Kişisel Statü – Miras Statüsü)*, Filiz Kitabevi, İstanbul 1987, p. 112; V. Doğan, 'Miras Hukukundan Doğan Kanunlar İhtilafı' (1990), 3 *SÜHFD* 181, 184 et seq.; F.B. Tanrıbilir, above n. 68, pp. 88 et seq.; R. Aybay and E. Dardağan, *Uluslararası Düzeyde Yasaların Çatışması (Kanunlar İhtilafı)*, 2nd ed., İstanbul Bilgi Üniversitesi, İstanbul 2008, p. 231; N. Baran Çelik, *Milletlerarası Unsurlu Ölüme Bağlı Tasarruflara Uygulanacak Hukukun Tayini*, Yetkin, Ankara 2011, pp. 106–107; N. Ekşi, above n. 30, p. 33; N. Ekşi, 'Comparison

Therefore, by adopting the application of the national law of the deceased in the field of succession law and excluding only the immovables in Turkey from the scope of this rule, the general approach of Turkish private international law on succession is, in principle, different from the conflict-of-laws rules of the treaties.

The Regulation, on the other hand, adopts a unitary approach and applies the law of the State in which the deceased had his habitual residence at the time of death to the succession as a whole (Article 21(1)). The difference between the systems on the general conflict rule can be demonstrated in a simple example. Assume, for instance, a Turkish citizen who was habitually resident in Germany and who dies there intestate, leaving in Germany some amount of money in a bank account and a house. From these assets, under the Turkish-German Treaty (**Treaty 19**), the money in Germany is governed by Turkish law, while the house in Germany is governed by German law. In the same hypothetical case, all the assets will be governed by Turkish law as the national law of the deceased under the Turkish Private International Law Act. If, on the other hand, the Regulation applies to this case, all the assets, irrespective of their location and nature, will be governed by German law as the law of the State of habitual residence of the deceased.

The question of which law is applicable to determine the movable and immovable nature of an asset is specifically dealt with only under Article 20(12) (3) of the Turkish-German Treaty (**Treaty 19**), providing that the *lex rei sitae* governs this question. Other treaties, however, are silent on this issue. The nature of the assets is indeed an important issue given that the conflict-of-laws rules in the treaties make a distinction between movable and immovable properties.[94] Due to the limited court practice on the treaties, it is highly likely that judges confronted by such a question would be inclined to apply the solution under their own law. A Turkish judge, therefore, can be expected to apply the *lex rei sitae* when determining the movable and immovable nature of an asset.[95]

An important issue with regards to the law applicable to immovable assets is that citizens of the other Contracting State are entitled to equal treatment with nationals in each other's territory for immovable property as provided under Article 20(14) (2) of the Turkish-German Treaty (**Treaty 19**). It is questionable

---

of Articles 20 and 43 of the Turkish Private International Law and Procedural Law Act ('PILA') with the EU Succession Regulation' in P. Beaumont and B. Yüksel (eds.), *Turkish and EU Private International Law - A Comparison*, On İki Levha, İstanbul 2014, p. 122; V. Doğan, above n. 84, p. 367; G. Tekinalp and A. Uyanik, above n. 19, p. 232; A.K. Altiparmak, *İngiliz, Avrupa Birliği ve Türk Hukukunda Mirasa Uygulanacak Hukuk*, On İki Levha, İstanbul 2017, pp. 19–20 and 105; A. Çelikel and B. Erdem, above n. 88, p. 334; E. Nomer, *Devletler Hususi Hukuku*, 22nd ed., Beta, İstanbul 2017, p. 293; C. Şanli, E. Esen and İ. Ataman Figanmeşe, above n. 84, p. 217–218, n. 272.

94 E. Nomer, above n. 93, p. 305.

95 Ibid.

under this provision whether rules such as those in the Land Registry Law of Turkey,[96] which are claimed to restrict the succession rights of foreigners in practice,[97] are applicable for German citizens in cases falling within the scope of the Treaty. This question also applies for other possible restrictions on immovable property, such as the law regarding farmhouses ('*Höfeordnung*')[98] in Germany. The wording of the provision seems to suggest that these restrictions could only be applicable to the citizens of the other Contracting State if they are also applied to nationals of the State where the estate is found. Nevertheless, it seems that a correct interpretation could only be made if the provision is read in conjunction with the Treaty of Establishment between the Republic of Turkey and Germany of 1927,[99] which specifically addresses the acquisition of immovable property

---

96 Above n. 16. See especially Arts. 35 and 36 of the Law imposing legal restrictions on the acquisition of real estate by foreigners in Turkey, which are considered as overriding mandatory rules. Other restrictions which may be relevant regarding the succession rights of foreigners exist in the Equivalent Retaliation Act ('*Hudutları Dahilinde Tebaamızın Emlakine Vaziyet Eden Devletlerin Türkiye'deki Tebaaları Emlakine Karşı Mukabelei Bilmisil Tedabiri İttihazı Hakkında Kanun*' – *Resmi Gazete* of 15.06.1927, No. 608) and the Law on the Closed Military and Security Zones ('*Askeri Yasak Bölgeler ve Güvenlik Bölgeleri Kanunu*' – *Resmi Gazete* of 22.12.1981, No. 2565). They are also considered as overriding mandatory rules. See, in this regard, N. Ekşi, *Türk Mahkemelerinin Milletlerarası Yetkisi*, 2nd ed., Beta, İstanbul 2000, pp. 221–223; N. Baran Çelik, above n. 93, pp. 205–207; Ekşi, above n. 30, pp. 73–74; H. Özdemir Kocasakal, *Doğrudan Uygulanan Kurallar ve Sözleşmeler Üzerindeki Etkileri*, Galatasaray Üniversitesi Yayınları, İstanbul 2001, p. 147; M. Erkan, 'Bir Tabu: Taşınmazın Aynına İlişkin Davalarda Münhasır Yetki' (2012) 20 *SÜHFD* 11, 45, n. 125; C. Şanli, E. Esen and İ. Ataman Figanmeşe, above n. 84, p. 9.

97 See, for example, Yargıtay 2. Hukuk Dairesi, T. 21.12.2005, E. 2006/4387 K. 2006/11476, above n. 14.

98 BGBl. I 1933. The last modification of the law was on 20.11.2015 (BGBl. I 2010). Similar rules also exist in Turkey, see Law on the Protection of Soil and the Use of Land ('*Toprak Koruma ve Arazi Kullanımı Kanunu*' – *Resmi Gazete* of 19.07.2005, No. 25880).

99 *Resmi Gazete* of 08.06.1927, No. 605. See, especially, Art. 1 and 3 of the Treaty. The Treaty was signed on 12 January 1927 in Ankara. Its application, likewise the Turkish-German Consular Treaty of 1929 (**Treaty 19**), was suspended during the Second World War in 1945. It was, however, put into force again after the war in 1952. See, in this regard, above nn. 59–60.
This Treaty, unlike the Turkish-German Consular Treaty of 1929, had much been used in Turkish legal practice for interpretation of the reciprocity requirement for the acquisition of real estate by foreign nationals under Art. 35 of the Land Registry Law before its abolition with the amendments made in 2012 (*Resmi Gazete* of 18.05.2012, No. 28296). For a decision of Yargıtay in this regard, see Yargıtay 8. Hukuk Dairesi, T. 21.10.1986, E. 1986/9681 K. 1986/10741 <http://www.kazanci.com> accessed 21.04.2019; Yargıtay Hukuk Genel Kurulu, T. 10.04.1989, E. 1988/8-556 K. 1989/69 <http://www.kazanci.com> accessed 21.04.2019.
The Treaty was also referred to in legal opinions given by the Turkish Directorate General for International Law and Foreign Relations to guide Turkish courts in cases regarding the issuance of succession certificates. Such legal opinions were personally reported to the author by the Justice Counsellor of Berlin, Aslan Özdemir. The author is thankful to Mr. Özdemir for this important contribution.

by nationals of both States in each other's territory.[100] Such a provision does not, however, exist in the Turkish-Italian or Turkish-Hungarian treaties.

4.2. SCOPE OF THE LAW APPLICABLE TO SUCCESSION

As mentioned earlier,[101] the law applicable to succession under the treaties governs all issues of succession. Whereas the two instruments are not always consistent as to which issues fall within the scope of the rules, such imprecision characterizes the Regulation as well. Nonetheless, the Regulation is certainly much clearer on the question of what is meant by succession, giving some examples under Article 23. Accordingly, *lex successionis* covers all questions relating to the succession from its opening to the sharing out of the estate. It also covers issues concerning the administration of estates and the liability for debts under succession.[102] Turkish Private International Law Act likewise aims for all the issues of succession to be covered by the general conflict-of-laws rule. Nevertheless, unlike the other instruments, the Turkish Act submits the provisions pertaining to the grounds for the opening, acquisition and sharing out of a succession – due to practical reasons[103] – to the law of the place where the estate is located (Article 20(2)). In addition, in order to prevent other States from claiming to be the final heir of an estate found in Turkey,[104] a further exception to the general rule has been provided in the Act clarifying that an heirless estate in Turkey will belong to the State (Article 20(3)).

4.3. THE LAW APPLICABLE TO THE FORMAL VALIDITY OF DISPOSITIONS OF PROPERTY UPON DEATH

Unlike the treaties with Italy and Hungary, the Turkish-German Treaty (**Treaty 19**) has a separate principle on the law applicable to the formal validity of dispositions of property upon death as set out in Article 20(16), which should be applicable both for movable and immovable property.[105] The rule stipulates that such dispositions are valid if they were made in accordance with the law of the State in which they were made or with the law of the national State of

---

100 See, for a short comment on this Treaty and its application to inherited properties, A.Y. Aydoğmuş, *AİHS EK 1 No'lu Protokole Göre Yabancıların Türkiye'de Taşınmaz Edinmesi*, On İki Levha, İstanbul 2016, pp. 239–240 and 365.

101 Above under sections 3.1.1, 3.2.1 and 3.3.1.

102 See Recital (42) of the Regulation.

103 G. Tekinalp and A. Uyanik, above n. 19, p. 232; E. Nomer, above n. 93, pp. 293–294.

104 E. Nomer, above n. 93, p. 296.

105 The rules regarding the formal validity of testamentary succession do not differentiate between movable and immovable property: E. Nomer, above n. 53, p. 525.

the deceased at the time of making the disposition. This law will also govern the annulment or revocation of such dispositions. With regards to testaments, both Germany[106] and Turkey[107] are party to the Hague Convention of 5 October 1961 on the Conflict of Laws Relating to the Form of Testamentary Dispositions. The Convention does not clarify its effect on the former bilateral or multilateral treaties of Contracting States covering the same issues. The general principle of '*lex posterior derogat legi priori*' regarding a conflict of treaties, also regulated under Article 30 of the Vienna Convention on the Law of Treaties,[108] should be applicable here. Hence, the Hague Convention replaces the rule of the Treaty between Turkey and Germany in respect of the formal validity of testamentary dispositions and their revocation.[109]

The rule of the Treaty is applicable for other forms of dispositions of property upon death, i.e. agreements as to succession under Turkish law.[110] This also appears to be disadvantageous for the nationals of both Contracting States considering the current rules in both jurisdictions. The Regulation sets out a variety of connecting factors for the formal validity of dispositions of property upon death, which are also applicable for agreements as to succession under Article 27. Pursuant to these rules, dispositions of property upon death will be formally valid if they are made in accordance with the law of: the State in which they are made; the national State; the State of domicile or the State of habitual residence of the testator or one of the persons whose succession is the subject of an agreement as to succession either at the time of making the disposition or at the time of death; and the State where the immovable property is located.

Even though the alternative connecting factors are as not as numerous as in the Regulation, the ambit of the rule provided in the Turkish Private International Law Act is also broader than Article 20(16) of the Treaty. The law applicable to the formal validity of dispositions of property upon death under Article 20(4) of the Turkish Private International Law Act is the national law of the deceased, or the law of the State where the disposition is made, or the law applicable to the succession (*lex causae*). Since the law governing succession issues is generally the national law of the deceased under Article 20(1) of the Turkish Private International Act, there are only two different connecting factors in most cases. The third alternative

---

106 BGBl. II 1966, 11.

107 See, above n. 18.

108 For the text of the Convention, see <https://treaties.un.org/doc/publication/unts/volume%20 1155/volume-1155-i-18232-english.pdf> accessed 21.04.2019.

109 This also applies to testamentary dispositions made before the entry into force of the Convention if the testator died after its entry into force. This is because Turkey did not make any reservations under Art. 13: G. Tekinalp and A. Uyanik, above n. 19, p. 249.

110 H. Dörner, above n. 63, 94–95.

only comes into play when there are immovable assets in Turkey that are under the authority of Turkish law as a consequence of the exception provided in the second sentence of the Article 20(1).[111] As a result, in a case where, for instance, a German national domiciled in Turkey makes an agreement as to succession in France in accordance with the formal requirements of Turkish law concerning his holiday home in Turkey, this agreement is valid under both the Turkish Private International Law Act and the Regulation but invalid under the Treaty. It is obvious from this basic example that the scope of the rule of the Treaty is too narrow considering the rules of both other instruments.

4.4. *RENVOI*

As they are international agreements, *renvoi* is not applicable in the treaties, and hence the substantive law of the Contracting States should be ultimately applicable to succession issues.[112] This is consistent with Article 2(3) of the Turkish Private International Law Act, providing that the application of *renvoi* is possible only for issues relating to personal status and family law. Succession issues are not covered by this provision.[113] The Regulation accepts *renvoi*, however, if the law of a third State whose law is applicable to the succession makes a reference to the law of a Member State or to the law of another third State which would apply its own law (Article 34).

4.5. *PROFESSIO IURIS*

An important aspect of the conflict-of-laws rules of the treaties is that the *professio iuris* is not allowed as in the Turkish Private International Law Act. Therefore, if a Turkish deceased habitually resident in one of the Contracting Member States makes a choice of law in favour of Turkish law as his national law, such a choice will not be recognized under the treaties. If, however, the Regulation applies, a choice in favour of the national law of the deceased will be valid in accordance with Article 22 and his succession will be governed by Turkish law as a whole. The choice will be valid even if this person has another nationality in addition to his Turkish nationality (Article 22(1)).

---

111 G. Tekinalp and A. Uyanik, above n. 19, p. 243; C. Şanli, E. Esen and İ. Ataman Figanmeşe, above n. 84, p. 232, n. 313.

112 H. Krüger, above n. 46, p. 148; S. Lorenz, above n. 72, para. 6; L. Kroiß, 'EGBGB Art. 25' in T. Heidel et al. (eds.), *NK-Bürgerliches Gesetzbuch-BGB Band 1: Allgemeiner Teil, EGBGB*, 3th ed., Nomos, Baden-Baden 2016, para. 8; F. Bauer, above n. 69, para. 16.

113 N. Ekşi, above n. 30, p. 84; G. Tekinalp and A. Uyanik, above n. 19, p. 37. See, however, A. Çelikel and B. Erdem, above n. 88, pp. 119–120.

4.6. *ORDRE PUBLIC*

There is no *ordre public* clause in the treaties, this is in contrast to the Regulation (Article 35) and the Turkish Private International Law Act (Article 5). In spite of the lack of a provision, it might be arguable that the parties have implicitly reserved their right to refer back to national provisions on *ordre public* in order to prevent the application of the law of the other contracting party. Nonetheless, the parties conclusively drafted conflict-of-laws rules in the treaties, and it is not desirable for them to prevent the application of the other party's law by resort to their national provisions. The use of the *ordre public* exception may still come into play, though, based on the general principles of international law in extreme cases such as an infringement of rights protected under the European Convention on Human Rights.[114]

5. PROCEDURAL ISSUES OF THE TREATY REGIMES

5.1. JURISDICTION

In parallel to the conflict-of-laws rules, jurisdictional rules of the treaties subject legal claims with regards to movable and immovable property to different regimes. All legal claims regarding movable property are to be settled by the courts of the national State of the deceased (Article 20(15) of the Turkish-German Treaty (**Treaty 19**), Article 21(11) of the Turkish-Italian Treaty (**Treaty 21**) and Article 18(3) (1) of the Turkish-Hungarian Treaty (**Treaty 24**)). On the other hand, all legal issues with respect to immovable property are to be settled by the courts of the State where the estate is found (Article 20(15) of the Turkish-German Treaty, Article 21(15) (4) of the Turkish-Italian Treaty and Article 18(3) (3) of the Turkish-Hungarian Treaty). By doing so, the treaties provide for a parallelism between *forum* and *ius* as in the Regulation.

The treaties also have a jurisdictional rule for claims of third parties made against the estate which confers jurisdiction to the courts of the State where the estate is found (Article 20(8) of the Turkish-German Treaty, Article 21(8) (1) of the Turkish-Italian Treaty, Article 18(3) (2) and (3) of the Turkish-Hungarian Treaty).

---

[114] H. Dörner, above n. 63, 91; F. Bauer, 'EuErbVO Art. 75 Anhang II-deutsch-türkisches NA' above n. 69, para. 17. See also H. Krüger, above n. 46, p. 148; A. Dutta, above n. 70, Art. 75, para. 21; J. v. Hein, 'EGBGB Art. 6' in F.J. Säcker et al. (eds.), *Münchener Kommentar zum Bürgerlichen Gesetzbuch*, vol. 11, 7th ed., C.H. Beck, Munich 2018, paras. 38–42.

5.1.1. Scope of the Jurisdictional Rules

Unlike the other treaties, the Turkish-German Treaty (**Treaty 19**) includes a list of the legal claims falling within the ambit of the rule. Pursuant to this, all legal claims regarding the entitlement to the estate, the ownership of an inheritance ('*hereditatis petitio*'/'*vindicatio hereditatis*' or '*miras sebebiyle istihkak davası*'), legacy, dispositions of property upon death and the reserved portion are covered by the jurisdictional rule. Other treaties have a general wording regarding the scope of jurisdictional rules. Article 21(11) of the Turkish-Italian Treaty (**Treaty 21**) refers to all the issues based on a title to inheritance and legacy and pertaining to the right or the sharing out of succession for movable property. Article 21(15) (4) of the Treaty uses a broader wording and refers to all the claims and disputes concerning immovable property. Similarly, Article 18(3) (1) and (3) of the Turkish-Hungarian Treaty (**Treaty 24**) makes a reference to all the conflicts arising out of succession and legacy. Whilst there are differences in the wording of these articles, they should be understood as covering all disputes relating to succession.

A broad interpretation of the rules would even suggest that jurisdiction to issue succession certificates is also covered by these rules, since issuing succession certificates is basically a process of determining the heirs and their respective shares. Yet while it is true that the rules employ a variety of terms, such as 'legal claims' ('*davalar*')[115], 'issues' ('*mesail*')[116], 'claims and objections' ('*talep ve itirazlar*')[117] and 'conflicts' ('*ihtilaflar*')[118], all these terms seem to make reference to contentious proceedings and do not cover the jurisdiction to issue succession certificates.[119]

5.1.2. Exclusive Jurisdiction?

An issue of utmost importance is whether the jurisdiction of Turkish courts is exclusive under the treaties. The only explicit rule in this respect is Article 21(15) (4) of the Turkish-Italian Treaty (**Treaty 21**), which states that the jurisdiction of the Contracting States' courts over immovable property

---

115 Art. 20(15) of the Turkish-German Treaty.

116 Art. 21(11) of the Turkish-Italian Treaty.

117 Art. 21(15) (4) of the Turkish-Italian Treaty.

118 Art. 18(3) (1) and (3) of the Turkish-Hungarian Treaty.

119 See, with regards to the Turkish-German Treaty, H. Dörner, above n. 63, 96; F. Bauer, above n. 15, 1252; LG Braunschweig 18.5.2009, *IPRax* 2010, 255, above n. 15; F. Bauer, above n. 69, para. 11; C. Rumpf, 'Erbrechtsfälle im deutsch-türkischen Rechtsverkehr' (2018) 27 *Informationsbrief der DTJV* 25, 31; R. Sieghörtner, 'FamFG § 105 Andere Verfahren' in M.-M. Hahne, J. Schlögel, R. Schlünder (eds.), *BeckOK FamFG*, 25th ed. (01.01.2018), para. 19.

is exclusive. Other provisions, by contrast, are not clear on the issue. Exclusive jurisdiction of Turkish courts comes into play only if the jurisdictional rule is laid down by the legislature with the intention that the dispute be handled solely by Turkish courts. In order to determine this, the initial inquiry should be an examination of the *ratio legis* of the rules.[120] It is obvious from the drafting history of the treaties that the rules were created in order to replace the capitulary regime – in which only the consular courts of foreign States had jurisdiction over succession cases on movable property – with a system based on the principle of reciprocity and other general principles of international law and also to ensure that the nationals of the contracting parties would not be discriminated against in each other's territory.

In addition, the legal background of the rules, especially for movable property, should also be considered to determine their nature. Rules conferring courts of the deceased's national State with jurisdiction over movable property can be traced back to the Turkish Private International Law Act applicable at that time (the Temporary Act) and to the Convention Respecting Conditions of Residence and Business and Jurisdiction[121] signed for seven years in 1923 as a part of the Treaty of Lausanne abolishing capitulations. Article 4 of the Temporary Act provides that Turkish courts have no jurisdiction in cases relating to the movable property of foreign nationals unless the parties bring the case before Turkish courts, or the case involves Turkish nationals, or there is a pending case before the Turkish courts.[122] Likewise, Article 16 of the Convention, to which

---

120 A. Çelikel, 'Yeni Kanuna Göre Yabancı Mahkeme Kararlarının Tenfiz Şartları' (1982) 2 *MHB* 7, 9; A. Sakmar, *Yabancı İlamların Türkiye'deki Sonuçları*, Fakülteler Matbaası, İstanbul 1982, p. 99; E. Nomer, 'Türklerin Kişi Hallerine İlişkin İhtilafları ve Türk Mahkemelerinin Münhasır Yetkisi' (1983) 3 *MHB* 11, 12; F. Sargın, *Milletlerarası Usul Hukukunda Yetki Anlaşmaları*, Yetkin, Ankara 1996, p. 152; N. Ekşi, above n. 96, p. 214; E. Esen, 'Türk Hukukunda Yabancı Mahkeme Kararlarının Tanınması ve Tenfizinde Münhasır Yetki Kavramı' (2002) 22 *MHB* 183, 187; C. Demir Gökyayla, 'Yabancı Mahkemelerden Alınan Mirasçılık Belgelerinin Türkiye'de Hüküm ve Sonuç Doğurması' in M. Ünal (ed.), *Prof. Dr. Fikret Eren'e Armağan*, Yetkin, Ankara 2006, p. 574; R. Aybay and E. Dardağan, above n. 93, p. 234; V. Doğan, above n. 84, p. 83; E. Nomer, above n. 93, p. 521; A. Çelikel and B. Erdem, above n. 88, p. 715; C. Şanlı, E. Esen and İ. Ataman Figanmeşe, above n. 84, pp. 535.

121 For the text of the Convention, see (1924) 18 *American Journal of International Law – Supplement: Official Documents* 67.

122 Another relevant provision could be found under Art. 18 of the former Turkish Code of Civil Procedure ('*Hukuk Usulü Muhakemeleri Kanunu*' – *Resmi Gazete* of 02, 03, 04.07.1927, No. 622, 623, 624). The article provides that in matters of personal status ('*ahkâm-ı şahsiye*') of Turkish nationals who are not domiciled in Turkey, Turkish courts at their last domicile, or failing that, courts of Ankara have jurisdiction. The jurisdiction under this provision was considered to be exclusive: O.F. Berki, 'Türk Hukukunda Ahkâmı Şahsiyeden Doğan Teşriî ve Kazaî Selâhiyet İhtilafı Esasları' (1952) 9 *AÜHFD* 452, 470; V.R. Seviğ, above n. 72, p. 14; S. Üstündağ, *Medeni Yargılama Hukukunun Esasları*, Sulhi Garan Matbaası, İstanbul 1973, p. 41; Y. Altuğ, *Devletler Hususi Hukukunda Yargı Yetkisi*, 2nd ed., Sermet Matbaası, İstanbul 1979, pp. 60 et seq; B. Kuru, *Hukuk Muhakemeleri Usulü*, vol. I, 5th ed., Evrim Basım Yayım Dağıtım, İstanbul 1990, p. 407. Nevertheless, whether the term 'personal status' also covers

Italy was also a party, states that the courts of the national State of the person whose personal status is in question have jurisdiction in matters of personal status, including testamentary and intestate succession to the movable property of non-Muslim nationals in Turkey. It was again clarified that the parties can submit their case in writing to the jurisdiction of the Turkish courts. In spite of the exceptions provided, both of the provisions seem to confer exclusive jurisdiction on the courts of the national State of the deceased consistent with the legal developments of that era.[123] The rule which grants jurisdiction to the courts of the national State of the deceased over movable property was later reiterated in the treaties and, unlike the former two instruments, no exception was provided.[124] This denotes that the parties intended in the treaties that the courts should be exclusively competent to hear succession issues.[125]

Hence, it seems that the jurisdiction of the courts within the treaties is exclusive for both movable and immovable property based on the *ratio legis* and legal history of the rules.[126] This, nevertheless, contradicts the current understanding of international procedural law, especially for movable property.[127] The treaties were drafted at a time when individuals were domiciled outside their national States only for a limited period of time and mostly without their families. Under such circumstances, it was believed that the courts of the national State of the deceased were in a better position to solve succession issues regarding the movable property of the deceased, as the heirs of the deceased often lived in that State. But this has changed over time, and it is now undesirable for Turkish nationals who have been living in the Contracting Member States for decades to go to Turkey in order to enforce their succession rights on movable property such as money held in the bank accounts of these States.[128]

---

succession issues on movable property was a matter of discussion among scholars. See, in this regard, V.R. Seviğ, above n. 72, pp. 12 et seq.; Y. Altuğ, p. 61; B. Kuru, p. 407, n. 689.

123 V.R. Seviğ, above n. 72, p.8; A. Çelikel, 'Yabancılara Ait Ahkamı Şahsiye ve Menkul Miras Davalarında "Birrıza Müracaat" Şartının Yorumu' (1976), 42 *İÜHFD* 245, 251–252 (with regards to Art. 4 of the Temporary Act).

124 It is noteworthy that such a jurisdictional rule has been kept in the field of succession law only in treaties signed after the adoption of the Turkish Civil Code in 1926: V.R. Seviğ, above n. 72, p. 9.

125 See, however, P. Franzina, section 2.2.7.1 in his report on Italy in this volume.

126 V.R. Seviğ, above n. 64, p. 191; V.R. Seviğ, above n. 72, p. 9; H. Dörner, above n. 63, 96; M. Atali, *Internationale Zuständigkeit im Deutsch-Türkischen Rechtsverkehr*, Peter Lang, Berlin 2001, p. 122; H. Krüger, above n. 46, p. 153; F. Bauer, above n. 15, 1251 et seq.; D. Damar, 'Deutsch-türkisches Nachlassabkommen: zivilprozess- und kollisionsrechtliche Aspekte' (2012) *IPRax* 278, 279; C.F. Majer, above n. 72, 184; N. Ekşi, above n. 30, p. 25 (with regards to the Turkish-Italian Treaty); S. Lorenz, above n. 72, para. 9; F. Bauer, above n. 69, para. 8. See also Yargıtay 2. Hukuk Dairesi, T. 27.1.1977, E. 401, K. 665, above n. 14; OLG Cologne 30.01.1986, *IPRspr* 1986, No. 109, 248–252; OLG Karlsruhe 17.06.2013, *ZEV* 2014, 158.

127 H. Dörner, above n. 63, 96; M. Atali, above n. 126, p. 123; H. Krüger, above n. 46, p. 153; E. Nomer, above n. 93, p. 523, n. 264 (with respect to the Turkish PILA).

128 H. Dörner, above n. 63, 96; M. Atali, above n. 126, p. 123; H. Krüger, above n. 46, p. 152.

Therefore, a restrictive interpretation of the rule allowing the courts of the other Contracting State to assume jurisdiction over movable property has been propounded.[129] This could be followed either when the parties have their habitual residence in one State, e.g. where all the heirs are Turkish nationals who are habitually resident in Germany,[130] or when the succession case is between German (or Italian and/or Hungarian) and Turkish nationals.[131]

5.2. RECOGNITION OF DECISIONS

With regards to the recognition of decisions in succession cases, Article 20(15) of the Turkish-German Treaty (**Treaty 19**) stipulates that the decisions of the Contracting State courts are to be recognized in the other Contracting State. A similar provision also exists in the Turkish-Italian Treaty (**Treaty 21**) with regards to movable property. Article 21(11) of the Treaty clarifies that the decisions of the courts of Contracting States on movable property is to be recognized in the other Contracting State. Although rules refer to the recognition, they do not specify the prerequisites or the procedure for recognition. Thus, it is important to clarify whether such decisions will be recognized in accordance with the procedure laid down under the Turkish Private International Law Act (Article 58) or automatically.[132] Consistent with the drafting history and the purposes of the parties when concluding such treaties, the decisions of the courts of one Contracting State will be recognized *ipso iure* in the other Contracting State.[133] Since there is no rule on the issue under the Turkish-Hungarian Treaty (**Treaty 24**), the domestic rules of the States will be applicable for the recognition of judgments rendered by the courts of the Contracting States. This applies also for the Turkish-Italian Treaty regarding immovable property.

The Turkish-German Treaty (**Treaty 19**) also lays down a rule for the effects of a certificate of succession or comparable documents. Article 20(17) of the Treaty prescribes that such documents issued by the competent authorities of

---

129 H. Dörner, above n. 63, 96; M. Atali, above n. 126, p. 124; H. Krüger, above n. 46, p. 153; H. Krüger, 'Erbrechtliche Probleme in den deutsch-türkischen Beziehungen' in H. Krüger and Y. Körtek (eds.), *Beiträge zum türkischen Recht – Erbrecht und Sozialrecht*, BWV, Berlin 2010, pp. 46–47; G. Hohloch, 'EGBGB Art. 25' in H.P. Westermann, B. Grunewald and G. Maier-Reimer (eds.), *Erman BGB*, 14th ed., Verlag Dr. Otto Schmidt, Cologne 2014, para. 57a; S. Lorenz, above n. 72, para. 9; C. Rumpf, 'Länderbericht Türkei' in M. Ferid and K. Firsching (eds.), *Internationales Erbrecht*, vol. VIII, C.H. Beck, Munich 2016, para. 109; cf. F. Bauer, above n. 15, 1256–1257. See, however, OLG Cologne 30.01.1986, above n. 123; LG Munich I 26.09.2006, above n. 15.

130 H. Dörner, above n. 63, 96.

131 H. Krüger, above n. 46, p. 153.

132 N. Ekşi, above n. 30, p. 96.

133 Ibid., pp. 96–97.

one Contracting State will be sufficient to invoke the status and the rights of heirs, legatees and testamentary executors on movable property in the other Contracting State, provided that they are approved by the consular staff or the diplomatic agents of the national State of the deceased. This means that German certificates of inheritance or other comparable documents could be used as rebuttable evidence before the Turkish courts and authorities.[134] Such a provision, however, does not exist in the Turkish-Italian and the Turkish-Hungarian Treaties.

5.3. CONSULAR COMPETENCES

In accordance with the drafting purpose of the treaties,[135] there are detailed rules on the rights of a Contracting State's consular staff over the movable property of a deceased from that Contracting State. In the event of the death of a national of one of the Contracting States in the territory of the other Contracting State, the consular staff and the local authorities are under a duty to inform each other.[136] If applicable under the relevant treaty, the consular staff are permitted to take appropriate measures for the preservation of estate assets;[137] notify the heirs and beneficiaries with regards to the opening of the succession;[138] conduct the liquidation process;[139] take possession of the property and all documents

---

134 H. Krüger, above n. 46, p. 155; N. Ekşi, above n. 30, pp. 95–96; E. Nomer, above n. 93, p. 548. See also Yargıtay 2. Hukuk Dairesi, T. 21.12.2004, E. 2004/13533, K. 2004/15443 <http://www.kazanci.com> accessed 21.04.2019. See also, on the effect of certificates of inheritance in cases of same-sex registered partnerships, H.S. Pürselim Doğan, 'Almanya'da Tescil Edilmiş Eşcinsel Hayat Ortaklığında Veraset İlamının Alınması ve bu İlama Dayanılarak Türkiye ve Almanya'da Bulunan Terekenin Paylaşılması' (2011) 31 *MHB* 243, 253 et seq.

135 Consular staff, whose main duty is to protect the rights of nationals of their own State who are abroad, was given broad rights over movable property. At that time the Treaty was drafted, local authorities had only a right of superintendence over the procedures regarding movable property. States concluded agreements in order to ensure this: A.K. Yörük, above n. 61, p. 439.

136 Art. 20(1) (1) and (2) of the Turkish-German Treaty (**Treaty 19**), Art. 21(1) of the Turkish-Italian Treaty (**Treaty 21**) and Art. 18(1) of the Turkish-Hungarian Treaty (**Treaty 24**).

137 Art. 20(6) of the Turkish-German Treaty, Art. 21(7) (1) of the Turkish-Italian Treaty, Art. 18(2) of the Turkish-Hungarian Treaty.
The issue of whether the consul is authorized to take appropriate measures for the preservation of the estate assets alone or together with the local authorities is not clear in the treaties. See, in this regard, with respect to the Turkish-German Treaty, D. Damar, above n. 126, 279 and with respect to the Turkish-Italian Treaty, A.K. Yörük, above n. 61, pp. 439–440. See, generally on this issue, Z. Kurşat, *Terekenin Korunması Önlemleri*, Filiz Kitabevi, İstanbul 2010, p. 348; E. Nomer, above n. 93, p. 300; G. Tekinalp and A. Uyanik, above n. 19, p. 238.

138 Art. 20(3) of the Turkish-German Treaty, Art. 21(4) of the Turkish-Italian Treaty and Art. 18(4) (3) of the Turkish-Hungarian Treaty.

139 Art. 20(4) – (10) of the Turkish-German Treaty, Art. 21(9) of the Turkish-Italian Treaty.

of the deceased, including dispositions of property upon death and collect debts of the deceased;[140] and administer the estate.[141] With regards to immovable property, however, the power to undertake such actions has been given to the local authorities of the State where the estate is found.[142]

6. THE FUTURE OF THE TREATIES

It is evident that the treaties were drafted almost a century ago under the political and legal environment of the time. Therefore they include rules that are incompatible with the current understanding of the private international law on succession in the Contracting States. For this reason, it has been contended that the treaties are superfluous[143] and pose challenges for Turkish nationals in the Contracting States.[144] Although the Turkish government has not voiced any plans in this regard, it has been underscored by certain scholars, following the views in German academic literature,[145] that they should be terminated[146] or at least reformed.[147]

---

140 Art. 20(5) of the Turkish-German Treaty, Art. 21(5) of the Turkish-Italian Treaty, Art. 18(4) (2) of the Turkish-Hungarian Treaty.

141 Art. 20(6) of the Turkish-German Treaty, Art. 21(7) (2) of the Turkish-Italian Treaty.

142 Art. 20(12) of the Turkish-German Treaty, cf. Art. 21(15) (4) of the Turkish-Italian Treaty.

143 H. Krüger, above n. 46, p. 158; H. Krüger, above n. 129, p. 49; H. Krüger, 'Neues zum Deutsch-Türkischen Nachlassabkommen – Zu einer Initiative des Nordrhein-Westfälischen Justizministers' (2013) 22 *Informationsbrief der DTJV* 4, 5; E. Nomer, above n. 93, p. 292, n. 128 (following H. Krüger).

144 B. Ercan, 'Deutsch-Türkische erbrechtliche Probleme' (1996) 5 *Informationsbrief der DTJV* 6, 9; C.F. Majer, above n. 72, 186; H. Krüger, above n. 143, 5; F. Sütçü, above n. 68, 45.

145 H. Krüger, above n. 46, p. 158; H. Krüger, above n. 129, p. 49; H. Krüger, above n. 143, 8; F. Bauer, above n. 15, 1257; Max Planck Report, above n. 12, 532 et seq.; C. Kohler, 'Die künftige Erbrechtsverordnung der Europäischen Union und die Staatsverträge mit Drittstaaten' in G. Reichelt and W.H. Rechberger (eds.), *Europäisches Erbrecht: Zum Verordnungsvorschlag der Europäischen Kommission zum Erb- und Testamentsrecht*, Jan Sramek Verlag, Vienna 2011, p. 126; S.G. Seyfarth, 'Wandel der internationalen Zuständigkeit im Erbrecht', Universität Konstanz, Konstanz 2011, p. 271 <http://kops.uni-konstanz.de/handle/123456789/19299> accessed 21.04.2019; S. Lorenz, 'Erbrecht in Europa – Auf dem Weg zu kollisionsrechtlicher Rechtseinheit' (2013) *ErbR* 39, 49; C.F. Majer, above n. 72, 186; 'Statement des Justizministers Thomas Kutschaty anlässlich des Sommerpressegesprächs zum Thema "Aktuelle Probleme des Erb- und Familienrechts von Bürgerinnen und Bürgern mit türkischer Staatsangehörigkeit, die ihren Wohnsitz in Deutschland haben" am 19. August 2013 in der Staatskanzlei des Landes Nordrhein-Westfalen' p. 3; H. Dörner, 'Zur Qualifikation des §1371 Abs 1 BGB – eine verpasste Gelegenheit (zu BGH, 12 9 2012 – IV ZB 12/12, unten S. 343, Nr. 28)' (2014) *IPRax* 323, 326; A. Dutta, above n. 70, Art. 75, para. 6; J. Müller-Lukoschek, *Die neue EU-Erbrechtsverordnung: Leitfaden mit Erläuterungen für die notarielle Praxis*, 2nd ed., Deutscher NotarVerlag, Bonn 2015, paras. 407–408; K. Lechner, above n. 72, p. 145; K. Lechner, above n. 72, 112; cf. R. Süß, above n. 72, p. 198.

146 E. Nomer, above n. 93, p. 292, n. 128; G. Tekinalp and A. Uyanik, above n. 19, p. 246, n. 44.

147 M. Atali, above n. 126, p. 123.

Although the non-application of the treaties by Turkish courts in cases falling within their scope[148] and their limited practical relevance in Turkey make it difficult to remonstrate with the views supporting the termination of the treaties, the future of the treaties should be re-evaluated for Turkey, particularly from the perspective of Turkish nationals in the Contracting States, whose number is considerably high.

It is undoubted that there are certain rules in the treaties, such as the exclusive jurisdiction rule for movable property, which present difficulties for these individuals.[149] Nevertheless, the termination of the treaties for the sake of European harmonization may result in further difficulties for the exercise of their succession rights in Turkey, particularly regarding immovable assets. This is because Article 4 and Article 10 of the Regulation allow Member State courts to rule on succession as a whole, including immovable assets located in Turkey. The jurisdiction of the Turkish courts over immovable assets located in Turkey, however, is considered to be exclusive by scholars[150] and by the Turkish Court of Cassation ('*Yargıtay*').[151] If this is indeed the case, judgments

---

148 Above n. 14.

149 It should be taken into consideration that this conclusion would not be applicable for the Turkish-Italian Treaty under P. Franzina's understanding of the exclusive nature of jurisdiction over movable property as highlighted above in n. 122.

150 E. Nomer, 'Devletler Hususi Hukukunda Milletlerarası Yetki Mefhumu' (1974) 40 *İÜHFM* 393, 416; Y. Altuğ, above n. 122, pp. 58–59; E. Nomer, above n. 14, 62; A. Çelikel, above n. 120, 9; A. Sakmar, above n. 120, p. 100; C. Şanlı, 'Türkiye'deki Gayrimenkullerle İlgili Bir Yabancı Boşanma Kararının Tenfizi' (1986) 6 *MHB* 40, 45; A. Uyanık, 'Türk Milletlerarası Usul Hukukunda Yetki Sözleşmeleri', Master Thesis, İstanbul Üniversitesi, İstanbul 1994, p. 71; M. Lale, 'Türk Milletlerarası Usul Hukukunda Türk Mahkemelerinin Milletlerarası Yargı Yetkisi', Master Thesis, Ankara Üniversitesi, Ankara 1996, p. 29; F. Sargın, above n. 120, p. 162; B. Erdem, 'Hukuki ve Ticari Konularda Mahkemelerin Yetkisi ve Mahkeme Kararlarının Tanınması ve Tenfizi Hakkında 1968 Tarihli Brüksel Antlaşmasının Hükümlerinin Türk Mahkemelerinin Milletlerarası Yetki Kuralları ile Karşılaştırılması' (1997) 17 *MHB* 183, 206; N. Ekşi, above n. 96, pp. 220 et seq.; E. Esen, above n. 120, 188; B. Huysal, '6100 Sayılı Hukuk Muhakemeleri Kanunu İle Getirilen Yenilikler Işığında Yabancı Mahkeme Kararlarının Tanınması ve Tenfizi Konusunda Bazı Tespitler' (2012) 32 *MHB* 71, 85; N. Ekşi, above n. 30, p. 140; V. Doğan, above n. 84, pp. 70–71; E. Nomer, above n. 93, p. 521; A. Çelikel and B. Erdem, above n. 88, p. 715; C. Şanlı, *Uluslararası Ticari Akitlerin Hazırlanması ve Uyuşmazlıkların Çözüm Yolları*, 6th ed., Beta, İstanbul 2016, p. 261; C. Şanlı, E. Esen and İ. Ataman Figanmeşe, above n. 84, p. 535. For a different view, however, see M. Erkan, above n. 96.

151 *Yargıtay* holds in its decisions that the jurisdiction of Turkish courts is exclusive with regards to immovable property by virtue of the fact that the law applicable to the succession in such cases is Turkish law pursuant to Art. 20(1) of the Turkish PILA, providing that Turkish law is applicable for immovable assets in Turkey. See, in this regard, Yargıtay 2. Hukuk Dairesi, T. 10.2.1986, E. 1986/808, K. 1986/1284 <http://www.kazanci.com> accessed 21.04.2019; Yargıtay 2. Hukuk Dairesi, T. 22.6.1990, E. 1990/6373, K. 1990/6410 <http://www.kazanci.com> accessed 21.04.2019; Yargıtay 2. Hukuk Dairesi, T. 12.7.2002, E. 2002/8254, K. 2002/9339 <http://www.kazanci.com> accessed 21.04.2019; Yargıtay 8. Hukuk Dairesi, T. 17.10.2014, E. 2013/23629, K. 2014/18556 <http://www.kazanci.com> accessed 21.04.2019;

rendered by European courts cannot be recognized and enforced in Turkey, since Article 54(b) of the Turkish Private International Law Act stipulates that only judgments on issues which do not fall within the exclusive jurisdiction of Turkish courts can be recognized[152] or enforced in Turkey. The only solution to this under the Regulation is the limitation of proceedings specified under Article 12. This is, nevertheless, insufficient to solve the problem as a whole.[153] The limitation of jurisdiction under Article 12 is possible only at the request of one of the parties and is subject to the discretion of the courts. There might still be many instances in which the courts will proceed and render a judgment on the succession as a whole, including immovable property in Turkey.

This can be illustrated with an example inspired from the plot of the hilarious movie '*Almanya: Willkommen in Deutschland*'.[154] A Turkish guest worker comes to Germany in the 1970s, as *Hüseyin* in the movie, and lives many years with his family there. He becomes a German citizen. A short time after that he buys a house in Turkey and moves there after working many years in Germany. However, after a year he dies in Turkey intestate, leaving behind a house in Turkey and a house in Germany. If a dispute were to arise between his wife and children, who have spent most of their lives in Germany, and they wish to bring the case before the courts of Germany, German courts have to decline jurisdiction as regards the house in Turkey, as Turkish courts have exclusive jurisdiction over it under Article 20(15) of the Turkish-German Treaty (**Treaty 19**). If, however, the Regulation were to apply to this case, German courts could assume jurisdiction as the last habitual residence of the deceased was in Germany. The decision rendered at the end of such an action, however, could not be recognized and enforced in Turkey due to the fact that the jurisdiction of Turkish courts in matters relating to immovable property in Turkey is considered to be exclusive. The same example could also be formulated for the other two treaties, as they have similar rules. Therefore, it appears that the treaties are still important under the current circumstances for the Turkish community in the Contracting Member States.

Moreover, the fact that the treaties are consular treaties and regulate many aspects of consular rights and functions, in addition to the rights of consular officers regarding movable property of nationals of the Sending State, cannot be disregarded. In this sense, a termination of the treaties only because they have

---

Yargıtay 14. Hukuk Dairesi, T. 04.04.2016, E. 2015/7541, K. 2016/3995 <http://www.kazanci.com> accessed 21.04.2019.

152 For the recognition, see Art. 58 of the Turkish PILA, which refers back to Art. 54 for the conditions allowing for recognition.

153 E. Lein, 'Die Erbrechtsverordnung aus Sicht der Drittstaaten' in A. Dutta and S. Herrler (eds.), *Die Europäische Erbrechtsverordnung, 20 Jahre DNotI 1993–2013*, C.H. Beck, Munich 2014, p. 220. Under the relevant articles, it is uncertain which criteria could be considered by European courts as a basis for declining jurisdiction: A. Dutta, above n. 70, Art. 12, para. 10.

154 Y. Şamdereli (dir.), *Almanya: Willkommen in Deutschland*, Eurovideo, Munich 2011.

conflict-of-laws and jurisdictional rules that differ from the Regulation seems to be disproportionate.[155] Additionally, there might be political reasons for keeping them by virtue of the consular nature of the treaties.[156]

For these reasons, termination of the treaties under the given circumstances does not seem to be advisable. Reform of the treaty rules, on the other hand, is undoubtedly needed. In the first place, there have been many changes that societies have experienced since the time when the treaties were initially concluded. The rules of the treaties now impose certain challenges for affected individuals, especially for Turkish nationals who have lived for decades in the Contracting States at issue. What is more, as one of the results of such a social change, there has been a reform of the private international law on succession in these States. Consequently, the rules of the treaties, albeit to different degrees within each body of law, contradict the Regulation and the Turkish Private International Law Act. The terms used in the treaties are outdated and ambiguous as compared to the domestic rules applicable in the Contracting States. There is, thus, a case for more precise and coherent rules on succession issues corresponding to current understanding of succession in all of the systems.

7. CONCLUSION

Bilateral treaties of EU Member States with Turkey which continue to be applicable under Article 75 of the Regulation are of much practical significance due to the significant number of Turkish nationals in those States. In particular, the Turkish-German Treaty (**Treaty 19**) results in a large number of succession cases not being governed by the Regulation. These treaties were signed in the first half of the 20th Century – consistent with the underlying legal and political atmosphere of that era – and thus include rules incompatible with the Regulation. Consequently, it has been argued that the treaties must be terminated.

Although it is difficult to challenge this assertion given the limited legal practice involving the treaties in Turkey, not to mention the non-application of those treaties by Turkish courts in a number of cases, it seems that the treaties are still important for the exercise of succession rights of Turkish nationals regarding immovable assets found in Turkey. Moreover, the treaties are consular treaties regulating many facets of consular rights and functions beyond the

---

155 C. Kohler, above n. 145, p. 126.

156 Even though Contracting States already have a right to terminate the treaties, they have not done so until now. See, in this regard, Art. 30(3) of the Turkish-German Treaty (**Treaty 19**); Art. 26(2) of the Turkish-Italian Treaty (**Treaty 21**); Art. 25(2) of the Turkish-Hungarian Treaty (**Treaty 24**).

rights of consular staff in respect of movable property owned by nationals of the contracting parties. There might also be broader political reasons for the States wishing to keep such treaties. Thus, terminating the treaties on the grounds that they contain conflict-of-laws and jurisdictional rules that contradict the Regulation appears to be unreasonable. There is, however, a need to reform their rules in order to eliminate those problems in legal practice resulting from both societal changes and an evolution of the legal atmosphere in these States.

PART III

THE PERSPECTIVE OF THE EUROPEAN UNION AND A COMPARATIVE OUTLOOK

THE PERSPECTIVE OF THE EUROPEAN UNION

Anatol DUTTA

1. THE INTERESTS OF THE EUROPEAN UNION

The country reports in this book show that the private international law treaties of the Member States with third States cannot be seen as being in the interest of the European Union (EU).[1] These bilateral or regional conventions diminish the harmonizing effects of European private international law, especially of the common rules on jurisdiction and applicable law, as based on Article 81(2)(c) of the Treaty on the Functioning of the European Union (TFEU). Only the recognition and enforcement provisions of the European Regulations are unaffected, at least as far as the Member State's conventions are restricted to the recognition of third State decisions in the Member States or Member States' decisions in third States: the private international law Regulations of the EU deal with the cross-border effects of European decisions only and leave the circulation of judgments between Member States and third States to the national law of the Member States, including their treaties. Third State treaties on recognition and enforcement might even be – as Stéphanie Francq and Julie Mary have stressed in the Belgian report[2] – in the interest of the EU, at least as far as the jurisdictional concepts of the Regulations are in fact transported to

---

1 See the evaluation of the third State treaties from a policy perspective by W. WURMNEST, section 5.

2 See S. FRANCQ and J. MARY, sections 2.1.1 and 5.

third States by reviewing the indirect jurisdiction of the third State under the European jurisdictional standards.

The fact that the treaties of the Member States limit the harmonizing effects of EU law is, as such, already not ideal. However, the interference with the harmonized choice-of-law rules in the area of the Succession Regulation is particularly damaging.[3] Here the European legislature has introduced an instrument whose functioning is in fact dependent on European decisional harmony: the European Certificate of Succession can operate effectively only if the certified position as an heir, as a legatee having direct rights in the succession, as an executor of wills or as an administrator of the estate (cf. Article 63(1) SR) is assessed in all Member States on the basis of the same applicable law.[4] Otherwise, a Certificate issued in one Member State might reflect information that is incorrect in other Member States – not due to factual reasons, such as unknown intestate heirs or wills, but due to legal reasons – if, for example, either the issuing Member State or the receiving Member State, where the Certificate is used, is obliged under Article 75(1)1 and (2) SR to give effect to a treaty previously entered with a third State. Then the position as heir, legatee, executor or administrator is no longer established by the Certificate in the entire EU against the background of the law determined by Chapter III of the Succession Regulation, but rather by the law applicable under the conflict rules of a third State treaty. The aim of having information provided in the European Certificate be correct in all Member States was also indicated by the Court of Justice of the European Union – in one of its first decisions on the new instrument – as one of the Succession Regulation's cornerstones.[5]

The reports demonstrate that the dimension of the problem cannot be overestimated. Many Member States – except Belgium[6] and most likely France[7] – are party to treaties which deviate considerably from the solutions established by the Succession Regulation. In some Member States these treaties apply to large groups of foreign nationals and, hence, to many cross-border cases which should have been targeted by the Succession Regulation. For example, in Germany the impact of the Succession Regulation on Turkish nationals might

---

3 J. Kohler, 'Die künftige Erbrechtsverordnung der Europäischen Union und die Staatsverträge mit Drittstaaten' in G. Reichelt and W. H. Rechberger (eds.), *Europäisches Erbrecht*, Jan Sramek Verlag, Wien 2011, pp. 109, 123 et seq., has previously concluded that the third State conventions could cause 'Systemstörungen'.

4 See in general, L. Konvalin, *Das Europäische Nachlasszeugnis ohne europäischen Entscheidungseinklang*, Wolfgang Metzner Verlag, Frankfurt am Main, 2018; see also A. Dutta, in F. J. Säcker, R. Rixecker, H. Oetker, and B. Limperg (eds.), *Münchener Kommentar zum BGB*, Vol. 11, 7th ed., C. H. Beck, München 2018, Vor Art. 62 EuErbVO paras. 9 and 10 with further references.

5 Cf. ECJ C-558/16, *Mahnkopf*, para. 42 et seq.; see also the case note by M. Fornasier, [2018] *Zeitschrift für das gesamte Familienrecht* 634.

6 See S. Francq and J. Mary, section 1.

7 See S. Fulli-Lemaire, section 1.

be rather small. Things will change only if an increasing number of Turkish nationals also acquire German nationality and might, thereby, no longer be covered by the German-Turkish Treaty (**Treaty 19**) – of course only if one follows the prevailing opinion on dual nationality as regards this treaty.[8] Apparently, the European legislature was not aware of the number of third State treaties – which comes as no surprise given how difficult it was for our project to discover and collect those treaties.

Hence, the interest of the EU – at least as far as it is convinced that its private international law instruments should be applied – clearly must be to do away with the third State treaties as soon as possible.

But what options does the EU have to protect its private international law against the existing third State treaties?

2. SUPERSEDING THE THIRD STATE TREATIES?

A first option could be to turn the tables and to oust the treaties of the Member States by an act of EU law. For example, the European legislature could delete Article 75(1)1 and (2) SR from a revised version of the Succession Regulation. As a consequence, the Succession Regulation would not preserve the application of the existing treaties of Member States. Rather, the Regulation would prevail. At least from a purely EU law perspective, EU law supersedes treaties entered into by Member States.[9]

On closer inspection, this solution is, of course, not an option. If such an approach were adopted, EU law would force Member States to violate their duties toward third States contrary to the principle of *pacta sunt servanda*, a basic tenet of public international law adhered to by the EU. In this regard, Article 351(1) TFEU provides that the 'rights and obligations arising from agreements concluded before 1 January 1958 or, for acceding States, before the date of their accession, between one or more Member States on the one hand, and one or more third countries on the other, shall not be affected by the provisions of the Treaties'. This clause is also applied, by analogy, to treaties of the Member States which were concluded before the EU gained legislative competence.[10] Hence, Article 351(1) protects the private international law treaties of the Member States with third States, or at a minimum the status quo upon the entering into force of the Amsterdam or Lisbon Treaty. As a consequence, abolishing Article 75(1)1 and (2) SR would trigger application of Article 351(1) TFEU. Only treaties concluded after the entering into force

8 Cf. D. Looschelders, section 2.3.2.3.

9 Cf. ECJ Case 235/87, *Matteucci*, ECR 1988, 5589, para. 22; ECJ Case C-158/91, *Levy*, ECR 1993, I-4287, para. 22.

10 Cf. the opinion of AG J. Kokott in Case C-188/07, *Commune de Mesquer*, para. 95.

of the Amsterdam or Lisbon Treaty could be excluded from Article 351(1), which could – at first sight – be the case for some of the treaties of the Czech Republic.[11] However, those treaties were adopted before the accession of the Czech Republic to the EU and are, therefore, also covered by Article 351(1).

3. ADJUSTING EUROPEAN PRIVATE INTERNATIONAL LAW TO THE THIRD STATE TREATIES?

As a second option the EU could come to an arrangement in respect of the third State treaties by adjusting the European private international law rules to the treaties.

However, this solution also has its limits. The EU could only achieve decisional harmony to a limited extent through an attempted accommodation of the existing treaties.

One possibility for enhancing decisional harmony under the treaties could be a revival of *renvoi*, not only – as under the current Article 34(1) SR – for references by the European conflict rules to the law of a third State, but also for references to the law of other Member States.[12] This would at least guarantee that if a Member State was bound by a third State treaty and the European conflict rules referred to the law of that Member State, decisional harmony within the EU would be restored. The price, of course, would be rather high: the scope of the European conflict rules would be reduced, and the conflict rules of a third State treaty exported to the other Member States. The succession of a Turkish national with last habitual residence in Berlin would not only from a German perspective but also from a European perspective – e.g. a French, Belgian or Finnish perspective – be governed by the German-Turkish Treaty (**Treaty 19**) rather than by German substantive law according to Article 21(1) SR. Given the considerable number of third State treaties, little room would be left for the Succession Regulation. Furthermore, a *renvoi* would not create a total harmony of decisions within Europe. No harmony is restored if, from the Succession Regulation perspective, the law of the Member State having the third State treaty is not applicable. Consider, for example, a Turkish national habitually resident in the Netherlands. In that scenario, in the absence of a choice of law, the German courts would still apply the German-Turkish Treaty whereas all other Member States – if not similarly bound by a treaty with

---

11 M. Pfeiffer, section 2.

12 A recognition of a *renvoi* by a third State treaty of the Member State whose law is applicable under the Succession Regulation has already been proposed by some authors *de lege lata*, see e.g. A. Köhler, '§4 Internationales Privatrecht' in W. Gierl, A. Köhler, L. Kroiss and H. Wilsch (eds.), *Internationales Erbrecht*, Nomos/Manz, Baden-Baden/Wien 2015, pp. 89, 148.

Turkey – would determine jurisdiction and applicable law on the basis of the Regulation.

There are also other remedies by which the European legislature could cure at least some of the symptoms caused by the third State treaties, especially regarding the efficiency of the European Certificate of Succession. One could, for example, think about restricting the European Certificate to cases where the conflict rules of the Regulation are not superseded by third State treaties of the forum Member State – a solution which has already been proposed by some authors *de lege lata*.[13] This would, of course, have rather harsh consequences. Turkish nationals might no longer be able to apply in Germany for a European Certificate, which could cause a denial of justice if, from the perspective of the Succession Regulation, only German courts had jurisdiction to issue a European Certificate.

4. TERMINATION OR REVISION OF THE TREATIES?

It appears that from a EU perspective there is only one option for protecting the European private international law instruments: the termination of the treaties,[14] which would solve the problem at its root. It would, at least, be in the interest of the EU if the treaties were reformed and brought in line with the solutions of the Succession Regulation, for example, by shifting the connecting factor from nationality to habitual residence (Article 21(1) SR) or by abolishing

---

13 See the so-called 'Grundlagentheorie' by R. Süss, 'Der Vorbehalt zugunsten bilateraler Abkommen mit Drittstaaten' in: A. Dutta and S. Herrler (eds.), *Die Europäische Erbrechtsverordnung*, C. H. Beck, München 2014, p. 181.

14 Cf. also e.g. Max Planck Institute, 'Comments on the European Commission's Proposal for a Regulation of the European Parliament and of the Council on jurisdiction, applicable law, recognition and enforcement of decisions and authentic instruments in matters of succession and the creation of a European Certificate of Succession', (2010) 74 *Rabels Zeitschrift für ausländisches und internationales Privatrecht* 522, 532 et seq.; F. Bauer, 'Anmerkung' [2007] *Zeitschrift für das gesamte Familienrecht* 1252, 1257; H. Dörner, 'Zur Qualifikation des §1371 Abs. 1 BGB – eine verpasste Gelegenheit' [2014] *Praxis des Internationalen Privat- und Verfahrensrechts* 323, 326; K. Lechner, *Verordnung (EU) Nr. 650/2012 über Erbsachen und die Einführung eines Europäischen Nachlasszeugnisses*, 2015, p. 34; S. Lorenz, 'Erbrecht in Europa – Auf dem Weg zu kollisionsrechtlicher Rechtseinheit' [2012] *Zeitschrift für das gesamte Erbrecht* 39, 49; C. F. Majer, 'Das deutsch-türkische Nachlassabkommen: ein Anachronismus' [2012] *Zeitschrift für Erbrecht und Vermögensnachfolge* 182, 186; P. Mankowski, 'Gelten die bilateralen Staatsverträge der Bundesrepublik Deutschland im Internationalen Erbrecht nach dem Wirksamwerden der EuErbVO weiter?' [2013] *Zeitschrift für Erbrecht und Vermögensnachfolge* 529, 530; S. Marino, 'La proposta di regolamento sulla cooperazione giudiziaria in materia di successioni', (2010) 93 *Rivista di diritto internazionale* 463, 467; K. Siehr, 'Ausländischer Erbschein für Nachlass in Deutschland?' [2013] *Praxis des Internationalen Privat- und Verfahrensrechts* 241, 245; L. Konvalin, above n. 4, p. 94 et seq.

the scission of the estate in favour of a monist approach universally covering all assets of the deceased (Article 21(1) and Article 23(1) SR).

Of course, from a public international law perspective, the EU would not be able to terminate the third State treaties (to the extent a termination is at all possible under public international law)[15] or to revise the treaties that are 'Succession Regulation friendly'. There is no provision in the European treaties which grants the EU a power of representation for the administration of Member State treaties with third States. The EU could, however, use its external competence in respect of private international law and conclude with a third State a treaty superseding the treaties of that third State with any Member States. Article 351(1) TFEU primarily aims to protect the public international rights of third States. Therefore, the Union can probably, within its external competence, even require Member States to terminate or to attempt to renegotiate the treaties. Such an approach by the EU would have at least one positive aspect: the individual Member States, when terminating or revising the third State treaties, could lay political blame on Brussels.

It is, of course, a different question whether primary EU law allows the individual Member States to terminate their third State treaties on their own, without permission of the EU. The question, in particular, is whether the EU has exclusive competence to decide on the future of the third State treaties. This could be the case if one interprets Opinion 1/2013 of the Court of Justice of the European Union[16] extensively.[17] In this decision the Court of Justice held that the EU has, according to Article 3(2) TFEU, exclusive competence for the administration of the Hague Child Abduction Convention, which was endorsed and – as between the Member States – modified by the Brussels IIbis Regulation.[18] The Court of Justice thus came to the conclusion that individual decisions of the Member States regarding the Hague Convention may affect the common rules contained in the Brussel IIbis Regulation. Nevertheless, I doubt that one can interpret Opinion 1/2013 as meaning that the Member States, with the adoption of the Succession Regulation, have lost their competence to *terminate* the third State treaties in total or limited to their private international law parts.[19]

---

15 See Art. 54 et seq. of the 1969 Vienna Convention on the Law of Treaties. The fact that a third State no longer applies the treaty (cf. B. S. Güneş, section 1) is likely to be regarded as a 'material breach of a bilateral treaty by one of the parties', thereby allowing for a termination of the treaty under Art. 60(1) of the 1969 Vienna Convention.

16 See the comprehensive evaluation of the opinion in P. Franzina (ed.), *The External Dimension of EU Private International Law after Opinion 1/13*, Intersentia, Cambridge 2017.

17 Favouring an external competence of the EU, F. Bauer, 'Art. 75 EuErbVO Anh. I' in A. Dutta and J. Weber, *Internationales Erbrecht*, C. H. Beck, München 2016, para. 6; cf. also K. Lechner, above n. 14, p. 34.

18 Council Regulation (EC) No. 2201/2003 of 27 November 2003 concerning jurisdiction and the recognition and enforcement of judgments in matrimonial matters and the matters of parental responsibility, repealing Regulation (EC) No. 1347/2000 [2003] OJ L338/1.

19 Cf. A. Dutta, 'Anmerkung', [2015] *Zeitschrift für das gesamte Familienrecht* 24.

Of course, the termination of the third State treaties 'may affect common rules or alter their scope', as provided by Article 3(2) TFEU. The Succession Regulation would become applicable to cases that it would not otherwise govern if the treaty remained in force. This, however, would be a rather formalistic view. In effect, the termination would broaden the scope of the European rules and would make them more efficient, a by no means inappropriate step, given that the Member States are required by Article 351(2)1 TFEU to 'eliminate the incompatibilities established' by third State treaties. It is true that this duty is not explicitly mentioned in Article 75 SR, unlike in Article 62(1) of the Matrimonial Property Regulation for spouses[20] and Article 62(1) of the Property Regulation for registered partners.[21] Nevertheless, one cannot readily argue that Article 75 SR, as a provision of secondary EU law, relieves the Member States of a duty created by primary EU law.[22] Also, it is rather unclear whether and, if yes, to what extent Article 351(2)1 TFEU alone creates a duty to revise or even terminate third State treaties which deviate from the private international law of the EU.[23] However, a Member State terminating a third State treaty ought to at least follow the spirit of Article 351(2)1 TFEU.

The situation might be different regarding a *revision* of an existing third State treaty as to its private international law content. The conclusion of a new treaty in general would definitely fall within the exclusive competence of the EU under Article 3(2) TFEU because such a new treaty would affect the scope of the Succession Regulation. However, at least a 'Succession Regulation friendly' revision of a treaty remains within the competence of the Member State, for example, by adjusting the jurisdiction or choice-of-law rules to the solutions of the Succession Regulation, be it by adopting a monist approach, using habitual residence as the primary connecting factor or allowing a choice of law in favour of the deceased's nationality. Such a revision of a treaty would contribute to an elimination of the incompatibilities between the treaties and EU law, even if a complete harmony with the Succession Regulation were not attained and compromises with the third State became necessary. Hence, with an 'EU law friendly' revision of their third treaties, the Member States would only be following the mission of Article 351(2)1 TFEU, and one cannot assume that

---

20 Council Regulation (EU) 2016/1103 of 24 June 2016 implementing enhanced cooperation in the area of jurisdiction, applicable law and the recognition and enforcement of decisions in matters of matrimonial property regimes [2016] OJ L183/1.

21 Council Regulation (EU) 2016/1104 of 24 June 2016 implementing enhanced cooperation in the area of jurisdiction, applicable law and the recognition and enforcement of decisions in matters of the property consequences of registered partnerships [2016] OJ L183/30.

22 See also J. Kohler, 'Die Güterrechtsverordnungen der Europäischen Union und die vorrangigen Staatsverträge mit Drittstaaten' in: A. Dutta and J. Weber (eds.), *Die Europäischen Güterrechtsverordnungen*, C. H. Beck, München 2017, pp. 163, 166.

23 For a thorough analysis, especially against the background of ECJ case law, see J. Kohler, above n. 22, pp. 173 et seq.; cf. furthermore J. Kohler, above n. 3, pp. 119 et seq.

Article 3(2) TFEU aims at preventing the Member States from doing so. Furthermore, Article 351(2)2 TFEU would in any event oblige the other Member States to assist a Member State when fulfilling its duties under Article 351(2)1 TFEU, cf. also Article 4(3) TEU. One could even argue that Article 351(2) TFEU, as a kind of *lex specialis*, grants Member States the external competence to revise their treaties with third States.[24] Hence, a Member State planning to revise its third State treaties could, for example, assert in the Council that the other Member States support its plans.

If one comes to a different conclusion and vests in the EU the exclusive competence, based on Article 3(2) TFEU, to terminate or revise the third State treaties, the European legislature should empower the Member States to terminate or revise those treaties. The EU has granted the Member States in other areas of private international law the power to conclude new treaties.[25] It could therefore also do the opposite: transferring the power to revise or terminate treaties.

5. AGREEMENTS OF THE EUROPEAN UNION WITH THIRD STATES

The termination of a treaty is a potentially unfriendly act towards the third State at issue. The question is whether the EU could offer the third States something in exchange, for example, by opening the Succession Regulation to third States on a treaty basis.

Conventions of the EU with third States deviating from the private international law approaches of the Succession Regulation would, however, not be sensible from an EU perspective (and also from the perspective of the other Member States not bound by a treaty with the third State). First, the border between the conflict and jurisdictional rules of such a deviating convention and the Succession Regulation might be quite difficult to determine; the delimitation

---

24 J. Kohler, above n. 3, p. 127.

25 See Regulation (EC) No. 662/2009 of the European Parliament and of the Council of 13 July 2009 establishing a procedure for the negotiation and conclusion of agreements between Member States and third countries on particular matters concerning the law applicable to contractual and non-contractual obligations [2009] OJ L200/25; Council Regulation (EC) No. 664/2009 of 7 July 2009 establishing a procedure for the negotiation and conclusion of agreements between Member States and third countries concerning jurisdiction, recognition and enforcement of judgments and decisions in matrimonial matters, matters of parental responsibility and matters relating to maintenance obligations, and the law applicable to matters relating to maintenance obligations [2009] OJ L200/46; see as to those instruments J.-J. Kuipers, 'Regulations (EC) Nos. 662/2009 and 664/2009: Can exclusivity be successfully reconciled with flexibility?' in: P. Franzina (ed.), *The External Dimension of EU Private International Law after Opinion 1/13*, Intersentia, Cambridge 2017, p. 149.

could probably only be based on the habitual residence or the nationality of the deceased. Further, deviating from the Succession Regulation would weaken the European private international law solution in certain third State cases.

Nevertheless, offering third States the chance to accede to the Succession Regulation by means of a treaty is tempting only at first sight; such an 'orbit' approach would in fact be rather problematic. Third States are not bound by the decisions of the Court of Justice of the European Union, and some of the provisions of the Succession Regulation, especially the European Certificate of Succession, are an expression of the mutual trust between the Member States, to name only some of the obstacles to such 'orbit' instruments.[26]

Hence, an informal cooperation between the EU, the Member States and third States might be a better solution. The integration of the Succession Regulation in the Nordic Inheritance Convention (**Treaty 14**) has shown how European solutions can be extended to third States so as to create decisional harmony beyond the EU borders.[27] The developments in respect of the Balkans also demonstrate that, especially regarding conflict and jurisdictional rules, informal harmonization is possible; in North Macedonia this has led, as we have seen, to the odd result that practically the same rules will apply in the Member State (Succession Regulation) and the third State (rules inspired by the Succession Regulation) – for some Member States, however, this manner of spontaneous harmonization is superseded by an outdated treaty.[28] The same type of informal harmonization could be achieved by Switzerland and Italy, bearing in mind that Swiss lawmakers are thinking about approximating their private international law to the Succession Regulation, which is ousted by the Italian-Swiss Treaty (**Treaty 20**).[29] One could, at least from a European perspective, consider applying Article 75(2) SR in such a scenario by analogy. This provision clarifies that the Regulation 'as between Member States, take[s] precedence over conventions concluded exclusively between two or more of them'. It is true, North Macedonia and Switzerland are not 'Member States', but, to the extent they adopt the solution of the Succession Regulation, they could be regarded as 'quasi Member States' at least for purposes of the Succession Regulation and Article 75(2) SR.

Hence, from an EU perspective the optimal solution would be to encourage Member States to terminate their third State treaties while at the same attempting to export the European rules informally.

---

26 See for more details A. Dutta, 'Orbitrechtsakte – eine Idee für das internationale Privatrecht der Europäischen Union?', [2017] *Zeitschrift für das Europäische Privatrecht* 553.

27 See M. Helin, section 3.2, stressing, however, that it was mainly the bargaining power of the EU which compelled the Nordic states to give precedence to the Succession Regulation.

28 See S. Đorđević and Z. Meškić, sections 2.2 and 2.3.

29 See Franzina, section 2.1, and Bonomi, section 2.

6. CONCLUSION

This brief survey of the options has shown that – although the political goal of the EU is rather clear: the termination of the third State treaties – the division of competence as to those treaties gives rise to many questions. Hence, there lurks a danger that the status quo will persist. The EU must therefore overcome the 'deafening silence' that one commentator has described as characterizing the approach the EU has followed so far in respect of third State relations in the area of private international law.[30]

30 See J. Kohler's quote referring to the 'dröhnendes Schweigen' of the EU, cf. the discussion report of S. Graf, 'Diskussionsbericht' in A. Dutta and J. Weber (eds.), *Die Europäischen Güterrechtsverordnungen*, C. H. Beck, München 2017, pp. 181, 182.

COMPARATIVE REPORT AND POLICY PERSPECTIVES

Wolfgang WURMNEST

1. INTRODUCTION

The final contribution of this book will first provide an overview of the treaty law and its historical background, topics discussed in great detail in the various country reports (section 2). It then analyzes the impact of the treaty law on the functioning of the Succession Regulation (section 3). As the treaty law affects the functioning of the Succession Regulation in various ways, this contribution will examine the question of whether there are any compelling reasons for those EU Member States that do not plan to terminate or adapt the treaties concluded with third States, to keep the rules on jurisdiction and/or applicable law as enshrined in the treaties (section 4). As these rules are – at least from the perspective of the European Union[1] as opposed to that of (most) third States – based on outdated concepts of private international law which create frictions with the Succession Regulation, various policy options are discussed to improve the law and the working of this Regulation (section 5). A summary concludes this contribution (section 6).

2. INSTRUMENTS TAKING PRECEDENCE OVER THE SUCCESSION REGULATION: A SURVEY

2.1. MAPPING THE LAW

The country reports have revealed that not all EU Member States scrutinized in this book have concluded bilateral agreements or multilateral conventions that take precedence over the EU Succession Regulation. As a rule of thumb, the further east one looks, the more agreements one finds between EU Member States and third States covering succession issues, at least partly.

Starting in the west, *Belgium* is not party to a single agreement that could be in conflict with the Succession Regulation. There are only two general instruments on the recognition and enforcement of judgments with Switzerland and the United Kingdom. However, neither of these instruments affects the respective rules in the Succession Regulation as they concern the recognition and enforcement of Belgian judgments in Switzerland and in the United Kingdom and vice versa,[2] an issue which is not covered by the Succession Regulation. This Regulation deals exclusively with the free movement of decisions in succession matters amongst the participating Member States.

---

1 European Union Perspective, A. Dutta, section 1. (Note that all references to the country reports in this book refer to the numbering of the headings).

2 For details see Belgium, S. Francq and J. Mary, sections 2.1 and 2.2.

The situation in *France* is ambiguous. Even though the treaty between France and Iran from 1964 contains a rule on the law applicable to the '*statut personnel*', it does not – in the understanding of the French rapporteur – extend to succession upon death, but only to family matters.[3] In contrast, a similarly worded rule in a Judicial Convention concluded with Tunisia in 1957 (**Treaty 16**) should be interpreted as encompassing succession matters. Even though it is discussed whether this treaty has lapsed, and it seems that the conflict-of-law rule is not applied in practice, it cannot be excluded that this treaty takes precedence over the Succession Regulation for the determination of the applicable law.[4]

Moving further east, the landscape changes considerably. *Germany* has concluded three bilateral treaties that take precedence over the Succession Regulation.[5] The Treaty on Establishment with Iran (**Treaty 17**) contains a conflict-of-law rule covering succession cases. The consular agreements concluded with Turkey (**Treaty 19**) and with the former Soviet Union (**Treaty 18**) (the latter continues to apply to many of its successor States outside the EU) deal with jurisdiction and applicable law. Additionally, in *Austria* three treaties take priority over the EU rules.[6] The Treaty of Friendship and Establishment with Iran (**Treaty 1**), which is modelled in a similar fashion as its German-Iranian counterpart, contains a general rule on the applicable law in succession cases. The Treaty on Mutual Assistance with Yugoslavia (**Treaty 3**), which nowadays applies to all those successor States that have not (yet) joined the EU, deals, *inter alia*, with jurisdiction, choice of law and recognition and enforcement of judgments in succession matters. The Consular Treaty with the Soviet Union (**Treaty 2**) contains, *inter alia*, rules on jurisdiction and applicable law in succession matters. Nowadays, this agreement binds the Russian Federation as one of the successor States to the former Soviet Union.

Looking south, *Italy* has entered into a Consular Treaty with Turkey (**Treaty 21**) that contains rules on jurisdiction and the applicable law. Further, it has agreed on a Consular and Establishment Treaty with Switzerland (**Treaty 20**) that contains a rule for jurisdiction for certain succession disputes. It is silent on the issue of the applicable law, at least according to the prevailing (Italian) view, even though Swiss courts have held otherwise in the past.[7]

In the north(east), *Sweden* and *Finland* are party to the Nordic Inheritance Convention (NIC) (**Treaty 14**), which also binds Denmark, Iceland and Norway,

---

3 France, S. Fulli-Lemaire, section 5. From the perspective of Iran, the French-Iranian treaty could, however, include succession matters, see Iran, N. Yassari, section 3.4.1.1.

4 France, S. Fulli-Lemaire, section 3.

5 For details see Germany, D. Looschelders, section 2.1 et seq.

6 For details see Austria, C. Rudolf, section 1.1 et seq.

7 For details see Italy, P. Franzina, section 1.2.2 et seq. On the Swiss judgments see Switzerland, A. Bonomi, section 2.1.2.

hereby unifying matters of jurisdiction, applicable law and recognition and enforcement of judgments in succession matters among the Nordic countries. This regional instrument was reformed recently and, as a consequence, has barely any impact on the functioning of the European Succession Regulation (see below section 2.3). Finland had also concluded an agreement of legal assistance with the Soviet Union (**Treaty 15**). It contains a provision on the applicable law with regard to the form of wills. In today's practice, this instrument is only relevant between Finland and the Russian Federation.[8]

Looking eastwards, and south-eastwards, all the countries analyzed in this book entered into various agreements that precede the Succession Regulation. *Estonia*[9] concluded legal assistance treaties with the Russian Federation[10] and with Ukraine[11] which contain rules on jurisdiction and applicable law. In the *Czech Republic*, a large number of agreements on legal assistance are in force.[12] These agreements are of a general nature. Out of these, the treaties with Albania (**Treaty 5**), Cuba (**Treaty 6**), Mongolia (**Treaty 8**), North Korea (**Treaty 7**), the former Soviet Union (**Treaty 9**), Ukraine (**Treaty 10**), Uzbekistan (**Treaty 11**), Vietnam (**Treaty 12**) and former Yugoslavia (**Treaty 13**) contain rules on international jurisdiction and applicable law in succession matters. The treaties with Afghanistan, Algeria, Switzerland, Syria, Tunisia and Yemen deal with the recognition and enforcement of judgments of these States in the Czech Republic (and vice versa) and are thus outside Succession Regulation's scope of application. The treaty on legal assistance binding (now) *Croatia* and the Russian Federation (**Treaty 4**) deals with jurisdiction, applicable law and recognition and enforcement of judgments in succession cases. Finally, even though this jurisdiction is not covered in detail in this book, it is worth noting that *Greece* has concluded a treaty with Switzerland (**Treaty 23**) which contains a rule on the law applicable to certain succession matters.[13]

---

8 For details see Finland and Sweden, M. Helin, section 2 et seq.

9 All information in this contribution on the legal situation in Estonia, including translations of the relevant rules in bilateral treaties, is based on the work of M. Torga, who for personal reasons could not submit an entry to this volume as had been initially planned. Any errors or oversights, however, are mine alone.

10 Treaty between the Estonian Republic and the Russian Federation on Comprehensive Legal Assistance of 26.01.1993, RT II 1993, 16, 27, also available at <https://www.riigiteataja.ee/akt/13141764> accessed 08.04.2019.

11 Treaty between the Estonian Republic and Ukraine on Comprehensive Legal Assistance of 15.02.1995, RT II 1995, 13/14, 63, also available at <https://www.riigiteataja.ee/akt/13119066> accessed 08.04.2019.

12 For details see Czech Republic, M. Pfeiffer, section 2 et seq.

13 For details see Switzerland, A. Bonomi, section 3. As this book does not contain a country report on Greece, it cannot be ruled out the Greece has concluded other treaties that take precedence over the Succession Regulation.

2.2. THE HISTORIC BACKGROUND OF THESE INSTRUMENTS

2.2.1. *Friendship, Reciprocity, Commerce*

The various instruments were concluded in different historical settings which sometimes overlap. A first group of treaties was set up to establish friendly relations with certain third States based on an equal footing. These instruments were also adopted to foster commerce between the contracting States. They contain only rules on the applicable law and not on jurisdiction. One of these agreements was the German-Iranian treaty on establishment of 1929 (**Treaty 17**),[14] which was coupled with a Friendship Treaty.[15] This instrument grants the citizens of both States the right to engage in commerce in the other State within the legal framework prescribed by that State.[16] Further, the treaty grants citizens of both States equal treatment according to the laws of the other State, including access to courts.[17] This 'reciprocity approach' was an important point for Iran: wanting to end the capitulation regime, under which Iranian courts had no jurisdiction over certain disputes involving foreigners (whereas Iranians in the then German Reich did not enjoy the same privileges), the quest for equal treatment drove the conclusion of the agreement.[18] The rules on the applicable law in family and succession matters, which are based on nationality as connecting factor, seem to have been incorporated in that agreement to ensure that German citizens living in the Persian Empire were treated according to German law and vice versa. Market access and reciprocity also induced the treaty between Austria and Iran (**Treaty 1**).[19] Negotiations were taken up in the 1930s, but due to the '*Anschluss*' of Austria to the German Reich in 1938, the negotiated instruments never entered into force. After World War II, Austria resumed negotiations and entered into the Treaty of Friendship and Establishment.[20]

---

14 Earlier agreements with other European nations were not extended; see Iran, N. Yassari, section 2.

15 See Freundschaftsvertrag zwischen dem Deutschen Reich und dem Kaiserreich Persien vom 17.02.1929 nebst Schlussprotokoll, RGBl. 1930 II, 1002.

16 Art. 3 German-Iranian Establishment Treaty states in part: 'Die Angehörigen jedes vertragschließenden Staates haben im Gebiet des anderen Staates, sofern sie die Landesgesetze und -verordnungen beobachten, das Recht, in gleicher Weise wie die Inländer jede Art von Gewerbe und Handel zu betreiben und jedes Handwerk und jeden Beruf auszuüben, soweit es sich nicht um ein Staatsmonopol oder um die Ausbeutung eines vom Staate verliehenen Monopols handelt ….' ['The nationals of each Contracting State have the right – as far as they respect the laws and bylaws – to pursue every trade and commerce and to perform every craft and profession on the territory of the other State like the nationals of that other State, as far as the activity does not relate to a State monopoly or to the exploitation of a monopoly granted by the State ….') (author's translation).

17 Art. 8 German-Iranian Establishment Treaty.

18 Iran, N. Yassari, section 2.

19 Austria, C. Rudolf, section 1.4.1.

20 Austria, C. Rudolf, section 1.4.1.

2.2.2. *Consular Relations and Establishment*

A second group of treaties containing rules on jurisdiction and/or applicable law for succession matters had the formation of consular relations as the main purpose or the right of establishment. Sometimes these agreements were concluded to deal with a strong flux of emigrants from one country to another.

The first agreement of that kind was concluded in 1868 between Italy and Switzerland (**Treaty 20**). At that time, many Italians were emigrating to Switzerland. The two States, therefore, negotiated an instrument dealing with consular powers to assist emigrants. This instrument, however, goes beyond a traditional consular treaty. It also grants the citizens of both contracting States the right to enter and work in the respective other contracting State, and it deals with the issue of jurisdiction in case a national of one contracting State dies in the other State. Given that the heirs often had their habitual residence in the 'home country' of the deceased emigrant, the treaty provides that disputes between the heirs of a person that has died in the other contracting State can be brought before the courts of the place where the deceased had his or her last domicile in his or her country of origin. Thus, heirs of an Italian emigrant deceased in Switzerland can litigate before Italian courts and vice versa in the case of a Swiss emigrant dying in Italy. The purpose of that agreement was, therefore, to facilitate access to courts, mainly having the family of the deceased emigrant in mind.[21]

The consular treaties concluded by Turkey in 1929 with Germany (**Treaty 19**) and with Italy (**Treaty 21**) and in 1938 with Hungary (**Treaty 24**) were concluded in a similar political setting as the treaties that Iran concluded with several European powers (above, section 2.2.1). A capitulation regime, under which citizens of the European powers did not generally fall under the jurisdiction of Turkish courts, was also present in the Ottoman Empire. Consequently, consuls adjudicated private law disputes between foreigners and were also involved in the administration of the movable estate of foreign citizens dying in Turkey.[22] After the end of the Ottoman Empire, the Republic of Turkey concluded various treaties with European powers that ensured the same rights and privileges of consuls in both countries, thereby ending the capitulation system. Following the traditional role of consuls in succession matters, rules on private international law following the scission principle were incorporated into the treaties: the nationality of the deceased was chosen as connecting factor for the movable estate, the *lex rei sitae* governs succession to immovable property. To ensure the harmony of forum and *ius*, all treaties

---

[21] For details see Italy, P. FRANZINA, section 2.1.6.

[22] Turkey, B. GÜNEŞ, section 2.

further provide that the courts of the country in which the estate is located are exclusively competent to hear (certain) claims regarding the succession to immovable property.[23] The courts of the State whose nationality the deceased possessed at the time of death are competent to adjudicate claims regarding movable assets. Whether or not jurisdiction is exclusive in the latter case is disputed with regard to the Turkish-Italian agreement (see below, section 5.3). Claims of third parties against the estate must be brought before the courts of the country in which the estate is located.[24] In addition, the consular staff were granted various powers to administrate the estate of the deceased.[25]

The agreements between Germany and Austria with the former Soviet Union (**Treaties 18** and **2**) that were signed in 1958 and 1959, respectively, were an attempt to ensure a closer relationship between the countries after World War II.[26] These agreements could build upon prior consular treaties between the contracting States and contain rules on succession matters in line with the traditional tasks and powers of consular staff to assist in administrating the estate of foreigners dying in the host State. The treaty between Germany and the Soviet Union provides only a rule on the succession to immovable property. It calls for the application of the law of the country where the property is located.[27] The treaty concluded by Austria is broader as it deals with international jurisdiction and applicable law. The rules on private international law are based on the scission principle. The succession to immovable property is governed by the *lex rei sitae* rule,[28] whereas the succession to movable property located in the 'receiving State' is (only) 'upon application' governed by the law of that State if the deceased was a citizen of the sending State but was last domiciled in the receiving State.[29] The rules on international jurisdiction are modelled along the same principles to ensure harmony between forum and *ius*.[30]

Finally, even though it does not concern consular relations, the 1927 treaty between Greece and Switzerland (**Treaty 23**) on establishment and the equality of legal protection should also be mentioned here. It contains provisions for cases in which citizens of one country die in the other State. Local authorities are to inform the consular or diplomatic staff of the deceased's home country

---

23 Germany, D. Looschelders, section 4.1 (German-Turkish Treaty); Italy, P. Franzina, section 2.2.7.1 (Italian-Turkish Treaty); Turkey, B. Güneş, section 5.1.2 (Hungarian-Turkish Treaty).

24 See Art. 20(15) German-Turkish Treaty; Art. 21(8) Italian-Turkish Treaty; Art. 18(3)(2), (3) Hungarian-Turkish Treaty, see Turkey, B. Güneş, section 5.1.

25 For details see Turkey, B. Güneş, section 5.3.

26 See generally Germany, D. Looschelders, section 2.4.1; Austria, C. Rudolf, section 1.3.1.

27 Art. 28(3) German-Soviet Consular Treaty.

28 Art. 26 Austrian-Soviet Consular Treaty.

29 Art. 23(1) Austrian-Soviet Consular Treaty.

30 Arts. 23, 26 Austrian-Soviet Consular Treaty, for details see Austria, C. Rudolf, section 3.1.2.

if no heirs are known and are to take measures to safeguard the possessions of the deceased.[31] In addition, the treaty deals with the matter of applicable law but not with the issue of jurisdiction. Under the treaty, the *lex patriae* of the deceased governs the succession. This rule, however, covers only the determination of legal heirs and their shares as well as the question of forced heirship rights.[32] This conflict-of-law rule was a compromise between the private international law of Switzerland, which had already established domicile as the relevant connecting factor, and the Greek rules which were based on the *lex patriae*, but not for all issues of the succession.[33] Therefore, the treaty enshrines the nationality of the deceased as connecting factor, but the rule's scope of application is limited to certain issues (legal heirs and their shares as well as forced heirship rights).

2.2.3. Regional Cooperation

The third setting for international treaties on (or including rules for) cross-border succession matters is the context of regional cooperation. Such cooperation exists between the Nordic countries of Denmark, Finland, Iceland, Norway and Sweden. Given their common history and culture as well as close political ties, these countries established a comprehensive cooperation in legal matters between them from the second half of the 19th century onwards. Many agreements were concluded to provide an adequate framework for cross-border family and succession matters, including the Nordic Inheritance Convention of 1934 (**Treaty 14**).[34] This convention unifies the rules on international jurisdiction, applicable law and recognition and enforcement of judgments in cross-border succession cases. The convention deals further with the issue of legal assistance regarding an estate's administration.

---

31 Art. 10(1) Swiss-Italian Treaty states: 'Si un ressortissant de l'une des parties contractantes vient à décéder, sur le territoire de l'autre partie, sans laisser d'héritiers connus ni d'exécuteurs testamentaires, les autorités du lieu du décès en aviseront le représentant diplomatique ou consulaire du pays d'origine, afin qu'il transmette aux intéressés les informations nécessaires.' ['If a citizen of one of the contracting parties dies on the territory of the other party, without leaving known heirs or executors of his will, the authorities at the place of death shall inform the consular or diplomatic representative of the deceased's home State, so that this person can transmit the necessary information to the interested parties.']; Art. 10(2) Swiss-Italian treaty states in part: 'Les autorités qualifiées à cet effet du lieu du décès ou du lieu où se trouvent situés des biens du défunt prendront, à l'égard de ces biens toutes les mesures conservatoires que la législation du pays prescrit pour les successions des nationaux.' ['The competent authorities at the place of death or at the place where property of the deceased is located shall take all protective measures allowed under local law for successions of nationals of this State'] (author's translation).

32 Switzerland, A. Bonomi, section 3.

33 Switzerland, A. Bonomi, section 3.

34 Finland and Sweden, M. Helin, section 3.1.

2.2.4. *Legal Assistance*

The creation of a comprehensive architecture of legal assistance between the contracting States was another driver for the conclusion of bilateral agreements which now precede the Succession Regulation. Such agreements on legal assistance may come in various shapes and sizes. They might contain rules on legal aid and service of documents or the taking evidence abroad alongside rules on international jurisdiction and the applicable law for succession matters as well as general rules for the recognition and enforcement of judgments. Usually, these treaties are not restricted to civil and commercial matters and include other fields of law, for example, criminal matters.

Austria concluded such an agreement with Yugoslavia in 1954 (**Treaty 3**), and a forerunner to this treaty dates back to 1928.[35] After World War II, legal assistance agreements were very popular amongst states of the 'Eastern Bloc' and also between those countries and other socialist countries. Yugoslavia concluded such agreements with Bulgaria in 1956 (**Treaty 22**), with Poland in 1960 (**Treaty 26**), with the Soviet Union in 1962 and with Hungary in 1968 (**Treaty 25**). Similarly, Czechoslovakia established many such agreements from 1959 onwards. After the end of the East-West divide, the Czech Republic continued to conclude these kinds of treaties, entering into agreements with Ukraine in 2001 (**Treaty 10**) and with Uzbekistan in 2002 (**Treaty 11**).

As far as these agreements contain rules on matters of private international law, they are usually based on connecting factors and approaches that prevailed at the time of their conclusion in one or both contracting States. Given that these principles differed across the globe and that compromises had to be found, the adopted rules differ significantly. A few remarks shall suffice to prove this point.

Regarding the applicable law, some treaties follow the monist approach, using one connecting factor to determine the applicable law for the succession to both movable and immovable property. Against this background, the treaties between Yugoslavia and Bulgaria (**Treaty 22**), Hungary (**Treaty 25**) and Poland (**Treaty 26**) lay down nationality as the general connecting factor.[36] This general rule is supplemented by special conflict rules (which differ to some extent in the three treaties), for example on the validity of wills or on an estate without a claimant (*bona vacantia*), deviating in part from this approach.[37] The treaties concluded by Czechoslovakia with Yugoslavia (**Treaty 13**) and Cuba (**Treaty 6**) follow a similar approach even though their special conflict rules

---

35 Austria, C. Rudolf, section 1.2.1.

36 For details see Bosnia and Herzegovina, Serbia, North Macedonia and Montenegro, S. Đorđević and Z. Meškić, section 4.

37 For details see Bosnia and Herzegovina, Serbia, North Macedonia and Montenegro, S. Đorđević and Z. Meškić, section 4.

vary to some degree.[38] Most treaties on legal assistance scrutinized in this book, however, follow the scission principle by prescribing different connecting factors for the succession to movable and immovable property. In line with the traditional approach, all treaties scrutinized in this book call for the application of the *lex rei sitae* to determine the succession to immovable property. The connecting factor for the succession to movable property is sometimes the concept of domicile, for example in the treaties between the (now) Czech Republic and Uzbekistan (**Treaty 11**) as well as with the former Soviet Union (**Treaty 9**).[39] Most treaties, however, call for the application of the *lex patriae*, for example the treaties between the (now) Czech Republic and Albania (**Treaty 5**), Mongolia (**Treaty 8**), Vietnam (**Treaty 12**), North Korea (**Treaty 7**) and Ukraine[40] (**Treaty 10**), or the treaty between former Yugoslavia and the former Soviet Union (**Treaty 4**).[41] The rules of international jurisdiction are modelled along similar lines. As a general rule, many treaties confer international jurisdiction for disputes over succession to immovable property upon the judicial authorities of the contracting party on whose territory the property is located. With regard to succession to movable property, jurisdiction is awarded to either the courts of the State whose national the deceased was at the time of death (treaties between the (now) Czech Republic and Albania, Cuba, North Korea, Vietnam, former Yugoslavia and Ukraine) or those at his or her last domicile (treaties between the (now) Czech Republic and Uzbekistan as well as with the former Soviet Union).[42]

Besides the fact that the rules on international jurisdiction and applicable law follow the traditional principles prevailing at the time of conclusion of the treaty, it seems that, at least in some negotiations, succession issues were not a primary concern given that some agreements deal only with selected issues. An example supporting this observation is the legal assistance agreement between Austria and former Yugoslavia of 1956 (**Treaty 3**). It has no general conflict-of law rule. It deals only with a very unique situation in which the deceased, being a national of one contracting State, is domiciled ('*Wohnsitz*') in the other contracting State with his or her heirs also living in the State of domicile. In this scenario, the heirs may request within certain time frames (three–six months) that the courts of the domicile State rule over the movable (not the immovable) property located in the State of domicile (unless there is an objection) and that the court apply the law of the nationality of the deceased.[43] This rule, which was already

38 Czech Republic, M. Pfeiffer, section 3.
39 Czech Republic, M. Pfeiffer, section 3.
40 Czech Republic, M. Pfeiffer, section 3.
41 Croatia, D. Babić and T. Hoško, section 3.
42 Czech Republic, M. Pfeiffer, section 4.
43 Art. 36 Austrian-Yugoslavian Legal Assistance Treaty, for details see Austria, C. Rudolf, section 2.1.1; Bosnia and Herzegovina, Serbia, North Macedonia and Montenegro, S. Đorđević and Z. Meškić, section 4.1.

enshrined in the Treaty between Austria and the Kingdom of Serbia, Croatia and Slovenia of 1928,[44] is especially remarkable because the agreement does not set forth which law applies to the succession to immovable property. A similar rule (coupled with more comprehensive conflict-of-law rules) can be found in the treaty between (former) Yugoslavia and the (former) Soviet Union.[45]

2.2.5. Border Changes and De-Colonialization

Finally, border changes occurring in the context of dissolution of States and the de-colonialization process led to the conclusion of agreements that affect the Succession Regulation today.

The 1957 Judicial Convention between France and Tunisia (**Treaty 16**) was concluded in the aftermath of Tunisia's struggle for independence. To safeguard the interests of France as the former colonial power, the treaty contains a rule on applicable law that applies to French nationals only. French nationals are governed by French law in personal and family matters as defined by a 1956 Tunisian decree which includes succession matters.[46]

The emergence of new States was also the historical background for the conclusion of the legal assistance agreement between the Republic of Estonia and the Russian Federation in 1993.[47] Despite being a comprehensive treaty on legal assistance drafted along lines similar to those of the treaties described in the preceding section, it seems that the reason for its conclusion was primarily the desire of Estonia to be recognized by the Russian Federation as an independent entity and only to a lesser extent the need to solve issues arising in cross-border private law matters. The same may be said about the legal assistance treaty concluded between Estonia and Ukraine in 1995.[48] The drafters of these agreements, however, also had to deal with the fact that many inhabitants of Estonia held passports issued by other States emerging from the dissolution of the Soviet Union.

The basic rule for the applicable law in succession matters in these treaties follows the traditional scission principle. The connecting factor for succession

---

44 Art. 26 Staatsvertrag zwischen der Republik Österreich und dem Königreiche der Serben, Kroaten und Slowenen über den wechselseitigen rechtlichen Verkehr vom 01.05.1928, Austrian BGBl. 1929, No. 100.

45 For details see Croatia, D. Babić and T. Hoško, sections 3, 4.1.

46 France, S. Fulli-Lemaire, section 3.

47 Treaty between the Estonian Republic and the Russian Federation on Comprehensive Legal Assistance of 26.01.1993, available at <https://www.riigiteataja.ee/akt/13141764> accessed 08.04.2019. This section on the legal situation in Estonia is based entirely on information provided by M. Torga, who also provided translations of the relevant rules of the treaties. Any errors or oversights are, however, mine alone.

48 Treaty between the Estonian Republic and Ukraine on Comprehensive Legal Assistance of 15.02.1995, available at <https://www.riigiteataja.ee/akt/13119066> accessed 08.04.2019.

to immovable estate is the *lex rei sitae*, and the law of habitual residence governs the succession to movable estate.[49] The rules on international jurisdiction are modelled in a similar fashion to ensure harmony between forum and *ius*.[50] Given that the general connecting factor for the movable estate is not the nationality of the deceased, the treaties ensure that the succession to movables of Russian/ Ukrainian citizens having their habitual residence in Estonia is governed by Estonian law.

2.3. MEASURES TAKEN IN ANTICIPATION OF THE SUCCESSION REGULATION

When the Succession Regulation was negotiated and drafted, some EU Member States reconsidered or re-visited their commitments vis-à-vis third States in order to prevent or ease tensions with the newly created EU system on cross-border succession cases.

The most prominent example was the amendment of the Nordic Inheritance Convention (**Treaty 14**). The adaptation of this instrument was somewhat forced by the EU Commission.[51] In 2006, the Nordic countries decided to amend the Inheritance Convention of 1934. A group of experts drafted a proposal for an amended version which was presented in 2009. The entire process was, however, put on hold when the EU Commission issued its proposal for the Succession Regulation that same year. In light of the principle of loyalty, Sweden and Finland did not want to adapt the Inheritance Convention to avoid frictions with the future EU system. When the Succession Regulation took shape, Finland and Sweden requested an exception for the Nordic Inheritance Convention in the form of the 2009 proposal to preserve the unity of law in the Scandinavian world. The EU rejected their request to a large extent. Priority for the Nordic Inheritance Convention over the rules of the Succession Regulation was granted only with regard to: (i) the rules on the procedural aspects of estate administration and related legal assistance issues; and (ii) procedures for the recognition and enforcement of decisions in succession matters.

---

49 Art. 42 Estonian-Russian Legal Assistance Treaty; Art. 34 Estonian-Ukrainian Legal Assistance Treaty.

50 Art. 45 Estonian-Russian Legal Assistance Treaty; Art. 37 Estonian-Ukrainian Legal Assistance Treaty. In cases in which the entire movable estate is located in the contracting State in which the deceased did not have his or her last habitual residence, the authorities/ courts of the State in which the movable estate is located are – upon application – competent to deal with the case, if all heirs agree, Art. 45(2) Estonian-Russian Legal Assistance Treaty; Art. 37(2) Estonian-Ukrainian Legal Assistance Treaty.

51 On this process see Finland and Sweden, M. Helin, section 3.2.

Against this background, the Nordic States had to discard the idea of amending the Convention, as agreed upon in 2009, given that the rules on applicable law and jurisdiction would not have prevailed over the Succession Regulation. Instead, the Convention was partly rewritten to reflect the basic choices of the Regulation. But embracing this (forced) import of the EU's approach was not due to the 'high quality' of the EU rules. Doing so was, as our country reporter for Finland and Sweden has pointed out, the only possible way of preserving coherence in the North.[52]

Less troublesome were the changes that Slovakia adopted in the course of the negotiations of the Succession Regulation. In 2014, it signed an additional protocol to the legal assistance treaty with Montenegro – that had previously been concluded between (former) Czechoslovakia and (former) Yugoslavia – to set aside the rules on jurisdiction and applicable law in succession matters as contained in that instrument.[53]

Other EU Member States that have concluded bilateral agreements which precede the Succession Regulation (Austria, Croatia, Czech Republic, Estonia, Germany, Greece, Italy) have not announced any plans to terminate or adapt their existing treaties. The impact of these agreements on the European Succession Regulation will be assessed in the following section.

3. IMPACT ON THE SUCCESSION REGULATION

3.1. GENERAL REMARKS

As the national treaties contain very different rules on the questions of jurisdiction and applicable law compared with the EU's set of rules (see above, section 2.1), the Regulation cannot achieve true harmonization within the Member States. The treaty law impairs decisional harmony within the European Union. In addition, the treaties preserve very traditional concepts of private international law, such as nationality as the general connecting factor, the exclusion of party autonomy or the scission principle, whereas the Succession Regulation is based on modern concepts of private international law. These differences also open the door to forum shopping.[54]

52 Finland and Sweden, M. Helin, section 3.2.

53 Bosnia and Herzegovina, Serbia, North Macedonia and Montenegro, S. Đorđević and Z. Meškić, section 4.3.

54 C. Kohler, 'Die künftige Erbrechtsverordnung der Europäischen Union und die Staatsverträge mit Drittstaaten' in G. Reichelt and W.H. Rechberger (eds.), *Europäisches Erbrecht: Zum Verordnungsvorschlag der Europäischen Kommission zum Erb- und Testamentsrecht*, Jan Sramek Verlag, Wien 2011, pp. 118 et seq.

3.2. FURTHER FRICTIONS WITH THE EU SYSTEM

Beside these general effects, there are also various frictions with the EU's system because the treaty law is not coordinated with the Succession Regulation. The German-Soviet Treaty (**Treaty 18**), for example, applies only to succession to immovable property, whereas succession to movable property falls under the Succession Regulation.[55] This causes a scission, which is not endorsed by EU law. Other effects of the treaty law are frictions concerning jurisdiction rules. If a Russian national having his or her habitual residence in France dies owning a house in Germany, the succession to that house would be governed by German law according to the consular treaty. German courts, however, under the Succession Regulation have no (general) jurisdiction to decide on this matter as the Regulation designates French courts (habitual residence of the deceased at the time of death) as exclusively competent (Article 4 SR).[56] Not being bound by the treaty with (today) Russia, the French courts would apply the rules of the Succession Regulation to the entire case and would judge the matter according to French law (Article 21 SR).[57] Enforcing the French decision in Germany, on the other hand, would amount to a violation of Germany's obligation under international law towards Russia.[58] As a way out of this dilemma, the idea of granting the heirs access to German courts through the forum of necessity (*forum necessitatis*) (Article 11 SR) has been discussed as a means of enforcing the provisions of the treaty.[59] Things can get even more complex if a treaty with a third State confers jurisdiction on the courts of a contracting EU Member State that would not be competent according to the Regulation. In such scenarios it is not clear how parallel proceedings are to be dealt with. There is thus a danger that two EU courts will decide on the same matter on the basis of two different applicable laws (if the treaty also provides for rules on the applicable law that differ from those laid down in the Regulation).

Another friction arises with regard to the European Certificate of Succession. Based on the law that the Succession Regulation designates as applicable, this Certificate is issued by a single court within the EU for all of the deceased's

---

55 For details see Germany, D. Looschelders, section 3.1.3.

56 German courts cannot base their international jurisdiction on Art. 10 SR as the deceased was habitually resident in a Member State at the time of death.

57 R. Magnus in B. Dauner-Lieb, T. Heidel and G. Ring (eds.), *NomosKommentar BGB*, Vol. 6, 2nd ed., Nomos-Verlagsgesellschaft, Baden-Baden 2015, Article 75 EuErbVO para. 11.

58 R. Süß, 'Der Vorbehalt zugunsten bilateraler Abkommen mit Drittstaaten' in A. Dutta and S. Herrler (eds.), *Die Europäische Erbrechtsverordnung*, C.H. Beck, München 2014, p. 190 (regarding a German-Iranian case).

59 C. Kohler, 'Die künftige Erbrechtsverordnung der Europäischen Union und die Staatsverträge mit Drittstaaten' in G. Reichelt and W.H. Rechberger (eds.), *Europäisches Erbrecht: Zum Verordnungsvorschlag der Europäischen Kommission zum Erb- und Testamentsrecht*, Jan Sramek Verlag, Wien 2011, pp. 116 et seq.

property. If certain States have treaty provisions that differ from the Regulation's conflict-of-law rules, it is not clear on what terms the European Succession Certificate should be issued. The effect of the treaty law depends on the treaty's scope. If a treaty between Member State A and third State B also applies to property located outside the contracting States, the outcome might be different than in cases in which the treaty covers assets in the contracting States only.[60] Given that the European Certificate of Succession is gaining in importance, the problem will become more pressing in the near future. Up to now, many cases covered by treaty law only concerned the contracting EU State and the third State.[61] An Iranian citizen habitually residing in Germany will often have property in Germany and Iran, and less likely in other EU States. Thus, issuing a European Succession Certificate might not become a necessity for the heirs. A German certificate will suffice. But given that human mobility in the EU is constantly on the rise, cases in which foreign citizens falling under treaty law own property in more than one Member State will certainly increase in the future. An example would be a couple from Iran that moved to Austria and bought a house there. Their children later move to Germany for work purposes, and the parents follow them when they are old to be closer to them. In such a scenario, it is likely that the parents will have assets in more than one Member State.

3.3. CONCLUSION

Summing up, the treaty law affects the Succession Regulation in different ways: the unification effect is hampered, decisional harmony within the European Union is impaired, the treaties cause frictions with the European rules and the functioning of the European Succession Certificate can be affected. The severity of the frictions caused by the treaty law on the Succession Regulation is difficult to assess empirically. But, given that some treaties concern significant minority groups within a country, the impact should not be underestimated. Examples of such treaties having a considerable impact on the functioning of the Succession Regulation are the German-Turkish Consular Treaty of 1929[62] (**Treaty 19**)

---

60 R. Magnus in B. Dauner-Lieb, T. Heidel and G. Ring (eds.), *NomosKommentar BGB*, Vol. 6, 2nd ed., Nomos-Verlagsgesellschaft, Baden-Baden 2015, Article 75 EuErbVO para. 12.

61 See Germany, D. Looschelders, section 5.

62 European Union Perspective, A. Dutta, 1. C. Kohler, 'Die künftige Erbrechtsverordnung der Europäischen Union und die Staatsverträge mit Drittstaaten' in G. Reichelt and W.H. Rechberger (eds.), *Europäisches Erbrecht: Zum Verordnungsvorschlag der Europäischen Kommission zum Erb- und Testamentsrecht*, Jan Sramek Verlag, Wien 2011, p. 113, points out that out of the 2.3 million Turkish emigrants in Europe, 1.7 million have their habitual residence in Germany. The practical importance stems also from the fact that many Turkish nationals with habitual residence in Germany have property in both countries,

(even though more and more residents of Turkish origin in Germany hold both German and Turkish nationality, so that the treaty does not apply according to the prevailing opinion[63]), the Legal Assistance Treaty between Austria and former Yugoslavia of 1956 (**Treaty 3**) and, presumably, the Estonian-Russian Legal Assistance Treaty of 1993.

4. ARE THERE COMPELLING REASONS TO MAINTAIN THE TREATY LAW AS IT IS?

4.1. AUSTRIA

The historic background that led to the conclusion of the treaty with Iran (**Treaty 1**) has changed significantly. Applying the *lex patriae* to succession cases was imperative at the time of its conclusion for the reasons described above (section 2.2.1). The shift towards habitual residence as the connecting factor and the possibility of choosing the applicable law, as ushered in with the Succession Regulation, brought a sweeping change to the rules of private international law in Austria.

If a Friendship and Settlement Treaty between Austria and Iran were negotiated today (and Austria had the power to do so), it would seem likely that the Austrian delegates would try to align the conflict-of-law rules with the European standards or to exclude choice of law from the scope of the treaty. Moreover, the argument that Austria needs to preserve the nationality principle to ensure that its citizens habitually residing in Iran fall under Austrian law instead of Iranian law is only a weak argument. First, one could ask why this rule is restricted to Austrians habitually resident in Iran, and why similar treaties were not concluded with other nations having a similar legal system as Iran. Second, also without special conflict-of-law rules in the Friendship Treaty, succession in respect of Austrian citizens having their habitual residence in Iran could be judged according to Austrian law as the Succession Regulation accepts a *renvoi* to the law of an EU Member State (Article 34 SR). Without a special conflict-of-law rule in the Establishment and Friendship Treaty, the Austrian judge would apply Iranian law (including its private international law) to Austrian citizens that are habitually resident in Iran. As under Iranian private international law, the nationality of the deceased is the connecting factor,[64] it would refer the case back to Austrian law which would accept the *renvoi*.

see M. Gebauer, 'Das deutsch-türkische Nachlassabkommen im Sog des Europäischen Kollisionsrechts', [2018] *IPRax* 345, 346.

63 See Germany, D. Looschelders, section 2.3.2.3.

64 Iran, N. Yassari, section 4.

The application of Austrian law would however be subject to the condition that Austrian courts have international jurisdiction. This is so because without the rules of the Friendship Treaty, an Iranian judge would, at least according to the law in the books, apply Iranian law to Austrians habitually resident in Iran. Even though the connecting factor of Iranian law (nationality) points towards Austrian law, Iranian law accepts a *renvoi* and the general connecting factor enshrined in the Succession Regulation (habitual residence of the deceased) points back to the law of Iran.[65]

It is, however, not unlikely that a number of such cases involving Austrians having their habitual residence in Iran will be brought before Austrian courts. Under the Regulation, Austrian courts would respect a choice of Austrian law by an Austrian citizen with a habitual residence abroad (Article 22 SR) and also choice-of-court agreements that designate Austrian courts as being exclusively competent to rule on any succession matter (Article 5 SR), so that persons attached to Austria could take precautionary steps.[66] Without such an agreement, Austrian courts can base jurisdiction on Article 10(a) SR provided that assets of the estate are located in Austria, which will often be the case. So in a number of cases (albeit not all), Austrian law could apply to Austrian citizens habitually resident in Iran if the Friendship Treaty were amended.

Despite this finding, it cannot be argued that the Friendship Treaty has lost its *raison d'être* entirely as it ensures decisional harmony in Austrian-Iranian succession cases. Furthermore, the treaty still makes sense from the Iranian perspective because it corresponds to the connecting factor used in Iranian private international law.[67]

With regard to the treaties with the former Soviet Union, the political background has changed. Nevertheless, Austria wants to maintain unchanged the treaty with the Russian Federation (**Treaty 2**) to keep the harmony of forum and *ius*.[68] Also, the treaty with former Yugoslavia (**Treaty 3**) shall remain as it is because its rules are well established.[69] A harmony of forum and *ius* is an important aspect for cross-border succession cases and seems – at least in theory – less ensured by the Succession Regulation, which is open to choice-of-law agreements. It is also true that established rules may facilitate the administration of cross-border cases. But given that the States of the 'Western Balkans' that are still bound by the treaty with former Yugoslavia (Bosnia and

65 Cf. Art. 873 Iranian Civil Code. On the concept of *renvoi* in Iranian private international law see N. Yassari, 'Iran' in J. Basedow, G. Rühl, F. Ferrari and P. de Miguel Asensio (eds.), *Encyclopedia of Private International Law*, Edward Elgar Publishing, Cheltenham 2017, pp. 2173, 2178.

66 It is, however, doubtful whether Iranian courts would respect the choice-of-court agreement if one of the heirs brought the matter before a court in Iran.

67 Iran, N. Yassari, section 4.

68 Austria, C. Rudolf, section 4.

69 Austria, C. Rudolf, section 4.

Herzegovina, Kosovo, North Macedonia, Montenegro and Serbia) wish to join the EU in the long run or want to establish close relations, it is likely that at least some of these States will adapt their national rules to the ones in the Succession Regulation in the future as a 'pre-accession strategy', to the extent they have not already done so, like Montenegro.[70] Once that is done, it does not make sense to stick to outdated rules if both contractual partners have moved on in their national codes. So striking out the relevant provisions of the treaty law binding Austria and the States of the 'Western Balkans' is an option for the future.

4.2. CROATIA

The treaty binding Croatia and the Russian Federation (**Treaty 4**) contains private international law provisions that deviate from the Succession Regulation as well as from Russia's private international law code, as the Croatian rapporteurs point out.[71] It is thus difficult to argue that the treaty rules are 'set in stone' given that the concepts of the treaty obviously do not reflect special national interests. The Croatian rapporteurs therefore see some room for changes that would bring the treaty law closer to both Russian private international law and the Succession Regulation.[72]

4.3. CZECH REPUBLIC

The treaties binding the Czech Republic are legal assistance treaties that were concluded in the context of establishing or deepening amicable relations between the contracting States. The Czech rapporteur points out that the interest of the Czech Republic to preserve friendly relations with its contractual partners outweighs the frictions these treaties cause and that even an attempt to modify the treaties could hamper the good relationships between the contracting States. Therefore, the Czech Republic does not seek any changes as all attempts to modify the existing framework might be detrimental to stable political ties.[73] However, the report also stresses that the treaty with North Korea (**Treaty 7**) has little practical relevance and that there are no longer any strong political ties with this contractual partner.[74] Against this background, only few treaties might be put up for revision. But a closer look at the rules reveals that the Czech Republic

---

70 For details see Bosnia and Herzegovina, Serbia, North Macedonia and Montenegro, S. Đorđević and Z. Meškić, section 2.3.

71 Croatia, D. Babić and T. Hoško, section 5.

72 Croatia, D. Babić and T. Hoško, section 5.

73 Czech Republic, M. Pfeiffer, section 5.

74 Czech Republic, M. Pfeiffer, section 1 ('non-functioning treaty').

has no paramount interests in maintaining special private international law rules, apart from the general interest regarding stable political ties. As explained above (section 2.2.4), the Czech Republic has accepted a broad variety of private international law rules within the treaties (monist approach, scission principle, different connecting factors, etc.). It thus cannot be argued that certain rules for the designation of jurisdiction and applicable law are imperative to the Czech Republic. If the Czech Republic were to conclude an agreement with a third State today (and had the power to do so), one may assume that it would try to incorporate rules resembling those in the Succession Regulation. From the third States' perspectives, the current versions of the treaties are more meaningful, as it can be presumed that these States still follow more traditional approaches in private international law than the Succession Regulation does.

4.4. ESTONIA

Estonia has concluded legal assistance treaties in the aftermath of its independence with the Russian Federation and the Ukraine.[75] As far as these treaties concern succession matters, they follow the outdated scission principle with the effect that different laws might apply in a single succession case. In addition, the treaties are silent with regard to important issues, for example with regard to the law according to which an asset is to be qualified as movable or immovable. Against this background, there is no need to maintain the outdated treaty law in its current shape in support of particular Estonian national interests, apart from ensuring decisional harmony with the Russian Federation and Ukraine.

4.5. FRANCE

The 1957 Judicial Convention (**Treaty 16**) was concluded in the aftermath of Tunisia's independence from France. France had an interest in ensuring that its nationals living in the newly founded State would be governed by French law in the era's politically troubling times, and accordingly a single conflict-of-law rule ensuring this aim was incorporated into the treaty.[76] Given that the relationship between Tunisia and France is politically stable today, there is no need to cling to nationality as key connecting factor from a French perspective.

Moreover, the treaty cannot ensure true decisional harmony between France and Tunisia given that the conflict-of-law rule applies only to French nationals. Whereas both French and Tunisian courts will apply French law in

---

[75] This section is based entirely on information provided by M. Torga.

[76] France, S. Fulli-Lemaire, section 3.

succession cases concerning French citizens, and therefore ensure a measure of decisional harmony, the situation is different for Tunisian citizens. Here, French courts are bound by the Succession Regulation as succession matters involving Tunisian citizens would not fall under the scope of the Judicial Convention. Consequently, whereas French courts will – unless provided otherwise by the Regulation – apply the law of the habitual residence of the deceased (Article 21 SR), Tunisian courts will decide the succession in principle based on the *lex patriae* (Article 54 Tunisian Private International Law Act).[77] In this respect, the Judicial Convention does not ensure decisional harmony.

Finally, the fact that it is not settled whether the Convention is still in force today or whether it has lapsed also indicates that there is no pressing need to maintain this outdated conflict-of-law provision.

4.6. GERMANY

The historical settings that led to the conclusion of the treaties with Iran (**Treaty 17**), Turkey (**Treaty 19**) and the former Soviet Union (**Treaty 18**) have changed significantly. Similar to Austria (above, section 4.1), it is unlikely that Germany would try to preserve the existing conflict-of-law rules of the treaties if it had the power and the possibility to negotiate these agreements today. But that does not mean that Germany's contracting partners would accept different rules given that their private international law systems are still based on traditional concepts.[78] In addition, the *raison d'être* of these treaties nowadays is to maintain decisional harmony in cross-border cases between Germany and its contractual partners, which would be hampered were these agreements repealed. Nevertheless, not all of the rules ease the management of cross-border cases with third States. The rule of the German-Turkish Consular Treaty according to which the courts of the State whose nationality the deceased possessed at the time of death have exclusive jurisdiction over issues of succession to movable estate has been correctly depicted as a harsh rule for those citizens of one contracting State who have had their habitual residence in the other State.[79] Amending this treaty to additionally grant jurisdiction to the courts of the State in which the deceased had his or her habitual residence at the time of death would improve the fate of

---

77 Art. 54 Code de droit international privé (Loi n° 98–97 of 27.11.1998, JORT n° 96 of 01.12.1998, 2332) states: 'La succession est soumise à la loi interne de l'Etat dont le de cujus a la nationalité au moment du décès ou à la loi de l'Etat de son dernier domicile ou à la loi de l'Etat dans lequel il a laissé de biens. …'

78 Germany, D. Looschelders, section 5 (regarding Iranian and Turkish private international law).

79 Germany, D. Looschelders, section 5; Turkey, B. Güneş, section 6.

many families of Turkish citizens living in Germany as well as German citizens domiciled in Turkey.

4.7. GREECE

With regard to the one treaty concluded by Greece that was covered in this book,[80] the conflict-of-law rule contained in the 1927 establishment treaty with Switzerland (**Treaty 23**) is outdated. At the time the treaty was concluded, Greece still followed the *lex patriae* approach with regard to movable property, an approach that was abandoned with the coming into force of the Succession Regulation. Consequently, none of the contracting States uses nationality as a connecting factor anymore. Moreover, the rule can complicate succession cases unnecessarily because its narrow scope of application may lead to the application of different laws to different aspects of the succession. Against this background there seems to be no valid reason to cling to the outdated rule.[81] Even decisional harmony will not be an issue, given the close relation of the general connecting factors otherwise applicable under Swiss private international law (domicile of the deceased, Article 90 Swiss Private International Law Act) and European private international law (habitual residence of the deceased, Article 21(1) SR).

4.8. ITALY

The consular (and establishment) agreements Italy has concluded with Turkey (**Treaty 21**) and Switzerland (**Treaty 20**) are regarded as outdated when it comes to the private international law rules. Their rules, as the Italian rapporteur points out, are unable to handle the complexity of cross-border succession cases.[82] With regard to the Swiss-Italian Treaty, this view is shared essentially by the Swiss contribution, which suggests renegotiation of Article 17 of the Swiss-Italian Treaty to ensure a better coordination between Swiss and Italian courts and to avoid parallel proceedings.[83] With regard to the consular convention concluded with Turkey, the Turkish contribution similarly advocates amending the treaty, especially the exclusive jurisdiction rule for movable property.[84] Thus, from the perspective of private international law, the contracting States have no interests arguing for maintaining the treaty rules as they are.

---

80 See Introduction, A. Dutta and W. Wurmnest, fn. 4.

81 Switzerland, A. Bonomi, section 3 (with further arguments in favour of a repeal).

82 Italy, P. Franzina, section 3.3.

83 Switzerland, A. Bonomi, section 2.3.

84 Turkey, B. Güneş, section 6.

4.9. CONCLUSION

The rules on jurisdiction and applicable law in the various treaties are often based on traditional and – indeed – outdated concepts compared with modern concepts of European private international law. Moreover, it is difficult to argue that the shape of the rules on jurisdiction and applicable law in the treaties is essential for the EU Member States. A different picture emerges, however, if one takes the interests of the third States into consideration. Their conflict-of-law rules are often still consistent with treaty law, so that the treaty rules are still considered to be 'good law'. More importantly, the treaty law ensures decisional harmony between EU Member States and third States, which would vanish to a certain extent if the Succession Regulation governed these cases and no reforms of the third States' rules of private international law were undertaken. At the same time, some treaties deal only with selected issues of cross-border cases, making this aim of decisional harmony – which is also in the interest of the Member States that have concluded treaties with third States – difficult to achieve. In addition, the question must be raised as to the circumstances in which the interest of an EU Member State in achieving decisional harmony with third States is greater than the achievement of decisional harmony based on a European system.

Even though there are, from a theoretical private international law perspective, no compelling reasons to adhere to the treaty law as it is shaped today, Member States do have an interest in maintaining the overall treaties. This is so because the rules affecting the Succession Regulation are enshrined in very general treaties on friendship, consular relations, establishment and legal assistance.

5. POLICY PERSPECTIVES

5.1. TERMINATION OF THE TREATIES OR PARTS THEREOF

For the sake of optimally preserving unity and the integrity of EU law, all rules in the agreements with third States preceding the Succession Regulation and creating frictions with the European system should be abolished.[85] This approach would, however, completely disregard the interests of certain EU Member States and of the third States. It would also ignore the fact that these treaties ensure (at least in some cases) decisional harmony regarding cross-border succession cases with third States.

For political reasons, one can practically exclude that many EU Member States that have not terminated or amended existing treaties to date will do

85 See European Union Perspective, A. Dutta, section 1.

so in the years to come. Many of these agreements have been concluded with third States that play an important role in international relations. In addition, those rules affecting the function of the Succession Regulation are elements of treaties that deal with broader matters, such as consular relations, market access or legal assistance. This background makes it difficult to approach the contractual partner and ask for major reforms or even a termination of parts of a treaty. Some examples will underline this point. Turkey plays a major role in administrating the refugee influx for Europe. At the same time, in the aftermath of the attempted military coup, various tensions between some EU Member States and Turkey have developed. This general political environment will probably bar countries like Germany or Italy from entering into talks with Turkey to terminate or amend the existing treaty law to ease frictions with the Succession Regulation.

Iran is an important international actor with regard to various crises in the Middle East. In addition, over the last years, intense negotiations on Iran's nuclear power programme have taken place in the international arena. After the withdrawal of the United States from the previously agreed upon nuclear deal, the negotiations continue to mitigate the effect of economic sanctions imposed by the United States against Iran. Against this background, the problems discussed with Iran at the diplomatic level do not currently leave any room for a termination of the agreements concluded by Austria and Germany or for talks on their modification.

Finally, some European States are currently experiencing diplomatic disputes with the Russian Federation such that revising the treaties on consular relations or legal assistance would be difficult.

But not all treaties analyzed in this book face such political obstacles. The jurisdiction rule of the Swiss-Italian treaty of 1868 (**Treaty 20**), for example, could be repealed without creating a diplomatic crisis or making life harder for the families of former Italian emigrants. The same holds true for the conflict-of-law rule in the Greek-Swiss treaty of 1927 (**Treaty 23**). Also the conflict-of-law rule enshrined in the French-Tunisian Convention of 1957 (**Treaty 16**) could be repealed without causing political trouble if one does not follow the view that this treaty has already lapsed anyway.

Currently, however, the EU Member States have no incentive to terminate these treaties. Assisting EU efforts to make the EU Succession Regulation work better is not an aim national ministries seem eager to fulfil.

5.2. RESHAPING THE TREATY LAW

If the frictions cannot be remedied bilaterally in the short and medium term by repealing the treaty law or parts of it, one has to think of other options. One option could be to export the European rules to third States informally. To this extent, efforts must be undertaken to convince third-State scholars, institutions and legislatures that the monist approach, choice of law, choice of forum and the connecting factor of habitual residence (for determining forum and *ius*) are useful doctrines worthy of being incorporated into their national private law codes. This approach seems sensible, as one obstacle to amending the treaty law in conflict with the Succession Regulation is the fact that not many third States have similarly advanced rules of private international law as contained in the Succession Regulation. Potential changes in the treaty law would be facilitated if third States could be convinced of the merit in – at least partly – adapting their national rules on jurisdiction and applicable law to resemble the approaches taken by the Succession Regulation. Once these States have changed their national rules, their openness to discussing changes in the treaty law seems very likely, given that the treaty rules would then be in conflict with the national private international law codes of both contracting partners. And even if sweeping changes like the introduction of habitual residence as the connecting factor for the determination of applicable law in countries like Turkey, Russia or Iran, which still consider nationality as the connecting factor representing the closest connection in succession cases, are unlikely to occur in the near future, it would already help to ease frictions if third States accepted the possibility of choosing the law of the habitual residence. Even without changes in domestic private international law, incorporating provisions for the choice of law in these treaties would, for instance, grant Iranian nationals habitually residing in Germany or Austria the possibility of choosing the laws of these countries (and correspondingly allow German and Austrian nationals habitually residing in Iran to choose Iranian law).

Lobbying for changes in foreign private international law is, however, a long-term strategy. In addition, it is unclear whether any changes will occur at all in countries like Iran, Russia or Turkey, as these countries have currently few incentives to adopt the EU's approach. Chances for changes are better in the area of the 'Western Balkans'. Many EU Member States have concluded treaties affecting the Succession Regulation with those States of former Yugoslavia that have not (yet) joined the EU. These States seem more open to adapting their private international law rules consistent with the Succession Regulation, as is demonstrated by the example of Montenegro.[86] If the EU Commission convinced the respective Member States to renounce those patchwork rules in their treaty law and convinced the third States to align their private international law rules to the rules of the Succession Regulation, it would already improve the law

[86] Bosnia and Herzegovina, Serbia, North Macedonia and Montenegro, S. Đorđević and Z. Meškić, section 2.3.

compared to how it stands today.[87] Alternatively, one could think of establishing an international convention, replacing the existing treaty law, between the EU and the States of the 'Western Balkans' – even though the respective scopes of application of such a convention and the Succession Regulation might be quite difficult to determine.[88] In all cases, the interests of the third States must be taken into account. For example, the treaty binding Austria and the states of former Yugoslavia that are not EU Member States (**Treaty 3**) ensures that decisions rendered in one State can be enforced in the other contracting State. Given that under Austrian law a foreign judgment from a third State can be enforced only when reciprocity is ensured by a treaty or a regulation, countries such as Bosnia and Herzegovina, Serbia, North Macedonia and Montenegro have a strong interest in maintaining either this treaty or another instrument having a similar effect, as it ensures that judgments from these countries can be enforced in Austria.[89]

5.3. INTERPRETATION PROTOCOLS

The book has also shown that the treaties are not always interpreted in a consistent manner. Conflicts concern, *inter alia*, the scope of the treaties (e.g. whether a treaty applies to citizens holding dual or multiple nationalities). An example is the interpretation of the Turkish-Italian consular treaty (**Treaty 21**). If the deceased is, for instance, a national of France and Turkey, the Turkish rapporteur suggests that the principle of effective nationality be applied to decide whether the deceased falls under the Turkish-Italian consular treaty.[90] The Italian rapporteur, in turn, argues that this approach would not accord with international law.[91] Another issue concerns the interpretation of the jurisdiction rules. Whereas the Turkish report argues that the jurisdiction rule on movable estate (Article 21(11) Turkish-Italian Consular Treaty) is exclusive (as is the rule on immovable property),[92] the Italian report argues that one can derogate from the rule on jurisdiction over movable property by agreement or submission.[93] The 'outdated and ambiguous' wording of the treaty thus calls for clarification.[94]

---

87 This would be the optimal scenario from the EU perspective, see in general European Union Perspective, A. Dutta, section 5.

88 See European Union Perspective, A. Dutta, section 5.

89 Bosnia and Herzegovina, Serbia, North Macedonia and Montenegro, S. Đorđević and Z. Meškić, section 6.

90 Turkey, B. Güneş, section 3.2.3.

91 Italy, P. Franzina, section 2.2.5.1 (fn 66).

92 Turkey, B. Güneş, section 5.1.2.

93 Italy, P. Franzina, section 2.2.7.1.

94 Turkey, B. Güneş, section 6.

In some cases, the courts of one or both contracting States have had no chance to clarify disputed issues yet. With regard to the German-Iranian Establishment Treaty (**Treaty 17**), the prevailing view in Germany would be to not apply this instrument to cases where the deceased held a German and an Iranian passport. If, however, the deceased held an Iranian passport and a passport of a third State, a German court would probably apply the provisions of the treaty if the Iranian citizenship is the effective one, i.e. if the deceased had a closer relationship with Iran than with the third State.[95] A similar approach is advocated by scholars regarding the parallel agreement between Austria and Iran, although this issue is equally disputed, and courts have not yet had an occasion to rule on this matter.[96] In turn, the Iranian report points out that it is unclear whether courts would look at the effective nationality to determine the scope of the German-Iranian or German-Austrian Establishment Treaty.[97] Similarly, the application of the Austrian-Yugoslavian Legal Assistance Treaty (**Treaty 3**) to persons with more than one nationality is not yet settled.[98] The legal uncertainty surrounding many issues with regard to the application of the German-Turkish Treaty (**Treaty 19**) have even led a scholar to argue that this treaty should be repealed.[99]

To overcome these and other disputes and to achieve greater legal clarity, the contracting States could adopt interpretation protocols. It is submitted that the power to conclude such instruments still lies with the individual EU Member States, as such a text only clarifies what has been agreed upon by the parties prior to the enactment of the Succession Regulation. Given that such a protocol would also help to determine the reach of Article 75(1) SR, the EU Member States would be following their obligations arising under Article 351 TFEU by concluding such agreements. It goes without saying that the power to conclude interpretation protocols does not go as far as to allow a renegotiation or modernization of an entire convention or large parts thereof.[100]

---

95 Germany, D. Looschelders, section 2.2.2.3.

96 Austria, C. Rudolf, section 1.4.2 (following the interpretation of the German-Iranian Establishment Treaty voiced by the AG Hamburg-St. Georg 13.04.2015, *ZEV* 2015, 580).

97 Iran, N. Yassari, section 3.4.3 ('The actual assessment of an effective nationality by Iranian courts remains, however, largely hypothetical as no case law could be retrieved dealing with this issue.').

98 Austria, C. Rudolf, section 1.2.2 (pointing out that treaties with third States generally do not apply to citizens possessing multiple nationalities); Bosnia and Herzegovina, Serbia, North Macedonia and Montenegro, S. Đorđević and Z. Meškić, section 3.2.1 (stressing that none of the bilateral agreements concluded by (then) Yugoslavia expressly deal with individuals having multiple nationalities).

99 M. Gebauer, 'Das deutsch-türkische Nachlassabkommen im Sog des Europäischen Kollisionsrechts', [2018] *IPRax* 345, 351.

100 M. Gebauer, 'Das deutsch-türkische Nachlassabkommen im Sog des Europäischen Kollisionsrechts', [2018] *IPRax* 345, 350.

A side effect of interpretation agreements could be a lessening of the detrimental impact that the treaty law has on the Succession Regulation. This would be the case if the contracting parties interpret the treaty rules rather narrowly.

6. CONCLUSION

This book has revealed that the treaty law with third States raises complex issues to which there are no simple answers or quick solutions.

The country reports have demonstrated that the treaty law is often not interpreted consistently and that some treaties are not applied by third States. If the treaties are not abolished or amended in the near future, it is indispensable that the respective EU Member States conclude interpretation protocols to ensure a uniform interpretation of the treaty law in both contracting States. This endeavour should also help to ease frictions with the Succession Regulation.

The important political question regarding the future of this treaty law cannot be answered definitively on the basis of this book. This book has focused on selected EU Member States and selected third States. It is therefore essential to commission a comprehensive study that analyzes the treaty law of all Member States and also its application in many third States.

Based on this study, it seems clear, however, that the frictions between the treaty law and the Succession Regulation will not disappear in the near future. All EU Member States that abstained from adapting their law when the Succession Regulation was negotiated have either indicated that they want to keep the treaties as they are or have thus far not responded to calls for change. Even though the treaty law is largely outdated from the perspective of European private international law, the rules enshrined in the treaties work and do not cause harm to the people covered by them to such an extent that political intervention seems imperative. This encourages inactivity by the EU Member States. In addition, the rules are laid down in agreements addressing broader issues, such as consular relations, legal assistance or friendship and market access, meaning the Member States are – for good reasons – hesitant to induce changes since the relations with the affected third States are built upon them. This is true even more when political tensions with the contractual partner exist. But these concerns do not hold for all treaties. Some could be revised or partly amended to ease frictions with the Succession Regulation without creating a diplomatic crisis.

Against this background, the EU should not just sit and wait for the problem to disappear over time. In addition, this book has demonstrated that there is no hard and fast solution regarding the future of the treaty law. Rather, one has to look at each country and each concluded treaty to determine the best way of ending or at least easing the frictions it creates. Spreading the approach laid down in the Succession Regulation to the national private international law codes of third States that have concluded treaties with EU Member States in the area of succession law would certainly help ease frictions caused by the treaties. A partial termination or adaption of the treaty law would become more likely if both contracting parties followed similar concepts in their general private international law. Inducing such changes in foreign private international law is certainly a long-term strategy – and a strategy with an unclear outcome. For some regions, a convention between the EU and certain third States might therefore be a better strategy to improve the status quo.

ANNEX

TREATIES AND CONVENTIONS TAKING PRECEDENCE OVER THE SUCCESSION REGULATION

The members of the working group have discovered various agreements between Member States and third States that touch upon the areas harmonized by the Succession Regulation. The treaties and conventions are listed below under the name of the EU Member State that has concluded it. As many countries have concluded more than one agreement, all agreements of one country are reproduced in alphabetical order following the common name (as opposed to the official name) of the contracting state and not in chronological order, even though some country reports analyze the respective instruments in the order of their conclusion. The texts are reprinted in (one of) the language(s) of the EU Member State that concluded it and in an (unofficial) English translation. If the authentic language is a language other than the language of the EU Member State that has concluded it, the text is reproduced in the agreement's authentic language together with an English translation. Treaties concluded by third States with EU Member States that are not covered by country reports in this book ('other EU Member States') are reproduced in the language of the third State together with an (unofficial) English translation. The treaties are referred to throughout the volume by their number.

AUSTRIA

TREATY 1: AUSTRIA–PERSIAN EMPIRE

Freundschafts- und Niederlassungsvertrag zwischen der Republik Österreich und dem Kaiserreich Iran vom 9. September 1959*

Artikel 10

Die Angehörigen einer Hohen Vertragschließenden Partei genießen auf dem Gebiet der anderen Partei, was den gerichtlichen und behördlichen Schutz ihrer Person und ihres Eigentums anbelangt, die gleiche Behandlung wie die Angehörigen der meistbegünstigten Nation.

Sie haben insbesondere freien, ungehinderten Zutritt zu den Gerichten und können vor diesen unter denselben Bedingungen auftreten, wie die Angehörigen der meistbegünstigten Nation. Die Fragen, betreffend das Armenrecht und die Prozeßkostensicherstellung, sind Gegenstand einer besonderen Gegenseitigkeitserklärung, die dem vorliegenden Vertrag angeschlossen ist.

In Angelegenheiten der Eheschließung, des ehelichen Güterrechtes, der Ehescheidung und Ehetrennung, der Mitgift, der Vaterschaft, der Abstammung, der Annahme an Kindesstatt, der Rechts- und Handlungsfähigkeit, der Großjährigkeit, der Vormundschaft, der gesetzlichen und testamentarischen Erbfolge bleiben die Angehörigen einer Hohen Vertragschließenden Partei auf dem Gebiete der anderen Partei den Bestimmungen des in ihrem Heimatstaat geltenden Rechtes unterworfen.

Treaty of Friendship and Establishment between the Republic of Austria and the Persian Empire of 9 September 1959**

Article 10

The citizens of one of the High Contracting Parties enjoy on the territory of the other Party the same treatment as citizens of the most favoured nation in matters concerning the judicial and official protection of their person and property.

They especially enjoy free and unimpeded access to tribunals and can appear before a tribunal under the same conditions as citizens of the most favoured nation. Questions concerning the assistance to the poor and the caution judicatum solvi are the object of a special declaration of reciprocity attached to the present treaty.

In matters of marriage, matrimonial property regimes, divorce and legal separation, dowry, paternity, descent, adoption, legal capacity, majority, tutelage, intestate succession and testate succession the citizens of one of the High Contracting Parties remain, on the territory of the other Party, subject to their national law.

---

* Austrian BGBl No. 45/1966.

** The English translation has kindly been prepared by Claudia Rudolf and Sarah Kohlweg.

Von der Anwendung dieser Gesetze kann die andere Vertragschließende Partei nur in Ausnahmefällen und lediglich insoweit abweichen, als dies einer allgemeinen, auch allen anderen ausländischen Staaten gegenüber gepflogenen Übung entspricht. Die Tatsache, daß eine Ehe gemäß den Formvorschriften des Eheschließungsortes abgeschlossen wurde, oder daß ein Testament gemäß den Formvorschriften des Errichtungsortes verfaßt wurde, und nicht gemäß den Formvorschriften des Rechtes des Heimatstaates, berührt nicht die Gültigkeit dieser Handlungen.

The other Contracting Party can derogate from the application of this law only in exceptional cases and only to an extent which is in accordance with the general practice exercised in relation to all other foreign States. The fact that a marriage was entered into in compliance with the formal requirements of the law of the State in which it was entered into or the fact that a testamentary disposition was made in compliance with the formal requirements of the law of the State in which it was made instead of in compliance with the formal requirements of national law has no impact on the validity of those acts.

Artikel 11

Wenn ein österreichischer Staatsangehöriger im Iran oder ein iranischer Staatsangehöriger in Österreich Vermögen hinterläßt, und wenn die am Nachlaß Berechtigten unbekannt, abwesend oder nicht vertreten sind, haben die zuständigen konsularischen Vertreter das Recht, die Versiegelung oder Entsiegelung aller Einrichtungsgegenstände, Effekten und Papiere zu verlangen; sie können die Liquidation des Nachlasses selbst vornehmen oder hierzu einen Verwalter bestellen, insbesondere wenn der Nachlaß leicht verderbliche Gegenstände enthält. Die konsularische Intervention ist nicht mehr zulässig, sobald feststeht, daß Berechtigte, die die Staatsangehörigkeit des Erblassers besitzen, nicht vorhanden sind.

Keinesfalls darf jedoch dieser Artikel dahin verstanden werden, daß hiedurch den Gerichten des Staates, in dem sich die Vermögenswerte befinden, Geschäfte entzogen werden, die in ihre eigene Zuständigkeit fallen.

Article 11

If an Austrian citizen leaves property on Iranian territory, or if an Iranian citizen leaves property on Austrian territory and those entitled to the estate are unknown, absent or are not represented, the competent consuls are entitled to demand the sealing or unsealing of all furniture, securities and papers; they can undertake the liquidation of the estate and appoint an administrator for these proceedings, especially if the estate contains perishable goods. Consular intervention becomes inadmissible as soon as it is certain that no persons possessing the same nationality as the deceased are entitled to the estate.

Under no circumstances shall this article be understood in a way pursuant to which courts of the State in which the estate is located cannot exercise jurisdiction in relation to matters which fall under their own jurisdiction.

TREATY 2: AUSTRIA–USSR

Konsularvertrag zwischen der Republik Österreich und der Union der Sozialistischen Sowjetrepubliken vom 28. Februar 1959*

Artikel 19

Die Konsuln haben das Recht, in den Konsulaten oder in ihren Wohnungen wie auch auf Wunsch der Staatsangehörigen des Sendestaates in deren Wohnungen sowie an Bord der unter der Flagge des Sendestaates fahrenden Schiffe folgende Handlungen vorzunehmen:

1. von den Staatsangehörigen des Sendestaates Erklärungen entgegenzunehmen und sie zu beurkunden;
2. letztwillige Verfügungen und andere einseitige Rechtsgeschäfte sowie sonstige Erklärungen der Staatsangehörigen des Sendestaates abzufassen, zu beurkunden und diese Urkunden in Verwahrung zu nehmen;
3. Verträge, die zwischen Staatsangehörigen des Sendestaates geschlossen wurden, abzufassen oder zu beglaubigen, sofern solche Verträge den Rechtsvorschriften des Empfangsstaates nicht widersprechen. Die Konsuln dürfen jedoch keine Verträge über die Begründung, Abänderung oder Aufhebung von dinglichen Rechten an Liegenschaften, die im Empfangsstaat gelegen sind, abfassen oder beglaubigen;
4. Verträge zwischen Staatsangehörigen des Sendestaates einerseits und Staatsangehörigen des Empfangsstaates oder Staatsangehörigen dritter Staaten andererseits abzufassen oder zu beglaubigen, soweit diese Verträge sich ausschließlich auf Gegenstände oder Rechte im Gebiete des Sendestaates beziehen oder Angelegenheiten betreffen, die in die Zuständigkeit der Behörden des Sendestaates fallen, und soweit diese Verträge nicht den Rechtsvorschriften des Empfangsstaates widersprechen;
5. Unterschriften von Staatsangehörigen des Sendestaates auf Urkunden jeglicher Art zu beglaubigen;

Treaty on Consular Relations between the Republic of Austria and the Union of Soviet Socialist Republics of 28 February 1959**

Article 19

The consuls have a right to undertake the following acts in the consular offices or in their residences as well as in the residence of a citizen of the sending State or on board a ship sailing under the flag of the sending State if the citizen of the sending State so wishes:

1. receive and register declarations by citizens of the sending State;
2. draw up, register and take into safekeeping dispositions of property upon death, other unilateral acts and other declarations made by citizens of the sending State;
3. draft or authenticate contracts between citizens of the sending State, provided these contracts do not infringe the law of the receiving State. The consuls are not entitled to draft or authenticate contracts on the creation, modification or termination of rights in immovable property;
4. draft or authenticate contracts between citizens of the sending State on one side and citizens of the receiving State or a third State on the other side, provided the contracts concern goods or rights located on the territory of the sending State or concern matters falling within the competence of the authorities of the sending State. The contracts must not infringe the law of the receiving State;
5. authenticate any kind of signature of citizens of the sending State;

* Austrian BGBl No. 21/1960.

** The English translation has kindly been prepared by Claudia Rudolf and Sarah Kohlweg.

6. Urkunden von Behörden oder Amtspersonen des Sendestaates oder des Empfangsstaates zu legalisieren sowie auch Abschriften dieser Urkunden zu beglaubigen;
7. Schriftstücke jeder Art zu übersetzen und diese Übersetzungen zu beglaubigen;
8. Urkunden, Geld, Wertgegenstände und sonstige im Eigentum von Staatsangehörigen des Sendestaates stehende Sachen von diesen in Verwahrung zu nehmen;
9. andere konsularische Amtshandlungen vorzunehmen, sofern diese nicht den Rechtsvorschriften des Empfangsstaates widersprechen.

6. legalize official documents drafted by authorities or officials of the sending State or of the receiving State and authenticate copies of such documents;
7. translate any documents and authenticate these translations;
8. take into safekeeping official documents, money, valuables and other property of citizens of the sending State;
9. undertake other consular acts in accordance with the law of the receiving State.

Artikel 22

(1) Den Konsuln stehen bezüglich des Nachlasses nach einem Staatsangehörigen des Sendestaates und zum Schutze der Rechte von Erben, die Staatsangehörige des Sendestaates sind, folgende Rechte zu:

a) an der Aufnahme eines Inventars des Nachlasses teilzunehmen;
b) mit den Gerichten oder den sonst zuständigen Behörden des Empfangsstaates wegen Maßnahmen zur Erhaltung des Nachlasses sowie zur Vermeidung seiner Beschädigung und seines Verderbs oder, nötigenfalls, wegen des Verkaufes von Nachlaßsachen in Verbindung zu treten.

(2) Diese Rechte der Konsuln können auch von einem Bevollmächtigten des Konsuls ausgeübt werden.

Article 22

(1) The consuls have the following rights regarding property left by a citizen of the sending State and for the purpose of the protection of heirs who are citizens of the sending State:

a) participation in the drawing up of the inventory of the estate;
b) contacting the courts or other competent authorities about measures for the purpose of the conservation of the estate and the prevention of its damage or spoilage or, in case it is necessary, the selling of the estate.

(2) These rights can also be exercised by representatives of the consuls.

Artikel 23

(1) Hatte ein Staatsangehöriger des Sendestaates seinen letzten Wohnsitz im Empfangsstaat, so haben die Behörden dieses Staates mit Bezug auf seinen im Empfangsstaat befindlichen beweglichen Nachlaß die Rechtsvorschriften dieses Staates anzuwenden, wenn dies die gesetzlichen oder testamentarischen Erben oder Vermächtnisnehmer, die ihren Wohnsitz im Empfangsstaat oder in einem dritten Staate haben, innerhalb von sechs Monaten nach dem Tode des Erblassers beantragen.
(2) Andernfalls ist der bewegliche Nachlaß nach Maßgabe des Artikels 24 dem Konsul zu übergeben. Dieser verfährt mit dem Vermögen gemäß den Rechtsvorschriften des Sendestaates.

Article 23

(1) Upon application by the statutory or testamentary heirs or the legatees domiciled in the receiving State or a third state the authorities of the sending State shall apply the law of this State in matters concerning movable property located in the receiving State left by a citizen of the sending State. The application must be filed within six months of the death of the decedent.

(2) Otherwise, the movable property shall be handed over to the consul pursuant to Article 24. The consul then proceeds in accordance with the law of the sending State.

Artikel 24

(1) Für die Anmeldung von den Nachlaß betreffenden Ansprüchen von Erben, sofern Artikel 23 Absatz 1 nicht zur Anwendung gelangte, und von Gläubigern oder anderen interessierten Personen, die ihren Wohnsitz oder Sitz im Empfangsstaat oder in einem dritten Staate haben, gilt die im Artikel 23 Absatz 1 festgesetzte Frist.

(2) Der Teil des Nachlasses, der innerhalb von drei Monaten nach Ablauf der im Artikel 23 Absatz 1 festgesetzten Frist nicht zur Berichtigung oder Sicherstellung der angemeldeten Ansprüche verwendet worden ist oder der in keinem Zusammenhang mit den Ansprüchen steht, derentwegen ein Verfahren zu ihrer Geltendmachung eingeleitet worden ist, ist dem Konsul zu übergeben.

(3) Die Übergabe des Nachlaßvermögens nach Absatz 2 oder dessen Verbringung durch den Konsul erfolgt unter Bedachtnahme auf die devisenrechtlichen Vorschriften des Empfangsstaates.

Article 24

(1) The period of time stipulated in Article 23(1) is applicable to the registration of claims to the estate by heirs, provided Article 23(1) does not apply, and to the registration of claims by creditors or by other interested parties domiciled in the receiving State or a third State.

(2) A share of the estate which was within three months after expiry of the period provided for in Article 23(1) not used for the purposes of satisfying or safeguarding claims that were registered or is not linked to these claims is to be issued to a consul.

(3) The issuing of the estate provided for in paragraph 2 and the subsequent transfer by the consul must be in accordance with exchange restrictions imposed by the receiving State.

Artikel 26

Im Empfangsstaat gelegenes unbewegliches Vermögen eines Erblassers, der Staatsangehöriger des Sendestaates war, ist von den Gerichten oder den sonst zuständigen Behörden des Empfangsstaates nach den Rechtsvorschriften des Ortes, wo das Vermögen gelegen ist, der Nachlaßregelung zu unterziehen.

Article 26

Courts and other competent authorities of the receiving State shall apply the law of the State in which the estate is located to immovable property of a deceased who was a citizen of the sending State if the estate is located in the receiving State.

TREATY 3: AUSTRIA–YUGOSLAVIA

Vertrag zwischen der Republik Österreich und der Föderativen Volksrepublik Jugoslawien über den wechselseitigen rechtlichen Verkehr samt Schlußprotokoll vom 16. Dezember 1954*

Artikel 29

(1) Die Angehörigen des einen vertragschließenden Staates können letztwillig oder durch Schenkung auf den Todesfall über das gesamte Vermögen, das sie auf dem Gebiete des anderen vertragschließenden Staates besitzen, nach ihrem Heimatrecht oder nach dem Recht des anderen vertragschließenden Staates verfügen
(2) Die Angehörigen des einen vertragschließenden Staates können im anderen vertragschließenden Staat auf Grund der gesetzlichen Erbfolge und des Pflichtteilsrechtes, auf Grund letztwilliger Verfügungen oder durch Schenkung auf den Todesfall Vermögensrechte unter denselben Voraussetzungen und im gleichen Ausmaßerwerben wie die Angehörigen dieses Staates

Artikel 30

Die Abhandlung des unbeweglichen Nachlaßvermögens und die Entscheidung über die dieses Vermögen betreffenden streitigen Erb-, Pflichtteils-und Vermächtnisansprüche stehen ausschließlich den Gerichten des vertragschließenden Staates zu, auf dessen Gebiete dieses Nachlaßvermögen gelegen ist.

Agreement between the Republic of Austria and the Federal People's Republic of Yugoslavia on Mutual Legal Assistance Including the Final Protocol of 16 December 1954**

Article 29

(1) Citizens of one Contracting State have the right to make dispositions on all property located on the territory of the other Contracting State by declaration of a last will and by testamentary gift. These dispositions are valid if they are in compliance with their national law or the law of the other Contracting State.
(2) The citizens of one Contracting State can acquire property by statutory succession, reserved share, disposition by declaration of the last will or testamentary gift in the other Contracting State under the same preconditions and to the same extent as citizens of this Contracting State.

Article 30

The courts of the Contracting State in which the estate is located shall have jurisdiction to rule on the liquidation of immovable property and on contentious proceedings on succession, reserved shares or legacies regarding immovable property.

* Austrian BGBl No. 224/1955.

** The English translation has kindly been prepared by Claudia Rudolf and Sarah Kohlweg.

Artikel 31

(1) Die Abhandlung und die Entscheidung über streitige Erb-, Pflichtteils- und Vermächtnisansprüche hinsichtlich der beweglichen Nachlässe von Angehörigen der vertragschließenden Staaten stehen, soweit im folgenden nichts anderes bestimmt ist, den Gerichten des Heimatstaates des Erblassers zu. Die Gerichtsbarkeit des anderen vertragschließenden Staates ist jedoch in den Fällen nicht ausgeschlossen, in welchen die im Absatz 2 vorgesehene Vollstreckung nicht mehr möglich ist.

(2) Die vertragschließenden Staaten verpflichten sich, die über den Nachlaß und über streitige Erb-, Pflichtteils- und Vermächtnisansprüche von den Gerichten des Heimatstaates des Erblassers getroffenen Verfügungen und Entscheidungen, soweit sie sich auf den in ihrem Gebiete befindlichen beweglichen Nachlaß eines Angehörigen des anderen Staates beziehen, anzuerkennen und hinsichtlich dieses Nachlasses zu vollstrecken, wenn nicht

1. aus dem folgenden sich etwas anderes ergibt oder
2. ein Verstoß gegen die Grundsätze der Gesetzgebung des Staates, in dem sich der Nachlaß befindet, vorliegt.

(3) Hinsichtlich der bei Anträgen auf Vollstreckung (Absatz 2) vorzulegenden Aktenstücke sind die Bestimmungen des Artikels 3 Absatz 2 sinngemäß anzuwenden; bei Streitsachen ist jedoch eine Ausfertigung der Entscheidung samt Entscheidungsgründen vorzulegen.

(4) Zwecks Durchführung der Abhandlung im Sinne des Absatzes 1 werden die Gerichte der vertragschließenden Staaten auf Ersuchen den Heimatbehörden des Erblassers die beweglichen körperlichen Nachlaßsachen ausfolgen, soweit nicht
1. im folgenden etwas anderes bestimmt ist oder
2. Ausfuhrverbote oder devisenrechtliche Bestimmungen entgegenstehen.

Article 31

(1) The courts of the Contracting State of which the decedent was a national shall have jurisdiction to rule on the liquidation of movable property left by a citizen of one of the Contracting States and on contentious proceedings on succession, reserved shares or legacies regarding such property save as otherwise provided in the following paragraphs. Jurisdiction of the other Contracting State is not precluded in case the enforcement provided for in paragraph 2 is no longer possible.

(2) The Contracting States commit themselves to recognizing and enforcing dispositions on the estate and decisions given in contentious proceedings on succession, reserved shares or legacies by the courts of the State of which the deceased was a national to the extent to which they concern the movable property of a citizen of the other State located on their territory, save as

1. otherwise provided in the subsequent paragraphs or
2. this violates the legal principles of the State in which the estate is located.

(3) The provisions of Article 3(2) are applicable mutatis mutandis to documents necessary for an application for enforcement (paragraph 2); contentious proceedings nevertheless require the submission of the decision including the grounds for the decision.

(4) Upon application the courts of the Contracting States will issue movable corporeal property to the authorities of the State of which the deceased was a national for the purpose of the liquidation within the meaning of paragraph 1, save as
1. otherwise provided in the subsequent paragraphs
2. the transfer is prohibited by a ban on exports or by exchange restrictions.

Artikel 34

(1) Auf Antrag von Erben, Pflichtteilsberechtigten oder Vermächtnisnehmern, die Angehörige des vertragschließenden Staates sind, in dem sich Nachlaßvermögen befindet, oder die sich auf dessen Gebiet aufhalten, ist das Gericht berechtigt, das ganze Nachlaßvermögen oder einen hinreichenden Teil hievon zurückzubehalten, bis über den Erb-, Pflichtteils- oder Vermächtnisanspruch von dem zuständigen Gerichte des Heimatstaates des Erblassers rechtskräftig entschieden ist.

(2) Die gleichen Verfügungen kann das Gericht auf Antrag von Gläubigern treffen, die Angehörige des vertragschließenden Staates sind, auf dessen Gebiete sich Nachlaßvermögen befindet, oder die sich auf dessen Gebiet aufhalten, sofern ihre Ansprüche angemeldet und nötigenfalls geltend gemacht werden.

Article 34

(1) The court can, upon application by heirs, persons entitled to a reserved share or legatees who possess the nationality of the State in which the estate is located or reside in that State, retain the whole or at least a sufficient share of the estate until such time as the competent court of the State of which the deceased was a national has given a final decision on succession, reserved shares or legacies.

(2) The court can make those same dispositions upon application by creditors possessing the nationality of the Contracting State in which the estate is located or residing in that State provided their claims have been registered and, if necessary, filed.

Artikel 35

(1) Zur Stellung der im Artikel 34 angeführten Anträge ist mittels Edikt eine Frist von drei bis sechs Monaten festzusetzen, während welcher die Ansprüche der oben erwähnten Personen angemeldet und nötigenfalls geltend gemacht werden müssen. Wurden sie innerhalb dieser Frist nicht angemeldet oder geltend gemacht, so kann die Ausfolgung des beweglichen Nachlaßvermögens nicht mit Berufung auf die Bestimmungen des Artikels 34 verweigert werden.

(2) Eine Ausfertigung des Ediktes ist der Konsularbehörde des Heimatstaates des Verstorbenen zu übersenden.

Article 35

(1) A period of three to six months shall be stipulated in an edict within which the applications mentioned in Article 34 must be filed. Within this period claims must be registered or filed by the persons mentioned above. Where they are not registered within this period, the issuing of the estate cannot be refused by invoking Article 34.

(2) A copy of the edict shall be issued to the consular office of the State of which the deceased was a national.

Artikel 36

(1) Wenn der Erblasser, der Angehöriger des einen vertragschließenden Staates war, seinen letzten Wohnsitz im Gebiete des anderen vertragschließenden Staates gehabt hat, können Erben oder Pflichtteilsberechtigte, die im Gebiete dieses Staates wohnen, innerhalb der gemäß Artikel 35 Absatz 1 festgesetzten Frist die Abhandlung des dort befindlichen beweglichen Nachlasses durch die Gerichte dieses Staates beantragen. Dem Antrag ist Folge zu geben, wenn weder ein Erbe noch ein Pflichtteilsberechtigter oder ein Vermächtnisnehmer innerhalb einer vom Gericht mit einem bis drei Monaten festzusetzenden Frist nach gehöriger Verständigung dagegen Einspruch erhebt. In einem solchen Falle sind die Gerichte dieses Staates auch zur Entscheidung über streitige Erb-, Pflichtteils- und Vermächtnisansprüche zuständig.

(2) Ist gemäß Absatz 1 der bewegliche Nachlaß von den Gerichten des Staates abzuhandeln, in dem er sich befindet, so sind die erbrechtlichen Bestimmungen des Heimatstaates des Erblassers sowohl bei der Abhandlung als auch bei der Entscheidung über streitige Erb-, Pflichtteils- und Vermächtnisansprüche anzuwenden.

Article 36

(1) Heirs or persons entitled to a reserved share residing on the territory of one of the Contracting States can request, within the period stipulated in Article 35, the liquidation of movable property located in this State by the courts of this State if the deceased was last domiciled in this State but was a citizen of the other Contracting State. This application shall be granted if neither an heir nor a person entitled to a reserved share nor a legatee enters an objection within a period of one to three months set by the court after being notified of the request. In this case the courts of this State shall have jurisdiction to rule on contentious claims concerning succession, reserved shares and legacies.

(2) If, in accordance with paragraph 1, movable property falls under the jurisdiction of the State in which it is located, the succession law of the State of which the deceased was a national is applicable to the liquidation of the estate and to contentious proceedings on succession, on reserved shares and on legacies.

Artikel 38

In streitigen und nichtstreitigen Nachlaßangelegenheiten, die im Gebiet eines der vertragschließenden Staaten durchgeführt werden, ist die Konsularbehörde des anderen Staates berechtigt, ihre Staatsangehörigen zu vertreten, sofern sie abwesend sind und keinen anderen Bevollmächtigten ernannt haben; innerstaatliche Bestimmungen über den Anwaltszwang bleiben unberührt.

Article 38

The consular office of a Contracting State is entitled to represent their citizens in contentious and non-contentious proceedings held on the territory of the other Contracting State in case they are absent and have failed to appoint other representatives; this Treaty shall not affect domestic law regarding the obligation to be represented by a lawyer.

Artikel 39

Was als bewegliches Vermögen anzusehen ist, richtet sich nach den Vorschriften des Staates, in dem sich dieses Vermögen befindet

Article 39

The law of the State in which the goods are located shall determine whether or not the goods constitute movable property.

CROATIA

TREATY 4: CROATIA–USSR

Ugovor između Federativne Narodne Republike Jugoslavije i Saveza Sovjetskih Socijalističkih Republika o pravnoj pomoći u građanskim, porodičnim i krivičnim stvarima od 24. februara 1962*

3. Zaostavštine

Član 36

Načelo jednakosti

1. Državljani jedne Strane ugovornice mogu sticati dobra i prava na teritoriji druge Strane ugovornice na osnovu zakonskog ili testamentalnog nasleđivanja pod istim uslovima i u istom obimu kao i domaći državljani
2. Državljani jedne Strane ugovornice mogu testamentom raspolagati svojom imovinom koja se nalazi na teritoriji druge Strane ugovornice.

Član 37

Primena naslednog zakona

1. Pravo nasleđa pokretne imovine reguliše se po zakonu one Strane ugovornice čiji je državljanin bio ostavilac u vreme smrti.

2. Pravo nasleđa nepokretne imovine reguliše se po zakonu one Strane ugovornice na čijoj teritoriji se imovina nalazi.

Treaty between the Federal People's Republic of Yugoslavia and the Union of Soviet Socialist Republics on Legal Assistance in Civil, Family and Criminal Matters of 24 February 1962**

3. Succession

Article 36

Principle of equal treatment

1. Nationals of one Contracting Party can acquire goods and rights on the territory of the other Contracting Party *ex lege* or on the ground of testamentary succession, under the same conditions and scope as domestic nationals.
2. Nationals of one Contracting Party can dispose by testament of their property which is situated on the territory of the other Contracting Party.

Article 37

Applicable law

1. The succession to movable property shall be governed by the law of the Contracting Party whose nationality the deceased possessed at the time of death.
2. Succession to immovable property shall be governed by the law of the Contracting Party on whose territory the property is located.

---

* Službeni list Socijalističke Federativne Republike Jugoslavije – Dodatak: Međunarodni ugovori i drugi sporazumi, br. 5/63.

** The English translation has kindly been prepared by Davor Babić and Tena Hoško. The translators are thankful to their research assistants Barbara Bolonja and Petar Kovačević for helping to prepare the translation.

Član 38

Forma testamenta

Forma testamenta i opozivanja istog određuje se po zakonu Strane ugovornice čiji je državljanin bio zaveštalac u vreme sastavljanja i opozivanja testamenta ili po zakonu Strane ugovornice na čijoj je teritoriji testament sastavljen odnosno opozvan.

Član 39

Nadležnost u ostavinskim stvarima

1. Za raspravljanje pokretne zaostavštine, osim u slučaju predviđenim u stavu 4. ovog člana, nadležan je organ one Strane ugovornice čiji je državljanin bio ostavilac u vreme smrti.

2. Za raspravljanje nepokretne zaostavštine nadležan je organ Strane ugovornice na čijoj se teritoriji nalazi nepokretna imovina.

3. Odredbe st. 1. i 2. ovog člana važe i za raspravljanje nasledno-pravnih sporova.

4. Ako je ostavilac, koji je bio državljanin jedne Strane ugovornice, imao poslednje prebivalište na teritoriji druge Strane ugovornice, mogu naslednici koji imaju prebivalište odnosno boravište na teritoriji te druge Strane ugovornice, zahtevati, u roku od šest meseci od smrti ostavioca, da nadležan organ te Strane ugovornice sprovede raspravu pokretne zaostavštine koja se nalazi na njezinoj teritoriji. O ovom zahtevu obavestiće se naslednici i legatari. Ako u roku od tri mjeseca od obaveštenja nijedan od naslednika ne prigovori, udovoljiće se tom zahtevu. U tom slučaju primjenjuje se zakon Strane ugovornice čiji je državljanin bio ostavilac u vreme smrti.

Član 40

Ako državljanin jedne Strane ugovornice umre za vreme putovanja na teritoriji druge Strane ugovornice, gde nije imao mesto prebivanja ili boravka, onda se stvari koje je nosio sa sobom predaju po spisku, bez ikakvih formalnosti, diplomatskom ili konzularnom predstavništvu Strane ugovornice čiji je on državljanin bio.

Article 38

The form of a will

The form and revocation of a will shall be governed by the law of the Contracting Party whose national was the testator at the time of death or revocation, or by the law of the Contracting Party on whose territory the will was made or revoked.

Article 39

Jurisdiction in succession matters

1. For proceedings relating to the succession to movable property, authorities of the Contracting Party whose nationality the deceased possessed at the time of death shall have jurisdiction, except in cases defined by paragraph 4 of this Article.

2. For proceedings relating to the succession to immovable property, the authorities of the Contracting Party on whose territory the assets are located shall have jurisdiction.

3. The rules contained in paragraphs 1 and 2 of this Article shall also be applied to succession disputes.

4. If the deceased, who was a national of one of the Contracting Parties, had his last domicile on the territory of the other Contracting Party, heirs who have their domicile or residence on the territory of the latter Contracting Party may request, within six months of the death of the deceased, that the competent authorities of that Contracting Party conduct a succession proceeding for movable property which is located on its territory. The heirs and legatees shall be informed about the request. If no objection is raised by the heirs within three months of notice, the request shall be carried out. In this case the law of the Contracting Party whose nationality the deceased possessed at the time of death shall be applied.

Article 40

If a national of one Contracting Party dies when travelling on the territory of the other Contracting Party, where he had no domicile or residence, property which he had on his person shall be listed and handed over without any formalities to the diplomatic or consular representative of the Contracting Party whose national he was.

Član 41

Izveštavanje o smrti

1. Ako na teritoriji jedne Strane ugovornice umre državljanin druge Strane ugovornice, nadležan organ će o tome odmah obavestiti diplomatsko ili konzularno predstavništvo te Strane ugovornice i saopštiti sve što mu je poznato o naslednicima, o njihovom prebivalištu ili boravištu, o sastavu i vrednosti zaostavštine kao i da li postoji testament. Ovako će se postupiti i u slučaju kad nadležan organ jedne Strane ugovornice sazna da je državljanin druge Strane ugovornice, koji je umro van teritorije obeju Strana ugovornica, ostavio imovinu na teritoriji njegove države.

2. Ako diplomatsko ili konzularno predstavništvo ranije sazna za smrt svoga državljanina dužno je da o tome izvesti nadležan organ druge Strane ugovornice radi preduzimanja mera za očuvanje zaostavštine.

3. Ako organ jedne Strane ugovornice u postupku za raspravljanje zaostavštine sazna da je za nasleđe zainteresovan državljanin druge Strane ugovornice, obavestiće o tome diplomatsko ili konzularno predstavništvo te Strane ugovornice.

Article 41

Notice of death

1. If a national of one Contracting Party dies on the territory of the other Contracting Party, the competent authorities of the latter shall immediately notify the diplomatic or consular representative of the former of the death of its national and inform it about heirs, their domicile or residence, about the composition of the estate and its value, and whether there was a will. The same proceeding shall take place when the competent authorities of one Contracting Party acquire knowledge that a national of the other Contracting Party, which died outside of the territory of both Contracting Parties, has left property on the territory of the other Contracting Party.

2. If the diplomatic or consular representative has previously acquired knowledge of the death of its national, it is under the obligation to inform the competent authorities of the other Contracting Party in order to take measures for preservation of the estate.

3. If the authorities of one Contracting Party, during the succession proceeding, acquire knowledge that a national of the other Contracting Party has an interest in the succession, they shall inform the diplomatic or consular representative of that Contracting Party.

Član 42

Mere za očuvanje zaostavštine

1. Organi Strana ugovornica izvršiće popis i preduzeti, u skladu sa svojim zakonom, druge neophodne mere za očuvanje i upravljanje zaostavštine, koju je na njihovoj teritoriji ostavio državljanin druge Strane ugovornice.

2. O merama koje se preduzimaju po stavu 1. ovog člana obavestiće se odmah diplomatsko ili konzularno predstavništvo druge Strane ugovornice, koje može da učestvuje u sprovođenju ovih mera. Na predlog diplomatskog ili konzularnog predstavništva, ove mere mogu se izmeniti, ukinuti ili odložiti.

3. Na zahtev diplomatskog ili konzularnog predstavništva predaće se istom pokretna zaostavština i lične i druge isprave umrlog.

Article 42

Measures for preservation of the estate

1. The authorities of the Contracting Parties shall make an inventory of the estate and, in accordance with the domestic law, take other measures necessary for the preservation and administration of the estate that was left on their territory by a national of the other Contracting Party.

2. The diplomatic or consular representative of the other Contracting Party shall be informed immediately about measures taken under paragraph 1 of this Article and can take part in their performance. Upon proposal of the diplomatic or consular representative, these measures can be modified, revoked or prolonged.

3. At the request of the diplomatic or consular representative, the movable property and personal or other documents of the deceased shall be handed over to that representative.

Član 43

Proglašenje testamenta

1. Otvaranje i proglašenje testamenta spada u nadležnost organa Strane ugovornice na čijoj se teritoriji testament nalazi.
2. Ako je organ jedne Strane ugovornice proglasio testament državljanina druge Strane ugovornice, overen prijepis testamenta, zajedno sa podacima o stanju testamenta, a po potrebi i originalni testament, dostaviće se nadležnom organu Strane ugovornice čiji je državljanin bio zaveštalac. Ovako će se postupiti i u slučaju ako je za raspravljanje zaostavštine nadležan i organ druge Strane ugovornice.

Article 43

Opening of a will

1. Authorities of the Contracting Party on whose territory a will is located have jurisdiction for opening and reading of a will.
2. If the authorities of one Contracting Party have opened and read a will of a national of the other Contracting Party, a certified copy of the will, together with information on the state of the will, and, where applicable, the original will, shall be submitted to the competent authorities of the Contracting Party whose nationality the testator possessed. The same shall be done in cases where the authorities of the other Contracting Party are also competent for a succession proceeding.

Član 44

Ovlašćenja diplomatsko-konzularnog predstavništva u ostavinskom postupku

U svim naslednim predmetima po kojima se raspravlja na teritoriji jedne Strane ugovornice, diplomatsko ili konzularno predstavništvo druge Strane ugovornice ima pravo da zastupa svoje državljane pred nadležnim organima bez posebnog punomoćja, ako su oni odsutni i ako nisu ovlastili druge lice da ih zastupa.

Article 44

Power of the diplomatic and consular representative in a succession proceeding

In all succession proceedings which are conducted on the territory of one Contracting Party, the diplomatic or consular representative of the other Contracting Party has the right, without any special authorization, to represent its nationals before the competent authorities if these nationals are absent and where they did not already authorize another person to represent them.

Član 45

Predaja nasledstva

Ako po okončanju ostavinskog postupka treba predati pokretne stvari nasledniku državljaninu druge Strane ugovornice, koji ima prebivalište odnosno boravište na teritoriju te Strane ugovornice ova imovina predaće se diplomatskom ili konzularnom predstavništvu Strane ugovornice čiji je državljanin naslednik pod uslovom da je:

a) nadležan organ pozvao, ukoliko je to predviđeno propisima Strane ugovornice na čijoj se teritoriji nalazi imovina, poverioce zaostavštine da prijave svoja potraživanja;

b) plaćena nasledna taksa odnosno da su namirena ili obezbeđena prijavljena potraživanja;
c) nadležan organ suglasan sa iznošenjem stvari.

Article 45

Transfer of the estate

Where after the closing of a succession proceeding movable property needs to be transferred to the heir, who is a national of the other Contracting Party and has his domicile or residence on the territory of that Contracting Party, that property shall be transferred to the diplomatic or consular representative of the Contracting Party whose national the heir is, provided that:

a) the competent authorities have invited creditors to lodge their claims, if such a proceeding is provided by the law of the Contracting Party on whose territory the property is located;
b) the succession tax is paid, and the lodged claims are settled or secured;

c) the competent authorities have approved the transfer of the property.

Član 46

Zaostavština bez naslednika

Pokretna imovina bez naslednika predaje se Strani ugovornici čiji je državljanin bio ostavilac u vreme smrti, a nepokretna imovina pripada Strani ugovornici na čijoj se teritoriji imovina nalazi.

5. Priznanje i izvršenje sudskih odluka

Član 48

1. Strane ugovornice priznaće i izvršiće na svojoj teritoriji, pod uslovom predviđenim ovim ugovorom, sljedeće sudske odluke donete na teritoriji druge Strane ugovornice:

a) pravosnažne i izvršne odluke u građanskim i porodičnim stvarima;
b) poravnanja zaključena pred sudom u građanskim stvarima;
c) pravosnažne i izvršne odluke u krivičnim stvarima u delu koji se odnosi na naknadu štete pričinjene krivičnim delom.

2. Odredba tač. a) i b) stava 1. ovog člana primenjuju se i na odluke o nasleđivanju ako su donete od strane notarijalnih organa Strana ugovornica.
3. Sudske odluke jedne Strane ugovornice navedene u tač. a) i b) stava 1. ovog člana priznaće se i izvršiće se na teritoriji druge Strane ugovornice samo ako je pravni odnos po kome je doneta sudska odluka, nastao posle stupanja na snagu ovog ugovora.

4. Odluke navedene u tač. c) stava 1. ovog člana priznaće se i izvršiti samo ako su postale pravosnažne i izvršne posle stupanja na snagu ovog ugovora.
5. Odredba stava 3. ovog člana ne odnosi se na sudske odluke o razvodu ili nevažnosti braka, o proglašenju nestalim ili umrlim, o utvrđivanju činjenice smrti i o poslovnoj sposobnosti.

Article 46

Estates without a claimant

Movable property without a claimant shall be transferred to the Contracting Party whose nationality the deceased possessed at the time of death, and immovable property shall belong to the Contracting Party on whose territory the assets are located.

5. Recognition and enforcement of judgments

Article 48

1. The Contracting Parties will recognize and enforce on their territory, under the conditions set out in this Treaty, the following judgments rendered on the territory of the other Contracting Party:

a) final and enforceable judgments in civil and family matters;
b) court settlements in civil matters;

c) final and enforceable judgments in criminal matters in part related to compensation for damage caused by a criminal act.

2. Provisions of points a) and b), paragraph 1 of this Article, are also applied to succession decisions if given by notaries of the Contracting Parties.
3. Judgments of one Contracting Party listed in points a) and b) of paragraph 1 of this Article will be recognized and enforced on the territory of the other Contracting party only if the legal relationship on which the judgment is based on came into existence after this Treaty came into force.
4. Judgments listed in point c) of paragraph 1 of this Article will be recognized and enforced only if they became final and enforceable after this Treaty came into force.
5. Paragraph 3 of this Article is not applicable to judgments on divorce or the invalidity of marriage, on declaration of death or declaration of death in absentia, or on determining the fact of death or legal capacity.

Član 49

Sudske odluke navedene u članu 48. ovog ugovora priznaće se i izvršiće se:

a) ako je potvrđena pravosnažnost i izvršnost odluke;
b) ako je po propisima Strane ugovornice na čijoj se teritoriji zahteva priznanje ili izvršenje sud na čijoj je teritoriji odluka doneta mogao da postupa u toj stvari;
c) ako se priznanje ili izvršenje sudske odluke ne protivi osnovnim načelima zakonodavstva one Strane ugovornice na čijoj teritoriji odluka treba da se prizna ili izvrši;

d) ako stranka protivu koje je doneta odluka nije bila lišena mogućnosti odbrane svojih prava, odnosno ako je u slučaju parnične nesposobnosti bila pravilno zastupana;

e) ako po istoj stvari i između istih stranaka ne postoji pravosnažna odluka koju je ranije doneo sud Strane ugovornice na čijoj se teritoriji zahteva priznanje ili izvršenje ili ako kod suda te Strane ugovornice nije ranije pokrenut postupak u toj stvari;

f) ako je, u slučaju kada je trebalo primeniti zakon Strane ugovornice na čijoj se teritoriji traži priznanje ili izvršenje, primenjen zakon te Strane ugovornice ili zakon koji se u suštini ne razlikuje od zakona Strane ugovornice na čijoj se teritoriji traži priznanje ili izvršenje.

Article 49

Judgments listed in Article 48 will be recognized and enforced:

a) if the judgment's finality and enforceability is certified;
b) if pursuant to the law of the Contracting Party on whose territory recognition or enforcement is sought, the court of origin had jurisdiction in that matter;
c) if recognition or enforcement of the judgment is not contrary to the fundamental principles of the law of the Contracting Party on whose territory it should be recognized or enforced;
d) if the party against whom the decision was brought was not deprived of the possibility to defend himself, or in cases of procedural incapacity the party was appropriately represented;
e) if in the same matter and between the same parties there is no final judgment previously brought by a court of the Contracting Party on whose territory recognition or enforcement is sought or if the proceeding in such a matter was not previously initiated before a court of that Contracting Party;
f) if, in cases where the law of the Contracting Party on whose territory recognition or enforcement is sought was to be applied, the law of that Contracting Party was applied or a law which is essentially not different from the law of the Contracting Party on whose territory recognition or enforcement is sought.

Član 51

1. Sud Strane ugovornice na čijoj teritoriji treba priznati ili izvršiti odluku suda druge Strane ugovornice priznaće odnosno dozvoliće prinudno izvršenje te odluke, ako postoje uslovi predviđeni ovim ugovorom.

2. Zahtev za priznanje ili izvršenje podnosi se sudu koji je u toj stvari doneo odluku u prvom stepenu. Ovaj sud će zahtev dostaviti nadležnom sudu druge Strane ugovornice na način predviđen u članu 3. ovog ugovora.

Article 51

1. The court of the Contracting Party on whose territory a decision of the court of the other Contracting Party is to be recognized or enforced will recognize or allow enforcement of that decision under conditions provided by this Treaty.
2. Request for recognition or enforcement shall be submitted to the court which handed down the judgment in that matter in the first instance. This court will deliver the request to the competent court of the other Contracting Party in a way foreseen in Article 3 of this Treaty.

3. Ako lice koje traži prinudno izvršenje ima prebivalište ili boravište na teritoriji Strane ugovornice u kojoj treba sprovesti izvršenje, zahtev za priznanje ili izvršenje može se podneti i neposredno nadležnom sudu te Strane ugovornice.

4. Uz zahtev za priznanje ili izvršenje treba priložiti i overen prevod istog.

3. If the person requesting enforcement has his domicile or residence on the territory of the other Contracting Party where the enforcement is to be performed, the request for recognition or enforcement can be submitted directly to the competent court of that Contracting Party.

4. With the request for recognition or enforcement an authenticated translation also needs to be submitted.

Član 52

Uz zahtev za priznanje ili izvršenje mora se priložiti:

a) prepis sudske odluke i službena potvrda o njenoj pravosnažnosti i izvršnosti, ako to ne proizlazi iz same odluke;
b) potvrda da je stranka, koja nije učestvovala u postupku i protiv koje je doneta odluka, bila svojevremeno, saglasno propisima Strane ugovornice na čijoj je teritoriji odluka doneta, pozvana da učestvuje u postupku;

c) overen prevod isprava navedenih u tač. a) i b) ovog člana.

Article 52

Alongside the the request for recognition or enforcement, the following has to be submitted:

a) a transcript of the judgment and an official certificate of its finality and enforceability, if that is not derived from the judgment itself;
b) a certificate that a party who did not take part in the proceeding and against whom the judgment was brought was previously, pursuant to the laws of the Contracting Party on whose territory the judgment was rendered, invited to participate in the proceeding;
c) an authenticated translation of documents listed in points a) and b) of this Article.

Član 53

1. Sud Strane ugovornice na čijoj teritoriji odluka treba da se prizna ili izvrši rešava o dozvoli i preduzima mere za izvršenje po sopstvenim propisima.

2. Sud može zatražiti od lica koje je podnelo zahtev da otkloni nedostatke ili da pruži objašnjenje u vezi sa zahtevom. Isto tako, sud može zatražiti i objašnjenje od suda koji je doneo odluku.

Article 53

1. The court of the Contracting Party on whose territory the judgment is to be recognized or enforced decides on the permissibility of this request and takes measures for enforcement under its own law.

2. The court can invite the person who submitted the request to remedy shortcomings or to explain the request. Equally, a court can ask for an explanation from the court which rendered the judgment.

CZECH REPUBLIC

TREATY 5: CZECHOSLOVAKIA-ALBANIA

Smlouva mezi Československou republikou a Albánskou lidovou republikou o právní pomoci ve věcech občanských, rodinných a trestních ze dne 16. ledna 1959*

Oddíl IV

Dědictví

Článek 31

Zásada rovného postavení

Občané jedné smluvní strany jsou co do způsobilosti zřídit nebo zrušit závěť o majetku, který je na území druhé smluvní strany, nebo o právech, která se tam mají uplatnit, jakož i co do způsobilosti nabývat dědictvím nebo odkazem takového majetku nebo takových práv postaveni na roveň občanům druhé smluvní strany. Majetek a práva přecházejí na ně za podmínek stanovených pro vlastní občany žijící na území této smluvní strany.

Článek 32

Dědické právo

1. Dědění movitostí se spravuje právním řádem té smluvní strany, jejímž občanem byl zůstavitel v době smrti.

2. Dědění nemovitostí se spravuje právním řádem té smluvní strany, na jejímž území nemovitosti jsou.

Treaty between the Czechoslovak Republic and the People's Republic of Albania on Legal Assistance in Civil, Family and Criminal Matters of 16 January 1959**

Part IV

Succession upon death

Article 31

Principle of equal treatment

Nationals of one Contracting Party enjoy equal capacity to make or revoke a will with respect to their property located on the territory of the other Contracting Party or with respect to rights to be exercised therein, as well as equal capacity to acquire such assets by succession or legacy as nationals of the other Contracting Party. Assets and rights are transferred to them under the same conditions as to nationals living in the territory of this Contracting Party.

Article 32

Law applicable to succession upon death

1. The succession to movable property shall be governed by the law of the Contracting Party of which the deceased was a national at the time of death.
2. The succession to immovable property shall be governed by the law of the Contracting Party in whose territory the immovable property is located.

* Vyhláška ministra zahraničních věcí č. 97/1960 Sb.

** The English translation has kindly been prepared by Magdalena Pfeiffer.

Článek 33

Závěť

1. Způsobilost zřídit nebo zrušit závěť, jakož i právní účinky vad vůle spravují se právním řádem smluvní strany, jejímž občanem byl zůstavitel v době zřízení nebo zrušení závěti. Tento právní řád je také rozhodný pro určení, které druhy pořízení pro případ smrti jsou přípustné.

2. Forma zřízení a zrušení závěti se spravuje právním řádem smluvní strany, jejímž občanem byl zůstavitel v době zřízení nebo zrušení závěti; stačí však, byl-li zachován právní řád smluvní strany, na jejímž území byly tyto úkony učiněny.

Article 33

Will

1. The capacity to make or revoke a will, as well as the legal consequences for the absence of intent to testate, shall be governed by the law of the Contracting Party of which the deceased was a national at the time of making or revoking the will. This law shall also apply to the admissibility of dispositions of property upon death.

2. The form of making and revoking a will shall be governed by the law of the Contracting Party, of which the deceased was a national at the time of making or revoking the will; it shall however be sufficient for the formal validity if the will complies with the law of the Contracting Party in whose territory the will was made or revoked.

Článek 34

Pravomoc

1. Movité dědictví projednají bez újmy ustanovení odstavce 4 tohoto článku justiční úřady smluvní strany, jejímž občanem byl zůstavitel v době smrti.

2. Nemovité dědictví projednají justiční úřady smluvní strany, na jejímž území je dědictví.

3. Ustanovení odstavců 1 a 2 tohoto článku platí obdobně i o sporech, které vzniknou z dědických nároků.

4. Je-li celé movité dědictví po občanu jedné ze smluvních stran na území druhé smluvní strany a souhlasí-li s tím všichni dědici, projedná je na návrh dědice nebo odkazovníka justiční úřad této smluvní strany.

Article 34

Jurisdiction

1. Subject to the exception referred to in paragraph 4 of this Article, the judicial authorities of the Contracting Party of which the deceased was a national at the time of death shall have jurisdiction to rule on the succession to movable property.

2. The judicial authorities of the Contracting Party in whose territory immovable property is located shall have jurisdiction to rule on succession to this immovable property.

3. Paragraphs 1 and 2 of this Article shall also apply in contentious proceedings regarding succession claims.

4. Provided that all movables of the deceased national of one Contracting Party are located in the territory of the other Contracting Party and provided that all heirs agree, the judicial authority of this Contracting Party shall, upon request of an heir or a legatee, have jurisdiction to rule on the succession to these movables.

Článek 35

Sdělování úmrtí

1. Zemře-li na území jedné smluvní strany občan druhé smluvní strany, uvědomí příslušný úřad bez odkladu diplomatický nebo konzulární úřad druhé smluvní strany o úmrtí a sdělí mu vše, co je známo o dědicích a odkazovnících a o jejich bydlišti nebo pobytu, o rozsahu a ceně dědictví, jakož i o tom, zda tu je závěť. Totéž platí, doví-li se příslušný úřad jedné ze smluvních stran o tom, že občan druhé smluvní strany, který zemřel mimo území obou smluvních stran, zanechal jmění na území jeho státu.

2. Doví-li se diplomatický nebo konzulární úřad o úmrtí dříve, je povinen o něm zpravit justiční úřad příslušný k zajištění dědictví.

Článek 36

Oprávnění diplomatického nebo konzulárního úřadu při projednávání dědictví

1. Ve všech dědických věcech, které se vyskytnou na území jedné ze smluvních stran, jsou členové diplomatického nebo konzulárního úřadu druhé smluvní strany oprávněni zastupovat před justičními nebo jinými úřady vlastní občany, pokud jsou nepřítomni a neustanoví-li si jiného zmocněnce; zvláštní plné moci není třeba.

2. Zemře-li občan jedné smluvní strany cestou územím druhé smluvní strany a neměl-li tam bydliště ani pobyt, budou věci, které měl u sebe pro vlastní potřebu, odevzdány bez dalšího řízení diplomatickému nebo konzulárnímu úřadu smluvní strany, jejímž byl občanem.

Article 35

Notice of death

1. If a national of one Contracting Party dies in the territory of the other Contracting Party, the competent authority shall, without delay, notify the diplomatic or consular office of the other Contracting Party about the death and communicate any available information about the heirs or the legatees, their domicile or residence, the extent and value of the estate as well as information on any wills. The same applies if the competent authority of one Contracting Party learns that a national of the other Contracting Party, who died outside of the territory of both Contracting Parties, had assets in its territory.

2. If a diplomatic or consular office learns about a case of death before the competent authority does, it shall be reported to the judicial authority competent to preserve the inheritance.

Article 36

Powers of a diplomatic or consular office in succession matters

1. Members of a diplomatic or consular office of one Contracting Party shall be entitled to represent their own nationals before judicial or other authorities of the other Contracting Party in all succession matters provided that the represented nationals are absent and had not issued any power of attorney to any person or agent; a special power of attorney is not required.

2. If a national of one Contracting Party dies when travelling in the territory of the other Contracting Party, in whose territory he had neither domicile nor residence, his personal possessions shall be handed over to the diplomatic or consular office of the Contracting Party of which the deceased was a national without further proceedings.

Článek 37

Otevření a vyhlášení závěti

K otevření a vyhlášení závěti je příslušný justiční úřad smluvní strany, na jejímž území je závěť. Ověřený opis závěti a protokolu o stavu a obsahu závěti, podle okolností ověřený opis protokolu o otevření a vyhlášení závěti a na žádost i prvopis závěti je třeba zaslat justičnímu úřadu státu zůstavitele nebo justičnímu úřadu druhé smluvní strany, který ve věci koná řízení.

Article 37

Opening of the will

The opening of the will falls within the competence of the authority of the Contracting Party in whose territory the will is located. A duly certified copy of the will and of the minutes on its condition and content, and if necessary a duly certified copy of the minutes on its opening, and upon request the original must be sent to the judicial authority of the State of which the deceased was a national or to the judicial authority of the other Contracting Party that initiated succession proceedings.

Článek 38

Opatření k zajištění dědictví

1. Úřady obou smluvních stran učiní podle svého právního řádu opatření, která jsou nutná k zajištění nebo ke správě dědictví, které na jejich území zanechal občan druhé smluvní strany.

2. O opatřeních, která byla učiněna podle odstavce 1 tohoto článku, je třeba bez odkladu uvědomit diplomatický nebo konzulární úřad druhé smluvní strany, který může při těchto opatřeních spolupůsobit. Na návrh diplomatického nebo konzulárního úřadu mohou být opatření učiněná podle odstavce 1 změněna, zrušena nebo odložena.

3. Úřad smluvní strany, jejímž občanem je zůstavitel a který je příslušný podle článku 34 odstavec 1, může navrhnout, aby byla zrušena opatření učiněná podle odstavce 1.

Article 38

Measures to preserve the estate

1. The authorities of both Contracting Parties shall take all measures necessary pursuant to their own law to preserve and administer the property of the deceased national of the other Contracting Party that is located in their territory.

2. The measures taken pursuant to paragraph 1 of this Article shall be notified to the diplomatic or consular office of the other Contracting Party, which can take part in performing those measures, without delay. The measures taken pursuant to paragraph 1 may be modified, revoked or postponed at the request of the diplomatic or consular office.

3. The measures taken pursuant to paragraph 1 may be revoked at the request of the authority of the Contracting Party of which the deceased was a national and that has jurisdiction in matters of succession pursuant to Article 34 paragraph 1.

Článek 39

Vydání dědictví

1. Jestliže má být movité dědictví nebo výtěžek z prodeje movitého nebo nemovitého dědictví po projednání dědictví na území jedné smluvní strany odevzdáno dědicům nebo odkazovníkům, kteří mají bydliště nebo pobyt na území druhé smluvní strany, odevzdá se dědictví nebo výtěžek z jeho prodeje diplomatickému nebo konzulárnímu úřadu této druhé smluvní strany, jestliže:

a) justiční úřad vyzval, je-li tak stanoveno v právním řádu smluvní strany, kde dědictví je, věřitele zůstavitele, aby do tří měsíců přihlásili své pohledávky;

b) veškeré dědické poplatky a všechny přihlášené pohledávky byly zaplaceny nebo zajištěny;

c) příslušné úřady daly souhlas, jehož je případně třeba, k vývozu dědických věcí nebo převodu výtěžku jejich prodeje.

[...]

Article 39

Releasing inherited property

1. In a situation where, after the succession proceedings have been terminated in the territory of one Contracting party, movable property or proceeds from the sale of movable or immovable property shall be released to the heirs or legatees that have their domicile or residence in the territory of the other Contracting Party, it shall be handed over to the diplomatic or consular office of this other Contracting Party provided:

a) the judicial authority, if required by the law of the Contracting Party in whose territory the estate is located, has invited the creditors of the deceased to lodge their claims within three months;

b) inheritance tax and all outstanding lodged claims have been paid or secured;

c) the competent authority has given consent to the export of assets or to the transfer of proceeds from their sale.

[...]

TREATY 6: CZECHOSLOVAKIA–CUBA

Smlouva mezi Československou socialistickou republikou a Kubánskou republikou o vzájemné právní pomoci ve věcech občanských, rodinných a trestních ze dne 18. dubna 1980*

Kapitola 4

Věci dědické

Článek 34

Zásada rovnosti

1. Děděním ze zákona nebo ze závěti mohou občané jedné smluvní strany nabýt majetku a práv na území druhé smluvní strany za stejných podmínek a ve stejném rozsahu jako její vlastní občané.

2. Občané jedné smluvní strany mohou v závěti nakládat se svým majetkem nacházejícím se na území druhé smluvní strany.

Článek 35

Právní poměry dědické se řídí právním řádem té smluvní strany, jejímž občanem byl zůstavitel v době své smrti.

Článek 36

Závěť

1. Způsobilost zřídit nebo zrušit závěť, jakož i řízení o námitkách proti závěti na základě vad vůle zůstavitele nebo jejího projevu nebo na základě jiných nedostatků závěti, se řídí právním řádem smluvní strany, jejímž je zůstavitel občanem v době zřízení nebo zrušení závěti.

Treaty between the Czechoslovak Socialist Republic and the Republic of Cuba on Mutual Legal Assistance in Civil, Family and Criminal Matters of 18 April 1980**

Chapter 4

Matters of succession upon death

Article 34

Principle of equal treatment

1. Nationals of one Contracting Party may acquire property or rights in the territory of the other Contracting Party by testate or intestate succession under the same conditions and to the same extent as its own nationals.

2. Nationals of one Contracting Party are entitled to draw up a will with respect to their property located in the territory of the other Contracting Party.

Article 35

Succession upon death shall be governed by the law of the Contracting Party whose nationality the deceased had at the time of death.

Article 36

Will

1. The capacity to make or revoke a will, as well as proceedings contesting the will on grounds of the absence of intent to testate or on other deficiencies of the will shall be governed by the law of the Contracting Party of which the deceased was a national at the time of making or revoking the will.

* Vyhláška ministra zahraničních věcí č. 80/1981 Sb.

** The English translation has kindly been prepared by Magdalena Pfeiffer.

2. Forma zřízení nebo zrušení závěti se řídí právním řádem smluvní strany, jejímž je zůstavitel občanem v době zřízení nebo zrušení závěti. Závěť je platná, jestliže byla dodržena ustanovení právního řádu smluvní strany, na jejímž území k těmto úkonům došlo.

2. The form of making or revoking a will shall be governed by the law of the Contracting Party of which the deceased was a national at the time of making or revoking the will. It shall be sufficient for the validity if the will complies with the law of the Contracting Party in whose territory the will was made or revoked.

Článek 37

Odúmrť

Jestliže podle právního řádu smluvní strany, jímž se řídí dědické právní poměry, není dědiců, připadne movité dědictví té smluvní straně, jejímž byl zůstavitel občanem v době smrti, nemovité dědictví smluvní straně, na jejímž území nemovitost leží.

Article 37

Estates without a claimant

If according to the law of one Contracting Party governing the succession upon death there is no claimant, the movable property shall pass to the Contracting Party of which the deceased was a national at the time of death, the immovable property shall pass to the Contracting Party in whose territory the immovable property is located.

Článek 38

Příslušnost v dědických věcech

1. S výjimkou případu uvedeného v odstavci 2 tohoto článku je k řízení o movitém dědictví příslušný orgán té smluvní strany, jejímž občanem byl zůstavitel v době své smrti.

2. Jestliže je celé movité dědictví, které zanechal občan jedné smluvní strany, na území druhé smluvní strany, projedná je na návrh dědice orgán této smluvní strany, jestliže s tím souhlasí všichni známí dědicové.

3. K projednání nemovitého dědictví je vždy příslušný orgán té smluvní strany, na jejímž území nemovitost leží.

4. Ustanovení odstavců 1 a 3 tohoto článku platí také pro projednání dědických sporů.

5. Posouzení, zda jde o majetek movitý nebo nemovitý, se řídí právním řádem smluvní strany, na jejímž území je majetek.

Article 38

Jurisdiction in matters of succession

1. Subject to the exception referred to in paragraph 2 of this Article, the judicial authority of the Contracting Party of which the deceased was a national at the time of death shall have jurisdiction to rule on the succession to movable property.

2. Provided that all movables of the deceased national of one Contracting Party are located on the territory of the other Contracting Party and provided that all known heirs agree, the judicial authority of this Contracting Party shall, upon request of an heir, have jurisdiction to rule on succession to these movables.

3. The judicial authority of the Contracting Party in whose territory immovable property is located shall have jurisdiction to rule on succession to this immovable property.

4. Paragraphs 1 and 3 of this Article shall also apply in contentious proceedings regarding succession claims.

5. The issue of whether the property is movable or immovable is governed by the law of the Contracting Party in whose territory the property is located.

Článek 39

Zajištění dědictví

1. Orgán smluvní strany, na jejímž území je dědictví po občanu druhé smluvní strany, učiní podle právního řádu svého státu opatření potřebná k zajištění dědictví a k jeho správě. To platí také v případech, kdy dědictví může nabýt občan druhé smluvní strany.

2. O opatřeních, která byla učiněna podle odstavce 1 tohoto článku, příslušné orgány bezodkladně uvědomí diplomatickou misi nebo konzulární úřad druhé smluvní strany, které mohou při výkonu opatření k zajištění dědictví spolupůsobit přímo nebo prostřednictvím zmocněnce. Na návrh diplomatické mise nebo konzulárního úřadu mohou být učiněná opatření odložena, změněna nebo zrušena.

3. Na návrh orgánu příslušného k projednání dědictví musí být opatření učiněná podle odstavce 1 zrušena.

Article 39

Preserving the estate

1. The authority of the Contracting Party where the property belonging to the deceased, if a national of the other Contracting Party, is located shall take all measures necessary to preserve and administer the estate pursuant to its own law, even if the potential heir is a national of the other Contracting Party.

2. The measures taken pursuant to paragraph 1 shall be notified by the competent authority to the diplomatic or consular office representative of the other Contracting Party, which either directly or through an agent may take part in performing those measures if it is deemed necessary to preserve the estate. Upon request of the diplomatic or consular representative the measures may be postponed, modified or revoked.

3. The measures taken pursuant to provisions of paragraph 1 shall be revoked at the request of the authority that has jurisdiction in matters of succession.

Článek 40

Vyhlášení závěti

K otevření a vyhlášení závěti a ke zjištění jejího stavu a obsahu, jakož i k řízení o její platnosti je příslušný orgán smluvní strany, na jejímž území se závěť nachází. Jestliže zůstavitel byl v době své smrti občanem druhé smluvní strany, bude příslušnému orgánu této smluvní strany zaslán ověřený opis závěti a listina, v níž bude uveden stav a obsah této závěti. Na žádost se zašle originál závěti.

Article 40

Opening of the will

The opening of the will, ascertaining its condition and content, and ruling on its validity falls within the competence of the authority of the Contracting Party in whose territory the will is located. A duly certified copy of the will and the minutes on its condition and content must be sent to the competent authority of the Contracting Party of which the deceased was a national at the time of death. The original shall be sent upon request.

Článek 41

Vydání dědictví

1. Jestliže je movité dědictví na území jedné smluvní strany, bude toto dědictví za účelem projednání předáno příslušnému orgánu nebo diplomatické misi nebo konzulárnímu úřadu té smluvní strany, jejímž byl zůstavitel občanem v době své smrti, za podmínky, že budou dodržena ustanovení odstavce 4 písm. b) tohoto článku.

Article 41

Releasing inherited property

1. Movable property located in the territory of one Contracting Party shall be released to the competent authority or diplomatic or consular office of the Contracting Party of which the deceased was a national at the time of death for the purposes of succession proceedings, provided that the conditions set in paragraph 4 letter b) of this Article are fulfilled.

2. Poplatky z nemovitého dědictví vybere smluvní strana, na jejímž území nemovitost leží. Pokud není v této smlouvě stanoveno jinak, vybere poplatek z movitého dědictví smluvní strana, jejímž občanem byl zůstavitel v době smrti.

2. Inheritance tax on immovable property shall be collected by the Contracting Party in whose territory the immovable property is located. Unless provided otherwise in this Treaty, the tax on inheritance of movable property shall be collected by the Contracting Party of which the deceased was a national at the time of death.

3. Jestliže podle výsledků projednání dědictví toto nabývají dědicové, kteří mají bydliště nebo pobyt na území druhé smluvní strany, a není možno předat dědictví uvedeným dědicům nebo jejich zmocněncům, předá se toto dědictví diplomatické misi nebo konzulárnímu úřadu této smluvní strany.

3. In a situation where the estate is acquired by heirs domiciled or resident in the territory of the other Contracting Party, and the property cannot be handed over to the heirs or their agents, it shall be handed over to the diplomatic or consular office of this Contracting Party.

4. Dědictví se vydá za podmínek, že:

a) jsou zaplaceny všechny daně a poplatky s dědictvím spojené nebo jejich zaplacení je zajištěno,
b) příslušný orgán vydal povolení nutné k vývozu předmětů tvořících dědictví nebo k převodu peněžních částek,
c) byly zaplaceny nebo zajištěny všechny pohledávky věřitelů zůstavitele přihlášené ve lhůtě stanovené právním řádem smluvní strany, na jejímž území je dědictví.

4. The assets shall be released provided:

a) inheritance tax has been paid or secured,

b) the competent authority has given consent to the export of assets or to the transfer of money,
c) all outstanding claims of creditors of the deceased lodged within the time limit set by the law of the Contracting Party in whose territory the estate is located have been paid or secured.

TREATY 7: CZECHOSLOVAKIA–NORTH KOREA

Smlouva mezi Československou socialistickou republikou a Korejskou lidově demokratickou republikou o vzájemné právní pomoci ve věcech občanských, rodinných a trestních ze dne 11. září 1988*

Článek 25

Dědické věci

1. Občan jedné smluvní strany může dědit majetek na území druhé smluvní strany ze zákona nebo ze závěti a zřizovat nebo rušit závěť za stejných podmínek a má stejná práva jako občan druhé smluvní strany.

2. Dědické právo k movitostem se řídí právním řádem smluvní strany, jejímž občanem byl zůstavitel v době smrti. Dědické právo k nemovitostem se řídí právním řádem smluvní strany, na jejímž území se nemovitost nachází. Určení, jde-li o majetek movitý nebo nemovitý, se řídí právním řádem smluvní strany, na jejímž území se majetek nachází.

3. K projednání movitého dědictví je dána pravomoc orgánu smluvní strany, jejímž občanem byl zůstavitel v době smrti, a k projednání nemovitého dědictví orgánu smluvní strany, na jejímž území se toto dědictví nachází.

Treaty between the Czechoslovak Socialist Republic and the Democratic People's Republic of Korea on Mutual Legal Assistance in Civil, Family and Criminal Matters of 11 September 1988**

Article 25

Matters of succession upon death

1. A national of one Contracting Party may acquire property in the territory of the other Contracting Party by testate or intestate succession, may make or revoke a will under the same conditions and has the same rights as a national of the other Contracting Party.

2. Succession to movable property shall be governed by the law of the Contracting Party of which the deceased was a national at the time of death. Succession to immovable property shall be governed by the law of the Contracting Party in whose territory the immovable property is located. The issue of whether the property is movable or immovable shall be governed by the law of the Contracting Party in whose territory the property is located.

3. The judicial authority of the Contracting Party of which the deceased was a national at the time of death shall have jurisdiction to rule on the succession to movable property, and the judicial authority of the Contracting Party, in whose territory immovable property is located, shall have jurisdiction to rule on succession to this immovable property.

* Vyhláška ministra zahraničních věcí č. 93/1989 Sb.

** The English translation has kindly been prepared by Magdalena Pfeiffer.

4. Forma závěti, způsobilost zřídit nebo zrušit závěť a právní účinky vad projevu vůle se řídí právním řádem smluvní strany, jejímž občanem byl zůstavitel v době projevu vůle. Forma závěti a její zrušení se však může řídit i právním řádem smluvní strany, na jejímž území byla závěť zřízena.

4. The form of a will, the capacity to make or revoke a will as well as legal consequences for absence of intent shall be governed by the law of the Contracting Party of which the deceased was a national at the time of the declaration of the will. However, the form of making and revoking a will may also be governed by the law of the Contracting Party in whose territory the will was drawn up.

5. Není-li dědiců podle právního řádu smluvní strany, kterým se řídí dědění, přechází movitý majetek na smluvní stranu, jejímž občanem byl zůstavitel v době smrti, a nemovitost na smluvní stranu, na jejímž území se nachází.

5. If according to the law of one Contracting Party governing the succession upon death there is no heir, the movable property passes to the Contracting Party of which the deceased was a national at the time of death, and the immovable property passes to the Contracting Party in whose territory the immovable property is located.

TREATY 8: CZECHOSLOVAKIA–MONGOLIA

Smlouva mezi Československou socialistickou republikou a Mongolskou lidovou republikou o poskytování právní pomoci a o právních vztazích v občanských, rodinných a trestních věcech ze dne 15. října 1976*

Treaty between the Czechoslovak Socialist Republic and the Mongolian People's Republic on Legal Assistance and Legal Relations in Civil, Family and Criminal Matters of 15 October 1976**

DÍL ČTVRTÝ

Dědění

Článek 38

Zásada rovnosti

1. Státní občané jedné smluvní strany mohou nabývat majetek a práva na území druhé smluvní strany děděním ze zákona nebo ze závěti za stejných podmínek a v takovém rozsahu jako vlastní státní občané.

2. Státní občané jedné smluvní strany mohou závětí nakládat se svým majetkem nacházejícím se na území druhé smluvní strany.

Článek 39

Dědické právo

1. Dědické právo k movitému majetku se řídí právním řádem té smluvní strany, jejímž státním občanem byl zůstavitel v době své smrti.
2. Dědické právo k nemovitému majetku se řídí právním řádem té smluvní strany, na jejímž území se majetek naléză.

Článek 40

1. Způsobilost zřídit nebo zrušit závěť, jakož i právní účinky vad projevu vůle se řídí právním řádem smluvní strany, jejímž státním občanem byl zůstavitel v době projevu vůle.

PART FOUR

Matters of Succession upon death

Article 38

Principle of equal treatment

1. Nationals of one Contracting Party may acquire property or rights in the territory of the other Contracting Party by testate or intestate succession under the same conditions and to the same extent as its own nationals.
2. Nationals of one Contracting Party are entitled to draw up a will with respect to their property located in the territory of the other Contracting Party.

Article 39

Law applicable to succession upon death

1. Succession to movable property shall be governed by the law of the Contracting Party of which the deceased was a national at the time of death.
2. Succession to immovable property shall be governed by the law of the Contracting Party in whose territory the immovable property is located.

Article 40

1. The capacity to make or revoke a will, as well as the legal consequences for the absence of intent to testate shall be governed by the law of the Contracting Party of which the deceased was a national at the time of making or revoking the will.

* Vyhláška ministra zahraničních věcí č. 106/1978 Sb.

** The English translation has kindly been prepared by Magdalena Pfeiffer.

2. Forma závěti a forma jejího zrušení se řídí právním řádem smluvní strany, jejímž státním občanem byl zůstavitel v době pořízení nebo zrušení závěti. Pokud jde o formu pořízení nebo zrušení závěti, stačí, jestliže se postupovalo podle právního řádu smluvní strany, na jejímž území byla závěť pořízena nebo zrušena.

Článek 41

Jestliže podle právního řádu smluvní strany, jímž se řídí dědické právo, zůstalo dědictví a není dědiců, připadá movitý majetek ve prospěch té smluvní strany, jejímž státním občanem byl zůstavitel v době smrti a nemovitý majetek přechází do vlastnictví té smluvní strany, na jejímž území se nalézá.

Článek 42

Příslušnost v dědických věcech

1. K projednání dědictví k movitému majetku je příslušný orgán smluvní strany, jejímž státním občanem byl zůstavitel v době smrti, pokud se touto smlouvou nestanoví jinak.

2. K projednání dědictví k nemovitému majetku je příslušný orgán smluvní strany, na jejímž území se tento majetek nalézá.

3. Ustanovení odstavců 1 a 2 tohoto článku platí obdobně i pro projednávání sporů, které vznikly na základě dědického práva.

4. Jestliže předmětem dědictví je movitý majetek, který zůstal po smrti státního občana jedné ze smluvních stran na území druhé smluvní strany, a jestliže s tím souhlasí všichni dědicové, projedná dědictví na návrh dědice nebo zůstavitele příslušný orgán této smluvní strany.

Článek 43

Posouzení, zda jde o movitý nebo nemovitý majetek, se řídí právním řádem té smluvní strany, na jejímž území se tento majetek nalézá.

2. The form of a will and the form of its revocation shall be governed by the law of the Contracting Party of which the deceased was a national at the time of making or revoking the will. It shall be sufficient for the formal validity if the will complies with the law of the Contracting Party in whose territory the will was made or revoked.

Article 41

If according to the law of one Contracting Party governing the succession upon death there is no heir, the movable assets pass to the Contracting Party of which the deceased was a national at the time of death, and immovable assets pass to the Contracting Party in whose territory the immovable assets are located.

Article 42

Jurisdiction in matters of succession

1. The judicial authority of the Contracting Party of which the deceased was a national at the time of death shall have jurisdiction to rule on the succession to movable property, unless provided otherwise in this Treaty.

2. The judicial authority of the Contracting Party in whose territory immovable property is located shall have jurisdiction to rule on succession to this immovable property.

3. Paragraphs 1 and 2 of this Article shall also apply in contentious proceedings regarding succession claims.

4. Provided that all movables of the deceased national of one Contracting Party are located in the territory of the other Contracting Party and provided that all heirs agree, the competent authority of this Contracting Party shall, upon request of an heir or the deceased, have jurisdiction to rule on succession to these movables.

Article 43

The issue of whether the property is movable or immovable is governed by the law of the Contracting Party in whose territory the property is located.

Článek 44

Oznamování úmrtí

Jestliže státní občan jedné smluvní strany zemře na území druhé smluvní strany, je příslušný orgán povinen neprodleně o tom uvědomit diplomatickou misi nebo konzulární úřad druhé smluvní strany a oznámit mu vše, co je mu známo o dědicích, jejich bydlišti nebo pobytu, o rozsahu a hodnotě dědictví, jakož i o tom, zda byla pořízena závěť. Je-li příslušnému orgánu jedné ze smluvních stran známo, že po zemřelém zůstal majetek na území třetího státu, je povinen to oznámit druhé smluvní straně.

Článek 45

Opatření k zajištění dědictví

Orgán smluvní strany, na jejímž území je dědictví po státním občanu druhé smluvní strany, je povinen neprodleně uvědomit diplomatickou misi nebo konzulární úřad druhé smluvní strany o opatřeních provedených k zajištění ochrany dědictví. Zástupci těchto úřadů se mohou přímo nebo prostřednictvím svých zmocněnců zúčastňovat provedení těchto opatření. Opatření přijatá k ochraně dědictví mohou být na návrh diplomatické mise nebo konzulárního úřadu změněna nebo zrušena.

Článek 46

Otevření závěti

K otevření a vyhlášení závěti je příslušný orgán smluvní strany, na jejímž území se závěť nalézá a do jehož působnosti náleží řízení o dědických věcech. Žil-li zůstavitel na území druhé smluvní strany, bude zaslán příslušnému orgánu smluvní strany, na jejímž území probíhá řízení, opis závěti a protokol o stavu a obsahu dědictví a podle okolností i protokol o otevření závěti. Na žádost bude zaslán i originál závěti a též protokol o otevření a vyhlášení závěti.

Article 44

Notice of death

If a national of one Contracting Party dies in the territory of the other Contracting Party, the competent authority shall, without delay, inform the diplomatic or consular office of the other Contracting Party of the death and communicate any available information on the heirs, their domicile or residence, the extent and value of the estate as well as information on any wills. If the competent authority of one Contracting Party knows that the estate of the deceased is located in the territory of a third State, it shall be reported to the other Contracting Party.

Article 45

Measures to preserve inheritance

The authority of the Contracting Party where the assets belonging to the deceased, if a national of the other Contracting Party, is located shall notify, without delay, the diplomatic or consular office of the other Contracting Party on measures taken to preserve the estate. The representatives of these offices may take part in taking such measures directly or through agents. The measures taken to secure the estate may be modified or revoked at the request of the diplomatic or consular office.

Article 46

Opening of the will

The opening of the will falls within the competence of the authority of the Contracting Party in the territory of which the will is located and which has jurisdiction in matters of succession. If the deceased lived in the territory of the other Contracting Party, a copy of the will together with the minutes on the condition and content of the inheritance and, if necessary, the minutes on its opening, shall be sent to the competent authority of the Contracting party in whose territory the proceedings were opened. The original of the will as well as the minutes on its opening shall be sent upon request.

Článek 47

Oprávnění diplomatické mise nebo konzulárního úřadu v dědických věcech

1. Pracovníci diplomatické mise nebo konzulárního úřadu smluvních stran jsou oprávněni zastupovat před orgány druhé smluvní strany, bez zvláštního zmocnění, vlastní státní občany, pokud tito jsou nepřítomni nebo si neustanovili zástupce.

2. Zemře-li státní občan jedné smluvní strany na území druhé smluvní strany, kde neměl bydliště nebo pobyt, budou odevzdány věci, které u sebe měl, bez dalšího řízení a po úhradě jeho dluhů spolu s jejich seznamem diplomatické misi nebo konzulárnímu úřadu smluvní strany, jejímž byl státním občanem.

Článek 48

Vydání dědictví a dědické poplatky

1. Jestliže se na území jedné smluvní strany nalézá movitá pozůstalost, bude vydána orgánu příslušnému k provedení dědického řízení nebo diplomatické misi nebo konzulárnímu úřadu té smluvní strany, jejímž státním občanem byl zůstavitel, pokud jsou splněny podmínky uvedené v článku 49 odst. 2 písm. b) této smlouvy.

2. Dědické poplatky z nemovitého majetku náleží smluvní straně, na jejímž území se tento majetek nalézá.

3. Dědické poplatky z movitého majetku náleží smluvní straně, jejímž státním občanem byl zůstavitel v době smrti.

4. Jestliže dědické řízení podle článku 42 odst. 4 této smlouvy uskutečňuje orgán smluvní strany, na jejímž území se majetek nalézá, vybírají se poplatky podle právních předpisů této smluvní strany. Smluvní strana, která v těchto případech vydá podle svého právního řádu movitý majetek druhé smluvní straně, nevybírá dědické poplatky z vydávaného majetku.

Article 47

Powers of a diplomatic or consular office in succession matters

1. Members of the staff of a diplomatic or consular office of the Contracting Parties shall be entitled to represent their own nationals, without a special power of attorney before the authorities of the other Contracting Party, provided that the represented nationals are absent or had not issued a power of attorney to any person or agent.

2. If a national of one Contracting Party dies in the territory of the other Contracting Party, where he had neither domicile, nor residence, his personal possessions, together with an inventory, shall be, without further proceedings and after payment of his debts, handed over to the diplomatic or consular office of the Contracting Party of which the deceased was a national.

Article 48

Releasing inherited property and inheritance tax

1. Movable property located on the territory of one Contracting Party shall be released to the authority competent to rule on succession or to the diplomatic or consular office of the Contracting Party of which the deceased was a national, provided the conditions laid down in Article 49 paragraph 2 letter b) of this Treaty are fulfilled.

2. The inheritance tax on immovable property falls to the Contracting Party in whose territory the immovable property is located.

3. The inheritance tax on movable property falls to the Contracting Party of which the deceased was a national at the time of death.

4. If the proceedings in matters of succession are initiated in accordance with Article 42 paragraph 4 of this Treaty by an authority of the Contracting Party, in whose territory the property is located, the tax shall be collected pursuant to the law of this Contracting Party. The Contracting Party which releases movable property to the other Contracting Party pursuant to its law shall collect no inheritance tax on the released assets.

Článek 49

1. Movité dědictví nebo výtěžek získaný prodejem movitého nebo nemovitého majetku na území jedné smluvní strany se vydá po ukončení dědického řízení dědicům, kteří mají bydliště nebo pobyt na území druhé smluvní strany. Pokud dědictví nebo jeho výtěžek nelze odevzdat přímo dědicům nebo jejich zmocněncům, vydá se diplomatické misi nebo konzulárnímu úřadu druhé smluvní strany.

2. Podle ustanovení odstavce 1 tohoto článku odevzdání může být uskutečněno pod podmínkou, že:

a) byly zajištěny nebo zaplaceny všechny dědické poplatky a všechny přihlášené pohledávky;
b) příslušné orgány daly souhlas k vývozu věcí náležejících k dědictví nebo k převodu výtěžku získaného jejich prodejem;
c) byly zaplaceny nebo zajištěny všechny pohledávky věřitelů zůstavitele, přihlášené ve lhůtě stanovené právním řádem smluvní strany, na jejímž území se dědictví nalézá.

Article 49

1. Once proceedings in matters of succession have been terminated, movable property or proceeds from the sale of movable or immovable property in the territory of one Contracting Party shall be released to the heirs domiciled or resident in the territory of the other Contracting Party. If assets or proceeds from their sale cannot be handed over directly to heirs or their agents, they shall be handed over to the diplomatic or consular office of the other Contracting Party.
2. Pursuant to the provisions of paragraph 1 of this Article, property shall be released provided that:

a) inheritance tax and all outstanding lodged claims have been secured or paid;

b) the competent authorities have given consent to the export of the property or to the transfer of proceeds from its sale;
c) all outstanding claims of creditors of the deceased, lodged within the time limit set by the law of the Contracting Party in whose territory the estate is located, have been paid or secured.

DÍL 6

Uznání a výkon rozhodnutí

Článek 55

1. Smluvní strany budou podle této smlouvy uznávat a vykonávat na svém území tato rozhodnutí soudů a jiných orgánů vydaná na území druhé smluvní strany:
[...]

2. Za soudní rozhodnutí ve smyslu ustanovení odstavce 1 tohoto článku se považují i rozhodnutí ve věcech dědických vydaná orgány smluvní strany, které jsou podle právního řádu této smluvní strany příslušné k řízení ve věcech dědických.
[...]

SECTION 6

Recognition and Enforcement of Decisions

Article 55

1. The Contracting Parties shall, under the conditions laid down in this Treaty, recognize and enforce in their territory the following decisions rendered in the territory of the other Contracting Party:
[...]
2. Decisions on matters of succession upon death rendered by the authority of one Contracting Party that has jurisdiction pursuant to its own law to hear matters of succession shall also be considered as court decisions within the meaning of paragraph 1 of this Article.
[...]

TREATY 9: CZECHOSLOVAKIA–USSR

Smlouva mezi Československou socialistickou republikou a Svazem sovětských socialistických republik o právní pomoci a právních vztazích ve věcech občanských, rodinných a trestních ze dne 12. srpna 1982*

Část IV

DĚDICKÉ VĚCI

Článek 39

Zásada rovnosti

Občané jedné smluvní strany mohou nabývat majetek nebo práva na území druhé smluvní strany děděním ze zákona nebo ze závěti za stejných podmínek a ve stejném rozsahu jako její vlastní občané.

Článek 40

Dědické právo

(1) Dědění movitého majetku se řídí právním řádem té smluvní strany, na jejímž území měl zůstavitel poslední bydliště.

(2) Dědění nemovitého majetku se řídí právním řádem té smluvní strany, na jejímž území se nemovitý majetek nachází.

(3) Posouzení toho, zda majetek, který je předmětem dědění, se považuje za movitý nebo za nemovitý, se řídí právním řádem té smluvní strany, na jejímž území se majetek nachází.

Článek 41

Odúmrť

Není-li podle právního řádu smluvní strany, kterým se řídí dědění, dědiců, přechází movitý majetek, který je předmětem dědění, na smluvní stranu, jejímž občanem byl zůstavitel v době smrti, a nemovitý majetek, který je předmětem dědění, na smluvní stranu, na jejímž území se nachází.

Treaty between the Czechoslovak Socialist Republic and the Union of Soviet Socialist Republics on Legal Assistance and Legal Relations in Civil, Family and Criminal Matters of 12 August 1982**

Part IV

MATTERS OF SUCCESSION UPON DEATH

Article 39

Principle of equal treatment

Nationals of one Contracting Party may acquire property or rights in the territory of the other Contracting Party by testate or intestate succession under the same conditions and to the same extent as its own nationals.

Article 40

Law applicable to succession upon death

(1) Succession to movable property shall be governed by the law of the Contracting Party in whose territory the deceased had his last domicile.

(2) Succession to immovable property shall be governed by the law of the Contracting Party in whose territory the immovable property is located.

(3) The issue of whether the property is movable or immovable is governed by the law of the Contracting Party in whose territory the property is located.

Article 41

Estates without a claimant

If according to the law of one Contracting Party governing the succession upon death there is no heir, the movable assets pass to the Contracting Party of which the deceased was a national at the time of death, and the immovable assets pass to the Contracting Party in whose territory the immovable property is located.

* Vyhláška ministra zahraničních věcí č. 95/1983 Sb.

** The English translation has kindly been prepared by Magdalena Pfeiffer.

Článek 42

Závěť

(1) Způsobilost zřídit nebo zrušit závěť, právní účinky vad projevu vůle, jakož i způsoby popření platnosti závěti se řídí právním řádem smluvní strany, jejímž byl zůstavitel občanem v době zřízení nebo zrušení závěti.

(2) Forma závěti se řídí právním řádem smluvní strany, jejímž občanem byl zůstavitel v době, kdy závěť učinil. Stačí však, vyhoví-li právnímu řádu smluvní strany, na jejímž území byla závěť učiněna. Totéž platí o formě zrušení závěti.

Článek 43

Pravomoc v dědických věcech

(1) K projednání movitého dědictví je dána pravomoc justičních orgánů smluvní strany, na jejímž území měl zůstavitel bydliště v době své smrti.

(2) K projednání nemovitého dědictví je dána pravomoc justičních orgánů smluvní strany, na jejímž území toto dědictví je.

(3) Ustanovení odstavců 1 a 2 platí také pro projednání sporů, které vzniknou v souvislosti s projednáváním dědictví.

Článek 44

Oprávnění diplomatické mise nebo konzulárního úřadu v dědických věcech

V dědických věcech včetně dědických sporů jsou diplomatické mise nebo konzulární úřady smluvních stran oprávněny zastupovat, s výjimkou práva odmítnout dědictví, bez zvláštní plné moci, před orgány druhé smluvní strany občany svého státu, pokud jsou tito občané nepřítomní nebo si neustanoví zástupce.

Article 42

Will

(1) The capacity to make or revoke a will, the legal consequences for the absence of intent to testate as well as grounds for contesting its validity shall be governed by the law of the Contracting Party of which the deceased was a national at the time of making or revoking the will.

(2) The form of a will shall be governed by the law of the Contracting Party of which the deceased was a national at the time of making the will. It shall however be sufficient if the will complies with the law of the Contracting Party in whose territory the will was drawn up. The same applies to the form of a revocation of a will.

Article 43

Jurisdiction in matters of succession

(1) The judicial authorities of the Contracting Party in whose territory the deceased had his domicile at the time of death shall have jurisdiction to rule on the succession to movable property.

(2) The judicial authorities of the Contracting Party, in whose territory immovable property is located shall have jurisdiction to rule on succession to this immovable property.

(3) Paragraphs 1 and 2 shall also apply in contentious proceedings regarding succession claims.

Article 44

Powers of a diplomatic or consular office in succession matters

Diplomatic or consular offices of the Contracting Parties shall be entitled to represent their own nationals without a special power of attorney before the authorities of the other Contracting Party in succession matters, with the exception of the right to waive the succession, including succession disputes, provided that such nationals are absent and had not issued any power of attorney to any person or agent.

Článek 45

Opatření k zajištění dědictví

(1) Orgány obou smluvních stran učiní podle svého právního řádu opatření nutná k zajištění nebo ke správě dědictví, které na jejich území zanechal občan druhé smluvní strany.

(2) O opatřeních učiněných podle odstavce 1 bude bezodkladně uvědoměna diplomatická mise nebo konzulární úřad druhé smluvní strany, který může být přítomen provedení těchto opatření. Na návrh diplomatické mise nebo konzulárního úřadu mohou být opatření učiněná podle odstavce 1 změněna, zrušena nebo odložena.

(3) Na žádost justičního orgánu, jehož pravomoc k projednání dědictví je dána, mohou být opatření učiněná podle odstavce 1 změněna, zrušena nebo odložena.

Článek 46

Zemře-li občan jedné smluvní strany v době krátkodobého pobytu na území druhé smluvní strany, věci, které měl u sebe, se po provedení jejich soupisu předají, bez jakéhokoli řízení, diplomatické misi nebo konzulárnímu úřadu smluvní strany, jejímž byl občanem. Tyto věci mohou být vyvezeny ze státu, ve kterém občan zemřel, pouze v souladu s právním řádem tohoto státu.

Článek 47

Otevření závěti

Otevření a vyhlášení závěti provádí justiční orgán smluvní strany, na jejímž území závěť je. Je-li k řízení o dědictví dána pravomoc justičního orgánu druhé smluvní strany, zašle se mu ověřená kopie závěti a protokol o jejím otevření a vyhlášení.

Article 45

Measures to preserve the estate

(1) The authorities of both Contracting Parties shall take all measures necessary pursuant to their own law to preserve or administrate the assets of the deceased national of the other Contracting Party that are located in their territory.

(2) The measures taken pursuant to paragraph 1 shall be notified without delay to the diplomatic or consular office of the other Contracting Party, which may take part in performing these measures. The measures taken pursuant to paragraph 1 may be modified, revoked or postponed at request of the diplomatic or consular office.

(3) The measures taken pursuant paragraph 1 may be modified, revoked or postponed at request of the judicial authority that has jurisdiction in matters of succession.

Article 46

If a national of one Contracting Party dies during a short-term stay in the territory of the other Contracting Party, his personal possessions shall be, after having been inventoried, handed over to the diplomatic or consular office of the Contracting Party whose national the deceased was without further proceedings. The possessions may be exported from the State in which the national died in accordance with its law.

Article 47

Opening of the will

The opening of the will falls within the competence of the judicial authority of the Contracting Party in the territory of which the will is located. A duly certified copy of the will and the minutes on its opening shall be sent to the judicial authority of the other Contracting Party that has jurisdiction in succession matters.

Článek 48

Vydání dědictví

Má-li být po skončení dědického řízení na území jedné smluvní strany movitý majetek, který je předmětem dědění, nebo částka získaná prodejem movitého nebo nemovitého majetku, který je předmětem dědění, předána dědicům, jejichž bydliště nebo přechodný pobyt je na území druhé smluvní strany, a nelze-li jim nebo jejich zástupcům tento majetek nebo tuto částku přímo vydat, předá se majetek, který je předmětem dědění, nebo částka získaná jeho prodejem diplomatické misi nebo konzulárnímu úřadu této smluvní strany za podmínek, že:

a) státní notářství vyzvalo zůstavitelovy věřitele, je-li to stanoveno právním řádem státu, kde je majetek, který je předmětem dědění, aby uplatnili své nároky ve lhůtě tří měsíců;
b) všechny dědické poplatky a všechny uplatněné nároky byly zajištěny nebo zaplaceny;
c) příslušné orgány daly souhlas k vývozu věcí náležejících do dědictví nebo k převodu částek získaných jejich prodejem, je-li takový souhlas nutný.

Article 48

Releasing inherited property

In a situation where, after the termination of proceedings in succession matters in the territory of one Contracting Party, the movable property or proceeds from the sale of movable or immovable property shall be released to the heirs that have their domicile or temporary residence on the territory of the other Contracting Party, or if they cannot be handed over to the heirs or their agent directly, they shall be handed over to the diplomatic or consular office of this Contracting Party, provided that:

a) the State notary, if required by the law of the Contracting Party in whose territory the property is located, has invited creditors of the deceased to lodge their claims within three months;
b) inheritance tax and all lodged claims have been secured or paid;

c) the competent authorities have given consent, if required, to the export of assets or to the transfer of proceeds from their sale.

TREATY 10: CZECH REPUBLIC–UKRAINE

Smlouva mezi Českou republikou a Ukrajinou o právní pomoci v občanských věcech ze dne 28. května 2001*

Oddíl IV

Dědické právo

Článek 37

Zásada rovnosti

1. Občané jedné smluvní strany mohou nabývat majetek nebo práva na území druhé smluvní strany formou dědění ze zákona nebo ze závěti, za stejných podmínek a ve stejném rozsahu jako vlastní občané druhé smluvní strany, pokud v této smlouvě není stanoveno jinak.

2. Občané jedné smluvní strany při sepsání závěti mohou disponovat se svým majetkem, který se nachází na území druhé smluvní strany, stejně tak jako občané této druhé smluvní strany, pokud tato smlouva nestanoví jinak.

Článek 38

Právní předpisy o dědění

1. Právní poměry dědické ohledně movitého majetku se řídí právním řádem té smluvní strany, jejímž občanem byl zůstavitel v době úmrtí.
2. Právní poměry dědické ohledně nemovitého majetku se řídí právním řádem té smluvní strany, na jejímž území se nachází nemovitost.
3. Posouzení toho, zda majetek, který je předmětem dědění, se považuje za movitý nebo nemovitý, se řídí právním řádem té smluvní strany, kde se movitý majetek nebo nemovitost nacházejí.

Treaty between the Czech Republic and Ukraine on Legal Assistance in Civil Matters of 28 May 2001**

Part IV

Law applicable to succession upon death

Article 37

Principle of equal treatment

1. Nationals of one Contracting Party may acquire property or rights in the territory of the other Contracting Party by testate or intestate succession under the same conditions and to the same extent as its own nationals, unless provided otherwise in this Treaty.

2. Nationals of one Contracting Party are entitled to draw up a will with respect to their property located in the territory of the other Contracting Party under the same conditions as its own nationals, unless provided otherwise in this Treaty.

Article 38

Law applicable to succession matters

1. Succession to movable property shall be governed by the law of the Contracting Party of which the deceased was a national at the time of death.
2. Succession to immovable property shall be governed by the law of the Contracting Party in whose territory the immovable property is located.
3. The issue of whether the property is movable or immovable is governed by the law of the Contracting Party in whose territory the movable or immovable property is located.

---

* Sdělení Ministerstva zahraničních věcí č. 123/2002 Sb.m.s.

** The English translation has kindly been prepared by Magdalena Pfeiffer.

Článek 39

Připadnutí dědictví státu

Nenabude-li dědictví žádný z dědiců, připadne movitý majetek té smluvní straně, jejímž občanem byl zůstavitel v době úmrtí. Majetek nemovitý připadne té smluvní straně, na jejímž území se nachází nemovitost.

Článek 40

Závěť

1. Způsobilost osoby pořídit závěť nebo ji zrušit, jakož i právní účinky vad projevu vůle pořizovatele závěti se řídí právním řádem smluvní strany, jejímž občanem byl zůstavitel v době pořízení či zrušení závěti.

2. Forma pořízení nebo zrušení závěti se řídí právním řádem smluvní strany, jejímž občanem byl zůstavitel v době pořízení nebo zrušení závěti. Stačí však, bylo-li postupováno podle právního řádu smluvní strany, na jejímž území byla závěť pořízena nebo zrušena.

3. Ustanovení odstavců 1 a 2 se použijí obdobně na vydědění.

Článek 41

Pravomoc justičních orgánů ve věcech dědických

1. Pravomoc k projednání dědictví u movitého majetku mají justiční orgány té smluvní strany, jejímž občanem byl zůstavitel v době úmrtí, s výjimkou případů uvedených v odstavci 3 tohoto článku.

2. Pravomoc k projednání dědictví ohledně nemovitého majetku mají justiční orgány té smluvní strany, na jejímž území se nemovitost nachází.

Article 39

Estates without a claimant

If there is no heir, the movable property passes to the Contracting Party of which the deceased was a national at the time of death. The immovable property passes to the Contracting Party in whose territory the immovable asset is located.

Article 40

Will

1. The capacity to make or revoke a will, as well as the legal consequences for the absence of intent to testate, shall be governed by the law of the Contracting Party of which the deceased was a national at the time of making or revoking the will.

2. The form of making or revoking a will shall be governed by the law of the Contracting Party of which the deceased was a national at the time of making or revoking the will. It shall however be sufficient for the formal validity if the will complies with the law of the Contracting Party in whose territory the will was drawn up or revoked.

3. The provisions of paragraphs 1 and 2 shall apply to disinheritance accordingly.

Article 41

Jurisdiction of judicial authorities in matters of succession

1. The judicial authorities of the Contracting Party of which the deceased was a national at the time of death shall have jurisdiction to rule on the succession to movable property, subject to the exception referred to in paragraph 3 of this Article.

2. The judicial authorities of the Contracting Party in whose territory immovable property is located shall have jurisdiction to rule on succession to this immovable property.

3. Jestliže je veškerý movitý majetek zůstavitele, který byl občanem jedné smluvní strany, na území druhé smluvní strany, má pravomoc projednat dědictví, pokud všichni známí dědicové s tím souhlasí, na žádost kteréhokoliv dědice či jiné osoby, která má práva anebo nároky na dědictví, justiční orgán této druhé smluvní strany.

4. Ustanovení odstavců 1 a 2 tohoto článku se použijí i při řešení dědických sporů.

Článek 42

1. V případě, kdy občan jedné smluvní strany zemře na území druhé smluvní strany, příslušný justiční orgán smluvní strany neprodleně uvědomí o jeho úmrtí diplomatickou misi nebo konzulární úřad státu, jehož byl zemřelý občanem, a zároveň mu sdělí všechno, co je mu známo o dědicích, jejich bydlišti nebo pobytu, o hodnotě pozůstalosti, jakož i o závěti, pokud tato existuje.
2. Ustanovení odstavce 1 tohoto článku se uplatní i v případě, kdy je příslušný justiční orgán jedné smluvní strany informován o tom, že občan druhé smluvní strany, který zemřel na území třetího státu, zanechal jmění na území první smluvní strany.

3. Diplomatická mise nebo konzulární úřad jedné smluvní strany, která disponuje informací o úmrtí občana svého státu, jehož majetek zůstal na území druhé smluvní strany, vyrozumí o tom justiční orgán této smluvní strany.
4. Jestliže na území jedné smluvní strany dojde k zahájení dědického řízení a přitom se zjistí, že dědicem je občan druhé smluvní strany, příslušný justiční orgán o tom neprodleně uvědomí diplomatickou misi nebo konzulární úřad této smluvní strany.

3. Provided that all movable property of the deceased national of one Contracting Party is located in the territory of the other Contracting Party and provided that all known heirs agree, the judicial authorities of this Contracting Party shall, upon request of an heir or another person that has inheritance rights or claims, have jurisdiction to rule on succession to these movables.
4. Paragraphs 1 and 2 of this Article shall also apply in contentious proceedings regarding succession claims.

Article 42

1. If a national of one Contracting Party dies in the territory of the other Contracting Party, the competent authority of the Contracting Party shall, without delay, inform the diplomatic or consular office of the Contracting Party of which the deceased was a national of the death and communicate any available information on the heirs, their domicile or residence and the value of the estate as well as information on any wills.
2. Paragraph 1 of this Article applies also in the situation when the competent judicial authority of one Contracting Party learns that the national of the other Contracting Party, who died outside of the territory of both Contracting Parties, has left property in its territory.
3. The diplomatic or consular office of one Contracting Party that has information on the death of its own national whose property is left in the territory of the other Contracting Party shall inform the judicial authority of the other Contracting Party.
4. In a situation where succession proceedings are opened in the territory of one Contracting Party and the heir is a national of the other Contracting Party, the competent judicial authority shall, without delay, inform the diplomatic or consular office of the other Contracting Party.

Článek 43

Zemře-li občan jedné smluvní strany v době krátkodobého pobytu na území druhé smluvní strany, kde neměl bydliště, věci, které měl u sebe, se po provedení jejich soupisu předají diplomatické misi nebo konzulárnímu úřadu smluvní strany, jejímž byl občanem.

Article 43

If a national of one Contracting Party dies during a short-term stay on the territory of the other Contracting Party, where he had no domicile, his personal possessions shall, after having been inventoried, be handed over to the diplomatic or consular office of the Contracting Party of which the deceased was a national.

Článek 44

Práva diplomatických misí a konzulárních úřadů ve věcech dědických

V dědických věcech na území jedné smluvní strany má diplomatická mise nebo konzulární úřad druhé smluvní strany právo v případě, kdy její vlastní občané nejsou přítomni a neurčili svého zmocněnce, učinit všechna opatření k tomu (s výjimkou práva odmítnutí dědictví), aby byli zastoupeni před kterýmkoli justičním orgánem přijímacího státu. K výkonu tohoto práva není třeba zvláštního pověření.

Article 44

Powers of diplomatic and consular offices in succession matters

A diplomatic or consular office of one Contracting Party shall be entitled to take all measures necessary to ensure representation of its own nationals before any judicial authority of the other Contracting Party in succession matters (with the exception of the right to waive the succession), provided that the represented nationals are absent and had not issued any power of attorney to any person or agent. A special power of attorney is not required.

Článek 45

Opatření k ochraně dědictví

1. Justiční orgány obou smluvních stran budou činit podle svých právních řádů veškerá nezbytná opatření k ochraně nebo zajištění pozůstalostního majetku, který zůstal na jejich území po úmrtí občana druhé smluvní strany.
2. O opatřeních učiněných podle odstavce 1 tohoto článku budou vždy bezodkladně uvědoměny diplomatická mise nebo konzulární úřad druhé smluvní strany, které se budou rovněž podílet na uskutečňování těchto opatření. Na návrh diplomatické mise nebo konzulárního úřadu mohou být opatření učiněná podle odstavce 1 tohoto článku změněna nebo zrušena.
3. Opatření učiněná podle odstavce 1 tohoto článku mohou být změněna, zrušena, případně odložena na žádost justičního orgánu, který má pravomoc k projednání dědictví.

Article 45

Measures to preserve inheritance

1. The judicial authorities of the Contracting Party where assets belonging to the deceased, if a national of the other Contractingy Party, are located shall take all measures necessary to preserve and administrate the estate pursuant to their own law.
2. The measures taken pursuant to paragraph 1 of this Article shall always be notified, without delay, to the diplomatic or consular office of the other Contracting Party, which takes part in performing these measures. Upon request of the diplomatic or consular representative the measures taken pursuant to paragraph 1 of this Article may be modified or revoked at their request.
3. The measures taken pursuant to paragraph 1 of this Article may be modified, revoked or postponed at request of the judicial authority that has jurisdiction in matters of succession.

Článek 46

Otevření a prohlášení závěti

K prohlášení závěti je dána pravomoc justičního orgánu smluvní strany, u něhož je závěť uložena. Ověřený opis závěti a doklad o jejím otevření nebo seznámení se s jejím obsahem budou zaslány příslušnému justičnímu orgánu druhé smluvní strany, pokud zůstavitel byl jejím občanem nebo pokud je justiční orgán této smluvní strany podle této smlouvy příslušný k projednání dědictví.

Article 46

Opening of the will

The opening of the will falls within the competence of the judicial authority of the Contracting Party in the territory of which the will is located. A duly certified copy of the will and the minutes on its opening must be sent to the competent judicial authority of the other Contracting Party, if the deceased was its national or if the judicial authority of this Contracting Party has jurisdiction in succession matters according to this Treaty.

Článek 47

Vydání dědictví

1. Movitý majetek nebo peněžní částky získané prodejem pozůstalostního movitého nebo nemovitého majetku, které jsou na území jedné ze smluvních stran a jež náležejí dědicům, kteří jsou občany druhé smluvní strany a mají bydliště nebo pobyt na území jedné ze smluvních stran, nebo na území třetího státu, budou předány po ukončení dědického řízení těmto dědicům. Jestliže se tito dědicové nedostaví osobně nebo prostřednictvím zmocněnce, aby převzali majetek nebo výše uvedené peněžní částky, budou tyto předány diplomatické misi nebo konzulárnímu úřadu smluvní strany, jejímiž občany jsou tito dědicové.
2. Výše uvedený majetek může být předán dědicům anebo diplomatické misi či konzulárnímu úřadu, jestliže:

a) byly zaplaceny dědické poplatky nebo daně,
b) byly uspokojeny veškeré nároky věřitelů zemřelého týkající se dědictví, ve lhůtě stanovené zákony té smluvní strany, na jejímž území se majetek nachází,
c) příslušné orgány vydaly souhlas, jehož je případně třeba, pro vývoz dědictví nebo pro převedení prostředků v souladu s právním řádem smluvní strany, na jejímž území se majetek nachází.

Article 47

Releasing inherited property

1. After proceedings in matters of succession have been terminated, movable property or proceeds from the sale of movable or immovable property in the territory of one Contracting Party shall be released to the heirs, if they are nationals of the other Contracting Party, having domicile or residence in the territory of one Contracting Party or in the territory of a third State. In a situation where the heirs do not appear either in person or through an agent to take possesion of the assets or the above-stated proceeds, they shall be handed over to the diplomatic or consular office of the Contracting Party of which the heirs are nationals.
2. The above-mentioned assets may be released to the heirs or the diplomatic or consular office provided that:

a) inheritance tax has been paid,
b) all outstanding claims of creditors of the deceased have been settled within the time limit set by the law of the Contracting Party in whose territory the asset is located,
c) the competent authorities have given consent, if needed, to the export of assets or to the transfer of money pursuant to the law of the Contracting Party in whose territory the asset is located.

TREATY 11: CZECH REPUBLIC–UZBEKISTAN

Smlouva mezi Českou republikou a Republikou Uzbekistán o právní pomoci a právních vztazích v občanských a trestních věcech ze dne 18. ledna 2002*

ČÁST V

DĚDĚNÍ

Článek 41

Zásada rovnosti

Občané jedné smluvní strany mohou nabývat majetek nebo práva na území druhé smluvní strany děděním ze zákona nebo ze závěti za stejných podmínek a ve stejném rozsahu jako občané této smluvní strany.

Článek 42

Dědické právo

1. Právní poměry dědické, s výjimkou uvedenou v odstavci 2 tohoto článku, se řídí právním řádem smluvní strany, na jejímž území měl zůstavitel poslední bydliště.

2. Dědění nemovitého majetku se řídí právním řádem smluvní strany, na jejímž území se nemovitý majetek nachází.

3. Posouzení toho, zda majetek, který je předmětem dědění, se považuje za movitý nebo nemovitý, se řídí právním řádem té smluvní strany, na jejímž území se majetek nachází.

Treaty between the Czech Republic and the Republic of Uzbekistan on Legal Assistance and Legal Relations in Civil and Criminal Matters of 18 January 2002**

PART V

MATTERS OF SUCCESSION UPON DEATH

Article 41

Principle of equal treatment

Nationals of one Contracting Party may acquire property or rights in the territory of the other Contracting Party by testate or intestate succession under the same conditions and to the same extent as its own nationals.

Article 42

Law applicable to succession upon death

1. Succession upon death shall be governed by the law of the Contracting Party, where the deceased had his last domicile, subject to the exception referred to in paragraph 2 of this Article.

2. Succession of immovable property shall be governed by the law of the Contracting Party in whose territory the immovable property is located.

3. The issue of whether the property is movable or immovable is governed by the law of the Contracting Party in whose territory the property is located.

---

* Sdělení Ministerstva zahraničních věcí č. 133/2003 Sb.m.s.

** The English translation has kindly been prepared by Magdalena Pfeiffer.

Článek 43

Připadnutí dědictví státu

Jestliže podle právního řádu smluvní strany, kterým se řídí dědění, má dědictví připadnout státu, pak movitý majetek, který je předmětem dědění, přechází na smluvní stranu, jejímž občanem byl zůstavitel v době smrti, a nemovitý majetek přechází na smluvní stranu, na jejímž území se tento majetek nachází.

Article 43

Estates without a claimant

If according to the law of one Contracting Party governing the succession upon death the estate shall be acquired by the State, the movable property passes to the Contracting Party of which the deceased was a national at the time of death, and the immovable property passes to the Contracting Party in whose territory the immovable property is located.

Článek 44

Závěť

1. Způsobilost pořídit nebo zrušit závěť, právní účinky vad projevu vůle, jakož i způsob popření platnosti závěti se řídí právním řádem smluvní strany, jejímž občanem byl zůstavitel v době pořízení nebo zrušení závěti.

2. Forma závěti se řídí právním řádem smluvní strany, jejímž občanem byl zůstavitel v době pořízení závěti. Stačí však, vyhoví-li právnímu řádu smluvní strany, na jejímž území byla závěť pořízena. Totéž platí i o formě zrušení závěti.

3. Otevření a vyhlášení závěti provádí justiční orgán smluvní strany, na jejímž území je závěť uložena. Je-li k řízení o dědictví dána pravomoc justičního orgánu druhé smluvní strany, zašle se mu ověřená kopie závěti a protokol o jejím otevření a vyhlášení.

Article 44

Will

1. The capacity to make or revoke a will, legal consequences for the absence of intent to testate, as well as the grounds for contesting the validity of a will, shall be governed by the law of the Contracting Party of which the deceased was a national at the time of making or revoking the will.

2. The form of a will shall be governed by the law of the Contracting Party of which the deceased was a national at the time of making the will. It shall however be sufficient for the formal validity if the will complies with the law of the Contracting Party in whose territory the will was drawn up. The same applies to the form of a revocation of a will.

3. The opening of the will falls within the competence of the judicial authority of the Contracting Party on the territory of which the will is located. A duly certified copy of the will and the minutes on its opening must be sent to the judicial authority of the other Contracting Party if it has jurisdiction in succession matters.

Článek 45

Pravomoc v dědických věcech

1. K projednání movitého dědictví je dána pravomoc justičních orgánů smluvní strany, na jejímž území měl zůstavitel bydliště v době své smrti.

Article 45

Jurisdiction in matters of succession

1. The judicial authorities of the Contracting Party in whose territory the deceased had his domicile at the time of death shall have jurisdiction to rule on the succession to movable property.

2. K projednání nemovitého dědictví je dána pravomoc justičních orgánů smluvní strany, na jejímž území se nemovitost nachází.

3. Ustanovení odstavců 1 a 2 tohoto článku se použijí rovněž při projednání sporů, které vzniknou v souvislosti s dědickým řízením.

Článek 46

Oprávnění diplomatických misí a konzulárních úřadů v dědických věcech

V dědických věcech včetně dědických sporů jsou zastupitelské nebo konzulární úřady smluvních stran oprávněny zastupovat bez zvláštní plné moci, s výjimkou práva odmítnout dědictví, před justičními orgány druhé smluvní strany občany svého státu, pokud jsou tito nepřítomni nebo si neustanovili zástupce.

Článek 47

Oznámení faktu smrti

Jestliže občan jedné smluvní strany zemře na území druhé smluvní strany, příslušný orgán smluvní strany neprodleně tuto skutečnost oznámí zastupitelskému nebo konzulárnímu úřadu státu, jehož občanem byla zemřelá osoba, a zároveň mu sdělí údaje o dědicích, o místě jejich bydliště nebo pobytu, o rozsahu a hodnotě dědictví, jakož i o závěti, pokud existuje.

Článek 48

Opatření k zajištění dědictví

1. Justiční orgány smluvních stran učiní podle svého právního řádu opatření nutná k zajištění nebo ke správě dědictví, které na jejich území zanechal občan druhé smluvní strany.

2. The judicial authorities of the Contracting Party in whose territory immovable property is located shall have jurisdiction to rule on succession to this immovable property.

3. Paragraphs 1 and 2 of this Article shall also apply in contentious proceedings regarding succession claims.

Article 46

Powers of diplomatic and consular offices in succession matters

Diplomatic or consular offices of the Contracting Parties shall be entitled to represent their own nationals without special powers of attorney before the judicial authorities of the other Contracting Party in succession matters, with the exception of the right to waive the succession, including succession disputes, provided that the represented nationals are absent and had not issued any power of attorney to any person or agent.

Article 47

Notice of death

If a national of one Contracting Party dies in the territory of the other Contracting Party, the competent authority of the Contracting Party shall, without delay, notify the diplomatic or consular ofice of the other Contracting Party about the death and communicate any available information about the heirs, their domicile or residence, the extent and value of the estate as well as information on any wills.

Article 48

Measures to preserve inheritance

1. The judicial authorities of the Contracting Party where the property belonging to the deceased, who was a national of the other Contracting Party, is located shall take all measures necessary to preserve or administer the estate pursuant to its own law.

2. O opatřeních učiněných podle odstavce 1 tohoto článku bude bezodkladně uvědomena diplomatická mise nebo konzulární úřad státu, jehož občanem je zůstavitel. Uvedený úřad nebo justiční orgán se může provádění těchto opatření zúčastnit.
3. Na žádost justičního orgánu, jehož pravomoc k projednání dědictví je dána, mohou být opatření učiněná podle odstavce 1 tohoto článku změněna, zrušena nebo odložena.

Článek 49

Vydání dědictví

1. Má-li být po skončení dědického řízení na území jedné smluvní strany movitý majetek, který je předmětem dědění, nebo částka získaná prodejem movitého nebo nemovitého majetku, který je předmětem dědění, vydána dědicům, kteří se zdržují na území druhé smluvní strany, a nelze-li jim nebo jejich zákonným zástupcům tento majetek nebo částku přímo vydat, předá se majetek, který je předmětem řízení, nebo částka získaná jeho prodejem diplomatické misi nebo konzulárnímu úřadu této smluvní strany.
2. Justiční orgán příslušný v dědickém řízení vydá rozhodnutí o předání dědictví diplomatické misi nebo konzulárnímu úřadu.

3. Tento majetek může být vydán dědicům, jestliže:

3.1. byly zaplaceny nebo zajištěny veškeré nároky věřitelů zůstavitele, uplatněné ve lhůtě stanovené právním řádem smluvní strany, na jejímž území se dědictví nachází;

3.2. byly zaplaceny nebo zajištěny veškeré dědické poplatky a daně;
3.3. příslušné orgány smluvních stran vydaly povolení k vývozu dědictví, je-li ho třeba.

4. Převod peněžních částek se uskutečňuje podle právního řádu smluvních stran.

2. The measures taken pursuant to paragraph 1 of this Article shall be notified without delay to the diplomatic mission or consular post of the State of which the deceased was a national. This office or a judicial authority may take part in performing these measures.
3. The measures taken pursuant to provisions of paragraph 1 of this Article may be modified, revoked or postponed at the request of the judicial authority that has jurisdiction in matters of succession.

Article 49

Releasing inherited property

1. If, after the proceedings in matters of succession have been terminated in the territory of one Contracting Party, the movable property or proceeds from the sale of movable or immovable property shall be released to the heirs resident in the territory of the other Contracting Party, and if these assets cannot be handed over to the heirs or their agents directly, they shall be handed over to the diplomatic or consular office of this Contracting Party.

2. The judicial authority that has jurisdiction in succession matters renders the decision about handing over the assets to the diplomatic or consular office.
3. These assets may be released to the heirs provided:

3.1. all outstanding claims of creditors of the deceased lodged within the time limit set by the law of the Contracting Party in whose territory the estate is located have been paid or secured;
3.2. inheritance tax has been paid or secured;

3.3. the competent authorities of the Contracting Parties have given their consent, if required, to the export of assets.
4. The transfer of money is made pursuant to the law of the Contracting Parties.

TREATY 12: CZECHOSLOVAKIA – VIETNAM

Smlouva mezi Československou socialistickou republikou a Vietnamskou socialistickou republikou o právní pomoci ve věcech občanských a trestních ze dne 12. října 1982*

Kapitola 4

Věci dědické

Článek 34

Zásada rovnosti

(1) Děděním ze zákona nebo ze závěti mohou občané jedné smluvní strany nabýt majetku a práv na území druhé smluvní strany za stejných podmínek a ve stejném rozsahu jako její vlastní občané.

(2) Občané jedné smluvní strany mohou v závěti nakládat se svým majetkem nacházejícím se na území druhé smluvní strany.

Článek 35

(1) Dědění movitého majetku se řídí právním řádem té smluvní strany, jejímž občanem byl zůstavitel v čase smrti.

(2) Dědění nemovitého majetku se řídí právním řádem té smluvní strany, na jejímž území se nemovitý majetek nachází.

(3) Posouzení toho, zda majetek, který je předmětem dědění se považuje za movitý nebo nemovitý, se řídí právním řádem té smluvní strany, na jejímž území se majetek nachází.

Treaty between the Czechoslovak Socialist Republic and the Socialist Republic of Vietnam on Legal Assistance in Civil and Criminal Matters of 12 October 1982**

Chapter 4

Matters of Succession upon death

Article 34

Principle of equal treatment

(1) Nationals of one Contracting Party may acquire property and rights in the territory of the other Contracting Party by testate or intestate succession under the same conditions and to the same extent as its own nationals.

(2) Nationals of one Contracting Party are entitled to draw up a will with respect to their assets located in the territory of the other Contracting Party.

Article 35

(1) The succession to movable property shall be governed by the law of the Contracting Party whose nationality the deceased had at the time of death.

(2) The succession to immovable property shall be governed by the law of the Contracting Party in whose territory the immovable property is located.

(3) The issue of whether the property is movable or immovable is governed by the law of the Contracting Party in whose territory the property is located.

* Vyhláška ministra zahraničních věcí č. 98/1984 Sb.

** The English translation has kindly been prepared by Magdalena Pfeiffer.

Článek 36

Závěť

(1) Způsobilost zřídit nebo zrušit závěť, jakož i řízení o námitkách proti závěti na základě vad vůle zůstavitele nebo jejího projevu nebo na základě jiných nedostatků závěti, se řídí právním řádem smluvní strany, jejímž je zůstavitel občanem v době zřízení nebo zrušení závěti.

(2) Forma zřízení nebo zrušení závěti se řídí právním řádem smluvní strany, jejímž je zůstavitel občanem v době zřízení nebo zrušení závěti. Závěť je platná, jestliže byla dodržena ustanovení právního řádu smluvní strany, na jejímž území k těmto úkonům došlo.

Article 36

Will

(1) The capacity to make or revoke a will, as well as proceedings contesting the will on grounds of the absence of intent to testate or on grounds of other deficiencies of the will, shall be governed by the law of the Contracting Party of which the deceased was a national at the time of making or revoking the will.

(2) The form of making or revoking a will shall be governed by the law of the Contracting Party, of which the deceased person was a national at the time of making or revoking the will. It shall be sufficient for the validity if the will complies with the law of the Contracting Party in whose territory the will was made or revoked.

Článek 37

Odúmrť

Jestliže podle právního řádu smluvní strany, jímž se řídí dědické právní poměry, není dědiců, připadne movité dědictví té smluvní straně, jejímž byl zůstavitel občanem v době smrti, nemovité dědictví smluvní straně, na jejímž území nemovitost leží.

Article 37

Estates without a claimant

If according to the law of one Contracting Party governing the succession upon death there is no claimant, the movable property passes to the Contracting Party of which the deceased was a national at the time of death, and immovable property passes to the Contracting Party in whose territory the immovable asset is located.

Článek 38

Příslušnost v dědických věcech

(1) S výjimkou případu uvedeného v odstavci 2 tohoto článku je k řízení o movitém dědictví příslušný justiční orgán té smluvní strany, jejímž občanem byl zůstavitel v době své smrti.

(2) Jestliže je celé movité dědictví, které zanechal občan jedné smluvní strany, na území druhé smluvní strany, projedná je na návrh dědice justiční orgán této smluvní strany, jestliže s tím souhlasí všichni známí dědicové.

Article 38

Jurisdiction in matters of succession

(1) The judicial authority of the Contracting Party of which the deceased was a national at the time of death shall have jurisdiction to rule on the succession to movable property, subject to the exception referred to in paragraph 2 of this Article.

(2) Provided that all movables of the deceased national of one Contracting Party are located in the territory of the other Contracting Party and provided that all known heirs agree, the judicial authority of this Contracting Party shall, upon request of an heir, have jurisdiction to rule on the succession to these movables.

(3) K projednání nemovitého dědictví je vždy příslušný justiční orgán té smluvní strany, na jejímž území nemovitost leží.

(4) Ustanovení odstavců 1 a 3 tohoto článku platí také pro projednání dědických sporů.

(3) The judicial authority of the Contracting Party in whose territory immovable property is located shall have jurisdiction to rule on succession to this immovable property.

(4) Paragraphs 1 and 3 of this Article shall apply also in contentious proceedings regarding succession claims.

Článek 39

Zajištění dědictví

(1) Orgán smluvní strany, na jejímž území je dědictví po občanu druhé smluvní strany, učiní podle právního řádu svého státu opatření potřebná k zajištění dědictví a k jeho správě. To platí také v případech, kdy dědictví může nabýt občan druhé smluvní strany.

(2) O opatřeních, která byla učiněna podle odstavce 1 tohoto článku, příslušné orgány bezodkladně uvědomí diplomatickou misi nebo konzulární úřad druhé smluvní strany, které mohou při výkonu opatření k zajištění dědictví spolupůsobit přímo nebo prostřednictvím zmocněnce. Podle návrhu diplomatické mise nebo konzulárního úřadu mohou být učiněná opatření odložena, změněna nebo zrušena.

(3) Podle návrhu justičního orgánu příslušného k projednání dědictví musí být opatření učiněná podle odstavce 1 tohoto článku odložena, změněna nebo zrušena.

Article 39

Measures to preserve the estate

(1) The authority of the Contracting Party where the property belonging to the deceased who was a national of the other Contracting Party is located shall take all measures necessary to secure and administer the estate pursuant to its own law. This applies also if the potential heir is a national of the other Contracting Party.

(2) The measures taken pursuant to paragraph 1 of this Article shall be notified by the competent authorities without delay to the diplomatic or consular office of the other Contracting Party, which directly or through an agent may take part in performing measures to preserve the estate. Upon request of the diplomatic or consular representative the measures may be postponed, modified or revoked.

(3) The measures taken pursuant to paragraph 1 of this Article shall be postponed, modified or revoked at request of the judicial authority that has jurisdiction in matters of succession.

Článek 40

Vyhlášení závěti

K otevření a vyhlášení závěti a ke zjištění jejího stavu a obsahu, jakož i k řízení o její platnosti je příslušný justiční orgán smluvní strany, na jejímž území se závěť nachází. Jestliže zůstavitel byl v době své smrti občanem druhé smluvní strany, bude justičnímu orgánu této smluvní strany zaslán ověřený opis závěti a listina, v níž bude uveden stav a obsah této závěti. Na žádost se zašle originál závěti.

Article 40

Opening of the will

The opening of the will, ascertaining its condition and content, and initiating proceedings on its validity fall within the competence of the judicial authority of the Contracting Party in whose territory the will is located. A duly certified copy of the will and minutes on its condition and content shall be sent to the judicial authority of the other Contracting Party if the deceased was its national at the time of death. The original shall be sent upon request.

Článek 41

Vydání dědictví

(1) Jestliže je movité dědictví na území jedné smluvní strany, bude toto dědictví za účelem projednání předáno justičnímu orgánu nebo diplomatické misi nebo konzulárnímu úřadu té smluvní strany, jejímž byl zůstavitel občanem v době své smrti, za podmínky, že budou dodržena ustanovení odstavce 4 písm. b) tohoto článku.

(2) Poplatky z nemovitého dědictví vybere smluvní strana, na jejímž území nemovitost leží. Pokud není v této smlouvě stanoveno jinak, vybere poplatek z movitého dědictví smluvní strana, jejímž občanem byl zůstavitel v době smrti.

(3) Jestliže podle výsledků projednání dědictví toto nabývají dědicové, kteří mají bydliště na území druhé smluvní strany, a není možno předat dědictví uvedeným dědicům nebo jejich zmocněncům, předá se dědictví diplomatické misi nebo konzulárnímu úřadu této smluvní strany.

(4) Dědictví se vydá za podmínek, že:

a) jsou zaplaceny všechny daně a poplatky s dědictvím spojené nebo jejich zaplacení je zajištěno,

b) příslušný orgán vydal povolení nutné k vývozu předmětů tvořících dědictví nebo k převodu peněžních částek,

c) byly zaplaceny nebo zajištěny všechny pohledávky věřitelů zůstavitele přihlášené ve lhůtě stanovené právním řádem smluvní strany, na jejímž území je dědictví.

Article 41

Releasing inherited property

(1) In a situation where movable assets are located in the territory of one Contracting Party, they shall be released for the purposes of succession proceedings to a judicial authority, diplomatic or consular office of the Contracting Party of which the deceased was a national at the time of death, provided that the conditions laid down in paragraph 4 letter b) of this Article are fulfilled.

(2) The inheritance tax on immovable property is collected by the Contracting Party in whose territory the immovable property is located. Unless provided otherwise in this Treaty, the inheritance tax on movable property is collected by the Contracting Party of which the deceased was a national at the time of death.

(3) In a situation where the estate is acquired by heirs domiciled in the territory of the other Contracting Party and the assets cannot be handed over to the heirs or their agents, they shall be handed over to the diplomatic or consular office of this Contracting Party.

(4) The inheritance shall be released provided:

a) inheritance tax has been paid or secured,

b) the competent authority has given its consent to the export of assets or to the transfer of money,

c) all outstanding claims of creditors of the deceased lodged within the time limit set by the law of the Contracting Party on whose territory the estate is located have been paid or secured.

TREATY 13: CZECHOSLOVAKIA–YUGOSLAVIA

Smlouva mezi Československou socialistickou republikou a Socialistickou federativní republikou Jugoslávií o úpravě právních vztahů ve věcech občanských, rodinných a trestních ze dne 20. ledna 1964*

Oddíl 4

Věci dědické

Článek 35

Zásada rovnosti

1. Občané jedné smluvní strany mohou nabývat jmění nebo jiných práv na území druhé smluvní strany děděním ze zákona nebo ze závěti za stejných podmínek a ve stejném rozsahu, jako občané vlastní.

2. Občané jedné smluvní strany mohou závětí nakládat svým jměním nacházejícím se na území druhé smluvní strany.

Článek 36

Použití dědického práva

Dědické poměry se řídí právním řádem smluvní strany, jejímž občanem byl zůstavitel v době smrti.

Článek 37

Odúmrť

Jestliže podle právního řádu smluvní strany, jímž se řídí dědické poměry, není dědiců, movité jmění se odevzdá smluvní straně, jejímž občanem byl zůstavitel v době smrti, nemovité jmění smluvní straně, na jejímž území nemovitost leží.

Treaty between the Czechoslovak Socialist Republic and the Socialist Federal Republic of Yugoslavia on Legal Relations in Civil, Family and Criminal Matters of 20 January 1964**

Part 4

Matters of Succession upon death

Article 35

Principle of equal treatment

1. Nationals of one Contracting Party may acquire property or other rights in the territory of the other Contracting Party by testate or intestate succession under the same conditions and to the same extent as its own nationals.
2. Nationals of one Contracting Party are entitled to draw up a will with respect to their assets located in the territory of the other Contracting Party.

Article 36

Law applicable to succession upon death

Succession upon death shall be governed by the law of the Contracting Party whose nationality the deceased had at the time of death.

Article 37

Estates without a claimant

If according to the law of one Contracting Party governing the succession upon death there is no heir, the movable property passes to the Contracting Party of which the deceased was a national at the time of death, and the immovable property passes to the Contracting Party in whose territory the immovable property is located.

---

* Vyhláška ministra zahraničních věcí č. 207/1964 Sb.

** The English translation has kindly been prepared by Magdalena Pfeiffer.

Článek 38

Závěť

1. Způsobilost zřídit nebo zrušit závěť, jakož i právní následky vad vůle se řídí právním řádem smluvní strany, jejímž občanem byl zůstavitel v době, kdy závěť zřídil nebo zrušil.

2. Forma závěti se řídí právním řádem smluvní strany, jejímž občanem byl zůstavitel v době, kdy závěť zřídil. Stačí však, jestliže se postupovalo podle právního řádu smluvní strany, na jejímž území byla závěť zřízena. Totéž platí i pro zrušení závěti.

Article 38

Will

1. The capacity to make or revoke a will, as well as the legal consequences for the absence of intent to testate, shall be governed by the law of the Contracting Party of which the deceased was a national at the time of making or revoking the will.

2. The form of a will shall be governed by the law of the Contracting Party of which the deceased was a national at the time of making the will. It shall however be sufficient for the formal validity if the will complies with the law of the Contracting Party in whose territory the will was drawn up. The same applies to revocation of a will.

Článek 39

Příslušnost v dědických věcech

1. K projednání movitého dědictví je s výjimkou případu uvedeného v odstavci 4 tohoto článku příslušný orgán smluvní strany, jejímž občanem byl zůstavitel v době smrti.

2. K projednání nemovitého dědictví je příslušný orgán smluvní strany, na jejímž území nemovitost leží.

3. Ustanovení odstavců 1 a 2 platí i pro projednání dědických sporů.

4. Jestliže zůstavitel, který byl občanem jedné smluvní strany, měl poslední bydliště na území druhé smluvní strany, mohou dědicové, kteří mají bydliště nebo pobyt na území této smluvní strany, žádat do šesti měsíců po zůstavitelově smrti, aby movité dědictví nacházející se na tomto území bylo projednáno příslušným orgánem této smluvní strany. Jestliže do tří měsíců od vyrozumění o takové žádosti žádný z dědiců nevznese námitky, žádosti bude vyhověno.

5. Posouzení, zda jde o majetek movitý nebo nemovitý, se řídí právním řádem smluvní strany, kde se majetek nachází.

Article 39

Jurisdiction in matters of succession

1. The judicial authorities of the Contracting Party of which the deceased was a national at the time of death shall have jurisdiction to rule on the succession to movable property, subject to the exception referred to in paragraph 4 of this Article.

2. The judicial authorities of the Contracting Party in whose territory immovable property is located shall have jurisdiction to rule on succession to this immovable property.

3. Paragraphs 1 and 2 shall also apply in contentious proceedings regarding succession claims.

4. Provided that the deceased, who was a national of one Contracting Party, had his last domicile in the territory of the other Contracting Party, heirs domiciled or resident in this State can request no later than six months after the death of the deceased that the judicial authority of this Contracting Party shall have jurisdiction to rule on succession to movables located in the territory of this State. If no objections are raised by any of the heirs within three months of notification of such a request, the request is granted.

5. The issue of whether the property is movable or immovable is governed by the law of the Contracting Party in whose territory the property is located.

Článek 40

Opatření k zajištění dědictví

1. Orgán smluvní strany, na jejímž území je dědictví po občanu druhé smluvní strany, učiní podle právního řádu svého státu opatření nutná k zajištění dědictví a k jeho správě. Příslušné orgány smluvních stran budou stejně postupovat i v případech, kdy jako dědic přichází v úvahu občan druhé smluvní strany.
2. O opatřeních, která byla učiněna podle ustanovení odstavce 1, je třeba uvědomit diplomatickou misi nebo konzulární úřad druhé smluvní strany, které mohou při výkonu opatření k zajištění dědictví přímo anebo prostřednictvím zmocněnce spolupůsobit. Na jejich návrh mohou být učiněná opatření odložena, změněna nebo zrušena.
3. Na návrh orgánu příslušného k projednání dědictví budou opatření učiněná podle ustanovení odstavce 1 změněna nebo zrušena.

Článek 41

Sdělování úmrtí

Zemře-li občan jedné smluvní strany na území druhé smluvní strany, uvědomí příslušný orgán bez odkladu přímo diplomatickou misi nebo konzulární úřad druhé smluvní strany o úmrtí a sdělí vše, co je známo o dědicích, o jejich bydlišti nebo pobytu a o předmětu dědictví, jakož i o případné závěti. Je-li tomuto orgánu známo, že po zemřelém zůstal majetek i v jiném státě, podá zprávu i o tom.

Article 40

Measures to preserve the estate

1. The authority of the Contracting Party where assets belonging to the deceased, who was a national of the other Contracting Party, are located shall take all measures necessary to preserve and administer the estate pursuant to its own law, even if the potential heir is a national of the other Contracting Party.

2. The measures taken pursuant to paragraph 1 shall be notified to the diplomatic or consular office of the other Contracting Party, which may directly or through an agent take part in performing the measures deemed necessary to preserve the estate. The measures may be postponed, modified or revoked at its request.
3. The measures taken pursuant to provisions of paragraph 1 shall be modified or revoked at request of the authority that has jurisdiction in matters of succession.

Article 41

Notice of death

If a national of one Contracting Party dies on the territory of the other Contracting Party, the competent authority shall, without delay, inform the diplomatic or consular office of the other Contracting Party of the death and communicate any available information about the heirs, their domicile or residence and the estate as well as information on any wills. If the authority knows that the estate of the deceased is located in another State, it shall also be reported.

Článek 42

Oprávnění diplomatické mise nebo konzulárního úřadu v dědických věcech

V dědických věcech včetně dědických sporů jsou diplomatické mise a konzulární úřady smluvních stran oprávněny zastupovat bez zvláštní plné moci před orgány druhé smluvní strany vlastní občany, pokud tito občané jsou nepřítomni a neustanoví si zmocněnce.

Article 42

Powers of a diplomatic or consular office in succession matters

Diplomatic or consular offices of the Contracting Parties shall be entitled to represent their own nationals without special powers of attorney before the authorities of the other Contracting Party in succession matters, including succession disputes, provided that the represented nationals are absent and had not issued any power of attorney to any person or agent.

Článek 43

Zemře-li občan jedné smluvní strany v době přechodného pobytu na území druhé smluvní strany, věci, které měl u sebe, budou bez dalšího řízení a po úhradě jeho dluhů odevzdány spolu s jejich seznamem diplomatické misi nebo konzulárnímu úřadu smluvní strany, jejímž byl občanem.

Article 43

If a national of one Contracting party dies during a temporary stay in the territory of the other Contracting Party, his personal possessions including an inventory shall be, without further proceedings and after payment of his debts, handed over to the diplomatic or consular office of the Contracting Party of which the deceased was a national.

Článek 44

Vyhlášení závěti

K vyhlášení závěti je příslušný orgán smluvní strany, na jejímž území je závěť. Orgánu příslušnému k projednání dědictví je třeba zaslat ověřený opis závěti a protokolu o jejím vyhlášení a na žádost i originál závěti.

Article 44

Opening of the will

The opening of the will falls within the competence of the authority of the Contracting Party on the territory of which the will is located. A duly certified copy of the will and the minutes on its opening must be sent to the authority that has jurisdiction in succession matters, including, upon request, also the original will.

Článek 45

Vydání dědictví

1. Jestliže movité dědictví nebo výtěžek z prodeje movitého nebo nemovitého dědictví má být po projednání dědictví vydán dědicům, kteří mají bydliště nebo pobyt na území druhé smluvní strany, a jestliže není možno dědictví nebo jeho výtěžek odevzdat přímo dědici nebo jeho zmocněnci, vydá se diplomatické misi nebo konzulárnímu úřadu této smluvní strany.

Article 45

Releasing inherited property

1. In a situation where, after the succession proceedings have been terminated, movable property or proceeds from the sale of movable or immovable property shall be released to the heirs that have their domicile or residence in the territory of the other Contracting Party, and if they cannot be handed over to the heir or his agent directly, they shall be handed over to the diplomatic or consular office of this Contracting Party.

2. Dědictví se vydá za podmínek, že

a) byly zaplaceny nebo zajištěny všechny pohledávky věřitelů zůstavitele přihlášené ve lhůtě stanovené právním řádem smluvní strany, na jejímž území dědictví je,

b) byly zaplaceny nebo zajištěny dědické poplatky a
c) příslušný orgán dal souhlas k vývozu věcí nebo k převodu peněz.

Oddíl 6

Uznání a výkon rozhodnutí

Článek 50

1. Smluvní strany za podmínek stanovených v tétoSmlouvě uznávají a vykonávají na svém území tato rozhodnutí vydaná na území druhé smluvní strany:
[...]

2. Za soudní rozhodnutí ve smyslu ustanovení odstavce 1 se pokládají též rozhodnutí o dědictví vydaná orgánem jedné smluvní strany příslušným podle právního řádu svého státu k projednávání věcí dědických.
[...]

2. The assets shall be released provided that:

a) all outstanding claims of creditors of the deceased lodged within the time limit set by the law of the Contracting Party, in whose territory the estate is located, have been paid or secured;
b) inheritance tax has been paid or secured and
c) the competent authority has given consent to the export of assets or to the transfer of money.

Section 6

Recognition and Enforcement of Decisions

Article 50

1. The Contracting Parties shall, under the conditions laid down in this Treaty, recognize and enforce in their territory the following decisions rendered in the territory of the other Contracting Party:
[...]
2. Decisions on matters of succession upon death rendered by the authority of one Contracting Party that has jurisdiction pursuant to its own law to hear matters of succession shall also be considered as court decisions within the meaning of paragraph 1.
[...]

FINLAND

TREATY 14: NORDIC INHERITANCE CONVENTION

Suomen, Islannin, Norjan, Ruotsin ja Tanskan kesken 19 päivänä marraskuuta 1934 tehty perintöä, testamenttia ja pesänselvitystä koskeva sopimus*

I. Perintö ja testamentti

1 artikla

Tämän sopimuksen säännöksiä sovelletaan perintöä ja testamenttia koskeviin asioihin, jos henkilö oli kuollessaan sopimusvaltion kansalainen ja hänellä oli asuinpaikka sopimusvaltiossa, ellei Euroopan parlamentin ja neuvoston asetuksesta (EU N:o 650/2012) toimivallasta, sovellettavasta laista, päätösten tunnustamisesta ja täytäntöönpanosta ja virallisten asiakirjojen hyväksymisestä ja täytäntööpanosta perintöasioissa sekä eurooppalaisen perintötodistuksen käyttöönotosta muuta johdu.

2 artikla

Perimykseen sovelletaan sen sopimusvaltion lakia, jossa perittävällä oli kuollessaan asuinpaikka, ellei perittävä ole määrännyt toisin 3 artiklan mukaisella tavalla.

Convention between Denmark, Finland, Iceland, Norway and Sweden Comprising Private International Law Provisions on Succession, Wills and Estate Administration of 19 November 1934 (partly amended in 2012)**

I. Inheritance and wills

Article 1

The provisions in this Convention apply to issues concerning inheritance from, and the will of, a citizen of a Contracting State who, at the time of death, had his or her habitual residence in a Contracting State, unless otherwise provided in the European Regulation (EU) No. 650/2012.

Article 2

The law applicable to the succession shall be the law of the Contracting State in which the deceased had his habitual residence at the time of death, unless the deceased had designated another law in accordance with Article 3.

---

* Suomen asetuskokoelman sopimussarja 21/1935, amendments Suomen asetuskokoelman sopimussarja 36/1976 and Suomen säädöskokoelman sopimussarja 60/2015.

** The English translation has kindly been prepared by Markku Helin based on an (unofficial) translation of the proposed 2009 amendments carried out by the Nordic delegates for the negotiations of the Succession Regulation.

Jos poikkeuksellisesti tapaukseen liittyvistä kaikista seikoista ilmenee, että perittävällä oli kuollessaan selvästi läheisempi yhteys toiseen sopimusvaltioon kuin siihen valtioon, jonka laki tulisi sovellettavaksi 1 kohdan nojalla, perimykseen sovellettava laki on tuon toisen valtion laki.

Where, by way of exception, it is clear from all the circumstances of the case that, at the time of death, the deceased was manifestly more closely connected with another Contracting State than the State whose law would be applicable under paragraph 1, the law applicable to the succession shall be the law of that other State.

3 artikla

Perittävä voi määrätä, että hänen perimykseensä sovelletaan sen sopimusvaltion lakia, jonka kansalainen hän on valinnan tehdessään tai kuollessaan.

Henkilö, joka on useamman sopimusvaltion kansalainen, voi valita minkä tahansa sopimusvaltion lain, jonka kansalainen hän on valinnan tehdessään tai kuollessaan.

Jos perittävä on valinnut sovellettavaksi muun kuin sopimusvaltion lain, arvioidaan lainvalinnan pätevyys kussakin sopimusvaltiossa voimassa olevien yleisten säännösten nojalla.

Article 3

A person may choose as the law to govern his succession the law of the Contracting State whose nationality he possesses at the time of making the choice or at the time of death.

A person possessing multiple nationalities of Contracting States may choose the law of any of the States whose nationality he possesses at the time of making the choice or at the time of death.

Had the deceased chosen the law of a State other than a Contracting State, the validity of the choice in each Contracting States depends on the general provisions in force in that State.

3a artikla

Ollakseen pätevä perittävän tekemä määräys sovellettavasta laista edellyttää, että se on annettu testamentille säädetyssä muodossa tai että se käy ilmi testamentin ehdoista. Lainvalinnan peruuttaminen on tehtävä testamentin peruuttamista koskevia muotomääräyksiä noudattaen, jotta se olisi pätevä. Lainvalinnan tai sen peruuttamisen pätevyyttä harkittaessa on otettava huomioon, mitä 8 artiklassa sanotaan.

Article 3a

A provision on applicable law must be made in the form that applies to wills in order to be valid or shall be demonstrated by the terms of such a disposition. A revocation of the provision must be made in the form that applies for revocation of a will in order to be valid. When examining the formal validity of a provision or revocation, consideration must be given to what is stated in Article 8.

3b artikla

Sopimusvaltio, jossa perittävällä oli asuinpaikka tehdessään 3 artiklassa tarkoitetun lainvalinnan, voi säätää, että lainvalinta on siinä sopimusvaltiossa toimitettavassa perinnönjaossa pätevä perittävän aviopuolisoa tai avopuolisoa kohtaan vain, jos se on annettu hänelle tiedoksi.

Article 3b

Each Contracting State may decide that when an estate is distributed in that State, such a choice of law provision, as referred to in Article 3, made by a deceased person who had his or her habitual residence in the State at the time the provision was made, shall only be effective against the deceased's spouse or cohabitee if the spouse or cohabitee has been informed of the provision.

8 artikla

Perittävän testamentti katsotaan muodoltaan päteväksi, jos se täyttää testamentin muodolle sen paikkakunnan lain asettamat määräykset, jolla testamentti tehtiin tai jossa testamentintekijällä oli asuinpaikka testamentin tehdessään tai kuollessaan taikka sellaisen valtion lain määräykset, jonka kansalainen testamentintekijä oli testamentin tehdessään tai kuollessaan. Milloin testamentti koskee kiinteää omaisuutta, se katsotaan muodoltaan päteväksi myös, jos se täyttää testamentin muodolle säädetyt edellytykset siinä valtiossa, missä omaisuus sijaitsee.

Mitä 1 kappaleessa on sanottu, sovelletaan vastaavasti myös testamentin muuttamiseen tai peruuttamiseen. Peruuttaminen katsotaan muodoltaan päteväksi myös, jos peruuttaminen muotonsa osalta täyttää sellaisen lain määräykset, jonka mukaan testamentti, joka on peruutettu, oli 1 kappaleen nojalla muodoltaan pätevä.

Jos testamentintekijällä oli muun kuin sopimusvaltion lain mukaan domisiili (domicile) tässä valtiossa, voidaan domisiiliin vedota asuinpaikan asemesta 1 tai 2 kappaleessa tarkoitetuissa tapauksissa.

Milloin 1, 2 tai 3 kappaleen mukaan on kysymys muun kuin sopimusvaltion lain soveltamisesta, on noudatettava tästä kussakin sopimusvaltiossa voimassa olevia yleisiä säännöksiä.

Article 8

The deceased's will is deemed formally valid if the will meets the formal requirements prescribed in the law in the place where the will was made or where the testator had his or her habitual residence when drawing up the will or at his or her death, or the requirements prescribed in the law of the State in which the testator was a citizen when drawing up the will or at his or her death. Insofar as the will refers to real property, it shall also be deemed formally valid if the will meets the formal requirements prescribed in the law in the place in which the property is located.

The first paragraph applies correspondingly to issues concerning amendments to, or revocation of, a will. A revocation shall also be deemed formally valid if the revocation meets the formal requirements prescribed in the law under which the revoked will was formally valid on the grounds of what is stated in the first paragraph.

If the testator, under the law of a non-contracting State, had his or her domicile in that State, this domicile may be invoked instead of habitual residence in cases referred to in the first or second paragraph.

If, under the first, second or third paragraph, the law applicable is the law of a non-contracting State, the relevant general rules that apply in each Contracting State shall apply.

9 artikla

Perittävän kelpoisuus tehdä tai peruuttaa testamentti määräytyy sen sopimusvaltion lain mukaan, jota 2 tai 3 artiklan nojalla sovelletaan perimykseen.

Perittävällä katsotaan lisäksi olleen kelpoisuus tehdä tai peruuttaa testamentti, jos hänellä oli siihen kelpoisuus sen sopimusvaltion lain mukaan, jossa hänellä oli asuinpaikka testamenttia tehdessään tai peruuttaessaan. Jos perittävän asuinpaikka oli tuolloin muussa kuin sopimusvaltiossa, on noudatettava kussakin sopimusvaltiossa voimassa olevia yleisiä säännöksiä.

Article 9

A question concerning the deceased's authority to make or revoke a will shall be determined by the law of the Contracting State, the law of which shall apply to issues concerning the right to inherit from the deceased under Article 2 or 3.

The deceased shall also be deemed to have had the authority to draw up or revoke the will if he or she had such authority under the law of the Contracting State in which he or she had his or her habitual residence at the time the will was made or revoked. If, at the point in time in question, the deceased had his or her habitual residence in a non-contracting State, the general rules that apply in each Contracting State shall apply.

10 artikla

Kysymys testamentin tai sen peruuttamisen pätemättömyydestä testamentintekijän mielentilan perusteella tai petoksen, erehdyksen, pakottamisen tai muun epäoikeutetun vaikuttamisen vuoksi ratkaistaan sen sopimusvaltion lain mukaan, missä hänellä testamentin tehdessään tai peruuttaessaan oli asuinpaikka. Jos testamentintekijän asuinpaikka oli tuolloin muualla kuin sopimusvaltiossa, on noudatettava tästä kussakin sopimusvaltiossa voimassa olevia yleisiä säännöksiä.

Article 10

A question concerning the invalidity of the will or the revocation on the grounds of the testator's state of mind or on the grounds of fraud, delusion, coercion or other undue influence shall be determined by the law of the State in which the testator had his or her habitual residence at the time of making or revocation of the will. If, at the point in time in question, the testator had his or her habitual residence in a non-contracting State, the general rules that apply in each Contracting State shall apply.

11 artikla

Jos sopimusvaltion kansalaisella kuollessaan oli asuinpaikka Suomessa tai Ruotsissa, on testamentin moittimiseen sovellettava siellä voimassa olevaa lakia.

Norjan lain säännöksiä, joiden mukaan testamenttiin perustuva oikeus on saatettava voimaan ja väitteet testamentin pätevyyttä vastaan on tehtävä tiettyjen määräaikojen kuluessa, sovelletaan myös toisen sopimusvaltion kansalaisen tekemään testamenttiin, jos hänellä kuollessaan oli asuinpaikka Norjassa.

Article 11

If a citizen of a Contracting State had his or her habitual residence in Finland or Sweden at the time of death, the law that is in force there shall apply to issues concerning the contesting of a will.

Provisions in Norwegian law stating that rights based on a will and objections to the validity of a will must be asserted within certain time limits also apply to issues concerning the will of a citizen of another Contracting State if he or she had his or her habitual residence in Norway at the time of death.

12 artikla

Perittävän tekemän perintösopimuksen tai kuoleman varalta antaman lahjan sitovuus ratkaistaan sen valtion lain mukaan, jota oikeustointa suoritettaessa olisi 2 tai 3 artiklan mukaan sovellettu hänen perimykseensä.

Saman lain nojalla ratkaistaan, onko perillisen perittävältä tämän eläessä saamaa omaisuutta pidettävä ennakkoperintönä.

Jos 1 tai 2 kappaleen nojalla sovellettavaksi tulee muun kuin sopimusvaltion laki, sovelletaan tästä kussakin sopimusvaltiossa voimassa olevia yleisiä säännöksiä.

Article 12

If the deceased has entered into an inheritance agreement or given a bequest on death, the binding nature of the agreement or the bequest shall be determined by the law of the State that at that time applied, under Article 2 or 3, to the right to inherit from him or her.

The same law applies to whether property that an heir has received from the deceased during the latter's lifetime shall be considered an advancement on inheritance.

If, according to paragraph 1 or 2, the applicable law was the law of a non-contracting State, the general rules that apply in each Contracting State shall apply.

13 artikla

Milloin sopimusvaltiossa on jonkun perillisen oikeudesta kiinteään omaisuuteen tarpeistoineen tai perinnönjättäjän oikeudesta määrätä tällaisesta omaisuudesta testamentilla jonkun perillisen hyväksi voimassa erikoismääräyksiä, on näitä noudatettava siinä valtiossa olevan omaisuuden osalta.

Oikeus testamentilla antaa sääntöperintömääräyksiä kiinteästä omaisuudesta tai muuten syntymättömien hyväksi määrätä tällaisesta omaisuudesta määräytyköön niin ikään sen sopimusvaltion lain mukaan, missä omaisuus on. Oikeuteen antaa tällaisia määräyksiä irtaimesta omaisuudesta ei tätä sopimusta sovelleta.

Article 13

If special rules apply in a Contracting State concerning a certain heir's right to real property with fixtures or concerning the deceased's authority to provide in a will that such property shall go to a certain heir, the aforementioned rules shall be complied with concerning property in that State.

Concerning the right to make a fidei commissum entailing real property or otherwise dispose of such property for the benefit of unborn persons, the law of the Contracting State in which the property is located shall apply. This Convention does not concern the right to thus dispose of personal property.

14 artikla

Jos sopimusvaltion kansalaiselta jää eloon ottolapsi, olkoon milloin päätös lapseksiottamisesta on annettu tällaisessa valtiossa ja päätöksessä on lapseksiottajalle varattu oikeus jäämistönsä määräämiseen, tämä varaus voimassa kaikissa sopimusvaltioissa.

Article 14

If a citizen of a Contracting State leaves adopted children, and if the adoption order was delivered in such State and contains a clause on the right of the adopter to have entire disposal over the property he or she leaves, this clause will apply in each of the States.

16 artikla

Perintöä tai testamenttia koskevan oikeuden vanhentumiseen perittävän kuoleman jälkeen sovelletaan sitä lakia, jota 2 tai 3 artiklan nojalla sovelletaan hänen perimykseensä.

Article 16

Concerning the issue of time limits on the right to inherit from, or benefit from the will of a deceased person, the law of the State that applies under Article 2 or 3 to the right to inherit from him or her shall apply.

II. Vainajan velka

17 artikla

Perillisen tai testamentinsaajan vastuu sopimusvaltion kansalaiselta jääneestä velasta tai legaatin tai käyttömääräyksen täyttämisestä vainajan testamentin mukaisesti määräytyy sen sopimusvaltion lain mukaan, missä vainajalla oli kuollessaan asuinpaikka.

II. The deceased's debts

Article 17

Issues concerning an heir's or beneficiary's liability for debts left by the deceased, who was a citizen of a Contracting State or for the execution of legacies or of a testamentary request, are determined by the law of the Contracting State in which the deceased had his or her habitual residence at the time of death.

18 artikla

Pesänselvityksen yhteydessä haettu julkinen haaste tuntemattomien velkojien selvittämiseksi on tehoton, jos kyse on tunnetusta saamisesta ja velkojalla oli asuinpaikka toisessa sopimusvaltiossa, ellei velkoja ole ajoissa saanut eri ilmoitusta haasteesta ja sen vaikutuksesta tai hänellä muuten ollut siitä tietoa.

Article 18

A proclamation for unknown creditors issued during estate administration is of no legal effect if the claim was known about and the creditor had his or her habitual residence in another Contracting State, unless the creditor received a timely special communication about the advertisement and its effects or otherwise knew about it.

III. Pesänselvitys, omaisuuden ositus ja perinnönjako

III. Estate administration, division of matrimonial property and distribution of the estate

19 artikla

Pesänselvitys, omaisuuden ositus ja perinnönjako sopimusvaltion kansalaisen jälkeen toimitetaan sen sopimusvaltion lain mukaan, missä vainajalla oli asuinpaikka. Jos tuon valtion lain mukaan asiassa tarvitaan tuomioistuimen tai muun viranomaisen myötävaikutusta, kuuluu se tuon valtion tuomioistuimen tai viranomaisen tehtäviin.

Milloin eloonjäänyt puoliso, joka on sopimusvaltion kansalainen, on elänyt jakamattomassa pesässä ja pesä on jaettava, toimitetaan jako sen valtion lain mukaan, missä hänellä on tai kuollessaan oli asuinpaikka. Jos sanotun lain mukaan asiassa tarvitaan tuomioistuimen toimenpiteitä, kuuluvat ne tuon valtion tuomioistuinten tehtäviin.

Pesänselvitys, omaisuuden ositus ja perinnönjako kattavat pesään kuuluvan omaisuuden muissakin sopimusvaltioissa.

Article 19

Estate administration, division of the matrimonial property and distribution of the estate of a citizen of a Contracting State shall be carried out under the law of the Contracting State in which the deceased had his or her habitual residence. If, under this law, a court or other authority is to assist, this will be the responsibility of a court or authority in that State.

If a surviving spouse, who is a citizen of a Contracting State, has stayed in an undistributed estate and the property is to be divided, procedures must follow the law in the State in which he or she has or at the time of death had his or her habitual residence; and if measures are to be taken by a court under the aforementioned law, the measures shall be the responsibility of a court in that State.

Estate administration, division of matrimonial property and distribution of the estate shall also include property belonging to the estate that is located in another Contracting State.

20 artikla

Osituksessa, jota 19 artiklassa tarkoitetaan, on kysymykseen eloonjääneen puolison oikeudesta ottaa pesästä tiettyä omaisuutta, joko vastiketta vastaan tai ilman vastiketta, sovellettava sanotussa artiklassa määrättyä lakia. Saman lain mukaan ratkaistaan, onko puolisolla oikeus vaatia, että perillisen osituksessa saama perintöoikeus jää puolison haltuun ja perilliselle annetaan tästä saamisestaan panttioikeus, kuitenkin siten, että panttioikeus toisessa sopimusvaltiossa olevaan omaisuuteen voidaan perustaa vain siellä voimassaolevan lain mukaisesti.

Article 20

In the event of division of matrimonial property referred to in Article 19, the law stated in Article 19 shall apply to the surviving spouse's right to, with or without compensation, take out certain property. The same applies to whether the spouse is entitled to demand that property that, in the division of matrimonial property, is distributed to an heir should remain with the spouse and that the heir enjoy a lien; but that a lien on property located in another Contracting State may not be granted in any other way than under the law that applies there.

21 artikla

Riita sellaisen henkilön jättämästä perinnöstä tai tekemästä testamentista, joka oli sopimusvaltion kansalainen ja jolla oli asuinpaikka jossakin sopimusvaltiossa, eloonjääneen puolison oikeudesta taikka saamisesta kuolinpesältä on sen valtion käsiteltävä, jonka lakia noudattaen pesänselvitys, omaisuuden ositus ja perinnönjako on 19 artiklan mukaan toimitettava.

Jos asianosaiset siitä sopivat, voidaan riita ottaa käsiteltäväksi muussa sopimusvaltiossa, ei kuitenkaan milloin kuolinpesää koskeva asiaa käsittelee tuomioistuin, testamentin toimeenpanija, pesänhoitaja (bobestyrer) tai tuomioistuimen määräämä pesänselvittäjä tai pesänjakaja taikka jos riita koskee tällaisessa pesässä toimitetun osituksen tai perinnönjaon tai jonkun sellaisen henkilön tekemän testamentin moitetta, jolla oli kotipaikka Suomessa tai Ruotsissa, eikä myöskään, kun riita tarkoittaa sellaisen henkilön jälkeen toimitetun osituksen tai perinnönjaon moittimista, jolla oli Suomessa asuinpaikka.

[...]

Article 21

Disputes over inheritance from, or the will of, a citizen of a Contracting State, who had his or her habitual residence in such a State, or over the surviving spouse's rights or claims on the estate shall be examined by a court in the State, the law of which shall apply to the estate administration, division of matrimonial property and distribution of the estate under Article 19.

If the parties are in agreement, the dispute may be examined in another Contracting State, but not where the estate is the subject of consideration by an inheritance court or an estate executor, trustee or an official estate administrator appointed by a court or a special estate distributor, or if the dispute concerns contestation of a division of matrimonial property or distribution of such an estate or contestation of the will of a person who had his or her habitual residence in Finland or Sweden, or of a division of property or distribution of the estate of a person who had his or her habitual residence in Finland.

[...]

IV. Yleisiä määräyksiä

27 artikla

Jos sopimusvaltion tuomioistuin on päättänyt, että tuomioistuimen, perinnönjako-oikeuden, pesänselvittäjän, pesänhoitajan (bobestyrer) tai testamentin toimeenpanijan on otettava 19 artiklassa tarkoitettu kuolinpesä hoitoonsa, että pesänselvitys ja -jako tapahtuu osakasten toimesta tai että pesän jako toimitetaan pesänjakajan myötävaikutuksella, on päätös voimassa muissakin sopimusvaltioissa.

IV. General provisions

Article 27

If a court in a Contracting State has decided that an estate referred to in Article 19 shall be taken in charge by an inheritance court, estate administrator, trustee or executor, or that the property is to be subject to administration and distribution of the shareholders, or distributed with the assistance of a special estate distributor, the decision applies in the other Contracting States.

28 artikla

Sellaisen tuomion tai sovinnon tunnustamisessa tai täytäntöönpanossa, joka koskee perintöön tai testamenttiin perustuvaa oikeutta, eloonjääneen puolison oikeutta, pesänselvitystä tai kuoleman johdosta toimitettua jakoa taikka vastuuta vainajan velasta, on noudatettava sen valtion lakia, missä tunnustamista tai täytäntöönpanoa pyydetään.

Article 28

Concerning recognition and enforcement of a judgment or settlement regarding a right based on an inheritance or will, a surviving spouse's right, estate administration or distribution of property in connection with a death or liability for the deceased's debt, the law of the State in which recognition or enforcement have been requested shall apply.[***]

[***] Remark: 'The law of the State' in this Article refers in fact to uniform Nordic laws on recognition and enforcement of Nordic judgments concerning claims in private law. The title of the Finnish law is 'Laki yksityisoikeudellista vaatimusta koskevien pohjoismaisten tuomioiden tunnustamisesta ja täytäntöönpanosta (588/1977)'. According to it, the judgments given in accordance with the Nordic Inheritance Convention are recognized and enforceable in other Nordic states. Grounds of refusal which are relevant in this context concern mistakes in service of documents and situations where parallel proceedings are pending in different Contracting States.

TREATY 15: FINLAND–USSR

Sopimus Suomen Tasavallan ja Sosialististen Neuvostotasavaltojen Liiton välillä oikeussuojasta ja oikeusavusta siviili-, perhe- ja rikosasioissa, tehty 11 päivänä elokuuta 1978*

25 artikla

Testamentin muoto

Sopimuspuolen kansalaisen testamentti katsotaan muodoltaan päteväksi, jos sitä tehtäessä oli noudatettu:

a) sen valtion lainsäädäntöä, jonka alueella testamentti oli tehty; tai
b) sen sopimuspuolen lainsäädäntöä, jonka kansalainen perinnönjättäjä oli testamentin tehdessään tai kuollessaan tai sen valtion lainsäädäntöä, jonka alueella hänellä oli kotipaikka jonakin mainittuna hetkenä.

Siltä osin kuin testamentti koskee kiinteätä omaisuutta, testamentti katsotaan muodoltaan päteväksi, jos sitä tehtäessä oli noudatettu sen valtion lainsäädäntöä, missä kiinteä omaisuus sijaitsee.

Tämän artiklan 1 kappaleen määräykset koskevat myös testamentin peruuttamista.

Treaty between the Republic of Finland and the Union of Soviet Socialist Republics Concerning the Provision of Legal Protection and Legal Assistance in Civil, Family and Criminal Cases of 11 August 1978**

Article 25

Form of the testament

A will made by a citizen of a Contracting State is deemed to be valid as regards form if its form complies with

a) the law of the State in the area of which the will was made; or
b) the law of the Contracting State whose citizen the deceased was at the time when he made the will or at the time of his death, or the law of the State where he was habitually resident at a time mentioned above.

As far as immovable property is concerned, the will is deemed to be valid as regards form if its form complies with the law of the State where the property is situated.

Paragraph 1 of this article shall also apply to revocation of such a will.

* Suomen asetuskokoelman sopimussarja 48/1980.

** The English translation has kindly been prepared by Markku Helin.

FRANCE

TREATY 16: FRANCE-TUNISIA

Convention judiciaire entre la France et la Tunisie du 9 mars 1957*

Article 1

Dès l'entrée en vigueur de la présente convention, les juridictions françaises de Tunisie sont supprimées et toutes les compétences qui leur étaient attribuées sont dévolues aux tribunaux tunisiens.

Article 2

En matière de statut personnel, tel qu'il est défini par le décret beylical du 12 juillet 1956, les personnes de nationalité française sont régies par leur loi nationale.

Dans toutes les matières civiles et commerciales et à défaut de texte tunisien, le texte français en vigueur en Tunisie à la date d'application de la présente convention continuera à être appliqué devant les juridictions tunisiennes.

Judicial Convention between France and Tunisia of 9 March 1957**

Article 1

Upon the entry into force of the convention, all French courts in Tunisia are abolished and their jurisdiction is transferred to Tunisian courts.

Article 2

In matters of personal [and family] status, as defined by the 12 July 1956 decree of the [ruling] Bey, persons of French nationality are governed by French law.

In all civil and commercial matters, and unless there is an applicable Tunisian text, Tunisian courts will continue to apply the French text as it existed in Tunisia on the date this convention was implemented.

* JORF, 2 February 1958, p. 1266.

** The English translation of this treaty (and the 1956 Decree of the Bey reproduced as annex below) has kindly been prepared by Samuel Fulli-Lemaire.

Annexe

Article 2 du Décret fixant le statut personnel des Tunisiens non musulmans et non israélites du 12 juillet 1956 (3 doul hidja 1375)***

Le statut personnel comprend les contestations relatives à l'état et à la capacité des personnes, au mariage, aux régimes matrimoniaux, aux droits et devoirs réciproques des époux, au divorce, à la répudiation, à la séparation, à la filiation, à la reconnaissance et au désaveu de la paternité, aux relations entre ascendants et descendants, à l'obligation alimentaire entre parents et autres alliés, à la légitimation, à l'adoption, à la tutelle, à la curatelle, [...] à l'émancipation, aux successions, eu testament et autres dispositions à cause de mort, à l'absence et à la présomption de décès.

Annex

Article 2 of the Decree setting out the personal [and family] status of non-Muslim and non-Jewish Tunisian citizens of 12 July 1956 (3 doul hidja 1375)

Personal [and family] status includes disputes relating to the status of persons, capacity, marriage, matrimonial property, the reciprocal rights and duties of spouses, divorce, repudiation, separation, parentage, acknowledgment of paternity, procedures for disclaiming paternity, the relationship between ascending and descending relatives, maintenance between parties related collaterally or by affinity, legitimation, adoption, guardianship, curatorship, [...] emancipation, donations, successions, testaments and other dispositions of property upon death, declarations of absence and presumptions of death.

*** Journal Officiel Tunisien, 13 July 1956, p. 987.

GERMANY

TREATY 17: GERMANY-PERSIAN EMPIRE

Niederlassungsabkommen zwischen dem Deutschen Reich und dem Kaiserreich Persien vom 17. Februar 1929*

Artikel 8

Die Angehörigen jedes vertragsschließenden Staates genießen im Gebiet des anderen Staates in allem, was den gerichtlichen und behördlichen Schutz ihrer Personen und Güter angeht, die gleiche Behandlung wie Inländer.

Sie haben insbesondere freien und völlig ungehinderten Zutritt zu den Gerichten und können vor Gericht unter den Bedingungen wie Inländer auftreten. Jedoch werden bis zum Abschluss eines besonderen Abkommens die Voraussetzungen für das Armenrecht und die Sicherheitsleistung für Prozesskosten durch die örtliche Gesetzgebung geregelt.

In Bezug auf das Personen-, Familien- und Erbrecht bleiben die Angehörigen jedes der vertragsschließenden Staaten im Gebiet des anderen Staates jedoch den Vorschriften ihrer heimischen Gesetze unterworfen. Die Anwendung dieser Gesetze kann von dem anderen vertragsschließenden Staat nur ausnahmsweise und nur insoweit ausgeschlossen werden, als ein solcher Ausschluss allgemein gegenüber jedem anderen Staat erfolgt.

Treaty on Establishment between the German Reich and the Persian Empire of 17 February 1929**

Article 8

The nationals of each Contracting State in the territory of the other State shall enjoy the same treatment as nationals of that State in all matters concerning the judicial and official protection of their person and property.

In particular, they shall have free and unrestricted access to the courts and may be a party to legal proceedings under the same conditions as nationals. But, until the conclusion of a special agreement the conditions regarding legal aid and security for legal costs shall be regulated by local legislation.

However, regarding the law of persons, family and succession, the nationals of each Contracting State in the territory of the other State shall remain subject to the provisions of their national law. The other Contracting State may only exceptionally exclude the application of these provisions and only insofar as the preclusion applies to any other State.

* Reichsgesetzblatt 1930 II, 1002.

** The English translation has kindly been prepared by Dirk Looschelders.

Schlussprotokoll zu Art. 8 Absatz 3

Die vertragsschließenden Staaten sind sich darüber einig, dass das Personen-, Familien- und Erbrecht, das heißt das Personalstatut, die folgenden Angelegenheiten mitumfasst: Ehe, eheliches Güterrecht, Scheidung, Aufhebung der ehelichen Gemeinschaft, Mitgift, Vaterschaft, Abstammung, Annahme an Kindes Statt, Geschäftsfähigkeit, Volljährigkeit, Vormundschaft und Pflegschaft, Entmündigung, testamentarische und gesetzliche Erbfolge, Nachlassabwicklungen und Erbauseinandersetzungen, ferner alle anderen Angelegenheiten des Familienrechts unter Einschluss aller den Personenstand betreffenden Fragen.

Final protocol to Article 8 paragraph 3

The Contracting States agree that the law of persons, family and succession, i.e. the personal statute, includes the following matters: marriage, matrimonial property regime, divorce, legal separation, dowry, paternity, filiation, adoption, legal capacity, age of majority, legal and nominated guardianship, deprivation of legal capacity, testate and intestate succession, administration and all distribution of the estate, and all further matters relating to family law and personal status.

TREATY 18: GERMANY–USSR

Konsularvertrag zwischen der Bundesrepublik Deutschland und der Union der Sozialistischen Sowjetrepubliken vom 25. April 1958*

Artikel 28 Absatz 3

Hinsichtlich der unbeweglichen Nachlassgegenstände finden die Rechtsvorschriften des Staates Anwendung, in dessen Gebiet diese Gegenstände belegen sind.

Consular Treaty between the Federal Republic of Germany and the Union of Soviet Socialist Republics of 25 April 1958**

Article 28 paragraph 3

Matters regarding the immovable parts of the estate shall be determined by the law of the State in whose territory these parts are located.

* Bundesgesetzblatt 1959 II, 233.

** The English translation has kindly been prepared by Dirk Looschelders.

TREATY 19: GERMANY–TURKEY

Konsularvertrag zwischen dem Deutschen Reich und der Türkischen Republik vom 28.5.1929*

Artikel 20

In Ansehung der in dem Gebiete des einen vertragsschließenden Staates befindlichen Nachlässe von Angehörigen des anderen Staates haben die Konsuln die aus der Anlage dieses Vertrages ersichtlichen Befugnisse.

Anlage zu Art. 20 des Konsularvertrages

§12

(1) In Ansehung des unbeweglichen Nachlasses sind ausschließlich die zuständigen Behörden des Staates, in dessen Gebiet sich dieser Nachlass befindet, berechtigt und verpflichtet, alle Verrichtungen nach Maßgabe der Landesgesetze und in derselben Weise vorzunehmen wie bei Nachlässen von Angehörigen ihres eigenen Staates. Beglaubigte Abschrift des über den unbeweglichen Nachlass aufgenommenen Verzeichnisses ist sobald als möglich dem zuständigen Konsul zu übersenden.

(2) Hat der Konsul eine Verfügung von Todes wegen in Besitz genommen, worin Bestimmungen über unbeweglichen Nachlass enthalten sind, so hat er der Ortsbehörde auf ihr Ersuchen die Urschrift dieser Verfügung auszuhändigen.

(3) Das Recht des Staates, in dem sich der Nachlass befindet, entscheidet darüber, was zum beweglichen und zum unbeweglichen Nachlass gehört.

Consular Treaty between the German Reich and the Republic of Turkey (with an Agreement on Succession Matters) of 28 May 1929**

Article 20

With respect to the estates of nationals of one Contracting State located in the territory of the other Contracting State the consuls have the powers specified in the Annex of this Treaty.

Annex to Article 20 of the Consular Treaty

Section 12

(1) With respect to the immovable part of the estate, the competent authorities of the State in whose territory the immovable part is located shall exclusively be entitled and obliged to perform all measures pursuant to the domestic law and in the same manner as in cases of estates of their nationals. A certified copy of the register in which the immovable part of the estate is listed shall be transmitted to the competent consul as soon as possible.

(2) If the consul has taken possession of a disposition of property upon death containing provisions related to immovable parts of the estate, he shall hand over the original document to the local authority upon request.

(3) The law of the State in whose territory the part of the estate is located shall determine whether it is to be qualified as movable or immovable.

* Reichsgesetzblatt 1930 II, 747.

** The English translation has kindly been prepared by Dirk Looschelders.

§13

In allen Angelegenheiten, zu denen die Eröffnung, Verwaltung und Regelung der beweglichen und unbeweglichen Nachlässe von Angehörigen des einen Staates im Gebiet des anderen Staates Anlass geben, soll der Konsul ermächtigt sein, die Erben, die seinem Staate angehören und keinen Bevollmächtigten in dem anderen Staate bestellt haben, zu vertreten, ohne dass er gehalten ist, seine Vertretungsbefugnis durch eine besondere Urkunde nachzuweisen. Die Vertretungsbefugnis des Konsuls fällt weg, wenn alle Berechtigten anwesend oder vertreten sind.

Section 13

In all matters to which the opening, administration and settlement of the movable and immovable estates of nationals of the one State in the territory of the other State have given rise, the consul shall be authorized to represent the heirs who belong to his State and who have not appointed an authorized representative in the other State, without being obliged to prove his power of representation by a special certificate. The Consul's power to representation is lost if all the persons entitled are present or represented.

§14

(1) Die erbrechtlichen Verhältnisse bestimmen sich in Ansehung des beweglichen Nachlasses nach den Gesetzen des Landes, dem der Erblasser zur Zeit seines Todes angehörte.
(2) Die erbrechtlichen Verhältnisse in Ansehung des unbeweglichen Nachlasses bestimmen sich nach den Gesetzen des Landes, in dem dieser Nachlass liegt, und zwar in der gleichen Weise, wie wenn der Erblasser zur Zeit seines Todes Angehöriger dieses Landes gewesen wäre.

Section 14

(1) As far as the movable part of the estate is concerned, the legal relationships relating to succession shall be determined by the law of the State of which the deceased was a national at the time of death.
(2) As far as the immovable part of the estate is concerned, the legal relationships relating to succession shall be determined by the law of the State in whose territory the immovable part is located, in the same manner as if the deceased had been a national of this State at the time of death.

§15

Klagen, welche die Feststellung des Erbrechts, Erbschaftsansprüche, Ansprüche aus Vermächtnissen sowie Pflichtteilsansprüche zum Gegenstand haben, sind, soweit es sich um beweglichen Nachlass handelt, bei den Gerichten des Staates anhängig zu machen, dem der Erblasser zur Zeit seines Todes angehörte, soweit es sich um unbeweglichen Nachlass handelt, bei den Gerichten des Staates, in dessen Gebiet sich der unbewegliche Nachlass befindet. Ihre Entscheidungen sind von dem anderen Staate anzuerkennen.

Section 15

Actions concerning a declaratory judgment on the entitlement to an estate, claims to an inheritance, claims arising from a legacy and claims to a reserved share shall – as far as the movable part of the estate is concerned – be brought before the courts of the State of which the deceased was a national at the time of death, and – as far as the immovable part of the estate is concerned, before the courts of the State in whose territory the immovable part is located. Their decisions shall be recognized by the other Contracting State.

§16

(1) Verfügungen von Todes wegen sind, was ihre Form anlangt, gültig, wenn die Gesetze des Landes beachtet sind, wo die Verfügungen errichtet sind, oder die Gesetze des Staates, dem der Erblasser zur Zeit der Errichtung angehörte.
(2) Das gleiche gilt für den Widerruf solcher Verfügungen von Todes wegen.

Section 16

(1) Dispositions of property upon death shall be formally valid if their form complies with the law of the State in which the dispositions were drawn up or the law of the State of which the deceased was a national at the time of the drawing up.
(2) The same shall apply to the revocation of dispositions of property upon death.

§17

Ein Zeugnis über ein erbrechtliches Verhältnis, insbesondere über das Recht des Erben oder eines Testamentsvollstreckers, das von der zuständigen Behörde des Staates, dem der Erblasser angehörte, nach dessen Gesetzen ausgestellt ist, genügt, soweit es sich um beweglichen Nachlass handelt, zum Nachweis dieser Rechtsverhältnisse auch für das Gebiet des anderen Staates. Zum Beweise der Echtheit genügt die Beglaubigung durch einen Konsul oder einen diplomatischen Vertreter des Staates, dem der Erblasser angehörte.

Section 17

As far as the movable part of the estate is concerned, a certificate of a legal relationship relating to succession, especially a certificate of the right of an heir or an executor of the will, issued by the competent authority of the State of which the deceased was a national shall be sufficient for the proof of this legal relationship in the territory of the other Contracting State, too. The attestation by a consul or a diplomatic representative of the State of which the deceased was a national at the time of death shall be sufficient to prove the authenticity of the certificate.

§18

Die Bestimmungen der §§1 bis 17 finden entsprechende Anwendung auf bewegliches oder unbewegliches Vermögen, das sich im Gebiet des einen Teils befindet und zu dem Nachlass eines außerhalb dieses Gebietes verstorbenen Angehörigen des anderen Teils gehört.

Section 18

The provisions of sections 1 to 17 shall apply mutatis mutandis to movable or immovable property located in the territory of one of the Contracting States but belonging to the estate of a deceased who died outside that territory and has the nationality of the other Contracting State.

ITALY

TREATY 20: ITALY–SWITZERLAND

Traité d'établissement et consulaire entre l'Italie et la Suisse du 22 juillet 1868*

Article 17

3. Les contestations qui pourraient s'élever entre les héritiers d'un Italien mort en Suisse, au sujet de sa succession, seront portées devant le juge du dernier domicile que l'Italien avait en Italie.
4. La réciprocité aura lieu à l'égard des contestations qui pourraient s'élever entre les héritiers d'un Suisse mort en Italie.

Establishment and Consular Treaty between Italy and Switzerland of 22 July 1868**

Article 17

3. The disputes that may arise between the heirs of an Italian who died in Switzerland, in respect of his or her succession, shall be brought before the courts for the place of the Italian's last domicile in Italy.
4. Reciprocity shall apply to such disputes as may arise between the heirs of a Swiss who died in Italy.

---

* Gazzetta Ufficiale del Regno d'Italia, No. 145 of 29 May 1865.

** The English translation has kindly been prepared by Pietro Franzina.

TREATY 21: ITALY–TURKEY

Convention consulaire entre le Royaume d'Italie et la République Turque du 9 septembre 1929*

Article 21 - Succession

I. En ce qui concerne les successions mobilières des sujets de l'une des Hautes Parties Contractantes sur le territoire de l'autre, les consuls généraux, consuls et vice-consuls du Pays du défunt auront les attributions suivantes [...]

VI. Le fonctionnaire consulaire conservera comme dépot soumis aux lois du Pays de sa résidence les objets inventoriés, le produit de la vente des meubles, si elle a eu lieu, et le montant des créances rentrées, pendant les trois mois qui suivront la dernière publication sur l'ouverture de la succession ou, a défaut d'une pareille publication, pendant les quatre mois qui suivront le décès. Au cours de ce délai il recouvrera, soit à l'amiable, soit par voie judiciaire, les créances, rentes, dividendes d'action, intérêts d'inscription de la dette publique, et tous autres sommes et revenus dûs à la succession, et en donnera bonne et valable quittance aux débiteurs. [...]

VIII. Si au cours du délai fixé au 1er álinéa du paragraphe VI, il s'élève des contestations à l'égard des réclamations qui pourraient se produire contre la succession de la part des sujets de n'importe quel Etat, la décision concernant ces réclamations, en tant qu'elles ne reposent pas sur le titre d'hérédité ou de legs, appartiendra aux tribunaux du Pays. [...]

Consular Convention between the Kingdom of Italy and the Republic of Turkey of 9 September 1929**

Article 21 - Succession

I. As regards succession to movable property belonging to the subjects of one of the High Contracting Parties on the territory of the other, the consuls general, consuls, and vice-consuls of the country of the deceased shall have the following powers [...].

VI. The consular officer shall keep as a deposit in accordance with the law in force in the receiving State the items inventoried, the proceeds of the sale of goods, if any, and the payments received, for a period of three months following the latest publication of the opening of the succession or, lacking such a publication, for a period of four months from death. During this time, the officer shall recover, either amicably or by means of judicial proceedings, any sum, rent, dividend, interest accrued on public loans, and generally sums of money or income due to the estate, and shall provide debtors with a proper receipt. [...]

VIII. If, during the time referred to in the first subparagraph of paragraph VI, a dispute arises as to possible claims towards the estate by persons of whatever nationality, the courts of the country [where the property is located] shall have jurisdiction to decide the said claims, insofar as the subject matter of the dispute is not the title to an inheritance or legacy. [...]

* Gazzetta Ufficiale del Regno d'Italia, No. 265 of 14 November 1930.

** The English translation has kindly been prepared by Pietro Franzina.

XI. Le droit successoral et le partage de la succession mobilière seront soumis à la loi nationale du défunt. Toutes les questions reposant sur le titre d'hérédité ou des legs et touchant le droit à ladite succession ou à son partage, seront décidées par les tribunaux ou autres autorités compétentes se trouvant sur le territoire du Pays dont relevait le défunt et conformément à ses lois nationales. Ces décisions seront reconnues dans l'autre Pays.

XV. Les dispositions des paragraphes II à XIV ne s'appliquent pas aux successions immobilières. [...]

Les questions reposant sur le titre d'hérédité ou de legs et touchant le droit à la succession immobilière ou à son partage seront soumises aux lois du Pays dans lequel les immeubles sont situés.

La connaissance de toutes demandes ou contestations concernant les successions immobilières appartiendra exclusivement aux tribunaux ou autres autorités compétents de ce Pays. Les tribunaux et autorités susvisés sont tenus de prendre à l'égard des biens immeubles du défunt les mêmes mesures conservatoires qu'ils doivent prendre d'après la législation du Pays à l'égard des successions immobilières de leurs nationaux.

L'administration des immeubles faisant partie de la succession appartiendra exclusivement au fonctionnaire consulaire ou à ses délégués, lesquels se conformeront aux lois du Pays où ces immeubles sont situés. [...]

XVI. Les dispositions du présent article seront appliquées par analogie aux biens meubles et immeubles qui se trouvent sur le territoire de l'une des Parties et qui appartiennent à la succession d'un sujet de l'autre Partie décédé hors de ce territoire.

XI. Succession to, and the sharing out of, movable property shall be governed by the national law of the deceased. All questions based on title to an inheritance or legacy and relating to the right to benefit from the succession or the sharing out of the estate shall be decided by the courts or other competent authorities of the country of which the deceased was a national and in accordance with his national law. The resulting decisions shall be recognized in the other country.

XV. The provisions in paragraphs II to XIV do not apply to succession to immovable property. [...]

Questions based on title to an inheritance or legacy and relating to the right to benefit from the succession or the sharing out of the immovable property shall be governed by the law of the country where the property is situated.

Any claims and disputes concerning succession to immovable property shall be decided exclusively by the courts or other competent authorities of this country. The aforesaid courts and authorities shall take, in respect of the immovable property of the deceased, the same protective measures as they are required to take under the law of their country in respect of the immovable property of their nationals.

The administration of the immovable property of the deceased shall be exclusively exercised by the consular officer or his delegates, in compliance with the law of the country in which property is situated. [...]

XVI. The provisions in this article shall apply by analogy to such movable and immovable property as is located on the territory of one contracting party, insofar as they belong to the estate of a national of the other party who died outside that territory.

OTHER EU MEMBER STATES

TREATY 22: BULGARIA-YUGOSLAVIA

Ugovor između Federativne Narodne Republike Jugoslavije i Narodne Republike Bugarske o uzajamnoj pravnoj pomoći od 23. marta 1956. godine*

Zaostavštine

Član 19

1. Državljani jedne Države ugovornice mogu, saglasno odredbama ovog Ugovora, izjavom poslednje volje (testamentom, zaveštanjem), raspolagati svojom imovinom koja se nalazi na teritoriji druge Države ugovornice.
2. Državljani jedne Države ugovornice mogu sticati u drugoj Državi ugovornici imovinska prava na osnovu zakonskog ili testamentalnog nasleđivanja pod istim uslovima i u jednakom obimu kao i državljani te Države.

Član 20

1. Nasledno-pravni odnosi određuju se po zakonodavstvu Države ugovornice čiji je državljanin bio ostavilac u momentu smrti.
2. Ako nema naslednika, nasleđivanje pokretne imovine vrši se po zakonu Države ugovornice čiji je državljanin bio ostavilac u momentu smrti, a nasleđivanje nepokretne imovine – po zakonu Države ugovornice na čijoj se teritoriji imovina nalazi.

Treaty between the People's Republic of Bulgaria and the Federal People's Republic of Yugoslavia on Mutual Legal Assistance of 23 March 1956**

Succession

Article 19

1. Nationals of one Contracting State may, in accordance with the provisions of this Agreement, dispose of their property located on the territory of the other Contracting State by last will (testament).
2. Nationals of one Contracting State may acquire in the other Contracting State property rights by testate or intestate succession under the same conditions and to the same extent as the nationals of that State.

Article 20

1. Succession relations shall be governed by the law of the Contracting State of which the deceased was a national at the time of death.
2. If there are no heirs, the succession to movable property shall be governed by the law of the Contracting State of which the deceased was a national at the time of his death and the succession to immovable property by the law of the Contracting State where the property is located.

* Službenilist Federativne Narodne Republike Jugoslavije – Dodatak: Međunarodniugovori i drugisporazumi, br. 1/57.

** The English translation has kindly been prepared by Slavko Đorđević and Zlatan Meškić.

Član 21

U pogledu sposobnosti za sastavljanje ili opozivanje testamenta kao i u pogledu pravnih posledica nedostatka volje (prevara, greška itd.) primenjuje se zakonodavstvo Države ugovornice čiji je državljanin bio ostavilac u momentu sastavljanja odnosno opozivanja testamenta.

Article 21

The capacity to make or revoke the testament as well as legal consequences for the absence of intent (fraudulent misrepresentation, fault, etc) shall be governed by the law of the Contracting State of which the deceased was a national at the time the testament was made or revoked.

Član 22

U pogledu forme u kojoj se sastavlja ili opoziva testament primenjuje se zakonodavstvo Države ugovornice, čiji je državljanin bio ostavilac u momentu sastavljanja odnosno opozivanja testamenta. Ipak je dovoljno ako pu bili poštovani propisi zakonodavstva Države ugovornice, na čijoj je teritoriji testament bio sastavljen odnosno opozvan.

Article 22

As to the form in which the testament is to be made or revoked, it shall be governed by the law of the Contracting State of which the deceased was a national at the time the testament was made or revoked. However, it is sufficient if the provisions of the law of the Contracting State on whose territory the testament was made or revoked are complied with.

Član 23

Za raspravljanje o nepokretnim stvarima iz zaostavštine i za rešavanje zahteva na nasledstvo, nužni deo ili legat koji se na te stvari odnose, isključivo su nadležni sudovi one Države ugovornice na čijoj se teritoriji te stvari nalaze.

Article 23

To rule on the immovable estate and to resolve inheritance claims, reserved shares or legacies related to these assets, the courts of the Contracting State on whose territory these assets are located shall have exclusive jurisdiction.

Član 24

1. Za raspravljanje o pokretnim stvarima iz zaostavštine državljana Država ugovornica, kao i za rešavanje spornih zahteva na nasledstvo, nužni deo ili legat koji se na te stvari odnose, nadležni su sudovi Države čiji je državljanin ostavilac ukoliko u ovom Ugovoru nije drukčije određeno. Međutim, nadležnost sudova druge Države ugovornice ne isključuje se u slučajevima u kojima izvršenje predviđeno u stavu 2. ovog člana nije više moguće.

Article 24

1. The courts of the State of which the deceased was a national shall have jurisdiction to rule on the movable estate of nationals of the Contracting States, as well as to rule on contentious inheritance claims, reserved shares or legacies related to those assets, unless this Agreement provides otherwise. However, the jurisdiction of the courts of the other Contracting State is not excluded in cases in which the enforcement provided by paragraph 2 of this Article is not possible any longer.

2. Svaka Država ugovornica obavezuje se da će priznavati i dopustiti izvršenje odluka o nasleđu i spornim zahtevima na nasledstvo, nužni deo ili legat koje donesu sudovi Države čiji je državljanin ostavilac, ukoliko se te odluke odnose na pokretnu zaostavštinu koja se nalazi na njenoj teritoriji, a radi se o zaostavštini državljana druge Države ugovornice, i to:

a) ako iz sledećih odredaba ne proizlazi što drugo; ili
b) ako se te odluke ne protive osnovnim načelima zakonodavstva Države u kojoj se zaostavština nalazi.
3. U pogledu pismena koja treba priložiti uz predlog za izvršenje primenjivaće se odredbe člana 45. ovog Ugovora.

4. Sudovi Država ugovornica predavaće radi sprovođenja rasprave zaostavštine u smislu stava 1. ovog člana, na molbu nadležnih organa Države čiji je državljanin bio ostavilac pokretne stvari iz njegove zaostavštine, ukoliko:

a) u sledećim odredbama nije drukčije određeno, odnosno
b) ukoliko se tome ne protive zabrane izvoza ili devizno-pravni propisi.

Član 25

1. Ako na teritoriji jedne Države ugovornice umre državljanin druge Države ugovornice, nadležni sud (organ) treba odmah da obavesti diplomatsko ili konzularno pretstavništvo druge Države o smrti i da mu saopšti sve što mu je poznato o naslednicima, o njihovom prebivalištu (boravištu) i adresi, o karakteru i vrednosti zaostavštine, a isto tako i o testamentu ako postoji. To isto važi i kada nadležni sud (organ) dozna da je u njegovoj Državi ostala imovina državljana druge Države ugovornice koji je umro van teritorije dveju Država ugovornica.

2. Every Contracting State is obliged to recognize and enforce the decisions on succession and contentious inheritance claims, reserved shares or legacies, issued by the courts of the State of which the deceased was a national, in cases where those decisions relate to movable estate located on its territory and they concern the estate of the national of the other Contracting State, provided that:

a) the following provisions do not provide otherwise; or
b) those decisions are not contrary to fundamental principles of the legislation of the State where the estate is located.
3. With regards to the written documents that need to be attached to the request for enforcement, the provision of Article 45 of this Agreement is applicable.
4. The courts of the Contracting States will, at request of the competent authorities of the State of which the deceased was a national, hand over the movable estate for the purpose of conducting the succession proceedings in the meaning of paragraph 1 of this Article, provided that:

a) the following provisions do not provide otherwise, or
b) it is not contrary to export bans or provisions on foreign currency.

Article 25

1. If the national of one Contracting State dies in the territory of another Contracting State, the competent court (authority) shall immediately inform the diplomatic or consular representative of the other State about the death and shall communicate everything that is known about the heirs, their domicile (residence) and address, the composition and value of the estate, and about the testament if it exists. The same applies if the competent court (authority) finds out that in its State there is property from the national of another Contracting State who died outside of the territory of both Contracting States.

2. Ako diplomatsko ili konzularno pretstavništvo Države čiji je državljanin bio umrli, sazna o smrti ranije, dužno je da o tome izvesti nadležni sud (organ) druge Države ugovornice.

Član 26

1. Ako se u jednoj Državi ugovornici nalazi zaostavština državljana druge Države ugovornice, sud ili drugi nadležni državni organ, preduzeće, na predlog ili po službenoj dužnosti mere koje su potrebne za obezbeđenje i korisno upravljanje zaostavštinom, kao i za sprečavanje njenog smanjenja ili nanošenja kakve druge štete.
2. Sud ili drugi nadležni državni organ preduzeće mere navedene u stavu 1. ovog člana po propisima koji važe u njihovoj sopstvenoj Državi. Međutim, te mere sprovešće se, po molbi druge Države, i u nekoj naročitoj formi ako ovo nije u protivnosti sa osnovnim načelima zakonodavstva zamoljene Države.

3. Ako je u mestu gde se nalazi zaostavština sedište diplomatskog ili konzularnog pretstavništva Države čiji je državljanin bio umrli, onda se mere navedene u stavu 1. ovog člana mogu preduzeti samo ako je diplomatsko ili konzularno pretstavništvo bilo o tome blagovremeno obavešteno; diplomatsko ili konzularno pretstavništvo ima pravo da učestvuje kod preduzimanja službenih radnji i da stavlja predloge.
4. U ostalim slučajevima treba bez odlaganja izvestiti diplomatsko ili konzularno pretstavništvo o ovim merama koje su preduzete za obezbeđenje i za upravljanje zaostavštinom. Na predlog diplomatskog ili konzularnog pretstavništva ove se mere mogu izmeniti ili ukinuti bez štete po prava trećih lica.

2. If the diplomatic or consular representation of the State of which the deceased was a national finds out about the death before the other State, it is obliged to inform the competent court (authority) of the other Contracting State about the death.

Article 26

1. If the estate of a national of one Contracting State is located on the territory of another Contracting State, the court or another competent authority shall, on request or on its own motion, take measures necessary to secure and administer the estate, as well as to preclude its diminishment or some other form of damage.
2. The court or some other competent authority shall take measures mentioned in paragraph 1 of this Article in accordance with the provisions of its own law. However, those measures have to be, on request of the other State, conducted in some special form if this is not contrary to the fundamental principles of the legislation of the requested State.
3. If the estate is located at the seat of the diplomatic or consular representative of the State of which the deceased was a national, the measures provided for in paragraph 1 of this Article may be taken only if the diplomatic or consular representative was timely informed about them; the diplomatic or consular representative is entitled to participate when the official measures are performed and to make requests.
4. In other cases, the diplomatic or consular representative shall be, without delay, informed about those measures taken to secure or administer the estate. Upon request of the diplomatic or consular representative these measures may be altered or annulled without damaging the rights of third persons.

Član 27

Proglašenje testamenta vrši sud (organ) Države ugovornice na čijoj se teritoriji nalazi testament. Overeni prepis testamenta i zapisnika o stanju i sadržini testamenta, a prema okolnostima i zapisnik o njegovom proglašenju dostavljaju se sudu Države čiji je državljanin bio ostavilac, nadležnom za raspravu zaostavštine, ukoliko po odredbama ovog Ugovora nije nadležan sud Države ugovornice u kojoj je zaveštanje proglašeno. Pod istim uslovima na molbu suda Države čiji je državljanin bio ostavilac može se dostaviti i originalni testament.

Article 27

The opening of the testament is conducted by the court (authority) of the Contracting State on whose territory the testament is located. A duly certified copy of the testament and the minutes on the condition and content of the testament, and according to the circumstances also the minutes on its reading, shall be delivered to the competent court of the State of which the deceased was a national, unless according to the provisions of this Agreement the court of the Contracting State, in which the testament was opened, is competent. Under the same conditions, upon request of the court of the State of which the deceased was a national, the original testament may be delivered.

Član 28

1. Na zahtev naslednika, ili legatara, koji su državljani Države ugovornice u kojoj se nalazi zaostavština ili koji borave na njenoj teritoriji, može sud da zadrži celu zaostavštinu ili dovoljan deo iste, dok nadležni sud Države čiji je državljanin bio ostavilac, pravosnažno ne odluči o zahtevu naslednika ili legatara.

2. Iste mere može sud preduzeti i na zahtev poverilaca ostavioca koji su državljani Države ugovornice na čijoj teritoriji se nalazi zaostavština, ili koji na toj teritoriji borave, ako svoja potraživanja prijave i, po potrebi, pokrenu postupak za njihovo priznanje.

Article 28

1. At the request of the heirs or legatees that are nationals of the Contracting State on whose territory the estate is located or that reside on its territory, the court may retain the whole estate or sufficient part of it, until the competent court of the State of which the deceased was a national, adopts a final decision about the request of the heir or legatee.

2. The same measures may be taken by the court upon request of creditors of the deceased that are nationals of the State on whose territory the estate is located or that reside on that territory, if they register their claims and, if needed, initiate proceedings for their recognition.

Član 29

1. Radi stavljanja zahteva navedenih u članu 28. ovog Ugovora odrediće se oglasom rok od tri do šest meseci u kome se zahtevi gore pomenutih lica moraju prijaviti i, po potrebi, pokrenuti postupak za njihovo priznanje. Ako se ti zahtevi u ovom roku ne prijave, odnosno ako se ne pokrene postupak za njihovo priznanje, ne može se odbiti prodaja pokretne zaostavštine pozivanjem na odredbe člana 28. ovog Ugovora.

Article 29

1. In order to file requests named in Article 28 of this Agreement, a term of three to six months shall be determined by public notice, within which the requests of the abovementioned persons need to be registered, and if needed, proceedings for their recognition have to be initiated. If those requests are not registered within this time frame, or if proceedings for their recognition are not initiated, the handing over of the movable estate cannot be refused by reference to Article 28 of this Agreement.

2. Objavljivanje oglasa iz stava 1. ovog člana izvršiće se u službenim listovima obeju Država ugovornica ("Službeni list Federativne Narodne Republike Jugoslavije" odnosno "Izvestija na Presidiuma na Narodnoto s'branie" Narodne Republike Bugarske). Overen prepis oglasa mora se poslati diplomatskom ili konzularnom pretstavništvu Države čiji je državljanin bio ostavilac.

2. The notice under paragraph 1 of this Article shall be published in the Official Journal of both Contracting States ("Službeni list Federativne Narodne Republike Jugoslavije" odnosno "Izvestija na Presidiuma na Narodnoto s'branie" Narodne Republike Bugarske). A certified copy of the notice needs to be sent to the diplomatic or consular representative of the State of which the deceased was a national.

Član 30

1. Ako je ostavilac koji je bio državljanin jedne Države ugovornice, imao poslednje prebivalište na teritoriji druge Države ugovornice, mogu naslednici, koji stanuju na teritoriji te druge Države, zahtevati u roku iz člana 29. stav 1. ovog Ugovora da sud te Države sprovede raspravu pokretne zaostavštine koja se nalazi u istoj Državi. Ovom zahtevu udovoljiće se ako tome ne prigovori koji naslednik, ili legatar, u roku od tri meseca po isteku roka iz člana 29. stav 1. ovog Ugovora. Ako nema prigovora sudovi te Države nadležni su i za rešavanje spornih zahteva na zaostavštinu.

2. Ako u smislu stava 1. ovog člana treba da o pokretnoj zaostavštini raspravlja sud Države u kojoj se ta zaostavština nalazi, primenjivaće se odredbe naslednog prava Države čiji je državljanin bio ostavilac i to kako kod rasprave zaostavštine, tako i pri rešavanju spornih zahteva na zaostavštinu.

Article 30

1. If the deceased who was a national of one Contracting State had his last domicile on the territory of another Contracting State, the heirs that live on the territory of that second State may request within the term of Article 29 paragraph 1 of this Agreement that the court of that State conduct the proceedings on the movable estate that is located in the same State. This request shall be approved if an heir or legatee does not object to it within three months from the end of the term under Article 29 of this Agreement. If there is no objection, the courts of that Contracting State are competent for deciding upon contentious inheritance claims.

2. If within the meaning of this Article the proceedings on the movable estate shall be conducted before the court of the State where that estate is located, the provisions on succession law of the State of which the deceased was a national shall be applicable to the succession proceedings as well as to contentious inheritance claims.

Član 31

1. Ako državljanin jedne Države ugovornice umre za vreme putovanja na teritoriji druge Države ugovornice, a tamo nema prebivališta ni uobičajeno boravište, onda će se stvari, koje je nosio sa sobom, po spisku, bez drugih formalnosti predati diplomatskom ili konzularnom pretstavništvu njegove Države.

Article 31

1. If the national of one Contracting State dies during his travel on the territory of the other Contracting State, and he has no domicile or habitual residence there, the items that he carried with him and that are listed in an inventory shall, without further formalities, be handed over to the diplomatic or consular representative of his State.

2. Diplomatsko ili konzularno pretstavništvo postupiće sa tim stvarima po propisima svoje Države, pošto bude regulisalo dugove koje je umrli napravio za vreme boravka u Državi u kojoj je umro.

2. The diplomatic or consular representative shall deal with those items under the law of its State, after it has paid the debts that the deceased made during his residence in the State where he died.

Član 32

U parničnim i vanparničnim stvarima zaostavština, po kojima se raspravlja na teritoriji jedne Države ugovornice, diplomatsko ili konzularno pretstavništvo druge Države ugovornice zastupa njene državljane ako su ovi otsutni i nisu odredili punomoćnika.

Article 32

In litigious or non-litigious succession proceedings conducted on the territory of one Contracting State, the diplomatic or consular representative of the other Contracting State represents its nationals if they are absent and they have not appointed an agent.

Član 33

Koja se imovina ima smatrati pokretnom ili nepokretnom, određuje se po zakonodavstvu Države u kojoj se nalazi ta imovina.

Article 33

The issue of whether property is considered to be movable or immovable is governed by the law of the Contracting State in whose territory the property is located.

Član 34

Dok se između obe Države ugovornice ne zaključi sporazum radi izbegavanja dvostrukog opterećenja porezom i taksama na nasleđe, svaka Država ugovornica pridržava sebi pravo da, pre predaje pokretne zaostavštine organima druge Države ugovornice, naplati sve poreze i takse kojima podleže nasleđe po njenom akonodavstvu.

Article 34

Until between both Contracting States an agreement is concluded with the purpose to avoid a double burden of taxes and fees, each Contracting State reserves its right to charge all taxes and fees that are due for succession under its legislation before the movable property is handed over to the authorities of the other Contracting State.

TREATY 23: GREECE–SWITZERLAND

Convention d'établissement et de protection juridique entre la Suisse et la Grèce du 1 December 1927*

Article 10

[3.] La succession du ressortissant d'une des parties contractantes décédé sur le territoire de l'autre partie sera régie par la loi nationale du défunt en vigueur au moment du décès pour ce qui concerne la question de savoir quels sont les héritiers légaux et leurs quotes-parts et dans quelle mesure ils sont réservataires.

Treaty between Greece and Switzerland on Establishment and Legal Protection of 1 December 1927**

Article 10

[3.] The succession of a national of one of the contracting parties, deceased in the territory of the other party, will be governed by the national law of the deceased in force at the time of his/her death, for the purpose of establishing who the heirs are in case of intestacy and their shares, and to what extent they are entitled to forced heirship rights.

* RS 0.142.113.721.

** The English translation has kindly been prepared by Andrea Bonomi.

TREATY 24: HUNGARY–TURKEY

Türkiye Cumhuriyeti ile Macaristan Krallığı Arasında Konsolosluk Mukavelesi, 18 Haziran 1938*

Madde 18 – Veraset

Yüksek Âkid Taraflardan birinin, diğer taraf ülkesinde bulunan tebaasına aid ve menkul muhallefata taallûk eden hususlarda, mütevaffanın tâbi olduğu Devletin başkonsolos, konsolos ve muavin – konsolosları, millî kanunlarile mezun bulundukları takdirde atideki salâhiyetleri haiz olacaklardır:

§:3

Salâhiyettar merci ve tatbik edilecek kanun

1. Menkul muhallefatta veraset veya hibeden mütevellit bütün ihtilâflar, müteveffanın tâbi olduğu Devlet mahkemelerinde ve bu Devlet kanunlarına göre halledilecektir.

2. Diğer taraftan, menkul muhallefatta veraset ve hibeden gayri bir sebebden çıkan bütün ihtilâflar muhallefatın bulunduğu ülkedeki Devlet mehakiminde ve bu Devletin kanunlarına göre tesviye olunacaktır.

3. Gayrimenkule müteallik bütün ihtilâflar, veraset ve hibeden tehassül etse dahi gayrimenkulun bulunduğu ülkedeki Devlet mahkemelerinde ve o Devletin kanunlarına göre hal ve fasledilecektir.

Consular Treaty between the Kingdom of Hungary and the Republic of Turkey of 18 June 1938**

Article 18 – Succession

As regards matters concerning the movable estate belonging to the nationals of one of the High Contracting Parties in the territory of other, consul generals, consuls and vice consuls of the State whose nationality the deceased possessed shall have the below-mentioned functions, provided that they are competent pursuant to the law of their respective State:

Section 3

Jurisdiction and applicable law

1. All conflicts arising out of succession or legacy on the movable property shall be settled by the courts of the State whose nationality the deceased possessed in accordance with the law of that State.
2. However, all conflicts on the movable property arising out of areas other than succession or legacy shall be settled by the courts of the State where the property is located in accordance with the law of that State.
3. All conflicts concerning the immovable property, even if they arise out of succession and legacy, shall be settled by the courts of the State where the property is found in accordance with the law of that State.

* Resmi Gazete of 27 December 1939, No. 4395.

** The English translation has kindly been prepared by Biset Sena Güneş.

TREATY 25: HUNGARY–YUGOSLAVIA

Ugovor o uzajamnom pravnom saobraćaju između SFR Jugoslavije i NR Mađarske od 7. marta 1968. godine*

Glava IV

Zaostavštine

Član 40

1. Državljani jedne strane ugovornice mogu sticati imovinska prava na teritoriji druge strane ugovornice na osnovu zakonskog ili testamentarnog nasleđivanja pod istim uslovima i u istom obimu kao i državljani te strane ugovornice.
2. Državljani jedne strane ugovornice mogu izjavom poslednje volje (testamentom) raspolagati svojom imovinom koja se nalazi na teritoriji druge strane ugovornice.

Član 41

Nasledno-pravni odnosi regulišu se po zakonu one strane ugovornice čiji je državljanin bio ostavilac u vreme smrti.

Član 42

Ako je prema pravu iz člana 41. ovog ugovora naslednik država, pokretna imovina pripada državi čiji je državljanin ostavilac u vreme smrti, a nepokretna imovina državi na čijoj se teritoriji imovina nalazi.

Treaty between the People`s Republic of Hungary and the Socialist Federal Republic of Yugoslavia on Mutual Legal Relations of 7 March 1968**

Chapter IV

Succession

Article 40

1. Nationals of one Contracting State may acquire property rights in the territory of the other Contracting State by testate or intestate succession under the same conditions and to the same extent as the nationals of that Contracting State.
2. The nationals of one Contracting State may with their last will (testament) dispose of their property located on the territory of the other Contracting State.

Article 41

Succession relations shall be governed by the law of the Contracting State of which the deceased was a national at the time of his death.

Article 42

If there are no heirs, the succession to movable property shall be governed by the law of the Contracting State of which the deceased was a national at the time of his death, and the succession to immovable property shall be governed by the law of the Contracting State on whose territory this property is located.

* Službeni list Socijalističke Federativne Republike Jugoslavije – Dodatak: Međunarodniugovo riidrugisporazumi, br 3/68.

** The English translation has kindly been prepared by Slavko Đorđević and Zlatan Meškić.

Član 43

1. Sposobnost za pravljenje ili opozivanje testamenta, kao i ništavost testamenta zbog nedostatka u volji zaveštaoca (prinuda prevara, zabluda i dr.) procenjuju se po zakonu strane ugovornice čiji je državljanin bio ostavilac u vreme sastavljanja odnosno opozivanja testamenta.

2. Testament sastavljen od strane državljanina jedne strane ugovornice punovažan je u pogledu forme ako odgovara:

a) zakonu države u kojoj je sačinjen, ili
b) zakonu one strane ugovornice čiji je državljanin bio zaveštalac u vreme sastavljanja testamenta ili smrti ili zakonu one države u kojoj je zaveštalac u navedenom vremenu imao prebivalište ili boravište, ili

c) zakonu mesta gde se nepokretnost nalazi.

3. Pitanje da li je zaveštalac imao prebivalište ili boravište u određenom mestu procenjuje se prema zakonu tog mesta.
4. Odredbe st. (2) i (3) ovog člana odnose se i na opozivanje testamenta.

Član 44

Za raspravljanje nepokretne zaostavštine i za rešavanje spornih zahteva na nasledstvo, nužni deo ili legat koji se odnose na nepokretnu zaostavštinu, isključivo su nadležni sudovi (organi) one strane ugovornice na čijoj teritoriji se nalazi nepokretna imovina.

Član 45

1. Za raspravljanje o pokretnim stvarima iz zaostavštine državljana strana ugovornica, kao i za rešavanje spornih zahteva na nasledstvo, nužni deo ili legat koji se na te stvari odnose, nadležni su sudovi (organi) one strane ugovornice čiji je državljanin ostavilac u vreme smrti, ako ovim ugovorom nije drukčije određeno.

Article 43

1. The capacity to make or revoke the testament as well as the nullity of the testament because of the absence of intent (compulsion, fraudulent misrepresentation, fault, etc) shall be governed by the law of the Contracting State of which the deceased was a national at the time the testament was made or revoked.
2. The testament made by the national of the other Contracting State is valid with regards to its form if its complies with:

a) the law of the State where it was made, or
b) the law of the Contracting State of which the deceased was a national at the time the testament was made or at the time of his death, or the law of the State in which the deceased at that time had his domicile or residence, or
c) the law of the place where the immovable is located.

3. The question if the deceased had his domicile or residence in a certain place shall be determined by the law of that place.
4. The provisions of paragraph (2) and (3) also apply to the revocation of the testament.

Article 44

The courts of the State where the immovable property is located shall have exclusive jurisdiction to rule on contentious inheritance claims, reserved shares or legacy related to the immovable estate.

Article 45

1. The courts of the State of which the deceased was a national shall have jurisdiction to rule on movable assets of the estate of nationals of the Contracting States, as well as to rule on contentious inheritance claims, reserved shares or legacies related to those assets, unless this agreement provides otherwise.

2. Pokretna zaostavština državljana jedne strane ugovornice koja se nalazi na teritoriji druge strane ugovornice predaće se radi sprovođenja ostavinskog postupka diplomatskom ili konzularnom predstavništvu ili nadležnom organu strane ugovornice čiji je državljanin bio ostavilac, izuzev u slučajevima predviđenim u čl. 49. i 51. ovog ugovora i ukoliko su ispunjeni uslovi iz člana 55. stav (2) tačka b) ovog ugovora.
3. Strane ugovornice zadržavaju pravo da pre predaje pokretne zaostavštine po stavu (2) ovog člana naplate dažbine predvidene svojim propisima za sticanje po osnovu nasledstva.

Član 46

1. Ako na teritoriji jedne strane ugovornice umre državljanin druge strane ugovornice, sud (organ) treba odmah da obavesti o smrti diplomatsko ili konzularno predstavništvo druge strane ugovornice i da saopšti sve što mu je poznato o naslednicima, i njihovom prebivalištu i adresi, o sastavu i vrednosti zaostavštine, kao i o testamentu ako postoji. Sud (organ) će isto tako postupiti i kad dozna da je u njegovoj zemlji ostala imovina državljanina druge strane ugovornice koji je umro u svojoj ili u trećoj državi.

2. Ako je postupak za raspravljanje zaostavštine pokrenut na teritoriji jedne strane ugovornice pa se utvrdi da je naslednik državljanin druge strane ugovornice o tome će se obavestiti diplomatsko ili konzularno predslavništvo te strane ugovornice.
3. Ako je diplomatsko ili konzularno predstavništvo jedne strane ugovornice ranije obavešteno o smrti državljanina te strane ugovornice, radi obezbeđenja zaostavštine obavestiće o tome nadležni organ druge strane ugovornice.

2. The movable estate of the nationals of one Contracting State located on the territory of the other Contracting State shall be handed over to the diplomatic or consular representative or the competent authority of the Contracting State of which the deceased was a national, except in cases provided for in Article 49 and 51 of this Agreement and if the conditions of Article 55 paragraph 2 letter b) of this Agreement are fulfilled.
3. The Contracting States reserve the right to charge the fees provided for by their rules on the acquisition of property by succession before the handing over of the movable estate under paragraph 2 of this Article.

Article 46

1. If a national of one Contracting State dies on the territory of another Contracting State, the court (authority) shall immediately inform the diplomatic or consular representative of the other State about the death and shall communicate everything that is known about the heirs, their domicile or residence, the composition and the value of the estate, and about the testament – if it exists. The court (authority) shall do the same if it finds out that on its territory there is property of a national of the other Contracting State who died in his State or a third State.
2. If a succession proceeding is initiated on the territory of one Contracting State, and if it is determined that the deceased is a national of the other Contracting State – the diplomatic or consular representative of the other Contracting State must be informed.
3. If the diplomatic or consular representative of one Contracting State has been informed earlier of the death of its national, it shall send this information to the competent authority of the other Contracting State in order to safeguard the estate.

Član 47

1. Ako se na teritoriji jedne strane ugovornice nalazi zaostavština državljanina druge strane ugovornice, sud (organ) će na predlog ili po službenoj dužnosti, preduzeti mere koje su potrebne za obezbeđenje i upravljanje zaostavštinom. U ovim slučajevima mora se sastaviti popis pokretnih stvari i po potrebi, postaviti pogodno lice za staraoca zaostavštine.
2. Sud (organ) će preduzeti mere navedene u stavu (1) ovog člana po propisima koji važe u njegovoj zemlji. Mere obezbeđenja sprovešće se, na traženje druge strane ugovornice i u nekoj naročitoj formi ako ova nije u suprotnosti sa načelima zakonodavstva zamoljene strane ugovornice.

3. Ako je u mestu gde se nalazi zaostavština sedište diplomatskog ili konzularnog predstavništva strane ugovornice čiji je državljanin bio umrli, onda se mere navedene u stavu (1) ovog člana mogu preduzeti samo ako je diplomatsko ili konzularno predstavništvo bilo o tome blagovremeno obavešteno, osim u slučajevima koji ne trpe odlaganje. Diplomatsko ili konzularno predstavništvo može da učestvuje kod preduzimanja službenih radnji i da stavlja predioge.
4. U ostalim slučajevima treba bez odlaganja izvestiti diplomatsko ili konzularno predstavništvo o merama koje su preduzete za obezbeđenje i za upravljanje zaostavštinom. Na predlog diplomatskog ili konzularnog predstavništva, ove mere mogu se izmeniti ili ukinuti bez štete po prava trećih lica.

Article 47

1. If the estate of the national of the other Contracting State is located on the territory of the other Contracting State, the court (authority) shall, at the request or on its own motion, undertake the measures necessary to safeguard and manage the estate. In such cases an inventory of all movable assets shall be made and, if needed, an appropriate custodian for the estate shall be appointed.
2. The court (authority) shall undertake the measures provided for in paragraph 1 according to the rules provided for in its law. Those measures will be, upon request of the other State, also conducted in some special form if it is not contrary to the fundamental principles of the legislation of the requested State.
3. If the estate is located at the seat of the diplomatic or consular representative of the State of which the deceased was a national, the measures named in paragraph 1 of this Article may be taken only if the diplomatic or consular representative was timely informed about them, unless the measures may not be postponed. The diplomatic or consular representative has the right to participate in official actions that are being undertaken or to make requests.
4. In other cases, the diplomatic or consular representative shall be, without delay, informed about those measures taken to secure or administer the estate. Upon request of the diplomatic or consular representative these measures may be altered or annulled without damaging the rights of third persons.

Član 48

1. Ako je sud (organ) jedne strane ugovornice proglasio testament državljanina druge strane ugovornice, overeni prepis testamenta, zapisnik o stanju i sadržini testamenta i zapisnik o njegovom proglašenju dostavljaju se sudu (organu) strane ugovornice čiji je državljanin bio ostavilac, ako po ovom ugovoru za raspravljanje zaostavštine nije nadležan sud strane ugovornice u kojoj je testament proglašen. Na isti naćin će se postupiti i u slučaju ako je za raspravljanje zaostavštine nadležan i sud druge strane ugovornice

2. Sud koji je proglasio teslament može, na traženje suda (organa) druge strane ugovornice, dostaviti ovom i originalni teslament.

3. Odredbe st. (1) i (2) ovog člana primenjuju se i na isprave o usmenom testamentu.

Član 49

1. Na zahtev naslednika ili legatara, koji su državljani strane ugovornice na čijoj se teritoriji nalazi zaostavština ili koji borave na njenoj teritoriji može sud (organ) da zadrži celokupnu pokretnu zaostavšiinu ili dovoljan deo iste dok nadležni sud (organ) strane ugovornice čiji je državljanin bio ostavilac pravnosnažno ne odluči o zahtevu naslednika ili legatara.

2. Iste mere može sud (organ) preduzeti i na zahtev poverilaca koji su državljani strane ugovornice na čijoj se teritoriji nalazi zaostavština, ili koji na toj teritoriji borave, ako svoja potraživanja prijave i, po potrebi, pokrenu postupak za njihovo priznanje.

Article 48

1. If the court (authority) of one Contracting State opens the testament of the national of another Contracting State, a certified copy of the testament, the minutes on the condition and content of the testament, as well as the minutes on its reading, shall be delivered to the court (authority) of the State of which the deceased is a national, if under this agreement the court that read the testament does not have jurisdiction for the succession proceedings. It will proceed in the same manner if the court of the other Contracting State also has jurisdiction for the succession proceedings.

2. The court that opened the testament may, upon request of the court of the other Contracting State, deliver to it the original testament.

3. The provisions of paragraph (1) and (2) of this Article also apply to deeds on oral testaments.

Article 49

1. At the request of the heirs or legatees, who are nationals of the Contracting State on whose territory the estate is located or who reside on its territory, the court (authority) may retain the whole movable estate or a sufficient part of it, until the competent court (authority) of the State of which the deceased was a national adopts a final decision about the request of the heir or legatee.

2. The same measures may be taken by the court (authority) at the request of creditors of the deceased who are nationals of the State on whose territory the estate is located, or that reside on that territory, if they register their claims and, if needed, initiate proceedings for their recognition.

Član 50

1. Radi stavljanja zahteva navedenih u članu 49. ovog ugovora, sud (organ) će oglasom odrediti rok od tri do šest mescci u kome poverioci i naslednici treba da prijave svoje zahteve i, po potrebi, pokrenu postupak za njihovo priznanje. Ako se ti zahtevi u pomenutom roku ne prijave, odnosno ako se ne pokrene postupak za njihovo priznanje, ne može se odbiti predaja pokretne zaostavštine pozivanjem na odredbe člana 49. ovog ugovora.

2. Objavljivanje oglasa po stavu (1) ovog člana vrši se po zakonu one strane ugovornice na čijoj teritoriji se nalazi pokretna zaostavština.

Član 51

1. Ako je ostavilac, koji je bio državljanin jedne strane ugovornice, imao poslednje prebivalište na teritoriji druge strane ugovornice, mogu naslednici koji stanuju na teritoriji te druge strane ugovornice, zahtevati u roku od šest meseci po smrti ostavioca da sud (organ) te strane ugovornice sprovede raspravu pokretne zaostavštine koja se nalazi na teritoriji te strane ugovornice. Ovom zahtevu udovoljiće se samo ako tome ne prigovori koji od naslednika, lice koje ima pravo na nužni deo ili legatar, i to u roku od tri meseca od obaveštenja suda (organa) da je zahtev podnet.

2. Ako se sve pokretne stvari nalaze na teritoriji jedne od ugovornih strana, ostavinski postupak se, na molbu bilo kog naslednika ili legatora, može voditi kod organa te strane ugovornice ako svi poznati naslednici ili legatori za to daju svoj pristanak.

3. Nasledno-pravni odnosi u slučaju iz st. (1) i (2) ovog člana regulišu se po zakonu strane ugovornice čiji je državljanin bio ostavilac.

Article 50

1. In order to file requests named in Article 49 of this Agreement, a term of three to six months shall be determined by public notice of the court (authority), within which the requests of creditors and heirs need to be registered, and if needed, proceedings for their recognition initiated. If those requests are not registered within this term, or if proceedings for their recognition are not initiated, the handing over of the movable estate cannot be refused by reference to Article 49 of this Agreement.

2. The publication of the notice under paragraph 1 of this Article shall be conducted under the rules of the Contracting State where the movable estate is located.

Article 51

1. If the deceased who was a national of one Contracting State had his last domicile on the territory of another Contracting State, the heirs that live on the territory of that other Contracting State may request within six months of the death of the deceased that the court (authority) of that State conduct the proceedings on the movable estate that is located in the same State. This request shall be approved if a heir, a person who has a right to reserved share or a legatee does not object to it within three months from the notice of the court (authority) that the request was filed.

2. If all movable assets are located on the territory of one Contracting State, the authorities of that Contracting State may conduct the succession proceedings upon request of any heir or legatee, provided that all known heirs and legatees have given their consent to it.

3. The succession relations under paragraphs (1) and (2) of this Article shall be governed by the law of the State of which the deceased was a national.

Član 52

Ako državljanin jedne strane ugovornice, za vreme privremenog boravka, umre na teritoriji druge strane ugovornice, onda će se stvari koje je nosio sa sobom, po spisku, bez drugih formalnosti, predati diplomatskom ili konzularnom predstavništvu njegove zemlje.

Article 52

If the national of one Contracting State dies during his temporary residence on the territory of the other Contracting State, the items that he carried with him and that are listed in an inventory shall, without further formalities, be handed over to the diplomatic or consular representation of the Contracting State of which he was a national.

Član 53

U parničnim i vanparničnim stvarima zaostavština o kojima se raspravlja na teritoriji jedne strane ugovornice, diplomatsko ili konzularno predstavništvo druge strane ugovornice zastupa svoje državljane bez posebnog punomoćja, ako su oni odsutni i nisu odredili svoje zastupnike.

Article 53

In contentious and non-contentious succession proceedings conducted on the territory of one Contracting State, the diplomatic or consular representative of the other Contracting State represents its nationals without special authorization if they are absent and they have not appointed an agent.

Član 54

Koja se imovina ima smatrati pokretnom ili nepokretnom određuje se po zakonu strane ugovornice na čijoj teritoriji se nalazi ta imovina.

Article 54

The issue of whether property is considered to be movable or immovable is governed by the law of the Contracting State on whose territory the property is located.

Član 55

1. Ako pokretnu zaostavštinu ili protivuvrednosti dobivenu prodajom pokretne ili nepokretne zaostavštine treba po okončanju ostavinskog postupka predati naslednicima koji imaju prebivalište ili boravište na teritoriji druge strane ugovornice, a nije moguće zaostavštinu ili njenu protivuvrednost predati neposredno nasledniku ili njegovom punomoćniku, zaostavština ili njena protivuvrednost predaće se diplomatskom ili konzularnom predstavništvu te strane ugovornice.
2. Po odredbama slava (1) ovog člana postupiće se:

a) ako poverioci u roku od šest meseci posle objavljivanja oglasa ne prijave potraživanja, odnosno ako su prijavljena potraživanja namirena ili obezbeđena;
b) ako su plaćene ili obezbeđene odgovarajuće nasledne dažbine;
c) ako je nadležni organ dao saglasnost za iznošenje stvari ili za transfer novca.

Article 55

1. If the movable estate or the money from the sale of the movable or the immovable estate after the end of the proceedings needs to be handed over to the heirs having their domicile or residence on the territory of the other Contracting State, and it is not possible to hand over the estate or the sums of money directly to the heir or its agent, the estate or the money shall be handed over to the diplomatic or consular representative of that Contracting State.

2. It will proceed as provided in paragraph (1) of this Article if:

a) creditors did not register their claims or these claims have not been secured or paid within the period of six months from the publication of the notice;
b) the fees for succession are either paid or secured;
c) the competent authority gave its consent for the removal of the assets or the money transfer.

TREATY 26: POLAND–YUGOSLAVIA

Ugovor između Federativne Narodne Republike Jugoslavije i Narodne Republike Poljske o pravnom saobraćaju u građanskim i krivičnim stvarima od 6. Februara 1960. godine*

Zaostavštine

Član 35

1. Državljani jedne Strane ugovornice mogu, izjavom poslednje volje na slučaj smrti (u daljem tekstu: testament), raspolagati svojom imovinom koja se nalazi na teritoriji druge Strane ugovornice.
2. Državljani jedne Strane ugovornice mogu stucati u drugoj Strani ugovornici imovinska prava na osnovu zakonskog ili testamentalnog nasleđivanja pod istim uslovima i u jednakom obimu kao i državljani te Strane ugovornice.

Član 36

Nasledno pravni odnosi određuju se po zakonodavstvu Strane ugovornice čiji je državljanin bio ostavilac u momentu smrti.

Član 37

U pogledu sposobnosti za sastavljanje ili opozivanje testamenta, kao i u pogledu pravnih posledica nedostatka volje primenjuje se zakonodavstvo Strane ugovornice čiji je državljanin bio ostavilac u momentu sastavljanja odnosno opozivanja testamenta.

Član 38

U pogledu forme u kojoj se sastavlja ili opoziva testament primenjuje se zakonodavstvo Strane ugovornice čiji je državljanin bio ostavilac u momentu sastavljanja odnosno opozivanja testamenta. Ipak je dovoljno ako su bili poštovani propisi zakonodavstva Strane ugovornice na čijoj je teritoriji testament bio sastavljen odnosno opozvan.

Treaty between the People's Republic of Poland and the Federal People's Republic of Yugoslavia on Mutual Legal Relations in Civil and Criminal Matters of 6 February 1960**

Succession

Article 35

1. Nationals of one Contracting State may dispose of their property which is located on the territory of the other Contracting State by last will (testament).

2. Nationals of one Contracting State may acquire in the other Contracting State property rights by testate and intestate succession under the same conditions and to the same extent as the nationals of that State.

Article 36

Succession relations shall be governed by the law of the Contracting State of which the deceased was a national at the time of death.

Article 37

The capacity to make or revoke the testament as well as legal consequences for the absence of will to testate shall be governed by the law of the Contracting State of which the deceased was a national at the time the testament was made or revoked.

Article 38

The form in which the testament is to be made or revoked shall be governed by the law of the Contracting State of which the deceased was a national at the time the testament was made or revoked. However, it is sufficient if the provisions of the law of the Contracting State on whose territory the testament was made or revoked are complied with.

* Službeni list Socijalističke Federativne Republike Jugoslavije – Dodatak: Međunarodni ugovori i drugi sporazumi, br. 5/63.

** The English translation has kindly been prepared by Slavko Đorđević and Zlatan Meškić.

Član 39

1. Ako se u jednoj Strani ugovornici nalazi zaostavština državljanina druge Strane ugovornice sud će preduzeti, na predlog ili po službenoj dužnosti, mere koje su potrebne za obezbeđenje i upravljanje zaostavštinom.

2. Sud će preduzeti mere navedene u stavu 1 po propisima svoje države. Međutim, te mere sprovešće se, po molbi suda druge Strane ugovornice, i u nekoj naročitoj formi ako ovo nije u suprotnosti sa osnovnim načelima zakonodavstva zamoljene Strane ugovornice.

3. Ako je u mestu gde se nalazi zaostavština sedište diplomatskog ili konzularnog predstavništva Strane ugovornice čiji je državljanin bio umrli, onda se mere navedene u stavu 1 preduzimaju uz jednovremeno obaveštenje diplomatskog ili konzularnog predstavništva.

4. U ostalim slučajevima treba bez odlaganja izvestiti diplomatsko ili konzularno predstavništvo o svim merama koje su preduzete za obezbeđenje i upravljanje zaostavštinom. Na predlog diplomatskog ili konzularnog predstavništva ove se mere mogu izmeniti ili ukinuti bez štete po prava trećih lica.

Article 39

1. If the estate of the national of one Contracting State is located on the territory of another Contracting State, the court shall, upon request or on its own motion, take measures necessary for the protection and administration of the estate.

2. The court shall take the measures mentioned in paragraph 1 in accordance with the provisions of its own law. However, those measures shall be, upon request of the court of the other Contracting State, conducted in some special form, if this is not contrary to the fundamental principles of the legislation of the requested Contracting State.

3. If the estate is located at the seat of the diplomatic or consular representative of the Contracting State of which the deceased was a national, a notice has to be given to the diplomatic or consular representative at the same time as the implementation of the measures provided for in paragraph 1.

4. In other cases, the diplomatic or consular representative shall be, without delay, informed about all measures taken to secure or administer the estate. Upon request of the diplomatic or consular representative these measures may be altered or annulled without damaging the rights of third persons.

Član 40

Otvaranje i proglašenje testamenta vrši sud Strane ugovornice na čijoj se teritoriji nalazi testament. Overeni prepis testamenta i zapisnika o stanju i sadržini testamenta, prema okolnostima i zapisnik o njegovom proglašenju, dostavljaju se sudu Strane ugovornice čiji je državljanin bio ostavilac, nadležnom za raspravu zaostavštine, ukoliko po odredbama ovog Ugovora nije nadležan sud Strane ugovornice u kojoj je testament proglašen. Pod istim uslovima na molbu suda Strane ugovornice čiji je državljanin bio ostavilac može se dostaviti i originalni testament.

Article 40

The opening of the testament is conducted by the court of the Contracting State on whose territory the testament is located. A certified copy of the testament and the minutes on the condition and content of the testament, and according to the circumstances also the minutes on its opening, shall be delivered to the court of the Contracting State of which the deceased was a national that is competent to hear the succession proceedings, unless according to the provisions of this agreement the court of the Contracting State, in which the testament was opened, is competent. Under the same conditions, upon request of the court of the Contracting State of which the deceased was a national, the original testament may be delivered.

Član 41

Nadležni sud Strane ugovornice, čiji je državljanin bio ostavilac, koji ima na čuvanju testament dužan je da na zahtev nadležnog suda za obezbeđenje zaostavštine izda ovome overen prepis testamenta.

Član 42

Za raspravljanje o nepokretnim stvarima iz zaostavštine i za rešavanje zahteva na nasledstvo, nužni deo ili legat koji se na te stvari odnose, nadležni su sudovi one Strane ugovornice na čijoj se teritoriji te stvari nalaze.

Član 43

1. Za raspravljanje o pokretnim stvarima iz zaostavštine državljana Strana ugovornica, kao i za rešavanje spornih zahteva na nasledstvo, nužni deo ili legat koji se na te stvari odnose, nadležni su sudovi Strane ugovornice čiji je državljanin ostavilac.

2. Međutim, ako je ostavilac, koji je bio državljanin jedne Strane ugovornice, imao poslednje prebivalište na teritoriji druge Strane ugovornice, mogu naslednici ili lica koja imaju pravo na nužni deo nasleđa, koji stanuju na teritoriji te druge Strane ugovornice, zahtevati u roku iz člana 46 stav 1 da sud te Strane ugovornice sprovede raspravu pokretne zaostavštine koja se nalazi u istoj državi. Ovom zahtevu udovoljiće se ako tome ne prigovori koji naslednik, legat ili lice koje ima pravo na nužni deo nasleđa, u roku od tri meseca po isteku roka iz člana 46 stav 1. Ako nema prigovora sudovi te Strane ugovornice nadležni su i za rešavanje spornih zahteva na zaostavštinu.

3. Isto tako ne isključuje se nadležnost suda Strane ugovornice u kojoj se stvari nalaze u slučaju kad izvršenje koje je doneo sud nadležan po stavu 1 nije više moguće.

Article 41

The competent court of the Contracting State of which the deceased was a national, which keeps the testament, has the duty to deliver a certified copy of testament to the court which is competent to protect the estate upon its request.

Article 42

The courts of the Contracting State on whose territory immovable estate is located shall have jurisdiction to rule on that immovable estate and resolve inheritance claims, reserved shares or legacies related to that estate.

Article 43

1. The courts of the Contracting State of which the deceased was a national shall have jurisdiction to rule on movable assets of the estate of nationals of the Contracting States, as well as to rule on litigious inheritance claims, reserved shares or legacies related to those assets.

2. If the deceased, who was a national of one Contracting State, had his last domicile on the territory of another Contracting State, the heirs that live on the territory of that second State, may request within the term of Article 46 (1) that the court of that State conduct the proceedings on the movable estate that is located in the same State. This request shall be approved if the heir or legatee does not object to it within three months from the end of the term under Article 46 (1). If there is no objection, the courts of that Contracting State are competent to decide on litigious inheritance claims.

3. The jurisdiction of the court of the Contracting State in which assets are located shall not be excluded in a case where the enforcement declared by the competent court in paragraph 1 is not possible anymore.

4. Ako u smislu stava 2 treba da o pokretnoj zaostavštini raspravlja sud Strane ugovornice u kojoj se ta zaostavština nalazi, primenjivaće se materijalne odredbe naslednog prava Strane ugovornice čiji je državljanin bio ostavilac i to kako kod rasprave zaostavštine tako i pri rešavanju spornih zahteva na zaostavštinu.

4. If within the meaning of paragraph 2 the proceedings on the movable estate shall be conducted before the court of the Contracting State where that estate is located, the provisions on succession law of the State of which the deceased was a national shall be applicable to the succession proceedings as well as to the litigious inheritance claims.

Član 44

Sudovi Strana ugovornica predavaće radi sprovođenja rasprave zaostavštine u smislu člana 43 stav 1, na molbu nadležnih sudova Strane ugovornice čiji je državljanin bio ostavilac, pokretne stvari iz njegove zaostavštine, ukoliko odredbama ovog Ugovora nije drugačije određeno.

Article 44

In order to conduct the succession proceedings within the meaning of Article 43 (1), the courts of the Contracting States shall hand over the movable estate to the courts of the Contracting State of which the deceased was a national upon their request, unless it is provided otherwise by this agreement.

Član 45

1. Na zahtev naslednika, legatara ili lica koja imaju prvo na nužni deo nasleđa, koji su državljani Strane ugovornice u kojoj se nalazi zaostavština ili koji borave na njenoj teritoriji, može sud da zadrži zaostavštinu ili odgovarajući deo iste, dok nadležni sud Strane ugovornice čiji je državljanin bio ostavilac, pravosnažno ne odluči o zahtevu naslednika ili legatara ili lica koja imaju pravo na nužni deo nasleđa.
2. Iste mere može sud preduzeti i na zahtev poverilaca ostavioca koji su državljani Strane ugovornice na čijoj teritoriji se nalazi zaostavština, ili koji na toj teritoriji borave, ako svoja potraživanja prijave i, po potrebi, pokrenu postupak za njihovo priznanje.

Article 45

1. Upon request of the heirs or legatees, who are nationals of the Contracting State on whose territory the estate is located or that reside on its territory, the court may retain the whole movable estate or sufficient part of it, until the competent court of the Contracting State of which the deceased was a national finally decides on the claims of the heir or legatee.

2. The same measures may be taken by the court upon request of creditors of the deceased who are nationals of the Contracting State on whose territory the estate is located or who reside on that territory, if they register their claims and, if needed, initiate proceedings for their recognition.

Član 46

1. Radi stavljanja zahteva navedenih u članu 45 odrediće sud oglasom rok od tri do šest meseci u kome se zahtevi gorepomenutih lica moraju prijaviti i, po potrebi, pokrenuti postupak za njihovo priznanje. Ako se ti zahtevi u ovom roku ne prijave, odnosno ako se ne pokrene postupak za njihovo priznanje, ne može se odbiti predaja pokretne zaostavštine pozivanjem na odredbe člana 45.

Article 46

1. In order to file requests named in Article 45, a term of three to six months shall be determined by public notice of the court, within which the requests of creditors and heirs need to be registered, and if needed, proceedings for their recognition initiated. If those requests are not registered within this term, or if proceedings for their recognition are not initiated, the handing over of the movable estate cannot be refused by reference to Article 45.

2. Overen prepis oglasa mora se poslati diplomatskom ili konzularnom predstavništvu Strane ugovornice čiji je državljanin bio ostavilac.

Član 47

Svaka Strana ugovornica pridržava sebi pravo da pre predaje pokretne zaostavštine naplati sve poreze i takse kojima podleže nasleđe po njenom zakonodavstvu.

Član 48

Koja se imovina ima smatrati pokretnom ili nepokretnom određuje se po zakonodavstvu Strane ugovornice u kojoj se ta imovina nalazi.

2. The certified copy of the public notice shall be delivered to the diplomatic or consular representation of the Contracting State of which the deceased was a national.

Article 47

Before handing over the movable estate, each Contracting State has a right to charge all succession taxes and fees in accordance with its own law.

Article 48

Whether property is to be considered movable or immovable is to be determined under the law of the Contracting State where that property is located.

TREATY 27: ROMANIA-YUGOSLAVIA

Ugovor između Federativne Narodne Republike Jugoslavije i Rumunske Narodne Republike o pravnoj pomoći od 18. oktobra 1960. godine*

Glava IV

ZAOSTAVŠTINE

Član 34

1. Državljani jedne strane ugovornice mogu sticati dobra i prava na teritoriji druge strane ugovornice na osnovu zakonskog ili testamentalnog nasleđivanja pod istim uslovima i u istom obimu kao domaći državljani.
2. Državljani jedne strane ugovornice mogu testamentom raspolagati svojim pokretnim i nepokretnim dobrima koja se nalaze na teritoriji druge strane ugovornice.

Član 35

1. Sposobnost za pravljenje ili opozivanje testamenta, kao i pravne posledice nedostatka volje određuju se po zakonu strane ugovornice čiji je državljanin bio zaveštalac u vreme sastavljanja odnosno opozivanja testamenta.

2. Forma sastavljanja ili opozivanja testamenta određuje se po zakonu strane ugovornice čiji je državljanin bio zaveštalac u vreme sastavljanja odnosno opozivanja ili po zakonu strane ugovornice na čijoj je teritoriji testamenat sastavljen odnosno opozvan.

Treaty between the Romanian People's Republic and the Federal People's Republic of Yugoslavia on Legal Assistance of 18 October 1960**

Chapter IV

Succession matters

Article 34

1. Nationals of one Contracting State may acquire property and rights in the territory of the other Contracting State by statutory or testamentary succession under the same conditions and to the same extent as its own nationals.
2. The nationals of one Contracting State may dispose of their property located on the territory of the other Contracting State upon death by a will.

Article 35

1. The capacity to make or revoke a testament as well as legal consequences for the absence of intent to testate shall be governed by the law of the Contracting State of which the deceased was a national at the time the testament was made or revoked.
2. The form in which the testament is to be made or revoked shall be governed by the law of the Contracting State of which the deceased was a national at the time the testament was made or revoked or by the law of the Contracting State on whose territory the testament was made or revoked.

* Službeni list Federativne Narodne Republike Jugoslavije – Dodatak: Međunarodni ugovori i drugi sporazumi, br. 8/61.

** The English translation has kindly been prepared by Slavko Đorđević and Zlatan Meškić.

Član 36

1. Za raspravljanje o pokretnim stvarima iz zaostavštine državljana strana ugovornica, kao i za rešavanje sporova iz nasledno-pravnih odnosa u vezi sa ovim stvarima, nadležan je organ one strane ugovornice čiji je državljanin bio ostavilac u vreme smrti, ako ovim ugovorom nije drukčije određeno.
2. Za raspravljanje nepokretne zaostavštine državljana strana ugovornica, kao i za rešavanje sporova iz nasledno-pravnih odnosa u vezi sa ovim nepokretnostima, isključivo je nadležan organ one strane ugovornice na čijoj se teritoriji nalazi nepokretna imovina.

Article 36

1. The courts of the State of which the deceased was a national shall have jurisdiction to rule on the succession to movable property of nationals of the Contracting States, as well as to rule on contentious proceedings relating to those assets, unless this agreement provides otherwise.
2. The competent authority of the Contracting State on whose territory immovable property is located shall have exclusive jurisdiction to rule on the immovable estate and resolve inheritance claims related to that estate.

Član 37

Ako je ostavilac, koji je bio državljanin jedne strane ugovornice, imao poslednje prebivalište na teritoriji druge strane ugovornice, mogu naslednici koji imaju prebivalište odnosno boravište na teritoriji te druge strane ugovornice, zahtevati u roku od šest meseci od smrti ostavioca da nadležni organ te strane ugovornice sprovede raspravu pokretne zaostavštine koja se nalazi na njenoj teritoriji. O ovom zahtevu obavestiće se naslednici i legatari. Ako u roku od tri meseca od obaveštenja nijedan od naslednika ili legatara ne prigovori, udovoljiće se zahtevu.

Article 37

If the deceased, who was a national of one Contracting State, had his last domicile on the territory of another Contracting State, the heirs that have domicile or residence on the territory of that Contracting State may request within six months of the death of the deceased that the competent authority of that Contracting State conduct proceedings on the movable estate located on its territory. The heirs and legatees shall be informed about this request. If within three months after the notice none of the heirs or legatees objects to it, the request shall be granted.

Član 38

Da li se jedna stvar ima smatrati pokretnom ili nepokretnom određuje se po zakonu strane ugovornice na čijoj se teritoriji nalazi ta stvar.

Article 38

The issue of whether property is considered to be movable or immovable is governed by the law of the Contracting State on whose territory the property is located.

Član 39

1. Ako na teritoriji jedne strane ugovornice umre državljanin druge strane ugovornice, nadležan organ će odmah obavestiti o smrti diplomatsko ili konzularno predstavništvo te strane ugovornice i saopštiti sve što mu je poznato o naslednicima, o njihovom prebivalištu odnosno boravištu, o sastavu i vrednosti zaostavštine, kao i o testamentu – ako postoji. Ovako će ovaj organ postupiti i kad sazna da se na teritoriji njegove zemlje nalazi imovina državljanina druge strane ugovornice koji je umro bilo na teritoriji strane ugovornice čiji je državljanin bio, bilo na teritoriji treće države.
2. Isto tako, ako diplomatsko ili konzularno predstavništvo strane ugovornice čiji je državljanin bio umrli sazna o smrti izvestiće o tome nadležan organ druge strane ugovornice radi preduzimanja mera u cilju očuvanja zaostavštine.

Article 39

1. If the national of one Contracting State dies on the territory of another Contracting State, the competent authority shall immediately inform the diplomatic or consular representative of that State about his death and shall communicate everything that is known about the heirs, their domicile or residence, the composition and the value of the estate, and about a testament – if it exists. The competent authority shall do the same if it finds out that on territory of its State there is property of a national of the other Contracting State, who died in this State or in a third State.
2. If the diplomatic or consular representative of the Contracting State of which the deceased was a national is informed about the death, it will provide that information to the competent authority of the other Contracting State who shall undertake measures in order to protect the estate.

Član 40

Ako državljanin jedne strane ugovornice umre za vreme putovanja ili privremenog boravka na teritoriji druge strane ugovornice, gde inače nije imao prebivalište odnosno boravište, onda će se stvari koje je nosio sa sobom, po spisku, bez drugih formalnosti, predati diplomatskom ili konzularnom predstavništvu strane ugovornice čiji je bio državljanin.

Article 40

If a national of one Contracting State dies during his travel or temporary residence on the territory of another Contracting State, and he has no domicile or residence there, the items, that he carried with him and that are listed in an inventory shall without further formalities be handed over to the diplomatic or consular representatives of the State of which he was a national.

Član 41

1. Organi svake strane ugovornice, na predlog ili po službenoj dužnosti, saglasno svom zakonu, izvršiće popis i preduzeće potrebe mere za očuvanje i upravljanje zaostavštine koja je ostala na njenoj teritoriji posle smrti državljanina druge strane ugovornice.

Article 41

1. The authority of each Contracting State shall, upon request or on its own motion and in accordance with its own law, make an inventory of property of the deceased and undertake the measures necessary to protect and administer the estate which is located on its territory after the death of the national of other Contracting State.

2. Ako je u mestu gde se nalazi zaostavština sedište diplomatskog ili konzularnog predstavništva strane ugovornice čiji je državljanin bio umrli, mere navedene u stavu 1. ovog člana mogu se preduzeti samo ako je diplomatsko ili konzularno predstavništvo bilo o tome blagovremeno obavešteno, osim u slučajevima koji ne trpe odlaganja. Diplomatsko ili konzularno predstavništvo može da učestvuje u sprovođenju ovih mera i da stavlja predloge.
3. U ostalim slučajevima treba bez odlaganja izvestiti diplomatsko ili konzularno predstavništvo o merama koje su preduzete za obezbeđenje i za upravljanje zaostavštinom. Na predlog diplomatskog ili konzularnog predstavništva, ove mere se mogu izmeniti ili ukinuti bez štete po prava trećih lica.

Član 42

1. Ako po okončanju ostavinskog postupka pokretnu zaostavštinu koja se nalazi na teritoriji jedne strane ugovornice treba predati naslednicima koji imaju prebivalište odnosno boravište na teritoriji druge strane ugovornice, ista će se predati diplomatskom ili konzularnom predstavništvu te strane ugovornice:

a) ako su plaćena ili obezbeđena potraživanja poverilaca prema zaostavštini po odredbama člana 43. ovog ugovora;
b) ako su nadležni organi dali odobrenje za iznošenje stvari, ukoliko postoji zabrana iznošenja odnosnih stvari.

2. Novčani iznos, koji je deo zaostavštine, kao i novac dobiven prodajom pokretne ili nepokretne zaostavštine, a koji treba predati naslednicima koji imaju prebivalište odnosno boravište na teritoriji druge strane ugovornice, položiće se na njihovo ime kod banke strane ugovornice, na čijoj se teritoriji nalazi novac, a transfer ovog novca izvršiće se saglasno propisima te strane ugovornice.

2. If the estate is located at the seat of the diplomatic or consular representative of the Contracting State of which the deceased was a national, the measures provided for in paragraph 1 of this article may be taken only if the diplomatic or consular representation was timely informed about them, except for emergency cases; the diplomatic or consular representative may participate when these measures are performed or make requests.
3. In other cases, the diplomatic or consular representative shall be, without delay, informed about those measures taken for protection and administration (management) of the estate. Upon request of the diplomatic or consular representative, these measures may be changed or annulled without violating the rights of third persons.

Article 42

1. If, after the end of succession proceedings, the movable estate located on the territory of one Contracting State needs to be handed over to the hiers who have their domicile or residence on the territory of the other Contracting State, the estate shall be handed over to the diplomatic or consular representative of that Contracting State provided that:

a) the claims of creditors have been paid or secured in accordance with Article 43 of this agreement;
b) the competent authority has given its consent for the transfer of the assets in those cases in which a transfer without permission is forbidden.

2. Sums of money that are part of the estate and sums of money received by selling movable or immovable property, which have to be handed over to the heirs who have their domicile or residence on the territory of other Contracting State, shall be deposited in the heirs' name in the bank of the Contracting State where the money is located, and transfer of that money shall be performed in accordance with the law of that Contracting State.

Član 43

1. Na zahtev poverilaca koji imaju prebivalište odnosno boravište na teritoriji strane ugovornice gde se nalazi pokretna zaostavština umrlog državljanina druge strane ugovornice, nadležan organ može zadržati celokupnu zaostavštinu ili dovoljan deo iste dok se ne odluči o njihovim potraživanjima prema zaostavštini.
2. Radi stavljanja zahteva iz stava 1. ovog člana nadležan organ će oglasom pozvati poverioce da u određenom roku, koji ne može biti kraći od 30 dana ni duži od 6 meseci, prijave svoje zahteve prema zaostavštini i po potrebi pokrenu postupak za njihovo priznanje. Ako poverioci ne prijave svoje zahteve u tom roku, ili ako ne pokrenu postupak za priznanje svojih zahteva, ne može se sa ovog razloga odbiti predaja pokretne zaostavštine.

Article 43

1. Upon request of creditors who have their domicile or residence on the territory of the Contracting State where the movable estate of a deceased who was a national of other Contracting State is located, the competent authority may retain the whole estate or sufficient part of it until it decides upon their claims on the inheritance.
2. In order to file requests pursuant to paragraph 1 of this Article, the competent authority shall inform creditors by public notice that they need, within the term that shall not be shorter that thirty days and longer than six months, to register their claims and, if needed, to initiate proceedings for their recognition. If their claims are not registered within this time frame, or if proceedings for their recognition are not initiated, the handing over of the movable estate cannot be refused.

Član 44

1. Proglašenje testamenta vrši nadležan organ one strane ugovornice na čijoj se teritoriji nalazi testamenat.

2. Ako je organ jedne strane ugovornice proglasio testamenat državljanina druge strane ugovornice, overen prepis testamenta, zajedno sa podacima o stanju testamenta i prepisom zapisnika o proglašenju testamenta, dostaviće se nadležnom organu strane ugovornice čiji je državljanin bio zaveštalac. Na isti način postupiće se i u slučaju ako je za raspravljanje zaostavštine nadležan i organ druge strane ugovornice.

3. Organ koji je proglasio testamenat može, na zahtev organa druge strane ugovornice, dostaviti ovom i originalni testamenat.

Article 44

1. The opening of the will shall be performed by the competent authority of the Contracting State on whose territory the testament is located.
2. If the competent authority of one Contracting State has opened the will of a national of the other Contracting State, a duly certified copy of the testament together with details on its condition and a minutes on the content of the testament shall be delivered to the competent authority of the Contracting State of which the deceased was a national. The same applies when the competent authority of the other Contracting State has jurisdiction to rule on succession.
3. The competent authority which opened the will may, upon request of the authority of other Contracting State, deliver the original will to this authority.

Član 45

1. U svim naslednim predmetima po kojima se raspravlja na teritoriji jedne strane ugovornice, diplomatsko ili konzularno predstavništvo druge strane ugovornice je ovlašćeno da zastupa svoje državljane bez posebnog punomoćja, ako su ovi odsutni i nisu odredili svoje punomoćnike.
2. Odredbom stava 1. ovog člana ne dira se u odredbe o obaveznom zastupanju od strane advokata.

Član 46

Pokretna vakantna zaostavština predaje se strani ugovornici čiji je državljanin bio ostavilac u vreme smrti, a u pogledu nepokretne vakantne zaostavštine primeniće se zakon strane ugovornice na čijoj se teritoriji ta imovina nalazi.

Article 45

1. In all succession proceedings, conducted on the territory of one Contracting State, the diplomatic or consular representative of the other Contracting State is entitled to represent its nationals without special authorization if the represented nationals are absent and have not appointed an agent.
2. Paragraph 1 of this Article does not prejudice the application of the provisions on mandatory representation by an attorney.

Article 46

The movable estate without claimant shall be handed over to the Contracting State of which the deceased was a national at the time of his death, and the immovable estate without claimant to the Contracting State on whose territory this estate is located.

INDEX

ABOUT THE EDITORS

Anatol Dutta holds a Chair of Private Law, Private International Law and Comparative Law at the Ludwig Maximilians University Munich. Previously, he was Fellow at the Max Planck Institute for Comparative and Private International Law in Hamburg (2003–2014) and Professor at the University of Regensburg (2014–2017). Anatol Dutta is a member of the editorial board of the Zeitschrift für das gesamte Familienrecht (FamRZ), a leading family law journal for practitioners and academics in Germany, and a member of the German Council of Private International Law (Federal Ministry of Justice). He has a special interest in family and succession law, from a private international law as well as a comparative and interdisciplinary perspective.

Wolfgang Wurmnest holds the Chair of Private Law, Commercial Law, Private International and Comparative Law at the University of Augsburg. Previously, he was Fellow at the Max Planck Institute for Comparative and Private International Law in Hamburg (2002–2008, on leave during the 2003/04 academic year) and Professor at the University of Hannover (2009–2013). Wolfgang Wurmnest is a member of the *Redaktionsausschuß* of the Rabels Zeitschrift für ausländisches und internationales Privatrecht (RabelsZ), a leading academic private international law journal in Germany, and an associate member of the International Academy of Comparative Law.

Lightning Source UK Ltd.
Milton Keynes UK
UKHW031844310719
347165UK00001B/1/P

9 781780 686646